family
insp
loft
enhouse
easy
renewable
kids
discover
gate
decking
la
socket
relax
wallpaper
recycle
window
insulate
comfort
chisel
drill
style
bathroom
create
escape
energy saving
kitchen
flooring
entertain

Making it easier **B&Q**

you can
do it

the complete **B&Q** step-by-step
book of home improvement

with 2400 colour illustrations

Be safe

All home improvement activities involve a degree of risk. Skills of individual readers and site conditions vary widely. Although B&Q has made every effort to ensure that the instructions in this book are accurate, they are provided for general information only and you should always read and follow any manufacturer's instructions and, where appropriate, seek the advice of professionals.

In particular:
- All work on gas fittings and appliances must by law be carried out by a qualified professional.
- Before working with electricity or water you should consult an appropriate professional. When working with electricity always turn the power off at the mains.
- It is essential that you check the latest Building Regulations before proceeding with any electrical work. Contact your local authority's Building Control Department for guidance.
- All electrical advice in this book assumes that you have an up-to-date system that complies fully with the latest IEE Wiring Regulations, or the Scottish Building Regulations in Scotland. If you are not sure whether your system is compliant you should get it checked by a qualified professional.
- Always read any relevant manuals or instructions for using tools and follow the safety instructions.
- The law concerning Building Regulations, planning, local byelaws and related matters can be complicated and you should take professional advice where appropriate. In connection with building work, B&Q cannot advise on planning permission or Building Regulations issues.

The techniques suggested in this book should not be used by anyone less than 18 years of age. To the extent permitted by law, B&Q accepts no liability for any loss, damage or injury arising as a consequence of the advice contained in this book. References to legislation and regulations are correct at the time of going to press.

Feedback and further advice
B&Q welcomes your comments on this book and suggestions for improvements. Contact us by sending an email to: thebook@b-and-q.co.uk

To find your local B&Q store, or for design and planning advice, indoors and out, visit **diy.com**

You Can Do It
The Complete B&Q Step-by-Step Book of Home Improvement

B&Q Project Managers Ruth Harrison-Wood, Geoff Long

Project Director and Writer Nicholas Barnard
Consulting Editor Ken Schept
Managing Editor Amanda Vinnicombe
Designer Aaron Hayden
Production Manager Philip Collyer
Photographer Lucy Pope
Illustrator Peter Bull Art Studios

Edited, designed and produced by Thames & Hudson Ltd, London, and B&Q plc

First published in the United Kingdom in 2003 by B&Q plc, Portswood House, 1 Hampshire Corporate Park, Chandlers Ford, Eastleigh, Hampshire SO53 3YX, and Thames & Hudson Ltd, 181A High Holborn, London WC1V 7QX, www.thamesandhudson.com

Fourth edition 2010

British Library Cataloguing-in-Publication Data
A catalogue record for this book is available from the British Library
ISBN: 978-0-9535243-4-1 (B&Q edition)
ISBN: 978-0-500-51551-8 (Thames & Hudson edition)

This book is printed on 135gsm Royal Roto Matt, Vol. 1.0, FSC, produced by Sappi Fine Paper Europe, which has environmental accreditation ISO 14001.

Printed and bound in Italy by Rotolito Lombarda

Introduction

Know your home

Inside the home

Outside the home

Home systems
and services

The **basics**

Fionnuala **Johnston** Natalie **Etherington** Stephen **Hansford**

Ellen **Morgan** Kieron **Moore** Richard **Wesley** Matt **Beirne** Nick **Rickard**

Richard **Cullen** John **Mayson** Allison **Burdett** Amy **Mumford**

Kevin **Poulter** Sarah **Greenaway** Ruth **Harrison-Wood**

Tony **Bevan** Tony **Crease** Daniel **Smith** Tony **Man** Julia **Wickham**

Nix **Attia** Sarah **O'Brien** Ellie **Marshall** Hayley **Straker** Gemma **Board**

Louise **Fowen** Dee **Gittins** Tessa **Ireland** Mark **Turner**

Sarah **Brogan** Stacey **Welsh** Mike **Attwell** Catherine **Robinson**

Gin **Tidridge** Roy **Miller** Emily **Johnson**

Lisa **Hosni** Kevin **Walker** Susannah **Webber** Hana **Baker**

Claire **Veck** Gemma **Taylor** John **Badley** Stephanie **Neron**

Julie **Souch** Rachel **Warren** John **Humphreys** Elaine **Walter**

Chris **Poucher** Sophie **Mayes** Keith **Bibby** Vicky **Saunders** Laura **Simonett**

Joe **Sweeney** Debbie **Cave** Beth **Trzoska** Lesley **O'Doherty**

Ian **Purkis** Kate **Exton** Sam **Woodcock** Alan **Fisher** Lorian **Coutts**

Paul **Johnson** Stuart **Baker** Caye **Ocina** Murray **Fraser**

Debbie **Berry** Geoff **Menage** Dan **Bird** David **Westacot**

Mark **Lopez** Robyn **Barnes**

Claire **Mitchell** Jayne **Adamson** Sam **Fowler**

Barry **Batley** Carol **Bellwood** Sally **Gant**

Arthur **Weir** Jenny **Woodyer** Hugh **Bracey**

Mark **Lane** Angela **Lambert** Jackie **Watson** Geoff **Long** Alan **Pearce**

Adrian **Clark** Keith **Dooley** Tony **Royales**

Steve **Davis** Martin **Cooper** James **Smith**

Daryl **Shaw** Steven **Groves** Ray **Shaw** Jo **Morley** Jim **Chapman**

Keith **Traynor**

Andy **Ritchie** David **Humphreys**

Scott **Trayhorn** David **Boswell** Peter **Daniel** Darren **Kay** Brian **Wiggins**

Angie **Shawcroft** Jerry **Walker** David **Jennings** Nina **Jones**

Barry **Greening** Gary **Howells** Derek **Spears** James **Eden** Geoffrey **Evans**

George **Siaperas** Bob **Hesford** Janine **Dewar**

Paul **Town** Nicki **Spurr**

Philip **Taylor** Bernard **Buckley** Neil **Howarth** Mark **Turner**

Fiona **Bashford** Gary **Hatch** Simon **Bristow** Paul **Bagnall**

Peter **Cox** Tony **Rossi** Peter **Marten** Alex **Day** Ed **Brown** Steve **Guy**

Stuart **Watt**

Alison **Morrisey** Paul **Mulready** Phil **Duddridge** Stephen **Savage**

Sharon **Driscoll** Daz **McDermid** Dan **Fernandes**

Chris **Smith** Claire **Cooper**

Simon **Murphy** Sam **Park**

INTRODUCTION

Making it easier

You Can Do It is the UK's most trusted guide to home repair, upkeep and decoration. With over a quarter of a million copies sold, it has already helped a generation to mend, maintain and makeover their homes more easily.

This brand new edition has been expanded and updated for a new decade. Times have changed: 'don't move, improve' is the new motto of homeowners facing a more uncertain financial climate. Thousands of people are rediscovering the pleasures and satisfactions of doing things for themselves – from traditional arts and crafts, to home improvements, to growing their own fruit and veg.

No matter what kind of home you live in, **You Can Do It** is a book for how we live today. In easy-to-follow steps it shows you how to fix the problems and realise the potential of any property. And with wide-ranging practical advice on making your home more energy efficient, it reflects our shared desire to live well while reducing our impact on the environment.

This award-winning book presents knowledge gained from over forty years in the home improvement business. It includes all the features that you, our customers, told us meet your needs:

- An encyclopedic approach to basic and more advanced home improvement and repair
- Design options that inspire dreams and practical advice on how to achieve them
- Friendly, jargon-free language that is easy to understand and inspires confidence
- Colour photography and modern drawings that illustrate step-by-step instructions in a logical, easy-to-follow way

Above all, this is a book dedicated to **making it easier**. From decoration to insulation, plumbing, patios or ponds, **You Can Do It** offers expert tips, time-saving hints and all the most up-to-date innovations to enable you to achieve a successful result more quickly, more confidently and more easily.

You Can Do It is the result of an extraordinary partnership. B&Q's buyers, customer advisers and in-store experts – opposite – contributed to every page, drawing upon extensive customer feedback and their own in-depth knowledge. Thames & Hudson is the world's leading publisher of illustrated books with a long list of titles that present complicated subjects with clarity, authority and style.

You Can Do It – in our stores, on our website, **diy.com**, and now with this new edition of **You Can Do It** The Complete B&Q Step-by-Step Book of Home Improvement, part of our commitment to keep home improvement affordable and help you make yours a home to be proud of.

We make it easier...

Warren Scarr, Marketing Director

Good for you, good for the planet

If everyone on the planet used as many resources as we do in the West, we would need three planets to sustain us – and of course we only have one. That's why B&Q is supporting BioRegional's global **One Planet Living** campaign, designed to reduce the impact we are all having on the world's resources.

B&Q is working to become a One Planet Living business by reducing its stores' consumption of electricity and water, working with local community groups, and cutting the amount of waste it sends to landfill. In collaboration with independent sustainability experts, we have also developed the One Planet Home product range that helps customers manage their eco footprints at home.

Look out for the new **One Planet Home** features in this book that will help you to:

- save energy by using power and heating more efficiently and improving insulation in your home
- save water by harvesting rainwater and reducing your overall water consumption
- conserve nature by encouraging wildlife into your garden and supporting sustainable forestry and natural habitats across the world
- recycle and use recycled materials
- make your home healthier by reducing your family's exposure to pollutants such as VOCs

For more information visit **diy.com/eco**

Know your home

Take a look at your house – at the architectural lines and details, brickwork, wall finishes or tiling. Get a feel for the character of your house as a house – not just as your home. Find out what period it belongs to, and get to know how it was built – how the roof, walls and floors were put together and what they are made of. This investigation can be fun. And it will help you assess what improvements can be made – and what improvements really should be made. It can reveal unforeseen problems, making it easier to plan and budget for maintenance work. Learning a little about your house before you start work on a project will make you a more knowledgeable homeowner, and could save you time and money too.

When was your home built?

Over half of us live in relatively modern suburban houses built in the past fifty or sixty years. Home improvement often is an opportunity to add a bit of character to dwellings designed for maximum efficiency. Those of us in period houses, however, sometimes face the opposite challenge of increasing efficiency without diminishing character. In general, improving living space while respecting architectural heritage will enhance both the quality and the market value of a property.

1714–1837 Late Georgian and Regency

A popular style of architecture with classical proportions. Original Georgian houses, whether terraced or detached, can be expensive to buy and costly to restore, but you can be fairly sure you'll get your money back. They will probably be listed, however, so you will have to take a conservative approach to home improvements. The kind of alterations you are allowed to make will be limited.

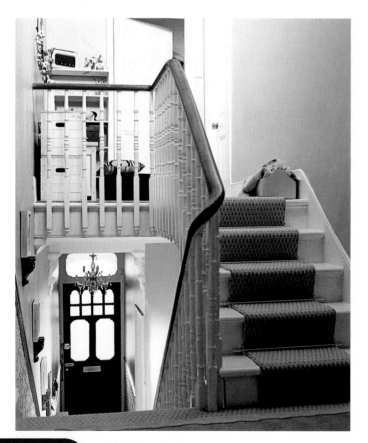

1837–1901 Victorian

Although Queen Victoria reigned from 1837, the term 'Victorian' is generally used to indicate the style of house popular from 1860 to the turn of the century, and in fact construction techniques for domestic buildings did not change significantly until the end of the First World War. Industrialisation led to a boom in house-building in towns and cities. The Health of Towns Act of 1848 initiated a series of housing acts that from 1875 prescribed minimum distances between dwellings, the inclusion of damp-proof courses in walls, and the provision of adequate natural lighting and ventilation. Doors, windows (sash rather than casement), and decorative details were mass-produced for the first time. One of the most popular styles of house was red brick with a plaster ground floor. Terraces, urban and suburban flats and detached villas flourished in this period. Their good, solid nature has ensured them lasting popularity.

1901–1939 Edwardian and Early Modern

After the Victorian era, the first significant changes in the materials and methods of domestic construction came with the large-scale private and public house-building after the First World War. The later Victorian development of back extensions, with porches and bay windows at the front, became universal in this period. The semi-detached house that still dominates suburbia first appeared in the 1920s, often in a mock-Tudor, half-timbered style.

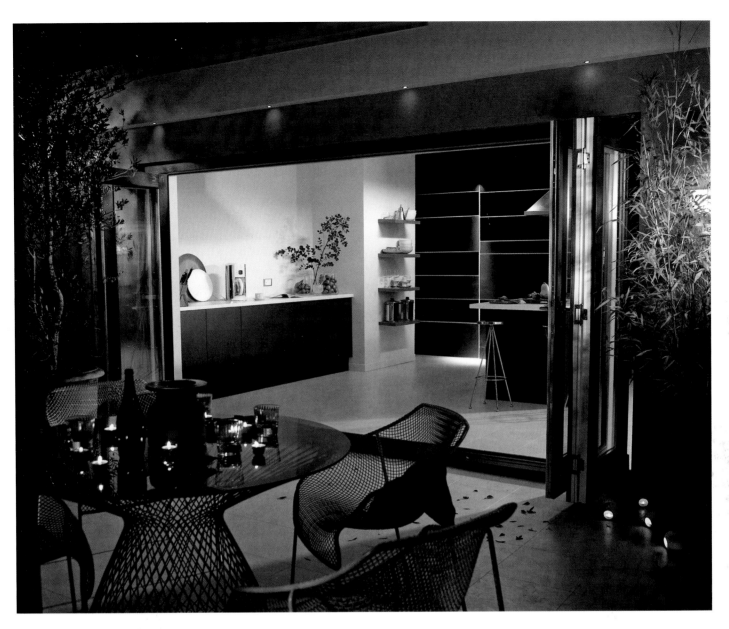

Postwar to New Millennium

The level of home ownership in the United Kingdom grew following the Second World War, as new houses began to be more affordable. Less expensive materials were used and certain building modifications, such as thinner walls, also reduced costs. Semi-detached houses, compact easy-to-run flats, or bungalows, these properties usually offer plenty of scope for home improvement ideas. Modern flats, purpose-built and often budget-priced as part of an estate, are constructed of steel, concrete and glass in rectangular, geometric shapes.

In the 1960s and 1970s house design became more geared to informal, open-plan living, and at the end of the century natural materials and styles became fashionable again. New-build properties have state-of-the-art furnishings and fittings in more traditional-looking settings. Natural stone, brick and wood provide a warmer, softer-looking environment.

Retaining the character of an older house

Unless you are planning a total transformation, in which case you will want advice from a professional (see pages 378–81), aim to make improvements that are in keeping with the type of home that you have. Unsympathetic additions or changes can look ugly, and may cost you. If you change the windows in your Georgian terrace house to PVCu, for example, you will certainly bring the value of your property down, and probably flout conservation regulations. As far as possible, materials

and finishes in older houses should be retained and cherished. Don't be tempted to add stone cladding or to paint brickwork, tile-hung bays and facades. Painting not only destroys the look of mellow brick and tile, but can also prevent these natural materials from breathing, and it is an unnecessary expense that will require continuous maintenance.

Creative salvage

Original features will enhance the aesthetics and value of your house. But if you decide to eliminate them don't throw them out – someone else is bound to want them. You can usually sell such items as iron fireplaces or old bathroom and kitchen fittings to a specialist company, which will probably come to remove them and give you some money for the privilege. Conversely, if you want to restore your property to its original condition, salvage yards can be a treasure-trove, and will no doubt fill you with inspiration for new projects.

CREATING A HOME THAT WORKS FOR YOU

The uncertain economic climate means that fewer people are moving house, and more are looking to make more of the home they already have. But there is also a trend across the UK of people rediscovering the joy and satisfaction of traditional crafts and home improvements, of making and growing things, and of doing it for themselves.

Don't move, improve!

Most UK houses were built in more traditional times, but life has changed and today individuals living alone comprise nearly a third of British households. And many of us work from home offices or joint bedroom/offices. Home improvement is increasingly about making spaces built for yesterday accommodate the way we live today. It's also about making our homes work more efficiently and less wastefully. That might mean switching to energy saving light bulbs or installing loft insulation, fitting water-saving taps and shower in the bathroom, or building a raised bed to grow vegetables in the garden.

Make the most of your home

You could well be living in your dream home right now. It may be waiting to be discovered under frayed carpet and layers of paint. You can dramatically enhance the character of your home by restoring existing features or adding architectural mouldings and other details. A disused fireplace can be revamped and wooden floors made good by stripping and waxing, staining or painting. New lighting can transform the atmosphere and usefulness of a room. Built-in storage solutions will enable you to clear your living space of clutter. If you want a home office, a kitchen makeover, even another bathroom, shower room or bedroom, you can do it – and it will be a lot cheaper and easier than moving. Don't forget the garden in any improvements as an attractive garden can be used like an extra room.

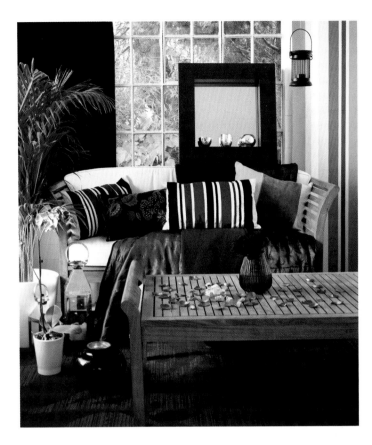

Express yourself

A coat of paint will spruce up any room but gone are the days of wall-to-wall magnolia. Go for some colour or make a style statement with designer wallpaper. A feature wall in a contrasting colour or bold pattern is a quick and easy way to give a room a stunning new look. And remember paint isn't just for walls – if you can't afford new furniture, try revamping old pieces with a fresh coat of paint.

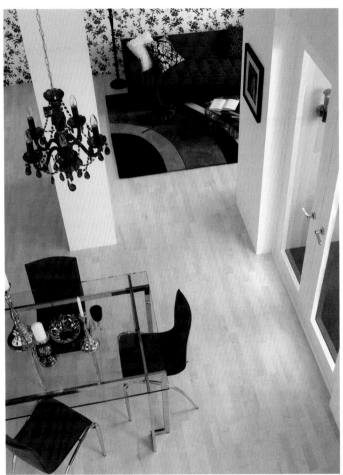

Enhancing value

Most home improvements will enhance the resale value of your home. But some are more profitable than others. Loft conversions, surprisingly, are not guaranteed to add value unless your house is in a fashionable area of a prosperous city. On the other hand, a kitchen or bathroom upgrade is likely to pay for itself in added market value. The same is true for investment in the garden.

But remember, the impact on resale value is only one consideration when contemplating a home improvement project. The first questions to ask are: is this what I want, will it make me happy, and can I afford it? If the answer is yes and you're ready to move ahead, then bear in mind the following dos and don'ts if you are eventually hoping to resell and recoup your costs.

Do

- Paint and decorate
- Replace outdated bathroom suites
- Choose a simple fitted kitchen
- Fit or expose wooden floors
- Increase natural light
- Maximise views of the garden
- Add an extension to create a spacious kitchen
- Convert a cellar into living or storage space
- Make your home more energy efficient

Don't

- Rip out period features such as fireplaces
- Use textured plaster or woodchip to cover uneven walls
- Create windowless rooms
- Install double glazing that doesn't open
- Split rooms to make more bedrooms, unless they are huge
- Economise by living with dated wallpaper or furnishings

Energy Performance Certificates (EPCs)

The energy efficiency and environmental impact of a property are increasingly important considerations for buyers. The legal requirement for house sellers to provide a Home Information Pack (HIP) was scrapped in May 2010. However, it is still compulsory to commission an Energy Performance Certificate (EPC) from an accredited energy assessor when putting a property on the market. This certificate records how energy efficient a property is and provides an A–G rating, similar to those given to new domestic appliances such as refrigerators and washing machines. This allows prospective buyers to understand the property's energy efficiency and carbon emissions, and to factor these in as part of their investment. An EPC is accompanied by a report that lists measures that could be taken to improve the property's energy rating, with an indication of what rating could be achieved if all the recommendations were implemented.

IMPROVEMENT BY DESIGN

Sometimes we just need a change to our surroundings – a makeover can help to revive flagging spirits. A redesign can be a quick and easy way to renew and update a home without having to spend a lot of money. Be creative. Have fun. And don't hesitate to ask for advice – that's what the experts are there for. A good starting point when dreaming up a new decorative scheme are the two essential ingredients of colour and light.

Designing with colour

Look at the neighbouring colours on the colour wheel. They harmonise and produce a sense of tranquillity. Imagine placing opposite colours together. They clash and produce tension. It's easy to blend harmonising colours; more difficult to use the dramatic opposites, known as complementary colours. Let nature be your guide. Think of a meadow dotted with vivid red poppies: splashes of a complementary colour will spice up a scheme dominated by similar shades.

Colour gives shape to spaces. Need to make a small room feel larger? Ceilings lift and walls recede with pale, cool colours. Want something cosier? A warm-coloured finish will make a room feel snug. Colour also creates character. Use bold shades or daring contrasts for heightened drama; calm, harmonious, pale colours for understated elegance. The choice depends on the mood you want to create and the size, shape, lighting, and character of the interior.

Pattern

Today's fashionable designer wallpapers can bring real glamour and wow-factor to a room. Covering an entire room with pattern can feel claustrophobic – especially large-scale pattern in a small room. But you could avoid that by turning a single wall into a striking feature by using bold stripes, geometric designs or ornate prints, then enhance the special effect with plain complementary wallpaper or paint on the other walls.

Self-adhesive wall stickers are another option for livening up plain decor. There are fun, colourful stickers for children's rooms, as well as sophisticated designs for the stylish grown-up. And many of them peel off easily, so you never need get bored of them.

 Making it easier

Try your new style online
B&Q has developed an online interactive room planner that lets you see how your room might appear with a new look. Choose the type of room you want to decorate and then try out different combinations from the extensive range of paints and wallpapers. You can save your design online for up to 90 days, giving you plenty of time to canvass the opinions of family and friends. Online calculators can even work out how many rolls of paper or cans of paint you will need. Visit **diy.com** and begin experimenting now.

Designing with light

Light and colour are very closely related. Dark colours absorb nearly 90% of light, while pale shades reflect over 80%. Begin by thinking about natural light, and how to make the best of what's available to you. In a room used mainly at night, you can compensate for the effect of a dark colour scheme with artificial lighting. But during the day, a room decorated in dark shades will be very gloomy without plenty of natural light.

Lighting is as important as colour when planning your home's design. Light can change a room completely, adding atmosphere and making it feel cosy and welcoming. Different parts of the home need different treatments, so always start by thinking about the purpose of the room, and when and how it is used by you or your family. Once you are sure that lighting levels meet your practical needs, you can add the finishing touches that will make the room come alive.

Kitchen

Good lighting is essential in the kitchen. Sharp knives and hot pans mean this is one room where you really need to see what you are doing. Aim spotlights at the areas you use the most, like the hob, sink and work surfaces. Fit lights under wall cabinets to shine on to work surfaces, and consider installing the latest LED spotlights along plinths (see page 293). Don't use plug-in lamps, which may clutter work surfaces or get wet.

Dining room

Dining should be a pleasurable experience, something to linger over, so you don't want a dining room to have a cold atmosphere. You need a light over the table, but control it with a dimmer switch so that you can adjust the light level; that way, you will be able to see what you are eating without being bathed in harsh glare. Again, picking out features in the room with accent lighting will provide added interest, and pastel-coloured bulbs will soften the atmosphere and enhance a colour scheme.

Lighting for effect

By introducing a variety of light fittings, either in combination with a pendant or instead of it, you can change a room completely. There are four key types of lighting:

- **Ambient light** for general illumination. Different rooms will require different levels of ambient light.
- **Task lighting**, which is directed and functional and is often provided by desk or bedside lamps. In a kitchen, task lighting can help to eliminate shadow on worktops, making it a safer place to work.
- **Accent lighting**, which is directed but decorative, for example a narrow beam to illuminate and draw attention to a painting or sculpture.
- **Mood lighting**, which uses lower light levels or colour to create an ambience. This can be very effective if combined with accent lighting.

Living room

Here you need to cater for a range of family requirements: reading, watching television, entertaining, children's play. So the general diffused lighting of overhead fittings is a start, but add directional lighting with spotlights and reading lamps; use recessed or surface-mounted spotlights to accent features or pictures, or 'wash' walls with light. Table and standard lamps can be used to provide soft pools of light to create a relaxing atmosphere, while dimmer switches will allow you to control the overall light levels.

Hallway and stairs

In a hallway, choose lamps that will provide a warm welcoming glow for visitors – table and standard lamps or wall lights. Stairs, though, must be well lit to prevent anyone missing a step.

Bedroom

Make the most of lighting to create a cosy atmosphere in a bedroom. Use recessed spotlights, wall lights and table lamps to generate a soft light, but provide task lighting for reading in bed and using a dressing table. Freestanding uplighters can also provide soft ambient lighting, though they are best avoided in children's bedrooms, where they can be a safety hazard.

IMPROVEMENT IN ACTION

Ask yourself some questions about how you use – or underuse – your living space. Is the kitchen the hub of family life? Is the table piled with work clutter? Could you convert a spare room into a study? Is there a spot for proper storage cabinets? Might some decking, a table and chairs and a sun umbrella be as good as building a dining room extension, at least for part of the year? Take a fresh look at your home: you may be amazed by how much unrealised potential it offers.

Kitchen

If, like so many of us, you live in the kitchen, then why not make it comfortable? Expand it to accommodate a table and chairs. Rearrange it to take advantage of a view. Whether from the sink or the cooking area, a view of the outside world, especially the garden, can be an uplifting distraction from the chores. Add windows or glazed doors to increase natural light. Tile the wall above your units to create an attractive waterproof splashback, or fit one of the latest purpose-designed splashback panels. Install good task lighting over the work surfaces. If an existing fitted kitchen is adequate but unattractive, consider giving it a decorative makeover by painting the units, or changing their doors and handles. These are only some of the possibilities for achieving your dream kitchen: see pages 156–65 for many more. But whatever you do, plan carefully, and take into account safety, convenience and efficient use of space.

Living room

Arranging the sofa and chairs to form a comfortable cluster will instantly make a living room feel more relaxing. Lighting a living room is another challenge. You may want to combine ambient lighting with table lamps to read by as well as spotlights to accentuate a special feature in the room. This is a good space to express your sense of style too, using textures, colours and patterns on the walls and furnishings.

Dining area

Enjoying food in company is one of life's great pleasures, so make the colours and lighting in a dining room match the desire for relaxation and calm. Lighting, as in a bedroom, should be versatile so that you can adjust the totally different levels of illumination required during daytime and evening with the flick of a switch.

Bathroom

We spend a surprising amount of our lives bathing and washing, and the bathroom can be a wonderful space for relaxation. It needs to be easy to clean and comfortable to use: consider tiles or mosaic finishes, moisture-proof downlighters, a heated towel rail and a well lit mirror. If you haven't room for a shower cubicle, look at installing a modern shower screen and shower over the bath – taking a shower saves water and time. Don't forget to make room for storage too. Though if you are making significant changes to the bathroom, keep the plumbing as simple as possible by planning around the existing waste outlets.

Bedrooms

More storage space is number one on many people's bedroom wish list. Fitted cupboards offer the most efficient storage, and are now available with a variety of extremely useful accessories for stowing shoes and clothes. When lighting a bedroom, you will need to combine ambient lighting to illuminate the entire room with task lighting, such as bedside lamps. Finally, the bedroom is usually the one room where even those who prefer exposed wooden flooring find the warmth and comfort of carpeting or rugs irresistible. See pages 154–55 for more inspiration on planning your dream bedroom.

Home office

Setting up an efficient home office requires planning, particularly in terms of services. You will be surprised how much storage and desk space an office needs, so prepare to install, and if necessary disguise, filing cabinets, computer equipment and a mess of cables. Make sure that you have an adequate electrical supply and good lighting for working. Think too about extra heating or cooling; sitting immobile at a desk can be chilly in winter and sweltering in summer – particularly if you have converted an attic or a shed.

Garden

Altering the landscape of your garden also takes careful planning and preparation. Look at photographs taken throughout the year and try to imagine how any improvements will be affected by the changing seasons. Draw an outline plan of the garden, make copies, and then experiment with sketching new ideas. There are any number of ways to increase the usefulness of your outdoor living space throughout the year: installing a deck, garden lighting, a dining area, a greenhouse, workshop, playhouse or shed. A new fence will increase your privacy, while a pond will add interest – and life.

It is becoming increasingly clear that if we want our children and grandchildren to continue to enjoy the good quality of life we have had, we will all need to help to look after the planet. But the good news is that small actions make a difference and lots of small actions add up. So we can all do our bit – and can often save money in the process.

The One Planet Home

If everyone in the world lived the lifestyle we enjoy in the West, we would need three planets to support us. Obviously we only have one. To help us all stay within our fair share of the earth's resources, B&Q has joined forces with the environmental charity BioRegional to develop a new initiative called the One Planet Home.

The One Planet Home lifestyle means achieving a better quality of life for you and your family by using energy more efficiently, saving water, recycling, reducing pollutants and conserving nature. It's good for your quality of life, your health and your bank balance – and it's also good for the planet.

Keeping in the heat

Effective insulation is one of the easiest ways of saving energy in the home. And it makes perfect sense: a well-insulated house feels cosy in winter, cooler in summer, and costs less to heat.

Since heat rises, the place to begin is at the top, in the loft. Loft insulation should be at least 270mm thick; if yours is less than that, topping it up will make a significant difference to your comfort and your heating bills. And it's a surprisingly straightforward and quick DIY job.

Heat can also disappear straight through the outside walls. Installing cavity wall insulation is a professional job, but it can be done in just a couple of hours for a typical three-bedroom house. Solid walls can be insulated by adding extra cladding either inside or out, though this is a bigger and more expensive job. If you have a cellar, insulation under the floorboards on the ground floor will help seal out draughts. Even simple measures can help keep heat in: fit reflective foil behind a radiator to reflect heat into the room rather than heating the wall behind it.

When it comes to windows, double glazing can cut heat loss by half. It works by trapping air between two panes of glass (three in the case of triple glazing) to create an insulating barrier that helps to stop heat escaping. Fit draught excluder strips around windows, or doors, if you can feel draughts – where cold air can get in, warm air can get out.

An unlagged cylinder in an airing cupboard squanders a surprising amount of energy, so fitting a hot water tank jacket will save you money. Lagging your pipes will also keep your water hot for longer.

Facing up to climate change

In the past when the earth's climate has changed it has done so very slowly. Today most leading scientists believe that global temperatures are rising at an unnaturally fast rate because of the amount of greenhouse gas emissions we're releasing into the atmosphere.

Greenhouses gases occur naturally in the earth's atmosphere, retaining heat like the glass walls of a greenhouse to give us temperatures suitable for life on earth. The problem is that human activities involving the burning of fossil fuels (coal, oil and natural gas) are releasing increasing amounts of carbon dioxide (CO_2). Carbon dioxide is the main greenhouse gas, and it is causing the earth to heat up. At the same time we are cutting down the rainforests that absorb carbon dioxide. The result could be changes in climate that will create more extreme weather conditions, raise sea levels, and might make parts of the planet uninhabitable. Consuming less energy from fossil fuels is one of the best ways to reduce the greenhouse gas pollution – and it is something we can all help with.

Energy efficient heating

Controls that enable you to fine-tune your heating are much more energy efficient. A room thermostat automatically turns the heating off when the temperature reaches a pre-set level. It should be well away from any heat source to give an accurate reflection of the temperature. Thermostatic radiator valves allow you to control the level of heat on individual radiators. You can set the temperature at which each radiator will come on, and a 'frost protection setting' protects your home if temperatures plunge in winter.

Boilers are rated in a band from A to G, according to their energy efficiency, with A the most efficient (converting over 90% of energy into heat) and G the least (below 70%). Replacing an old G-rated boiler with a new energy-efficient, A-rated condensing boiler with heating controls will significantly cut your home's carbon dioxide emissions as well as saving as much as £200 a year on your heating bills.

Quick tips to save energy

- Wash clothes at 30°C
- Turn down your heating thermostat by 1°C – you won't notice the difference
- Dry clothes on a washing line or clothes airer instead of in the tumble dryer whenever possible
- Boil only the water you need in your kettle
- Turn off televisions, computers and other gadgets rather than leaving them on stand-by. Some appliances use up to two-thirds of the power on stand-by that they use when on.

Energy efficient lighting

There are over 60 million people in the UK and if we all changed just three light bulbs in our home to energy saving bulbs, we would save enough energy to power every streetlight in the country. Energy saving bulbs produce the same amount of light as traditional ones and they do it using about 80% less electricity. LEDs (light-emitting diodes) are also extremely energy efficient. Very low wattage LED lights are perfect for accent or mood lighting but you can also get lights bright enough to read by and for general use.

Maximise natural light by keeping windows clean so you don't need to use electric lights during the day. Trim overgrown plants if they are blocking light. A reflective sun tunnel running from the roof is a very effective way of bringing natural daylight into a room, reducing the need for artificial lighting.

Appliances and gadgets

Choose appliances with the best energy efficiency rating. All European manufacturers and retailers must provide clear information about the energy consumption and performance of household electrical appliances such as fridges, freezers, washing machines, dishwashers and ovens. Like boilers, products are rated on a scale from A++ (the most energy efficient) to G (the least energy efficient).

ONE PLANET HOME®

Find out more
www.diy.com/eco
www.1010global.org/uk
www.bioregional.com
www.carbontrust.co.uk
www.energysavingtrust.org.uk
www.fsc-uk.org
www.recyclemore.co.uk
www.recyclenow.com
www.startuk.org
www.waterwise.org.uk

Secondary, double or triple glazing

Draught excluders

Cavity wall insulation

Garden irrigation system

Energy efficient light bulbs

Thermostatic radiator valves

Room thermostat

Programmer for central heating

Energy monitor

Heat reflecting radiator foil

Sun tunnel

Solar water heating panels

Loft insulation

Insulated water tanks

FSC wallpaper

FSC flooring

Lagged pipes

Flueless fire

Low VOC paint

Water efficient shower

Solar powered lighting

Eco click taps

Dual flush toilet

A-rated appliances and condensing boiler

Insulated hot water cylinder

Rainwater butt

Bird box

Timer on hose

Recycling bins

Compost bin

Rainwater butts

Mulched borders

Drought resistant plants

Bird feeding station

Peat free compost

Patio vegetables

Natural pesticides

Vegetable patch

Targeted sprinkler

FSC garden furniture

Pond to encourage wildlife

Wildlife area

Water is the earth's most precious resource and we are using it at a greater rate than ever before. On average, each of us uses about 150 litres every day; that's 30% more than in 1970, and a lot of it is wasted. All of that water has to be processed and purified, which requires energy. So what can we do to use less of it?

Why worry about water?

It might seem to rain the whole time, but hosepipe bans during recent dry summers have already shown that our water supplies are under strain. In cities, lots of concrete means much rainfall runs off into overflow systems. In rural areas, when there's too much rain, flooding can shut down water treatment plants, cutting off our supply of fresh water. Experts predict that water will become an increasingly precious commodity in the future as population density grows in many areas, single-person households increase, and summers get hotter and drier.

So we all need to do our bit to cut back our water consumption. If you are already on a meter, then reducing your use will directly save you money. If you are not on a water meter but do manage to take steps to reduce your consumption, then you may save money on your water bills by requesting one. And everyone can save money on energy bills by using less hot water.

Saving water indoors

Make sure any leaks or dripping taps are fixed as these just waste water as well as possibly causing damage. Then tackle the two rooms in the house where we use the most water – the bathroom (nearly two-thirds) and the kitchen (over a quarter).

Bathroom

New watersaving products can make a massive difference to your water use and you will barely notice the difference. Showers are much more water-efficient than baths, as long as you don't stay in them too long. Though be wary of power showers, which can use as much as the average bath (80 litres) in just four minutes. Challenge yourself to stay

Conventional mixer showerhead

Water-saving aerating showerhead

clean and green by cutting a minute off your shower time. If you have a mixer shower, install an aerating showerhead, which mixes water with air to give the same shower performance with up to 75% less water.

Toilet flushing alone accounts for 30% of our water use in the home, but this can be reduced by switching to a dual flush toilet that uses as little as 2.6 litres per short flush or 4.5 litres per full flush. You can convert your existing toilet to a dual flush using a cistern conversion kit (see page 314).

Turning the tap off while brushing your teeth is an easy way to reduce your water use. Many new taps have an eco click mechanism. When a tap is turned on, it flows at a rate ideal for rinsing a toothbrush or facecloth; for a higher flow, you turn the tap beyond the click.

Kitchen

There are lots of easy, practical steps you can take immediately to save water in the kitchen:
- Avoid running your washing machine or dishwasher until you have a full load. Use the water saving option if you have one.
- Fill the kettle with only as much water as you need; this saves you energy as well as water.
- Wash vegetables in a bowl rather than under a running tap.

You can make big savings by choosing water-efficient appliances. A-rated appliances use a lot less energy – and a lot less water, too. Check the rating if you're buying a new dishwasher or washing machine.

Saving water outdoors

Outdoor use only accounts for 7% of average household consumption through the year, but this peaks in summer, when water reserves are at their lowest. Garden watering can account for as much as 70% of the water we use in a hot spell. Fortunately, there are plenty of ways to keep your garden blooming without wasting water or breaking a hosepipe ban.

Watering wisely

Plants need water to survive, but you don't need to water as a matter of routine. Only water plants when they show signs of needing a drink or if they are newly planted. Use a watering can instead of a sprinkler so you can target the water at the plants' roots, or install an automatic watering system. If a border really does need watering then it should be done either early morning or preferably late evening to minimise the water lost to evaporation and prevent scorching.

When you do water, make sure the plants are given a thorough drenching, otherwise you will simply moisten the top few centimetres of soil and the roots will grow upwards in search of it. This creates a vicious circle: shallow-rooted plants require regular watering, whereas deep-rooted ones are capable of seeking out their own supply further down.

Mulch and soil conditioner
A layer of mulch over exposed soil helps slow down the loss of water from the ground through evaporation. Working in a soil conditioner such as home-made compost can help to retain more moisture in a light chalky or sandy soil (as well as improving drainage in a heavy clay soil).

Drought-tolerant plants
Some plants thrive in hot, dry conditions that mimic their native climate. The flavour and scent of many herbs is enhanced by dry growing conditions.

Automatic watering
An automatic watering system is an efficient means of delivering water exactly where it is needed. Controlled by a timer, it can be set to come on in the evening or at night, when you will lose less water to evaporation.

Collecting rainwater
Rainwater is free, and better for your plants. Water butts are easy to connect to a downpipe (see page 169), and you can even join two together to collect twice the amount of water.

How much to water

The amount of water plants need varies widely: those that thrive in full sun and free-draining soil require very little; large-leaved, luscious ones a great deal more. Hebes, lavenders, thymes and alyssums don't need much watering once established – and they can all help to support native British wildlife.

New lawns require watering throughout their first season, but established lawns will survive dry summers perfectly well without being watered, unless there are extreme drought conditions – at which point there will be a hosepipe ban anyway. In a long hot summer lawns will go brown, but when cooler, damper weather returns they will recover. Drought-resistant lawn seed can help to establish a lawn that requires less water. Setting your lawnmower so that grass is allowed to be longer in summer can help the lawn to retain moisture.

Grey water

Every home produces large quantities of waste water that can safely be used in the garden. This kind of domestic waste water is called grey water – completely different from black water, which is sewage. Alternate the use of grey water with rainwater or mains water. Just bear in mind that you should not use grey water:

- that is contaminated by an excess of detergents, soaps or cooking residues
- that contains bleach, disinfectants or strong cleaning products
- for filling ponds
- on edible plants
- on container-grown or newly propagated plants
- for conservatory or greenhouse-grown plants

From recycling, to choosing biodegradable cleaning products, to growing your own food, there are many ways you can reduce your impact on the planet. At the same time you will make your home healthier, improve your quality of life and often save money too.

Choosing sustainable timber

When buying wood or wood-based products – whether it is decorative bark or wood chip mulch for the flowerbeds, deck timbers, furniture, sheds, fencing or even wallpaper – always check that the raw materials have came from well-managed sources.

The Forest Friendly logo represents B&Q's commitment to ensuring that all of our wood and wood-containing products are from sustainable sources. We work in close collaboration with leading global timber certification schemes such as FSC (Forest Stewardship Council), PEFC (Programme for the Endorsement of Forest Certification) and TFT (Tropical Forest Trust). By the end of 2010 all B&Q wood and wood-containing products will be certified by one of these schemes.

So you can rest assured that B&Q have done the work to ensure that the product you are buying is not contributing to the destruction of the world's forests.

Recycle and reuse

Every year over 50% of the UK's waste goes to landfill sites. Landfills are large holes in the ground where we dump rubbish, some the size of football stadiums. As it decomposes, the waste creates yet more greenhouse gases. By recycling paper, plastic, metal and glass you make sure they are used more than once in their lifetime. Check with your local council to see what they will recycle.

Buying recycled goods wherever possible helps to reduce waste as well as consumption of raw materials and energy. From doormats made out of old car tyres to tumblers made from recycled glass, you can find a wide range of new products for your home made from all sorts of recycled materials.

Recycling bin
A recycling bin with separate compartments will help you and your family to sort recyclables from other rubbish.

Avoiding harmful chemicals

Man-made chemicals are in everything from plastics to household cleaners to garden fertilisers. Many of them are harmless to humans and the environment, but some are not.

VOCs stands for Volatile Organic Compounds, which are chemicals found in paints, cleaning products and some household furnishings. VOCs evaporate into the air at room temperature and are thought to harm our health and the environment. Choosing minimum-level or zero VOC products will make the indoor air in your home fresher, and could alleviate allergy symptoms, headaches and respiratory problems. The average VOC level of the paints sold at B&Q now is considerably lower than 10 years ago, and VOC content is shown in a clear graphic so you know exactly what you are buying.

Many household cleaning products also contain VOCs and other harmful chemicals. Thankfully alternative products are available that do just as good a job with fewer chemicals.

Safe disposal

Unwanted paint should never be poured into drains or watercourses. Contact your local Environmental Health Department for details of disposal or recycling facilities for paint.

Avoiding harmful chemicals in the garden

In the past, people were quick to combat pests and weeds with hazardous chemicals and pesticides. Britain now has some of the world's toughest pesticide regulations, and many once common products have been removed from the shelves. Even so, scientists and gardeners remain concerned about the 'cocktail effect': when chemicals seem perfectly safe in isolation, but cause unpredictable problems if combined. There are also worries about the build-up of chemicals in the soil.

So before using a pesticide, ask yourself whether there is an alternative method – removing slugs or snails when they come out at night, or digging up the odd dandelion in the lawn with a garden fork.

Organic gardeners use natural methods to help control pests without pesticides. A dish of beer, sunk into the ground, or upturned grapefruit skins will attract slugs and snails, which can then be disposed of. Marigolds ward off a variety of insect pests, and attract hoverflies, which feast on aphids. Growing flowering herbs such as santolina, lavender, sage or rosemary attracts ladybirds, lacewings and hoverflies, which all prey on greenfly and other pests. Useful visitors also include tits, which love aphids, and thrushes, which feast on slugs and snails.

Choosing peat-free composts

Be sure to choose peat-free composts and soil improvers for your garden and pot plants. Peat bogs form over hundreds of years, and many support a diversity of insects, birds and plants, as well as scores of different mosses, liverworts, lichen and fungi. They are drained of their water to harvest peat, often causing the fragile habitats these species depend on to be destroyed. What's more, peat bogs also act as a great store of CO_2, so it's best to leave them untouched.

Making your own compost

Food and garden waste thrown on landfill sites decomposes in a way that emits greenhouse gases. A well-managed compost heap or bin works differently, turning food and garden waste into nutrient-rich compost without the emissions. Garden compost can be made from any organic matter that will rot down, including:

- Uncooked kitchen waste: vegetable trimmings, tea bags, coffee grounds and eggshells
- Annual weeds (before seedheads form)
- Spent bedding plants and flowers
- Soft hedge clippings
- Soft prunings
- Lawn clippings
- Shredded natural fibre materials such as newspapers, paper, cotton and wool fabrics
- Shredded woody stems
- Cardboard, sawdust and straw

Growing your own food

Home-grown fruit and vegetables are great for the planet, travelling from plant to plate with no packaging waste or carbon emissions from food miles. Lots of herbs, fruit and vegetables grow well in containers, so you can easily turn your patio into a kitchen garden. Grow bags are great for tomatoes, but you can also grow cucumbers, chillies and peppers in them. The potato sack is an easy way to grow delicious potatoes on a patio. And even a small garden can accommodate a raised bed made with a simple framework of pre-treated timber.

Raised bed
A raised bed is perfect for growing vegetables. It takes up less space than a vegetable patch, is easy to manage and looks good in any size of garden.

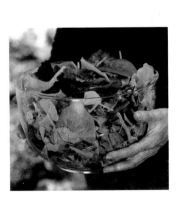

From garden to plate
The fresher the food, the more nutrients it has and the better it is for you. By growing your own, you can also choose what chemicals do and don't go on your food.

Encouraging wildlife

Native species are declining in the UK because their natural habitat is being lost to roads, construction sites and farmland. Creating a wildlife-friendly space in your garden offers native wildlife a refuge and it connects you to nature. Choose plants that attract birds and insects, and encourage different bird species to visit with simple feeders and a regular supply of good quality bird food. Try putting up a nest box. A pond in your garden, or a birdbath on your patio, will also attract birds.

Birds love plants that produce berries and seeds – plants like rowan, spindle, hawthorn, cotoneaster, honeysuckle, holly and ivy. Bullfinches like forsythia buds and the seeds of honesty. Goldfinches especially like teasel, sunflower and lavender seeds. If you have enough space, plant native trees like willow, oak and birch as they can support huge numbers of insects and caterpillars.

Compost bin
A purpose-designed compost bin with a hatch at the bottom will quickly recycle organic waste materials into rich, natural compost.

Birdlife
Birds will be attracted into your garden by a bird feeder or nest box, and by plants that produce berries and seeds.

Once your home is as energy efficient as possible, you might like to go a step further and consider renewable energy. Nowadays there is a choice of microgeneration schemes by which individuals or communities can generate zero or low carbon energy on a small scale. What's more, under the new feed-in tariff scheme, you will be paid for every unit of renewable electricity you generate – even if you use it yourself.

Renewable energy tariffs
If you are not in a position to invest in your own renewable scheme, you can still help to reduce the UK's carbon emissions by switching to a renewable energy tariff. The big energy suppliers all offer green tariffs, most of which cost no more than the standard tariffs. In return the company either makes a commitment to supply some or all of your energy (via the National Grid) from renewable sources, or to invest in research and development of sustainable energy projects.

Feed-in tariffs

Feed-in tariffs (FITs) came into effect in the UK on 1 April 2010 as an incentive to householders and communities to move to low carbon living – which is important if the UK is to reach its target of 15% of total energy from renewable sources by 2020.

The approved systems that can profit from the feed-in tariffs include solar electricity panels, wind turbines, hydroelectricity and micro combined heat and power (mCHP).

These systems do require a substantial initial investment, but once installed, you will be paid by your energy supplier for all the electricity generated, even if you use it yourself. Produce more than you need and you can export the surplus to the grid and receive an additional payment. If you don't produce enough electricity for your household, you simply import the extra from the grid and pay your supplier in the normal way.

Solar electricity panels

These panels, usually placed on the roof, consist of photovoltaic (PV) cells that convert the energy in sunlight into an electric current. They need to be sited on a south-facing roof or wall that is not shaded by buildings or trees. The stronger the sunshine, the more electricity they generate, but they can still produce some on a cloudy day.

The electricity produced by the cells is direct current (DC) while our homes use alternating current (AC). A device called an inverter connected to the panel and to the consumer unit (fuse box) converts the electricity. Transparent PV cells can be used on conservatories and others are made into solar tiles that look like roof tiles.

Wind turbines

Small wind turbines can generate enough electricity from the wind to power lights and electrical appliances. Their large blades turn when the wind blows, driving a turbine that produces electricity. Careful siting is essential: micro wind turbines are generally not effective in built-up areas, or any location where buildings, trees or hills will reduce wind speed or create turbulence. However, if you have enough unobstructed land, then you could consider a turbine mounted on a pole or mast fixed into the ground. An inverter converts the power into AC electricity for domestic use.

Small-scale hydro

If you have a stream or river on your property, then you could harness the energy of water to generate electricity through a small-scale hydroelectric system. The water must flow from a high level to a lower level, over a waterfall for instance, to turn a turbine that produces electricity. The amount of electricity produced will depend on the amount of water and how fast it flows.

Micro combined heat and power (mCHP)

Micro combined heat and power (mCHP) is very new technology, but if you are planning to replace your gas boiler it is something you can now consider. These boilers generate electricity as a by-product of burning gas to provide heating and hot water. They only produce electricity while the heating is on, but it is enough to power lights and small appliances.

Other renewable energy schemes

In addition to the FIT schemes, there are other heating systems that use renewable energy. Always check to see if building regulations approval is needed for a particular project.

Solar hot water systems ▾

Solar water heating panels can be integrated into most types of hot water systems, including combi boilers. The panels, called collectors, must be fitted on a roof that has sunlight for the main part of the day. They collect the sun's heat, which is used to warm water stored in a hot water cylinder. You will still need a boiler or immersion heater to make the water hot enough for general use, and to provide hot water when the sun isn't shining, but a solar system can typically fulfil up to a third of your hot water requirements using free energy from the sun. The panels will also prolong the life of your boiler and could add value to your house.

Ground source heat pumps

The ground stores the heat from the sun (solar energy) and maintains a fairly constant temperature all year round. Ground source heat pumps extract this heat and use it to warm water for underfloor heating systems, radiators or even hot water systems. They work in the same way as a refrigerator, except in reverse. A loop of pipe, known as a heat exchanger, is filled with water mixed with some antifreeze and buried in the garden. A heat pump inside the house pumps the water around the loop where it absorbs heat from the ground. When it comes back to the pump, a compressor increases its temperature before its heat is distributed within the house.

Air source heat pumps

Air source heat pumps work in a similar way to ground source pumps but extract heat from the outside air. The pump, which looks a bit like an air conditioning unit, is fixed on the exterior of the house. The pump's heat exchanger absorbs heat from the air and then the compressor raises the temperature of the air so it can either heat water for an underfloor heating system or produce warm air for circulation by fans. These pumps are cheaper to install than ground source heat pumps, but are less energy efficient when the weather is cold and the pump has to work harder to heat the air.

Wood-fuelled stoves and boilers ▾

Wood is classed as a carbon-neutral fuel. This is because the carbon dioxide emitted when it is burned is equal to that absorbed by the tree in its lifetime. As long as the tree is replaced, and its wood is not transported over long distances, this is a sustainable source of energy.

Woodburners generate far more heat than an open fire (which loses much of its heat up the chimney). Larger ones may be fitted with a back boiler to provide hot water. Stoves designed to burn wood pellets made from waste wood products have heating controls and thermostats. A woodburning boiler burning logs, wood chips or pellets can heat water and radiators.

Inside
the home

The ground floor of a house may be a solid floor sitting on a base of concrete and hardcore laid on the ground, or it may be a suspended floor built above the ground on joists. Floors on the first storey and above are always suspended.

Foundations

The floors of a house rest on the foundations, a solid base that supports the whole weight of the house. The loadbearing strength of the soil on which the house is built determines the type and depth of the foundations. Trench foundations are made by digging out trenches and filling them with concrete, then the external walls are built on top of them and a slab of concrete about 100mm–150mm thick is laid within the walls. Raft foundations consist of a reinforced-concrete slab laid on a layer of hardcore (coarse rubble), which covers the whole ground area and forms a base on which the walls are built.

Solid floors

A solid floor normally consists of several layers, although some old houses have flagstones or quarry tiles laid straight on top of the ground.

Screed

On top of the concrete there is a smooth screed of sand and cement. This is covered with the surface flooring, which may be wooden floorboards, man-made boards, tiles or carpet.

Insulation

Newly built houses must have a layer of thermal insulation beneath the ground floor. In a solid floor, this consists of rigid slabs of glass wool or polyfoam, laid either above or below the concrete. A strip of the same material is usually also run vertically at the edge to minimise heat loss at the bottom of the wall.

Damp-proof membrane

The damp-proof membrane (DPM) is a layer of moisture-resistant material that is usually laid on the layer of hardcore, although sometimes the concrete slab is laid first. The membrane may be either a thick sheet of polythene or a liquid coating of asphalt or bituminous material. The damp-proof membrane must be joined to the damp-proof course (DPC) in the walls. The damp-proof course is a layer of impervious material, such as polythene or bituminous felt, built into a joint between brick courses 150mm above the ground to prevent moisture rising from the ground into the walls.

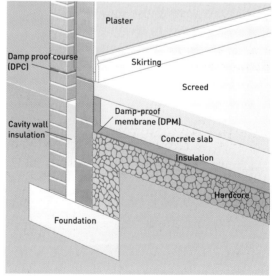

A solid floor on trench foundations

When the floor is built on trench foundations, it is constructed after the first few rows (courses) of bricks for the external walls have been laid above ground. The topsoil within the walls is removed, then hardcore is laid to level the ground. The rough surface of the hardcore is covered with a layer of sand before the damp-proof membrane, insulation, and concrete slab are laid.

Floor insulation
Thermal insulation under a solid or suspended ground floor helps to retain heat and keep your energy bills down.

Suspended floors

A suspended floor may be made of wooden floorboards or man-made boards set on timber beams called joists.

Ground floor

The joists supporting a ground floor sit on low sleeper walls inside the external walls. The bricks of the sleeper walls are laid in a honeycomb pattern to allow air to circulate freely. Alternatively, the ends of the joists slot into gaps or joist sockets in the outer walls, where they rest on timber beams called wall plates that are built into the wall. Often there will be sleeper walls in the middle of the floor space to give the joists extra support. Blocks of thermal insulation are positioned between the floor joists, supported by polypropylene netting. All the timbers are above the level of the damp-proof course to protect them from rising damp. Sleeper walls are also topped with a damp-proof course, then a timber wall plate to which the joists are secured.

Floorboards

Floorboards or chipboard are laid on top of the joists. Modern floorboards are most often tongue-and-groove design and slot together, while older ones are usually thicker and have straight edges that fit side by side. Flooring-grade chipboard may have either tongue-and-groove or straight edges.

Upper floors

Joists above the ground floor are fixed at each end but are unsupported in the middle. They may slot into sockets in the external walls or into metal joist hangers attached to the walls. Consequently upper floor joists need to be deeper than those on the ground floor to ensure they remain rigid without intermediate support; they also usually span shorter distances. For extra reinforcement, the joists may have wooden or metal supports called strutting nailed between them.

Suspended concrete floors

Timber is costly, and some houses have suspended concrete floors instead of wood. Rows of pre-cast concrete joists, which are shaped to hold concrete blocks, are placed on sleeper walls. Concrete blocks are set between the joists and covered with a concrete screed.

Flooring

A suspended floor made from soft- or hardwood boards can be sanded and sealed (see pages 40–41), or used as a sub-base for another flooring – carpet, laminate, vinyl or tiles. A concrete screed can serve as a sub-base (provided it is level and dry) or be covered first with flooring-grade plywood, chipboard or medium-density fibreboard (MDF).

A suspended ground floor

Plaster · Skirting · Solid wall · Floorboards · Damp-proof course (DPC) · Wall plate · Polypropylene netting · Block insulation · Floor joist · Damp-proof membrane (DPM) · Wall plate · Concrete slab · Honeycomb sleeper wall · Foundation

Underfloor heating
Heating pipes installed under the floor spread heat evenly around the room and create a luxurious warmth underfoot. Because there are no radiators, you can place furniture where you like and make more efficient use of the space. See also page 326.

Choosing flooring

Flooring is very much a matter of personal taste. But do give consideration to the practical pros and cons. If a family member is asthmatic, getting rid of carpets may make their life more comfortable; on the other hand, stripped wooden floors in a first-floor flat can be very noisy and may make you an unpopular neighbour.

CHOOSING FLOORING		
Flooring	**Advantages**	**Disadvantages**
Laminate and engineered real wood	Attractive, polished-wood look at less cost than new floorboards. Different finishes and wide range of colours.	May be damaged by heavy furniture. Not all types suitable for kitchens and bathrooms. Can be noisy if laid without sound-insulating underlay.
Solid wood	Attractive, timeless floor that will mellow with age and last a lifetime if properly cared for.	As above.
Carpet	Large range of colours, designs and prices. Warm feel.	Good quality carpet is expensive. Spills can stain. May trap dust and allergens.
Sheet vinyl	Cheap and easy to clean. Cushioned vinyl is more comfortable to walk on, but more expensive.	Smooth vinyl feels cold underfoot and is slippery when wet.
Vinyl tiles	Large range of colours and designs. Easy to clean.	Can be slippery when wet.
Cork tiles	Warmer than vinyl. Easy to clean if varnished or sealed.	Do not wear well in areas of heavy use unless you choose the more expensive PVC-coated type.
Hard tiles	Hardwearing, resistant to stains and spills. Easy to clean.	Cold to bare feet.

A staircase can be anything from a simple straight flight of steps running from one floor to the next, to a grand feature with intricately carved balustrades. Even in an ordinary house it may curve or change direction, and there may be one or more intermediate landings between floors.

Parts of a staircase

The flat part of each stair (the part that you walk on) is called the tread. The vertical pieces that close off the treads are the risers. Treads and risers slot into long timbers on each side of the stairs called strings. Vertical balusters fit between the outer string and a handrail. Wider staircases are supported by a length of timber (the central bearer, or 'carriage piece') fixed underneath the stairs.

Treads and risers

The treads and risers in a staircase may have tongue-and-groove joints, or they may be nailed or glued together. The joints between them are often reinforced from beneath with triangular wedges of wood that are glued in place. The rounded front edges of the treads are known as the nosings. Some staircases have moulding the same shape as the nosings fixed to the cut end of the treads. The treads of a straight staircase are all the same shape; but if a staircase changes direction at some point, specially shaped treads called winders are needed as it turns the corner.

Open-tread stairs are built without risers. The treads are likely to be thicker than in a standard staircase, and horizontal rods or rails are fixed across the gap to ensure that no child can squeeze through.

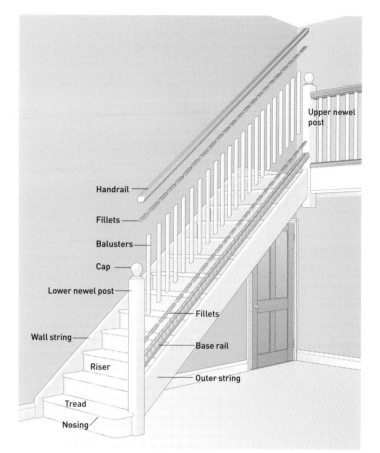

Upper newel post

Handrail

Fillets

Balusters

Cap

Lower newel post

Wall string

Riser

Tread

Nosing

Fillets

Base rail

Outer string

Strings

The strings run the full length of a staircase from one floor to the next, on each side of the stairs. The wall string is screwed to the wall beneath the treads. The outer string may be 'closed' or 'cut' (see below).

Handrail

Fillets

Wall string

Balusters

Fillets

Base rail

Tread

Riser

Closed outer string

◀ Closed string construction

A closed string has parallel top and bottom edges. The treads and risers are fitted into narrow channels (housings) cut in the inner face of the string. They are secured with wedges of wood driven in from the underside and glued in place. The balusters shown here are fitted to the handrail and base rail between small lengths (fillets) of wood.

Cut string construction ▶

A cut string follows the shape of the steps. The treads are nailed on to the horizontal sections and the outer ends of the risers are cut to fit the vertical edges of the string. Here the balusters fit into housings cut in the treads and the cut ends of the treads are covered by lengths of moulding matching the nosings on the front.

Tread

Riser

Moulding

Cut outer string

Balustrade

On the open side of the staircase vertical balusters are attached to the outer string at the bottom and a handrail at the top. They can be fitted in various ways (see below). Small wooden fillets may be fitted between the balusters to keep them evenly spaced. The handrail is held in place by newel posts. The balusters, handrail and string together make up the balustrade or banisters.

Butt-joint

Balusters may be simply butt-jointed and fixed to the handrail at the top and the string at the bottom by nails hammered through them at an angle.

Projecting stub

Some balusters have a projecting stub on each end (known as a stub-tenon) that fits into a corresponding recess (mortise) cut in the underside of the handrail, and in the edge of a closed string or tread of a cut string staircase.

Housed balusters

Alternatively, balusters may be 'housed' or fitted into slots cut in the underside of the handrail and in the edge of a closed string or the treads of a cut string staircase. Some balusters are housed at the bottom, but nailed at the top.

Handrail

Staircases normally have at least one handrail; some have one on both sides. A handrail along the wall is attached with screws or brackets. The outer handrail is fixed to newel posts at the top and bottom of the stairs.

Newel posts

The newel posts hold the outer handrail in place and make the staircase stronger. The newel post at the bottom of the stairs is fixed to the floor and the top one may be fixed to the ground floor or the landing. The handrail is bolted to the newel posts with special angled metal handrail brackets. When the bolts have been tightened, cover caps are fitted to hide the nuts.

Newel posts often have a decorative cap on top, and grander staircases may feature beautifully carved newel posts.

Newel post bracket

Under the stairs

The space below the staircase is known as the spandrel, and it is often enclosed to make a cupboard. If the underneath of the stairs is not plastered, you can gain access to them from inside the cupboard.

safety first

A stair balustrade should be no less than 900mm high and no more than 1m, with the measurement taken vertically from the pitch line – the line formed by the front of the treads. A balustrade edging a landing or upper floor must also be no less than 900mm high. The spaces between the balusters should not allow a 100mm-diameter sphere to pass between them, and the construction must not allow a child to climb over. The width of the treads, from back to front, must be at least 220mm.

Over the years, floorboards and stairs can work loose from their fittings, or dry out and shrink slightly, causing creaks and squeaks when you walk on them. If you take up a carpet in order to sand and seal a wooden floor, be sure to check for loose boards first – carpet and other floorcoverings can muffle a potentially infuriating problem.

Fixing creaking stairs

The way to fix a creaking stair depends on whether you can do the repair from underneath. If that would involve removing plaster from the underside of the stairs, it may be easier to work from above the stairs.

Fixes under stairs

Locate any loose steps by getting someone to walk up the stairs while you listen from underneath. Mark them with chalk. If the tread or riser has become loose in its string housing, the glued wedge securing the joint may have worked loose. Remove the wedge, clean it, apply PVA wood adhesive, then replace it.

Check the triangular blocks that fit in the angle between the treads and the risers. If they are not securely glued, remove them and scrape off the old adhesive. Prise open the tread/riser joint slightly and inject some adhesive. Apply adhesive to the block and press it in place, or screw it in place. If blocks were not fitted to the stairs, make some, each about 75mm long, and glue and screw them in place.

The joint between the back of a tread and the bottom of a riser can be strengthened by injecting PVA adhesive into the gap. Then drive three evenly spaced screws up through the tread and into the edge of the riser.

Screw through tread into riser

Screw triangular reinforcing blocks in place

Prise open joint and inject adhesive

Replace/renew wedges

Attach metal angle brackets

Screw down through tread into top of riser

Glue moulding into angle of tread and riser

Fixes above stairs

Another way to cure creaking stairs is to screw down the front of the tread on to the riser. Drill clearance holes (for the thick part of the screws – the shank) through the tread and thinner pilot holes (for the point of the screws) into the top of the riser. Then drill the clearance holes with a countersink bit so that the screws will be just below the surface when they are screwed in place. Inject some PVA wood adhesive into the holes then screw the screws in tightly. Cover the heads with filler, using wood filler if the stairs are uncarpeted.

If the loose joint is at the back of the tread, you can strengthen it by gluing a length of triangular moulding, 12mm x 12mm, into the angle between the tread and the riser (as long as it does not make the tread narrower than the regulation 220mm). Alternatively, screw two thin metal brackets into the angle between the tread and the riser. For a completely flush surface, cut out a recess for the brackets using a sharp chisel and mallet.

Fixing creaking floorboards

A floorboard creaks when some of its fixing nails have worked themselves loose, so that it is no longer firmly attached to the joists. If the board is in good condition, you can prise out the nails and screw it down using the existing nail holes. In older houses, where floorboards may have been lifted many times before, the board may be badly damaged at the sides and corners so it is usually best to make new holes for the screws. Before drilling new holes in a floorboard, first lift the board to check for pipes and cables.

1 Find the part of the floorboard that is loose by treading all over it and looking for movement. If the board is damaged and cannot be re-nailed in the old holes, prise out the nails with pincers, then lift the board to check for cables and pipes. Mark the top of the board in pencil to show their positions.

2 Drill a clearance hole in a sound part of the board, as near to the edge as you can. Insert the screw in the hole and screw it down firmly, seeing that it sits below the surface.

3 If the screw head projects above the surface, take it out, countersink the hole, and screw the board down again.

4 If you still have squeaks after re-fixing the boards, try sprinkling talcum powder along the joint and work it in with a knife. After a while, the squeaking should stop.

Timber treatment

Woodworm and dry rot can do great harm to structural timbers such as joists and roof timbers. Localised areas of woodworm infestation can be treated using a chemical insecticide. Major infestations should be treated by a specialist contractor, as should dry rot, which is far more serious.

1 Lift the floorboards. Wearing gloves, pour some timber treatment into a pot and brush it on to the affected joists according to the manufacturer's instructions.

2 Brush the underside of any floorboards showing signs of woodworm.

3 Turn the boards over and brush the top side with more of the insecticide.

 Making it easier

Spotting infestation
Woodworm holes are about 2mm in diameter. If dark in colour, they may have been treated before. Pale dust around the edge of a hole is a sign of recent activity and should be treated immediately. Wood that is infested with dry rot appears dry and spongy, with the fibres breaking down. Dry rot can do serious damage, and is best treated by a professional.

Over the years, floorboards may split, warp, shrink or break, and will need replacing. Or you may need to lift a board temporarily in order to access cables or pipes beneath. How you do this depends on whether your floor is made of tongue-and-groove boards, which are slotted together before being nailed to the joists, or square-edged boards, which are simply butted together.

Square-edged boards

Square-edged boards are easiest to take up. To remove a whole board that fits beneath the skirting at each end, however, you will have to saw through the board near the centre, or remove the skirtings (see page 78).

First locate any underfloor pipes and cables (see MAKING IT EASIER). Begin by driving a wide-bladed bolster chisel into the joint between the boards, close to one end. The blade will spread the load and keep damage to adjacent boards to a minimum.

Push down on the handle of the bolster chisel to prise the board up. Do the same on the other side until you can lift the end of the board high enough to insert a cold chisel or wooden wedge under it, to hold it clear of the joist.

Working on alternate sides of the board, insert the claw of your hammer under the edges and lever it higher. You can protect adjacent boards by placing a thin scrap of wood beneath the hammer head. Gradually work your way along the board.

When you have pulled most of the nails from the joists, you should be able to lift the free end of the board and lever up the remainder.

Replacing a section of board

If the damage affects only a small area of a floorboard, or if the board continues under the skirting, you may find it easier to cut out and replace a section rather than the whole board.

safety first

As soon as you lift a board, drive any projecting nails back through the wood, then prise them out with a claw hammer. This way you can't step on them. Any nails left in the joists should also be removed.

Prise the board up just enough to slide a length of wood beneath. Mark cutting lines with a try square and pencil, making sure they run along the centre-line of joists below.

Use a tenon saw to cut the section out, taking care not to damage adjacent boards and making sure that your cuts are square. Measure up for the replacement board. If the existing boards are not of a standard size, you may have to cut down a larger board to fit. If necessary, you can always notch the underside of a thicker board to fit over the joists.

Position the new board and secure with 50mm cut floor brads or ring-shanked nails, avoiding the existing holes in the joists. Drill pilot holes for the nails to prevent splitting. Alternatively, use 50mm countersunk screws (4mm or 5mm gauge).

Tongue-and-groove boards

A floor made from tongue-and-groove boards is more rigid and less likely to creak. However, to remove a board you will have to cut through the tongue. If replacing it, you will need a square-edged board.

First locate any underfloor pipes and cables (see MAKING IT EASIER). One way of freeing a board is to use a sharp, wide-bladed (at least 25mm) wood chisel and mallet to cut down through the tongues on each side.

Alternatively, use a floorboard saw (see IDEAL TOOL). To begin, hold the saw upside-down and work the curved tip of the blade back and forth to cut into the tongue.

project essentials

- pipe and cable detector
- wood chisel
- mallet
- floorboard saw
- padsaw
- narrow-bladed tool
- pencil
- try square
- ruler
- power drill with large wood bit

- 50mm x 25mm softwood batten
- 50mm cut floor brads or ring-shanked nails, or 50mm (4mm or 5mm gauge) countersunk screws

Once you have broken through the tongue, turn the saw over and continue cutting with the long edge of the blade. If the cut passes over a cable or pipe, use the curved edge of the blade again; work very slowly and apply minimal pressure so that you can control the blade as it breaks through the wood.

ideal tool

Floorboard saw

This saw will make lifting tongue-and-groove boards easier. In addition to teeth along one long edge, the blade has a curved tip with more teeth. This allows a cut to be started directly down into the tongue. It also permits cuts to be made across boards without lifting them or damaging adjacent boards.

Once you have sawn through the tongues each side of the board, you should be able to see the joists below. If not, feel for them with a narrow-bladed tool. Using a pencil and try square, mark cutting lines across the board, in line with the edges of the joists.

B&Q Making it easier

Locating underfloor pipes and cables

If you are lucky, you will find any pipes and cable runs already marked on the floorboards. Failing that, go over the area of floor you intend working on with an electronic pipe and cable detector. Look for signs that boards have been lifted before (damaged edges or multiple fixing holes). Mark the locations of any pipes or cables you find directly on the boards. Or if the boards are to be left exposed, draw up a paper plan and keep it somewhere safe.

Using a large wood bit and electric drill, bore a hole near one edge of the board so that it just touches the cutting line across the board.

safety first

Keep pets well out of the way whenever you lift floorboards. Before you nail the boards back down again double-check they haven't slipped underneath – getting trapped can be traumatic and dangerous for an animal.

Insert the blade of a padsaw into the hole and cut along the line to free the end of the board from the joist. Do the same at the other end. Now the board can be levered up in the same manner as a square-edged board (see Steps 1–4, opposite).

Having cut the ends of the board flush with the joists there will be nothing to nail or screw the board back into. Get around this by nailing or screwing 50mm x 25mm battens to the sides of the joists, making sure they are tight against the undersides of the neighbouring boards.

A change of floorcovering, be it vinyl, carpet or even ceramic tiles, can give a room a new lease of life. But before you start work, you must make sure that the underlying surface is sound and level. If it is not, the defects are likely to show through, spoiling the look of the new floor, and eventually resulting in uneven patterns of wear. Fortunately, there are simple ways of dealing with problem floors.

project essentials

- **old paint brush or plant spray bottle**
- **claw hammer**
- **plane or sanding block**
- **long-nosed pliers**
- **nail spacing stick**
- **panel saw**

- 3mm-thick 600mm x 1220mm hardboard sheets
- 19mm ring-shanked nails

Levelling a wood floor

Hardboard sheets will not only level a boarded floor but will also reduce draughts from below. Buy 3mm-thick sheets, which you must first condition by brushing or spraying water over the textured side before stacking them on the floor of the room, back to back, for 48 hours. This expands them very slightly and means they will dry and tighten rather than expand and buckle once laid. Before laying them, drive all floorboard nails below the surface and plane or sand down any boards that are proud of the rest. Fix the sheets in place with 19mm ring-shanked nails, which are too short to penetrate right through the floorboards and damage any pipes and cables below.

ideal tool

Long-nosed pliers

Use a pair of long-nosed pliers to hold a nail in position as you start it – not your fingers.

Lay the hardboard sheets textured side up (unless the instructions for the flooring that will cover them specify otherwise), as this will provide a key for the adhesive and accommodate the nail heads. Start in a corner of the room, setting the nails about 13mm in from the edges of the sheet in a pyramid pattern (see MAKING IT EASIER). Cut scraps of wood as nail spacing guides.

Butt the sheets tightly together, nailing along each meeting edge first, before continuing in pyramid fashion. When you reach the end of the first row of sheets, you will have to cut the last one to size.

Use the off-cut from the last sheet in the first row to start the second row. This will prevent wastage and ensure that the joints are staggered (see diagram, below). Continue in this way until you have finished the floor.

Staggered joints

By staggering the panel joints in adjacent rows, you will prevent the possibility of continuous undulations forming in the floor and showing through the floorcovering.

B&Q Making it easier

Pyramid nailing
To prevent hardboard sheets buckling as you nail them down, position nails in an expanding pyramid pattern, starting in the middle of one edge and gradually working across to the other side. Around the edge nails should be spaced at 150mm intervals, while in the centre they can be 225mm apart.

Replacing a wood floor

If a lot of floorboards are damaged, it will be cheaper and easier to pull them all up and fit tongue-and-groove chipboard flooring panels. These will provide a firm foundation for the final floorcovering.

project essentials

- claw hammer
- pencil
- try square
- panel saw or electric circular saw
- mallet

- tongue-and-groove chipboard flooring panels
- 50mm ring-shanked nails
- PVA wood adhesive

Start in the corner of the room. Lay the first panel so that its long side spans the joists and its end rests on a joist – if you need to cut it down, do so on the skirting edge. Position the board about 9mm from the wall to allow for expansion. Nail along the joists, beginning about 18mm from the edge, using 50mm ring-shanked nails spaced at 300mm intervals. Remember to mark on the boards the location of any pipes or cables beneath.

Check the fit of the next panel. If its tongued end does not meet a joist, cut it back as necessary. Then apply PVA wood adhesive to the end tongue of the first panel, slot the end groove of the second over the tongue, aligning the long edges, and nail down the second panel. Wipe off excess glue with a damp cloth.

If you shortened the second panel to meet a joist, the grooved end of the next will also need cutting off so that you can butt and glue them together over the joist. Cut the last board in the row to size, remembering to leave a 9mm expansion gap at the wall. Lay the first panel of the second row against the last panel of the first so the joints are staggered.

Make sure the panels fit tightly by driving each into place with a grooved panel off-cut. Continue until you reach the far side of the room, staggering the joints and allowing an expansion gap at the wall. Measure and cut the last row of boards to fit.

Levelling a concrete floor

Provided a solid concrete floor is basically sound, the simplest way of levelling it is with a latex self-levelling compound. This is poured on to the floor and trowelled fairly smooth. Any cracks or holes should be repaired first.

project essentials

- **old paint brush**
- **small trowel**
- **bucket**
- **stirring stick**
- **plasterer's trowel**

- sand/cement mortar
- latex self-levelling flooring compound

B&Q Making it easier

Smooth it over
If your trowel marks are still visible after a couple of minutes, sprinkle water on them and smooth the compound again.

Dampen cracks or holes by brushing them with water. This will stop your filler from drying out too quickly and cracking.

Fill large cracks or holes with a sand/cement mortar mix. Smaller ones can be treated with self-levelling compound. Trowel smooth and leave to harden. Once the floor has set, prepare it for the compound by pouring a little water on to the floor and brushing it out to dampen the surface. Do not flood it!

Mix the compound as instructed. Starting in the corner furthest from the door, pour it on to the floor and spread it to a thickness of about 3mm with a plasterer's trowel, using long, sweeping strokes. While you are doing this, get a helper to mix the next bucketful of compound.

Work quickly, but carefully; it will set in about 15 minutes, and you should be able to walk on the floor in a few hours.

You can greatly enhance the look of a room by stripping a boarded floor back to the bare wood and sealing it with a varnish, so that the beauty of the wood grain shows through. It is a dusty and noisy job, however, and as with so many home improvement projects the quality of the finish will largely depend on the effort you put into the preparation.

Preparing the floor

Before you begin sanding a floor, you must make sure that it is ready to be sanded, and that it will look good when finished. The boards must be in good condition, with no wide gaps or protruding nails.

1 Drive all the nails below the surface with a hammer and punch; protruding nails will tear a sanding sheet. Nail down loose boards and replace damaged ones, ideally using boards of similar age – you may be able to take these from other rooms in your home where the floorboards are not exposed.

2 Fill the gaps between the boards (see MAKING IT EASIER). If the gaps are very wide, you may be better off lifting and re-laying the boards more tightly, filling the final gap with an extra board. Otherwise, you can glue in narrow strips of wood, as illustrated.

3 Leave the filler strips slightly proud, and let the glue dry. Then plane or sand down the strips until they are flush with the surrounding boards. Sweep the floor clean.

Sanding the boards

To sand floorboards effectively, you will need to hire a heavy-duty industrial drum sander and rotary edge sander; make sure you are shown how to change the abrasive sheets. Sanding produces a lot of dust, so seal doors to other parts of the house with masking tape, and sweep up after each sanding pass.

1 Fit a coarse abrasive sheet to the drum sander and work across the floor in overlapping diagonal strips. Sweep up the dust and repeat the process, working at right angles to the first sanding pass.

2 Each time you start or stop the machine, tilt the drum clear of the boards to stop it damaging them.

B&Q Making it easier

Mind the gaps
Papier mâché makes a good filler for gaps between floorboards. Mix a stiff paste with torn strips of newspaper (not coloured) and wallpaper adhesive. Colour this with a little water-based wood dye to match the sanded floor. Force the papier mâché into the gaps and smooth off flush with the boards. Allow to dry before sanding.

Having levelled the boards by sanding diagonally, fit medium-grade paper to the drum and sand parallel to the boards, again overlapping each pass. Then finish off with fine-grade paper in the same manner. Do not work across the grain of the boards, as this will leave visible marks.

The drum sander will not sand right up to the skirting – for this you need the rotary edge sander. Use coarse, medium and fine grades of abrasive paper and keep it moving, otherwise it will score deep marks in the floor. Tilt the machine as you start and stop the disc.

Finish the corners and inaccessible areas with abrasive paper wrapped around a sanding block or – much easier – a powered hand sander (see IDEAL TOOL).

Sealing the boards

You can use a clear or tinted varnish to seal the sanded floorboards. Apply three coats for a really hardwearing finish. Make sure the brush is completely clean before you start.

Sweep the sanded floor thoroughly, then vacuum it. Finally, go over it with a lint-free cloth dampened with white spirit.

Thin the varnish for the first coat with 10% white spirit to make it more workable. The first coat seals the wood; working towards the door, brush out the varnish in the direction of the wood grain, making sure no pools form.

When the first coat has dried, remove any lumps or specks with fine abrasive paper and wipe clean with a lint-free cloth dampened with white spirit. Apply a second, unthinned coat and allow to dry. Then apply the final coat.

FLOORS LAMINATE AND WOOD FLOORING

Laminate flooring is available in a wide range of colours and decorative effects to suit any style of interior, and is surprisingly quick and easy to install. Engineered real wood flooring is laid in exactly the same way but has a surface layer of real wood that brings an authentic natural finish to your interior. Solid wood flooring has a unique natural beauty and character that, if properly cared for, can last a lifetime.

Choosing laminate flooring

Laminate flooring is extremely hard-wearing and virtually maintenance-free, making it ideal in the busiest parts of the house such as the hallway and living room. Whether you prefer a pale contemporary finish or the rich tones of tropical hardwood, there is a wood-effect laminate to suit you. You don't have to just use one shade: you could mix different colours to complement your interior and subtly partition the space. Not all laminate flooring has a wood finish. There are also tile-effect laminates on the market – terracotta, slate or ceramic – that look absolutely convincing but are warmer and gentler underfoot than a true tile floor.

When choosing flooring, it's important to take into account where it will be installed and how much traffic and moisture it will have to withstand. For a kitchen or bathroom, choose a splash-resistant laminate flooring with a water-resistant core (though be aware that even this will not take a soaking).

Laminate flooring

- Overlay
- Printed decoration
- High-density fibreboard
- Counterbalance

Choosing real wood flooring

Engineered real wood flooring adds an extra touch of luxury and style to a room. It combines the authentic look of solid wood with the speed and ease of installation of laminate flooring. The multi-layer construction makes the boards very stable and helps to minimise expansion and contraction. The real wood veneer is slightly less hardwearing than laminate, but it can be lightly sanded and relacquered two to three times and can also be polished to an attractive lustre. Engineered real wood flooring is particularly suited to a bedroom, study or conservatory – dry living spaces that generally aren't subjected to the heaviest wear.

Engineered real wood flooring

- Lacquer
- Real wood veneer
- Cross-laid spruce or high-density fibreboard
- Counterbalance

Choosing solid wood flooring

Solid wood flooring is, as the name suggests, made from solid wooden planks or boards. The natural grain of the wood is lacquered or oiled to produce a range of different finishes including smooth, brushed, hand scraped and sculpted. Solid wood floors mark and mellow over time, enhancing their look with age and adding to their natural charm. They can be sanded and relacquered up to four times.

Laying flooring

Any smooth, flat surface is suitable for laying laminate or wood flooring, as long as it is dry, firm and level. In most cases you need to strip away all existing floor coverings to reach the concrete or wooden sub-floor, though you can lay laminate or wood flooring over ceramic or vinyl tiles (but not over carpet, sheet vinyl or matting). For durability, noise reduction and comfort, it is essential to lay an appropriate underlay before installing the boards. A damp-proof membrane is recommended in any area where damp could become a problem. See pages 44–45 for more detail on preparing to lay new flooring.

Laminate and wood flooring is laid 'floating', which means there are no fixings attaching it to the floor below. It requires an expansion gap around all the edges of the room, including across doorways. This allows it to expand and contract slightly without buckling.

You can lay laminate or wood flooring up to existing skirting-boards and cover the expansion gap at the edges with special flooring trim (see page 47), or you could remove and replace the skirting.

Tongue-and-groove fitting systems

As well as the LOC system, solid wood flooring is available with more traditional tongue-and-groove edges which push together to create a simple joint. Because the joints can easily come loose, this type of flooring does need extra fixing. The boards can be laid on self-adhesive underlay, which holds them together without the need for glue or nails. Alternatively you can secure the boards to a timber sub-floor by secret nailing. Or you can glue them to the sub-floor (which must be dust-free and perfectly level). Underlay is not required when nailing or gluing to the sub-floor.

Glueless locking systems

The innovative LOC system is the perfect choice for quick and easy installation. The boards have long and short tongues on their sides and ends which lock together to create tight joints that need no glue. You can walk on the floor as soon as it is laid. The boards can easily be taken up again if you make a mistake while laying the floor, or if at any stage you want to move them or replace a damaged board.

All three types of flooring – laminate, real wood and even solid wood – are now available with the easy-fit LOC system.

Caring for flooring

Always lift and move furniture carefully to avoid scratches. Felt pads and/or castor cups under the feet of chairs and heavy furniture will help prevent dents. In a home office or any room where you use a desk chair, place a mat under the chair to protect the flooring from damage by the wheels. Place a rug or mat inside the front and back doors and in front of a hand basin or sink to protect from marks or spills. Any spills that do happen can be simply wiped away with a damp cloth.

Specially formulated cleaners provide a quick and easy way to clean a laminate floor, and repair kits are available for filling any chips. Don't wash, wax or varnish a laminate floor.

Protecting forestry
All B&Q wood flooring comes from sustainably managed forests certified by independent organisations such as the Forest Stewardship Council (FSC). So you can rest assured that the product you are buying has not contributed to the destruction of the world's forests.

As with all home-improvements, preparation pays when laying laminate or wood flooring. The sub-floor needs to be smooth, dry and level. And before the flooring goes down, you need an underlay, which will make the flooring easier to fit and longer lasting, as well as improving sound insulation.

Laying over a concrete floor

If you are installing over an existing concrete floor, the concrete must be checked for moisture. This is most easily done with a moisture meter. Alternatively, you can tape a sheet of polythene of about 1 square metre to the surface of the concrete. Tape all four edges to the floor and leave overnight. Presence of moisture will be confirmed either if the concrete is discoloured, or condensation has appeared on the underside of the polythene. If this is the case, you will need to seek specialist advice from a damp-proofing expert.

A newly concreted floor must be completely dry before you lay new flooring: allow one day per 1mm thickness of new concrete. If an old concrete floor is uneven, level it with self-levelling compound (see page 39).

How much to buy?

Before you start make sure you have sufficient packs to complete the project. To work out how many you need, calculate the area of your room. Measure the room's length (A) and width (B) in metres and multiply these together to find the area in square metres. If you have an irregularly shaped room, divide it into separate rectangular areas and calculate each individually. Add the figures up to get the total room area and divide this by the coverage per pack as stated by the manufacturer. You should allow an extra 10% for wastage. Unopened packs can be returned for a refund.

You also need to measure the perimeter of the room – the distance around the edge – to find out how much flooring trim or skirting to buy. Again, allow an extra 10% for wastage.

Laying over floorboards

If you are laying over floorboards, make sure all the boards are firmly screwed down and flatten nails with a hammer. Wide gaps between floorboards can be filled with mastic or thin wedges of wood glued in place and planed flush with the boards when dry. If the existing floor is very uneven, you will need to level it with plywood or hardboard sheets (see page 38). Your new flooring should be laid over an underlay at 90° to the existing floorboards. When laying over an existing wooden floor a damp-proof membrane is not required.

Acclimatising new flooring

To prevent warping, the flooring should be allowed to acclimatise for 48 hours in the room in which it is to be fitted. Stack the boards flat, in their packaging, in such a way that air can circulate between the packs. Raise them off the floor on off-cuts of wood. Don't be tempted to lean them against the wall: this could cause them to bow.

Choosing underlay

All sub-floors need to be fitted with an underlay before laminate flooring can be laid. Concrete, asphalt, vinyl, quarry or similar tiled sub-floors should be covered first with a plastic-film moisture barrier (a damp-proof membrane), in addition to any damp-proof course that may be present in the sub-floor. Or you could choose a combined underlay and damp-proof membrane (see below). Never lay laminate or wood flooring over carpet underlay, which is totally unsuitable for the job. Sweep or vacuum the prepared floor thoroughly before laying underlay.

Combined underlay and damp-proof membrane

The advantage of combined underlay is that whatever your sub-floor, you only have to fit one layer rather than two. It is thicker than poly foam underlay so will absorb very slight irregularities in the floor, and it provides good sound insulation.

1 Prepare the floor. Lay the underlay over the entire floor area, placing the lengths side by side. Trim to fit with scissors or a knife.

2 Tape the joins securely, making sure the lengths do not overlap.

Wood fibre

This is the thickest of the underlays used beneath laminate flooring, and the one you will need to use if you have a slightly uneven sub-floor. Because they are more substantial, wood fibre boards also give good heat and sound insulation, though they are not suitable for splash areas.

Prepare the floor and if necessary lay a damp-proof membrane. Tape any joints with a waterproof jointing tape. If you are removing old skirtings lap the damp-proof membrane about 50mm up the walls.

The underlay boards should be left to acclimatise in the room for 24 hours. Stagger the joints and leave a 10mm expansion gap around the edge of the room and 5mm between the boards. The boards should be loose laid at 90° to the intended direction of the new flooring. They can be cut to fit easily with a knife and straightedge over an off-cut of wood.

Poly foam underlay

This is the thinnest of the underlays used beneath laminate flooring, and is suitable for any firm, dry and level sub-floor, such as a wooden floor. Prepare the floor and if necessary lay a damp-proof membrane. Lay the poly foam underlay over the entire floor area. Trim to fit with scissors or a knife, allowing a 10mm gap around pipes. Lay lengths side by side and secure with masking tape.

Setting out

First decide in which direction you want to lay the boards. Lengthways towards a light source is ideal, as this makes the joins less visible. Laying boards in the direction of the longest wall can create an illusion of length; or you can make a room feel wider by running the boards widthways. However, if laying over a timber sub-floor you should lay the new floor at 90° to the direction of the sub-floor boards for the most stable and solid result.

Obstacles and cuts

Next think about any obstacles such as radiator pipes that you will have to cut the flooring to accommodate. Such cuts will be easier and tidier if they fall in the middle of a board's length or width rather than on a join.

You also want to avoid the last row being less than a third of the width of a board. Divide the total length of the room by the width of the boards (remember to allow for the expansion gap at each wall: see page 46). If the last row will be very narrow, it will be easier to cut the first row to less than a full width. Also loose lay the first row to check that you won't be left with a very short strip at the end.

safety first

Protect yourself
Laying flooring is very hard on the knees, so let a pair of knee pads take some of the strain. Wear a dust mask and safety goggles while you cut the boards, and ear defenders when using power tools. Ensure the room is properly ventilated.

The glueless LOC system makes easy work of fitting new flooring. It is quick, clean and needs no specialist tools. You will need to cut boards to fit and to accommodate obstacles like radiator pipes. This isn't difficult, especially if you always follow the old motto: measure twice, cut once.

Creating an expansion gap

Laminate and wood flooring expands and contracts with changes in temperature and humidity, so it's essential to leave an expansion gap of at least 10mm all around the edges of the floor, including across doorways and around any fittings such as a basin pedestal or toilet, and 15mm in the case of solid wood flooring. Otherwise you could find that your floor begins to buckle. Specially designed fitting wedges or expansion spacers make it easy to create this gap. Adjustable spacers (pictured) can compensate for slight irregularities in walls or skirting. Don't worry about the gap, which can be hidden with flooring trim or new skirting.

Fitting locking laminate

It's important to acclimatise the boards before you fit them, or they could warp: see page 44. There is no need to remove the skirting, but if you do, damp-proof membrane should be allowed to lap about 50mm up the walls (see page 48). The joints between boards should be staggered, random and more than 300mm apart for the best result. Locking systems do vary slightly between manufacturers, so always check the fitting instructions supplied with your flooring.

project essentials

- **knee pads**
- **try square**
- **pencil**
- **ruler**
- **dust mask**
- **safety goggles**
- **ear defenders**
- **workbench and clamps**
- **hardpoint handsaw or jigsaw with laminate blade**
- **mitre saw or trim cutters**

- locking laminate flooring
- expansion spacers
- reusable tack
- radiator pipe hole covers
- flooring trim
- grab adhesive
- threshold bar

1 Lay the first board in a left-hand corner over the underlay, the end with the short tongue against the wall. Insert expansion spacers against the end of the board and at intervals along the wall, including at the point where boards are joined.

2 Lay the next board end-on, placing its short tongue into the long tongue of the first board at a 30° angle. Lower the board and lock it into place. Continue to the end of the row, where you will probably have to cut a board to fit.

3 To measure the last board, turn it 180° and lay it next to the previous one, with an expansion spacer against the skirting. Using a try square and pencil, draw a line across the board level with the end of the previous one. Check the fit, then cut to size and insert to complete the first row. If the off-cut is more than 300mm, it can be used to start the next row; otherwise cut a board in half.

4 To start the next row, angle the cut board against the first board of the previous row, with the cut end against the wall. Press forward and down to lock it in place. Repeat along the row.

Alternatively, clip a whole row of boards together. Then with a helper lift the row to an angle of roughly 30° and push down to lock the long edges together.

5 To cut boards to fit the last row, place one at a time directly over the previous row, in the direction that it will be laid. Hold it in place with a little reusable tack. Then align a third board on top with its tongue touching the skirting. Use the edge of this board to mark the cutting line with a pencil on the board beneath.

Cutting the boards

Ideally you should do all your cutting in another room, a workshop, or outdoors if the weather is dry. This will prevent dust and debris getting on your sub-floor or underlay.

It is easiest to clamp boards to a work bench to cut them. You can use a handsaw or jigsaw (below left). Cut them face up when using a handsaw or a jigsaw with a laminate blade, but face down if using a jigsaw with a wood blade. A laminate blade will give the best results, and it's a good idea to have several spares to hand as your cuts will get rougher as the blade deteriorates.

If you are doing a lot of cutting, a fixed saw such as a compound mitre pull saw (right) will cut with accuracy and minimal effort.

Cutting around pipes

Most rooms contain at least one radiator, supported by pipes. It's straightforward to cut notches into the boards to fit around the pipes: see page 48. You can cover the holes with pipe hole covers.

Flooring trim

Once the flooring is laid, remove the expansion spacers and cover the gap around the room with a laminate flooring trim, chosen to match your floor. The trim should be glued to the skirting, not the floor.

Measure and cut lengths of laminate flooring trim. For a really neat finish use a mitre saw, as shown, to cut the corners to a 45° angle. Alternatively you could use an ordinary tenon saw and mitre block, or trim cutters.

Apply a suitable grab adhesive to the back of a length of flooring trim (not the base) so that it will stick to the skirting-board rather than the floor. Press the trim in place and hold it firm with a couple of heavy books while the adhesive dries. Or you can use panel pins to tack it in place as it dries.

ideal tool

Trim cutters

With a built-in guide for a range of different cutting angles, these trim cutters make quick, neat work of cutting flooring trim.

Fitting around door frames

If the door opens into the room, check that it will open over the new flooring and threshold bar: if not, you will need to remove it and cut or plane a strip off the bottom (see page 124).

If the architrave extends beyond the skirting, don't try to cut the flooring to fit around it. You'll achieve a neater finish by trimming the architrave so the underlay and flooring will fit below it. Don't forget to allow a 10mm expansion gap at the wall beneath the architrave.

Lay a board on a piece of underlay beside the door frame. Then place a panel saw flat on the board and cut through the bottom of the architrave.

Use a wood chisel to remove the waste piece of wood.

Finishing touches

Don't worry if your cutting is slightly less than perfect: radiator pipe hole covers, threshold bars and flooring trim can help to hide untidy edges, as well as the essential expansion gap all around the room.

Radiator pipe hole covers

These wood-effect discs cover any untidiness around holes cut for radiator pipes. Some clip into place around the base of the pipe, while others are flat discs that are glued down. Look for natural wood pipe covers and trims to complement engineered real wood and solid wood flooring.

Threshold bar

This is fitted in a doorway to make a neat join between the new floor and the flooring in the next room. Even if you are fitting laminate across the threshold, you still need a threshold bar to cover the essential expansion gap across the doorway. There are bars designed for joining laminate or wood to vinyl, carpet or to other common floorings (see page 61). Some have a base and a cover, others are a single strip. They are simply cut to the width of the doorway and glued or screwed in place, depending on the design.

project essentials

- knee pads
- try square
- pencil
- dust mask
- safety goggles
- ear defenders
- workbench and clamps
- hardpoint handsaw
- jigsaw with new hardwood blade
- power drill with 32mm spade bit or 32mm holesaw
- hacksaw

- solid wood flooring
- expansion spacers
- reusable tack
- wood adhesive
- radiator pipe hole covers
- threshold bar
- skirting, if required
- architrave, if required

Thanks to the glueless locking system, solid wood flooring is now as easy to lay as laminate. It is a bigger investment, but with proper care it will give you a lifetime's good looks and character. Don't forget to acclimatise the boards before fitting them, and be sure to lay a suitable underlay over a flat, level floor surface (see pages 44–45).

Starting in a left-hand corner, begin laying the boards with their short tongue against the wall. Lower and click boards end to end to form a row. Insert expansion spacers at regular intervals along the wall, including at the points where the boards join.

Laying a locking solid wood floor

Arrange the different-sized boards in a random pattern, ensuring that the joints are staggered and there is an expansion gap of 15mm around all the edges of the room. If removing skirting-boards, as here, then you should allow the damp-proof membrane to lap up the walls by 50mm. See pages 78–79 for how to remove and replace skirting-boards.

At the end of a row, turn the final board 180° and lay it next to the previous one, with an expansion spacer against the wall. Using a try square and pencil, draw a line across the board level with the end of the previous one. Cut to size. If using a jigsaw cut the board face down; if using a handsaw cut face up.

To fit the last row, place one board at a time directly over the previous row. Hold it in place with a little reusable tack. Align a third board on top with its tongue touching the wall. Use the edge of this board to mark the cutting line on the board beneath. Cut the board and ease into position.

Cutting around pipes

It's likely you will have to cut boards to fit around radiator pipes. This simple technique will give you an almost invisible result. Standard radiator pipes are 15mm in diameter, so a 32mm drill bit or holesaw will create a hole big enough for the pipe and the expansion gap.

Lay the board in position next to the pipe. Measure and mark the centre point of the pipe position on the board, remembering the expansion gap at the wall.

Use a power drill with 32mm spade bit or 32mm holesaw to cut a hole at the pipe position.

Draw two lines from the hole to the edge of the board, each on a slight outward angle. Cut neatly along the pencil lines with a handsaw and retain the wedge-shaped off-cut.

Fit the board, then glue the wedge in place. Wipe any excess adhesive immediately. Hide the cut with a pipe hole cover.

Making it easier

The last row

The final row of boards should be at least 50mm wide. You may need to cut the first row to avoid a narrow strip. See Setting out, page 45.

Making difficult cuts

You may well need to cut boards to fit around an alcove, or in a recess or bay. Be especially careful to take precise measurements, remembering to allow for the 15mm expansion gap.

Carefully measure and mark the shape to be cut on the board using a try square and pencil.

Transfer the measurements to the reverse of the board and cut using a jigsaw.

Neat doorways

If you are not replacing the architrave, cut a slot at the bottom on each side for a neat finish (see page 47). Choose a threshold bar that will match your new floor and is designed to join a wooden floor to the type of flooring in the next room (see page 61). The join should be positioned so that it is invisible when the door is closed. Profiling the threshold bar to fit snugly around the doorstops, as shown here, will give a really professional look.

Carefully measure and mark a notch to be cut from each end of the threshold bar so that it will fit perfectly against the doorstops on each side.

Cut the notches with a hacksaw and fit the bar in place in accordance with the manufacturer's instructions.

Finishing touches

You can reuse your old skirting provided it is wide enough to cover the expansion gap. But if it is old or damaged, this is a great opportunity to replace it. Skirting and architrave is available to match some flooring ranges. But don't worry if not: you can always buy softwood or hardwood skirting and architrave, and then stain and varnish it to match your new floor. Be sure to test the colour on an off-cut first.

New skirting

Replacement skirting can either be nailed or glued to the walls (not the floor), covering the expansion gap and any visible damp-proof membrane. A skirting-board mitre tool will make easy work of cutting mitres for both internal and external corners. See pages 78–79 for how to replace skirting.

Architrave

Matching architrave – the timber moulding that hides the joint between door frame and wall – will really complete the look. See page 127 for how to fix architrave.

Caring for your new floor

Everyday marks can be wiped away with a damp cloth. Never wash a wood floor or use abrasive cloths. If you wish, you can restore its shine by polishing once or twice a year.

FLOORS LAYING SOFT TILES

Soft vinyl floor tiles are very versatile and make an excellent hardwearing floor in any room. The tiles can be stuck to the floor with tile adhesive or they may have a self-adhesive backing, so all you do is peel off the paper covering it. Tiles pre-coated with adhesive are quicker to lay, and there is no mess. They are light to work with and if you make a mistake, you only ruin one tile rather than a whole – and expensive – sheet of vinyl.

What to buy

When you are calculating the area of your room, remember to measure any alcove or bay separately and add it to the total. Also be aware that the size and number of tiles per pack do vary. Buy all your tiles at the same time. Check that the batch and item numbers are the same on each pack, since there may be slight colour differences between batches. When you get home, stack the tiles in the room where you are going to lay them for 24 hours, so they become acclimatised.

Preparing the existing floor

The old floor must be sound, dry and level. If you want to lay new tiles over old ones, these must be firmly stuck down – otherwise, remove them. If you have a timber floor, screw down any loose boards and then lay hardboard or plywood over it (do not lay tiles directly on floorboards – the boards may start to show through and cause premature wear). Lay hardboard smooth side up, and fix it with 25mm ring-shanked nails. Timber treated with wood preservative is not suitable as a sub-floor, even if overlaid; you must replace it (see page 39). Make sure there are no proud nail heads. Seal porous surfaces such as cement, plywood, hardboard or chipboard with a suitable primer.

Setting out

Don't be tempted to start laying tiles along one wall and then work your way round the room. The wall may not be straight and the room is unlikely to be square. It is better to find the centre point of the room and work from there towards the wall in each direction. You will then have a symmetrical design, with no unsightly narrow gaps at the skirting.

Line 1 drawn between mid-point of opposite walls

Line 2 intersecting mid-point of line 1 at exactly 90º

project essentials

- **tape measure**
- **pencil**
- **chalk line**
- string

1 First measure one wall, calculate its mid-point and mark this on the floor. Repeat with the opposite wall. With a helper, stretch a chalk line between the two marks and snap a line across the floor. Calculate and mark the mid-point of this line. Tie about 1m of string to a pencil, and while your helper holds the end of the string firmly on the mid-point of the line, pull it taut and scribe an arc on the line either side.

2 Now get your helper to hold the end of the string on the point that one arc intersects the line, and with the string pulled taut draw arcs at a roughly 45º angle either side of the centre line. When you repeat this from the other side, the arcs should intersect.

3 Stretch a chalk line between these intersecting arcs and snap a line across the floor. You now have two lines intersecting at a perfect right-angle in the centre of the room.

B&Q Making it easier

Tiling awkwardly shaped rooms
If the dimensions of your room are irregular, the chalk lines will need to be snapped from a different place – the first line centred on a strong focal point such as a fireplace or patio doors, for instance. The room will still be divided into sections, but they will be different from one another.

Laying self-adhesive vinyl tiles

project essentials

- **straightedge**
- **pencil**
- **chinagraph pencil**
- **craft knife**

- cushioned vinyl tiles

Once the intersecting lines have been marked, you need to decide the position of the first (key) tile, which will determine where the other tiles will go. To do this, dry-lay some of the tiles from the centre line to check how they fit at the skirting.

1 Starting at the centre line, dry-lay a row of tiles from the line to one of the walls.

2 When you reach the wall, check to see if you are left with a narrow gap (as above). This should be avoided – a thin strip of tile at the skirting will look ugly and may not stick well.

3 To avoid such a narrow gap, move the starting line back the width of half a tile. Repeat the dry-laying from the start line in the opposite direction and then towards the other two walls. Adjust the start line as necessary, until there is a reasonable gap of about half a tile all round the room.

4 Peel the backing paper off the first tile and press its edge against the start line. Lower the rest of the tile on to the floor and press down.

5 Lay the next tile on the other side of the chalk line, butting against the first tile. Form a square with two more tiles, and then lay tiles around the square to form a pyramid shape. Continue positioning the tiles until half the room is covered (except for the gaps at the skirting). Then tile the other half of the room. Position all the whole tiles before filling in the gaps at the edges and tackling the areas where there are fittings (see page 52).

6 To cut the tiles for the gaps at the skirting, place the tile to be cut exactly on top of the last full tile. Place another tile on top, with its edge touching the wall. Using a chinagraph pencil, mark along the edge of the top tile on the face of the tile below.

7 Put the marked tile on an old piece of board, place a straightedge along the marked line and cut part-way through the tile with a craft knife.

8 Break the tile by bending it at the cut line until it snaps.

9 With the backing paper still on, check that the cut tile will fit into the gap without being forced, then remove the backing paper and stick it in place. Repeat the marking and cutting process all the way around the edge of the floor.

Once all the whole tiles are in place, you can deal with the awkward areas – round radiator pipes or lavatory and basin pedestals, for instance.

Tiling around basins and lavatories

To cut a tile to fit around a large awkward shape such as a basin pedestal, you need to make a template out of very thin card or paper to use as a cutting guide. Depending on your tiles, the object you are tiling around, and the layout of the room, you may require templates for more than one tile.

project essentials

- **scissors**
- **blunt knife**
- **tape**
- **pencil**
- **craft knife**
- **round metalworking file**
- **off-cut of copper pipe**
- **hammer**

- vinyl floor tile
- thin card or paper
- block of wood

1 To make a template, cut a piece of thin card or paper the size of one of the tiles. Cut slits on the side where the pedestal will fit. Position the template against the pedestal with the flaps fringing it. Press the flaps against the pedestal with a blunt knife. Tape the paper to the floor and draw a pencil line where the pedestal and the floor meet.

2 Remove the template and cut away the flaps, leaving the pencil guideline.

3 Place the template on a tile. If the tiles have a directional pattern, make sure the tile you are going to cut is the right way round. Draw the guideline on the tile and then cut it with a craft knife. Peel off the backing paper and fit the tile.

Cutting around pipes

The best way to cut a hole in a soft tile for a radiator pipe is to make a home-made punch from an off-cut of copper pipe the same diameter as the central heating pipe. You need a piece about 150mm long. Sharpen the inside of one end with a round metalworking file.

1 Hold the tile against the pipe and draw a line on it each side of the pipe to mark its width.

2 Move the tile so the marked edge touches the wall. Mark on the tile the distance to the front of the pipe.

3 Rest the tile on a block of wood. Position the sharpened off-cut of copper pipe where the lines meet. Hit the other end of the pipe with a hammer to punch a neat hole through the tile.

4 Cut a straight slit between the hole and the edge of the tile. Dry-lay to check the fit, then stick the tile firmly in place.

Laying non-adhesive vinyl tiles

If you've chosen non-adhesive tiles, use the glue recommended by the manufacturer and apply it according to the instructions. The floor must be level and free from any sign of damp. Work out the start line in the same way as for self-adhesive tiles (see page 50).

(see page 50)

project essentials

- **paintbrush**
- **notched spreader**
- **small roller**
- **damp cloth or sponge**

- primer
- adhesive recommended by the tile manufacturer
- non-adhesive vinyl floor tiles
- white spirit

1 If you are laying the tiles on a porous surface such as concrete, apply primer with a paintbrush to seal it.

2 Working from the centre line, spread the tile adhesive evenly over the floor with a notched spreader. Check with the manufacturer's instructions, but for most adhesives you should cover an area big enough for about 15 minutes' work.

3 Carefully lay the tiles over the adhesive while it is still wet. Press the tiles into the adhesive, ensuring that every part of each tile is in contact with the sub-floor. Check that the tiles are level and butted tightly up against each other.

4 Roll a small roller over the tiles, particularly at the edges and corners, to make sure they are well stuck down.

5 If any adhesive comes through the joins, wipe it from the surface of the tiles immediately with a damp cloth or sponge. Adhesive that has started to set can be removed with white spirit. To measure up the edging tiles, turn to Step 6 page 51. Cut the tiles and stick them in place.

turn to Step 6 page 51.

safety first

Take care when using adhesives for these tiles – the solvent- and spirit-based ones are highly flammable. Their fumes soak into clothing, so keep away from any fire and hang clothes outdoors when you have finished. If there is a pilot light in the room, turn it off while you lay the floor. Open all windows. Some manufacturers recommend wearing gloves when applying floor-tile adhesive: check the guidelines on the tin.

B&Q Making it easier

Create your own floor pattern
Try combining different coloured tiles. Patterns can range from a simple chessboard of dark and light to more dramatic combinations of two or more colours. Draw a scale plan of your design before starting to lay a patterned tile floor.

Hard ceramic and quarry tiles make an attractive floorcovering in kitchens, bathrooms, hallways or conservatories, and they are easy to care for and hardwearing. They can be expensive, however, so take care when laying them.

Preparing the existing floor

Hard tiles can be laid directly on a dry and level concrete floor, but a timber floor must be strengthened first with 13mm-thick exterior grade plywood fixed with countersunk 25mm screws (4mm gauge) or ring-shanked nails at 300mm intervals. Clean a concrete floor with detergent mixed with water; if it is uneven, level it (see page 39). New tiles can be laid over old quarry or vinyl tiles as long as they are securely stuck down. Vinyl tiles should be coated with primer. For best results, choose a tile adhesive specially formulated for the surface you are working on, particularly if tiling directly onto wood or concrete.

How many tiles to buy

Tiles are sold in packs and the size and number of tiles they contain will determine the area of floor they will cover. When you calculate the area of your floor, remember to include the dimensions of any alcove or bay. Round up the total to the nearest whole number to establish the number of packs of tiles you need.

Starting out

The first tile – the 'key' tile – determines the position of all the others, so it is very important that this tile is in the right place. Because rooms are seldom completely square, and the walls may not be straight, you cannot start by laying tiles right up against one wall and working your way out from there – you would end up with an untidy mess. The best way to ensure you have a symmetrical design is to start from the centre of the room and work out to the walls in each direction.

Positioning the key tile

First, find the centre of the room (see Setting out, on page 50). Starting at one of the centre lines, dry-lay a row of tiles from the line to the wall. When you reach the wall, make sure that you are not left with a narrow gap because a very thin strip of tile at the skirting will look very odd and may not stick very well. If necessary, move the line away from this wall the width of half a tile to create a larger gap. Repeat the dry-laying from this centre line in the opposite direction and then in both directions perpendicular to it. Adjust the key tile position, as shown below, until there is an equal gap of about half a tile at all the edges of the room.

Position the central key tile so that there is an equal gap of about half a tile along all four edges of the room.

If necessary, shift the key tile by half a tile's width in one or more directions to avoid a narrow strip along one wall.

Laying the tiles

Start with the key tile, and work out towards one of the walls. Fix the tiles using a standard floor tile adhesive. When you have finished, you must let the adhesive set for 24 hours before you walk on the newly laid floor tiles. If you are laying them in a kitchen, tile half the room at a time so the whole kitchen is not out of action, and check you have left yourself an exit passage so you don't have to step on any tiles.

ideal tool

Notched trowel
Use the smooth side of this rectangular tool to spread the tile adhesive on the floor. Then draw its notched or serrated edge back through the adhesive to form ridges that leave the correct amount of adhesive needed to secure the tiles.

1 Starting in the centre of the room, pour out enough adhesive to cover about a square metre of floor. Spread the adhesive evenly using a notched trowel or spreader. The ribbed pattern leaves just the right amount of adhesive to make the tiles stick. Make sure you can still see enough of the chalk line to position the key tile. If you wish, nail a guide batten against one line to help align the first row of tiles.

2 Place the key tile in position, giving it a slight twist to bed it into the adhesive and to make sure that there is no air trapped underneath. Continue working out towards one of the walls to complete a row of whole tiles, fitting plastic spacers between them so they are evenly spaced. Check from time to time that the tiles are level using a spirit level. If you are laying thick handmade tiles, this may not be possible – you will need to rely on eye and judgment. Lay the next row of tiles out from the key tile, working at right angles to the first row. Continue working in rows in this quarter of the room.

4 Using a trowel, clean out any adhesive remaining in the gaps around the walls before it sets. Leave the tiles for 24 hours before cutting and laying the edge tiles at the walls (see page 56).

3 When the first section of the room is complete, repeat the process until all but the cut tiles at the edges are laid. Wipe the tiles regularly with a damp sponge to remove any adhesive on the surface.

B&Q Making it easier

Tile spacers
Using tile spacers will give even grout lines between the tiles and a professional-looking finish to the floor. They come in different sizes, suitable for floor and wall tiles. Cross-shaped spacers are for use with standard square or rectangular tiles, while special Y-shaped spacers are for laying octagonal tiles. Press them well below the surface of the tile so that they do not protrude through the finished grout.

Cutting and fitting edge tiles

Hard floor tiles are thicker than ceramic wall tiles, and to cut them you will need a heavy-duty tile cutter. Large tiles are easier to cut than smaller ones. If using a lever-action flat-bed cutter (see Step 1, below), make a single score line in one pass and then snap the tile smartly. Hesitation will produce bad results.

1 To measure an edging tile, place it over the last full tile; align a third tile on top, with one edge touching the wall; use the inside edge as a guide to draw a line on the face of the tile below (see Step 6, page 51). Use a chinagraph pencil rather than an ordinary pencil, which may stain. Cut the tile just short of the marked line to allow space either side for the grout and sealant (see below).

2 Apply a layer of adhesive to the back of each cut border tile. Place in position and leave to set for 24 hours.

ideal tool

Diamond-wheel tile cutter

An electric tile cutter with super-sharp diamond wheel blade will make precise and accurate cuts in your tiles. More versatile than a flat-bed cutter, it cuts thin strips and diagonals as well as straight lines, and will also shape mitred edges for tiling around corners. Water stored in a small reservoir beneath the cutting bed keeps the blade and tile cool while you work. Different models will cut tiles to different maximum depths, so check before you buy.

Grouting

The finished look of a tiled floor depends on careful grouting. Use floor tile grout and mix it thoroughly with water, making sure there are no lumps. Most grouts are best left to stand for a few minutes before use. Around the edge of the room use a similar-coloured flexible sealant instead of grout.

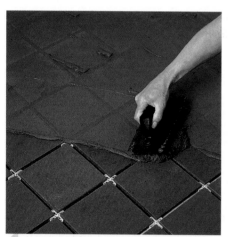

1 When the adhesive has set, mix the grout into a paste with water. If the surface of the tiles is glazed, you can pour the grout over them and spread it with a rubber-edged grout spreader, as here. If the surface of your tiles is absorbent, however, you should mix a very dry grout and press it into the joints one by one, taking care to keep the tiles as clean as possible to avoid staining.

2 When the grout begins to set, press and smooth it into all the joints with a striking tool or a wooden dowel to compact it and make it water-resistant. Clean off the surplus grout with a damp sponge as you proceed.

3 Leave the grout to harden for about an hour, wipe it again with a damp cloth and then polish the tiles with a dry cloth. Seal around the edge of the floor with a matching flexible sealant. Avoid giving the floor any heavy use for at least 48 hours after grouting.

Decorative border tiles

Count decorative border tiles as the last row of full tiles, and cut plain tiles to fit the gap around the edge of the room. Lay all the whole, plain tiles and allow the adhesive to set, then fit the decorative border tiles and the cut edging tiles the next day. Start by dry-laying all the border tiles. Measure a plain edging tile by first placing it exactly on top of the adjacent border tiles (aligned with their outer edge). Then position another plain tile on top, with one edge touching the wall. Use its inside edge as a guide to draw a line on the tile below with a chinagraph pencil (see Step 6, page 51). Cut the tile just short of the line to allow space for grout and sealant.

1 Spread enough adhesive for a few border tiles and edging tiles at a time, using a notched trowel or spreader. Some manufacturers recommend wearing gloves when applying floor-tile adhesive: check the guidelines on the tin.

2 Carefully place the decorative tiles in position, making sure they align with the plain tiles. Insert spacers between them.

3 Position the plain, cut edging tiles, taking care that they align with the decorative tiles.

4 Leave the adhesive to set for 24 hours, then mix the grout and spread it over the border and edging tiles with a rubber-edged grout spreader.

5 Smooth and compress the grout into the joints with a striking tool or a wooden dowel when the grout begins to set. Clean off the surplus grout with a damp sponge as you proceed. When the grout has hardened for about an hour, wipe it with a damp cloth and then polish the tiles with a dry cloth.

6 Seal around the edge of the floor with a flexible sealant that matches the colour of the grout. Avoid giving the floor any heavy use for at least 48 hours after grouting.

FLOORS LAYING SHEET VINYL

Sheet vinyl is quicker to lay than tiles. Unless your room is very large, you can usually lay it in one seamless piece, which looks better than two or three strips, though it can be more difficult to fit. Calculate the area of the room and add 50mm–100mm to each edge. Don't forget to measure right into any alcoves and up to the halfway point in the doorway.

Sheet vinyl is available in different widths. If you do opt to lay it in strips, work out how many you need by measuring the wall that their narrow ends will meet. Measure the room in the other direction and multiply this by the number of strips to find the total length. Add 75mm to each end for trimming, and more if there is a pattern. In small rooms with lots of obstacles, you may be able to use the old flooring as a template. Just remember to leave 50mm–100mm all round the edge for final fitting.

1 Unroll the vinyl and start by fitting the longer side of the sheet parallel to the longest clear wall, about 25mm away from the skirting. To make a scribing gauge, take an off-cut of wood and hammer a nail into it about 30mm from one end until the point is just protruding from the other side. Carefully move the gauge along the skirting so the nail traces the outline of the skirting on to the vinyl. Cut the sheet along this line with a knife or scissors, then slide the vinyl against the skirting.

ideal tool

Bolster
A bolster chisel can apply a good deal of pressure in the junction between the skirting and the floor, creating a precise crease in the vinyl to act as a cutting guide. Hold the vinyl in place with a straightedge while you make the cut.

2 To get the vinyl to lie as flat as possible, cut a triangular notch at each internal corner with the scissors. The cut is made in the extra allowed along each wall.

5 At external corners, make a straight cut from the edge of the vinyl down to the floor level. Cut away the excess vinyl, leaving 50mm–100mm turned up at the skirting.

Laying sheet vinyl flooring

Keep the roll of vinyl in the room where it will be laid for 48 hours to bring it up to room temperature. If the weather is cold, put the heating on to stop it becoming brittle. Skirting is rarely completely straight, and to cut the vinyl to fit the first wall – the longest clear wall – you will need to trace the skirting profile on to the vinyl using a home-made tool known as a scribing gauge.

3 Press the vinyl into the angle between the skirting and floor with a bolster chisel, to make a sharp crease.

6 Use a bolster chisel to press into the angle between the skirting and floor. Hold the straightedge against each crease and cut along it with the knife held at a slight angle to give a neat finish.

4 Holding a metal straightedge pressed against the crease, cut carefully along it with the knife held at a slight angle.

7 When the vinyl sheet has been fully laid, lift the edges and stick them to the sub-floor with double-sided tape or adhesive.

To fit the vinyl around a lavatory or washbasin pedestal, lay it as far as the front of the pedestal, then fold it back on itself. Using scissors, cut in from the edge in a straight line to the centre of the pedestal.

To fit the vinyl around a door frame, make a series of vertical cuts to the point where the vinyl meets the floor. Cut off the excess, leaving 50mm–100mm turned up at floor level for more accurate trimming.

Fitting difficult areas

Most rooms have architraves and radiator pipes, and there will be lavatory and basin pedestals to deal with in the bathroom. It is a good idea to seal the edges of the bathroom floor with silicone sealant to create a waterproof barrier.

Make a series of cuts in the vinyl around the base of the pedestal until the sheet lies flat. Take care not to cut too far in, or to tear the vinyl.

Use the bolster chisel to make a sharp crease in the vinyl all the way round the base of the pedestal.

Cut around the crease, carefully trimming off each flap of vinyl until it fits. Then peel back the vinyl, apply adhesive to the floor around the pedestal, and press it back into place. You may wish to seal the edges with silicone sealant.

Press the vinyl into the angle between the door frame and the floor and cut along the crease. Cut the vinyl straight across the line of the door so it ends halfway under the door. Fit a threshold bar to hold down and protect the edge of the vinyl.

To fit vinyl around a pipe, make a straight cut in line with the pipe to the edge of the vinyl, then make a series of small cuts at the pipe end of the slit until the vinyl lies flat around the pipe. Trim the slit pieces for a neat fit.

B&Q Making it easier

Gluing vinyl

Not all vinyl has to be glued to the floor. Heavy-duty 'stay flat' vinyl does not shrink or lift, so it can be laid without glue. Cushioned vinyl, however, should be glued around the edges and at joins. Thinner non-cushioned types need to be stuck down all over: once fitted, roll back half the vinyl and apply adhesive to the floor (use the adhesive supplied or recommended by the manufacturer). Fit the vinyl back in place and repeat for the other half of the room. When it is all back in place, press the vinyl flat with a soft broom.

Joining vinyl

In a large room you may have to join two or more sheets to cover the whole floor. These should be from the same roll – different rolls may vary slightly in colour. Don't have a join in the doorway where it will get heavy wear.

To join patterned sheets, slide the second sheet along until the pattern matches the first sheet. If this will be difficult, overlap the sheets until the pattern matches exactly, then make a cut through both sheets using a straightedge and a knife.

Without moving the sheets, fold back the edges and use double-sided tape or adhesive to secure them to the floor. Press down well with both hands to glue the join.

project essentials

- **pipe and cable detector**
- **heavy-duty gloves**
- **small saw or tinsnips**
- **tape measure**
- **carpenter's pincers**
- **hammer**
- **long bar**
- **knee pads**
- **hammer tacker or staple gun**
- **craft knife**
- **dolphin-handled flooring knife**
- **carpet tucker**
- **carpet stretcher**
- **hacksaw**
- **bradawl**
- **power drill and masonry bit, if needed**
- **screwdriver**

- gripper
- gripper adhesive, if needed
- floor lining paper
- underlay
- heavy-duty cloth tape or carpet tape
- hessian-backed carpet
- threshold bar
- wallplugs, if needed

All carpet benefits from a good quality cushioned underlay, which makes it more comfortable underfoot and helps it to last longer. Here a hessian-backed carpet is laid on a rubber underlay. Hessian- and woven-backed carpets are generally better quality than foam-backed carpets, and must be stretched and attached to gripper. Measure the room at its widest and longest points, including any alcoves, and buy a piece of carpet with a minimum 50–75mm excess on all four sides.

Check for hidden wires or pipes with a pipe and cable detector and mark their positions on the floor. If you do find any, or if you need to fit gripper in places where hammering is awkward, you will need to secure it with gripper adhesive instead.

Fitting gripper

Gripper consists of long thin pieces of wood with small sharp pins that hold the carpet in place once it is stretched. Wear gloves to handle it, as the pins are very sharp. It is fitted all the way around the edge of the room except for across the doorway, where you need a threshold bar instead. Gripper can be fitted to both concrete and wooden floors and comes supplied with nails already in place for fixing it to the floor.

Where necessary, cut gripper to length with a small saw or a pair of tinsnips. Butt lengths together. Gripper is angled on one edge: this should face the skirting-board. Leave a gap of 7mm (or roughly ¾ the thickness of the carpet) between the skirting-boards and gripper.

First secure any lengths that are to be stuck down. Pull out the nails using carpenter's pincers and then apply gripper adhesive. Hammer the remaining gripper in place, taking care not to damage the skirting.

Laying underlay

Good carpets are only as good as their underlay, so it's worth investing in quality. A floor lining paper prevents the underlay from sticking to the floor and keeps dust and dirt from passing through to the carpet, making your carpet last longer. It also improves insulation. Fitting carpet is hard on the knees, so protect yours by wearing knee pads.

Roll out the floor lining paper and secure it in place using a hammer tacker or heavy-duty staple gun. Alternatively, it can be sprayed with adhesive around the edges to fix it. Slightly overlap the rows.

Loose lay the underlay, rubber side face down. Using a craft knife, cut it flush with the gripper rods.

Butt the rows and join with a heavy-duty cloth or carpet tape. Don't overlap the underlay: it needs to be smooth and level.

Gripper in awkward areas
For hard-to-reach areas, such as under a radiator, reposition the nails closer to the edge of the gripper and hold in place with a long bar, which you can hit with the hammer further back, avoiding the radiator.

Fitting the carpet

Careful storage of a carpet before it is fitted is essential. Keep it rolled not folded to avoid problems laying it flat and stretching it. Carpet is very heavy and hard to manoeuvre, so do have someone on hand to help you carry and position it. A carpet stretcher, or knee kicker, is used to stretch hessian-backed carpet onto the gripper. At one end it has a flat plate with teeth that grip the carpet and at the other end a padded cushion that the carpet fitter pushes (rather than kicks) with one knee.

Lay the carpet loosely in position, starting from one corner. Stand in the corner with one foot under the carpet then smooth and push the carpet into place using your other foot. Cut the carpet to size if necessary, leaving 50–75mm extra lapping up at each edge.

Cut a vertical line in the excess directly above the corners, then trim the overlapping triangles so you can lay the carpet flat to the gripper.

Start fitting the carpet from the longest wall and work back towards the doorway. Using a carpet tucker, firmly crease the carpet against the skirting to mark a fold line for cutting along the first wall.

Using a dolphin-handled knife with a new sharp blade held flat to the floor, cut along the carpet edge. Your cut needs to be slightly higher than the carpet surface (about 5mm). Be careful not to mark the skirting-board.

Position the carpet stretcher, teeth downwards, about 25mm from the skirting, and push firmly against the padded end with your knee to hook the carpet onto the gripper either side of the corner. Push the excess carpet down between the skirting and the gripper with the carpet tucker. Repeat all along the first wall. Then trim, stretch and fix the carpet along the two adjacent walls and finally the opposite wall.

For difficult shapes such as around a door frame make several vertical cuts down the edge, then trim the carpet flush with the knife.

To fit the carpet around a pipe, make a straight cut from the edge of the carpet to the centre of the pipe. Press the carpet around the pipe, then trim it by running the knife around the base of the pipe at a 45° angle until the carpet lies flat.

Across a doorway, cut the carpet in line with the edge of the flooring in the next room. Fit a suitable threshold bar (see below) and push the carpet edge beneath it with a bolster or screwdriver.

Door thresholds

A door threshold bar creates a neat and safe transition from the flooring of one room to the next. There is a wide choice available, in a variety of finishes. Some are designed to be used where floors of equal height meet, others for joining floors of slightly different heights and with different surfaces. A threshold bar should be positioned centrally under the door so it cannot be seen on either side when the door is closed. Measure and cut it to length with a hacksaw. Check for hidden pipes and cables under the floor. On a concrete floor, drill holes with a power drill and masonry bit, and insert wallplugs first. For wooden floors make pilot holes with a bradawl and screw the strip to the floor.

Carpet to carpet

Carpet to wood/laminate/tile

WALLS INSIDE AND OUT

B&Q Making it easier

Supporting a window
A window frame is not strong enough to support the weight of the structure above it in a loadbearing wall, so a rigid beam called a lintel must be installed. This spans the gap above the opening, transmitting the weight to the walls each side. A lintel may be wood, stone, brick, concrete or steel, depending on the opening and the weight overhead; calculating this is a job for an architect or structural engineer.

The majority of houses are built from a combination of bricks, concrete blocks and timber on a solid base known as the foundations. Older houses may be made of local natural stone. The construction of the walls depends on whether they are external or internal, and whether they are loadbearing or non-loadbearing.

The external walls of a house are all loadbearing – they support the weight of the roof, floors and internal walls. Internal walls divide the floor space into rooms and are generally made of less heavyweight materials. Many internal walls are not structural (ie they do not support the structure); these are known as non-loadbearing walls. Not all internal walls are non-loadbearing, however, some may partly support floor and ceiling joists while others add to the stability of the building. Never assume an internal wall is non-loadbearing – always seek professional advice before attempting major alterations.

Solid external walls

External walls can be either of solid or cavity (hollow) construction. Solid external walls, made of natural stone or brick, are mostly found in houses built before the 1920s. Traditional brick and stone walls vary in thickness depending on the age and size of the building, but they are usually at least 225mm thick (the length of a standard brick), and are often a brick and a half thick in places where houses are exposed to severe weather. These days when solid walls are required, concrete blocks will normally be used. Solid walls provide good sound insulation, but do not retain heat efficiently.

Natural stone

In solid stone walls the entire depth, approximately 300mm–510mm, is made up of natural stone. In the days when houses were built this way, the best stone was used for the outer facing layer of the wall, which was left uncovered, and the inside of the wall was usually made from less attractive pieces of stone which were rendered (coated with a mix of builder's sand and cement) and plastered. Older houses may have lath and plaster on the inside, dating back to the days before plasterboard. Thin strips of wood (laths) were nailed horizontally to vertical timbers to act as a key for a covering of plaster. Many stone walls are rendered on the outside to improve their weatherproofing.

Concrete blocks

External walls made from concrete blocks usually have the external face of the wall covered with render, which is painted. The internal wall is rendered and plastered.

Bricks

With a solid brick wall the entire thickness of the wall is made from bricks, two or three bricks deep. The bricks are laid with mortar in overlapping bonding patterns. The outer wall is left as bare brick unless the brickwork has become shabby, in which case it may have been rendered and painted with masonry paint. The interior of the wall is normally covered with a coat of render, then plastered.

Natural stone wall

Concrete block wall

Brick wall

ONE PLANET HOME

Solid or cavity?
Uninsulated cavity brick walls can have insulating material blown between them, making your house much cosier and more energy efficient (see page 340). If you are not sure whether a brick external wall is solid or not, look at the pattern of the brickwork. If some of the bricks are laid end-on, then it is likely to be solid. If all the bricks are side-on, it is likely a double-leaf wall with a cavity in the middle.

Solid

Cavity

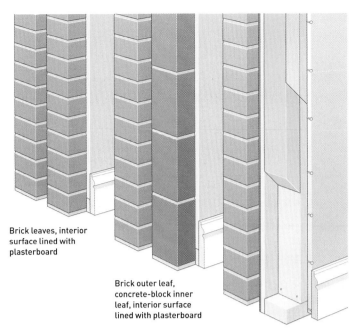

Brick leaves, interior surface lined with plasterboard

Brick outer leaf, concrete-block inner leaf, interior surface lined with plasterboard

Brick outer leaf, timber-frame inner leaf fitted with thermal insulation, the cavity side lined with plywood sheeting and the interior surface lined with plasterboard

Cavity external walls

Most modern houses have external walls that are constructed with a cavity in the middle. Typically the leaves (walls) are each about 100mm thick, separated by a gap of at least 50mm. The leaves are tied together with metal wall ties to make them stable. This type of wall is more effective in preventing moisture penetration and heat loss. For it to work as a moisture barrier, mortar must not drop on the ties during construction as this would bridge the gap. Cavity walls are built from bricks, concrete blocks or timber framing, or a combination of these.

Brick and block cavity walls

These walls have an outer leaf of brick and an inner leaf of either brick or concrete blocks. The inner wall may be rendered and plastered; alternatively, plasterboard may be attached directly to the wall or to a wooden batten framework.

Timber-framed cavity wall

With timber-framed walls the outer leaf is brick, or sometimes stone or wooden boarding, and the inner leaf is constructed of a timber framework with plywood sheeting on the cavity side and plasterboard attached to the inside. Thermal insulation may be fitted between the plywood and plasterboard.

Internal walls

There are two types of internal walls in a house: party walls and partition walls. Party walls are shared walls between neighbouring houses, detached or semi-detached. Partition walls divide up the floor space within a property into rooms and they are usually – though not always – non-loadbearing. Internal walls may be made from a variety of materials, including stone in older houses, brick and concrete blocks, and plasterboard or wallboard fixed to frames made from timber or metal. Lightweight internal walls can even be made from glass blocks.

Solid internal walls

In houses with stone external walls, the internal walls may be made from the same stone. Other solid internal walls may be constructed from bricks or lightweight concrete blocks, usually one brick or block thick. The grey blocks widely used for modern partition walls are made from cement and lightweight aggregate. They provide good sound and heat insulation and are fireproof. Their relatively large size (225mm x 450mm and anything from 75mm to 350mm thick) makes building a wall with blocks quick and simple. Solid internal walls may be plastered on both sides (in older stone-built houses, there may be a lath-and-plaster finish). Or plasterboard may be attached, either to timber battens or directly to the bricks or blocks.

Stud partition walls

Hollow partition walls called stud walls are a very common type of internal wall, and they may or may not be loadbearing. The cavity in the middle is ideal for running concealed water pipes and cables. In newer homes stud walls consist of plasterboard sheets fixed to each side of a timber frame. The vertical timbers in the frame are known as studs. In older houses, built before the days of plasterboard, thin strips of wood, called laths, were nailed to the studs. The laths provided a surface for the plaster to stick to. Some modern stud wall frames are made of metal rather than softwood.

Cellular-core wallboards

These wallboards are used to make a lightweight, non-loadbearing wall. They have plasterboard on each side and a centre of cardboard in a hollow grid pattern. They can be decorated as they are, or plastered first then decorated.

Laths nailed horizontally to each side of vertical studs to provide a key for plastering

Plasterboard fitted to a timber frame

Internal walls of concrete blocks plastered on both sides

WALLS REPAIRS

Wear and tear and slight movement in a building will often damage the plastering. Small cracks and holes can be repaired with filler. Where an area of plaster is seriously damaged or has come away from the wall ('blown'), it is better to repair it with plaster. If the entire wall is in a bad condition it may need completely replastering – a job for the professionals. Put down dust sheets before you start any repair work.

Filling holes and cracks

You can choose from various fillers for minor repairs:
- Interior filler: a general-purpose cellulose filler available ready-mixed in tubs or as a powder for mixing to a stiff paste with water.
- Fine-surface filler: an ultra-smooth fine-particle filler for minor cracks and surface imperfections.
- Deep-repair filler: a ready-mixed lightweight filler for holes up to 20mm deep.
- Fast-setting filler: a filler that sets in 10–20 minutes.
- Flexible acrylic fillers: for gaps between plaster and woodwork.
- Foam or expanding filler: for large holes or gaps. Once dry, it needs trimming back with a craft knife.

For more extensive repairs there are two main types of plaster that can be used:
- Gypsum plasters: these are the ones used by professional plasterers. They are mixed with water and applied in two coats – an undercoat and a finishing coat. They are quick-setting and generally the most economical, but they are also the most difficult plasters to use.
- General plasters: these are available as two coats – an undercoat or 'repair' plaster, and a finishing coat – either ready-mixed or as powder to mix with water. If a wall is to be papered, plaster undercoat will give a good enough finish; if it is to be painted, you need a plaster finish (also known as plaster skim) as well. The finishing plaster is applied before the undercoat is completely dry. Application methods vary for finishing plasters, so check the manufacturer's instructions.

B&Q Making it easier

Make it stick
If you are mixing your filler from a powder, add a squirt of PVA adhesive to make a smooth yet sticky paste.

Patching corners

Corners are particularly vulnerable to wear and tear and often need patching. There are two ways to do this. You can repair the damage with undercoat plaster, using a nailed-on piece of board to achieve a neat edge. Or if a longer stretch is damaged, it is better to reinforce the corner with metal or plastic corner beading. In either case, cut back crumbling plaster to a firm surface with a cold chisel and hammer first.

Using plaster and a board

Hammer two nails into a piece of board slightly larger than the damaged area on one side of the corner, making sure that the nails will fit into firm plaster beyond the damaged area. Position the board's edge so that it is flush with the plaster surface on the adjacent wall. Nail the board to the wall. Dampen the broken edges on the uncovered wall with a large paintbrush and apply the plaster undercoat with a trowel. When the plaster has set, pull the board away from the wall. Once the plaster has completely hardened, nail the board to the repaired side and fill the other side of the corner in the same way. Leave the plaster to dry, remove the board then sand the corner to a smooth edge. Fill and sand the holes made by the nails.

Using metal corner beading

Cut the expanded metal corner beading to the required length with a hacksaw. Paint the cut ends with metal primer to seal them. Wet the wall and apply patches of plaster undercoat each side of the corner, using a plasterer's trowel. Press the beading into position, allowing the plaster to squeeze through the mesh. Build up the undercoat plaster, then scrape it back to 2mm below the old finished level with the trowel. Apply a top coat of finishing plaster in a wide band and feather in the new plaster level with the existing surface. Take care not to damage the metal beading's coating or rust may come through later. To be on the safe side, brush metal primer over the corner before decorating.

project essentials

- **hammer**
- **cold chisel**
- **hacksaw**
- **plasterer's trowel**
- **small paintbrush**
- **large paintbrush**

- metal corner beading
- metal primer
- plaster undercoat and finishing coat

project essentials

- **hammer**
- **cold chisel**
- **large paintbrush**
- **plasterer's trowel**
- **sanding block**

- wooden board
- nails
- plaster undercoat
- medium-grade abrasive paper

Cracks and holes in plaster

A deep crack can be filled with screwed-up newspaper to make a base for the filler. With larger holes you may need to build up several thin coats of filler rather than one thick one, letting each coat dry before adding the next.

project essentials

- **filling knife or scraper**
- **small paintbrush**
- **sanding block**

- plaster filler
- medium-grade abrasive paper

1 Rake loose plaster from the crack with the corner of a filling knife or scraper. Using a small paintbrush, dampen the crack with water to make the filler dry slowly – this helps to stop it shrinking and falling out of the crack.

2 Load some filler onto a filling knife and draw it across the hole at right angles to the crack, firmly pressing it in until the filler is just proud of the surface. Leave to dry, then smooth with medium-grade abrasive paper wrapped around a sanding block.

Lath-and-plaster repairs

As long as the laths are secure, you can fill small holes in a lath-and-plaster wall in the same way as ordinary plaster. Broken laths can often be the reason for plaster crumbling; if this is the case, they need to be reinforced with expanded metal mesh under the new plaster.

1 Remove any debris until you get back to an edge where the plaster is still firmly attached to the laths. Using tinsnips, cut a piece of mesh the size of the hole.

2 Position the mesh and secure it in place around the edges with plaster undercoat. (Nailing or stapling on to the laths may cause further damage to the surrounding plaster and lath.)

Repairing holes in plasterboard

Small holes in plasterboard can be repaired in the same way as holes and cracks in plaster, but a hole bigger than about 125mm needs to have a plasterboard patch fitted into it otherwise the filler will simply fall into the cavity.

project essentials

- **craft knife**
- **padsaw or hole saw**
- **power drill**
- **filling knife or scraper**

- off-cut of plasterboard
- string
- nail
- plaster filler
- pencils or timber off-cut

1 Neaten the edge of the damaged area with a craft knife. From an off-cut of plasterboard, cut a patch that will fit through the hole but is just larger than it. Drill through the centre and thread a piece of string through. Tie a nail to the end of the string at the back of the patch (the grey side). Make a loop in the string on the front side and apply filler around the front edge. Keeping hold of the string, push the patch through the hole.

2 Pull on the string to manoeuvre the patch into place, with the filler side facing you. Holding it taut, add more filler to the hole. To hold the patch in place while it sets, tie your string to a pencil or timber off-cut and 'wind' it taut against the wall. When the filler is set, cut the string flush with the wall and apply a finishing coat of filler.

project essentials

- **tinsnips**
- **small plasterer's trowel**

- expanded metal mesh
- plaster undercoat and finishing coat

ideal tool

Tinsnips
Snips are made in different sizes and cut through sheet metals like scissors.

3 Dampen the laths and apply a plaster undercoat using a plasterer's trowel. Force the plaster between the laths to make sure it sticks well. Score the surface in a diamond pattern to create a key for the finishing coat. Allow it to set, then apply a finishing coat of plaster.

Problems with painted and wallpapered surfaces are commonplace in many homes. They spoil the look of the surface and need attention. If you try a 'quick fix' by redecorating over damaged areas the finish will soon deteriorate again. It's much better to tackle the problem head on.

Curing paint problems

Problems on a painted surface are usually caused by poor preparation, incompatible paints on top of one another, and trapped moisture. Generally the only cure is to strip off the paint and redo it.

Paint blisters

Sometimes blisters will appear on painted woodwork. If pricking the blisters releases water then you know the surface is damp. Strip the paint with a hot-air gun, and when the wood is dry, prime and repaint.

Air can be trapped under the painted surface of open-grained wood. Strip the paint, and fill the grain with epoxy-based wood filler. This filler flexes with the natural expansion and contraction of the wood. Alternatively, repaint with microporous acrylic paint.

Paint flaking

Paint will flake off a surface that is already flaky, or is incompatible – emulsion over a gloss, for instance. The flaking paint must be stripped off with a wide stripping knife, sanded with medium-grade abrasive paper around a sanding block, then washed with sugar soap and water and repainted. Emulsion will also flake if painted over distemper – old-fashioned water-based paint containing glue. In this case you must treat the whole area with special stabilising solution before repainting.

Paint runs

Too much paint applied to the wall too quickly will result in runs. You can simply brush runs out of wet paint. Rub dry paint with fine abrasive paper until the surface is smooth. Then dust and wipe with a damp cloth, and carefully apply a new top coat.

Tackling damp
Damp patches should be looked at by a professional, as there may be a problem that needs to be addressed (see page 342). When you are ready to redecorate, apply a specially formulated damp sealant or oil-based undercoat over the stain first. You can also help to keep damp at bay with microporous acrylic paint, which is a water-based paint that allows the wall surface to breathe.

safety first

Lead in paint
Paint with a high lead content can cause poisoning. Most paint you buy nowadays contains little or no lead, and any that does must bear a clear warning. But before stripping old paint, especially pre-1960s paint, you must use a lead-testing kit on it first. If the result is positive, you should use a specially formulated chemical stripper: don't dry-strip the paint either with a hot-air gun or a sander. Keep the windows open and children well out of the way.

Problems on wallpapered walls

Problems with wallpaper are often down to human error – rushing the job when hanging the paper, using too little paste, or not being careful enough with the paper. Take your time! ... but if it's too late, try these solutions.

Lifting seams

Seams can open up if too little paste has been applied at the edges, particularly with vinyl and relief papers. Lift the seam with a round-bladed knife and apply fresh paste with a fine brush. Run down the seam with a seam roller to press the edges together.

Shiny patches

Shiny patches can appear on matt wallpaper if it was rubbed too hard when it was hung. Try gently rubbing the shiny areas with a ball of white bread to dull the shine. Bread can be used to remove dirty marks too. Next time you hang matt wallpaper, smooth it carefully with a clean dry sponge to avoid this problem.

Bubbles under paper

Small bubbles should disappear as wallpaper dries. If the paper was not left to soak for long enough, however, it may expand on the wall and create air bubbles. Simply cut small bubbles with a razor blade and insert some wallpaper paste behind the flaps with a fine brush. Press the paper into place, then wipe off the excess paste with a damp rag.

Damaged vinyl wallpaper

Since you can't tear vinyl paper, cut a square larger than the damaged area. Tape the square over the damage, then with a trimming knife cut within it (through both layers) a square large enough to take out all of the damaged area. Remove the old square of vinyl, apply paste to the patch, and fit it into the gap.

Gaps at seams

Sometimes gaps appear at wallpaper seams, generally due to poor hanging, but occasionally because of shrinkage while the paper was drying. White gaps can be filled with felt-tip pen the same colour as the base colour of the paper. Some paper manufacturers sell special pens for this purpose.

Torn patches

Remove all the damaged paper, leaving only paper that is firmly attached. Tear around the edges of a patch of fresh wallpaper – this will make a less noticeable repair than a square-cut patch – and paste it over the damaged area so that the pattern exactly matches. Smooth it down with a sponge.

Putting up a wall to create an extra bedroom, en-suite bathroom or home office is much easier and cheaper than moving house to get another room. A stud wall consists of a frame of timber or metal studs secured to the floor, ceiling and walls, which is then covered with plasterboard; once decorated, it looks like an integral part of the house. While it is a fairly straightforward job, there are things that have to be considered before you start.

- Check with your local authority to make sure that the work involved conforms to the current building regulations relating to fire resistance, light and ventilation.
- Organise lighting, heating and, if necessary, plumbing for the new room.
- If the wall is going to have a doorway, buy a door and frame that matches the thickness of the timber and plasterboard you are using.

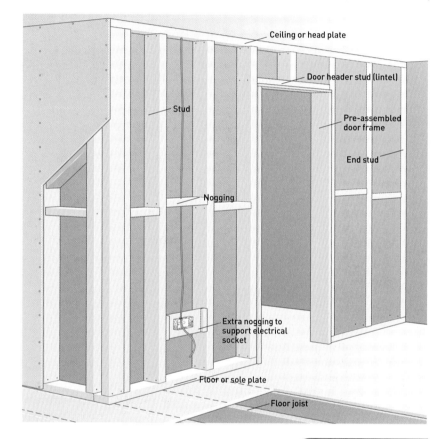

Ceiling or head plate

Door header stud (lintel)

Stud

Pre-assembled door frame

End stud

Nogging

Extra nogging to support electrical socket

Floor or sole plate

Floor joist

Making a frame

The stud wall frame can be made from 75mm x 50mm or 100mm x 50mm sawn timber. It consists of a ceiling or head plate, which is fixed to the ceiling joists; a matching length nailed to the floor, called the floor or sole plate; studs that stand vertically between the plates, equally spaced and fixed with nails; and noggings, which are short, horizontal braces that give extra support and keep the frame rigid.

1 Decide where to position your wall, and use an electronic detector to trace joists, cables and pipes in the walls, ceiling and floor. If the new wall is to run at right angles to the floor and ceiling joists, it can be fixed at any point. If the wall is to run parallel with the joists, it must stand directly over one of them. (If the partition wall must be installed between joists, lift the floorboards below and above and secure 100mm x 50mm timbers at right angles between two joists at 1m intervals to support the new wall.) Measure from both ends of a wall in the room and mark the position for one edge of the stud wall on the floor or skirting-board.

2 Suspend a plumb line to the mark you have made and draw a line up the wall to the ceiling, following the plumb line.

ONE PLANET HOME

Insulating your wall
Improve sound and heat insulation by fitting slab insulation between the studs before applying plasterboard to the second side (see page 335). To prevent electric cables from overheating, run them inside PVC conduit clipped to the studs or noggings, and passed through notches rather than holes.

B&Q Making it easier

Metal stud partitioning
Metal-frame stud partitions are available as a kit, including floor and ceiling fixings. They are quicker to assemble and make less mess than timber.

project essentials

- **joist, pipe and cable detector**
- **pencil**
- **tape measure**
- **plumb line**
- **chalk line**
- **bradawl**
- **panel saw**
- **power drill and twist bits**
- **hammer**
- **tenon saw**
- **spirit level**

- off-cut of wood
- 75mm x 50mm or 100mm x 50mm sawn timber
- 100mm countersunk cross-head wood screws (5mm gauge)
- 100mm nails
- wallplugs

Mark the ceiling line, using an off-cut of wood.

Knock a nail into the ceiling close to the wall junction at what will become the side edge of the ceiling plate. Measure and mark the opposite ceiling/wall junction. Make a guideline to show the ceiling plate position by snapping a chalk line between the two points. Use the detector to find the joists if they are at right angles to the new wall – you need to locate the joists so that the ceiling plate can be secured to them.

If the detector does not indicate the joist positions, use a bradawl to probe the ceiling along the length of the chalk line to find the joists. The holes you make will be hidden by the ceiling plate. Mark the positions for the fixing points on the ceiling adjacent to the chalk line.

Measure and cut the length of timber for the ceiling plate – it must fit exactly between the walls at the ceiling. Holding the plate in position, mark the fixing points along its length. If the wall runs directly underneath a parallel joist, these should be at 400mm intervals. Take it off the ceiling and drill clearance holes for the screws at the marked points. Fix the ceiling plate in position along the edge of the chalk line using 100mm countersunk cross-head wood screws (nails may crack the ceiling plaster). It's best to have some assistance, but failing that, use a wooden prop to help you to hold the ceiling plate in position.

Measure and cut the timber for the floor plate so that it fits exactly between the opposite walls (or skirting). If you're having a door, find the width of the opening you need by laying the pre-assembled door frame on the floor against the plate. Mark and cut the floor plate so that the frame will fit the gap exactly. Nail the floor plate to the floor at approximately 400mm intervals. If the joists run at right angles to the wall, follow the line of their fixings (or use the detector to find them) so that you can drive the nails into them (see diagram below). If the floor is solid, drill holes with a masonry bit and use plugs and screws.

Measure the distance between the ceiling and floor plates at each end of the frame and cut two studs to length; these end studs should be a tight fit. Place each one alongside the guideline you have drawn down the wall, and mark the clearance required for the skirting-board. Remove and use a tenon saw to shape a notch to fit around the skirting-board.

Drill clearance holes for the screws along the length of the end studs, and mark the positions of the holes on the walls. The first fixings should be approximately 100mm up from the floor (just above the skirting-board) and 100mm down from the ceiling. The remaining fixings should be 410mm–450mm apart. Drill the marked points on the walls, fit wallplugs, and then reposition and screw home the two end studs.

B&Q **Making it easier**

Positioning a door
Stud walls are non-loadbearing, so you can make a doorway or opening exactly where you wish, in whatever shape you wish. Although it's a good idea to put a door hard up against one end stud, as this braces the frame more securely, it really is up to you. Think about how you are going to use your new room, and where you want to put furniture.

Filling in the frame

Your frame is now ready to be filled in with timber studs and noggings. First, mark the floor plate at intervals to show the position of the vertical studs, which should be 600mm apart. If you need a doorway, start measuring at the wall and work towards where you want the frame – the doorway will be better braced by an adjacent vertical stud.

1 It is much easier to fix the vertical studs if you nail a supporting off-cut block of timber to one side of each vertical stud guideline on the floorplate.

2 Measure and cut your vertical studs. Hold them steady at the base, against the block supports. Fix them to the floor plate with 100mm nails skewed at an angle from both sides of the stud (see detail above). Fix to the ceiling plate in the same way, using a spirit level to make sure that each one is vertical.

3 To reinforce the vertical studs, take a measurement at the ceiling plate and cut short lengths of timber (noggings) to fit horizontally between them. Fit the noggings about half-way between the floor and ceiling, staggering their positions so that nails can be driven straight through the studs into the ends of the noggings. If you are using a metal box to mount a socket outlet or switch, fit an extra nogging to support it, or else use a cavity socket box (see page 279). Noggings also need to be fitted if you intend to mount a heavy item such as a washbasin, WC cistern, radiator or kitchen cupboard on the wall.

Making it easier

Creating a doorway

Use the pre-assembled door frame to measure the width of the header stud that will run horizontally across the top of the door. Cut and nail in place the vertical stud to which the door frame will be fixed.

Tack (lightly nail) the door frame in place, checking it is vertical with a spirit level and packing out with off-cuts of wood or hardboard if necessary. Mark the position of the door frame header stud. Remove the frame and fit the header stud.

Cables and pipes

Position all electric cables and plumbing pipes before enclosing the wall with plasterboard. Remember to mark the pipe and cable runs on the outside of the plasterboard on one side.

1 Plan the runs of plumbing pipes by marking the faces of the studs with a tenon saw. Carve out the pipe runs with the saw, or a chisel and mallet. Make the notches slope backwards very slightly, so they will hold the pipes while they are fitted. If you need a deep notch – for a waste pipe, for instance – reinforce the stud with a bridging piece.

2 Drill holes for cable through the middle of the noggings. Allow a generous air gap around the cable to prevent overheating. Don't run electric cables and plumbing pipes through the same holes.

safe electrics

• Never take risks with electrical safety. Before you start any kind of electrical work, see page 268.

• All new or modified installations must comply with the latest IEE Wiring Regulations. New or replacement cables or sockets may require RCD protection.

• If you plan to make changes to a power or lighting circuit in a bathroom, you must inform your local authority's Building Control Department first (see page 268).

Strengthen the doorway by fixing a short vertical stud centrally between the door header stud and the ceiling plate, using skewed nails. Then nail the frame securely in place.

Working with plasterboard

Once the stud wall framework is in place, it needs to be covered with 12.5mm thick plasterboard. This comes in different widths, lengths and types, including acoustic-check plasterboard (see page 369), which will give enhanced sound insulation. Tapered-edge boards will make it easier to achieve a smooth finish using tape and jointing compound (see page 75). Plasterboard sheets can be fixed horizontally or vertically (which is easier, as they are heavy and can be rested on the floor). Whichever way you choose, you should start at the doorway and work outwards at either side.

project essentials

- tape measure
- pencil
- craft knife with plasterboard blades
- bolster chisel
- power drill with twist bits
- tenon saw
- chisel
- mallet

- 2400mm x 1200mm plasterboard sheets or 220mm x 600mm handy boards (plaster lath sheets)
- off-cut of wood
- 32mm plasterboard nails

Using handy boards (plaster lath sheets)

If you're worried that you'll have trouble transporting or handling full-size plasterboard sheets, you can use 1220mm x 600mm handy boards instead. As these are smaller, they need many more fixings and therefore result in a patchwork finish. So although they are easier to manage, securing them is very time-consuming. And think twice before you attempt to finish handy boards with tape and jointing compound, as it's difficult to achieve a smooth surface. You'll be better off getting in a good plasterer to complete the job with a full plaster coat.

Vertical or horizontal?

If you are fixing your plasterboard sheets vertically, position each width so that the joins align at the centre of a stud. If you are fixing your sheets horizontally, start by nailing the bottom row of boards to the frame and stagger the vertical joints.

Vertical fixing

Cutting plasterboard

Standard plasterboard has a grey side and an ivory side, which faces outwards. The sheets need to be cut to fit, especially where walls and ceilings are not completely straight. Be warned – your knife blade will become blunt very quickly, so a knife with replaceable blades is a useful tool for this job. If cutting a lot of plasterboard, specialist plasterboard blades will be quicker, safer and produce cleaner cuts.

Fixing plasterboard

Get someone to help you attach the plasterboard to the frame – it's much easier with two people. A wood off-cut used as a 'floor lifter' will enable you to raise each board tight up against the ceiling as you fix it. The plasterboard should be fitted with the ivory side outwards. Finish the joints with tape and jointing compound (see page 75).

1 Measure the sheets to 12mm less than the floor-to-ceiling height. Mark the cutting line on the ivory side of the plasterboard, then cut along it using a craft knife and straightedge.

2 Turn the plasterboard over and fold the end along the cut to snap the board. Use a craft knife to cut through the paper backing.

1 Starting at the door studs, carefully position a full-size board vertically, ivory side outwards, to cover half the width of the door stud and half of one other stud. Wedge a bolster chisel at the foot of the board, slide a wood off-cut underneath and use your foot to press down and force the board hard up against the ceiling.

2 Fix the board in place with 32mm plasterboard nails at roughly 150mm intervals, 15mm away from the edges. Continue to fit whole boards in the same way before cutting boards to fit above the doorway and against the adjacent walls. If there is a skirting-board, notch the plasterboard to fit around it.

WALLS DRY-LINING

Dry-lining, or attaching plasterboard to a wall surface, provides a smooth finish for decorating. It is much easier for the non-professional to achieve a good quality result than with wet plaster, and can be decorated straight away.

Setting out

To ensure the plasterboard is straight on the wall, first mark guidelines on the walls and ceiling to help you position the boards in the right place.

1 Start by measuring out board widths, working away from the window opening. Place an off-cut of plasterboard against the window reveal and measure a plasterboard width across, allowing an extra 10mm for the adhesive that will fix the window sections to the reveal.

2 Using a laser level or a spirit level, mark a vertical plumb line from the floor to the ceiling, extending the marks onto the ceiling and the floor.

3 Snap a vertical chalk line down the marked line. This will be your guideline for the first board. Continue across the room, marking the board positions.

project essentials

- tape measure
- laser level or spirit level
- pencil
- chalk line
- combination square
- plasterboard padsaw
- marker spray
- straightedge
- craft knife
- bucket
- builder's float
- pointing hawk
- board lifter or bolster chisel and wood off-cuts
- plasterboard rasp

- 12.5mm plasterboard sheets
- plasterboard adhesive

4 Mark a line across the top, which will be the finish line, allowing 12.5mm for the thickness of the board and 10–15mm for the adhesive.

Making difficult cuts

For a professional finish, it's important to make neat cuts in the plasterboard to fit it around obstacles such as window sills. Make any cuts before applying the adhesive. A plasterboard padsaw has a pointed, narrow blade that is ideal for cutting out awkward shapes, and its coarse teeth cut easily through plasterboard.

1 Make a mark on the wall where the plasterboard sheet finishes and measure from that mark to the window sill, using a combination square and a tape measure. Make a note of the measurements.

2 Transpose those measurements to the plasterboard, adding a little extra so you have room for positioning the plasterboard. This extra space can be filled once the plasterboard is fitted.

3 Cut out the shape using a plasterboard padsaw.

ideal tool

Combination square

A combination square can be used to measure a level and to check 90° and 45° angles. It incorporates a small spirit bubble for checking a level surface.

Attaching the plasterboard

Plasterboard adhesive is rapid setting so it is a good idea to do just one area of the wall at a time. Mark on the wall where you want the dabs of adhesive to go before you start. There should be lines of dabs from the top to bottom of the wall but don't bridge the joins between sheets of plasterboard with dabs of adhesive.

Use a marker spray to mark the position of the adhesive dabs 400mm apart, or according to the adhesive manufacturer's instructions. Mix the plasterboard adhesive in a bucket.

Check that the board is perfectly vertical with a spirit level.

Cutting holes for sockets

Run a marker pen or old lipstick around the rim of a socket mounting box.

Hold the plasterboard accurately in position against the mounting box to leave an outline. Make a pilot hole in each corner, then turn the board around and join up the holes with a pencil. Cut the square with a plasterboard padsaw.

Using a builder's float and pointing hawk, apply dabs of adhesive to the walls.

Make sure that the board is fitting tightly against the ceiling. If it is not, lift it with a board lifter or a bolster and wood off-cuts. Repeat the process for the next sheet of plasterboard.

Lift the plasterboard into place, in line with the chalk lines on the wall and ceiling.

Dry-lining a timber frame
If a wall is very uneven or in poor condition, attach a framework of timber studs to it before dry-lining. Fix the plasterboard to the studs with nails rather than adhesive. You can install thermal insulation between the timber studs before applying plasterboard, as well as using sound-deadening plasterboard (see page 369) to provide acoustic insulation.

Use a heavy batten to tap the board flat against the wall. A long piece of 50x100mm timber is ideal.

Fitting a corner

Walls and corners are rarely absolutely straight, so for a neat fit you will need to scribe and cut a plasterboard sheet to the shape of the wall. Measure the gap between the wall and the closest sheet of plasterboard. Cut a sheet of plasterboard 250mm wider than the gap and cut a small piece the same width as the gap.

Position the plasterboard sheet 200mm away from the corner. Place one end of the small piece against the corner at the top of the wall and the other overlapping the plasterboard sheet. Move the piece down to the floor, tracing the contour of the corner on the plasterboard.

Cut along the line and use a plasterboard rasp to neaten the cut edge.

WALLS DRY-LINING

Once all the walls have been dry-lined with plasterboard, the windows can be lined with pieces of plasterboard and then the corners and joins can be given a smooth finish with angle bead and jointing tape.

Measure the width and height of the window reveals. Cut pieces of plasterboard to size and stick them in place with adhesive.

Plasterboard in a window recess

For a neat look around a window, you need to cut pieces of plasterboard to fit the sides (reveals) and the top of the window.

Use masking tape to temporarily hold the pieces in position.

Measure the width and depth at the top of the window reveal. Cut a piece of plasterboard to size and stick it in place with adhesive.

project essentials

- **tape measure**
- **straightedge**
- **craft knife**
- **masking tape**
- **timber supports**
- **tinsnips**
- **bucket**
- **filling knife**
- **internal and external corner trowels**

- 12.5 mm plasterboard sheets
- plasterboard adhesive
- paper-faced metal angle bead
- plasterboard jointing compound

Use timber supports between the plasterboard and window sill to hold the top piece of plasterboard in place while the adhesive dries.

Finishing internal corners

For a perfect finish at an internal corner and along the join with the ceiling, use paper-faced metal angle bead stuck in place with jointing compound. A steel-bladed internal corner trowel will give the jointing compound a smooth finish.

Measure the height of the wall. Cut the angle bead 12.5mm shorter than the wall height with tinsnips, cutting first from one side then the other.

Mix the jointing compound in a bucket and apply it to the corner with a filling knife, extending it just beyond where the angle bead will fit.

Press the angle bead into position in the corner.

Cover with a top coat of jointing compound and smooth with an internal corner trowel.

Finishing along the ceiling

The joins between the plasterboard walls and the ceiling can be finished in the same way as internal corners. Stand on a stable stepladder to reach the ceiling.

1 Measure along the top of the wall, cut paper-faced metal angle bead to fit and stick it in place with jointing compound.

2 Cover the bead with a top coat of jointing compound and smooth it with an internal corner trowel.

Finishing external corners

Paper-faced metal angle bead is also used to create a strong join at an external corner. Here an external corner trowel will give a crisp angle to the jointing compound.

1 Measure the width and height of the corner. Cut the angle bead to fit. Apply jointing compound to the corner and stick the bead in place.

2 Cover with a top coat of jointing compound and smooth with an external corner trowel.

Smoothing the joints

For the smoothest possible finish, plasterboard should be plastered – a skilled job best left to a professional. However, plasterboard joints can be given a satisfactory finish with jointing compound and jointing tape. When all the joints are dry, fill the join with the adjacent wall and any other gaps with filler, then all you need to do is apply a drywall primer to the surface and you're ready to decorate.

1 Mix the jointing compound in a bucket. Smooth the compound down or along the joint with a filling knife or scraper.

2 Cut a piece of jointing tape the length of the joint with scissors and press the tape in place.

project essentials

- bucket
- filling knife or scraper
- scissors
- coating knife
- clean sponge
- sanding block

- plasterboard jointing compound
- jointing tape
- fine-grade abrasive paper

ideal tool

Pole sander

This sander is fitted on a lightweight extendable handle, which allows you to smooth off ceiling joins and other out-of-reach areas.

3 Using the blade of a coating knife, press jointing compound along the taped join flush with the surface of the tape. Immediately smooth the surface and feather the edges of the compound with a clean damp sponge. Keep rinsing the sponge and wringing it thoroughly, as excess moisture will weaken the joint.

4 Leave the compound to dry, then, if necessary, sand any bumps very lightly with a sanding block.

ONE PLANET HOME

Protecting forestry
Always choose timber that has been certified by an independent organisation such as the Forest Stewardship Council (FSC). That way you can rest assured that the product you are buying has not contributed to the destruction of the world's forests.

FOREST FRIENDLY Responsibly sourced wood products diy.com/forestfriendly

Tongue-and-groove panelling is both attractive and hardwearing. You can paint or stain it, or keep a natural wood finish. It is made from planks with a small tongue along one edge and a matching groove along the other. The tongue slots neatly into the groove of the neighbouring plank. The panelling can cover as much of the wall as you like – up to dado level is a popular height. It is usually easier to leave old skirting-boards in place and apply new skirting when you have finished panelling. Or, if the floor is uneven, it may be better to use a thin moulding and bend it to fit the contour of the floor as you fix it. The simplest way of covering the top edge of the panelling is to glue on L-shaped capping. Any switches and sockets will have to be moved forward and remounted.

Fixing the battens

The tongue-and-groove panels are nailed to horizontal battens which you should fit in place first. For panelling up to dado level, you will need to fit three battens, one at floor level, one level with the top of the panelling, and one half-way between the two. There should be approximately 400mm–500mm between them.

project essentials

- **tape measure**
- **pencil**
- **tenon saw**
- **spirit level**
- **power drill with masonry bit**
- **bradawl**
- **pipe and cable detector**
- **screwdriver**
- **long-nosed pliers**
- **nail punch**
- **hammer**

- 50mm x 25mm softwood battens
- tongue-and-groove panelling
- 50mm screws (5mm gauge) and wallplugs
- abrasive paper
- panel pins
- L-shaped capping
- wood adhesive
- skirting

1 Cut battens to fit the length of the wall you wish to panel. Decide on the height of the panelling and cut each tongue-and-groove plank to length. Using one of the cut planks, mark the height on the wall with a pencil. Use a tape measure and pencil to measure and mark the other levels. If there is skirting on the wall, the lower batten should be fixed just above it. If there is no skirting, mark the lower batten position about 50mm from the floor to leave a gap for air to circulate.

2 Using a spirit level, draw horizontal lines across the wall joining up the marks at the three batten levels. The top edge of the top batten should be exactly the same height as the top of the cut plank.

3 Drill the battens 50mm from each end and at about 400mm intervals in between. Hold each batten in position and mark the drill points on the wall with a bradawl. Check there are no hidden pipes or cables behind the fixing positions before you drill and plug the wall and screw the battens in place.

B&Q Making it easier

Filling gaps
If the wall is very uneven, you will need some packing, such as cardboard or wood off-cuts, to fill any gaps behind the battens.

Sand any rough edges at each end of the planks. Starting on the left, hold the first plank in place (tongue side on the right), level with the top batten. Nail a panel pin through the top left-hand side of the plank face into the batten.

Sink the pin heads below the surface of the plank using a nail punch and hammer. Slot the next plank into place with its groove covering the tongue of the previous plank. Repeat for each plank until you reach the end of the wall. Cut the last plank to fit, and nail through the face into the battens. If you are panelling the next wall too, leave a 3mm gap between the last plank and the wall at the corner. Butt the grooved edge of the first plank on the adjoining wall against this last plank, and nail it though the face into the battens.

Attaching the panelling

The design of tongue-and-groove panelling allows for 'secret nailing' (see cross-section, right). Panel pins are nailed through the tongue of each plank and covered by the groove of the next plank as it is slotted in place.

Use a spirit level to check the plank is vertical before fixing it to the remaining battens. Repeat this every 3 or 4 planks to make sure the panelling remains vertical.

Cut the capping to fit the top edge of the panelling. Apply wood adhesive to the panelling, attach the capping, and leave to dry.

▲ **Surface-mounted fitting**

A surface-mounted switch or socket sits on the panelling, but remember to fit short battens to to the wall behind to support its fixing screws. Turn off the mains power. Drill a hole, disconnect the cable and pass it through the hole. Screw the box to the battens, reconnect the cable and replace the faceplate.

To 'secret nail' the planks, hold a pin with long-nosed pliers and hammer it at an angle through the corner of the tongue into the batten behind it. Repeat for each batten.

Cut a length of skirting to fit and nail it to the bottom of the panelling with panel pins.

Remounting a power socket

◄ **Flush-mounted fitting**

Cut a hole for the mounting box as you fit the panels at that point. With the power switched off at the mains, unscrew the faceplate. Move the mounting box forward and pack the recess behind it with short pieces of wood. Screw the box to the wall using wallplugs inserted into the masonry. The screws should penetrate about 25mm. Fit the planks, reconnect the cable and replace the faceplate.

Skirting covers the joint between the wall and the floor. It makes a decorative border while hiding the gaps needed for the natural expansion and contraction that takes place in a house. It also suffers a lot of hard wear. Fortunately, replacing it is not complicated, and there is a range of profiles to choose from (see page 369). Or you may want to restore skirting to a property whose original mouldings have been stripped out, or fit it on a newly built stud partition wall.

Removing old skirting
Take care when prising away old skirting not to damage adjacent plaster. Tap the blade of a bolster chisel between the wall and the skirting using a hammer. Lever the top edge away enough to insert the blade of a crowbar. Place a thin piece of wood behind the crowbar to protect the wall.

Fitting new skirting

Coat the back of new skirting-board with wood preservative before fitting it. The type of fixing will depend on the construction of the wall and the previous fixings:

- masonry walls: use masonry nails or screws
- stud walls: use oval wire nails nailed into the studs (located with a stud detector, see page 68)
- grounds (timber blocks): if the old skirting was attached to these common fixing points, then use them again. Mark their position on your new skirting and fix onto them using lost-head nails.

You could just glue it in place with wood adhesive, and on damp-proofed walls you will have to in order to avoid penetrating the damp-proofing with nails or screws. It may be necessary to use a combination of methods. For long lengths, you will need a trestle on which to rest one end of the board.

Start at the longest wall with internal corners. Measure the wall and mark the top edge of a length of skirting to show where it should be cut. Fit the skirting-board mitre tool (see IDEAL TOOL) in a vice or workbench. Put the left-hand end of the skirting in the mitre tool and rest the other end on the trestle, making sure the trestle is level with the base of the mitre tool. Protect the board face with a piece of hardboard placed under the thumbscrews, then tighten the screws. Cut the mitre for the left-hand corner with the saw, then move the skirting and cut the right-hand corner.

If fixing the skirting with masonry nails or screws, fit them to existing points where possible; otherwise, fix them approximately every 600mm at the highest flat point on the skirting, checking first that there are no pipes or cables behind the fixing positions. If there are timber grounds, fix the skirting to them with lost-head nails. If using screws, drill pilot holes and insert plugs then screws. For stud walls, locate the studs using a stud detector and nail oval wire nails into them.

If gluing the skirting, apply adhesive evenly to the back. Press the piece in place and, if necessary, hold it in position with props made from off-cuts of wood until the adhesive has set.

ideal tool

Skirting-board mitre tool
This guiding tool is fixed in a vice or workbench, and the skirting is held steady in it by thumbscrews. It can be used for cutting left- or right-hand mitres, and for both internal and external corners.

Continue measuring, cutting and fixing skirting to one wall at a time. Turn the board the other way up in the skirting board mitre tool to cut mitres for external corners. To fix the skirting at external corners, use adhesive and then hammer two panel pins into the skirting each side of the corner for extra security.

When all the skirting is in place, sand the external corners and fill any gaps with filler. Sand them again when dry. Cover any nail or screw holes with filler.

Fill the gaps between the skirting and the wall with decorator's caulk. Leave to dry before applying primer, then undercoat and finally a top coat of paint. Or if you plan to varnish the new skirting, use an acrylic filler that matches the colour of your wood.

Cutting skirting profiles

Instead of cutting mitres for corners, you can fit boards at internal corners by profile cutting. The first board is fitted right into the corner, then the end of the second board is cut to fit around the profile of the first.

project essentials

- **profile gauge**
- **pencil**
- **workbench**
- **coping saw**

- new skirting

Fit one skirting-board right into the corner, with the end butting up against the wall. Hold a profile gauge against this skirting to take a copy of its shape.

Measure and mark the next length of skirting to be fitted. Hold the profile gauge against the mark and draw round the shape with a pencil.

Alternatively, hold an off-cut of the skirting at 90° to the piece to be fitted and trace its profile with a pencil.

Cut along the pencil mark with a coping saw.

Check the fit – you may have to make small adjustments to get it absolutely right.

ideal tool

Profile gauge
A simple profile gauge will make numerous tasks easier – not just tracing skirting profiles, but laying tiles or flooring or anything that needs to be cut to fit an awkward shape.

project essentials

- **tape measure**
- **pencil**
- **panel saw**
- **pipe and cable detector**
- **power drill**
- **screwdriver**
- **hammer**
- **trowel**
- **spirit level**
- **craft knife**
- **damp sponge**
- **striking tool**
- **grout raker**
- **soft cloth**

- glass blocks and frame
- 38mm screws or 50mm screws and wallplugs (4mm or 5mm gauge); or hollow-wall fixings
- 20mm nails
- foam expansion-joint strip
- glass-block mortar
- plastic spacers
- panel anchors
- panel grout
- silicone sealant

Glass blocks make an interesting alternative to more traditional building materials. You can choose from a vast array of sizes, colours and designs. They are especially good in kitchens and bathrooms as they are resistant to grease and humidity, and they can even be used to build a curved wall.

While glass blocks are not suitable for a structural wall, they are a stylish way of dividing a room while making good use of the light. The blocks are simply laid within a wooden frame, which is fixed to the floor, ceiling and walls at either end. Special glass block frames are available, which you cut to size. Choose a frame to fit your blocks with the width the same as the thickness of the blocks. A flexible foam expansion-joint strip is fitted between the frame and the glass blocks to allow for slight movement. Panel anchors (hidden by mortar) are screwed to the sides of the frame to secure the blocks. Fit them every row or alternate row according to the manufacturer's instructions.

Building the wall

To work out the dimensions of the frame, lay a single row of blocks on the floor with plastic spacers between them, including one at each end. Measure the total length, then do the same for the vertical dimension. Cut the frame to fit.

Fit the frame into place, packing it with small off-cuts of wood to ensure it is level and square if necessary. Fix it to the walls, ceiling and floor: drill holes in the frame, mark the wall, and check for hidden pipes and cables. Then drill the fixing holes and insert either 50mm wallplugs and screws into masonry; 38mm screws into wood (ceiling joists or the studs of a stud wall); or hollow-wall fixings into plasterboard (see page 376).

safety first

A wall of glass blocks is heavy, so you must check that the weight can be supported by the floor below, especially if building on a suspended wooden floor. If in doubt, seek professional advice before starting the project.

Nail the expansion strip to the sides of the frame at intervals, stopping just short of the bottom of the frame to allow a spacer to be fitted against the frame. Mix the mortar to a smooth consistency and lay a bed of mortar on the bottom of the frame (the sill). Use enough mortar to give a 10mm joint when the blocks are in place.

Starting at one corner, place an L-shaped spacer against the frame. Place a T-shaped spacer to support the other end of the block (use one of the blocks to mark out the right position).

Lay the first block in the corner and bed well down on spacers.

B&Q Making it easier

Spacers
The cross-shaped plastic spacers sold with glass blocks are three spacers in one, as you can snap them off to make T-shaped and L-shaped spacers to fit around the frame. The tabs are twisted off once the mortar has set. To work out how many you need, allow 1.5 spacers per block plus 10%.

Position the next T-shaped spacer. Apply enough mortar to the side of the second block to fill the cavity between the blocks. Sit the second block on the spacers and push it against the first block, ensuring it is snug on the spacers.

Continue until the first row is complete, checking from time to time with a spirit level to make sure it is straight. Lay mortar on top of the first row and bed in full spacers between the blocks. Lay the second row.

Using a craft knife, cut the expansion strip level with the second row of blocks.

Lift the expansion strip and screw a panel anchor to the side of the frame at either end of the row. Drop the strip back over the vertical arm of the anchor. Its horizontal arm should fit over the block and the spacers; cover it with mortar and continue laying the blocks.

Clean the face of the blocks with a damp sponge from time to time as you work.

Reinforcing the wall

If the span of the wall is greater than 1.4m, steel reinforcing bars must be laid between each row of blocks. Lay the mortar on top of the blocks and press the reinforcing bar into it. If you need more than one bar for the length of the wall, overlap them by 150mm.

Finishing

When all the blocks are laid, you should leave the mortar to set for about an hour and then smooth out all the joints. Apply panel grout (if your mortar is a dirty colour or the wall is for a shower) and finish with silicone sealant where the bricks meet the frame.

ideal tool

Striking tool

This metal or plastic tool consists of a handle and a set of curved blades in different sizes. Use the blade to smooth the mortar in the joints, compacting it and creating a moisture-resistant seal.

1 When the mortar has set, twist off the tabs on the spacers. Smooth the joints with a striking tool (see IDEAL TOOL). This compacts the mortar to create a moisture-resistant seal. After striking, all the joints should be full of mortar.

2 If the wall is being built for a shower, rake some of the mortar out of the joints with a small trowel so that a depth of 10mm remains, and leave for 24 hours. (You can also do this if your mortar is not white and you want a white finish.)

3 The next day, fill the joints with white panel grout, moulding and compacting them with a striking tool. Leave for 1–2 hours, then wipe the surface with a clean, soft cloth.

4 Apply silicone sealant in a continuous bead where the blocks join the frame, at the top, sides and bottom on both sides.

WALLS PREPARATION

Walls almost always need some surface preparation before you can apply paint. Even brand-new plaster needs sealing. Cracks and holes must be filled (see page 64), and surfaces must be clean, smooth and dry (for problems such as damp, see page 66). Emulsion-painted surfaces in good condition can be painted over; peeling paint should be stripped back or sanded. Only paint over wallpaper if it is very firmly stuck to the wall.

Stripping wallpaper

Before you begin any preparation or decoration work, clear the room as much as possible. Anything that has to stay should be moved into the centre of the room and covered with dust sheets. Use dust sheets to protect the floor too. Soaking wallpaper with hot water makes it much easier to remove. The water soaks in more easily if you perforate the paper first, either by scoring with the blade of a stripping knife or running an orbital scorer over the surface (see below). Be sure to stand on a stable stepladder to tackle the higher sections.

project essentials

- **dust sheets**
- **bucket**
- **large sponge**
- **protective gloves**
- **safety goggles**
- **orbital wallpaper scorer**
- **stepladder**
- **wide stripping knife**
- **wallpaper steam stripper**
- **hot-air gun, if removing cork tiles**

- hot water
- liquid detergent
- wallpaper paste

ideal tool

Steam stripper
An electric steam stripper consists of a tank and a pad, joined by a length of pipe. The tank is filled with water which is heated until it boils. Steam comes out of the pad, which is held against the wall to loosen the paper. Filling the tank with warm water will bring it to the boil faster. Don't hold the stripper over one spot for too long, as this can damage plaster.

Always use a steam stripper safely:

- Turn off the power and leave to cool for two minutes before refilling the tank.
- Do not use around electrical switches and sockets.
- Wear heat-resistant gloves and goggles.
- Never leave a steam stripper unattended when it is turned on.
- Keep the boiler on a level surface.
- Never move it by pulling the pipe, and don't detach the pipe while it is switched on.
- Always read the instruction leaflet before you start.

1 Run the orbital scorer over the paper, being careful not to damage the plaster behind. Fill a bucket with hot water and add some liquid detergent and a handful of wallpaper paste to thicken it a little.

2 Using a large sponge, wet the wall, covering a few square metres at a time. Leave it to soak for at least five minutes. Slide the edge of a wide stripping knife under the paper at a seam to see if it is ready to be stripped. It should come away in fairly large sections. If this doesn't happen even after a long and thorough soak, you will need to use wallpaper stripper solution (SEE MAKING IT EASIER) or a steam stripper.

3 Hold the stripper pad at the bottom of a wallpaper length for a minute or so, until the paper around it appears damp. Move the pad up onto the next section, while pulling off the damp paper below, loosening stubborn areas with a stripping knife. Strip each length from bottom to top. Take care not to damage the plasterboard or plaster with the blade of your stripping knife.

B&Q Making it easier

Wallpaper stripper solution
Specially formulated wallpaper stripper solution will enable you to remove wallpaper without the need for steaming.

Stripping cork tiles

Removing cork tiles is easy: simply lever them off the wall with a large stripping knife. The problem is the adhesive they leave behind, still firmly attached to the wall. The best way to get rid of this is to soften it with an electric hot-air gun, also known as a hot-air stripper. This is much safer than a blowtorch because there is no naked flame – it simply blasts hot air. Scrape the adhesive from the surface while it is still soft, using the stripping knife.

Smooth and clean surfaces

The difference between a good paint job and a disappointment is almost always down to the time and care spent in preparing the surface. It is often tempting to get quickly to the excitement of the final coat, but no paint can properly mask dirty or uneven surfaces. So you should always make sure you remove any dirt, grease and loose or flaking material from the surface to be painted, and fill any holes and repair defects (see pages 64–65). Even on new surfaces there may be small areas that need touching up. If a surface has been previously painted, you will need to remove or fill chips, blisters and bumps and strip back peeling paint. Be sure to allow any fillers to dry completely before carrying on.

Washing

Painted and wallpapered surfaces alike need to be washed down before being painted over. The less dirt or grease on a surface, the better the final paint job will look. Grease, damp, mould, nicotine stains, children's drawings and finger marks can all be removed using detergent or, better still, sugar soap. Wear waterproof gloves and safety goggles as you work, as sugar soap can irritate the skin. Always finish by rinsing with clean water and then leave to dry completely.

In older houses you still sometimes find distemper. This old-fashioned emulsion is often dusty or powdery to the touch, and will rub off as you wash the surface. Don't be tempted to paint or wallpaper over distemper, as neither will stick. You must wash and scrape off as much as possible, and then seal with a special stabilising solution.

PRIMERS FOR DIFFERENT SURFACES

Surface	Primer
Wood	Use a wood primer. This fills and levels the wood grain, and prevents the paint soaking in. Ensure wood is dry before applying.
Metal	Use metal primer. This is anti-corrosive and helps paint to bond to the smooth surface of the metal. Different primers may be required for ferrous and non-ferrous metals. Special primers can be used to prevent rust or can be painted onto rusty surfaces.
Radiators	Bare radiators or exposed areas should be primed using a metal or radiator primer. The primer helps prevent metal corrosion and improve paint finish. Prime when the radiator is cold.
MDF	Use MDF primer. MDF is highly absorbent; the primer seals the porous surface, helping prevent paint soaking in.
Bare plaster	Use plaster sealer. This will seal the porous surface, preventing paint from sinking in. Without it, you will need many more coats of paint. Be sure to allow new plaster to dry out completely first: this can take up to four weeks for a skim coat, and several months for a full new plaster. As it dries, the surface of the plaster will turn from dark to pale pink.
Multiple surfaces	If you have lots of small areas to prime, a multi-surface (or 3 in 1) primer can be very useful. Suitable for use on wood, metal or plaster, it will save you buying lots of separate products.
Tiles, melamine, PVCu	Use a specialist primer to ensure that paint bonds to the smooth, hard surface: tile primer, melamine (or cupboard) primer, or PVCu primer, as appropriate.

Sanding down

Sanding creates a smooth, even foundation that greatly enhances the final finish of paintwork. It gives a slight roughness – a 'key' – to surfaces such as varnish or paint, and this helps the primer or paint to stick. On stripped plaster, sanding levels out any repairs and also removes stubborn traces of old wallpaper or paste. When sanding wood, remember always to work in the direction of the grain.

Sanding produces a lot of dust, so be sure to protect yourself with a dust mask and good ventilation, and to cover anything vulnerable with dust sheets. Once finished, you will need to dust down the whole sanded surface from ceiling to floor, and vacuum thoroughly. It may sound like a lot of extra work, but the professional finish sanding creates really does make it all worthwhile in the end.

B&Q Making it easier

Liquid sander
On previously painted surfaces in good condition, a 'liquid sander' that you wipe on does a good job of cleaning thoroughly and providing a key. It is also much less messy.

Priming

You don't need to prime a surface that has previously been painted and is in good condition: washing and light sanding are usually enough. But you will achieve a better finish on most other surfaces by priming them first. Paint will cling firmly to a coat of primer, and not crack or flake. If you have stripped a previously painted surface back to the bare material, priming the exposed area will give a smoother final finish. On a porous surface, primer prevents the top coat from being absorbed, meaning you have to apply fewer coats of paint to achieve good coverage. On non-porous, shiny surfaces, paint often won't bond properly: a coat of primer gives it something to stick to.

Different surfaces need different primers, so be sure to select the right one and to follow the manufacturer's instructions carefully. If you are in a hurry, look out for quick-drying primer: some can be painted over in just an hour. Water-based primers are low odour and less damaging to the environment.

Once you have prepared the walls and cleared the room, you can start painting. This is one of the most pleasurable parts of decorating, but don't rush into it without thinking. Before you start, run through some final checks:

- Are you sure you have the right paint, and also enough of it (see below)?
- Do you have the right sort of cleaning fluid for your paint, and a good supply of it?
- Do you have the right tools for the job? Most paints can be applied with either a brush or a roller.
- Can you reach all the surfaces safely? You will certainly need a stepladder, and may have to hire or make a work platform (see pages 356–57).
- Have you allowed yourself enough time? Take account not only of the drying time, but also the period between coats of paint (see the chart below).
- Are there children and pets around? Keep them away from wet paint!

Choosing your paints

Large areas like walls and ceilings should be painted with water-based paint. You can choose between traditional emulsion or the latest multi-surface formulas, suitable for wood, metal and even radiators. See below, and also the tables on page 372.

Emulsion

Emulsion is a water-based paint for walls and ceilings available in a large variety of colours, which usually need two coats. It can be applied directly on to walls that have been previously painted, or on to paintable wall coverings such as lining paper and textured wallpaper. Emulsion paint generally comes in two finishes – matt and silk. Matt has a flat, non-reflective appearance, which is useful for disguising uneven surfaces. Traditional matt emulsion marks easily and is not washable, but new 'wipeable' matt paints have been introduced in many ranges. Silk emulsion has a shiny, reflective finish, and can be washed. It is useful for vulnerable areas such as halls, staircases and children's rooms. There is a third finish, often called soft sheen, satin or mid-sheen, which is basically half-way between matt and silk, with a wipeable surface.

One-coat emulsion

This special emulsion paint is thicker and has superior covering power. Just one coat will cover most surfaces. This paint usually comes in satin, mid-sheen and matt finishes. Always be sure to use a good quality roller with one-coat paint to ensure even coverage.

Kitchen and bathroom emulsion

These paints are specifically formulated for areas of high humidity. They have moisture- and grease-resistant properties, and give a tough, scrubbable surface.

Multi-surface acrylics

These paints can be applied to walls, ceilings, woodwork and radiators, meaning you only need one paint for the whole job. Like traditional emulsion paints they are water-based, quick-drying and low-odour, but their advanced formula means they are tougher and washable. They are available in matt finish for a solid, flat colour or satin for a subtle sheen.

Undercoat and base coat

Many modern paints are formulated to give good coverage on a properly prepared surface without a separate undercoat: check the manufacturer's advice. Often, however, an undercoat will ensure better results, especially if you are painting over a strong or dark colour. Look out for specially formulated base coat which includes fine, flexible fillers that will cover not just strong colour but filled areas and hairline cracks.

PAINTS FOR INTERIOR WALLS AND CEILINGS	Emulsion	One-coat emulsion	New-plaster emulsion	Multi-surface acrylic	Textured paint	Cement paint
Drying time (hours)						
Touch-dry	1–2	3–4	1–2	1–2	24	1–2
Recoatable	4		4	4		24
Number of coats						
Normal conditions	2	1	1–2	1–2	1	2
How far it spreads						
Sq metres per litre	12–14	8–10	11	12–14	2–3	
Sq metres per kg						1–6

Paint in sequence

Do you need to paint the ceiling? If so, paint it first, since you are bound to get some on the walls. Then paint the walls, and finally the woodwork. Start painting by the window or light source, and paint in bands away from and in parallel to it. Take a break when you reach the corner of a room, not in the middle of a wall. For a detailed guide to painting windows, see pages 134–35.

Paintbrushes

There is a vast range of paintbrushes to choose from, ranging from cheap ones that you use once then throw away to professional-quality brushes that will improve with use, careful cleaning and correct storage. You can also now buy high-quality synthetic brushes that minimise bristle-loss and have individually tapered fibres for a finer finish.

Taking a break?

Stop brushes or rollers drying out by wrapping them in cling film. If you make the wrap as airtight as possible, they will remain soft overnight.

Cleaning and storing

Brushes used with water-based paints are simply washed with water. Work a little soap into the bristles, rinse them clean and leave them to dry. Clean, dry brushes, rollers and pads can be stored wrapped in lint-free cloth, plastic bags, foil or brown paper. Brushes steeped in oil- or solvent-based paint can be stored immersed in an appropriate cleaner or solvent. However, resting the bristles on the bottom of a jar for any length of time is certain to ruin them, so suspend the brush, or use a specially designed cleaning tub.

Using a paintbrush cleaning tub

This is ideal for storing as well as cleaning brushes that have been used with oil- and solvent-based paints. With the lid on tight, store brushes with a small amount of cleaning fluid in the bottom. The vapours circulate, keeping the brush clean and fresh.

Snap the brushes into position.

Add enough cleaning fluid to cover just the bristles, fasten the lid and rock the container backwards and forwards several times to clean the brush. Dispose of the fluid as instructed, and replace with fresh fluid up to the mark. Keep the lid on while the brush is in storage.

Tricks of the trade

Buying paint in quantity can save you money, but only if you know how to store and decant it effectively.

Storing paint

Paint will not keep indefinitely, as it deteriorates over time. Solvent-based paints have a longer storage life than water-based ones. You can store small quantities in an airtight jar. Choose a size that leaves as little air in the jar as possible, and always label the container with the code number, name and type of paint, and note the room it was used in.

When storing paint in the tin, reduce the risk of a skin forming by turning it upside-down for a few seconds (first making sure that it is tightly shut) to 'seal' the lid with paint, or cut a round of foil to the size of the lid and press it down on to the paint to eliminate air.

Using a paint kettle

A large tin of paint may be more economical, but it is cumbersome to work with. Professionals always decant paint into smaller containers known as 'kettles'. These are available in metal or plastic. It takes a lot of white spirit to clean oil-based paint from a container, so it is a good idea to use a throwaway lining of aluminium foil (right). Mould the foil into the kettle and if necessary use more than one layer to make sure it is fully leak-proof.

ONE PLANET HOME

Recycling unused paint
Water-based paint is better for the environment than a solvent- or oil-based product, but whatever you use, never pour leftovers down the drain. Paint can pollute waterways. Contact your local authority to find out if there are any paint recycling schemes in your area.

WALLS PAINTING TECHNIQUES

Walls and ceilings are usually painted with emulsion, acrylic or water-based eggshell. Non-drip emulsion is also available, in jelly or solid form, and this is particularly good for ceilings. Never stir non-drip paint, however lumpy it looks. You will cause the gel structure to break down and it will lose its non-drip quality.

Applying liquid emulsion with a brush

Stir the paint and pour it into a paint kettle so that it is about a third full. Dip a 100mm–125mm brush into the paint to cover about one-third of the bristle depth. Press the brush against the rim to get rid of the excess; don't scrape it on the edge – you'll take off too much paint and create a build-up on the inside of the kettle.

1 Start at the top of the wall and apply the paint with short, overlapping horizontal and vertical strokes. Work in panels about 1 sq m at a time, allowing each area to merge into the next one while the edge is still wet.

2 Work systematically across the wall. Try and finish a complete wall before you take a break or there may be a visible change of tone where you stopped.

Beading where colours meet

You can use masking tape to get a neat edge where different colours meet, such as at the junction of walls and ceiling, or where adjacent walls are a different colour. But professionals use a technique called beading, which is not difficult, provided you have a reasonably steady hand. The adjacent colour must be dry before you start.

1 Load the brush with a little paint. Turn it edge-on and press it flat against the wall, a short way from the edge, so that the bristles are slightly splayed to create a bead of paint.

2 With a steady hand, draw the brush sideways or downwards along the surface, gradually working right to the edge to give a clearly defined line between the colours.

Painting edges

Rollers and larger paint pads are very good for covering whole walls, but they cannot reach all the way to the edges; you will need to finish off these areas with a brush or small paint pad – a process often referred to as 'cutting in'. This can be done before or after the main painting, but you will get the most uniform finish if you do it before the main area is painted.

1 Paint four or five overlapping strokes at right angles to the edge to fill the gap between the edge and the new paint.

2 Painting parallel to the edge, go over the first brush strokes in a long sweeping motion. Repeat until the whole edge is painted.

Known in the trade as a 'George', this is used to protect the skirting-board. Hold it at the bottom of the wall as you work your way along to stop the paint dripping down. When you are painting skirting-boards, you can use it to protect the floor and to ensure that no dirt or fluff sticks to the paintbrush.

B&Q Making it easier

Protective clothing
Wear something like cotton overalls when you are painting – don't wear wool because fibres will stick to the paint. A mask will protect you from the paint fumes. Wear a cap or hat to stop your hair getting speckled when painting a ceiling.

Painting with oil-based paint

Oil-based paint is slightly more difficult to apply and must be painted over an undercoat. Use a 75mm brush and work in 300mm-square areas. Clean brushes and any spillages with white spirit. It is not advisable to use oil-based paint on large areas like walls or ceilings (see SAFETY FIRST, below).

1 Paint three vertical, parallel strips, leaving a space slightly narrower than the brush between them.

2 Blend the strips together by painting horizontally, without reloading the brush with paint. With a nearly dry brush, make light vertical strokes over the painted area to give an even coating. Repeat the process on the area below, working the wet paint into the dry, so the sections marry into each other.

ideal tools

Specialised rollers

Rollers designed specifically for awkward areas will make your life much easier.

- An extension pole fitted to your roller lets you paint the ceiling from the floor.
- A special corner roller is perfect for painting corners where both walls are going to be the same colour.

- A mini roller with an extra-long handle allows you to paint the difficult-to-reach bits behind the radiator.

Using a roller

Applying emulsion with a roller is the quickest way of covering a large surface area, although you may need more coats than when painting with a brush because the paint goes on quite thinly. Roller sleeves are available in a variety of sizes and textures. Choose a short-pile sleeve for a smooth wall surface, and a shaggy sheepskin-style sleeve for a more textured surface. The areas the roller cannot reach will need to be finished with a brush. Solid non-drip emulsion, which comes in a tray, is also applied with a roller. As you apply the roller, the paint liquefies and allows the roller to pick up the right amount of paint.

1 Pour the emulsion paint into the paint tray reservoir – it should be about a third full. Dip the roller sleeve into the paint and roll it firmly up and down the tray's ribbed incline to spread the paint evenly. Don't overload the sleeve or paint will splatter everywhere.

2 Move the roller over the wall surface, using random strokes applied with a light, even pressure. Try not to work too fast or you will create a fine mist of paint spray. Each time the roller is dipped in the paint, move it to an adjacent unpainted area and work your way back to the painted area in overlapping strokes to blend in the wet edges.

Using paint pads

Paint pads come in different sizes. They are flat and rectangular with closely packed, short fibres bonded to a foam backing strip, which makes the pad flexible. Pads are good for painting large areas with liquid paint – the bigger the pad, the faster you cover the surface. They make less spray and mess than rollers, but they do need reloading more often. Use a paint pad tray with a built-in ribbed roller on which excess paint can be removed.

1 Pour the paint into the paint pad tray, then draw the pad over the built-in roller to distribute the paint evenly and remove any excess – a paint pad will give a patchy finish if it is loaded unevenly, and will drip if there is too much paint.

2 Start painting near a corner and work in strips about four times the width of your pad. Keeping the pad flat on the wall, move it up and down the surface with a gentle scrubbing action.

safety first

Oil- and solvent-based paints give off fumes that are harmful to your health and to the environment. Always make sure there is very good ventilation while applying them, and while they dry. Avoid using them on large areas like walls and ceilings.

WALLS PAINTING TECHNIQUES

There have never been so many different options for painting your walls. The latest power rollers such as the Dulux PaintPod are much quicker, cleaner and easier to use than a traditional roller and tray. The mains powered unit delivers just the right amount of paint to the roller at the press of a button. The roller tube can extend to 4m so there's no need for a ladder when painting the ceiling. Alternatively, you could experiment with a traditional painting technique such as sponging, or try some of the latest special effects paints.

Using a power roller

Clear the room and prepare the walls for painting (see pages 82–83). Set up the power roller in the room to be painted and load the paint pack into the unit as described below. Edges and corners are painted manually first with the triangular brush before the roller is used on the walls.

Plug in the unit. Gently shake the paint pack, unscrew the lid and peel off the foil seal. Lift the lid of the unit. Drop the paint pack in the chamber with the dip tube hole on the paint pack facing the front of the chamber.

project essentials

- **power roller**
- **stepladder**
- paint packs
- warm water

Close the chamber lid. Check the warning light: if it is illuminated, lift the lid and re-insert the paint pack in the correct position. Lift the dip tube cover and insert the dip tube (which is attached to the delivery tube), twisting clockwise to lock and click it into position. Close the cover. When ready to operate, press the 'paint' button and the blue light will illuminate.

The unit includes a triangular brush for painting wall edges and corners. Fit the spout onto the roller handle and squeeze the paint loading button to decant a small amount of paint into the edging cup. Press the pause button on the unit.

Paint the edges manually using the triangular brush and the paint in the edging cup.

Remove the spout by pressing the handle release button. Wipe the handle connector thoroughly before attaching it to the roller head in the docking station. Lift the roller head from the docking station. Ensure the 'paint' button is illuminated. Press the paint loading button to start applying paint to the wall. Roll evenly and reload as necessary.

Cleaning the unit

The unit has an integrated self-cleaning system that cleans the roller and unit at the same time. When you have finished, place the roller head back in the docking station and close the lid. Press the 'drain' button and the paint will drain back into the pack. Remove the dip tube and paint pack. Wipe the dip tube and place it on the dip tube rests. Take out the chamber and fill with 5 litres of warm water then follow the manufacturer's instructions for cleaning. This will take about 10 minutes. You may need to do it a second time for strong colours. Rinse the edging cup, brush and spout in warm water.

 Making it easier

Shielding ceilings and walls
When working close to the ceiling or into corners, shield them off with a paint shield (see page 86) or a piece of stiff thin card.

Sponging

Sponging is a simple decorative technique which can be created using one or more colours. It uses diluted matt emulsion over a solid and dry base colour. Always test your colour choice before you start on your walls. If you are using more than one colour it is a good idea to start with the darkest and finish with the lightest or white. This will create a sense of depth and the lighter colour will help correct any mistakes you might make. Dilute emulsion has a short drying time, so make sure the room to be decorated is not too hot or dry.

Mixing your colours

Buy tester pots of matt emulsion and thin with clean water by 50% or more, depending on the strength of colour you are looking for. Pour the emulsion into a jam jar then add a measured amount of water. Secure the lid and shake until completely mixed. All emulsion that is diluted will have its performance reduced when thinned, which means the surface will not be as washable as a standard coat of paint.

Special effects paints

Paint manufacturers are continually developing inspiring new products that expand the range of possibilities for decorating your home, as well as for transforming furniture and accessories.

Metallic-effect paints

Great for accessories as well as trim details and radiators, you can now also find metallic-effect paint suitable for woodwork and walls. It takes a little extra care to get a good finish with metallic paints over a large area as brushes and rollers are liable to leave marks. Paint a small cutting-in strip around the edges of the wall, then fill in with a short-pile roller in vertical strokes, working quickly. It can help to practise first on an out-of-the-way area or on lining paper until you are confident of your technique.

1 Pour a little colour mix on to a paint tray or plate and dip a natural sponge into it. The sponge should be washed in warm water first, to make it soft and pliable. Wipe any excess paint on a cloth or card. Experiment on an out-of-the-way patch of wall first.

2 Gently pat the sponge on the wall, constantly changing its angle and position. Don't press too hard or turn the sponge while it is in contact with the surface; this will cause smudges, which will stand out. From time to time step back to make sure your work is even. For a denser effect, go over the wall a second or third time.

Glitter glaze

Apply with stamps or a stencil, or paint onto marked-out shapes.

Chalkboard paint

An area of chalkboard paint on a wall or MDF gives a great space for writing or drawing in chalk. The surface wipes clean with a damp or dry cloth. Ideal in the kitchen – for shopping lists or messages – as well as in a children's room or study.

Suede paint

Textured emulsion with the sophisticated finish of soft suede, this will transform a feature wall, or create subtle contrasts when applied with stencils or in marked-out shapes on a matt wall surface.

▼ Glow-in-the-dark paint

Switch off the lights and this paint will glow in the dark for at least fifteen minutes.

▲ Pearl-finish paint and glaze

This luxurious paint is especially effective used on workwork and trim details, or applied with a stencil. As with metallic-effect paint, brush marks have a tendency to be visible, so take care to keep brush strokes all in one direction. Look out for transparent pearl glaze. Used as a top coat, this gives a soft shimmer to your colour. You can also apply it with a stencil to create transparent shimmering shapes and patterns.

Wallpapering is usually the final stage of decorating, as the ceiling, doors, windows and skirting-board should be painted first. Wallpaper allows you to change the colour, pattern and texture of your walls with immediate effect, and you can choose from an extensive range. Standard patterned wallpaper is ideal for most wall surfaces. It's available as traditional paste-the-back paper, or ready-pasted, or the newer paste-the-wall types. Textured wallpaper has a built-in relief pattern, making it suitable for rough wall surfaces. Vinyl paper can be wiped with a damp cloth, so it is good for kitchens and bathrooms.

project essentials

- **dust sheets**
- **stepladder**
- **bucket**
- **paper-hanging brush**
- **pasting brush**
- **pasting table**
- **tape measure**
- **plumb line**
- **pencil**
- **wallpaper scissors**
- **sponge**

- sugar soap
- wall size
- wallpaper paste
- wallpaper

Planning

Expect to make a mess! Move furniture and soft furnishings out of the room, and cover carpets and anything that can't be moved with dust sheets. Most wallpaper can be papered over, provided it's in good condition (but remove relief or washable paper). If it's in a poor state, strip it off and line the walls. You can paper directly over painted surfaces, but be sure to wash them thoroughly with sugar soap first. Your walls must be clean, dry and smooth before you can begin.

- Use the chart below to estimate the amount of wallpaper you are going to need – a standard roll of wallpaper is approximately 10.05m long and 530mm wide. When you measure around the room include the windows and doors – this allows for wastage when the paper is trimmed.
- Allow for extra when using a paper with a large repeat pattern – the size of the pattern is usually stated on the roll label.
- Make sure all the rolls you buy have the same batch number, to be certain the colours will match.
- Coat the wall surfaces with wall size, a special sealer that prevents them soaking up the wallpaper paste. Use a size recommended by the paste manufacturer. Or you can seal the walls with dilute wallpaper paste painted on with a large decorating or pasting brush.

Lining the walls

Lining paper helps to cover imperfections, giving you a smoother surface for the wallpaper. Lining paper is pasted and hung in the same way as wallpaper. Leave the lining paper to dry (this can take up to 12 hours) before applying the wallpaper. When hanging lining paper, always use a wall size and paste that are compatible with the manufacturer's recommended adhesive for the wallpaper.

HOW TO CALCULATE THE NUMBER OF ROLLS

Distance around room	Wall height 2.3–2.4m	Wall height 2.4–2.6m	Wall height 2.6–2.7m
10m	5	5	6
12m	6	6	7
14m	7	7	8
16m	8	8	9
18m	9	9	10
20m	10	10	11

Hanging lining paper horizontally

Wallpaper is usually hung vertically, so it's quite a good idea to apply the lining paper horizontally – that way the two lots of seams will not fall in the same place.

Hanging lining paper vertically

If you do want to hang the lining paper vertically, start from the place where you are going to hang the first length of wallpaper and hang a half-width of lining paper. Continue with full widths across the rest of the wall.

Cutting the paper

Wallpaper is expensive, so don't waste it by cutting the lengths too long or too short. Measure the wall at your starting point, from the ceiling to the top of the skirting board. If you are going to cut several lengths of paper before you start hanging it, check that the height of the wall is the same all the way around the room.

Measure the height of the wall in several places around the room with a steel tape measure. Add 100mm to the longest measurement, to allow for trimming at the top and bottom. Check which way round the wallpaper pattern goes and where any pattern should be in relation to the top of the wall. Unroll the paper on the pasting table, pattern-side down, and draw a straight line across the width at the measured point. Using wallpaper scissors, cut the first length.

Turn the cut length over. Unroll the next length, place it edge-to-edge with the first length, and match the pattern. Use the cut length as a guide to cut the second length. Continue cutting several lengths, numbering them at the top corner on the wrong side so that you know the hanging order. Mark the hanging direction, too.

Paste-the-wall wallpaper

There is one type of wallpaper – known as 'paste-the-wall' or 'dry-hanging' paper – that is hung 'dry' because the wall is pasted rather than the paper. The paper features a special backing that does not expand when wet, which means you can hang it straight from the roll on to the pre-pasted wall. This makes it much quicker to hang than traditional paper, which must be set aside for several minutes to allow the paste to soak in. It's also easier to avoid getting paste on the patterned side of the paper: this is especially helpful when working with paper that has a delicate or easily marked surface.

This type of paper also peels off easily, so there's no need for steaming or soaking when you want to redecorate. Simply lift a corner at the bottom of the wall and pull steadily upwards.

Don't paste the entire wall before starting to hang the paper. Just paste one section at a time. See page 99.

Pasting and folding the paper

The most common type of wallpaper is the traditional kind that you paste yourself. Use the paste recommended by the paper manufacturer and mix it according to the guidelines. Most lengths of wallpaper are longer than a pasting table. When the section on the table has been pasted, it should be pulled up and loosely folded over on to itself in a concertina shape. You can then carry on pasting the rest of the length.

Lay the cut length on the pasting table (pattern-side down), so that the paper hangs over the end of the table. If you are pasting a shorter length, use a weight to stop the end rolling up. Load the pasting brush, wipe off excess paste and begin applying paste along the centre of the length.

Work the paste from the middle to the edges of the paper in a herringbone pattern. It is easier to spot areas you have missed if you use coloured paste (which dries clear). Between lengths, wipe any paste spills off the table with a clean, damp sponge.

When the paper covering the table has been pasted, fold it over on itself, taking care not to crease it, and start a concertina. Move the concertina to one end of the table, using a weight such as a large brush to stop the unpasted end rolling up.

Paste the entire length, folding the paper as you go. Lift up the completed concertina and set it aside to allow the paste to soak into the paper for as long as the manufacturer recommends. The paper needs time to expand before it is hung. Soaking prevents bubbles appearing as the paper continues to expand on the wall. In the meantime, paste more lengths.

Walls and corners are rarely straight, so don't rely on them as a guide when hanging paper. Instead, mark a vertical guideline on the wall, using a plumb line or a spirit level, before you hang the first length. Always read the instructions to see if there are any specific requirements for your paper. Check the markings you made on the back when cutting the paper, to make sure that you hang the lengths in the correct order and the right way up.

Where to start

- Ideally, start at a corner and hang the first length of wallpaper on a wall that has neither door nor window, so you can hang a full length from the ceiling to the top of the skirting-board.
- Choose a wall to the right of the window if you are right-handed, to the left if you are left-handed.
- Work away from the window, so that the paper edges will not cast a shadow if they overlap slightly.
- Avoid having to hang narrow strips against a window or door. If necessary, cut the first length in half vertically along the edge that will overlap the corner.
- If your wallpaper has a large pattern, you should hang the first length over a fireplace or other focal point and then work away from it in both directions, so that the design is central and symmetrical. Complete this area before papering the rest of the room.

Making it easier

Wallplug markers
Unscrew all wall fixings before papering, leaving the wallplugs in place. Mark the position of each one by pushing a matchstick (with the head broken off) into the plug, leaving it slightly proud. As you hang the paper, bring it over the marked position and press the paper on to the matchstick, so it pierces the paper. Smooth the paper with a paper-hanging brush. When the paper is quite dry, remove the matchstick and replace the fitting.

Hanging the first length

You should always take your time hanging paper, but be particularly careful with the first length – it's very important to get that one straight.

1 To position the first length of wallpaper, draw a line from ceiling to skirting-board 480mm out from the corner, using a plumb line (see IDEAL TOOLS) or a spirit level. This allows a 50mm overlap on to the window wall.

2 Position the first pasted length at the top of the wall with its right-hand edge running down the vertical line. This is easier if you can keep the left-hand edge of the paper off the wall. Make sure about 50mm of excess paper is left above the top of the wall for trimming. Hold the paper at both sides and don't let the lower paper drop suddenly, as it may tear or stretch.

3 Once the right-hand edge is positioned, smooth the paper down with a paper-hanging brush. Work from the centre of the paper to the edges, making sure that there are no bubbles. Check the edge stays on the pencil mark.

project essentials

- stepladder
- tape measure
- plumb line or spirit level
- pencil
- pasting table
- paper-hanging brush
- wallpaper scissors
- seam roller

- lengths of pasted wallpaper

Plumb line

A plumb line will give you a true vertical guideline. Most plumb lines are a length of builder's string with a pointed weight (a 'bob') attached to the end. Hammer a small nail into the wall near the ceiling, and hang the plumb line. Use a pencil to mark the wall down the length of the line, then join up the marks with a ruler.

With the first length in place, crease the top and bottom of the paper against the ceiling and skirting-board junctions. Gently pull the paper away from the wall and cut along the creases with wallpaper scissors. Brush the trimmed edges back into place.

Butt the next length against the previous one, matching the pattern at eye level. When two or three pieces are in place, run the seam roller lightly down the joins. Don't press down heavily on textured paper or you'll flatten the pattern.

Keeping scissors clean
Occasionally dip your wallpaper scissors into a jar of clean, warm water to loosen the build-up of paste.

Cutting guide

Instead of creasing the paper at the skirting-board and trimming it with scissors, you can use an L-shaped piece of metal called a cutting guide. Hold the guide against the skirting-board (or picture rail or coving), tucking the paper into the crease of the guide, then trim the paper with a sharp knife.

High style, low environmental impact
Look out for the latest wallpapers designed with sustainability as well as style in mind. These are printed on 100% FSC paper using water-based inks and the packaging is totally biodegradable.

Wallpapering behind a radiator

Smoothing wallpaper behind a radiator is a fiddly job. Ideally, you should drain the radiator and take it off the wall. If that is not possible, turn off the heat and wait for the radiator to cool, then hoover out the inevitable cobwebs and dust behind it. You can either cut a standard length of paper to fit around the brackets (below); or cut the paper horizontally about 150mm below the top of the radiator and stick a separate, short length at the bottom (below right). Use a clean and dry radiator paint roller to push, guide and smooth the wallpaper into place.

Seam roller

This small, narrow roller is just the right size for running down the wallpaper seams to make sure they are flat and sticking to the wall. Though it should be used with care on textured paper, and not at all on flock paper.

Hang the length of paper on the wall, letting it cover the radiator. Mark the position of the fixing brackets on the paper, then cut from the bottom up to the pencil marks. Cut out a rectangular shape to accommodate the bracket. Push the paper into place each side of the supporting bracket using a narrow radiator paint roller. Trim the paper at the skirting.

Alternatively, cut the paper so that it covers approximately 150mm of wall behind the top of the radiator. Cut another length to fit the gap at the bottom of the radiator.

WALLS PAPERING CORNERS AND DETAILS

You will probably have started hanging your wallpaper on a straight wall without obstacles, but there's no way of papering all the way around a room without meeting corners, door frames and fittings such as light switches and sockets. However, if you know the right techniques, you can achieve a neat result.

Measure the distance between the edge of the last hung length and the corner, at the top, bottom and middle of the wall. Using the widest measurement, allow an extra 25mm for turning on to the next wall. Cut a length of paper to this width. Paste and hang the cut length, butting the paper to the edge of the previous strip and aligning the pattern at eye level. Allow the extra 25mm to stick lightly to the next wall. Use a paper-hanging brush to smooth the paper into the internal corner.

Internal corners

At an internal corner, it's much easier to cut a length of paper vertically and position the join at the corner – especially when you are papering a wall that is slightly crooked and your corner is not completely square. Measure and cut the paper so that it reaches slightly beyond the corner. If the off-cut of paper is half a width or more, then use it as the next length; if smaller than that, then start with a new length.

Make sure that the paper is firmly pressed against the wall by running the seam roller along its edge. Wipe excess paste from the roller before it dries. If any creases have formed, tear the paper and overlap the pieces so they lie flat – a tear will show less than if you cut the paper (although it is better to cut vinyl paper).

Hang the plumb line on the next wall at a distance from the corner that is either the width of the full paper roll or your off-cut, whichever you are using. Make pencil marks behind the vertical line at intervals down the wall. This will give you a completely vertical edge for starting the next wall.

 Making it easier

Uneven walls
If the lines and angles of your walls are uneven – which is typical of older properties, but is also true of many modern ones – it may be better to choose a plain paper or one with a small, frequently repeated pattern. In particular you should avoid striped papers, as these can make irregularities very obvious. Alternatively, just wallpaper a single feature wall – see pages 98–99.

Hang the next length with its right-hand edge aligned with the pencil marks, overlapping the paper turned from the previous wall. If the paper is patterned, match the two pieces as closely as possible. Use border adhesive along the overlapping strip.

ideal tool

Smooth finish
On non-textured paper, a wallpaper smoothing tool can be used to smooth out bubbles and help create a professional finish.

External corners

Walls and corners are often not absolutely straight or at perfect right angles. If this is the case, then you should also position an overlapping join at an external corner – as at an internal corner, above. Measure from the edge of the last full width to the corner, then allow an extra 25mm for the turn on to the next wall. Cut a length to this width. Hang it as far as the corner, then bend the excess paper around the corner onto the next wall. Use a plumb line to get a vertical start on the next wall (see Step 3, above), and lay the paper over the overlapping section of the previous length. Use border adhesive to stick paper to paper; this will be much more effective than wallpaper paste.

A mismatched pattern will be more obvious on an external corner, so this is best only done with small repeated patterns or plain wallpaper. See MAKING IT EASIER. The overlap will also be more obvious when using textured or flock papers.

Papering around a door frame

It is easier to paper around a door frame if you cut the wallpaper roughly to size before pasting it, as this makes it more manageable. Once the paper is on the wall, trim around the frame leaving at least 25mm overhang of paper.

Paste and hang the paper in the usual way until you reach the length that will meet the frame. Measure the distance between the edge of the last hung length and the door frame, at the top, bottom and middle of the wall. Using the widest measurement, allow an extra 25mm overlap, then cut a length of paper to this width. Paste and hang the cut length, aligning the pattern at eye level and butting the paper to the edge of the previous strip. Smooth the paper first up to an external corner, if there is one, and then up to the door frame.

Use a paper-hanging brush to smooth and press the paper into the edge of the door frame.

Gently press a line into the paper along the edge of the frame using the rounded back of the wallpaper scissors. Lift the edge of the paper off from the wall and trim neatly along this line with the scissors. Brush the paper back in place and wipe off any excess glue.

Papering around light switches or sockets

Every room has light switches and sockets – there's no avoiding them, so it's worth knowing how to deal with them. If you don't do a neat job, you'll notice every time you turn on the light. Always switch off the electricity at the mains before you start work.

Make sure the electricity is off. Hang the wallpaper from the top of the wall straight over the switch or socket. Brush gently over the fitting with a dry paper-hanging brush to make a slight impression on the paper, but take care not to tear it. Holding the paper over the fitting, make a small pencil mark from each corner into the centre of the faceplate. Pierce a hole in the paper at the centre point with a small pair of scissors. Cut the paper to the corners and pull back the flaps.

Trim the flaps just inside the outer edge of the switch or socket so there is an overlap of about 6mm covering the fitting. Partially unscrew the faceplate and pull it about 6mm away from the wall.

Carefully ease the faceplate through the hole in the paper. Use the brush to push the trimmed edges gently behind the faceplate and smooth away any air bubbles. Put the faceplate back in place and secure the screws. Let the paste dry before turning on the power.

Wallpapering around obstacles such as windows is a job that needs special care. As with door frames, it is best to cut lengths of wallpaper roughly to size before you apply the paste so that the amount of pasted paper is manageable.

Window frames

It is better to make small cuts and to try to fit the paper several times than cut away too much in one go. It helps if you apply wall size to the surface because this will make it easier to peel back and reposition the paper. The paper will be soft and tear easily when pasted – small scissors are the best tool for cutting around fiddly corners and mouldings. If there is a window reveal, as here, it is best to cut a separate strip for the inner part.

1 Paste and hang the wallpaper in the ordinary way as far as the frame. Push the paper around the window sill to form a highlight of the shape with the paper-hanging brush.

2 Make a diagonal cut down to the corner where the wall and window sill meet.

3 Smooth the paper with the paper-hanging brush around the corner of the window reveal. Make a vertical cut to the top of the reveal, leaving an extra 30mm for turnaround.

4 Make diagonal cuts in towards the next part of the moulding. Continue snipping around the corner of the sill. If necessary, press in with your fingers to mould the outline in the paper. Pull the paper away and cut along the outline using a small pair of sharp scissors.

5 Press the paper into the angle with rounded back of the scissors to mark a cutting line.

ideal tool

Smoothing/cutting tool
A combination wallpaper smoothing/cutting tool will help you cut paper close to a frame for a good fit. It works best along straight edges rather than around curves. Smooth the paper into a recess or corner so that it's easier to push the cutting knife along the crease to cut the paper. Peel away the unwanted paper.

Smooth the paper with the paper-hanging brush, using the bristles to press the paper around the corner. Measure the width of the window reveal and cut a new strip of wallpaper 30mm wider and 60mm longer than the reveal, taking care to match the pattern. To get a perfect straight line along the external corner cut with a metal straightedge and knife (see MAKING IT EASIER.)

Paste and hang the paper in the ordinary way, neatly trimming off all the excess paper. If the paste on the paper starts to dry before you have finished trimming, apply extra paste to the wall rather than the paper. Where you are sticking paper over paper use a stronger border adhesive.

Wipe the paste off the woodwork and any excess adhesive on the paper before it can dry.

Cut it
To make a quick and perfectly straight cut, loosely roll the wallpaper and press lightly with a metal straightedge then cut along the straightedge with a knife. This should be done before pasting.

Papering stairwells

Choose a good quality wallpaper with a non-matching pattern, as hanging long lengths can be difficult – they tear easily and tend to stretch. You are working with heavy lengths of pasted paper: if possible, get someone to stand on the stairs and hold the bulk of the paper while you hang the top part.

Making a platform

You need to be able to reach both the head wall and the well wall from a safe working platform (see diagram). Place a pair of steps on the top landing, lean a ladder against the head wall, with the ladder feet resting against a riser halfway down the stairs, and lay a scaffold board between them. Wrap the end of the ladder in a cloth to protect the wall. Tie the board to the ladders with rope to stop them slipping. Use one board on top of another if the gap between the steps and the ladder is more than 1.5m.

Hanging the paper

Paper the longest drop first. Cut the required length, remembering that the skirting will be at an angle. Begin attaching the paper at the top of the wall, allowing the folded length to hang. Unfold it as you work down the wall. If you have someone helping you, they can fix the lower half in place. If the stairwell is deep, you'll need to remove the ladder and place one end of the scaffold board on a stair tread and the other on steps at the bottom of the stairs so you can reach the lower half of the wall.

Well wall

Head wall

Ladder ends, wrapped in cloth

Use two boards if the platform spans more than 1.5m

Boards tied to the ladders with rope

WALLS CREATING A FEATURE WALL

Strong pattern covering every wall can easily overwhelm a room and make it feel smaller. Instead, consider wallpapering a single wall to create a striking design feature. Modern paste-the-wall paper is easy to apply, and to remove when you want a change, making it perfect for creating a feature wall.

 Making it easier

Delicate papers
Some wallpapers, such as flock, are very delicate and can mark easily. Take care not to damage the surface when cutting and smoothing flock papers. Don't use a seam roller on flock papers and avoid getting any paste on the surface.

Stripes on part of a wall

Choosing your design

Wallpapers come in designs to suit all tastes – dramatic florals, vibrant colours or bold stripes, including wall coverings created by top designers – and they are a great way to make a style statement. To create a feature you might paper a whole wall, part of a wall, a chimney breast or a recess.

Monochrome florals in a recess

Florals on a chimney breast

Positioning the first length

Ideally the first length should be positioned in the middle of the wall, as shown here, but do check that this won't leave you with tiny strips at the sides. Measure out wallpaper widths (usually 530mm) along the wall to be sure.

project essentials

- **stepladder**
- **tape measure**
- **pencil**
- **straightedge**
- **plumb line or spirit level**
- **pasting table**
- **pasting brush or roller and tray**
- **paper-hanging brush or sponge**
- **wallpaper scissors**
- **seam roller, if required**

- paste-the-wall wallpaper
- wallpaper paste

1 Find the centre of the wall by measuring the full width and dividing in half. Measure and mark the centre point with a pencil.

2 Check the width of a roll of wallpaper and make a pencil mark half this distance from the centre mark. Hang a plumb line at this second mark and use a pencil to mark the vertical at roughly 600mm intervals.

3 Join up the marks with a pencil and straightedge.

 Making it easier

Getting a straight cut
To be sure you cut each length in a straight line at the top and bottom, fold back about 300mm of paper and align the edges. Press down and cut along the fold line.

Matching the pattern

To get the best effect, a large-scale pattern needs to be positioned carefully. If there is a large or dominant motif, it should appear in the centre of the wall. You should also think about how the pattern will look at top and bottom. Stick up a sample length using masking tape to see how it looks. Most patterned wallpapers will have a pattern drop of roughly 530mm. For your second and subsequent lengths you will need to line up the pattern before measuring and cutting.

1 On a clean pasting table lay two pieces of paper together and work out the pattern drop. Measure your next length and cut to size.

2 To avoid confusion when hanging lengths, lightly mark the top on the reverse of each length.

Hanging the first length

Using a pasting brush or a roller, apply a generous, even layer of strong wallpaper paste to the wall where the first length of paper will hang. Cover the whole area and make sure the pasted area is slightly wider than the width of the roll.

1 Starting at the top of the wall, hang the first length of wallpaper, sliding it into position against the marked vertical line.

2 Smooth the paper with a brush or damp sponge towards the bottom of the wall. Gently press the paper into the angle of the ceiling and skirting and mark a cutting line with the rounded back of the scissors. Gently pull away the paper to cut along the line at the top and bottom. Smooth the trimmed edges into place.

Hanging the last lengths

Continue pasting across the width of the wall, matching the pattern at eye height and making sure there are no gaps between the lengths. Only use a seam roller (see page 93) on non-textured papers. At the edges of the feature wall you will probably meet either an internal or external corner, and be left with a strip of wall narrower than the wallpaper roll.

1 Measure from the last length to the corner of the wall. Add an extra 40mm to this measurement and mark on the reverse of the wallpaper (remembering which is top). Draw a vertical line down the length of the wallpaper using a pencil and straightedge.

2 Cut along this line with a pair of scissors.

4 Mark a vertical cutting line with the rounded back of the scissors, then cut neatly to trim off the excess paper. Smooth down the paper on the wall and wipe off any excess paste.

3 Carefully matching the pattern, push the paper into or around the corner, taking care not to get too much excess paste on the adjacent wall. Make a vertical cut in the excess paper at the top and bottom of the corner.

B&Q Making it easier

Easy pasting
When working with paste-the-wall papers, it is quicker and easier to use a paint roller to apply the paste. Use with a roller tray but make sure the paste on the roller doesn't dry out. Only paste a small area at a time, and take care not to flick paste onto adjacent walls or wallpaper.

Tiling is a skilled job, but with care there is no reason why you should not produce good results. The surface to be tiled must be clean, dry and flat. Strip wallpaper back to the plaster, remove any crumbling plaster and fill any holes. Allow new plaster to dry out completely – this will take at least two months. Prime porous surfaces with a PVA-based adhesive.

Lay out a line of tiles, inserting tile spacers between them. Place the batten alongside, lining up the end with the edge of the first tile.

Mark the positions of the tiles and gaps on the rod with a pencil. By numbering the tile positions, you will have a quick means of working out how many tiles you will need in each row.

Calculating quantities

Most modern ceramic tiles are supplied in packs that will cover 1 sq m. So to work out how many packs you need, simply measure the height and width of the area to be tiled and multiply the figures to obtain the area in square metres. Allow 5–10% extra for cutting and breakages. If your wall has doors, windows or fixed cupboards, calculate their area and subtract this from the total area to be tiled. It may help to draw a rough sketch of the wall and mark all the dimensions on it.

Vertical rows

The first job is to establish the position of the vertical rows. This will allow you to find the starting point, which should be near the centre of the area to be tiled. Measure the width of the area and mark its mid-point with a pencil.

Setting out

Because of the obvious grid pattern formed by the joints between tiles, finding the best starting point for the first row of tiles is crucial. It is no good simply starting in one corner and working across the wall – the corner may not be truly vertical and you may end up with tiny slivers of tile to cut at the far corner. It is much better to centre the grid on the wall, producing cut tiles of equal size at the ends of the rows and an overall symmetrical appearance.

project essentials

- **tape measure**
- **pencil**
- **gauge rod**
- **spirit level**
- **pipe and cable detector**
- **claw hammer**

- three 50mm x 25mm softwood battens
- tiles
- tile spacers
- 50mm masonry nails

1 Hold your gauge rod (see MAKING IT EASIER, left) so that one of its marks aligns with the centre-point on the wall. Step off the tile positions across the wall.

2 When you reach a corner, you will see if you need to cut the last tile in the row to fit. If this will be less than half a tile wide, it is best to reposition the starting point.

3 Reposition by aligning the rod with the centre-point as before, then pencil a new mark on the wall so that it falls halfway between two tile marks on the rod. This will be the actual starting position for tiling and will ensure that the cut tiles at each end are more than half a tile wide, and that the centre-line of the wall passes through the centre of a tile.

4 Hold the gauge rod against the new wall mark, using a spirit level to ensure that it is truly vertical, and draw a line from top to bottom.

Horizontal rows

Having established the positions of the vertical rows, you can check where the horizontal rows will fall and determine where the first row should be. Use wooden battens nailed to the walls as guides for positioning the tiles and to support them while the adhesive sets, so that they don't slide down the wall.

1 Position the gauge rod against the vertical pencil line on the wall, with its end touching the floor (or skirting). Put a pencil mark on the wall in line with the top tile mark on the rod. Now move the rod up the wall, still following the vertical pencil line, until it touches the ceiling. If you are very lucky, the pencil mark on the wall will align with one of the marks on the rod, indicating that you will not have to cut any tiles for the top and bottom rows. If there is no alignment, however, look at the mark on the rod below the wall mark; halving the distance between them will give you an idea of the size of the cut tiles required. As with the vertical rows, it is best if these are at least half a tile deep. If they will be narrower than this, make a mark on the wall in line with the next mark down on the rod.

2 Measure the distance between the two marks on the wall and make a third mark exactly halfway between them.

3 Hold your gauge rod so that the end is just clear of the skirting or floor, moving it until one of its marks aligns with the mark you have just made. Make another mark on the wall, level with the foot of the rod. This will be the starting point for the first horizontal row of whole tiles. Use a long straightedge and spirit level to draw a perfectly level line across the wall at this point.

4 Check there are no hidden pipes or cables behind the wall, then nail a 50mm x 25mm batten with its top edge aligned with the horizontal pencil line. Double-check with a spirit level that it is straight. If necessary, use more than one batten to span the wall. Then nail on another, this one aligned to the vertical line. Again, check for pipes or cables first, and ensure it is upright with a spirit level. Leave the nail heads slightly proud so the battens are easy to remove later.

Part-tiled walls

When part-tiling a wall, set out the horizontal tile rows so that the top row consists of whole tiles; this will look much better. Mark the position of the top row on the wall and use the gauge rod to determine the position of the lowest horizontal row. Fill the gap between this and the skirting with cut tiles. Move the top row up or down so that you don't have to cut narrow slivers of tile. You may even be able to avoid cutting tiles altogether, although if the skirting is uneven, some trimming will be necessary. In this case, you will need to start from the lowest point of the skirting. Find this by holding a long straight batten along it, levelled with the aid of a spirit level.

When you have a large area to tile, it is best to begin in the centre and work outwards, applying all the whole tiles – known as field tiles – first. Then you can fill in around the edges with cut tiles. Work on small areas at a time and pay particular attention to spacing and bedding the tiles properly. Your aim should be to achieve a perfectly flat tiled surface with a grid of uniform-thickness grouted joints.

Applying whole tiles

When applying the field tiles, it is essential to bed them so that their faces are level; any unevenness will spoil the overall effect. Lift any that are high or low, adding or scraping away adhesive as necessary.

1 Beginning in the corner formed by the two wall battens, scoop up a quantity of adhesive with a trowel and press it on to the wall. Then spread it out with a notched spreader, working away from the vertical batten with horizontal strokes and holding the blade at an angle of about 45°. The ridges produced will ensure that there is an equal quantity of adhesive behind each tile, making it easier to set them all level. Work on no more than 1 sq m at a time, or the adhesive may begin to harden before all the tiles are in place.

2 Set the first tile into the corner between the two battens, pressing its edges against them and the whole tile firmly against the wall. Add the tile above it and the one next to it, spacing them initially by eye and pushing them firmly into the adhesive.

3 Insert a tile spacer into the angles between the tiles and adjust the tile positions as necessary. Plastic tile spacers make it easy to obtain uniform joints. Push them in well so that they can be grouted over. (Alternatively, simply insert one leg of the spacer between two tiles and pull it out once the adhesive has set.)

4 Continue in this way, until you have tiled the area of adhesive. Apply more adhesive and tiles to the wall until you reach the point where you need to finish off with cut tiles. As you work, wipe off splashes of adhesive with a damp sponge. If you allow it to dry, it will be very difficult to remove.

5 Take off the vertical batten by prising out its nails. You may find that you need to remove hardened adhesive that has spread from under the tiles. Do this with the edge of a scraper. Continue adding field tiles to the rest of the wall. After that, you can finish off with cut tiles.

---

project essentials

- trowel
- notched spreader
- sponge
- claw hammer
- scraper
- felt-tip pen
- tile cutter
- tile file
- hacksaw

- tile adhesive
- tiles
- tile spacers
- corner trim

B&Q Making it easier

Glazed-edge tiles
If you buy tiles with bevelled or rounded glazed edges, you should be able to finish an external corner without using corner trim. Simply tile the first wall as normal, taking the tiles right up to the corner. Then tile the return wall, working away from the corner and allowing the tiles to overlap the edges of the tiles on the first wall. Make sure you provide a gap for grouting by inserting spacers between these tiles and the tiles on the first wall.

Internal corners

Corners between walls are rarely truly vertical, so resist the temptation to cut all the edge tiles to the same size – you will probably find that some do not fit. Instead, measure up for each tile separately. For a summary of tile-cutting techniques, see overleaf.

1 One way of marking a tile for cutting is to hold the tile exactly over the last whole tile in the row, then butt another against the wall, marking where it overlaps the one below with a felt-tip pen. Alternatively, take separate measurements at the top and bottom of the space to be filled.

2 After cutting, check the fit of the tile; you can make small adjustments with a tile file. If the adjoining wall is to be tiled, total accuracy is not crucial, since the edges will be hidden by the tiles on the adjoining wall; if only one wall will be tiled, make sure you allow room for a grouted joint at the corner.

3 Use the narrow end of the notched spreader to apply adhesive to the back of the cut tile, then press it into place so that it is level with the adjacent tile. Insert joint spacers as necessary.

4 When you have completed one wall, you can tile the next. Care is needed when cutting these edge tiles, to ensure a uniform grouted joint where they meet the tiles on the facing wall.

External corners

At an external corner, you can achieve a neat finish by using plastic corner trim. This comes in various sizes and colours, and normally has a quadrant shape. It has the added advantage of protecting the edges of the tiles from knocks, which could cause chipping.

1 Complete one wall. Use a hacksaw to cut the corner trim to length, apply a narrow strip of tile adhesive to the return wall and press the trim into it. Align the trim with the tiles of the first wall, using spacers to ensure there is a gap for grouting. Carefully apply more adhesive to the return wall with the notched spreader. Make sure that you apply it vertically, so that you are less likely to catch the teeth of the spreader in the corner trim's flange and dislodge it.

2 Begin tiling the return wall, working away from the corner trim. As you set the tiles in place, remember to allow a narrow grouting gap between them and the trim, inserting spacers and adjusting the tiles as necessary so that the gap is uniform. Make a final check to see that the trim has not moved.

Obstructions

The best way to deal with obstructions such as doors and windows is to work from the vertical centre of the most obvious feature. For example, with a single window or door, begin setting out from its centre-line; if there are two windows, use the centre of the space between them; if a window or door is near one end of the wall, work from the centre of the space between its frame and the far corner. Use the gauge rod to check for cutting problems around the feature, moving the starting point as required. The same applies for the horizontal rows.

WALLS CUTTING TILES

Unless you are tiling a small area, such as a splashback (see page 108), which you can restrict to whole tiles only, you will be faced with cutting tiles to fit. You can choose from a variety of hand and power tools to do this, and some will be easier to use than others. What you go for will depend on the size of the job and your budget.

Tile scribe

The simplest and cheapest tool for making straight cuts through tiles is the tile scribe, which has a specially hardened tip.

B&Q Making it easier

File your tiles
Any rough edges should be removed from a cut tile with a tile file. Hold it square on to the edge.

1 Having measured the gap to be filled, transfer the measurements to the tile, then use a steel rule and chinagraph pencil or felt-tip pen to mark a cutting line across the tile. Make sure that the rule does not slip as you make the mark.

2 Holding the rule firmly, score along the line with a tile scribe in one stroke, applying enough pressure to cut through the glaze. Place a pencil beneath the scored line and press down each side. The tile should snap cleanly in two.

Combined scorer/snapper

Snapping the tiles is not always easy with a tile scribe; a combined tile scorer/snapper is very effective and requires only a little pressure to operate successfully.

1 Mark the tile for cutting in the normal manner. Then, using the steel rule as a guide, run the cutting wheel of the tool along the line, pressing down firmly to score the glaze.

2 Insert the tile between the jaws of the tool, aligning the scored line with the centre mark. Squeeze the handles and the tile will snap in two.

Cutting curves

There are various methods of making curved cuts in tiles; one of the simplest is to use a tile saw, which has a round blade, allowing you to change direction easily.

1 Take a piece of paper or card of the same size as the tile and cut it to the required shape. Lay it over the tile and mark the shape on the face.

2 Clamp the tile securely and cut along the line with a tile saw. Check the fit of the tile, making any necessary adjustments with a tile file.

Tile-cutting machine

This robust lever-action device combines a scorer and snapper with a sturdy bed to support the tile. Some incorporate a removable gauge for measuring the tiles and will even make an allowance for a grout gap and tapered cut. They are relatively inexpensive and the easiest of all these tile-cutting tools to use.

1 Mark the tile for cutting and insert it into the machine, lining up the mark with the tool's guide. Lower the handle to bring the scorer into contact with the tile, press down and push the handle forward to score the tile.

2 Fit the tile into the slide of the handle, carefully aligning the scored mark with the guide. Lower the handle until you feel the snapper touch the tile's underside.

3 Apply firm pressure to the handle to snap the tile along the cutting line.

Cutting around pipes

If you are lucky, a projecting pipe may fall on the joint line between two tiles. If not, you will have to split a tile on the pipe's centre-line, then make cut-outs in each piece.

Tile the wall to one side of the pipe and just below it. Then, using another tile as a guide to ensure square lines, make pencil marks on the wall, level with the top, bottom and both sides of the pipe.

Now transfer the marks to the tile for cutting, using a felt-tip pen or chinagraph pencil. Support the tile on tile spacers while you do this, otherwise the marks will be in the wrong place.

Using a try square, or even another tile, join up the lines across the tile. Where they cross, they will form a square. Stand an off-cut of pipe (the same size as the wall pipe) in the square and draw around it. Then cut the tile in two, so that the cut passes through the centre of the circle.

To remove waste from the two pieces of tile, you could use a tile saw, a jigsaw fitted with a tile-cutting blade or a rotary cutter. With the last two, choose a slow speed, hold the tool still and rotate the tile around the blade. Keep inside the marked line, using a tile file to make final adjustments. Or you can simply break away small pieces with a pair of tile nippers until the cut-outs are of the correct size.

Check the fit of the two pieces of tile around the pipe. If all is well, apply adhesive to the back of each piece and stick to the wall. You should find that the joint between the two pieces is virtually invisible, while any gap around the pipe can be filled at the grouting stage.

Window recesses

Window recesses, being narrow, will need tiles cut to fit all round. Treat them in a similar manner to external corners. After tiling the face of the wall, tile the head of the recess, then the sides and lastly the bottom.

Glazed-edge tiles

If you are using glazed-edge tiles, you don't need corner trim. Tile the face of the wall up to the recess, then tile the recess, placing the tiles so that they cover the edges of those on the face of the wall. Work back towards the window frame.

Using corner trim

Tile the face of the wall, making sure that the edges of the tiles are flush with the window recess. Fit lengths of corner trim around the recess so that they are flush with the tile faces; mitre the ends for neatness. Then tile the recess, working back from the trim.

Supporting tiles above the recess

When tiling the wall face, you must provide support for the tiles above the recess. Do this by nailing a temporary batten to the wall so that its top edge is flush with the top of the recess.

Supporting tiles in the recess

When tiling a window recess, you must support the tiles at the head of the recess while the adhesive sets. The simplest way to do this is with a length of wood wedged in place by two more pieces.

WALLS GROUTING AND FINISHING TILES

Once you have applied all the tiles to the wall, they should be left for the adhesive to dry. How long depends on the product – check with the maker's instructions. Then you can finish off all the joints with grout, a special hard filler. To complete your tiling, you may also need to add a waterproof seal along the bottom of a splashback and possibly mount some fixtures.

Grouting

You can buy grout in powder form for mixing with water, or pre-mixed and ready to apply. Whichever you choose, check that you have enough for the job, and remember to use waterproof grout anywhere the tiles are likely to be splashed. You can also buy coloured grout to match or complement your tiles.

1 Press a small amount of grout on to the face of the tiles with a trowel. Use a grout spreader to spread it, making long, upward diagonal strokes and working it into the joints between tiles. Continue until you have grouted all the joints. Do this as quickly as possible, since the grout will soon begin to harden.

2 Immediately you finish applying the grout, go over the tiles with a damp sponge to remove any excess. It will be very difficult to shift once hard. Take care not to drag any grout from the joints.

3 After leaving the grout to harden slightly, use a grout shaper to finish off the joints and give them a neat appearance. Pull the shaper along the joints in one continuous movement. If any gaps appear in the joints, press in some more grout with the tip of your finger. Sponge off any excess grout.

4 As the grout dries, a powdery film will appear on the tiles. Simply polish this off with a soft, clean cloth to leave your tiles sparkling.

ideal tool

Grout shaper
Giving grouted joints a neat, uniform appearance is easy with a grout shaper. This simple plastic tool usually comes with interchangeable heads, offering a choice of profiles. Simply draw it along each joint so that it touches the tiles on each side, then wipe any grout from the faces of the tiles.

Replacing old grout

Moisture from baths and showers, or food spills in kitchens can stain grout, leaving it looking shabby while the tiles themselves are fine. Minor staining and fungal growths can be removed with grout cleaner, which contains detergents and biological agents to clean the grout and

discourage mould. But if your grout is particularly dingy, you may need to scrape out and replace it.

Use a grout raker to remove the old grout to at least half the thickness of the tiles, taking care not to scratch their edges. Do all the vertical joints first and then the horizontal ones, to make sure that you don't miss any. Then replace the grout as shown above.

ideal tool

Grout raker
Grout sets very hard, and it takes some effort to remove it. The only way is to scrape it out with a sharp point. A specially designed grout raker will miminise risk of injury to yourself as well as accidental damage to the tiles.

Wipe off any stray adhesive as you work – it is much easier to clean off when wet than dry.

Finish the upper and side edges of the splashback with matching glazed trim. Mark and cut the trim to match the length of your tiles so that the joins align neatly. Cut the corners at a 45° angle to create a neat mitre; use a tile file to refine the fit.

Remove the batten and measure the gap below. Cut the lowest row of tiles to fit, remembering to allow for a bead of silicone sealant between sink and tiles. When the adhesive is dry, grout the tiles and seal the gap at the bottom (see pages 106–7).

ideal tool

Tile file

If a cut tile is too big and doesn't quite fit, don't waste it – file it to size with a tile file. Cheap, durable and easy to use, this is an essential tiler's accessory.

Mosaic tiles

Setting out for mosaic tiles is much the same as for regular tiles (see pages 100–1) – just treat a panel of tiles as you would a whole tile. It isn't so important to centre the panels on the wall, since the individual tiles are so much smaller. But you should still establish horizontal and vertical starting lines, and work from the centre outwards for the neatest results. An adhesive specially formulated for mosaic tiles will give you a slightly longer working time than a general tile adhesive, allowing you to adjust and refine the placing of the tiles before they set hard. Once you have finished and the adhesive is dry, grout the tiles in the usual way (see page 106).

Applying mosaic tiles

Handling sheets of mosaic tiles takes a little practice, but the results are more than worth it.

Spread mosaic tile adhesive on the wall with a notched spreader, then place a panel of tiles onto it. Press evenly across the surface with spread fingers. You need to work accurately: once the backing paper or mesh is moistened by the adhesive it disintegrates, making the panel very difficult to adjust.

Hold a piece of scrap board over the tiles while the adhesive is wet and tap lightly with a wooden mallet. This will give the tiles a flat, even finish.

If you need to reduce the size of a panel, either use a craft knife to cut between two rows of tiles, or use tile nibblers to cut the tiles. There's no need to score them first.

project essentials

- **notched spreader**
- **wooden mallet**
- **craft knife or tile nibblers**

- mosaic tile adhesive
- mosaic tiles
- scrap board

ONE PLANET HOME

Insulating ceilings
The ceiling between the top floor of the house and the loft space should support a 270mm layer of insulation between and over the joists to prevent heat loss. See page 334.

In old houses the ceilings may well be constructed from lath and plaster, while in modern houses they are likely to be of plasterboard. It's not difficult to repair small areas of damage on a ceiling, and is well worth the effort, particularly before you decorate a room.

Ceiling structure

Both lath-and-plaster and plasterboard ceilings are fixed to the joists supporting the floor above. The depth of the joists varies according to the age of the building (older ones are often deeper than modern ones) and their length.

Lath and plaster ◢

This was a time-consuming method of building walls and ceilings, as individual laths (thin strips of wood) had to be nailed to the joists and then covered with layers of plaster. The plaster was squeezed between the laths so that 'nibs' formed – ridges of plaster that squeezed through the laths and set hard, holding the ceiling plaster in place. The room above would traditionally have had floorboards.

Floorboard floor nailed to joists

Laths nailed to joists

'Nibs' of plaster holding the ceiling plaster in place

Plaster (basecoat and finish)

B&Q Making it easier

Repairing plaster around a ceiling rose
First switch off the power at the mains and put the circuit fuse in your pocket, or switch off and lock the relevant circuit breaker and leave a sign at the consumer unit indicating that you are working on the circuit (see page 268). Use a voltage tester to check the circuit is dead. Unscrew the cover of the light fitting, and then the screws supporting the rose, so that the fitting drops away from the ceiling. Scrape away loose plaster and then apply new plaster with a trowel. Smooth it off and leave to dry for an hour before replacing the rose and then restoring the power.

Plasterboard ◢

Most modern ceilings are constructed from sheets of plasterboard nailed to the joists. The joints are taped with scrim – a very open-weave, self-adhesive tape. Wet plaster is then applied, or the ceiling is finished with jointing tape and compound, which seals the joints and creates a surface ready for decorating (see page 75). The floor of the room above a plasterboard ceiling may be laid with floorboards or chipboard.

Chipboard floor nailed to joists

Plasterboard ceiling nailed to joists

Suspended ceilings

Very high ceilings are sometimes lowered by fitting a suspended ceiling. Panels or tiles are fitted to a lightweight framework consisting of an outer frame – called the angle section – which is fixed to the walls, a main bearer section spanning the width of the room, and a cross-bearer section which fits between the main bearers. Wires fixed to angle brackets attached to the original ceiling hold the framework in place. Panels may be decorative and translucent or may have sound-proofing and/or thermal properties.

Ceiling repairs

Small areas of damage on a ceiling can be repaired in a number of different ways. Crumbling areas in a lath-and-plaster ceiling can be patched with conventional plaster (below) or a plasterboard patch (overleaf). Slight bulges can be repaired from the floor above. If a ceiling is damaged all the way through – for instance, if someone slips off a joist and puts a foot through it when walking in an unboarded loft – you can repair the hole with a plasterboard patch supported by noggings nailed between the joists.

Damaged area

1 Cut back damaged area, removing all loose plaster
2 Apply thin undercoat and key the surface
3 Apply second, thicker undercoat to bring surface level with ceiling
4 Skim in a finishing coat and polish smooth

Replastering a damaged section on a lath-and-plaster ceiling

Where the laths are still intact, damaged plaster can be repaired with new plaster. Carefully cut back the damaged area, removing all loose material, until you reach sound plaster. Dampen the laths and apply a thin coat of bonding undercoat plaster. Score the surface of the plaster in a diamond pattern with the side of the trowel to create a key for the next coat. Allow it to set, then apply a second coat of undercoat plaster. Scrape it back 2mm below the surface and lightly score it. When it has set, apply a finishing coat of plaster to bring it down level with the rest of the ceiling.

Repairing a lath-and-plaster bulge from above

An area of plaster that is sagging away from the laths can be repaired from above if you have good access to the upstairs floor. Prop up the sagging plaster using a flat piece of chipboard or plywood nailed to a length of 38mm-square timber that reaches from floor to ceiling (this is known as a 'deadman'). Lift the floorboards in the room above and vacuum between the joists over the bulge to collect up the loose plaster. Mix fairly runny bonding undercoat plaster and pour it over the damaged area to replace the broken plaster. Leave the supporting prop in place until the plaster has dried and bonded to the laths.

Pour plaster into damaged area
Lift floorboards to access sagging area
Joist
Upstairs floor
Prop up sagging area from below
Ceiling
Sagging plaster

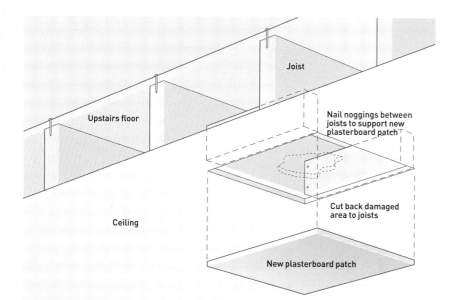

Joist
Upstairs floor
Nail noggings between joists to support new plasterboard patch
Cut back damaged area to joists
Ceiling
New plasterboard patch

Repairing a hole

Locate the joists each side of the hole with a stud detector. Draw a line along each joist, half-way across its width, with a straightedge and pencil, and then join them up to mark a square or rectangle around the damaged area. Cut away the laths and plaster or plasterboard inside the marked area with a padsaw. Remove any protruding nails in the joists with a claw hammer. Cut two noggings from 100mm x 50mm sawn softwood to fit between the joists and form the other two sides of the opening. Half the thickness of the noggings should project into the exposed area. Drive nails into the noggings at an angle to secure them to the joists. Using plasterboard that is slightly thinner than the ceiling depth, cut a piece the same size as the hole. Fix it in place with plasterboard nails along the joists and noggings. Fill the join with bonding undercoat plaster. When it is dry, apply multi-finish plaster to the patch to bring it level with the rest of the ceiling. If necessary, apply two thin coats rather than one thick coat.

The lath-and-plaster ceilings in older houses often crack with age and the plaster may bulge where it begins to break away from the laths. If only a small area of a ceiling is affected, a simple repair can be made with a plasterboard patch using dry-lining techniques that do not require plastering skills. Or it may be easier to overboard the entire ceiling with plasterboard sheets.

Making the patch

Remove the old plaster before you buy the plasterboard to make the repair patch, so that you can choose the thickness closest to the depth of plaster.

1 Areas of loose, bulging plaster should be dealt with promptly, as they are not only unsightly but also dangerous. Put on a dust mask, protective goggles and, preferably, a hard hat before you start. Open up one of the cracks with a filling knife or similar bladed tool until you can insert your fingers in it.

2 Pull away the loose sections of plaster to expose the wooden laths, continuing until you have reached sound plaster and have exposed the joists to which the repair patch can be nailed.

3 Undercut the edges of the plaster slightly with a filling knife. Then tape a sheet of newspaper over the hole, stretching it taut, and trace the edge of the plaster with a crayon or felt-tip pen.

4 Remove the newspaper and cut around the outline of the hole. Then lay it on a sheet of plasterboard and draw round it to obtain the shape of the patch.

5 Lay the plasterboard on a firm surface, such as a portable workbench, and cut out the patch. You can use a padsaw, a powered jigsaw or, as here, a plasterboard padsaw. Gently rub down any ragged paper edges with abrasive paper.

6 Check the fit of the patch; if necessary, scrape away more of the ceiling plaster to leave a gap of about 3mm. Prop the patch in place, or have someone support it, hold a straightedge across the ceiling and measure the vertical gap between it and the patch. This will show the thickness of packing needed to set the patch flush with the ceiling's surface.

7 The packing can be made from stiff card (make sure it cannot be compressed), hardboard, plywood or even plasterboard. Nail it to the joists.

project essentials

- **dust mask**
- **safety goggles**
- **hard hat**
- **filling knife**
- **crayon or felt-tip pen**
- **scissors**
- **pencil**
- **padsaw, jigsaw or plasterboard saw**
- **wooden props**
- **straightedge**
- **tape measure**
- **hammer**

- newspaper
- masking tape
- plasterboard
- abrasive paper
- packing pieces
- nails

ideal tool

Plasterboard padsaw
This saw is designed for cutting holes in plasterboard sheets (for electrical fittings, etc). Its pointed, tapering blade is inserted initially into a drilled hole, much like a padsaw, but its narrow blade also makes it ideal for cutting out an irregularly shaped patch. The coarse teeth will cut through the plasterboard quickly.

Fixing the patch

The edges of the repair can be disguised and reinforced by using plasterboard jointing tape and compound: see page 75.

project essentials

- **hammer**
- **pencil**
- **small brush**
- **coating knife**
- **sponge**
- **sanding block**

- plasterboard nails
- PVA adhesive
- ready-mixed filler
- abrasive paper
- plasterboard jointing compound
- jointing tape

1 Hold the patch in position and check that it is flush with the ceiling; adjust the packing if necessary. Then nail the patch to the joists with plasterboard nails. It may help to mark the positions of the joists with pencil on the surrounding plaster.

2 Brush a PVA solution on to the edges of the patch and surrounding plaster and allow it to dry. Then fill the gap around the patch with a ready-mixed filler, pressing it in well; the undercut edges of the plaster will help retain it. When dry, sand the filler lightly.

3 Spread a layer of plasterboard jointing compound over the joint and press jointing tape into it, applying another wide layer of compound with a coating knife.

4 Smooth the compound with a damp sponge, feathering the edges. When it has dried, sand it smooth before redecorating.

 Making it easier

Containing the mess
Removing damaged plaster creates a lot of dirt and dust. To reduce the mess, cut two holes in a rubbish sack and pass your arms through them. That way, the sack will catch most of the debris as you take it out.

Overboarding a ceiling

Removing crumbling plaster from a whole ceiling is an extremely messy and dusty job. Provided the ceiling is not sagging and most of the plaster is intact, it is much easier to overboard or dry-line the whole ceiling using plasterboard sheets. You could use acoustic-check plasterboard to improve sound insulation (see page 369).

First locate the joists using a joist, pipe and cable detector, or from the floor above, and measure the distance between joist centres – usually 400mm or 600mm. Check for pipes and cables, and then hammer nails into the ceiling in line with each joist centre along opposite walls. Snap chalk lines across the ceiling to mark the joist centres. Extend the lines a few cm down the wall so they remain visible as you fix the boards.

Secure tapered-edge plasterboard sheets with their long edges at right angles to the joists and the ivory side facing downwards. Butt-join the board ends in line with a joist, and stagger the joints. Use plasterboard nails long enough to drive securely into the joists. Take care to check for pipes and cables at each fixing point. You may need to scribe sheets to fit along the wall edges (see page 73). The ceiling can be finished with a skim coat of plaster, or with jointing tape and compound (see page 75).

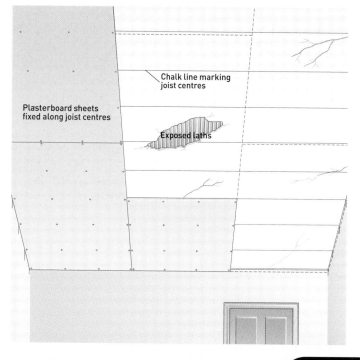

Chalk line marking joist centres

Plasterboard sheets fixed along joist centres

Exposed laths

You must have a solid platform from which to work when decorating a ceiling – scaffold board resting on trestles will do. If possible, construct a platform that allows you to paper or paint the length of the room without having to move it along. A ceiling surface should be prepared for papering or painting in the same way as walls (see pages 82–83).

project essentials

- **step-ladder**
- **tape measure**
- **pencil**
- **hammer**
- **chalk line**
- **pasting table**
- **wallpaper scissors**
- **bucket**
- **pasting brush**
- **paper-hanging brush**
- **seam roller**

- small nails
- lining paper, if necessary
- wallpaper paste
- wallpaper

Papering a ceiling

As with walls, it is particularly important to get the first length of paper absolutely straight. Ceiling/wall junctions are not usually true enough to use as a guide. It is better to mark a chalk line and then position the first length along it. Don't worry about a guideline for lining paper – just align the paper with the wall where you start and butt-join the edges (taking care not to overlap them).

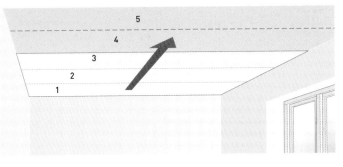

Choosing your direction

Start papering along a wall that is at right angles to the window wall. This way, if the joins overlap slightly they will not cast shadows. If the room has windows on two walls, you may not be able to avoid some shadows, so hang the paper across the narrowest part of the ceiling, as this will be easiest.

Decide where to hang the first length, and at either end of the ceiling measure out from the side wall a distance exactly 25mm less than the width of the paper. Hammer a small nail a little way into the ceiling at each point. If your ceiling is obviously uneven, measure its width at each end of the room, calculate the difference, and at the narrower end move the nail towards the wall junction by half of that amount. This will avoid the final strip of wallpaper appearing skewed.

Attach a chalk line between the two nails. From the centre of the trestle platform, pull and release the line to snap on to the ceiling. Remove the line and nails. Measure, cut and paste the paper (see pages 90–91).

Position the edge of the first length of paper against the chalk line and smooth the other edge into the ceiling/wall junction to give a 25mm overlap on to the wall. If the junction is not straight, the overlap will be uneven rather than the paper on the ceiling.

Brush out the bubbles with a paper-hanging brush, and then run wallpaper scissors along the ceiling/wall junction to make a sharp crease. Gently pull back the paper and cut along the crease. Brush the trimmed edge back into place, applying extra paste at the edges if needed. Butt the next length of paper against the first. Run a seam roller lightly along the joins.

B&Q Making it easier

Papering around a light fitting
When you reach a pendant light, turn off the power at the mains (switching off at the wall is not enough). Unscrew the cover and paper up to and over the base. With scissors, puncture the paper at the centre of the fitting and make a series of snips outwards, being careful not to cut beyond the fitting. Then trim away the flaps of paper, cutting just inside the rim of the base. Wipe away any paste. When the paper is completely dry, replace the cover and then turn the power back on.

Painting the ceiling

Paint a ceiling with a roller or a broad emulsion brush. To avoid having to stretch up continually, either construct a platform so that you can walk along the length of the room, or buy an extension pole to fit on to the end of your roller handle – some can extend to over 3m. If you are redecorating a room, you should paint the ceiling first. For general painting techniques, see pages 86–87.

safety first

Painting a ceiling need not be a particularly messy job, but you do tend to get speckled with paint when using a roller. Wear old clothes or protective clothing (including a hat) and clear vision safety glasses or goggles to keep the paint out of your eyes.

ideal tool

Roller with extension handle
This is an integrated roller and small telescopic extension handle tool – useful for both ceilings and walls.

Painting the edges

Either before or after you paint the bulk of the ceiling with the roller, you will need to paint into the edges of the room with a brush. If you are going to paint the walls after the ceiling, use a 25mm–50mm brush to carry a strip of paint on to the walls which you can later paint over. If you are not going on to paint the walls, bead the edges or use a 'George' (see page 86).

Painting with the roller

Dip the roller sleeve into the paint and roll it firmly up and down the tray's ribbed incline to spread the paint evenly, then apply it to the ceiling at an angle of about 45°. Experiment with the amount of paint on the roller. Too much and you will spray paint everywhere; too little and you will take forever! Move the roller over the wall surface, using random strokes applied with a light, even pressure. Each time you dip the roller in the paint, move it to an adjacent unpainted area and work back to the painted area in overlapping strokes to blend in the wet edges.

Fixing a plaster ceiling rose

When you have painted your ceiling, you can create an interesting focal point by adding a plaster ceiling rose. Lightweight ceiling roses can be secured with adhesive alone. If you want to fit a large one, you may need to use screws driven into the joists as well as adhesive. In that case, drill pilot holes for the screws through the rose into the joists above, then screw in place with brass screws.

project essentials

- **drill**
- **screwdriver**

- plaster ceiling rose
- adhesive
- damp sponge
- screws

Turn off the electricity at the mains (see page 268). Then disconnect and remove the light fitting. Drill a hole for the cable in the decorative rose (don't press down hard or you may crack it). Apply adhesive all round the edge on the back of the decorative rose.

Pass the lighting cable through the drilled centre hole. Position the rose on the ceiling and press it in place until the adhesive secures it.

Wipe off the excess adhesive with a damp sponge. When it has set completely, refit the light fitting using screws long enough to pass right through the rose and into the joist above. Drill pilot holes first. Reconnect the wires and then turn the power back on.

B&Q Making it easier

Painting with a brush
If you are using a brush instead of a roller, pour the paint into a paint kettle, so that it is about one-third full. Dip the brush into the paint to cover about one-third of the bristle depth. Apply the paint with short, overlapping strokes in different directions. Then, with a fairly dry brush, lightly draw the bristles across the painted surface, again in a criss-cross pattern, to remove any visible brush marks and achieve an even surface.

Coving or cornice is a prefabricated decorative moulding fitted at the junction of the wall and ceiling all the way around a room. As well as creating an elegant look, it is excellent for hiding any cracks that can open up between walls and ceiling. Traditionally coving has been made from plaster, but modern materials and manufacturing processes mean there are now more lightweight alternatives that can be easier to apply. Coving is available in a range of sizes and styles, from contemporary simplicity to the intricate and highly decorative cornices of yesteryear.

Before you start

B&Q Making it easier

Cutting coving
There are pre-mitred internal and external corner packs available to buy which you can use as a template. Cutting coving can be a complicated task and these guides will help you visualise the joins before you make the cuts.

Coving should be applied before you decorate a room. To mark out the area that it will cover, go around the room holding a piece of the coving in position, pencilling its upper and lower edge on the wall and ceiling. Coving can only be fixed to a sound, dry, clean surface, so remove all traces of distemper, loose plaster, wallpaper or flaking paint from this area. Strip off wall or ceiling paper by cutting through the paper 2mm inside the pencil guidelines with a sharp knife to give neat edges, and removing the paper between the marks with a scraper. Key the area between the guidelines by scoring the plaster with a series of criss-cross lines to give the coving adhesive a better grip. Brush away any loose particles.

project essentials

- **tape measure**
- **pencil**
- **mitre block**
- **fine-toothed panel saw**
- **scraper or trowel**
- **filling knife**
- **pipe and cable detector**
- **hammer**
- **sponge**

- coving
- fine-grade abrasive paper
- coving adhesive
- nails
- coving primer

Cutting corners

Check you have the coving the right way up before starting to cut or fix it. The edges are generally clearly marked on the reverse side.

Measure the length of the first wall and mark the coving where you need to cut mitres for the corners. Lay the coving on the mitre block with the wall edge of the coving upright against the side and the ceiling edge flat against the base. Use a panel saw to cut the mitres for the corners. Lightly sand the cut edges.

Apply coving adhesive all the way along the back edges of your length of coving. Use a scraper or trowel, as shown, or you can buy coving adhesive ready-mixed in a tube and apply it using a cartridge gun, which is easier. You don't need to apply it to the central area as this does not come into contact with the wall or ceiling.

Fixing coving

Always read the manufacturer's fixing instructions carefully before starting work – they may vary slightly, depending in the type of coving.

Press the coving into place along the pencil guideline. Allow excess adhesive to squeeze out, making sure there is firm contact along the entire length. Remove the excess with a filling knife or your finger and use it to fill in any gaps in the mitred corners and the joints between lengths. If any adhesive splashes on to the coving, wall or ceiling, wipe it away with a damp sponge.

Check there are no hidden pipes or cables then tap in nails just below the bottom edge of the coving to support it as the adhesive dries. You can remove the nails later, but if you are fixing plaster coving to a very uneven surface, you may have to reinforce the adhesive with galvanised nails or countersunk screws driven into wallplugs set in the wall. Continue to add lengths, butt-joining and gluing to the previous length.

When the room is complete, fill any gaps and joints with adhesive, then wipe with a damp sponge. Allow the adhesive to dry, then lightly sand the joints and corners with fine-grade abrasive paper.

Adding cornerpieces

Some manufacturers make coving cornerpieces, differently shaped to fit internal and external corners. They will give an elegant finish to your coving, and hide any less-than-perfect mitre joints. Simply apply adhesive to the back, hold the cornerpiece in place until it is secure, then wipe away any excess adhesive.

Decorating with coving

Coving can offer more than period elegance. By adding a lighter band at the highest point in a room, it can be a great way of making a ceiling seem higher, especially if you want to decorate the walls and ceiling in strong or dark colours. Modern designs are available that will give a bold lift to any design scheme. Before you paint coving, seal its porous surface with coving primer.

B&Q Making it easier

Mixing adhesive

Coving adhesive can come ready-mixed, or in powder form to be mixed with water. It sets very quickly, so if you are mixing it up yourself, check its setting time and only mix the amount you can use in that time.

The loft is a very handy storage place, but to make use of it you need to be able to access it easily. The best way to do this is via a fitted, extendable loft ladder, which folds back and is stored out of the way in the loft space.

Choosing a loft ladder

Loft ladders are made of wood or aluminium, and come in either fold-and-slide or concertina designs. They are made in different lengths (to suit heights of 2.3m, 2.5m and 2.9m–3m, measured from the floor of the landing to the top of the loft joists). All are hinged to the hatch; some have a handrail – which can be a real help when climbing into the loft – and some can be operated from inside the loft. The manufacturer will specify the size of hatch opening required and the pivoting height needed inside the loft (usually 1.1m above the loft floor). Make sure you have enough space.

A sliding ladder is simple to install and operate: it is lowered by means of a pole hooked over the bottom rail. It has two or three sections, with spring-locking catches to hold it in the fully extended or closed position. Some are fitted with a sprung power pivot arm to prevent the ladder from dropping down under its own weight. This also makes it easy to raise the ladder into the roof.

Making a hatch door

Some ladders come with a hatch door, but if yours does not, or if your old hatch door is not strong enough, you can make a new one quite easily. You can choose from 12mm or 19mm blockboard, MDF or plywood. The thicker board is very heavy to work with, but the thinner board may need a batten added to take the hinges.

1 Measure the hatch opening and cut a door from your blockboard, MDF or plywood. If the 12mm board is too thin to take the hinges, nail a strip of 50mm x 25mm batten to the hinge end of the board. Screw the hinges on to the door.

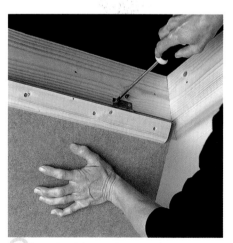

2 The door should open downwards, so fix the other side of the hinges the same side as the ladder will go, screwing through the hatch lining into the joist or trimmer.

project essentials

- **tape measure**
- **pencil**
- **tenon saw**
- **screwdriver**
- **adjustable spanner, if necessary**

- 12mm or 19mm blockboard, MDF or plywood
- 50mm x 25mm batten if required
- two 65mm or 75mm hinges and screws

3 Most ladders come with a push or turn lock/release catch which has to be fixed to the other side of the door. Follow the manufacturer's instructions for fitting it.

Fitting the loft ladder

Ladders will differ, so always follow the manufacturer's instructions. Don't be tempted to stand on the new loft ladder until it is fixed in place. You will need an ordinary ladder, securely positioned, to gain access to the loft to do the job.

project essentials

- **power drill with twist bits**
- **screwdriver**
- **bradawl**
- **adjustable spanner, if required**

- loft ladder and fittings

safety first

If you intend to store heavy items in your loft, be sure to keep them at the sides rather than in the middle of the loft space.

1 Lower the ladder to the floor. Fit the top stops on the ladder, according to the instructions. Drill pilot holes then screw the ladder hinge screws through the board into the joist or trimmer below and on to the front face. Fit the loft ladder guide assembly to the frame. You can fit the handrail now or, if you have a power pivot system, you may find it easier to fit it after this is installed.

2 If the ladder has a power pivot system, use the template supplied to mark the position for the pivot arm on the floor of the loft. Mark the position of the screws with a bradawl. The pivot system can usually be fitted to either side of the ladder.

3 Position the power pivot arm according to the manufacturer's instructions and screw it to the loft floor. With the ladder in fully stowed position in the loft, attach the pivot arm to one side of it.

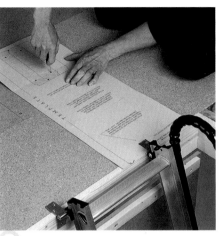

4 Follow the manufacturer's instructions for lowering and storing the ladder. This usually involves putting the hook on the end of the ladder's pole into the catch on the underside of the door and rotating the catch to lower the door. Then place the pole hook into the socket in the centre of the bottom rung on the middle section of the ladder and lower it until the stops are reached. Release the locking catches and lower all sections of the ladder.

5 To store the ladder, release the catches, move the ladder into a closed position and engage the catches. Slide the ladder upwards until it is able to swing through the loft opening and ease it into the loft space with the pole. Hook the end of the pole into the catch on the door, raise the door and twist the catch to close it.

ONE PLANET HOME

Insulating your loft door
The minimum recommended depth of insulation across the entire loft floor is 270mm (see page 334). To prevent heat escaping into the loft through the hatch door, you should cut and stick a square of insulation board to its underside. Or you can buy a ready-made insulated drop-down hatch door which simply screws in place.

There are plenty of styles and materials to choose from when you buy a new door. Most fall into one of two main categories: panel doors or flush doors. Houses built before the 1940s (and most built in the past decade or so) are likely to have panel doors; flush doors were popular in the post-war period.

Choosing a door

When buying a new door, choose one that matches the other doors in the house. Internal doors may be made from softwood or hardwood, and they may be painted or stained and varnished for a natural-wood look. Glazed doors are generally used for front and rear entrances, but are increasingly used for internal doors. The door frame may be made from timber, or aluminium if it's a PVCu plastic door.

Doors are sold in standard sizes of varying thicknesses to fit modern houses. Interior doors are thinner and less strong than exterior doors, which have to be weatherproof (see page 179). Older houses often have non-standard size doors so, if you have to replace one, you may need to have it made to measure. Alternatively, you may be able to buy a larger door and trim it to fit (see page 124), but check when you buy it how much can be safely removed without weakening the structure.

(see page 179) (see page 124)

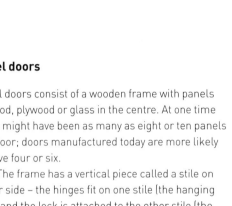

Panel doors

Panel doors consist of a wooden frame with panels of wood, plywood or glass in the centre. At one time there might have been as many as eight or ten panels in a door; doors manufactured today are more likely to have four or six.

The frame has a vertical piece called a stile on either side – the hinges fit on one stile (the hanging stile) and the lock is attached to the other stile (the shutting stile); three cross rails running horizontally at the top, centre and bottom of the door are jointed into the stiles; and the final piece of the framework is a vertical piece in the centre, called a muntin, which is joined to the cross rails. The panels fit into grooves in the frame and may have decorative moulded borders.

safety first

Fire safety

Fire-resistant doors can delay the spread of fire. They are primarily installed in multiple-storey buildings to prevent fire blocking the escape routes, but the door to a garage attached to a house must also meet fire-resistance requirements. Fire doors are usually the wooden flush type with a core of solid board material. Any window opening must be glazed with fire-resistant glass. Fire-resistant door frames have a recess containing a special strip that swells when hot and seals the gap around the door. If you are replacing an old fire door, make sure the new door is at least the same fire rating. Follow the instructions carefully and make sure the seals and special fittings are all properly installed. If you are considering fitting a new fire door, you should consult your local Fire Prevention Officer.

Bolection moulding

A bolection moulding is shaped so that it overlaps the door frame, making it less likely to shrink away from the frame.

Planted moulding

The inside edge of the frame is fitted with a planted moulding. This type can shrink away from the frame and cause cracks in the paint if the door is painted.

Plain moulding

The panel is slotted into a groove in the stiles and left without any moulding.

Panel door

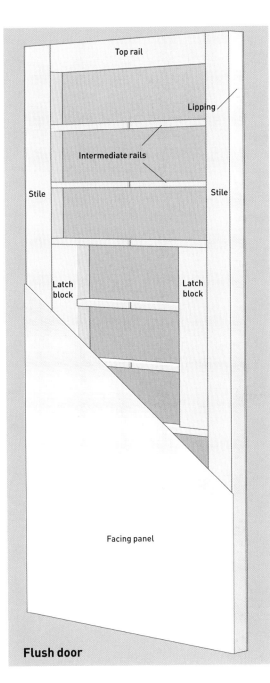

Flush door

Labels on diagram: Top rail, Lipping, Intermediate rails, Stile, Stile, Latch block, Latch block, Facing panel

Flush doors

Flush doors usually have completely flat facings of man-made board attached to a softwood frame. The frame consists of a stile on either side, and a top and bottom rail jointed into the stiles. A vertical block is glued to the inner side of each stile to take the door latch.

The frame is covered on both sides with sheets of plywood or hardboard, which may be painted or covered with a wood veneer. Some facings are embossed to look like a panelled door; others have mouldings fixed to them to look like panels. The edges of the door are covered with lipping.

Between these facing sheets, the core of the door can vary. The framework of a lightweight door may be filled with a honeycombed paper or cardboard material. Heavier alternatives include sheets of chipboard, laminated vertical strips of timber or horizontal timber rails, known as intermediate rails, attached to the stiles all the way down the door.

Door frames

An internal door is hung on a wooden frame screwed into the walls on both sides. If the door is in a masonry wall, a rigid beam called a lintel is set in the wall over the door to support the structure above the opening. Special brackets fix the frame to the walls. A door frame in a stud partition wall (see page 70) is attached to the timber studs supporting the plasterboard walls and extra studs are fitted over the doorway to strengthen it.

The top of the door frame is called the soffit casing and the sides are jamb casings. The door is attached to the frame with two hinges set in recesses cut out with a chisel. The line where the casings and the wall meet is covered with a decorative moulding called an architrave. The door closes against a doorstop, which is usually a separate piece of wood fitted to the frame.

Labels on diagram: Architrave, Soffit casing, Lintel, Recess for hinges, Doorstop, Jamb casing, Securing bracket attaching frame to masonry wall, Jamb casing, Recess for hinges, Threshold

Door frame casing

Panel door
A traditional panelled door, whether painted or stained and varnished, gives privacy and elegance.

Glazed pine door
Partially glazed doors are great for diffusing natural light through an interior.

Glazed french doors
Double doors with lots of glass look good leading onto a living room, conservatory or extension.

Folding doors
Concertina-style folding doors take up less space than conventional doors and can create a wider opening, making them ideal for access onto a balcony or terrace.

DOORS FIXING FAULTS

Doors can develop a variety of faults, any of which may prevent them opening and closing smoothly. Faults may be due to heavy wear and tear, age, previous damp or a build-up of paint layers over the years. Fortunately, they are quite easy to cure.

Door sticking on its opening edge

Loose or squeaking hinges

Latch doesn't engage

Lock hard to turn

Build-up of paint on frame, door or hinges, causing difficulties closing door

Door 'hingebound' by hinges set too deep

Door sticking or rubbing at bottom

Fixing a dropped door

A door may drop because its hinges have worn loose. Check all the hinge screws to make sure they are tight. If a screw will not tighten properly, you may need to replace it with a larger size or plug the existing hole with matchsticks.

1 Remove the screw. Apply wood adhesive to one end of some matchsticks and tap two or three into the screw hole.

project essentials

- **screwdriver**
- **wood chisel**
- **wooden mallet**

- wood adhesive
- matchsticks

2 When the adhesive has set, cut off the matchsticks level with the hinge flap, using a chisel and wooden mallet, then replace the screw.

Squeaks and stiffness

Squeaking hinges and a lock that is hard to turn can both usually be solved by a squirt of aerosol lubricant, either into the latch mechanism or on to the hinge pins. When you have sprayed the hinges, open and close the door a few times to allow the oil to flow through them, then wipe away any excess before it runs down to the floor.

Sticking door

A build-up of paint on the edge of the door and the frame can make the door stick or bind, either at the top, bottom or the side. You may be able to sand any high spots away, using coarse abrasive paper around a sanding block, but if it is sticking badly you will need to plane off the excess material.

project essentials

- **plane**
- **workbench, if required**

- abrasive paper
- sanding block
- wood primer
- paint

1 Marks on the paintwork will indicate where the door is sticking – in this case, the edge of the door. When a door is sticking along the top or upper side edge, you may be able to plane it without taking it off its hinges. If it is sticking near the floor, however, you will need to remove the door and secure it in a workbench in order to plane it.

2 Plane the edge, allowing sufficient clearance for repainting. Remove the lock first if you need to plane near it.

3 Sand the planed edge of the door and the top and bottom corners, using a sanding block. Prime the wood before repainting it.

1 If there is no clearance on the hinge side, remove the screws from one hinge at a time. Prise the hinge out of the recess – it helps to have an assistant holding the door steady while you do this. Cut some cardboard to fit the recess and pack it into the space.

Springing door

If a door springs open all the time, this usually means the hinges are set too deep in the door or frame and the door is straining against them. Alternatively, the door may not be closing properly against the doorstop, the thin strip of wood nailed on to the frame. Examine the paintwork around the door to locate the problem.

2 Screw back the hinge and repeat the process for the other hinge. The packed-out recesses will give the required clearance, but they may cause sticking on the lock side. If this happens, you will need to plane the edge of the door (see opposite).

3 If the door will not stay closed against the doorstop, tap a wood chisel into the joint between doorstop and door frame and lever the doorstop off.

4 Close the door, then reposition the doorstop to give the door enough clearance to close without catching. Nail it in place with 30mm nails roughly 300mm apart.

B&Q Making it easier

Jamming at the bottom
If the door is jamming at the bottom or there is insufficient clearance over the carpet, position the door where it is sticking the most. Rest a piece of thick card or a steel rule on the flooring against the door and mark a pencil line at that height along the bottom of the door. Take the door off its hinges and saw or plane off the excess material. Smooth the edges with abrasive paper and refit the door.

Misaligned lock

If the door latch is out of line with the striker plate, it will not engage. It may be possible to fix a very small misalignment without removing the plate by enlarging the cut-out area in the striker plate with a metal file. However, the plate may have to be taken off and repositioned.

1 Unscrew and remove the striker plate. Rub a pencil or crayon on the tip of the latch, then close the door and operate the handle several times. Open the door and you will see marks on the frame at the position of the latch. Mark over these with a pencil to show the new position for the striker plate.

2 Use a wood chisel to enlarge the cut-out area in the frame as far as the pencil marks.

3 Reposition the striker plate in the new position, making sure that its cut-out area fits over the cut-out area on the frame. If the plate has moved only a small distance, plug the old screw holes with small wooden pegs before drilling new pilot holes for the screws.

DOORS HANGING AN INTERNAL DOOR

Plane talking
When planing the top or bottom of a door, work from both sides towards the centre to avoid splitting at the outer edges.

Whether you are hanging a new door in a new frame or a new door in an existing frame, you must make sure that the door fits into it before fitting the hinges. Allow a clearance gap of about 2mm at the top and sides, and 6mm–12mm at the bottom, depending on the thickness of the flooring.

Fitting a new door in a new frame

New doors may have extensions to the stiles, known as horns, which prevent the corners being damaged. These should be sawn off before trimming the door.

project essentials

- tape measure
- pencil
- plane
- panel saw
- marking gauge (optional)
- wide-bladed wood chisel
- wooden mallet
- power drill with twist and wood bits
- screwdriver
- try square
- narrow chisel
- craft knife
- vice
- hacksaw
- mitre saw or mitre block
- long-nosed pliers
- nail punch

- new door
- abrasive paper
- two 100mm butt hinges and screws
- wooden wedges
- cardboard
- masking tape
- door latch and handles
- 30mm nails
- panel pins
- thin strip of wood for doorstop
- door architrave

1 Measure the door frame, allowing for the necessary clearance, and transfer the measurements to the door. Plane equal amounts from the two side edges of the door to a maximum of 5mm.

2 If you need to trim more than 6mm excess wood from the bottom edge of the door, use a saw, then finish with the plane. Sand the cut edges with abrasive paper until smooth.

ideal tool

Electric planer
This will make quick work of trimming a new door.

Fitting the door hinges

Two hinges are generally enough to support a standard internal door, though in the humid environment of a bathroom or kitchen fit three to help prevent bowing. Hinges fit into recesses of an equal depth in the door frame and the stile. You need a very sharp wood chisel with a wide blade for making them.

1 Mark the position of the upper hinge on the stile, 175mm from the top edge of the door. The lower hinge should be 250mm from the bottom edge of the door. Stand the door on its side edge with the hinge edge uppermost. Hold each hinge on its marked position with the knuckle protruding from the door. Draw round the hinge flap with a sharp pencil.

2 To mark the depth for the hinge recess, use a marking gauge or hold a hinge flap level with the edge of the door and mark the depth with a pencil.

3 Cut out the hinge recess using a sharp wide-bladed wood chisel and a wooden mallet. First cut the ends and then make a series of cuts along the length of the hinge to approximately the correct depth.

4 Use the chisel to pare away the surplus wood and trim the recess until it is level.

Testing the fit
Before test-fitting the door, partially hammer four nails into the frame at the depth of the door to prevent it from falling through.

ideal tool

Door/board lifter
Use this specially designed tool to lever the door into position with your foot, leaving your hands free to mark the hinge positions.

Fitting the latch

Door latches, locks, knobs and handles are available in a vast range of shapes and sizes, including reproductions of many traditional styles and designs. Here a brass door knob is fitted to a panelled door (Steps 1–12, below and on page 126).

Test-fit the hinge in the recess and trim it again as necessary. Repeat the process for the other hinge. Position each hinge flap in its recess and drill pilot holes in the screw positions. Screw in the screws with a screwdriver to secure the hinges to the door.

Get a helper to hold the door in the open position in the frame with the hinge flaps against the frame. Tap two screwdrivers or wooden wedges under the door to raise it to the required height to clear the flooring. Make sure the hinge knuckles are parallel with the frame, then mark the frame with a pencil. Remove the door. Chisel out the hinge recesses in the door frame in the same way as those in the door.

Wedge the door in the open position and check that the hinges fit into the recesses. Adjust them, if necessary. Drill pilot holes and screw the hinges to the frame using just one screw per hinge, then check to make sure the door closes smoothly. If it is straining against the hinges (hingebound), undo the screws and pack out the flaps with cardboard. If it rubs on the latch side of frame, make the hinge recesses slightly deeper. Screw in the remaining hinge screws.

Hold the latch in the correct position on the side of the door and, using a bradawl, mark the position of the handle spindle. Do the same on the other side of the door.

Measure and mark the middle point of the centre rail on the side of the door, using a pencil and a try square.

Centre the latch on this line. Holding it in place, draw round the latch. Use the try square to transfer the dimensions to the edge of the door.

Measure the depth of the latch then mark this measurement with a piece of tape on a wood cutting bit the same diameter as the latch (in this case 22mm). Drill a hole to the correct depth (as far as the tape) in the edge of the door, keeping the drill horizontal and in line with the door. Prise out the debris with a narrow chisel or suck it out with the nozzle of a vacuum cleaner.

Using a drill with a wood bit, drill a hole at the marked position large enough to give the handle spindle plenty of clearance. Drill from both sides into the latch hole already drilled.

Slide the latch into the hole on the edge of the door and mark the position of the rectangular edge plate with a pencil.

Score around the edge of the plate with a craft knife. Do use a knife for this – it is very easy to accidentally split the wood with a chisel.

Remove the latch and cut out a slight recess for the rectangular latch plate, using a chisel and mallet.

Door details
Door furniture isn't just about function – choose from a huge range to complement the style and materials of your interior.

Refit the latch. Fit the handle spindle and make sure that it will turn freely. Adjust the hole, if necessary. Screw the latch plate in position. Sand off the pencil marks.

To fix the handle plates to each side of door, start the screw holes with a bradawl, then screw in the screws. If the spindle is too long for the thickness of the door, secure it in a vice and saw to the correct length with a hacksaw.

Close the door so that the latch is touching the frame and mark its position on the frame with a pencil.

Hold the striker plate in position and mark the shape on the frame, including the central cut-out area. Use a narrow chisel to cut a recess for the latch and a wider one to cut around the outer shape and pare away the wood to the depth of the striker plate.

Measure and cut the doorstop for across the top of the door. With the door shut, position the strip and partially knock in some 30mm nails to hold it.

Fitting the doorstop

When the door is closed it should rest against the doorstop, fitting snugly. Allow enough clearance for coats of paint if you are planning to paint the door or frame.

Open the door and finish knocking in the nails. They should be roughly 300mm apart. Repeat the process for the strips at either side of the door.

Fitting the architrave

The architrave – the timber moulding that hides the joint between the door frame and the wall – is made from three lengths of moulding, a top and two sides, joined with mitred corners.

Hold a length of architrave beside the door frame and mark the internal height of the door frame plus 3mm. This is the position of the internal edge of the mitred corner. Cut the mitre at the marked point on the architrave, using a mitre saw or a mitre block and panel saw.

Nail the architrave in place with panel pins. Measure and fit the other two lengths of architrave in the same way.

Secure the mitred corners by nailing across them with a panel pin. To avoid hitting your fingers, hold pins with long-nosed pliers as you begin to drive them.

Tap the pin heads below the surface with a nail punch.

Fitting a new door to an existing frame

The doors in many older houses are not a standard size so you may need to trim a replacement door to fit, or even have one specially made. You should not cut more than 10mm off each side edge of a flush door, or 5mm off a panel door, or you will weaken the structure. Be aware that the old door frame may not be straight. Buy new hinges the same size as the existing ones or reuse the old hinges if they are in good condition.

Remove the old door. If it was a good fit, use it as a guide to measure and mark the new door; otherwise, hold the new door against the frame and mark where it needs to be trimmed. Shorten it, if necessary, before adjusting the width. Cut from both top and bottom if a large amount has to be removed so that you retain the symmetry of the panels. When the door is the correct height, position the hinge side in the door frame and insert two wedges or screwdrivers underneath to keep it in place.

It is much easier if two people mark the door width, one each side of the door. Run a pencil down the door against the frame on the lock side to mark the trimming line. Remove the excess equally from each side using a plane. Smooth the sharp edges with abrasive paper. Test-fit the door in the frame and trim again if necessary.

Measure the hinge positions on the door frame and transfer them to the new door. Hold each hinge in position and mark with a sharp pencil. Cut out the hinge recesses and fit the hinges to the door following Steps 2–5 on pages 124–25.

Use the existing striker plate if it will work with the new latch (otherwise fit a new one). Close the door and mark on it the latch position with a pencil. Fit a latch following Steps 1–12 on pages 125–26. Remove and reposition the doorstops if necessary.

If an old door has been painted and repainted many times, or if its paintwork is blistered or flaking, adding another layer will only exacerbate the problem. But stripping off the old paint can make a shabby door look like new. You could then repaint it or, if the wood is good quality, bring out its natural warmth by varnishing, or staining and varnishing.

Stripping with chemical stripper

Read the instructions, and take all the precautions recommended for the product you are using. If you can, take the door off its hinges and work in a garage or workshop, especially if you have small children or pets.

1 Apply paint stripper using an old paintbrush; remember to wear protective gloves and goggles. Stipple it into the mouldings and corners and brush liberally over the flat areas. Leave for the recommended length of time. The chemical will begin to react with the paint, and the surface will rupture and bubble.

2 Use a flat-bladed scraper to try scraping back the paint on a test patch. If the paint is several layers thick you may need to stipple in some more paint stripper and leave it a little longer. Once the stripper has done its job you can scrape back the paint to reveal bare wood.

3 Use a shave hook to scrape paint from mouldings. Draw the hook back towards you, removing paint from the crevices. Continue until all the paint has been removed.

4 Neutralise the surface using either white spirit or water (depending on the product – check the instructions on the tin). Work it into the surface with a cloth or brush to remove all traces of the stripping solution before sanding and finishing.

1 Strip paint from the flat areas first. Wearing protective gloves and goggles, direct the heat over a small area of paint, moving the gun slowly back and forth. Use a flat-bladed scraper to lift the paint as it softens.

Stripping with a hot-air gun

Hot-air guns usually come with a selection of nozzle attachments. Use the one that spreads the heat over a wide area, or use the gun with no attachment fitted. A conical nozzle is more likely to scorch the wood and should only be used when you are working next to an area that you don't want to damage.

2 Use a shave hook to strip paint from the mouldings. Keep the hot-air gun moving, or you will scorch the wood. Pull the shave hook towards you, working methodically on each section in turn.

Sanding and filling

A newly stripped door will usually reveal imperfections. Previously hidden cracks in the wood and blemishes may become apparent. Use wood filler to hide them. If you intend to stain or varnish the door, choose a filler to match the colour of the finished effect, since wood filler does not absorb stain or varnish in the same way as natural wood.

1 Wearing a dust mask, sand the flat panels with a medium-grade abrasive paper. Wrap the paper around a piece of wood or use a sanding block and work in the direction of the grain. Take care not to round off any sharp corners on mouldings. Or you could use a small hand-held electric sander (see page 41), but again take great care not to damage the mouldings. Go over the area a second time using a fine-grade abrasive paper.

2 Fold the abrasive paper into a suitable shape and work on the mouldings. You could wrap the paper around a piece of dowel. Take care when working on corners and edges not to damage the mouldings. Fine-grade wire wool can be used instead of abrasive paper (except on natural oak, which it will mark).

3 To sand into corners and crevices in mouldings, fold the abrasive paper and use the fold edge to reach into the joint.

Staining and varnishing

Wood stains and varnishes are available in a wide range of colours, though bear in mind that the final colour may differ from that shown on the tin, since it will look different on different woods. Wood stain can be mixed or diluted to achieve a particular shade. Test it on a piece of timber similar to the door before you begin.

1 Brush down the door and use a tack cloth to remove all traces of dust. Apply the stain with a paintbrush. Start with the panels, staining the mouldings first, then work around one half of the door and then the other. Follow the grain and pick up wet edges before they dry. Work quickly and apply the stain evenly, without overlap. While still damp, rub the door with a lint-free cloth to even out the stain and take off any excess.

2 Use a good quality clean brush to apply the varnish, and be sure to read the application instructions on the tin. Dip the brush to one third of the bristle length and touch the excess off on the inside of the container. Allow the first coat to dry thoroughly then go over the surface lightly with a fine-grade abrasive paper. Wipe the door using a tack cloth. Apply a second coat and, for a really tough finish, a third.

ideal tool

Tack cloths

These specially impregnated cloths are sticky to the touch – perfect for removing fine dust prior to painting or varnishing. They are cheap, reusable and endlessly useful.

As glass-making developed over the centuries, windows progressed from open slits in walls to the great variety of styles available today. Windows can have a dramatic effect on the appearance of a house, both from the outside and the inside. Choices range from old-fashioned windows in stained wooden frames to large single panes of glass that allow lots of natural light to flood indoors, with countless variations in between.

Choosing windows

The part of the window that opens is called the sash, and it consists of a fitted frame that either slides vertically or is hinged from one edge. Vertically sliding windows are usually known as sash windows, while hinged windows are called casements, and, although there are lots of styles to choose from, most windows are variations of these two main types.

When fitting new windows (see pages 184–85) be sure to choose ones that suit the style of your house and the neighbourhood.

Casement window

- Lintel
- Head
- Drip rail
- Handle
- Transom
- Jamb
- Mullion
- Jamb
- Window stay
- Sill
- Sill

Casement windows

Casements are the most common windows. They are often a mixture of fixed panes of glass and opening casements, which may be hinged either at the side or the top. Side-hinged casements are usually larger than the top-hinged ones. Wooden casement window frames have a vertical piece, called a jamb, at each side of the frame; there is a piece called a head at the top and a sill at the bottom, all joined by mortise-and-tenon joints. The frame may be divided vertically by a piece called a mullion or horizontally by a transom. The glazed areas of some windows are divided into smaller panes by moulded strips of wood called glazing bars.

Larger windows are conventionally fastened with a handle and mortise plate at roughly the mid-point and a window stay and locking peg at the bottom of the window; top-hinged windows may have just a window stay and locking peg.

Modern window frames are sometimes fitted with ventilators to give a constant supply of fresh air without having to open the window.

Pivot windows

Pivot windows are made like casement windows but they have a hinge mechanism on each side so the sash can pivot at its mid-point, allowing both sides of the glass to be cleaned from inside the house. Special weatherproof pivot windows, double-glazed and with ventilation in the frame, are made for installation in pitched roofs. These are often used in loft conversions.

Tilt-and-turn windows, which are usually made to measure, open inwards at the top or may open at the side.

Bay windows

A bay window is built into the external wall of the house, so the room extends into the bay. The window frames are built to fit the shape of the wall, and the sides of each frame may be set at an angle of 90° or less to the flat front of the house. They can be fitted with casement or sash windows. To make a curved bay, frames of equal size are set at a slight angle to each other.

Louvre windows

This type of window is usually found in a kitchen or bathroom. Horizontal strips of glass are attached to a frame with metal clips, and these enable the strips to pivot simultaneously to control the flow of air. With some windows the strips can be lifted out of the clips, which poses a security problem, but locking ones are available. Louvre windows are often fitted above or beside a fixed pane of glass.

Sash window

Inner lining
Outer lining
Parting bead
Inner staff bead
Pulley
Outer (upper) sash
Parting bead
Balance weight
Jamb
Sash cord
Meeting rail
Pulley stile
Inner staff bead
Inner (lower) sash
Pocket
Balance weight
Sill
Window sill

Sash windows

Traditional sash windows slide up and down, whereas some modern ones, especially those with metal frames, slide from side to side.

Traditional sash windows are operated by sash cords attached to cast-iron or lead weights. The cords and weights are concealed in a box-like compartment inside the vertical jambs at each side of the frame. These compartments consist of inner and outer linings and a pulley stile. The cords move over pulleys set in the pulley stiles. Access to the weights is through panels of wood, known as pockets, in the lower part of the stiles.

When both the top and the bottom sashes open, the window is known as a double-hung sash window. The sashes are held in runners formed by the outer lining of the jambs, parting beads – which keep the sashes apart – and inner staff beads. The beads can be removed if you need to carry out work on the sash mechanism. The upper sash moves up and down in the outer runner, and the lower sash in the inner runner. They overlap at horizontal meeting rails, and they are secured by fasteners which are screwed to the two meeting rails.

Modern sash windows have spring-action spiral balances which are not boxed in. Instead they are set into the frame and move up and down in grooves cut in the side of the sashes.

Bow windows

The frames for bow windows are ready-made from a series of casements set at an angle, so they form a curve. They may be fitted into a flat wall or a slightly bow-shaped one, but unlike bay windows the curve is too shallow to actually extend the size of the room.

French windows

These are really doors, hinged on the side, with the bottom of the frame level with the floor.

Window materials

Windows may be made of wood, plastic, steel or aluminium. These materials all require different amounts of maintenance.

Wood

Wooden windows look good but they do need regular maintenance. Cheaper softwood windows must be painted; hardwood and some better-quality softwood ones can be stained or painted. Modern wooden windows are often double-glazed. When buying new wooden windows, always check that they have been treated with preservative.

Steel

Steel windows have slim welded frames which make them strong and durable. Newer ones are galvanised before they are painted or given a polyester coating; in older ones, the galvanised coating can deteriorate, leaving them prone to rust.

Plastic

Plastic, or PVCu, windows are very practical and hardwearing. They do not warp, rot or rust, and aside from cleaning the glass they are virtually maintenance free.

Aluminium

Aluminium windows are often used in new houses and they are usually double-glazed. They require no maintenance unless they are fitted in a wooden frame, which will need regular painting or varnishing.

safety first

Safety glass
Glazed doors must be fitted with safety glass, which is reinforced or strengthened by a toughening process. Windows close to the ground and other vulnerable glazed areas, such as shower screens or large panes of glass, should also be fitted with safety glass.

WINDOWS PAINTING

Windows are constructed using lengths of wood with grain patterns that inevitably run in different directions. To achieve an even, professional-looking finish, free from brush marks, you need to paint them in a sequence that takes account of the grain. Think ahead when painting windows using oil-based paints, as they may take longer to dry than you expect. Or use water-based paint, which dries more quickly and releases much less odour and fumes.

Preparing to paint a window

Prepare the frame carefully before you begin to paint, stripping back old paint if necessary and filling any holes in the wood.

1 Remove catches and stays from the window frame before you begin. If you intend to fit new window furniture once the frame is repainted, fill the old fixing holes with wood filler and sand smooth.

2 Make a temporary stay to hold the window open while you are painting it (see MAKING IT EASIER).

4 Brush away dust and debris, paying particular attention to the corners.

5 If you don't have a steady hand, use a paint shield (see page 86) or cut some masking tape to fit around each pane of glass. Set the tape 2mm in from the frame so that paint will just overlap on to the glass.

ideal tool

Cutting-in brush
This has specially angled bristles that make it much easier to paint the rebates around a window pane and get a clean line along the glass.

3 Prepare the surface by lightly sanding over the old paintwork using medium-grade abrasive paper.

project essentials

- **screwdriver**
- **hammer**
- **soft brush**
- **paint shield or masking tape**
- **25mm paintbrush or paint pad**
- **cutting-in paintbrush**

- wood filler
- medium-grade abrasive paper
- stiff wire
- small nails
- combined primer/undercoat
- top coat paint

B&Q Making it easier

Temporary wire stay
It is tricky to paint a window once you have removed the stay, the metal bar that holds it open. Make a temporary window stay using stiff wire; an old coat hanger will do the job. Cut to length and bend the ends into a small loop just large enough to drive a nail through. Fix one end to the sill and the other end to the frame, using small nails.

Painting a casement window

You'll need an undercoat and a top coat for a hardwearing finish. Overlap the paint onto the glass by about 2mm to seal out water. For best results, you should paint in the sequence shown right. First paint the transoms (1), using a cutting-in brush against the glass. Next, paint the top and bottom cross rails (2) followed by the vertical mullions and jambs (3). Paint the edges (4) and then the frame (5) and lastly the sill (6). If the window must be closed before the paint is quite dry, rub a little talcum powder along the frame to prevent it sticking.

Temporary wire stay

Use a combined primer/undercoat and paint the frame in the painting sequence shown above. It will make the job easier if you use a cutting-in brush for the glazing bars.

When the first coat is dry, apply the top coat in the same sequence. Keep checking there are no runs, particularly at edges and corners.

Painting a sash window

Start by painting the bottom meeting rail of the upper sash (1). To expose it, raise the bottom sash and lower the upper one. Also paint the vertical bars (2) of the upper sash as far as you can. When it is touch-dry, raise the upper sash again, and lower the bottom, leaving a small opening top and bottom. Finish painting the upper sash (3,4). Now paint the bottom sash (5,6,7), including the underside of the cross rail (7), followed by the frame (8) and window sill (9). Wait until the paint is dry before you start painting the runners (10). Apply a thin coat to the inner runners and the upper section of the outer runners. Try not to get paint on the cords; pull them out of the way as you paint. Carefully check the sashes are running before the paint has dried.

Upper sash

Paint the sill last. Remove the masking tape when the paint is just touch dry. Once it is completely dry, remove the temporary wire stays.

ideal tool

Paint pad

You could use a paint pad instead of a brush. Its small square foam pad is designed to fit easily around mouldings and into corners. Pour some paint into a shallow bowl and dip the pad into the paint. It will produce a smooth painted surface with no visible brush strokes.

B&Q Making it easier

Painting windows

If you are not confident that you can keep a straight line, use a paint shield (see page 86) or masking tape to protect the glass. Set tape back 2mm from the edge of the glass and remove it before the paint is dry, or the paint may lift off at the same time. Or you can use a masking pen, which leaves a layer of wax on the glass. This can be removed (along with any drips of paint) with a window scraper once the paint is dry.

project essentials

- wood chisel
- wooden mallet
- table or workbench
- craft knife
- pincers
- old screwdriver or chisel
- plane or sander

- string
- new sash cord
- 50mm nail or screw
- 25mm or 32mm galvanised clout nails
- parting beads, if old ones are damaged
- 25mm oval nails
- wood filler

The most common repairs to sash windows are replacing broken sash cords and repairing damaged or loose beads. When a cord breaks you have to take the sash right out of the frame to replace it, so it's a good idea to replace both at the same time. You can be sure that if one breaks, the other will soon go too.

Sash cord

Sash cord is made from various materials, including waxed and unwaxed hemp and synthetic fibres, and is available in different diameters. Make sure your new cord is the same diameter as the old one – take a piece to the shop, if necessary. Most sash cord is sold in a pack containing enough for all types of window. Alternatively, measure from the top of the window to the sill and add about two-thirds as much again for each length of cord. Each sash – upper and lower – requires two lengths of cord. Don't cut it to length in advance.

Gaining access to the broken cord

If you remove both the sashes, label the weights so that you know which ones are from the upper (outer) sash and which from the lower (inner) one. Although they look the same, they may be slightly different and if you put them back the wrong way round, it could affect the smooth running of the sashes.

Pulley

Sash cord

Upper sash

Parting bead

Staff bead

Lower sash

To replace a lower sash cord, you must take out the lower sash window; to replace an upper sash cord, you will need to take out both the lower and then the upper sash.

2 Prise off the left- and right-hand staff beads from the inside of the frame. Start in the centre of each bead to avoid damaging the corners and tap a chisel into the joint using a mallet.

3 Once a staff bead has lifted in the middle, the rest of it should pull away from the frame and spring out from the mitred corners.

4 If either cord was unbroken, tie some string around it near the pulley; this will be used to pull the new cord into place. Cut through the old cord below the string and gently lower the weight to the bottom of its compartment, running the string over the pulley. Lift out the lower sash and support it on a table or workbench. Remove the piece of cord from each side of the sash, pulling out any securing nails with pincers.

5 Prise the narrow parting beads out of their grooves. They should be wedged in place, but may be nailed or screwed. Lift the upper sash into the room if you are replacing all the cords (otherwise it can stay in place). Cut and remove the cords in the same way as for the lower sash.

6 Use a chisel to prise off the pocket cover from each side of the frame. The covers should be just pushed in place but some may have been secured with screws or nails that you will need to take out.

7 Lift out the weights in the pockets and remove the old cords. If you have attached string to a cord, leave it in place over the pulley with one end in the pocket.

Replacing the cords

If you have removed both sashes, replace the cords on the upper sash first and fit it back in the frame, then do the same for the lower sash.

Where the cord was broken, tie a 50mm nail or screw to a piece of string and push it into the hole above the pulley. Feed the string through the hole so that it drops down into the weight compartment and you can retrieve it from the pocket.

Tie lengths of new cord – each at least one and a half times the depth of the window frame – to the ends of the strings hanging from the pulleys. Pull each cord over the pulley, down into the weight compartment and out through the pocket.

Remove the string from each cord, thread the cord through the hole in the top of the weight and tie it with a stop knot (see MAKING IT EASIER). Tuck the end into the cavity at the top of the weight. Put the weights back in the pockets and replace the pocket covers.

Reassembling the window

Before you can replace the lower sash in the frame, you will need to refit the parting beads – unless you have taken out the upper sash, in which case put that back in first.

Tap the parting beads back into their slots with a mallet. If necessary, use an old screwdriver or chisel to clean out any debris first. If the parting beads were nailed rather than pushed in, they are likely to have split when you removed them and you will need to replace them. Measure the window and cut new parting beads to the correct length. Plane or sand them if they are too thick, then tap them into place.

Rest the lower sash on the sill and get a helper to pull the cords and raise the weights to their highest position. Tie a knot in each cord level with the knot holes in the sides of the sash, then cut off the surplus cord. If the knot holes are damaged, as here, you will need to secure the cord with 3 or 4 galvanised clout nails. Then replace the sash in the frame.

Refit the staff beads on each side of the frame: tap them into place with the mallet, then nail with 25mm oval nails, but don't drive the nails all the way in. Check first that the sashes move up and down without sticking, and adjust the beads in or out accordingly.

When you are satisfied with the operation of the window, drive the nails fully home. Use wood filler to repair any damage before touching up or repainting the whole window (see page 133).

safety first

Before drilling into a wall always check for pipes and cables with an electronic detector. Never drill directly above or below a light fitting or power socket.

Curtains and blinds block out light and drafts and create privacy, but they can also be a distinctive design feature, introducing colour, pattern and texture into any room in the home. Curtain tracks and poles, too, come in many different designs to suit every style of interior. Ready-made curtains should be selected before buying a track or pole since many curtains are designed to be hung from a particular type of fitting.

Fitting a roller blind

Roller blinds come in a vast array of colours, designs and sizes. Decide if you want the blind to fit inside or across the top of the window recess and measure up before you go shopping. For a blind inside the recess (as shown here), remember that you will need a little clearance space either side for it to operate smoothly. Many blinds can be cut to fit a particular width of recess, as shown here, but do check that the manufacturer recommends this.

project essentials

- tape measure
- spirit level
- fine-tooth hacksaw
- straightedge
- pencil
- ruler
- scissors
- pipe and cable detector
- bradawl
- power drill with twist bits
- screwdriver

- roller blind and fixings

1 Measure the width of the recess, leaving sufficient clearance either side for the smooth operation of the blind (check the manufacturer's instructions on how much is required). Check for hidden pipes and cables then mark the positions for the brackets in the upper corners, using a spirit level to make sure they are level.

2 Unroll the blind and mark the width on the cardboard roller tube. Cut through the tube with a hacksaw, using an off-cut of wood to protect the surface below if necessary.

3 Measure and mark the width on the reverse of the blind with a pencil. Use a straightedge to draw a faint cutting line along the length of the blind. Carefully cut along the ruled line with a pair of sharp scissors.

4 Fit the side control into one end of the blind and the dummy pin into the other. Push home by pressing against a hard surface or tapping gently with a hammer.

ONE PLANET HOME

Stay cosy
Look out for the latest blinds with a special thermal coating that will help to insulate your home, keeping the heat in and your bills down.

5 Position the control bracket on the side from which you want to operate the blind. Use a bradawl to make starting holes, then drill into the window frame. Fix the brackets with the screws supplied. If fitting to a PVCu window frame you will need to use self-tapping screws.

6 Slot the blind into the two brackets and test it works freely.

safety first

Looped blind cords are a potential hazard to babies and small children. Fit a safety device to hold the cord taut or out of reach. Avoid placing a cot, bed, playpen or high chair within reach of a cord, or positioning any furniture near a window that a child could climb to reach a cord.

Putting up a curtain track

To let in plenty of light, curtains should draw back clear of the glass. To achieve that you will probably need to fit the track to the wall above the window recess, although it can also be fitted within the recess. Use flexible curtain track to hang curtains over a bay window. The screws supplied with your curtain track may not be long enough to achieve a secure fixing, particularly if your plaster is old and and slightly crumbly. In that case use longer screws and wallplugs, or screw into sound ceiling timber.

1. Measure the length of track needed to accommodate your curtains. If the window is wide and the curtains thick then the track will need to extend further than if the material is lightweight. Cut to length using a fine-tooth hacksaw. Mark the fixing position for the first bracket 25mm out from the vertical edge of the recess and 50mm up. Repeat at the other end, then mark the remaining bracket positions at equal intervals, measuring 50mm up from the top of the window recess each time. Use a long spirit level to check the marks are level.

2. Check there are no hidden pipes or cables, then drill the fixing holes and insert wallplugs of the correct size for your screws. Screw the brackets into position. The bracket latches that the track fits into should face forward.

3. To fit the end stops, slip one over each end of the track and tighten the retaining screws.

4. Place the track into the slot in one of the end brackets. Push into the bracket latch until you hear a click. Clip the track into each bracket in the same way.

Putting up a curtain pole

Curtain poles are available in metal, wood or plastic, and can make your curtain fittings more of a decorative feature than standard curtain track. The curtains hang from metal eyelets, rings or loops of fabric. The length of some curtain poles is adjustable; others you can cut to fit using a fine-tooth hacksaw. You may need to use longer screws than those supplied with the pole if you intend to hang very heavy curtains or your plaster is not completely sound.

1. The end brackets for a curtain pole should be at least 50mm from either end of the recess. Mark the positions for the two end brackets as in Step 1 above. Check they are level with a long spirit level.

2. Check there are no hidden pipes or cables then drill at the marked positions with a masonry bit. Insert wallplugs and screw the brackets into place.

3. Assemble the pole, cutting or adjusting the length as necessary, then slide it through the brackets. Leave one curtain ring on the outside of each bracket, with the remaining rings between them.

B&Q Making it easier

Matching holdbacks
Curtain holdbacks in a matching style will add an extra touch of sophistication to your room. Fix them after hanging your curtains to be sure of getting them in just the right position.

FIREPLACES AND FIRES

A fireplace with a glowing fire can be a real centrepiece to a room. Open fires can be a lot of work to maintain and some urban areas have restrictions on burning wood and coal. But there are many alternatives, including a huge range of cosy and stylish flame-effect gas and electric fires that will work with your existing fireplace and decor.

Wood-effect gas fire

Gas fires

Burning gas produces fumes which need a safe outlet. If your fireplace has a chimney, then a gas fire can easily be installed. If not, you must choose a flueless model with a catalytic converter to clean waste gases, or a balanced flue model, which expels gases via an outside wall. Either way, a Gas Safe registered gas fitter must do the installation. Before selecting a model to be set in an existing fireplace, make sure you measure the dimensions carefully.

Coal-effect gas fire

Wall-mounted gas fire

Electric fires

Because electric fires don't produce waste gases, they don't need a chimney or flue, making them very versatile. They can be wall-mounted, freestanding or fitted into an existing fireplace. Choose between radiant, convector or fan heaters.

Wall-mounted electric fire

Coal-effect electric fire

Stove-style electric fire

Wise choices

When choosing a new gas fire, check its energy efficiency. A firebox lined with ceramic panels can reduce heat loss by radiating more heat into the room. With up to 90% energy efficiency, some of the latest gas fires can significantly reduce your energy bills.

Sustainably sourced wood is an environmentally friendly choice for a solid-fuel stove. This is because wood is considered a carbon-neutral fuel, since the CO_2 released by burning it is equal to the CO_2 absorbed by the tree as it grew.

Solid-fuel stoves

Controlled-draught slow-burning fires and enclosed stoves are easy to clean, they burn all day without attention, and if you add a back boiler they can be used to heat water and for central heating. They do require a chimney, but are much more efficient than an open fire, which loses much of its heat straight up the chimney. Sustainably sourced firewood is a carbon-neutral fuel: see left. Don't forget that you will need to store logs in a dry, well-ventilated place.

Fire surrounds

A fire surround frames a fire and makes it an attractive focal point. Choose from wood, stone, marble or cast metal finishes, in a huge range of traditional and contemporary styles. For practical and safety reasons, you must set a fire on a heatproof hearth to protect the floor and against a back panel that will protect the chimney. These too are available in many finishes, so you can mix and match freely to create the perfect fireplace for your room.

If you have an unused fireplace, you can make it a decorative feature instead of sealing it up. To keep out debris and draughts, close off the flue with a piece of hardboard nailed to wooden battens screwed into the sides of the chimney opening, just out of sight. Cut some ventilation holes in the board to prevent damp. Then fit a fire surround and place a vase or ornament in the recess.

Mantel

Surround

Back panel

Hearth

FIREPLACES AND FIRES

Coal and wood fires produce a mixture of gas and solid waste products which are carried up the chimney. Some of these deposits settle in the chimney as soot. Too much soot will narrow the chimney and reduce the flow. If the build-up becomes too great, most likely at a bend in the chimney, a severe blockage may occur. This could cause a chimney fire or divert poisonous gases back into the room. Chimneys over an open fire should be swept annually and it is a good idea to sweep old chimneys and install a flue liner.

The working fireplace

To work efficiently, a fireplace needs a supply of oxygen and a means of removing smoke and fumes. Most fires have a barred grate where ash can fall through into a removable tray. The burning fuel produces gases which are lighter than air and so they rise up the chimney. This creates a draw, pulling fresh oxygen into the grate to feed the fire.

Occasionally a fire will smoke. This may be because the chimney needs cleaning; any partial blockage can prevent smoke being drawn up the flue. Double-glazing or draught-proofing can also prevent a fire from burning properly, as a constant supply of fresh oxygen is essential. Provide ventilation by inserting an airbrick into an outside wall or by fitting a window vent.

If the chimney is old and much used, it may have become damaged inside. The easiest way to prevent damp patches on walls or smoke seeping into the room is to put in a flexible flue liner. A flue liner may also be needed if you are installing a new gas fire into the fireplace. You will need a liner to suit the type of appliance you are fitting, so do consult a professional installer.

Mantelpiece · Flue · Lintel · Fire surround · Hardcore · Fireback · Hearth

Lintel · Airbrick

Removing a fireplace

Removing a fireplace from a room is a messy job that creates lots of dirt and dust. First you must remove the fire surround, hearth and adjacent skirting, then level the surrounding floor. If you suspect that you might want to use the chimney again in future, you can simply panel over the opening with a piece of plasterboard cut to the appropriate size and nailed to a wooden frame set within the fire opening. If you don't want to use the chimney again, you can brick it up then plaster over the top.

Whichever method you choose for enclosing your fireplace, it is crucial that you fit a ventilator in the opening, so that there is still a flow of air through the chimney. Otherwise, condensation could form in the chimney, which would eventually seep through and stain the wall. In the case of plasterboard, cut an opening just above skirting level and fit a ventilator into it. If you are bricking up the fireplace, fit an airbrick in the lowest course of bricks above the skirting.

Sweeping a chimney

Sweeping a chimney does not have to be excessively messy if you prepare the area carefully. Wear safety goggles and a dust mask to protect your eyes and lungs.

project essentials

- **dust sheets**
- **chimney sweeping brush and canes**
- **shovel**
- **safety goggles**
- **dust mask**

- plastic refuse sack

1 Roll back any carpet, remove nearby objects and cover everything in the vicinity with a dust sheet. Drape another dust sheet over the fire surround and use heavy objects to weight it down on the mantelpiece. Put a heavy object like a brick on each side of the opening against the fire surround to seal the chimney space. Screw the brush head to the first cane.

2 Lift the sheet and push the brush inside the flue above the fireplace.

3 Screw on another cane and push the brush up the flue. Continue adding canes and pushing the brush upwards. If the brush gets stuck, pull back a little and push up again, working to and fro. Don't use a screwing action or the canes might unscrew at a joint. You will be able to feel when the brush comes out at the top. If there is a cowl on the chimneypot, be careful not to push it off.

4 Pull the brush back down, unscrewing the canes as you go. Shovel the soot and debris from the grate and into a plastic refuse sack.

Repairing a cracked fireback

The extreme heat generated by a fire can easily damage a fireback over time. Fine cracks can be repaired quite simply, following the steps below. If the damage is severe, however, it may be better to replace the fireback.

1 Let the fireback cool for 48 hours. Spread a dust sheet around the fireplace and use a wire brush to clean away soot deposits and expose the damaged areas. Use the point of a trowel to clean out the cracks.

2 Brush dust out of the cracks with a wire brush and then brush water over the area using a paintbrush. This will help the fire cement to bond.

3 Use a small trowel to work fire cement into the cracks.

project essentials

- **dust sheet**
- **wire brush**
- **small trowel**
- **paintbrush**

- fire cement

4 Trowel away any surplus fire cement then brush the surface with a wet paintbrush to get a smooth finish. Leave the cement to harden for a few days, or light a small fire to warm the area and dry it more quickly (follow the instructions on the cement tin).

ideal tool

Wet and dry vacuum
Sweeping or repairing a chimney creates a lot of dust and mess. A wet and dry vacuum cleaner will be very useful for cleaning up afterwards.

STORAGE THROUGHOUT THE HOME

Nowadays there are ingenious, attractive and space-saving storage solutions for every room in the home. When everything has its place, it's much easier to stay tidy – and a tidy home is a calmer and more relaxing place to be.

Making use of every space

Are you making the most of your home's potential storage space? Look around and think afresh. It may be easier than you imagine to bring an end to the constant battle with household clutter.

Kitchen

Clutter in a kitchen is not just irritating, it can be dangerous, so this is a good room to start. Space-saving storage is vital in a small kitchen, and it will also make working in a larger kitchen more convenient. Fitted units and racks and pull-out cabinets give lots of storage space without taking up too much floor area.

Living room

Whether you want to store books, magazines, CDs and DVDs, or mount your flatscreen TV on the wall, you can choose from a wide variety of shelves, units and fixings.

Bathroom

Fitted or freestanding cabinets are a practical way of storing toiletries and allow you to keep harmful items out of reach of children. Open shelves and shower caddies are handy for bath and shower products. A towel radiator will keep your towels tidy as well as warm and dry.

Bedroom

Wardrobes with a mixture of rails, shelves and drawers will provide the maximum amount of storage space for all kinds of clothes. Items not in everyday use can be stored in wheeled boxes designed to fit under the bed.

Loft

The loft is a handy place to store things that are not in regular use. Plastic storage boxes will minimise the weight on the joists. To create a boarded storage area in your loft, see page 338.

Under stairs

The sloping space under the staircase is the ideal place to fit shelving for books and other bits and pieces. If the area is large enough, it can be turned into a compact office with a desk, shelves and filing cabinet.

Play space

A range of storage units and toyboxes will accommodate toys, books and games of all shapes and sizes.

Garage

Even if a car takes most of the garage space you can still mount ladder hooks and shelves on the walls, and may have space for a storage unit with drawers, or for stacking plastic trays.

Shed and garden

A garden shed is handy for storing the lawn mower, barbecue and garden furniture. Hang garden tools on hooks fixed to the wall. A bicycle lock-up in the garden will keep the family's bicycles secure and dry when not in use.

Bedroom storage: boxes for under beds

Shed storage: hooks for garden tools

Storage units and plastic boxes for children's toys

Shed for garden tools and furniture

Kitchen

Living room

Bathroom

Loft

Under stairs

Garage storage: ladder hooks

Freestanding metal shelving

Adjustable wall shelving

Lockable storage unit

Stacking plastic trays

Plastic storage boxes in loft

Home office shelves and boxes

Wall-to-wall sliding-door wardrobes with built-in shelves

Shelves for books, magazines, CDs and DVDs

Bathroom cabinets and drawers

Kitchen units

Wine rack

Pull-out larder

Under stairs shelving

Shoe cupboard

Bicycle lock-up

Garage with ladder hooks, shelves, lockable units and plastic trays

You can choose from a vast range of shelving and brackets, adjustable shelf systems, or flatpack sets of shelves with pre-drilled holes for easy assembling.

Shelving materials

Shelves can be made from a variety of materials, ranging from cheap chipboard to top quality hardwoods like oak and beech.

Chipboard

Consists of small pieces of wood glued together. Easy to cut and fix to brackets. Available with a wipe-clean melamine coating, or a wood veneer that needs to be sealed with varnish or wax. The cheapest material for shelves.

MDF

Medium-density fibreboard. Made from wood fibres stuck together under pressure. Has a smooth surface and edges. Can be painted, stained or varnished.

Blockboard

Cheaper than solid wood but very strong. Made from strips of softwood running parallel between two outer layers of veneer. Cut edges can be covered with veneer or wooden lipping.

Plywood

Thin wooden sheets glued together with the direction of the grain alternating at right angles in each layer. Edges can be left uncovered or covered as for blockboard.

Solid wood

The most traditional shelving material. Needs to be sealed with wax or varnish to protect from dirt.

Acrylic sheet or perspex

Sheets of minimum 12mm thickness can be used for shelves displaying light- to medium-weight objects. Cut edges can be smoothed with a fine file and abrasive paper.

Glass

Must be toughened and a minimum of 6mm thick. Glass is heavy, so shelves require medium- or heavyweight brackets.

Brackets

Brackets must be chosen and spaced according to the shelf material, its thickness and the load the shelf will be supporting. They may be fixed or be part of an adjustable shelf system. Both types are available in light-, medium- or heavyweight versions. It is vital that your shelves and brackets can support the weight they will have to bear. Use this table as a guide, but always read the shelving manufacturer's instructions as well.

Fixed brackets

The simplest shelf supports are non-adjustable fixed brackets, which are ideal for a single shelf. Fixed brackets may be made from aluminium, pressed steel, pressed and welded steel with an epoxy-coated finish, pressed steel with a snap-on coloured plastic cover, wrought iron or solid brass.

Repositioning fixed brackets ▶

If shelves with fixed brackets are sagging, you can fix this by moving the brackets further in so that the load at each end balances the central load. Unscrew the shelf from the bracket, take the brackets off the wall and reposition them following the steps opposite. Fill and sand the old holes and touch up with paint.

Adjustable shelving brackets

Adjustable shelving systems have tracks that are attached to the wall. Removable flanged brackets slot into these tracks to support the shelves. Cheaper, lightweight systems are often aluminium; medium- and heavyweight systems are made of steel or wood.

SPACING BRACKETS

Material	Thickness	Space between brackets (load)
Chipboard (coated)	16mm	610mm (medium)
	18mm	510mm (heavy); 700mm (medium)
Chipboard (veneered)	32mm	915mm (heavy)
MDF	18mm	510mm (heavy); 700mm (medium)
	25mm	700mm (heavy); 915mm (medium)
Blockboard	18mm	700mm (heavy); 750mm (medium); 800mm (light)
Plywood	18mm	700mm (heavy); 915mm (medium)
	25mm	915mm (heavy)
Softwood	16mm	400mm (heavy); 610mm (medium)
	18mm	510mm (heavy); 700mm (medium)
	25mm	700mm (heavy); 915mm (medium)
	32mm	915mm (heavy)
Hardwood	18mm	510mm (heavy); 700mm (medium)
	22mm	700mm (heavy); 915mm (medium)
	25mm	915mm (heavy)
Acrylic sheet	12mm	400mm (light–medium)
Toughened glass	6mm	400mm (light)

Getting a strong fixing

On masonry walls, you will need a hammer action drill with a masonry bit and at least 50mm screws and wallplugs, to go through the plaster and into the wall behind. For stud partition walls, the screws need to go directly into the timber noggings or studs (find them by tapping and listening, or by using an electronic stud detector). Use 38mm screws, or 50mm screws for heavy loads (there is no need for a wallplug). The screws should be the heaviest gauge that the holes in the bracket will take – generally 4mm gauge on small ones and 5mm or 5.5mm on larger ones.

Putting up a fixed shelf

Brackets are fitted with the longer arm against the wall and the shorter one under the shelf, so the length of the longer arm will determine how closely shelves can be fitted one above the other.

1 Check that the area is free from hidden pipes or cables (see SAFETY FIRST). Hold the shelf against the wall and mark where you want the bottom to go. Then mark where the first bracket should be, as well as the distance to the next bracket (see opposite). Check the marks are level with a spirit level.

2 Hold the first bracket up to the mark, checking it is vertical, and mark the wall through the fixing holes. Repeat with the second. If there are more than two brackets, fit them between the outer brackets, equal distances apart.

3 Drill into the wall, insert wallplugs if you have a masonry wall, and screw the brackets in place. Lay the shelf across, and make a mark through the holes in the brackets for the fixing screws underneath it. Take the shelf down and drill pilot holes for the short screws, but be sure not to go right through the shelf. Replace the shelf and screw home the fixing screws.

project essentials

- **pipe and cable detector**
- **pencil**
- **straightedge**
- **spirit level**
- **safety goggles**
- **power drill with masonry or twist bits**
- **screwdriver**

- shelf
- brackets
- 50mm or 38mm screws and wallplugs (4mm, 5mm or 5.5mm gauge)
- small screws for fixing the shelf to the brackets

Hidden fixture shelving

This is a storage system with no visible means of support. It comes as a kit with a ready-prepared shelf, available in different lengths. The shelf is supported by a metal strip you fix to the wall, from which project two or more bars that support the pre-drilled shelf. Some of these systems also have pre-drilled holes for small locating screws that go through the underside of the shelf into the bar to make the shelf more secure.

These systems look great, but they do have drawbacks: if your wall is not perfectly flat, the metal strip will not fit against it properly; the shelf itself looks overly thick, since it has to accommodate the bars; and it is really only strong enough for light objects.

project essentials

- **tape measure**
- **pencil**
- **spirit level**
- **power drill with masonry or twist bit**
- **screwdriver**

- hidden fixture shelf kit
- 50mm or 38mm screws and wallplugs (4mm, 5mm or 5.5mm gauge)
- small screws for fixing the shelf to the bars

1 Check there are no hidden pipes or cables (see SAFETY FIRST). Hold the metal strip on the wall, level it with a spirit level, and mark the fixing hole positions. Drill the holes, insert wall plugs and screw the strip in place.

2 Slide the shelf on to the bars. If your kit has pre-drilled holes in the underside of the shelf, fit small screws through them into the holes in the bar.

B&Q Making it easier

Shelves in alcoves
One of the most popular places for shelves is in an alcove, and here you need fixings on the side walls. Cut 50mm x 25mm wooden battens the width of the shelf and screw them horizontally to the side walls of the alcoves. If the shelf is long, a batten can be fixed to the back wall as well. For extra security, the shelf can be screwed to the battens by means of a metal plate positioned between batten and shelf.

If you need a stack of shelves, you can choose fixed shelves or an adjustable track system. Fixed shelving is usually cheaper, but a track system lets you adjust the height of the shelves.

Fitting a stack of fixed shelves

Stacks of fixed shelves are supported by brackets attached to wooden battens fixed vertically to the wall. If you want the backs of the shelves to touch the wall, the shelves must be cut to fit around each batten. The shelving material will determine the number of battens you need (see the table on page 144), and the length of the battens will depend on the number of shelves and the distance between them.

project essentials

- **tape measure**
- **pencil**
- **ruler**
- **panel saw**
- **abrasive paper**
- **paint brush**
- **pipe and cable detector**
- **bradawl**
- **power drill with twist or masonry bit**
- **spirit level**
- **screwdriver**
- **straightedge**
- **wood chisel**
- **wooden mallet**

- 50mm x 25mm battens
- paint or varnish for the battens
- 50mm or 38mm screws and wallplugs (4mm, 5mm or 5.5mm gauge)
- small screws for fixing the shelf to the brackets
- brackets
- shelves

Lay the battens side by side and mark and cut them to length (measure from the top of the top bracket to the bottom of the bottom bracket, plus about 30mm to prevent splitting when the screws are fitted). Mark the position of each bracket's top fixing hole on each batten, then mark the position for the wall fixings – these should go where they will be hidden by the brackets. Drill the fixing holes. Use three fixings per batten, or four if there are more than three shelves. Sand, paint or varnish the battens. Check for hidden pipes or cables (see SAFETY FIRST, page 145) before fixing the battens to the wall.

Hold the left batten in position and mark the place for the top fixing hole with a bradawl. Drill the hole and screw the batten loosely in place. Check it is vertical with a spirit level, and mark the other fixing holes. Swing the batten to one side to drill the holes, then screw it firmly in place. Measure the distance to the right batten and mark the wall. Position the right batten, using a spirit level to check it is level with the top of the left batten, and fix it as before.

Fix a third batten, if required, exactly mid-way between them, checking that all three are exactly level. Fix the brackets to the battens, starting at the top hole.

If you want the backs of the shelves to sit flush against the wall, you will need to cut slots in them to fit around the battens. Position each shelf in turn on its brackets, and mark where the sides of each batten are.

Remove the shelf. Use an off-cut of batten to mark the piece to be cut out. Make two saw cuts into the shelf and chop out the piece with a wood chisel and mallet. Repeat for all shelves except the top one (see MAKING IT EASIER).

Drill pilot holes for the screws, taking care not to go right through the shelf. If necessary, remove the shelf to drill it. Drive home the fixing screws.

Fit the shelves in place around the battens. Mark the positions for the fixing screws through the holes in the brackets on to the underside of the shelves.

Fitting adjustable shelves

Ready-made adjustable shelving sits on brackets slotted into metal tracks screwed into a wall. The track and brackets create a small gap behind the shelves, which can be useful for running electric cable for a lamp. If you prefer the shelves flush with the wall, you must cut notches in them (see Steps 4 and 5 opposite).

project essentials

- **pipe and cable detector**
- **spirit level**
- **pencil**
- **tape measure**
- **bradawl**
- **power drill with twist or masonry bit**
- **screwdriver**

- adjustable track and bracket shelving system
- 50mm or 38mm screws and wallplugs (4mm, 5mm or 5.5mm gauge)
- small screws for fixing the shelf to the bars

Check there are no hidden pipes or cables (see SAFETY FIRST, page 145). Using a spirit level, draw a vertical line down the wall the length of the track. Position the next track (manufacturer's guidelines will specify the distance between them), and draw another vertical line. Hold the left track on the wall and mark the top fixing hole. Drill the hole and screw the track loosely in place. Holding a spirit level to the side of the track to check it is vertical, mark the other fixing holes.

Swing the track to one side, drill the holes and fit wallplugs, then screw it in place. Slot in a bracket near the top of the track, and insert another in the same position in the second track. Hold the second track at the next marked vertical line. Lay a shelf across the two brackets and use a spirit level to get it exactly horizontal. Mark the top fixing hole for the second track, remove the shelf, and fix it in place at the top fixing hole.

Remove this shelf with its brackets and refit it at the bottom of the tracks. Mark the lower fixing holes of the second track and secure it to the wall. This way the tracks will be perfectly parallel and the shelves all interchangeable. Slot the remaining brackets into the tracks and screw the shelves to them.

Position the top shelf centrally on the brackets and use a bradawl to mark the drilling points for the small securing screws through the underside of the shelf. Drill pilot holes, removing the shelf if necessary, and screw home the shelf fixings to the brackets.

STORAGE ASSEMBLING FLATPACKS

Flatpacks have been available for many years but they just keep getting better. The choice is almost endless. Whether you need a fully fitted kitchen or just an extra set of shelves, you will find a flatpack to suit you.

Convenient

Flatpacks have become so popular because they are readily available and easy to transport. Most are packed so that they will fit into a normal family car.

Versatile

Flatpacks are a convenient way of creating attractive storage space, and many ranges are so versatile that with a little imagination you can create almost any design to suit the style of your home. They are made in a wide range of wood, coloured or glass finishes.

Flexible

B&Q flatpacks allow you to choose your own accessories. When you make your purchase, check what has been included in the pack. You may need to buy handles, drawer fronts or legs separately; this is a good opportunity to add your own design touches. You can even buy conversion kits to transform a simple cabinet into a filing cabinet, or a set of drawers. You can mix and match finishes, or replace the doors or drawer fronts to match a new colour scheme.

There is no need to feel limited by the size of unit available. Measure the space you wish to fill and then work out if a combination of units will fit the area. The units are designed to fit together horizontally, vertically, or both. Once they are secured to the wall, they will be perfectly stable and look just like fitted units.

Logical

All B&Q flatpacks follow the same basic principles. The steps are logical and each part will be numbered clearly on the accompanying instructions. The most important thing is to read them carefully first, check nothing is missing before you begin, and allow plenty of uninterrupted time for assembly.

Assembling a small cabinet

This compact cabinet is a typical building block in a flexible, modular storage system. You can fit drawers, or a shelf and door to make it into a cupboard. Buy several to make a unit that is purpose-built for your storage needs. Always read the manufacturer's assembly instructions too, since individual products may differ.

project essentials

- **cross-head screwdriver**
- **small hammer**
- **trimming knife**
- **power drill with 3mm twist bit**
- **ruler**
- **pencil**
- **bradawl**

- small cabinet flatpack
- shelf pack
- door pack
- handle pack

Lay panels out on the floor so that you can easily see each part. Use the packaging to protect the panels from scratches, if necessary. Keep screws and fixings inside their packaging until you need to use them.

Push the legs into the pre-drilled holes underneath the base panel. If you are using decorative legs that have been purchased separately, refer to the fixing instructions supplied with them.

Turn the base panel over so that it is standing on the legs. Using a screwdriver, screw four cam studs into the pre-drilled holes closest to each corner.

Apply a little of the PVA wood adhesive supplied to one end of four wooden dowels and insert them into the pre-drilled holes either side of the base panel.

Tap the dowels into place with a small hammer. They should fit snugly. Take care not to damage the end of the dowels; a light tap should be sufficient.

Insert a locking cam (see below) into each of the larger holes at the bottom of the side panels. The arrows embossed on the cams must point towards the end of the panel. Use a trimming knife to remove any excess edging at both ends of the grooves running along the length of the side panels. This is where the back panel will be fitted.

Apply a little PVA wood adhesive to the protruding end of each dowel.

Fit the first side panel to the base. It should slide neatly on to the already glued dowels. Keep the panel at right angles to the base, or you risk damaging the dowels. The grooves in the base and side panels should line up.

Locking cam

Cam stud

Base panel

Insert four locking cams into the holes on the top of the side panels, with their arrows pointing towards the end of the panel. Glue four wooden dowels and fit them into the top panel. Insert four cam studs into the pre-drilled holes and run a bead of glue into the groove. The top panel can now be fitted. Tighten the locking cams and fit cam covers to all of the exposed locking cams.

Slide the second side panel into position. Tighten the two locking cams.

You are now ready to fit the back panel. Run a bead of glue along the grooves in the side and base panel you have already assembled. Slide the back panel into place.

Secure the first side panel by tightening the two locking cams. Use a screwdriver, and turn them clockwise.

Fitting a shelf

This cabinet is supplied with a shelf, but you can fit shelves into any flatpack cabinet. Buy a shelf pack to match the cabinet and all the fixings you need will be included.

ideal tool

Cordless electric screwdriver

This rechargeable screwdriver is perfect for assembling a flatpack, or any job that involves a lot of screwing. Just press it onto the screw head and it will work automatically.

Decide on the height of the shelf. Use a screwdriver to fit two shelf support screws into each side panel. Make sure all four screws are at the same height. Avoid using any of the pre-drilled holes that you will need to fit door hinges to the cabinet.

Place the four shelf support inserts into the pre-formed holes in the shelf. You may need to use a small hammer to tap them into place.

Simply slide the shelf in and clip into place by pressing down. The shelf will rest on the exposed screw heads on the side panels.

Fitting door handles

If handles have not been supplied with the unit, you will need to buy them separately. Always drill at a 90° angle to the door, and select a drill bit that allows half a millimetre clearance around the screw.

1 Decide where you want the handle. It can be in the centre of the door or towards the upper corner if that's more convenient. Mark the position on the front of the door with a pencil (you can easily rub the marks out later if they are visible after the handle is attached).

2 Place the handle on the pencil marks. Tip the handle back a little and mark the position of the fixing holes.

3 Using the recommended drill bit (normally 3mm), drill the holes ready to attach the handle.

4 Place the handle on the front of the door. Line up the holes and insert screws from the back of the door to secure it.

5 Stick one door buffer to the front edge of the base panel and another to the front edge of the top panel. Position them both 15mm–20mm in from the side panel.

ideal tool

Bradawl
Bradawls are mainly used to start holes in a piece of wood in which you want to insert screws. They help to prevent the wood splitting or the drill bit slipping.

Fitting door hinges

Hinges are usually supplied with all the necessary fixings, and doors and cabinets have cut-outs and guide holes for easy fitting.

1 Use a bradawl to make guide holes in the pre-marked positions on the cabinet door. Insert the circular part of the hinge into the large hole in the door. Repeat with any other hinges.

2 Fix the hinges to the door using the screws provided. Make sure they are fitted squarely. Once all the hinges are in position on the door, fix them into the guide holes on the side panel of the cabinet. Do not overtighten the screws.

Adjusting door hinges

You may find that the doors need some adjustment after you have completed assembly of a new unit. On most modern cabinets, badly fitting doors can be adjusted in the same way.

1 If a door is hanging either too high or too low, use a screwdriver to loosen the top and bottom screws on the hinge mounting plates. Slide the door up or down until it is level with the top. Re-tighten the screws. To adjust the door to the left or right, turn the front screw on the arm of the hinge.

2 If a door does not fit flush against the cupboard front, loosen the screws at the back of all hinges. Reposition the door and re-tighten the screws. Adjust the screws at the front of the hinge if the door is not square with the cabinet. Re-tighten once you have a good fit.

Once you have grasped the basics, there's no end to what you can create by mixing and matching flatpack units, whether for bedroom, study, bathroom or kitchen.

B&Q Making it easier

Lay it out
When assembling any flatpack, it's a good idea to begin by laying out all the parts so that you can clearly see how they will fit together.

Drawer unit

Most flatpack systems give you the option of fitting drawers instead of a shelf and cupboard door to a small cabinet (see pages 149–50). You could of course create a combined drawer and cupboard unit by joining the two together either vertically or horizontally (see opposite); or use them as components of an entire built-in storage system, carefully designed to meet your own individual needs.

As always, do read the manufacturer's instructions as well, since different products are often assembled in slightly different ways.

project essentials

- **bradawl**
- **power drill with 3mm gauge twist bit**
- **screwdriver**

- small cabinet flatpack
- drawer pack
- drawer front pack

1 Push the drawer sides on to the drawer back to form a frame. The sides will be marked left and right. Make sure you fit them the right way around.

2 The drawer base has two different sides. Decide which you want to be visible, then slide it into the groove that runs around the lower part of the frame.

3 With the drawer upside down, make guide holes with a bradawl for the four screws that will hold the base in place. These holes are pre-drilled on some units. Screw the base panel into place.

4 Each drawer front will be marked top, bottom or middle, indicating the drawer's position in the finished cabinet. Take note of this order. Fix two retaining clips into the pre-drilled holes in the back of the drawer front. Each clip requires two screws. Swivel the clip round to cover the screws.

5 Push the drawer front into the drawer sides. Repeat Steps 2 to 5 for each drawer to complete the set.

6 Choose the position for the drawer handles. Measure accurately, so that the handles are neatly parallel. Use a bradawl to mark hole positions and then drill clearance holes for fixing. Insert screws from the back of the drawer and fix the handles in place.

7 There will be pre-drilled holes in the side panels of the cabinet to which the drawer runners will fit. Use two screws to fix each runner on to the side panels, making sure that you fit left- and right-hand runners on the correct sides. Make sure that opposite pairs of runners are at the same height.

8 Engage your assembled drawers on to the running mechanisms, making sure that the top, middle and bottom drawers are in the correct order. Check that the drawer fronts are aligned. If they need adjustment to left or right, turn the screws nearest to the drawer front. Do this at both sides, or you may create uneven pressure. To adjust up or down, turn the rear screws. Once you have completed all adjustments, fix the two locking plates into position.

Joining Units

You can join units vertically or horizontally using the same method. Three or more units joined vertically need to be secured to the wall with steel angle brackets for stability.

To join units vertically, locate the four joining points marked on the inside of the top panel. Wrap masking tape 30mm from the end of a 3mm bit and drill through the top of one unit into the base of the next, stopping when you reach the tape. Screw in 30mm screws and cover the heads with screw caps.

Position steel angle brackets on top of the uppermost unit 100mm in from the outer edges. Mark the screw positions then drill pilot holes into the wall with a 3mm drill bit. Don't drill right through the top panel. Screw the brackets to the units. Then put the units in position and mark the screw holes on the wall. Fix to the wall (see right).

project essentials

- **power drill with twist and masonry bits**
- **pipe and cable detector**
- **screwdriver**
- **bradawl**

- masking tape
- 30mm screws (3mm gauge) and screw caps
- steel angle brackets
- hollow-wall fixings or wallplugs

safety first

Safe drilling

Never drill directly above or below a light fitting or power socket. Always check for pipes and cables with an electronic detector before drilling into a wall.

Safe fixing

How you fix the units to the wall depends on what your wall is made from:

- Plasterboard: push a bradawl through at the fixing position. If you hit a stud, drill a pilot hole and fix with a 30mm screw; if not, use a special hollow-wall fixing (see page 368).
- Solid plaster: drill with a masonry bit, insert a wall plug and fix with a 30mm screw. If the plaster is old or crumbly, use longer screws and plugs.

Kitchen unit

You could adapt this kitchen unit to take a sink base, if you like, but the back would have to be altered to accommodate all the pipework. For more advice see Kitchens, pages 162–65.

project essentials

- **cross-head screwdriver**
- **small hammer**
- **power drill with 3mm gauge twist bit**

- kitchen unit flatpack
- plinth

Assemble the base unit as you would a small cabinet (see pages 149–50). Fit the central support and secure with four screws.

Position the leg brackets into the pre-drilled holes on the underside of the base panel. Ensure that the screw holes will not lie over panel joins.

Using a small hammer, tap in the central plastic lug.

Using a 3mm bit, drill pilot holes through the screw holes in the leg bracket and into the base panel. Then secure each bracket with three screws.

Fit the plastic legs into the brackets. Place the unit in position and adjust the legs until the unit is level at the correct height.

Push shelf supports into the pre-drilled holes at the required height. Turn the shelf on its side to feed it through the opening then rest it on the supports. To fit the doors, see page 151.

BEDROOM PLANNING

Planning a new bedroom gives you the chance to create a tranquil haven in an otherwise busy household; a place where you can relax and read, watch television or listen to music, as well as somewhere to sleep and store your clothes.

Designing your dream bedroom

Take a good look at your existing bedroom layout and see what works and what doesn't. Is the bed in the best place? Do you have enough storage space for your clothes? Be creative and play around with different ideas for making the most of the available space and for designing a bedroom that's both stylish and practical.

Get the most from the space

Clear away the clutter and immediately you create a more restful bedroom. The best bedroom plans put every inch of space to work to help you create as much storage as possible with the minimum of large pieces of furniture.

Think about the items you need to store. You will need hanging space for most of your clothes, internal shelves or drawers for jumpers, bridging cabinets for bulky items, and enough drawers for underwear and socks etc. Most clothes can hang in a short hanging space but three-quarter length and longer coats and dresses will need long hanging space. Think about the ratio of long hanging space to short: most women's clothes hang, while about half of men's clothes are better stored folded. Bridging cabinets on the wall over the bed are ideal for storing bulky items that you don't need that often.

Freestanding furniture

Freestanding furniture is very versatile, allowing you to arrange and rearrange your bedroom layout however you like. It is available flatpacked or ready-assembled, and you can add more pieces as your needs change.

Bedroom furniture

When it comes to bedroom furniture there's something to suit every taste and space, in styles from traditional to ultra contemporary.

Modular style

Whatever the shape and size of your room, you can really make the space work for you with modular furniture. You choose all the components – cabinets, doors, chests, handles and materials – from a wide range of styles and sizes of units to create your own individual furnishing solution, tailor-made for your bedroom.

Children's furniture

Freestanding kids' furniture means you can easily achieve a new look with a lick of paint and a change-around. If floor space is limited, consider a high sleeper bed; if sleep-overs are likely, look at Z beds; for homework choose a standard or pull-out desk.

Bedroom storage

Attractive storage systems can be freestanding or built-in. While freestanding wardrobes have the advantage of being moveable if you want to change the room, they do not hold as much as built-in ones. Built-in systems can also be fitted into alcoves and other irregular spaces.

Built-in storage with sliding doors

Wall-to-wall sliding-door wardrobes are elegant, practical and easy to install. Choose rails, shelves and drawers to suit your needs. Sliding door systems can be ordered off-the-shelf or made to measure. Look for soft-close sliding doors with a smooth and effortless closing action. Finishes range from wood to chic gloss panels or glass. If your room layout won't allow you to fit doors wall-to-wall, you can build a false end using plasterboard, MDF or a colour-matched decor panel.

Walk-in storage

If you have the space you could create the ultimate luxury, a dedicated walk-in storage area or dressing room, separated from the bedroom by wall-to-wall sliding doors.

Storage accessories

Bring order to your storage space with an extensive range of accessories, including shelves, hanging rails, drawers, shoe racks, a laundry bin, trouser or skirt rack, and storage boxes.

Colour

Colour plays a big part in creating a pleasing atmosphere as well as making a room appear larger or smaller, gloomy or sunny. An all-white room can look cold and stark whereas neutral shades such as cream add a touch of warmth; likewise, shades of pink are warmer than blues. If you want a strong colour or design you could have one feature wall and paint the other walls a complementary colour.

Give your bedroom furniture a stylish finish with colour-matched decorative panels and trims in cream or wood-effects such as maple, walnut and oak. The bedroom is also the perfect place for pretty fabrics – bed spreads, curtains and cushions – and colourful soft rugs.

Lighting

The right lighting in your bedroom can make all the difference to how it looks as well as how efficiently it functions. Stylish lighting options are available for everything from classic and contemporary ceiling lights and pretty bedside lamps to LED lighting for the insides of drawers and the plinths at the bottom of cabinets. You can even have an illuminated hanging rail fitted in a wardrobe. Using battery powered LED lighting, this requires no mains wiring.

Make a plan

As you develop your ideas, make a rough sketch of your bedroom and include all the fixed features like doors, windows, radiators and electrical sockets. Then take precise measurements of the room. Remember that walls are rarely completely straight so take measurements at three heights and widths, and always work with the smallest measurement. Draw a plan on graph paper, or use the interactive room planner on diy.com (see page 16).

Position furniture on your plan, starting with the bed, as it's the largest item. Avoid pushing it against a radiator and make sure you leave room for a bedside table or chest. Allow enough space for wardrobe doors and drawers to open (or choose sliding doors). Play around with a few different layouts to find the one that really works for you.

B&Q Making it easier

We do more...
B&Q offer a professional bedroom planning, design and installation service (see page 381). For further information, ask in store, or visit diy.com

KITCHEN PLANNING

The kitchen is evolving. For many of us it's no longer just a room for preparing food and doing chores. It's a place to dine, gather and entertain. It may even double as a living room, complete with television, radio or sound system. It is tempting when planning a new kitchen to keep the arrangement of appliances much the same as they already are. But there may be a better way. Start from scratch, consider your lifestyle and how you and your family use the room: you may discover all kinds of new possibilities.

A layout that works for you

It's important to design a kitchen that revolves around your needs. The layout you choose will depend on the size and shape of your room – and the position of windows and doors. Plumbing and electrical points can usually be moved, so there's no reason to let these restrict your design. Most kitchens fall into four basic designs: a single line of units, a double line (galley), and an L-shaped or U-shaped kitchen. By combining cabinets imaginatively in these arrangements it is easy to totally transform your kitchen to suit your lifestyle.

Most work in a typical kitchen revolves around the 'work triangle' of sink, fridge and cooker, so start with these elements when planning your layout. Try them in different arrangements. For maximum efficiency a work triangle should be neither too cramped nor too spread out: the combined distance of its three sides should be no less than 3.6m but no more than 7m.

If the kitchen doubles up as a dining area or faces a dining room, make sure that there is a clear path to the table – this will make it easier to serve food, as well as bringing together the diners with those hard at work preparing the meal.

Practical planning

Plan your kitchen around the most used elements: these may be a 'triangle' of sink, cooker and fridge, or a four-point arrangement including a serving and eating area. A hob and cooker should be positioned so as to minimise the distance it is necessary to carry hot pans across the kitchen walkways.

Lighting and flooring

It's worth thinking carefully about lighting. You will need directed task lighting over the work surfaces as well as overall illumination. There are so many options these days – from adjustable spotlights recessed into the ceiling or on tracks to lights installed under, on or inside cupboards. Consider mood too – bright white light creates a brisk, efficient atmosphere; pools of subdued illumination are more relaxing. Why not provide both, especially if you dine in the kitchen?

Finally, don't forget the flooring. This needs to be easy to clean and hardwearing. Water-resistant laminate or ceramic tiles are practical, popular choices.

Find your kitchen style

Gloss or matt, wood or glass, strong accent colour or calm neutrals; your choice of kitchen will reflect your own personal style as well as the period and style of your home. Even if you prefer to stick to a fairly neutral style with a view to reselling your home, you can still express your taste in easily replaceable elements such as unit doors.

Creating your kitchen plan

Start by making a rough sketch of the room showing fixtures, doors, windows, existing plumbing and electrical sockets, and gas outlet. Then take accurate measurements of every dimension and transfer them to the drawing. The walls and floor of your kitchen may not be regular. To measure the length and width, take three measurements at different wall heights and work with the smallest. Check the kitchen is square by measuring both diagonals (or measure and compare opposite wall lengths). Finally draw a plan of the room to scale on graph paper, or use the interactive room planner on diy.com (see page 16).

Appliances

- If using graph paper, cut out shapes to represent the kitchen appliances, sink and units that you want to include. Place them on the plan and move them around to experiment with different designs.
- Position the cooker at least 600mm from the sink.
- Leave at least 300mm of clear space each side of the hob to allow for protruding pan handles.
- Avoid placing the cooker or hob near to an inward-opening door or under a window, or next to a tall unit or corner.
- Allow for adequate access space around freestanding appliances (check the manufacturer's instructions).
- If possible, place washing machines and dishwashers close to a sink to keep the plumbing simple.
- Avoid placing appliances in a corner.
- Choose energy-efficient appliances to help reduce your energy use and bills.
- Don't put a fridge beside a hob or cooker, or it will have to work harder to keep food cold.

Units and sink

- Make sure there is easy access to cupboard doors and drawers, particularly in corners.

- Measure the height of window ledges and double-check that any units will fit underneath them.
- If you can, position the sink under a window to let in light and give you a view.
- Ensure that wall and floor units are of matching widths so that the doors and joins line up.
- Keep tall units to the end of worktop runs to maximise the working area.
- Check what the walls are made of to ensure that you buy the correct fixings for your units.

Ventilation and services

- Allow for adequate ventilation – an extractor fan is a must. It should be positioned on (or close to) an outside wall, and at least 750mm above a hob.
- Mark where you would like to install new sockets and light fittings. Allow for plenty of electrical sockets: you won't regret it. They should be a minimum of 150mm above worktops.
- Is your boiler in the kitchen? If it is in the way, could it be moved? Though don't be tempted to box in boilers or other gas appliances, as these require air flow to operate properly and safely.
- Avoid blocking existing air vents if there are gas appliances in the kitchen.

B&Q Making it easier

We do more...
B&Q offer a professional kitchen planning, design and installation service (see page 381). Our designers will take you through over 40 styles and details to find what really works for you. Products are quality-checked before being delivered in one go, ready for our qualified fitters. We can remove your old kitchen and dispose of it responsibly. All B&Q fitting work is guaranteed for two years. For further information, ask in store, or visit diy.com

safety first

Gas and electricity
Any fitting or moving of gas appliances must be carried out by a Gas Safe registered professional. Modifications to plumbing or electrics must be in accordance with the Wiring and Building Regulations; if in doubt, consult a professional.

Professional kitchen design

A professional kitchen designer will produce three-dimensional computer renderings showing how your kitchen could look with different layouts, units and details. They will also be able to show you some of the huge range of options available for everything from worktops, sinks and units to lighting, flooring and storage.

KITCHEN PLANNING

From worktops to units, appliances to storage solutions, there are endless stylish and innovative elements to help you create a quality kitchen that is good-looking, practical and will be great to work and live in for years to come.

Worktops

A hardwearing and hygienic worktop is essential in a modern kitchen. There are high-performance options in a wide range of finishes and profiles to suit every budget. Most can be cut to fit, though some must be templated and machine-cut as part of a professional fitting service.

Laminate, stone and granite

Laminate and composite stone worktops produced using the latest technologies are highly durable and maintenance free. The crystalline patterns of natural granite are unique to each individual worktop.

Natural wood

Solid wood ages beautifully over time, adding to its charm. You can sand away scratches or marks. Treating twice yearly with wax oil is recommended.

Dining

Eating in the kitchen is ever more the norm, so it's a good idea to plan a dining area. A table or breakfast bar with chairs or stools is also great for reading the morning paper, consulting a recipe book, or for the kids to do their homework while dinner is being prepared. But do be sure to position a dining area so that it does not create an obstruction, or block the walkways between sink, cooker and fridge.

Breakfast bar

A breakfast bar in the same material as the worktop is a stylish option, and ideal in a small kitchen without space for a separate table and chairs.

Table and chairs

Even if you have a separate dining room, a kitchen table and chairs will come in handy for everyday meals.

Be creative

Think afresh and experiment with different layouts, combinations, finishes and colours before you make your mind up on a new kitchen.

Island units

If you have sufficient space, an island can become the focal point of your kitchen. It can provide an additional work surface, or can house a cooker, hob or sink.

Combinations of units

Units come in a wide range of styles and dimensions, and can be combined in any number of different configurations. Experiment to see what works for you.

Accent colour

Interchangeable unit doors let you create your own unique design. Why not be bold and experiment with accent colours? You can easily change them in the future.

Splashback panels

A splashback doesn't have to be tiled. Purpose designed splashbacks are available in various finishes, including toughened glass and stainless steel. They are waterproof, easy to clean, and much quicker to fit than tiles.

Appliances

Eye-catching style statement or streamlined and integrated: the choice is yours when it comes to appliances.

Freestanding

Integrated

Cooker hoods

An extractor hood will help prevent the kitchen from steaming up and remove airborne grease and unwanted cooking smells. It can be wall-mounted or installed over an island, but ideally should be on or close to an outside wall.

Island hood

Chimney hood

Extraction or recirculation?

The most efficient way to keep the air fresh is by extraction, in which vapours and steam pass through ducting and are released outdoors. However, ducting should not run to more than 3m. If that is not possible, then you can operate the hood in recirculation mode. This draws the stale air through charcoal filters to purify it, then releases it back into the kitchen. Hoods can typically be run in either extraction or recirculation mode, though do check before buying.

Storage

Take the opportunity to incorporate lots of space-saving ideas to help keep worktops clear and cupboards and drawers neat and tidy. Base cabinets can have pull-out shelving or wire racks fitted, useful for all those odds and ends. Fit an integral swing bin into a base cabinet; it will open automatically when you open the door.

Corner carousel

A rotating corner carousel is a great way to make maximum use of space.

KITCHEN MAKEOVER

Bored with your kitchen? Want to change the style, but don't want the expense of a complete refit? There is no need to despair. You can completely alter the feel of your kitchen by changing the colour scheme and taking a critical look at all the accessories; with the choices available you can quickly make an older kitchen look like new.

Changing doors

The beauty of modular kitchen systems is that everything is made to mix and match. You may want to break up a solid run of cupboard doors by adding glass panelled ones for a softer look. Or convert cupboards to drawers or vice versa to make the most of the space. Base and wall units come in standard sizes, so doors, drawer fronts and worktops are interchangeable – though do check all measurements carefully before you buy.

Gloss

For a clean, bright, hardwearing modern kitchen, gloss units are hard to beat.

Matt

Matt-finish units are sophisticated and understated, and combine well with dramatic accent colour.

Wood veneer

The warm shades of natural woods work equally well in traditional and contemporary style kitchens.

Solid wood

Mellow tones and timeless quality: solid wood is a classic choice.

Black and white

Chic and contemporary: a black-and-white kitchen is a real stand-out option.

Focus on detail

Give your drawer or door fronts a facelift by changing the handles. You'll be surprised what a difference it can make.

Traditional ceramic

The large capacity of this timeless design makes it ideal for the busy family and it looks great in a traditional style kitchen.

Update your sink

As the mainstay of the kitchen, your kitchen sink should be good-looking as well as functional. See pages 165 and 316 for instructions on how to fit a sink.

Stainless steel

Tough, hygienic and functional, stainless steel looks good in any kitchen.

Bowl and drainer

A sink with a bowl plus separate, smaller drainer is a very popular and practical design.

Undermount sink

Sinks that sit below the work surface offer a seamless contemporary look. They aren't suitable for laminate worktops.

Repainting doors and drawers

Your melamine kitchen units may not be compatible with readily available replacement doors. Don't worry: painting cupboard doors and drawer fronts is a perfectly good option. Either buy a special paint designed for use on melamine, or apply a melamine base paint and then a topcoat of your choice. Provided you prepare all the surfaces carefully, a good result is easy to achieve. You can also repaint wooden doors and drawer fronts, but not the latest PVC foil finishes – if you have PVC foil doors, you will need to replace them.

project essentials

- **power drill with twist bit**
- **medium-grade abrasive paper**
- **screwdriver**
- **50mm paintbrush**
- **measuring tape**
- **pencil**

- timber off-cuts
- melamine paint, or melamine basecoat and topcoat of your choice
- handles, if required
- wood filler

B&Q Making it easier

Change your plinths
You can buy plinths, cornices, end panels and mouldings to match your kitchen units...but you don't have to. Take a look at other finishes and use a contrasting colour for a more unusual effect.

Remove all the handles and hinges, and rub down surfaces using a medium-grade abrasive paper. Carefully work into recesses and mouldings.

If you intend to change the handles, fill the fixing holes with wood filler; use an old screwdriver to work it well into the hole. When the filler is dry, sand the area smooth.

Apply the paint with a 50mm brush. Blend in wet edges and make your final brushstrokes in a consistent direction.

Light it up
The latest LED plinth lights create an atmospheric floor-level glow. What's more, they consume far less energy than standard light bulbs, leading to significantly reduced energy costs (see page 285).

Once the paint is thoroughly dry you can replace the drawer handles. Measure the width and depth of a draw front and mark the centre point very lightly in pencil. Centre the handle on your mark, ensuring it is level. Mark the fixing points. You can rub the guidelines out later.

Support the drawer front on two pieces of wood and drill clearance holes right through it for the handle screws. Make sure the drill is at exactly 90° to the surface or the handles won't fit properly.

Push the screws supplied through the holes from the back, and screw them into the handle.

Fit handles on all the cabinets and drawers. You will have to decide on the most convenient position for cupboard handles. On wall units, they are usually more practical at the bottom.

KITCHEN UNITS

Creating a new look for your kitchen is a great opportunity to stamp your personality onto the busiest room in the house. Base and wall units come in standard sizes and form the basis of a kitchen. Draw a detailed plan on graph paper and double-check all measurements before you begin. Products may differ, so do read the manufacturer's installation instructions too.

Fitting the base units

Remove the old units, disconnect power and water supplies and do any preparatory work necessary on the walls and ceiling. It is a good idea to apply the first coat of paint to the walls and ceiling before fitting the units. The top coat can be completed after they are in place. See page 153 for guidance on assembling kitchen units.

Using a spirit level as a straightedge, mark a horizontal guideline on the walls level with where the top of the units will be. Align them with any existing appliances. Remember to allow for the legs when working out the height of the units.

Assemble the base units (see page 153) and move them into position, starting with a corner cabinet. Rotate the legs of each unit to adjust the height until it aligns with the pencil guideline on the wall. Use a spirit level to check that the run of cabinets is level.

Clamp adjoining cabinets together to hold them securely. Wrap masking tape 20mm from the end of a 3mm twist bit as a depth guide. Drill between the two hinge holes, through one cabinet and 4mm into the next, stopping when you reach the tape. Do this at both hinge positions. Screw the units together using the 25mm screws supplied.

Screw two 30mm screws from behind through each bracket into the corner post. Drill two pilot holes through the side panel of the next unit, 13mm in from the outer edge. Keep clear of the hinge positions. Screw 30mm screws through the holes and into the corner post.

Each base is secured to the wall with two brackets. Mark the drilling positions in pencil on the wall and cabinet. Check for pipes and cables before drilling into the wall. On solid masonry use a drill with hammer action and a masonry bit, and fit a wallplug. On plasterboard use plasterboard fixings. Drill a pilot hole into the cabinet and secure the bracket with a 15mm screw. On end panels, angle the screws slightly downwards for ease of access.

To turn a corner with a run of cabinets, you need to fit a corner post or there will be an ugly gap. Screw two brackets at the top and bottom of the inside face of the central post of the cabinet that extends into the corner.

project essentials

- **tape measure**
- **pencil**
- **spirit level**
- **cross-head screwdriver**
- **power drill with 3mm twist bit**
- **pipe and cable detector**
- **masonry drill**
- **clamp**

- base cabinets
- base corner cabinet
- base corner post
- wall cabinet
- wall corner cabinet
- wallplugs or plasterboard fixings
- screws, 15mm, 25mm and 30mm
- masking tape

ideal tool

Pipe and cable detector
Whenever you need to drill into walls, you must make a thorough check for pipes or cables hidden behind the plaster. The simplest way of doing this is to use a battery-operated detector. Run it over the surface of the wall where you intend to drill a hole and it will indicate where hazards lie.

Planning the vertical layout

The distance between the top of the base units and bottom edge of wall units is up to you. However, wall units must not be directly above a hob, and you should check the hob manufacturer's instructions for the necessary clearance either side. Position all the wall units at the same height if possible and take into account the heights of the people who are likely to be using them. If you intend to tile between the base and wall units, calculate the gap in terms of whole tiles (plus grout and sealant) to make your life easier and the finish neater. As far as possible, align the doors and joins of base and wall units.

Fitting the wall units

The wall units hook onto brackets that must be very securely fixed to the wall.

Measure up from the top of the base unit and mark the bottom edge of the wall unit, allowing for the thickness of the worktop. Then use a spirit level to mark a horizontal guideline on the wall, stretching as far round as your wall units will go. Draw another line marking the top of the wall units. Then consult the kitchen plan and draw vertical lines where the cabinets will meet.

Check the manufacturer's instructions to find the correct position for the wall fitting brackets. Each unit will require two brackets, one in each top corner. Hold a bracket in place and mark the position of the fixing holes. How you fix the brackets to the wall depends on what kind of wall you have – see below.

Hook the wall cabinets onto the brackets. Use the adjustment block in the top internal corner to position them accurately. Lie a spirit level across the top of the cabinet and turn one screw to level it horizontally, then place the spirit level against the front face and adjust the other screw until it is vertical. Also check that the units are level with each other.

Join adjacent wall cabinets in the same way as base cabinets (see Step 3, opposite). Finally, decide on the best position for the shelves and push the shelf supports into the pre-drilled holes. Tilt the shelves and slide them into place.

Fixing units to different types of wall

Always check for pipes and cables before drilling into any wall. If you have solid plaster walls, then use a power drill with hammer action and insert wallplugs and then screws. If you have slightly crumbling plaster, use longer plugs and screws.

If you have plasterboard walls, use hollow-wall fixings to secure the brackets (see pages 376–77). But for safety you must add extra fixings to the wall units. Hang the cabinet on the brackets and adjust it as described above. Then unhook the cabinet. Use a stud detector to locate a stud or nogging behind the wall. Pack out the cavity at the back of the cabinet with a length of timber, rehang it on the brackets, and drill right through the back of the cabinet and packing to screw it firmly into the stud or nogging. Use two additional screws per cabinet.

KITCHEN WORKTOP, SINK AND PLINTH

project essentials

- **panel saw**
- **power drill with 4mm and 2mm twist bits and 12mm flat bit**
- **cross-head screwdriver**
- **hacksaw**
- **craft knife**
- **fine file**
- **pencil**
- **ruler**
- **power jigsaw with laminate blade**
- **try square**
- **bradawl**

- worktop
- profiled joining strip
- kitchen sink
- plinth with fixings
- masking tape
- 16mm (3.5mm gauge) and 38mm (5mm gauge) wood screws
- contact adhesive
- silicone sealant

It's the finishing touches – sinks, worktops and plinths – that will make your kitchen units look professionally designed and, most important of all, make them easy to work in and keep clean.

Fitting the worktop

Kitchen worktops can be made from a variety of materials, including wood, real or synthetic slate, stone, granite or marble, or laminated chipboard. Laminate worktop is the simplest to fit, and is available in a wide range of colours and textures. It also comes in different thicknesses; the worktop fitted here is 45mm thick. Use a panel saw to cut laminate board to the right length before you begin fitting. Factory-cut edges will inevitably be more accurate than those you cut yourself, so position factory cuts where the edge will show and hide your own cuts against wall junctions or under a joining strip.

 B&Q Making it easier

Curved-edge worktop jig

A worktop jig is a template for cutting perfect joins in round-edge laminate worktops using a router. Clamp it in position on the worktop before cutting, and be sure to practise on some off-cuts first.

Choose where to make the fixing positions for the worktop: three screws at the back and front of each unit will usually be about right. Using a 4mm gauge bit, drill clearance holes through the support panels on each unit.

Put the laminate worktop in position, checking it fits tightly against the wall, and that edges butt up snugly.

Where the run of units turns a corner, there has to be a join in the worktop. The front edge of a worktop is profiled, so to create a neat join you have to insert a specially profiled aluminium joining strip. Use a hacksaw to cut the strip to exactly the width of the worktop. Apply silicone sealant along the cut edge of the worktop, and then screw the strip in place using 16mm (3.5mm gauge) wood screws. Apply more sealant to the profiled edge of the adjoining worktop and slide the two sections together.

Now fix the worktop to the units. Wrap masking tape 38mm from the end of a 2mm gauge drill bit as a depth guide. Working from beneath the worktop and inside the cabinets, drill through each of the clearance holes you have already made, and into the worktop. Stop when you reach the masking tape so that the drill doesn't break through. Screw a 38mm (5mm gauge) wood screw through each fixing position.

Apply matching laminate strip to exposed worktop edges; this will be supplied with the worktop. Cut the strip to the right length. Apply contact adhesive to both the back of the edging strip and the worktop edge. Leave for the recommended time and then stick into place.

Once the glue has dried completely, trim the edge with a craft knife and file off rough edges with a fine file.

Fitting a sink into a laminate worktop

Although kitchen sinks come in a variety of designs, the basic technique for fitting them into a worktop remains the same. Check the instructions supplied with the sink for any variation.

Use the template supplied, or turn the sink upside down on the worktop (with the bowls in the right position – the sink may not be exactly rectangular). Make sure it is an equal distance from the front and back edges, and will fit into the base unit underneath. Trace its outline directly onto the work surface in pencil or – if pencil won't mark the laminate – stick masking tape on the surface beneath the sink edges and trace their outline onto it.

Take the sink away and measure the overlap required for the sink edge to rest on the worktop. The manufacturer's instructions should give you this measurement. Use a ruler to draw another line at this distance inside the first.

Using a 12mm gauge flat bit, drill a hole through the worktop at each corner of the inner line to enable you to insert the blade of a jigsaw. Be extremely careful that you don't stray over the line.

ideal tool

Laminate jigsaw blades
Blades designed for laminated materials cut only on the downstroke, minimising damage to the surface as you work.

Cut along the inner line using a power jigsaw with a laminate blade. Stick masking tape on the jigsaw plate to avoid scratching the surface. Support the piece you are cutting out as you get to the end, to prevent the worktop splitting. To plumb in a sink, see page 316.

Fitting the plinth

A plinth running round the bottom of your units will give a neat finish and make cleaning easier. It is held in place by special brackets that clip to the units' legs, shown below. Or look out for the latest plinth lock fixings, which attach plinth ends to adjacent panels and give a very tight, secure join.

Measure the distance of the run of units corner to corner, and cut the plinth to fit. Lie the plinth on the floor adjacent to the front edge of the units and, using a try square, draw lines level with either side of each leg.

Hold a fixing bracket between the two lines and use a bradawl to make a starting hole. Screw the bracket in place, parallel to the bottom edge, using the screws supplied. Fit the other brackets in line with each leg along the entire run of units.

Slide the plinth clips into the brackets then clip the plinth into place by simply pushing each bracket onto the legs of the unit.

B&Q Making it easier

Seal the joints

Kitchen surfaces endure a lot of cleaning and are often left wet. It's a good idea to seal all joints, particularly along the back of a worktop and around the sink. Sanitary silicone sealant is easy to apply, forms a flexible waterproof seal, and will prevent any water from penetrating.

Outside
the home

GUTTERING DRAINAGE AND WATER BUTTS

For a house to remain in a good condition it must be weatherproof. Rain that falls on the roof or is blown against the external walls must drain away efficiently, or it will penetrate the structure of the house and cause damp problems – or even leaks.

Walls

The external walls of a house are built with weather-resistant materials on the outside, normally stone, brick or concrete blocks. Stone is usually left in its natural state; concrete is most often covered with render – a weather-resistant finish of cement or cement and lime mortar; and brick may or may not be rendered, depending to a large extent on its condition. Some houses have a finish of timber boarding (also known as weatherboard cladding) or plastic cladding. Timber cladding must be protected by wood preservative or exterior paint.

The walls are shielded from rainwater that falls on the roof by the guttering, but all parts of the external walls, including doors and windows, must be maintained in good order so that any water that blows against them can run off the surfaces and drain away. Water will always find any cracks or gaps in render and mortar, and they must be repaired as soon as possible.

Roof

Guttering is the roof's drainage system. The size and layout of guttering is designed to enable it to cope with all the water that falls on a roof. It may be made of cast-iron, aluminium or – most often these days – plastic, and can have different shapes in cross-section (see below). If you need to replace a gutter, make sure the new one is the same size or even slightly larger than the old one and check that it can be joined to the old system – it's not always easy to join one manufacturer's guttering to another's and you may need a plastic adaptor.

Gutters must be kept clear of leaves and other debris or water will flow over the top rather than down the downpipe. Cast-iron downpipes can crack if damp material gets stuck inside and freezes. You can buy wire or plastic covers to prevent debris entering the downpipe at the guttering outlet.

Types of guttering

There are three different types of guttering: eaves, parapet and valley gutters.

Eaves gutters

These are the gutters found at the bottom edge of a sloping roof. They are usually attached to the fascia boards with brackets. They are available in different shapes and styles (see right), in plastic or metal. Old guttering is often cast-iron, whereas modern guttering is usually plastic, but aluminium is also used.

Parapet gutters

A parapet gutter drains a flat roof between parapet walls (which are walls that continue above the roof level by one or more courses of bricks). One of the parapet walls contains a gap or channel, and the roof slopes slightly towards it. This allows water to drain into a hopper fitted at the top of a downpipe.

Valley gutters

The junction between different sloping roofs – such as between a gable and hipped-end roof (see page 189) – is called a valley. Metal flashing runs the length of a valley and forms a watertight gutter that channels water into eaves or parapet guttering.

Gutter shapes and sizes

Gutters are available in several different shapes or profiles, both plain and decorative.

Half-round gutters

Standard 112mm half-round gutters are used with a 68mm circular downpipe for houses and large detached garages.

Square gutters

If you live in a larger house or in an area of high rainfall, you may need a gutter with a greater capacity, such as 116mm x 60mm 'square' guttering which has a straight back, front and base.

Ogee gutters

These have a straight back edge and a fluted front edge, which makes them wider at the top than at the bottom. They can be used with square or round downpipes.

Mini guttering

When fitting guttering on a shed, greenhouse or small detached garage, use 75mm half-round gutters and 50mm circular downpipe. This is smaller than the guttering on a house.

Fascia gutter brackets
90° angle fitting
Stop-end
Stop-end outlet
Running outlet
Half-round gutter
Offset bend
Downpipe
Union piece
45° angle fitting
Downpipe clip
Waste pipe
Downpipe
Hopper head
Downpipe connector
Shoe
Gulley grid

Guttering system

Lengths of guttering either have a socket at one end into which the plain end (the spigot end) of the next piece fits, or they are plain at both ends and two lengths are joined by a union piece, which contains gaskets to make the connections watertight.

- **Downpipe** The downpipe is the pipe running from the guttering to the drain at ground level. Special offset bends are added to the downpipe if it has to fit around overhanging eaves.

- **Outlets** A stop-end outlet is an end piece with an outlet to attach to a downpipe. A running outlet is attached to a downpipe positioned mid-way along a length of guttering.

- **Hopper head** Some downpipes incorporate a hopper head to take a wastepipe or pipes from another source. These can be replaced, if necessary, in an existing installation, but are no longer used in new installations (see page 303).

Installing a water butt

ONE PLANET HOME

Not only is rainwater free, but it is better for plants than tap water as it contains more nutrients. What's more, unlike hard mains water, rainwater will not leave limescale deposits or increase the alkalinity of the soil. The best way to collect rainwater is in a water butt connected to a downpipe. If you position it on a stand, you will be able to fill a watering can straight from its tap. If you have a big garden, you can connect two butts to a single downpipe using a flexible hose link kit.

(see page 303).

project essentials

- **power drill with hole saw**
- **hacksaw**

- water butt and stand
- rainwater diverter kit

Water butt pump
A plug-in pump will add pressure to stored water from a butt. This means you can use the water to feed sprinklers or irrigation systems.

B&Q Making it easier

1 Choose a suitable and convenient downpipe for the water butt and place the stand beneath it. Place the water butt on the stand and mark its height on the downpipe. Cut the downpipe 3cm below this point with a hacksaw.

2 Attach the rainwater diverter fitting to the downpipe; the cut section of downpipe fits onto the bottom of the diverter.

3 Measure 8cm down from the top of the water butt and drill a hole for the water butt connector.

4 Attach the connector to the water butt by pushing it through the drilled hole and screwing the fittings into place.

5 Attach the water butt connector to the rainwater diverter with the supplied fittings. Place the lid on the butt and lock it into place.

GUTTERING PROBLEMS

safety first

Working at heights

Take time to make sure that your ladder is secure before you start work, and never rest it against guttering. Use a ladder stand-off instead (see page 175). On uneven ground, use ladder stabilisers (see MAKING IT EASIER). A scaffold tower is not as easy to manoeuvre as a ladder but it provides a safe working platform and plenty of room for tools. Assemble the components carefully and check that the platform boards are secure. Construct a guard rail around the platform. On soft or uneven ground, stand the feet of the tower on level scaffold boards.

The exterior of the house takes a constant battering from the elements, especially wind and rain. This can take its toll on the masonry and guttering systems, and can sometimes overwhelm them.

Wall drainage problems

Masonry in good condition is waterproof; but if allowed to deteriorate, render, stone and bricks can let water through to the inside of the wall, and must be repaired.

Porous bricks or stones soaking up water

If the affected area is small, cut out the damaged bricks or stones and replace them (see page 177). This is impractical for a large area; in this case repoint the joints and coat the bricks or stones with silicone water-repellent fluid, which prevents water getting into the bricks but allows them to breathe so that the moisture that has already penetrated can evaporate.

Water seeping into cracks in the render

Fill cracks with exterior filler. If there is extensive damage, hack off the render in the damaged area and patch it with new render, then paint the wall with exterior paint.

Crumbling mortar joints

Rake out the mortar with a raking-out tool, or a cold chisel or plugging chisel and a club hammer, to a depth of 13mm. Clean out any dust and brush water into the joints before repointing them. Mix some mortar (see page 223); pick up a small amount on the back of a trowel and push it into the joints. Leave until semi-dry, then shape the joints to match existing brickwork (see page 227).

Water penetrating window or door frames

Wooden door and window frames tend to shrink and sometimes the mortar around the edges falls out, allowing rainwater into the gaps. Frames should be repaired, if necessary (see page 183), then cracks up to 10mm can be sealed with frame sealant; cracks more than 10mm wide should be filled with mortar.

Guttering problems

If the guttering does not work efficiently, water will overflow and saturate the wall below. Any problems with gutters should be remedied as soon as possible.

Rusted cast-iron gutter

Patches of rust can be smoothed off with an emery cloth but take care not to rub so hard that you make a hole. If there are large areas of rust, brush them off with a wire handbrush or use a round wire cup brush fitted in an electric drill. Then paint the affected area with a rust-inhibiting metal primer, then with black bitumen or gloss paint. If there are any small holes in the gutter fill them first with roof-and-gutter sealant. A bigger hole can be filled with glass-fibre filler, but if the guttering is in poor condition with a lot of holes you should replace it altogether (see pages 174–75).

ideal tool

Wire brush drill attachment

A wire cup brush attached to a drill will quickly clean off rust on old cast-iron guttering. It's also useful for cleaning paint off stone or concrete surfaces. Be sure to wear a dust mask and protective goggles while you work.

Overflowing hopper head

Water overflowing from a hopper head indicates leaves or other debris in the hopper head itself or a blockage in the downpipe below the hopper head. Scoop out any leaves in the hopper head. If the downpipe is blocked, try unblocking it from ground level. Cover the drain, turn on the water in a garden hose and push it up the pipe to dislodge the debris; if that doesn't work, use drain rods to unblock it from the top.

B&Q Making it easier

Ladder stabilisers

A ladder should only be positioned on level, firm ground (see page 357). If you do have to erect a ladder on an uneven surface, bolt stabilisers to the bottom on both sides to stop it rocking.

Leaking gutter joints

For a metal gutter, scrape any dirt out of the joint and dry it. Inject roof and gutter sealant into the joint with an applicator gun. If it is plastic guttering joined with a union piece, one of the gaskets (seals) may be damaged. Squeeze the gutter to release the union piece, peel the gasket away and replace it with a new one.

It may be that a loose or wongly positioned bracket has caused the guttering to sag, so that the water forms a pool rather than flows away. If the screw had worked loose, you should be able simply to insert a wallplug and rescrew the bracket; if the bracket was wrongly positioned, fill the hole and refix it. If the guttering still sags, fit extra brackets to support it.

Leaking from the end of a length of guttering

Water will run off the end of a length of guttering if the stop-end has come away, or one was never fitted. Check the dimensions and profile of your guttering, and buy one to fit.

Blocked outlet

Block the bottom of the downpipe with a rag to stop debris getting into the drain, then scoop out leaves and silt from the gutter with a small trowel. Remove the rag and rinse out the gutter and downpipe with water. To prevent the problem recurring, fit a leafguard cover over the outlet, and gutter guard (right) over the guttering. Gutter guard is simply cut to size and clipped in place.

Loose downpipes

If a plastic downpipe is loose, check to see if one of the clips has lost a connecting bolt, as here. Replace it with a galvanised bolt of the same size. Or the wallplugs may have worked loose: replace them and refix the screws or fit new 6.5mm gauge galvanised screws. If a cast-iron downpipe is loose, take out the fixing nails or screws and insert wallplugs. Then drive the nails back in or fit galvanised screws. If wooden plugs are loose, remove and replace them.

GUTTERING REPAIRS

Plastic guttering is lightweight and easy to replace if part of it goes wrong. But it is also quite straightforward to carry out minor repairs to old cast-iron guttering. Take care, though, because cast-iron guttering is very heavy. If it is in very poor condition, you would be better to replace it altogether (see pages 174–75).

project essentials

- **ladder, if required**
- **heavy-duty gloves**
- **wire brush**
- **scissors**

- joint repair tape

Repairing a leak with tape

You can use joint repair tape to fix minor leaks or cracks in a joint in cast-iron guttering or downpipes.

Clean around the area to be repaired with a wire brush to remove loose paint or rust. Cut off a length of repair tape a few centimetres longer than the diameter of the downpipe and remove the paper backing.

Wrap the repair tape around the joint and overlap the ends.

Press the tape firmly with your hand to mould it around the shape of the joint.

 Making it easier

Leaking downpipes
If a downpipe leaks during heavy rain, it may be a sign that the section of pipe below the leak is blocked by leaves or some other obstruction. You may be able to dislodge it with a garden hose: cover the drain, turn on the water, and direct it up the downpipe. If that doesn't work and the blockage is near the top of the pipe, use a length of wire to clear it. If it is near the bottom, you may need to use a drain rod or take a section of the pipe apart to clear it.

Repairing a leak with sealant

Roof and gutter sealant should be used to repair bigger leaks in metal guttering or a damaged union piece in plastic guttering. Protect your hands with heavy-duty gloves, especially while applying the sealant.

Clean around the area to be repaired with a wire brush to remove loose paint or rust.

Use an old screwdriver to dig out old jointing material.

Insert the nozzle of a sealant gun into the joint and run a bead of roof and gutter sealant around the pipe, making sure the cavity is filled.

project essentials

- **ladder, if required**
- **heavy-duty gloves**
- **wire brush**
- **old screwdriver**

- roof and gutter sealant

Smooth the sealant with your finger to leave a neat filling.

Repairing a leak in cast-iron guttering

Lengths of old cast-iron guttering may be joined together with bolts. If these have rusted in place, you will need to saw them off with a hacksaw.

project essentials

- **ladder**
- **spanner**
- **hacksaw**
- **nail punch**
- **hammer**
- **heavy-duty gloves**
- **wire brush**
- **screwdriver**

- roof and gutter sealant
- galvanised gutter bolt

Try to undo the old securing bolt with a spanner. If you can't, use a hacksaw to cut through the bolt then tap its shank upwards through the gutter with a nail punch and hammer.

Wearing heavy-duty gloves, separate the gutter joint – you will probably need to tap it to loosen the old putty or mastic. Clean the joint with a wire brush.

Run a bead of sealant into the joint.

Press the guttering into the sealant and fit a new galvanised gutter bolt. With gloves on, smooth the excess sealant with your finger.

Unblocking a drain

You will need special drain-cleaning rods to clear a blocked drain and some disinfectant to clean them afterwards.

project essentials

- **heavy-duty waterproof gloves**
- **rubber plunger**
- **drain rods**
- **hose-pipe**
- **watering can**

- disinfectant

Lift the inspection cover of the blocked drain. Fit a rubber plunger to the end of two drain rods and insert them into the bottom of the inspection chamber. Slide the rods into the drain outlet pipe – if the inspection chamber is full you will have to probe with the plunger to find it. Push the rods into the drain, adding more rods as required. Use a push and pull action as this will help to dislodge the blockage. Or turn them in a clockwise direction – but not anti-clockwise, or they may unscrew in the drain and add to the blockage.

Remove the rods from the drain and see if the waste water drains away. If not, repeat the process, adding more rods. When the drain is clear, dismantle the rods and stand them in the inspection chamber. Using a hose-pipe, wash the rods and flush the drain with clean water, then drench the rods and the gloves in diluted disinfectant, pouring it from a watering can.

Clearing a valley gutter

Valley gutters can be difficult to reach, but a long-handled garden hoe will help you clear any trapped debris.

project essentials

- **heavy-duty waterproof gloves**
- **garden hoe**
- **bucket**

Use a garden hoe to pull the debris towards you until you can reach it with your hand.

Hold a bucket beneath the end of the gutter and slide the debris into the bucket.

REPLACING GUTTERING

project essentials

- 2 ladders
- hammer
- hacksaw
- nail punch
- pincers or crowbar
- scraper
- paintbrush
- screwdriver
- builder's line or string
- plumb line
- pencil
- spirit level
- hammer action drill with masonry bits

- large nails
- rope
- filler
- paint or stain
- plastic guttering system
- wallplugs and screws (in sizes recommended by guttering manufacturer)

If you need to replace your guttering and plan to do the work yourself, new plastic guttering is the easiest type to fit. Measure all the way round the house to calculate the length of gutter you will need. Check the manufacturer's guidelines to determine the number of fittings you will need.

Removing the old guttering

Old plastic guttering is easy to remove but cast-iron guttering is extremely heavy and the edges can be sharp, so it takes two people to remove it.

Tie a rope around each end of the section of guttering to be removed. Break apart the gutter joint and unscrew the brackets holding the section to the fascia.

Cut through the bolts joining two sections of gutter with a hacksaw then tap them out with a nail punch and hammer.

Use the ropes to carefully lower the gutter section to the ground. Repeat the process to remove all the sections, then remove the downpipes. Use pincers to remove the pipe nails or, if they are rusted in, use a crowbar to lever them out of the wall. Remove downpipes one section at a time, starting from the top. Finally, repair the fascia board: fill in screw holes, strip off flaking finishes and repaint or restain.

Drive large nails into the fascia board beneath a section of guttering at either end to hold it and prevent it falling.

Fitting new guttering

Start by fitting the section of guttering with the outlet since this will be joined to the downpipe which must be positioned directly over the ground-level drain. It may be a stop-end outlet at the end of a run of gutter or a running outlet in the middle of the gutter.

Fit a gutter bracket near the top of the fascia board at one end of the run of guttering (the opposite end to the stop-end outlet, if you have one). Tie a builder's line or piece of string around the base of the bracket.

To position the gutter outlet accurately, hold a plumb line against the fascia directly over the drain. Mark the position on the fascia with a pencil. Fit the gutter outlet no more than 50mm below the level of the roof tiles, following the manufacturer's advice about the size and number of screws.

Stretch the string or builder's line from the bracket along the fascia board and tie it to the outlet. Using a spirit level, check that the string slopes towards the outlet: a slight fall (10mm every 6m of gutter), though not essential, will encourage water to drain efficiently.

Mark the position of the other brackets, spacing them no more than 1m apart and no more than 150mm from any joint or fitting. If the outlet is in the middle of the gutter, repeat the process with a bracket at the other end of the guttering run so that it too slopes towards the outlet.

Fit the rest of the brackets.

Fit a stop-end to the first length of gutter and clip the gutter into position on the brackets. The easiest way to do this is to tilt the gutter to fit under the back clip and then straighten it under the front clip. Line up the gutter end with the insertion depth mark on the bracket (see MAKING IT EASIER, opposite).

Fit a union piece at the other end of the first length and screw it into the fascia, then fit the next length of gutter into it. Continue joining lengths. Cut the last section to fit using a hacksaw and fit a stop-end. Make sure all joints line up with the insertion depth marks on the fittings.

Fitting a downpipe

Here, the downpipe is fitted directly into the outlet. If your eaves overhang, however, you will need to bridge the distance between the gutter and the house wall with two downpipe fittings called offset bends, with an off-cut of downpipe fitted between them (see page 169).

Using a spirit level or plumb line, mark a vertical line on the wall from the outlet to the drain.

Hold a downpipe clip centrally over the line and mark its fixing holes on the wall with a pencil. Repeat down the wall, spacing pipe clips and socket clips (see Steps 4 and 6) no more than 1.8m apart.

Drill the fixing holes with the size of drill bit recommended by the guttering manufacturer. Insert wallplugs into the holes.

Fit the first length of downpipe with its socket uppermost. Leave a 10mm gap between the end of the outlet and the bottom of the socket to allow for expansion in hot weather. Fix a socket clip over the join and screw it into the wallplugs.

Fit the clips to the pipe and screw them into the wallplugs. Continue fitting the pipe until you reach the bottom of the wall.

Fit the shoe to the bottom of the pipe so that it directs water into the drain. Secure the join with a socket clip.

ONE PLANET HOME

Choose water-based paint
Water-based masonry paint dries faster than solvent-based paint. It is less harmful to the environment, produces less odour, and you can wash your brushes in water.

Maintaining the exterior of your house in good condition helps to keep it weatherproof. There should be no need to paint brickwork. If the walls are porous, protect them with a clear waterproofer. If one brick becomes porous or damaged, it should be replaced to avoid damp problems developing. Render and pebbledash need regular painting with masonry paint, which is available in two basic versions – smooth and textured. Smooth masonry paint goes a lot further than textured, but textured paint is better for covering minor blemishes and hairline cracks.

Preparation

Good preparation before you start painting will make the finished surface much more durable.

- Trim back creepers and shrubs, or cover plants with dust sheets.
- Use a pressure washer to clean off dirt and mould from the walls. Start with the lowest pressure setting, and take care not to damage the surface.
- Scrape away any thick growths of mould with a spatula, then treat the masonry with fungicidal solution. Leave it on for 24 hours before washing the wall thoroughly with clean water.
- Fill cracks and holes in a rendered wall with fresh cement containing a little PVA adhesive to help it stick to the masonry.
- Fix gutters if they are loose or leaking. If you are painting the gutters as well, do this before you start on the walls.
- Paint powdery or chalky surfaces with a stabilising primer to bind the loose material to the wall.
- Cover extension roofs and porches, and wrap newspaper around drainpipes to protect them from paint splatters.

project essentials

- **ladder or scaffold tower**
- **100mm or 150mm paintbrush or a long-pile roller**
- **paint kettle or roller tray**

- newspaper
- adhesive tape
- masonry paint

Calculating the amount of paint

As a rough guide, smooth water-based masonry paint will cover 10–12 sq m of flat wall per litre, but may cover only 4 sq m of a very rough surface. Unpainted render will probably need more paint than render that has been painted before. To work out the area of your wall, multiply the length by the height. To calculate the height, climb a ladder, hold the end of a ball of string against the top of the wall and drop the ball to the ground (a helper is a good idea), then measure the length of the string. If you are not painting the whole house, work out the area of each section to be painted and deduct the combined area of the doors and windows. Some manufacturers recommend that the first coat of paint is thinned, so always read the instructions on the can.

Painting exterior walls

Pour the paint into a paint kettle (see page 85) – this will be lighter and easier to handle than a can of paint, and safer at the top of a ladder. A long-pile roller on an extension pole is faster than a paintbrush, but it can be difficult to work with a roller tray up a tall ladder. Only paint when the weather is fine and dry. Painting in direct sunlight can be difficult, especially if you are using white paint, so try and follow the shade. Divide each wall into manageable sections that you can finish in a single session – use features like windows and drainpipes as your boundaries.

B&Q Making it easier

Stipple action
When painting heavily textured walls, hold the brush at 90° and dab the bristles into the surface with a stippling action.

Wrap newspaper around the downpipes and secure it with tape. Start painting at the top of the house and work downwards so the newly painted surface does not get splashed. Push the brush carefully right behind downpipes.

Use short horizontal or vertical strokes, applying a loaded brush to an unpainted area and working back to a painted area.

Paint in the opposite direction to make sure that the surface is completely covered. On rough surfaces, it is better to rotate the brush in all directions to ensure even coverage. If using a roller, vary the angle of the strokes. Cut into corners and obstructions in the same way as you would when painting interior walls (see page 86).

Replacing a damaged brick

Keep an eye on your brickwork – the outer face of an old brick can break down and become porous, allowing rainwater to soak through to its inner face. Eventually a damp patch will appear on the plaster indoors. The same will happen when a brick gets cracked. Much better to fix the problem before the damage is done.

project essentials

- **hammer-action drill with 10mm gauge masonry bit**
- **heavy-duty gloves**
- **cold chisel or bolster chisel**
- **club hammer**
- **trowel**
- **raking tool**
- **old paintbrush**
- **soft brush**

- ready-mix mortar
- replacement brick

B&Q Making it easier

Seal out damp
Brick and masonry sealer forms a protective water-repellent barrier that can help prevent damage by water and damp, while allowing the surface to breathe and moisture to escape. Remove any moss, lichen or loose mortar with a stiff brush before applying, and ensure that the surface is completely dry.

Drill a series of 10mm holes into the mortar joints around the damaged brick.

Use a cold chisel or a bolster chisel and a club hammer to cut into joints until the brick becomes loose.

Tap and wriggle the brick until you can remove it.

Scrape out the old mortar in the cavity with a trowel or bolster chisel. Brush away the dust.

Use a jointing tool to rake out any loose or flaking mortar from the surrounding joints (see IDEAL TOOL, page 227).

Wet the surfaces of the cavity with an old paintbrush.

Spread mortar on the base and ends of the cavity with a trowel.

Wet the surface of the replacement brick and spread mortar on all sides.

Insert the brick into the cavity and tap it with the trowel handle until it aligns with the other bricks. Repoint the surrounding brickwork (see page 227).

When the mortar starts to harden, brush the surface of the bricks with a soft brush.

ideal tool

Mortar and grouting gun
Repointing brickwork is quicker and less messy with a mortar gun. Replace the copper nozzle with the smaller plastic one to use the gun for sealants, grouting, filler and adhesives.

Windows and doors have a big impact on the external appearance of your home. Their most important job is to keep heat in and moisture out, but it's also desirable that they are in keeping with the style of the house and you might decide to replace them as part of a general 'exterior facelift'. The way they are fitted depends on whether the exterior of the house is constructed with solid or cavity walls (see pages 62–63).

Windows in solid walls

In houses built with solid external walls of stone or brick, a wooden window frame often fits snugly in a slight recess (reveal) on the inner side of the opening in the wall. The window will either be flush with the inner wall surface or set back from it, depending on the thickness of the wall. The frame is held in place with nails or screws. Windows in old houses usually have a stone or concrete subsill which sits below the window frame and any wooden sill on the outside of the house.

Lintel

Sash window

Reveal (vertical recess)

Stone or concrete sill

Concrete lintel

Soffit

Reveal

Vertical damp-proof course

Cavity closing brick

Frame cramps

Wooden outer sill

Windows in cavity walls

These days most houses are built with cavity walls and window frames are attached to metal brackets, known as frame cramps, fitted into the walls as they are built. Special bricks are fitted between the window frames and the cavity to close the gap and prevent heat escaping. There also has to be a damp-proof course in line with the frame to prevent moisture transferring from the outer to the inner wall. On the inside wall, the sides and top of the window opening (the reveals and the soffit) are plastered once the window frame is in place to give a neat finish. The window frame's wooden sill sits on a wooden window board that is screwed or nailed directly to the masonry.

B&Q Making it easier

Preventing wet rot
The best way to protect wooden window frames against wet rot is to apply wood preservative, paint or varnish regularly. Always ensure that any new timber used for repairs or replacement is treated with wood preservative. You should also seal any gaps around the outside of window frames with frame sealant if it is a small gap, and mortar if the gap is more than about 10mm wide.

ONE PLANET HOME

Conserving warmth and energy
Make sure your windows are all draughtproofed to help retain warmth and conserve energy (see pages 340–41). New outside doors and windows must meet strict insulation standards in order to reduce heat loss and make your home more energy efficient. Look for products labelled 'Part L compliant.'

Door frames

Doors are usually fitted into a wooden frame consisting of a head at the top, a sill at the bottom and two side posts. The head has projections called horns supporting the frame joints and these are built into the masonry to secure the frame. The sides of the frame are fixed to the wall by wooden plates called pallets, or by metal brackets. Some aluminium and PVCu doors are supplied with their own frames.

Lintels

Where doors and windows are fitted in a loadbearing wall, a rigid horizontal beam called a lintel is installed over the window or door opening to support the masonry above. In an old house the lintels are often stone or wood, which cannot support a wide span. Some brick walls may have a decorative arch of bricks instead of, or as well as, a flat lintel. Each brick in the arch is narrower at the bottom than at the top so that they form a neat curve.

Nowadays, lintels are made from reinforced concrete or steel and they can support a much greater weight and span of masonry. The invention of plate glass coupled with stronger lintels means that single large panes of glass can be fitted safely into loadbearing walls.

Types of exterior doors

Besides a front door, a house may have many other kinds of door leading to the outside, including french doors, aluminium-frame glass doors, and up-and-over or sectional overhead garage doors.

Panelled and flush doors

Main front and back doors are generally panelled or flush wooden doors. Panelled doors may be made from expensive hardwoods or softwood, which may be solid, laminated or veneered.

Flush doors are cheaper than panelled doors. They are usually faced with plywood which needs to be painted to make it weatherproof. Some doors are fitted with panes of glass or leaded lights – small panes of plain or coloured glass held together with lead strips.

Doors often have a moulding called a weatherboard fitted at the bottom to encourage water to flow away from the doorway. Some frames have a weather bar – a metal or plastic strip fitted in the sill to stop rainwater leaking under the door. The door or weatherboard will have a rebate (recess) cut in the bottom in order to clear the bar.

Glazing

Window glass is secured in a bed of putty or glazing mastic in the frame. Small headless nails called glazing sprigs are tapped into the frame to hold the glass while the putty dries. Spring clips hold the glass in metal frames. More putty is smoothed over the top to make a neat finish.

Sometimes glass is secured with thin strips (beads) of hardwood instead of putty. The beads are cut and mitred individually, stuck in place with putty or glazing sealant, then secured with nails or brass screws.

Aluminium-frame glass doors

These doors are made from special double-glazed glass, which is sometimes opaque. The glass is fitted into an aluminium frame and may be one large single pane; if it is a front door, it will have a central aluminium rail fitted with a letter-box. At the back of the house, french doors often lead on to the garden or patio. One panel is fixed and the other slides horizontally on rollers. The panels are usually double-glazed for heat- and sound-insulation.

Garage doors

There are various types of garage doors. In the past, they were usually hinged, but modern garage doors are much more likely to be the up-and-over kind, which is lifted upwards and backwards to clear the opening. These operate either on vertical tracks to the sides of the door, or on horizontal tracks fixed to the garage ceiling. Most types of garage can be fitted with an automatic door-opening system that is operated by remote control from inside the car.

project essentials

- **protective gloves**
- **safety goggles**
- **tape measure**
- **craft knife**
- **hammer**
- **pincers**
- **old chisel or hacking knife**
- **putty knife**
- **paintbrush**

- thin hardboard or plywood
- panel pins
- wood primer paint
- putty

Cracked or broken glass in windows or doors can be very dangerous, especially if you have small children or pets. Security could be compromised and the glass will no longer be weatherproof. If you can't do a full repair straight away, you should at least make a temporary repair and ensure the area is safe. If you have to replace glass in an upstairs window, work from a scaffold tower rather than ladder and avoid working on a windy day. Carry panes on edge to prevent bending and always wear protective gloves. It will take two people to handle large pieces of glass safely.

Making a secure temporary repair

If security is not a problem, polythene sheeting will make a window opening temporarily weatherproof. Remove the broken glass, spread the polythene across the gap and secure it with thin wooden battens nailed to the edges of the frame. If the glass is cracked rather than broken, seal it with waterproof glazing tape. But on an accessible exterior window you will need a more secure repair.

Wearing protective gloves, remove any loose pieces of glass.

Measure the space and cut a piece of thin hardboard or plywood to fit.

Fit the cut board into the frame and tap panel pins into the surrounding wood.

B&Q Making it easier

Weatherproof repair
If weather conditions are bad and a full repair cannot be done straight away, use silicone sealant to make a temporary repair weatherproof.

Leave the broken glass in place and apply silicone sealant around the edge of the pane. Cut a piece of board to fit, and press into the silicone. Run another bead of silicone around the gap between board and frame.

Taking out a broken pane

Spread newspaper on the floor around the window to make it easier to clear up afterwards, and be sure to wear sturdy footwear. If the pane is only cracked, score it with a glass cutter about 25mm from the edge all the way round. Stick strips of adhesive tape across the cracks and scored lines and then tap each piece of glass free with a small hammer. The tape will hold the pieces safely together.

If the pane is smashed, remove jagged pieces still stuck in the putty by gripping each one in turn and working it loose. Wear protective gloves and goggles. Working from the top down, knock out the remaining glass by tapping it gently with a hammer.

Use a chisel or glazier's hacking knife and hammer to remove the old putty. Take out panel pins as you go using a pair of pincers.

Brush away any dust, then seal the wood with primer paint.

Buying replacement glass

A glazier will cut glass for you and advise on the best type of glass for the window to be replaced. If you are replacing glass in a large picture window, or within 800mm of the floor, use safety glass (see page 370).

Measuring pane size and thickness

It will help to ensure you buy the correct thickness if you take a piece of the broken glass with you, wrapped carefully in newspaper. If that isn't possible, measure the thickness of the pane to the nearest millimetre. You may not be able to find an exact match if the glass is old. If so, buy glass slightly thicker, as this will be safer. As a rough guide, use 3mm glass for very small panes, 4mm for windows up to 1 sq m, and 6mm for larger areas.

Measure the height and width of the area, measuring into the frame rebate on each side. Have the new glass cut to 3mm less than both the length and width measurements. Check that the window is square by measuring the diagonals. If they differ by more than a couple of millimetres, make a cardboard template of the window pane and take it to the glazier to use as a guide.

Types of putty

You will need about 500g of linseed oil putty to fill a rebate about 4m in length. Use linseed oil, all-purpose or acrylic putty when glazing painted wooden frames. Brown putty is available for use in stained and varnished wooden frames. For metal frames use all-purpose, acrylic or butyl rubber-based putty.

Installing a pane of glass

Working from outside, clean any debris from the rebate in the frame with a brush or old screwdriver. Rest the pane on a pad of newspaper away from where you are working. Don't stand it on a hard surface such as concrete or it may well crack. Linseed oil putty can be messy to work with. Wet your hands to prevent excessive sticking, and if necessary roll the putty on newspaper or card to remove some of the oil.

Run more putty into the rebate around the window, using your thumb to push the putty well into the edge. Use a putty knife to smooth the putty into a neat fillet running at an angle of 45°, covering the heads of the panel pins and lining up with the putty on the inside of the window. Wet the putty knife to get a really smooth finish and a clean angle at the corners. Allow the putty to harden for about two weeks before painting. When painting the frame, overlap paint from the new putty onto the glass by about 3mm to prevent water from penetrating.

Secure the glass in place by tapping in glazing panel pins at 200mm intervals with a small hammer. They should lie flat against the surface of the glass and protrude 5mm from the frame. Remove surplus putty from the other side of the glass with a putty knife.

Wearing gloves, sit the new pane of glass into the bottom edge and then gently push it into place. Exert gentle pressure around the edges of the glass – not in the middle, especially when working with a large pane, or it may break. Allow the glass to squeeze the putty until you have about a 2mm bed of putty behind the glass.

Knead the putty until it is soft and pliable. Take a palm-sized ball and squeeze a continuous band into the rebate, using your thumb to press it into place. It should be about 3mm thick all around the window.

ideal tool

Putty knife
Use a putty knife to create a neat moulding or fillet around the pane. The blade is shaped on one side to help you get a smooth finish.

Replacing a pane in a beaded casement

To repair a broken pane in a beaded casement window you will need to take out and replace the wooden beads – a slightly more complicated procedure, but not difficult.

Working from inside the room, prise off the beads. Using a large old screwdriver or chisel, start from the middle of the bead and work out, being careful not to damage the mitre joints at the corners.

As you remove the beads, lay them out carefully so that you can replace them in the same positions.

Remove the broken glass as described on page 180. Do remember to wear protective gloves and goggles.

Once all the glass is safely cleared, scrape out the old putty from the rebates with a hacking knife or old chisel. Brush away any dust and paint the rebate with wood primer or primer/undercoat. Allow it to dry thoroughly.

Measure up for the new pane. Take the horizontal and vertical dimensions to the inside of the rebates and reduce the measurements by 3mm to allow some tolerance when fitting.

Knead a palm-sized ball of putty until it is soft and pliable then press it into the rebate with your thumb. It should be about 3mm thick all round. Insert the new pane, slotting it into the bottom rebate first. Press the glass gently around the edges (not in the middle) until you have a 2mm bed of putty behind it.

Run another band of softened putty around the pane, pressing it well into the edges.

Press the casement beads into the putty in the same positions as before. Fit the top bead first, followed by the bottom, then the sides. Tap panel pins through the existing holes.

Clean away the excess putty on both sides of the glass with a putty knife. Repaint the woodwork in the sequence described on page 133.

Remove all rotten wood using an old chisel or narrow-bladed scraper. Dig into the frame until you reach firm, sound wood.

Repairing a rotten window sill

There are many wood repair compounds on the market that will make an effective repair to a rotten window sill. However, if the sill is stained or varnished rather than painted, the repair will remain visible unless the filler is the same colour as the wood.

Knead the repair compound until thoroughly mixed. Follow the manufacturer's instructions and wear protective gloves.

Press the compound into the damaged area with a narrow bladed scraper and smooth the surface to follow the sill profile.

project essentials

- **old chisel**
- **narrow bladed scraper**
- **protective gloves**
- **paintbrushes**

- exterior wood repair compound
- waterproof frame sealant
- paint or varnish

If there are gaps between window frame and wall, seal them using a waterproof frame sealant. Then repaint or varnish the window and frame (see pages 132–33).

Repairing a rusted window frame

Galvanised metal window frames will eventually succumb to rust. Most paints will slow down the rate of corrosion but cannot stop it altogether. When repainting the frame, use a good-quality primer and be sure to reach into any crevices and awkward areas. Pay particular attention to outer corners and edges.

Use a scraper to remove loose and flaking paint.

project essentials

- **scraper**
- **wire brush**
- **paintbrushes**

- medium-grade abrasive paper
- rust remover
- metal primer
- undercoat paint
- top coat paint

Go over the metalwork with a wire brush until you have removed all loose paint or rust.

Smooth the entire surface with medium-grade abrasive paper, paying particular attention to rough edges. Brush off the dust.

Paint the frame with a rust remover and allow it to dry thoroughly for the period advised on the tin. Next paint the frame using a zinc-based metal primer.

Repaint the frame. Apply an undercoat first then a top coat. Follow the sequence on page 133.

Replacement PVCu windows are available in standard sizes with add-on frame extenders so they can be adjusted slightly to fit, or they can be made to measure. Low maintenance, energy efficient and 100% recyclable, PVCu never needs painting and is available in different finishes – white, woodgrain and even oak effect.

Removing an old window and frame

Be prepared for this job to take more than a day. In that case you will need to cover the opening overnight with polythene sheet or hardboard. The most difficult part is removing the old window frame. Make sure you wear safety goggles and heavy-duty gloves, and take care to minimise damage to the surrounding masonry and plaster. If the sill is also old or decayed, then take the opportunity to replace it at the same time as the window. Interior sills are available in wood, MDF or PVCu, which needs no decorating.

1 Start by removing any opening windows. Unscrew them at the hinges, and have someone help you lift them out. Remove the beading and putty to take out any fixed panes. Then make an angled cut through the upright sections of the frame with a handsaw.

2 Use a long bar (or bolster chisel) and club hammer to remove the frame. Hammer the curved end of the long bar into the cut on one side of the window, then pull it upwards to open the joint and prise out the lower piece.

3 Use the curved end of the bar to remove the upper part of the frame. Repeat the process on the other sides of the frame. Prise out the sill too if you plan to replace it.

4 If the frame is fixed with screws, cut through them with a small close quarter hacksaw.

ideal tool

Close quarter hacksaw
This handy tool is ideal for making cuts that would be awkward or impossible with a conventional hacksaw.

Assembling the new window

Check the dimensions to make sure the window will fit; there should be a gap of about 5mm all round. Add frame extenders, if needed (see MAKING IT EASIER). Fit the handle(s) before installing the window.

1 To cut the outer sill of the window to size, measure the depth of the outer wall and cut a notch so the sill will fit snugly around the external brickwork. The sill comes with a protective wrapper so mark this with a pen or pencil and cut with a hacksaw.

2 Screw the outer sill to the window frame. Attach the frame fixers by sliding them evenly down the side track of the window frame.

3 Screw in the ventilator grille(s) on the internal face of the frame and fix the cover vent(s) in place.

B&Q Making it easier

Adjusting the frame size
If the new window isn't quite big enough you can add a total of 40mm to the width or depth by attaching frame extenders.

Fitting the window and sill

Pre-glazed casement windows can be heavy, so get someone to help you lift the new window into place, and if necessary remove the opening casement to do so. The window frame is fixed to the interior walls along both vertical edges. The interior sill is installed after the window.

Mark the fixing points and make a small notch in the internal plasterwork for each. Cut a notch each side for the sill, if replacing. Insert the prepared window and wedge it with spacers (shims).

Use a spirit level to check the window is level and adjust with spacers if necessary.

Check that the window is vertical using the spirit level, and add spacers to straighten it if needed.

Drill a pilot hole, insert a wallplug and screw the frame in place at each fixing point. Measure and cut the interior sill to fit around the window reveals. Check it is level: you might need to insert spacers to level it. Then secure it with a suitable grab adhesive, or masonry nails or screws.

Fill wider gaps around the window's exterior with expanding foam filler. Once dry, trim it flush using a sharp craft knife.

Use a frame sealant along smaller gaps for a neat finish.

 Making it easier

If fitting windows yourself, you must apply for Building Control approval and confirm the energy efficiency levels of the windows before installing them. Insulation levels are measured as U values (the lower the U value, the better the insulation level). All B&Q PVCu windows are Building Regulations compliant. If you live in a listed building or in a conservation area, additional regulations are likely to apply, so check with your local planning department before carrying out any work.

Trimming and finishing

There are trims and profiles in many different shapes and sizes to cover sealant and fixings and give a neat, professional finish, inside and out.

Wider gaps around the outside of the window can be covered with a PVCu scotia trim. Seal the frame behind the trim with frame sealant before fixing the trim. The trim can be stuck in place with frame sealant.

Inside, use a trim wide enough to cover the fixings. Secure in place with frame sealant.

Finishing touches

See pages 136–37 for how to fit curtains and a blind for your new window.

The procedure for fitting a letterplate or cat flap is similar. Both are simple jobs but always follow the instructions carefully and double-check all measurements before making the first cut.

Measuring up for a letterplate

Letterplates are available in a range of designs and materials. Some have a handle incorporated that doubles as a door-knocker. You can also fit an internal flap cover on the inside of the door, which will reduce draughts and look neater. If using solid brass screws, which are relatively soft, drill full-length pilot holes and don't use a power screwdriver or the screw slot may be damaged.

> ### project essentials
>
> - **long ruler**
> - **pencil**
> - **power drill with 6mm and 8mm gauge twist bits**
> - **padsaw or jigsaw**
> - **narrow chisel**
> - **mallet**
> - **small adjustable spanner**
> - **hacksaw**
>
> - letterplate with fixings
> - adhesive tape
> - medium-grade abrasive paper

1 Working from the outside of the door, measure the depth of the cross rail and make a pencil mark at the mid-point in two places, about 35mm apart.

2 Draw a horizontal line between the two marks.

3 Measure the width of the cross rail and find the centre point. Draw a short vertical line across the horizontal one you have already made.

4 Centre the letterplate over the intersection of the lines and mark the position of the fixing bolts on either side.

Fitting the letterplate

This job will be far quicker and easier if you use a power jigsaw to cut the opening (see IDEAL TOOL, opposite).

1 Drill clearance holes for the fixing bolts. Make the holes slightly larger than the diameter of the bolt shank – normally about 6mm.

2 With a pencil, mark where the opening will be cut. It should be a fraction larger than the hinged part of the letterplate.

3 Drill a hole at each corner of the slot. Select a drill bit large enough to create a hole into which you will be able to insert the blade of a padsaw or power jigsaw – normally about 8mm.

> ### ideal tool
>
> **Power jigsaw**
> A power jigsaw will make light work of cutting out difficult holes in wood. It is ideally suited for working in a restricted space. Blades are available with different numbers of teeth. Before use, check that the blade is fitted securely and that the roller guide is lubricated.

Insert the blade of a padsaw or power jigsaw into one of the corner holes and carefully cut around the rectangle all the way through the door.

After cutting the opening, use a narrow chisel and mallet to cut recesses for the hinge-pin. Clean out the corners of the opening and smooth the edges with abrasive paper.

Fit the letterplate into position using the nuts supplied. If the bolts are longer than the thickness of your door, shorten them with a hacksaw.

Fitting a cat flap

There are many types of pet door on the market. The majority have a simple locking mechanism but more sophisticated versions have a remote-controlled door operated by a collar worn by the resident pet. Whichever type you choose, it will come with a full set of fixing instructions, which you should read carefully before starting work.

Decide where to position the cat flap, taking into account ease of installation and ease of use. Stick the template supplied to the door with adhesive tape. Check it is level and drill through the four points indicated on the template. The holes need to be big enough to insert the blade of a padsaw or jigsaw to begin cutting – normally about 8mm.

Remove the template and, using a ruler, draw lines between the four holes. These mark the outline of the opening.

Hold both sides in place through the open flap and screw them together, fixing each screw through the clearance holes. Check that the flap is swinging freely.

Use a padsaw or power jigsaw to cut through the door along the line. Push out the piece and smooth rough edges with medium-grade abrasive paper.

project essentials

- **power drill with 8mm gauge twist bit**
- **long ruler**
- **pencil**
- **padsaw or power jigsaw**
- **screwdriver**

- cat flap with fixings
- adhesive tape
- medium-grade abrasive paper

Hold the cat flap in position, aligned with the hole. Check it is level and drill clearance holes for the screw fixing positions.

ROOFS CONSTRUCTION

Most houses have a pitched or sloping roof, made from a triangular-shaped wooden frame which is covered with tiles or slates. The weight of the tiles is supported by pairs of sloping rafters, whose heads meet at a central ridge board and whose lower ends are fixed to timber wall plates on the external walls of the house. Tiles are made from baked clay or concrete, and may be flat or moulded into various profiles. Slates are smooth flat pieces, either cut from rock (natural slate) or man-made. Pitched roofs can be constructed in several different ways, depending on the size and design of the house.

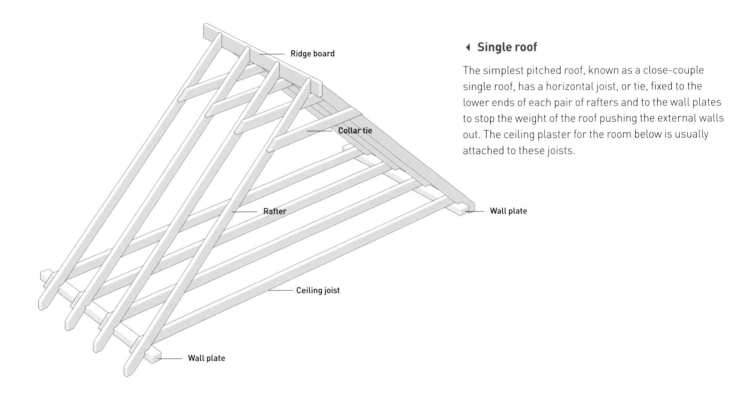

◄ **Single roof**

The simplest pitched roof, known as a close-couple single roof, has a horizontal joist, or tie, fixed to the lower ends of each pair of rafters and to the wall plates to stop the weight of the roof pushing the external walls out. The ceiling plaster for the room below is usually attached to these joists.

Double roof ▶

A roof spanning a large area may have horizontal beams called purlins fixed halfway down the rafters, in addition to the joists or ties across their lower ends. This type of roof is know as a double or purlin roof. A very large roof may have several purlins fitted at intervals down the rafters. Diagonal struts give extra support to the purlins. They are fixed at one end to the purlin and at the other end to the wall plate of a central, loadbearing partition wall. Horizontal timbers called binders and vertical ones called hangers may also be fitted to support the joists.

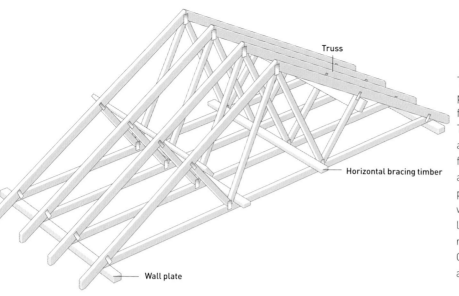

Truss

Horizontal bracing timber

Wall plate

◀ **Trussed roof**

This type of roof is constructed from individual prefabricated trusses. Each truss is a triangle made from a pair of rafters and a joist braced with struts. These trusses are linked to each other by horizontal and diagonal bracing timbers, which means that very few trussed roofs can be converted into living space, and you must not cut into one without seeking professional advice. The trusses are usually fixed to the walls with metal straps. Trussed rafters are relatively light, they allow for a fairly wide span, and there is no need for a ridge board or a loadbearing partition wall. Older houses with this type of roof may have purlins adding support to the rafters.

Covering a pitched roof ▶

Before the tiles or slates are fixed in place, a roof is lined with sarking, which may be bituminous roofing felt or other breathable material. To make sure it is waterproof, the sarking is laid horizontally in strips with each new section overlapping the one below it, working from the bottom of the slope up to the ridge. Sawn softwood battens are then nailed to the rafters, over the sarking.

Tiles and slates are laid across the roof in rows or courses, with the bottom of each course overlapping the one below. As with sarking, they are laid starting at the eaves and working up the slope to the ridge. Tiles have a nib that hooks over the battens and holds them in place, though some are fixed with nails or clips as well. Slates are held in place with nails alone or nails and copper rivets. The size and type of tiles and slates and the pitch of the roof all determine the fixings that are used.

Curved tiles are used for capping the ridge (or the hips of a hipped-end roof, see below), to keep the junction of the two slopes weatherproof. Where a tile or slate meets a wall or chimney, a strip of lead, zinc or mortar, known as flashing, covers the join to make it weatherproof. Flashing, or specially formed valley tiles, are fitted along the valley where two roofs meet.

Ridge

Tiles

Batten

Sarking

Gable roof

Hipped-end roof

◀ **Roof shape**

Gable and hipped-end roofs are the two most common pitched roof shapes. With a gable roof, the end walls of the house are built right up to the ridge, following the pitch of the roof and forming a triangular gable end. Hipped-end roofs slope down at the end as well as the sides, making them a more elaborate construction. They require additional timbers known as hip rafters, jack rafters, crown rafters and cripple rafters. A large house may well have both types of roof, and the junctions where they meet form 'valleys'.

ROOFS CONSTRUCTION AND REPAIRS

There are different types of eaves and verges protecting the edges of roofs where they meet the house walls. This is where guttering is attached, to drain water that falls on the roof (see pages 168–69). Flat roofs are usually covered in bituminous-based asphalt or roofing felt. Flat roofs tend to have a shorter life than pitched roofs and most problems should be left to the professionals, but you can buy a special sealant for making your own repairs to splits or blisters in the roofing felt.

Flush eaves

Eaves

The eaves are the bottom edges of the roof where the lower ends of the rafters join the external walls of the house. The ends of the rafters may be cut level with the walls, in which case they are called flush eaves. Fascia boards are nailed across the ends of the rafters to protect them from the elements and the guttering is fixed to the fascia boards. Alternatively, the ends of the rafters may project beyond the walls and the guttering is fixed to them. These are known as open eaves. Projecting rafters are sometimes boxed in by a fascia board and a soffit board, in which case they are called closed eaves.

Open eaves

Closed eaves

Flush verge

Ventilation

It's essential that air can circulate through a roof space so that condensation cannot build up and cause the timbers to rot. There may be vents at the eaves and ridge, in addition to breathable roofing felt and ventilation tiles at the upper edge of the roof slope.

Enclosed projecting verge

Verges

The sloping edges of a gable roof are called the verges and, as with the eaves, they may be level with the exterior walls or extend beyond them. If the verges are level with the walls, the last rafters are on the inside of the walls and the gap between the roof covering and the brickwork is sealed with mortar. Where the verges extend beyond the walls an outer rafter is fitted beyond each wall to cover the ends of the battens and wall plate. Long timbers called barge boards are fitted to the ends of these rafters, and the underside may be enclosed with soffit boards.

Flat roofs

Rear extensions and outbuildings often have a timber-framed flat roof covered with roofing felt. In fact no roof can be totally flat, or rainwater would just settle and cause it to collapse. Timbers in the roof frame called firring strips taper slightly so that the roof can drain. Roofing boards are laid on the firring strips, and three layers of roofing felt, bonded together with bitumen, are laid on top of the boards. The joint between a flat roof and an adjacent wall is sealed with metal flashing.

Vents at the eaves are essential so that air can circulate and moisture escape; there may also be vents through the roof alongside the junction with the house wall. Insulation is vital over a living space, either blocks of insulating material between the firrings, or sheet insulation laid on the ceiling.

Flashing

3 layers of roof felt

Firring strip

Roofing boards

Insulation

Air gap

Repairing roof felt

Flat roofs are not particularly durable, and it will pay you to keep a close eye on one. Besides weathering, the felt is prone to damage by careless feet and ladders. A prompt repair will stop rainwater seeping through and causing more serious structural damage.

If the edge of a strip of roofing felt is lifting from the surface, you can stick it down with specially formulated roof and gutter sealant. Wear protective gloves while you work to avoid getting the spray on your skin. If there is moss and lichen on the roof surface, treat the area with a fungicide before starting. Try to work on a warm day and avoid damp conditions.

Use a stiff brush to clean away loose chippings and dirt. Align a piece of card against the raised edge to protect the adjacent area from any stray sealant. Lift the flap of felt and spray the roof underneath with roof and gutter sealant. Leave to dry for the specified time then press the felt down firmly.

Patching a tear

Fix tears in roofing felt by inserting a patch of new felt underneath. Check the instructions and make sure you leave enough time for the sealant to dry before you stick the new patch down.

Lift the torn edge of felt and spray roof and gutter sealant underneath it and on the area adjacent to it. Allow to dry for the time specified by the manufacturer.

Cut a patch of matching felt, large enough to fit under the torn portion and cover the area around it. Slide the patch into place underneath the tear, and stick it down firmly.

Lift the torn section and spray sealant onto the upper surface of the new patch underneath it, and again leave it to dry.

Press the felt down and spray sealant liberally along all the joints.

ROOFS TILES AND SLATES

Check your roof regularly for broken tiles or slates. If you wait for it to spring a leak, you will find that much unnecessary damage has already been done. Provided you are comfortable working at heights, and you have proper, safe access equipment (see pages 356–57), there's no reason why you shouldn't make repairs yourself. When buying replacement tiles or slates, it will help if you can take one with you to get the best match.

Temporary repair of a roof tile

If you can't replace a cracked tile straight away, do a temporary repair to stop the leak.

1 Thoroughly clean the area around the crack using a wire brush and wipe away the dust and debris. Apply a coat of flashing strip primer to the crack and the area around it.

2 Cut off a piece of flashing strip to fit the length of the tile.

3 Peel off the backing from the flashing strip, lift the lower edge of the tile above the broken one and stick the flashing strip over the crack, making sure it is completely covered.

4 Press the flashing strip securely into place.

Replacing broken tiles

Tiles are usually simply hooked in place on nibs that fit over wooden battens. But occasionally alternate courses will be nailed or clipped to the battens: it depends on the type of roof you have and the weather conditions in your area. If so you may need to cut the tiles free with a special tool called a slater's ripper, which you can hire.

1 Take out the highest broken tile first. Slide the adjoining ones up, and tilt the broken one sideways to separate it. The tiles below that can simply be lifted off. Carry the tiles to the ground one at a time, or lower them in a bucket to a waiting helper. Replace the lowest course first, working from right to left. Carefully lift the adjacent tile and hook the nibs over the batten as you slide each one into place.

2 When you get to the last tile of the course, lift the tiles on either side and wiggle the new tile until it hooks over the batten and sits correctly.

3 Move to the next course up. When you get to the last tile you must raise the lower edge of the tile above and slide the new tile under the tiles on either side. This can be a bit awkward, but shift the tile from left to right and it should slot into place.

project essentials

- **wire brush**
- **scissors**
- **ladder with stand-off bracket**
- **roof ladder**
- **bucket on rope**
- **slater's ripper, if required**
- flashing strip primer
- self-adhesive flashing strip
- replacement tiles

safety first

Ladders and scaffolds
To make even minor roof repairs, you must have an ordinary ladder and a roof ladder (see page 356). The ladder to the roof should have a stand-off bracket, so that it rests against the wall not the guttering. A roof ladder has rubber wheels and hooks at one end. The wheels allow it to be pushed up the roof without dislodging loose tiles. When the top is level with the ridge, you turn the ladder over and hook it on the ridge. It must reach from the ridge all the way to the gutter so that you can step onto it easily from the ordinary ladder. For more extensive roof repairs you must have proper scaffolding – it's the law.

Temporary repair of a slate roof

Unlike roof tiles, slates are all nailed to battens below. If a slate has cracked and you are having difficulty finding a replacement, make a temporary repair to prevent water from seeping through. Wear protective gloves to avoid cutting yourself on sharp edges.

project essentials

- **ladder with stand-off bracket**
- **roof ladder**
- **heavy-duty gloves**
- **wire brush**
- **scissors**
- **bolster chisel**

- flashing strip primer
- self-adhesive flashing strip

Clean the crack and the area around it with a wire brush and apply flashing strip primer.

Cut a piece of self-adhesive flashing strip long enough to run the entire length of the slate.

Gently raise the lower edge of the slate above and insert a bolster chisel to hold it up. Peel off the backing and insert the strip.

Press the flashing strip firmly into place.

Replacing a slate

When you replace a single slate – or the last in a group of slates – you won't be able to nail it to the batten, so you will need to secure it with a metal strip. Removing broken slates can be tricky. If the nails are old and rusty, they may just pull out or break, but you might need to cut through them with a slater's ripper, which you can hire.

project essentials

- **ladder with stand-off bracket**
- **roof ladder**
- **heavy-duty gloves**
- **slater's ripper, if required**
- **bucket and rope**
- **hammer**
- **tinsnips**

- 25mm-wide strip of aluminium or copper
- 100mm large-head galvanised clout nails
- replacement slates

Remove the first broken slate carefully, wiggling it from side to side to dislodge it. Take it to the ground, or lower it in a bucket to a helper. Slates have sharp edges so don't risk letting any fall from the roof, which could be dangerous. Use tinsnips to cut the metal strip to the length of the slate plus about 100mm.

You should just be able to see the wooden batten between the two slates above the one you are replacing. Hammer a galvanised clout nail through the metal strip, about 25mm from the end, and fix it into the batten between the slates.

Slide the new slate under the two slates in the course above, with the bevelled edge facing outwards. Align the lower edge with the adjoining slates. Bend the end of the metal strip up and over the bottom edge of the new slate and press it down flat.

Whether you are looking for privacy from the neighbours, protection from wind or sun, to enhance the look of your property or to make your home more secure, there is a fence, gate or garden structure for you. Before investing, consider the location and period of your property. Choose something in keeping with the style of your home and environment.

Fencing

Fencing is the most popular way of marking a boundary. It is fairly easy to erect and cheaper than building a wall, though don't overlook the cost and effort of maintenance over the years – you will have to treat the timber regularly to protect it from insects and weathering. Privacy is likely to be your primary concern, and there are a number of options offering good screening. However, if the site of your fence is exposed to prevailing winds, take care not to choose one that offers so much resistance that it falls down. A fence with an open structure, such as a picket fence, would be a better option.

Planning your fence

Before putting up a fence discuss the plans with your neighbours. You need to check the exact line of the boundary and make sure the posts are positioned on your side. Before you take down an old fence first make sure it's yours. If it belongs to a neighbour and they won't allow you to take it down, you can erect another alongside provided it is on your side of the boundary. There is an unwritten rule that a good neighbour puts up a fence with the post and rails facing their own property, but this is not a legal obligation. Unless the boundary line meets a highway, you generally do not need planning permission for a fence less than 2m high.

Lap panel

Easy to put up, offering good screening and value for money, a lap panel fence is a popular choice. Ready-made panels are fitted between posts cemented into the ground. The panels usually come in standard 1.83m widths but can be cut down. They are available in heights of 0.6m–1.83m. Like all timber fences, a lap panel fence will need periodic treatment with wood preservative.

Combination trellis and lap panel

Add a trellis to the top of your panel fence to give increased height where you need it. The trellis is ideal for training climbing plants, creating a less stark effect than a solid fence, and offering more natural shade and privacy.

Closeboard

A closeboard fence consists of vertical featheredge boards (tapered on one side) which are nailed onto horizontal arris rails secured to the posts. It offers excellent screening and security – the vertical boards make a sturdy fence, good for keeping out intruders.

Picket

A picket fence is formed of a row of vertical pales with rounded or pointed tops. Available in panels usually no more than 1.2m high, this kind of fence is often used at the front of a house, where a boundary mark rather than screening is needed.

Willow or hazel panel

Panels of interwoven willow or hazel are ideal in a cottage garden, giving an informal, rustic feel. They are just one of a range of more unusual fencing options that can dramatically enhance your outdoor space.

Trellis

Trellis comes in a variety of forms and materials, including softwood, wood-effect synthetics and recycled material. It can be nailed between fence posts or fixed to the top of an existing fence or wall to give added height. It is perfect for supporting climbing plants, which will create their own natural leafy screen.

Trellis panels

Rigid panels of trellis made from softwood can be secured between fence posts to create a substantial and attractive freestanding screen. Or choose curved-profile trellis to create a striking garden feature.

Gates

Gates come in many different designs and may be made from wood or metal. They can be hung from timber posts, attached to a wall or hung on brick or concrete piers. Before you buy a gate, consider carefully your needs: how wide should it be and how will you hang it? You also need to establish which way the gate should open – both right- and left-handed gates are available. You may need one of each if you are putting up a pair of gates.

Entrance gate

An entrance gate needs to be sturdy enough to withstand continuous use. For additional strength, a wooden gate can be braced with a diagonal strut running from the latch to the opposite corner.

Metal gate

An ornate metal gate is an elegant feature that will complement brick or stonework equally well. They are often supplied with built-in hinge and latch fittings.

Boarded gate

Creating perfect privacy in a rustic-style garden, a boarded gate is also designed to form an unobtrusive entrance within a panel fence.

Picket gate

A picket gate will sit attractively alongside picket fencing, a wall or hedge. The pale tops can be square, rounded or pointed, and the wooden pales can be painted or stained.

Driveway gate

Choose a single gate or a pair that meet in the middle. Check you have space across the drive for it to swing fully open.

Structures

A pergola or an arbour can add a whole new dimension to even the smallest garden. Carefully situated, such a feature will draw the eye and entice visitors to explore. Climbing plants such as wisteria or honeysuckle can be trained to grow around the structure to create natural shade and a leafy retreat.

Timber pergola

A pergola, when supporting climbing plants, creates a natural 'roof' over a patio or walkway.

Timber arbour

An arbour provides a secluded spot and outlook from which to admire the garden.

FENCES AND GATES REPAIRS

Wooden gates and fences are prone to rot or attack by insects. To prolong their life, treat them regularly with wood preservative. You should also avoid piling earth up against a fence and where possible install gravel boards at its base.

Reinforcing a rotten fence post

The part of a wooden fence post most likely to rot is the section buried underground. If not reinforced in time, it will eventually collapse and pull down the fence.

Repairing an arris rail

A broken arris rail can be fixed with an arris rail bracket, a length of galvanised steel specially shaped to fit the rail and ready drilled with holes through which you secure it with galvanised screws or nails. If the arris rail is cracked near the post use a flanged bracket and fasten the flanges to the post.

Support the fence with lengths of timber on either side. Dig a hole around the base of the post, cut the rotten part away and remove any concrete. Coat sound wood with preservative. Place a concrete spur in the hole against the remains of the post. Insert coach bolts through the holes in the spur and tap them with a hammer to mark the post. Then drill holes through the post at the marked spots. Push the bolts through the post and spur so the tails appear on the spur side. Put on the nuts and tighten with a spanner. Brace the post with lengths of timber, checking it is vertical with a spirit level. Fill the hole with concrete, leaving the timber supports in place for 48 hours while it sets.

Replacing a panel or post

If a post or panel is rotten it may need replacing altogether. Panels come in a standard size so finding a new one to fit shouldn't be difficult.

project essentials

- **nail bar**
- **hacksaw**
- **hammer**
- **pincers**
- **power drill with twist bit**
- **spirit level**
- **long bar**
- **shovel**

- fence panel or post
- 75mm galvanised nails
- timber props
- cement and aggregate or post cement

1 Lever back the side frame of the panel with a nail bar to expose the nails joining it to the post.

2 Saw through the old nails with a hacksaw. Hammer in protruding nails or pull them out with pincers. If removing a panel, repeat at the opposite end. If the new panel isn't an exact fit, plane it a little each side, or close any gap with a thin fillet of wood. Drill six evenly spaced pilot holes horizontally through the framing batten at each end of the new panel, front and back, and fix it to the post with 75mm galvanised nails.

3 To remove a post, detach the panels on either side and pull them away from it. Dig out the base of the post and remove any concrete. If this proves difficult, cut a notch in the old post and lever it out with a long bar. Ensure the replacement post is the same size as the original and place it in the hole. Support the fence with timber props while you renail the panels either side (see Step 2). Check the post is vertical with a spirit level and concrete it in place, sloping the surface of the concrete away from the post to drain off rainwater. Leave the props in place for 48 hours while it sets.

Wood preservative
A coat of preservative will drastically extend the life of a fence or gate. Most treatments will keep fungi and insects at bay for several years. The wood needs to be completely dry, so the best time to apply it is in late summer after a dry period and when no rain is expected so. Paint it on with a block paintbrush or use a garden pressure spray; wear protective gloves and, if spraying, safety goggles and a mask.

Repairing a small area of rot

Small patches of rot on a wooden gate area easily treated without having to replace the whole gate.

With a small wooden mallet and a chisel, chip away the rot back to sound wood. Coat the area in preservative and allow to dry.

ONE PLANET HOME

Preserving wood without harming the environment
Old-fashioned wood preservatives made from tar oil were foul-smelling and could be harmful to plants. Modern preservers are much more pleasant to work with. They are usually solvent- or water-based. The odourless, water-based preservers are the least environmentally harmful. They are also available in a wide variety of stylish colours.

> ### project essentials
>
> - **wooden mallet**
> - **chisel**
> - **sanding block**
>
> - wood preservative
> - outdoor wood filler
> - abrasive paper

Fill the cavity with wood filler, which sets in about 15 minutes. Then sand it flush with the timber.

Adding a brace to a sagging gate

A gate may sag if it has no diagonal brace or if an existing brace is not strong enough. Lift and wedge the gate into its proper position

before measuring a new brace. The brace should fit snugly between the cross-rails on the back with the top pointing towards the latch. Cut it from a length of wood the same thickness as the cross-rails. Take the gate off its hinges, drill pilot holes, and fix the new brace to the pales with countersunk galvanised screws.

Strengthening a gate corner

If your gate sags, first check whether the hinges are loose. If not, the problem may be caused by the timber joints having worked loose at the corner of the gate.

Force waterproof adhesive into the loose joint and press it together with a sash clamp.

> ### project essentials
>
> - **sash clamp**
> - **screwdriver**
>
> - waterproof adhesive
> - metal bracket
> - galvanised screws

When the glue is dry, leave the sash clamp in place while you screw a metal bracket to the front of the gate to hold the joint.

Treating a rusting gate

Old metal gates and railings will quickly deteriorate once rust gets in, but you can give them a new lease of life with special rust-inhibiting metal paint.

One coat should be enough over a previously painted surface, but always read and follow the guidelines on the tin.

> ### project essentials
>
> - **wire brush**
> - **safety goggles**
> - **cloth**
> - **paintbrush**
>
> - medium-grade abrasive paper
> - white spirit
> - metal paint with rust inhibitor

Remove loose rust and paint with a wire brush or abrasive paper. Wear safety goggles, especially on a windy day.

Wipe down the surface with a cloth soaked in white spirit.

Apply one coat of rust-inhibiting metal paint.

If you are building a new fence with a gated opening, erect the gate and posts first and build the fence from them. If replacing an old gate, be sure to measure up precisely. Gates are sold in metric and imperial sizes and conversions are not always accurate, so note down the exact size you need and take a tape measure with you. Consider also which way you want it to open. Most gates open into a property rather than out.

Installing a picket gate

For a light gate the gateposts should be about 100mm square and 610mm longer than the gate height. For heavier gates – over 1.2m high or wide – posts should be thicker and at least 760mm longer than the gate height; check the manufacturer's specifications. Wooden gateposts should be treated with preservative before installing. They must be set in concrete since post spikes do not give enough support. Choose fittings that have been japanned (lacquered) or galvanised to deter rust.

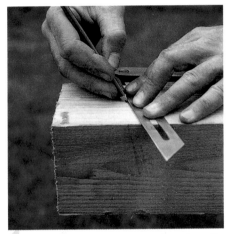

1 If your gate posts have not been 'weathered' – cut the top to a slant so that rainwater will run off – you will need to do this first. Use a sliding bevel to mark a 20° angle from the top of the post.

2 Continue the line square down the face of the post and saw neatly along it. Paint the cut edge with wood preservative; if the wood is untreated, paint the whole post.

3 When you have decided which way you want the gate to open, lay it face down on level ground. Position the posts either side with their tops 50mm higher than the top of the gate and a 5mm gap either side of the gate to allow it to open and close freely. Use two timber lengths to raise the gate slightly so that it sits flush with the gateposts. Adjust as necessary with timber off-cuts or wedges.

4 Place the hinges in position on the back of the gate. Mark the screw positions and drill one pilot hole. Test it by driving in a screw to check that the drill bit is not too large. Drill the remaining pilot holes.

5 Screw the hinges in place using galvanised screws. If you find it tricky to position them accurately on the post (see MAKING IT EASIER), wait to fit them and the latch until the gate is hung.

project essentials

- **panel saw**
- **sliding bevel**
- **pencil**
- **power drill with twist bits**
- **screwdriver**
- **trowel**
- **spade or post-hole borer**
- **spirit level**

- 2 gateposts
- wood preservative
- gate
- 5 lengths of timber (braces and supports)
- 2 hinges
- gate latch
- galvanised screws
- cement and aggregate or post cement

Drill pilot holes for the latch screws, then screw the latch in place. Don't forget to allow a 5mm gap between gate and post.

Brace the gate and posts with three lengths of timber to make sure the construction is solid. Use the braced gate to mark the position of the post holes.

Use a spade or post-hole borer to dig post holes roughly a spade and a half wide, and deep enough to leave a 50mm clearance gap beneath the gate so it can open freely. Check this is sufficient by laying a spirit level on the ground that the gate will open over. If necessary, level the ground. In soft ground, you should dig a trench between the post holes about 300mm wide and 200mm deep and fill it with concrete. This will help prevent the posts being pulled inwards by the weight of the gate. Lower the gateposts into the holes and check they are level with a spirit level.

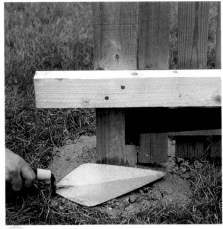

Use timber props to hold the gate and posts in position. Mix the concrete (see page 244) then concrete the posts into the ground, sloping the surface downwards to direct rainwater away from the wood.

Allow the concrete to set for 48 hours before removing the props and brace.

Fixing a gatepost to a wall

If you need to attach a gate to a wall, fix the first post using expanding masonry bolts. These have an expanding section that fits into a drilled hole in the masonry. The post is then fitted over the stud and the nut tightened, causing the expanding section to open out and grip the sides of the hole.

Use three fittings for a post 1.2m or higher; two for anything less. First use a flat wood bit to drill recesses in the post just deep enough for the nuts and wide enough to allow access for a socket spanner. Then change bits and drill clearance holes for the studs right through the timber. Take a long masonry bit of the same diameter and, holding the post against the wall, drill pilot holes into the masonry. Accuracy is crucial, or the bolts will not function! Remove the post and enlarge the holes in the wall using a masonry bit the same size as the expanding section. Insert the expanding section into the wall, hang the post on the studs, place the washers and nuts on the ends and tighten with a socket spanner, taking care not to overtighten.

Expanding masonry bolt

FENCES ERECTING A PANEL FENCE

safety first

Wear strong gloves to protect your hands from splinters. Take particular care when applying wood preservative, and wear safety goggles if recommended by the manufacturer.

The secret to a successful panel fence is in the preparation. Bear in mind that this project is hard work and you'll find it a lot easier if you have at least one helper. Clear away vegetation and pot any shrubs or plants that you will want to replant once the fence is up. To give your plants time to recover, the best time to erect a fence is early spring and late autumn. Prefabricated fence panels come in a standard 1.83m width and are generally available in four heights (900mm, 1.2m, 1.52m and 1.83m).

Marking out and digging post holes

First decide whether you want to set your posts in concrete or in post supports. The former produces a sturdier fence but is harder work and the posts need to be at least 600mm taller than the fence panels. Metal post supports (see MAKING IT EASIER) are a quicker and easier alternative, but the resulting fence will not be as solid. Fencing timbers come ready-treated, but it's still a good idea to soak the feet of your posts overnight in a bucket of wood preservative.

project essentials

- protective gloves
- long tape measure
- spade or post-hole borer
- club hammer
- spirit level
- 2 builder's lines
- panel saw
- power drill with twist bits
- trowel
- hammer

- canes
- fence posts and panels
- timber props
- bricks
- 75mm galvanised nails
- cement and aggregate or post cement
- post caps
- silicone sealant

Stretch a long tape measure taut from end to end along the line of the fence. Measure out the position for each post and mark it by pushing a cane into what will be the centre of each post hole. If you are using 1.83m-wide panels and your posts are 100mm wide, the centres of the posts will be 1.93m apart.

Dig all the post holes. If there are a lot, consider hiring a post-hole borer. A standard depth of 450mm is usually enough, though in soft ground you should dig deeper holes and use longer posts to compensate.

With a club hammer, drive in temporary wooden props to hold the first post in place, using a spirit level to make sure it is vertical.

Erect the last post the same way, checking it is vertical and supporting it with props. Run two builder's lines between the top and bottom of these posts, along the line of the fence. Rest the other posts loosely in their holes.

Cutting fence panels

Your fence run is unlikely to divide into an exact number of panels, so you will need to know how to cut one down to fit.

Carefully remove the framing battens from one end of a panel and move them in to the required width. Sandwich them either side of the panel and nail them in place.

Saw the panel flush with the outer edge of the repositioned framing battens.

B&Q Making it easier

Using post supports
Metal post spikes are an alternative to setting fence posts in concrete, provided the ground is firm. Buy supports that match the size of your fence posts.
Fit the driving tool or dolly (left) into the cup of the spike and hammer it into the earth with slow firm strokes. If you hit a rock, dig it out and start again or the finished post will not be true. Keep checking the spike is vertical with a spirit level. Continue driving into the earth until the top of the cup is level with the ground. Use a sledge-hammer to hammer the fence post into the cup.

Building the fence

Posts and panels should be erected alternately as you work down the line of the fence. Remember to keep checking that the panels are level and straight using a spirit level.

Fence clips

As an alternative to nailing panels directly to the fence posts you can use fence clips. First attach the fence clips to the post, then slide the panel between the jaws of the clips and nail or screw the panel to the clips. If at a later date you want to remove a panel, fence clips will make this a little easier. However, fence clips are very visible on a finished fence.

Drill six evenly spaced pilot holes into the batten framing of the panel on both sides and at each end. Raise the panel 50mm–75mm above the ground by temporarily supporting it on bricks. This gap will help prevent it rotting from the bottom up.

Lay a spirit level on the panel to check it is level, then nail it to the post with galvanised nails. The top of the panel should be a consistent distance (at least 25mm) below the top of the post.

Attach the second panel to the post, using temporary props to keep the fence vertical. Continue working this way until all the panels are in place.

Make sure each post is touching both builder's lines, and check that it is vertical using a spirit level. Mix the concrete (see page 244) and fill the post hole to just above ground level. Smooth the surface downwards so that rainwater will drain away from the wood.

Soak the post caps in a bucket of water – this will help prevent splitting as you nail them on. Apply a silicone-based sealant to the underside to reduce the chance of water seeping beneath and rotting the top of the post.

Nail a post cap to the top of each post.

Fencing on a slope

To erect a panel fence on a slope, you still need to fix the posts vertically and the panels horizontally, as you would on flat ground, but you should step the fence panels to match the gradient. Remember when ordering materials that longer posts will be required to compensate for the stepped panels. If you can, try and keep the steps even, if necessary digging out or building up the ground beneath to ensure the triangular gap below each section is roughly equal. Fill this gap with a length of gravel board, which is easily cut to fit.

Gravel board

Gravel boards are specially treated timbers that are fitted horizontally at the base of a fence. They protect the fence panels from rot by raising them off the ground. A rotten gravel board is much easier to replace than an entire fence panel. To fit gravel boards as you build a panel fence, leave a 150mm gap below the panels. Measure and cut 25mm-thick boards to fit between the posts. Fix them with galvanised screws or nails inserted at an angle into the posts. Countersink screws, or drill pilot holes for nails.

Post cap
Panel
Post
Gravel board
Concrete

A closeboard fence is a popular alternative to panel fencing. Featheredge boards, tapered on one edge, are nailed to horizontal arris rails which are secured to the fence posts. This kind of fence is very good for privacy and security but can be quite expensive.

Erecting the posts and arris rails

Some fence posts come with ready-made slots (housings) for the triangular arris rails; others will need to be notched prior to installation. Use three arris rails for a fence over 1.2m high; two for anything lower. Make sure each post is the right way round: the back of the fence is the side where the arris rail is visible. The distance between posts should be half the length of your arris rail sections, less 50mm (cut this off each rail). Mark out the line of your fence, dig the holes and run two builder's lines between the first and last posts as in Steps 1–4, page 200. Remember to position the posts on your side of the boundary.

Put the first three posts in their holes and prop each one up with temporary supports. Insert one end of the upper arris rail into the notch of the first post and the other end into the third post. Check the arris rail is level and mark and saw off any excess: the end of the rail should reach exactly half-way across the third post. Nail it in place using 75mm galvanised nails and fit the lower arris rail in the same way. Keep checking both are level.

The joins in the arris rail sections need to be staggered for added strength. Therefore measure and cut the central arris rail to the distance from the outer edge of the first post to the mid-point of the second.

Nail the central arris rail into position using galvanised nails. The next section of the central arris rail should be a standard two-post width.

As well as making sure each post touches your builder's lines, keep using a spirit level to check the fence is vertical and level.

Continue fitting posts and rails to create your skeleton fence, supporting it with timber props as you go. Mix the concrete (see page 244). Checking again that each post is vertical, concrete them into the ground and leave to set for 48 hours. Slope the concrete away from the post to drain off rainwater.

Fit gravel boards horizontally to the front of the posts across the base of the fence. Drill pilot holes for the nails before attaching the board to prevent the wood from splitting.

project essentials

- **spirit level**
- **panel saw**
- **hammer**
- **power drill with twist and wood bits**

- fence posts
- timber props
- arris rails (3 x length of fence)
- 50mm and 75mm galvanised nails
- cement and aggregate or post cement
- gravel boards
- featheredge boards
- capping strip

B&Q Making it easier

Post cement

Instead of aggregate and cement, consider using special rapid-setting post cement to secure your posts. It sets in 5–10 minutes.

Attaching the boards

The first featheredge board is fitted with its thicker edge aligned to the outer edge of the first post and the bottom standing on the gravel board. Cut all the boards to the correct length before you begin and treat the end grains with wood preservative. The boards should stand 25mm taller than the fence posts.

1 Using 50mm galvanised nails, nail the centre of the first board to the upper arris rail. Check the board is vertical before nailing it to the bottom rail and finally the central rail. Make a spacer by cutting an off-cut of timber to 20mm less than the width of a featheredge board. Align this to the thicker edge of the first board. Butt the second board up against it and fix it in the same way.

2 Continue fitting boards, using the spacer to maintain an identical overlap between them and checking that each is vertical with a spirit level. When you are six boards from the last post, measure how much space you have left and increase or decrease the overlap of the last few boards so that you meet the outer edge of the post neatly.

3 Run the capping strip across the top of the featheredge boards. Nail it in place using galvanised nails. If you find the wood is splitting, drill pilot holes before nailing.

Galvanised brackets
Another method of building a closeboard fence is to fix the arris rails in place using specially made galvanised brackets. These allow you to use standard fence posts without needing to

cut mortises to hold the arris rails. The brackets come ready-drilled with holes for nailing them in place. End brackets have additional flanges through which they are nailed to posts. These brackets are also ideal for reinforcing a broken arris rail.

Closeboard fencing on a slope

If you need to erect a closeboard fence on a slope, keep the posts and featheredge boards vertical, but slope the arris rails evenly parallel to the ground. When the boards are all in place, saw them across top and bottom in a line parallel to the arris rails. Finish the top of the fence with capping.

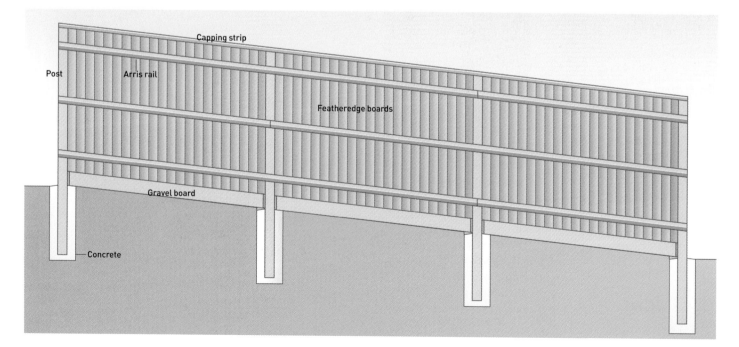

Capping strip

Post

Arris rail

Featheredge boards

Gravel board

Concrete

A pergola is basically an open roof set on posts or columns. Netting or trellis can be fixed to its timbers to encourage trailing plants such as wisteria or honeysuckle to spread up and over it and provide welcome shade in a sunny patch. Position it at the entrance to a garden, over a pathway or against a wall to shade a seating area or frame an ornament. If you want to pave the area beneath, it's best to do so after the structure is erected.

Side view

Front view

B&Q Making it easier

Hard surfaces
Post supports allow you to erect a pergola or other garden structure on a concrete terrace or patio. Use a hammer action drill and screw firmly in place with expanding masonry bolts (see page 199).

project essentials

- pencil
- panel saw
- wood chisel
- mallet
- power drill with twist bits
- hammer
- try square
- spirit level

- 6 posts 2.75m x 100mm x 100mm
- 2 rafters 3.14m x 100mm x 100mm
- 7 crossbeams 1.82m x 100mm x 75mm
- 4 trellis panels 1.83m x 1.22m
- cement and aggregate or post cement
- 65mm and 125mm galvanised nails
- timber props

Building a pergola

Pergolas can be bought in kit form but are also relatively easy to construct from scratch using treated softwood. Be sure to paint the cut ends of the timbers and the feet of the posts with wood preservative before you start.

1 Lay the three upright posts for one side of the pergola on the ground. Cut two lengths of timber to 1.22m and use them to mark the correct distance between the uprights, top and bottom.

2 Lay a rafter in position, jutting 200mm from the edges of the outer posts. Mark the outline of the post tops on the rafter. Since the timbers may not be identical, number each upright and the rafter in pencil so you can match them up again. Repeat this process with the other side of the pergola.

3 Mark up the rafter for a 25mm deep slot or housing for the top of each post. Saw down the side of the housing.

4 Cut out the housing with a wood chisel and mallet. It should be a neat, tight fit.

Profile the ends of the rafters and crossbeams. Measure 25mm down from the top and 75mm in from the outer edge. Draw a line between the points with a pencil and extend it square down the adjacent faces of the timber. Saw off the marked wedge. Or design a decorative profile of your own.

Use the 1.22m length of wood to space the uprights accurately and a try square to check they are square to the rafter. Then brace the structure with three lengths of timber.

Use the rafters as a guide to mark out the post holes. Square their ends with a length of timber and line them up exactly parallel using a 1.32m measure. This will give you the precise position for the centre of each post hole. Mark with canes, remove the timbers, and dig the holes to a depth of 450mm.

Raise one side of the pergola into the post holes and prop it up with temporary supports. Double check that the posts are vertical, in line with each other and the rafter is level.

Fit the posts into the housings in the rafters. Drill pilot holes and then secure with two 125mm galvanised nails.

Raise the other side of the pergola and use a spirit level to make sure both rafters are at the same height. You may have to adjust the depth of the holes. Concrete the posts in and leave to set for 48 hours.

Rest three crossbeams across the rafters at the post positions and nail into position. Then nail the remaining four crossbeams in place, evenly spaced between the first three.

Fitting cross bars and trellis

Trellis is optional on a pergola, but it will help plants to climb.

Drill pilot holes and nail the first trellis panel into position using 65mm galvanised nails, remembering to leave a gap between the bottom of the trellis and the soil to avoid rot.

Complete by nailing the final three trellis panels in place.

DECKING THE BASICS

A deck is essentially an open-air extension of your living space. Freestanding or built against a wall, it can be a place for barbecues or outdoor entertaining, a surround for a pool or sandpit, a play area for children or simply a place to relax outdoors. It can also create an ideal surface for an urban roof garden. A deck may also be a solution to a garden problem – occupying a shady area where the grass won't grow, for example, or levelling a slope and so removing the need for expensive landscaping.

Are decks easy to build?

Yes! You really don't need to be a carpenter to build a deck – only basic skills are required. Just make sure you plan very carefully and check and re-check all measurements both at the planning stage and as you build. A second pair of hands will often be useful. Choose decking timbers that have been pressure-treated to give years of protection against rot and insect attack, but do also remember to treat any cut timber ends with end-grain preserver.

Simple ground-level deck

Labels: Deck boards, Inner joists, Outer joist

Designing your deck

Start by drawing up a simple plan of the house and garden and mark where you intend to build the deck. The south-facing side of the house will give you maximum sunshine, but if that isn't an option, build it where it will be of most use. Take into account the view from the deck, privacy (your own and your neighbours'), access to the garden and proximity to the house.

If your deck adjoins the house make sure the exit door opens over it easily. Check for any amenities your deck will obscure such as a drain cover and if necessary install a hinged trap door to allow future access. You can always build around a tree – just remember to give it enough room to grow and to move with the wind. If necessary install temporary deck boards around the trunk that can be removed as it thickens.

An oversize deck can overwhelm a house. Planning permission may be required. If in doubt, always discuss your plans with the local Building Control office, since local restrictions can vary. And it may be a good idea to let your neighbours know too.

Ground-level deck with balustrade

Labels: Handrail, Baluster, Deck post, Baserail

Elevated deck with balustrade and steps

Labels: Metal joist hanger, Step tread, Step riser, Joist support post

Balustrade, steps and skirting

To make a deck safer and give it some style you can add posts and a balustrade. For peace of mind, fit a gate to stop children or pets straying.

Pre-cut treads and risers make easy work of adding steps to an elevated deck. A handrail will help prevent falls, and is essential if you have more than five steps, or they rise more than 600mm from the ground. Finally, if you don't need to use the space under an elevated deck for garden storage, you can finish it off with attractive latticed panels. Fit fine wire mesh behind them to prevent leaves and garden debris collecting beneath the deck.

Types of decking

There is a wide choice of deckboards available to suit every budget, garden and lifestyle. Some are more durable than others, and require more or less maintenance.

Softwood and hardwood

Softwood deckboards provide classic and highly affordable decking style. Hardwood is extremely durable, easy to maintain and weather resistant.

Heat-treated deckboards

The heat treatment gives these softwood boards a tough, water-resistant finish and a lifespan of 15 years or more.

Composite

Composite deckboards are produced from a mixture of recycled timber and PVC, which gives extra durability and makes them virtually maintenance-free.

Deck tiles

For ground-level decking, pathways and patios, deck tiles can be a very versatile alternative to deck boards. See page 209.

Grass effect

Providing a softer surface than traditional deckboards, grass effect decking is comfortable enough for sunbathing yet tough enough for children's play.

Lighting

Integrated deck lights will extend the use of your deck long into the evening. Flexible low-voltage kits are available that allow you to design a customised lighting system to suit your garden, and are simple and safe to install (see page 297). The latest LED spotlights are stylish, safe and offer dramatic energy savings over conventional lights (page 293). Or you can fit solar-powered lights, which take their energy from the sun's rays during the day and require no mains power supply at all.

A simple deck at ground level is a straightforward project – a perfect starting point if you are not completely confident of your carpentry skills. You can always add on features like posts and balustrade later. A walkway made from patio tiles looks great, and will prevent turf being worn away if your deck is accessed from a lawn.

project essentials

- tape measure
- builder's line
- wooden pegs
- hammer
- spade
- straightedge
- spirit level
- pencil
- protective gloves
- safety goggles
- panel saw or circular saw
- dust mask
- power drill with twist and countersink bits
- jigsaw, if required
- screwdriver
- socket set for coach screws and bolts
- paintbrush

- weed-control fabric
- gravel
- quick-drying concrete, if required
- damp-proof course, if required
- deck joists
- coach screws
- coach bolts
- 50mm or 63mm deck or galvanised screws (depending on thickness of deck boards)
- abrasive paper
- deck boards
- end-grain preserver

Horizontal
For standard right-angled decking, measure 400mm between the centre of one supporting joist and the next.

Deck boards

Deck boards are laid with a 3mm gap between to allow rainwater to run through. Reversible deck boards can be laid smooth or ridged side uppermost, or you can combine the two finishes for decorative effect. The easiest way to arrange them is at right angles to the supporting joists – but you don't have to. Decide on the pattern before you start, as the choice will affect the spacing and number of joists.

Diagonal
Boards laid diagonally need joists spaced 300mm centre-to-centre for the structure to be secure.

Chevron
For a chevron pattern, joists should measure 300mm centre-to-centre and you must lay a double joist where the boards meet in order to have space to fix them securely.

Preparing the site

A ground-level deck must be laid on even, level ground. Once you have decided on the size and location of your deck, mark out the area with pegs and builder's lines.

1 Clear away any turf, plants or weeds, taking care not to disturb any drains or underground cabling. Use a straightedge and spirit level to check that the whole area is level, and level out any slight unevenness in the ground.

2 To stop weeds growing back, cover the area in a layer of weed-control fabric and then 40mm–50mm of gravel.

Decking on damp ground

If drainage is a problem in your garden, you must raise your deck off the ground on concrete pads topped with a layer of damp-proof course. Dig holes roughly 150mm square and 150mm deep at intervals of 1.2m around the deck. Fill the holes with quick-drying concrete to just above ground level. Use a spirit level and straightedge to level the pads top-to-top while the concrete is

still semi-dry. When it is dry, cover the whole area with weed-control fabric (making cut-outs for the concrete pads) and a layer of gravel. Finally, cut squares of damp-proof course to sit between the concrete and the decking timbers.

Assembling the deck

Even a small deck will be very heavy, so do build it on site. A ground-level deck is basically an elevated deck without the deck support posts. Begin by assembling the sub-frame – the outer and inner joists – and then screw down the deck boards. Remember when measuring and cutting the outer joists that the timbers will overlap at the corners.

1 Drill holes and assemble the sub-frame with two countersunk coach screws at each corner and two through the outer frame into each end of all the inner joists. If you want to join the deck frame to a building (see page 210) or add balustrade, do so before laying the deck boards.

2 Use two deck screws or galvanised screws to fix the deck boards to every joist along the sub-frame. If you are using deck screws, you don't need to drill pilot holes; if galvanised screws, you do. Deck boards must be spaced 3mm apart to allow for drainage and expansion. A 3mm gauge deck screw makes an ideal spacer.

3 Position joins between deck boards exactly halfway across a joist, so that both boards can be screwed into it. Stagger the joins for greater strength, and arrange them in a regular pattern for an attractive finish.

4 Remember to coat all the cut ends with end-grain preserver.

 B&Q Making it easier

Joining joists

If you are extending your deck further than the length of a joist, you will need to join lengths. Clamp the joist sections end-to-end in a workbench. Place a joist off-cut about 600mm long across the join and clamp it temporarily to the joists. Secure it with eight coach bolts sunk from the outside of the frame. When joining lengths of internal joist, which will be hidden by the deck boards, use two 600mm sections of joist off-cut, sandwiched either side of the join.

A walkway of patio tiles

A series of patio tiles is a quick and easy way to construct an attractive walkway. The frame comes in a kit form, is simple to assemble and available in a variety of sizes. The corresponding patio tiles slot into place. You could lay it over a bed of gravel and weed-control fabric to deter weeds.

project essentials

- **power drill with twist bits**
- deck frame
- 50mm deck or galvanised screws
- patio tiles

1 Fit the frame together with deck screws or galvanised screws.

2 Add the cross-bars to the frame. The wooden struts are rebated to hold the tiles.

3 Drop the patio tiles in each of the square frames, creating an alternate or continuous pattern with the patio tiles as you wish. The frame will hold the tiles in place, but for a more secure structure and to prevent the tiles warping screw each one down using four deck screws per tile.

An elevated deck is a great way to take advantage of sloping or uneven land, and it will make an attractive and highly versatile addition to your house. Add balustrade, skirting, and steps for even greater usefulness and effect.

Protecting forestry
B&Q work in close collaboration with leading global timber certification schemes such as FSC (Forest Stewardship Council), PEFC (Programme for the Endorsement of Forest Certification) and TFT (Tropical Forest Trust). If a product is endorsed by one of these organisations, you can be confident that it is not contributing to the destruction of the world's forests.

Preparing the site

Begin by clearing away all vegetation, rocks and any trees not featuring in your deck design, taking care not to disturb any drains or underground cabling. If the site is lawned, take up the turf and make sure there is adequate drainage (see page 241).

According to your deck plan, measure out the site and hammer in four wooden pegs at each of the corners. Run a builder's line from each of the four pegs. This will help you visualise the site. Use a spade to lift the turf in manageable strips. Save some turf for making good around the site later. Level off the earth where necessary if the site is not quite flat.

Making it easier

Elevated decking on concrete
If part of your elevated deck extends over concrete, you don't have to take the concrete up. Instead position the posts in metal post supports, screwed down with expanding masonry bolts (see page 199). When marking out the site use chalk instead of pegs, and when squaring it drive in the wooden profiles beyond the concrete (even if this is some distance from the site).

Peg — Builder's line

Cleared area

project essentials

- **tape measure**
- **mallet**
- **builder's line**
- **spade**
- **protective gloves**
- **safety goggles**
- **dust mask**
- **panel saw or circular saw**
- **socket set for coach screws and bolts**
- **hammer**
- **line level**
- **spirit level**
- **builder's square**
- **pencil**
- **power drill with twist and wood bits**
- **workbench**
- **screwdriver**
- **quick-release clamps**
- **jigsaw**

- wooden pegs
- deck joists
- expansion bolts, if required
- 25mm x 100mm lengths of timber for profiles
- joist support posts
- quick-drying concrete
- weed-control fabric
- gravel
- end-grain preserver
- metal joist hangers and 50mm galvanised nails
- coach screws
- deck posts
- handrail and baserail
- balusters
- 50mm or 63mm deck screws or galvanised screws (depending on thickness of deck boards)
- masking tape
- 12mm wooden dowels, 75mm long
- exterior wood adhesive
- deck boards

Attaching a deck to a building

If you decide to adjoin your deck to the house, be careful not to block off any air bricks or interfere with the damp-proof course. You need to fix one joist directly to the masonry and then set out the rest of the sub-frame in alignment with it. Drill holes at 400mm intervals along the length of this joist. Arrange the holes alternately at the top and bottom so as not to weaken the joist, and make sure they do not coincide with the eventual positions of the joist hangers (see page 212). Check the joist is level and make a mark on the wall through each hole. Remove the board and drill through the masonry at the marked points. Place the board back in position and insert expanding masonry bolts (see page 199) into each of the holes, remembering to include the washers, and tighten with a spanner.

Expanding masonry bolt

ideal tool

Line level

This is a quick and easy method of checking that a line is level. Stretch the line taut and hang the level from a central position to take a reading.

Squaring the site

Time spent on careful measuring at this stage is well worth it in the long run. Use the 3–4–5 triangle method (see below) to ensure that the corners are accurate and the finished deck looks professional.

B&Q Making it easier

Corner to corner
As a final check, measure the diagonal distances from corner to corner. If they are the same, then each corner will be a right angle.

1 Make timber profiles to help you set out the deck sub-frame accurately. Cut three 600mm lengths of 25mm x 100mm timber for each profile. Two of them will form stakes that are driven into the ground; the third is a crosspiece. Cut the stakes to a point at one end and nail the crosspiece 50mm from the top of the stakes.

2 Take up the pegs and lines and hammer two profiles into the ground at each corner, about 450mm beyond the cleared area. Run a builder's line from each profile to its opposite and tie it taut. Place a line level in the middle and hammer the profiles in until you get a level reading. Use a spirit level to ensure each crossbeam is level.

3 To check that the lines are crossing directly at the corners, first lay a joist along the edge of the cleared area to represent the edge of the sub-frame. Then stand a spirit level vertically against it at the corner. Adjust the position of the lines on the profiles until they cross directly above the corner of the cleared deck area.

4 Use the 3–4–5 triangle method to square the corners, making any adjustments by sliding the string along the profiles. When the lines are perfectly level and square, mark the position of the string on each crosspiece with a pencil. Move it to one side and make a saw cut or hammer in a nail at the pencil mark. Then tie the line firmly in position.

Timber profiles

Lines crossing at corner of deck

Wall joist

3–4–5 triangle

It is vital at this stage of the project that the sides of the deck are square to each other. The easiest way to achieve this is by the 3-4-5 triangle method, which uses simple geometry to create perfect right angles at the corners. In a triangle with sides exactly 3, 4 and 5 metres long, a right angle will form at the corner where the shorter sides meet. Any multiples of 3, 4 and 5 will follow the same pattern.

First ensure that the lines between the profiles cross directly above the four corners of the site – use a spirit level or run a plumb line down to check that they do. Then either use a wooden builder's square (see page 225) or measure and stick masking tape 900mm from the corner on one line and 1200mm from the corner on the other. When the diagonal distance between these two marks measures exactly 1500mm, the corner is a true right angle. Make any necessary adjustments by sliding the string along the profiles.

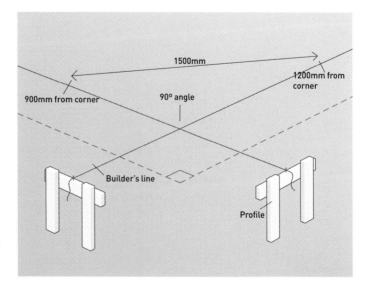

1500mm

1200mm from corner

900mm from corner

90° angle

Builder's line

Profile

Fixing the joist support posts

An elevated deck is raised on joist support posts. The corner posts don't sit right in the corners of the sub-frame but are offset by the width of a post to allow deck posts to be slotted in later. A lot of the work at this stage requires two pairs of hands.

Dig out 600mm deep holes for each of the joist support posts. Ideally the holes need to be about 300mm in diameter at the top and 400mm at the bottom. The gap between the centre of one post and the centre of the next must be a maximum of 1.2m. The corner posts should not be right in the corners but offset to one side (it doesn't matter which) by the width of a post.

Place the post in the hole and check it is vertical using a spirit level. Hold the post in position with temporary supports and pour quick-drying concrete into the hole.

When all the posts are in place and the concrete is firm, remove the lines and profiles.

Fit a sheet of weed-control fabric around the posts and cover it with gravel. This will stop weeds growing through and allow water to drain away. Then allow the concrete to set for 48 hours before building the sub-frame.

Building the joist sub-frame

The sub-frame forms the deck's outer skeleton. Remember that joists run in the opposite direction to the deck boards, so decide now which way you would like the deck boards to run.

Joist hangers
Galvanised metal joist hangers will enable you to fix the sub-frame joists quickly and securely to a wall joist (see page 210).

Cut the outer joists of the sub-frame to length, remembering to allow for overlapping corner joints. Paint the cut ends with end-grain preserver. Attach the sub-frame joists to the wall joist with metal joist hangers and 50mm galvanised nails.

Fix the side joists to the off-set corner posts, first checking that they are level. They need to protrude by the width of a deck post. Drill holes through the joist into the post and attach with two countersunk coach screws. Drive in two more coach screws at the corner to join the outer joists together.

Continue round the deck fixing the joists to each post with two countersunk coach screws.

To give extra strength to the sub-frame, screw two support beams onto every second post along the length of the deck. Position them immediately beneath the joists of the sub-frame.

Cut the inner joists to length and attach to the joist sub-frame with two countersunk coach screws at either end, or to the wall joist using joist hangers. If you plan to lay the deck boards in a horizontal pattern, the distance between the centre of one joist and the next should be 400mm; for diagonally laid boards, measure 300mm.

Fitting a balustrade

Attach railings to a deck after you have built the sub-frame but before you lay the deck boards. Work out how high you would like the railings to be and cut the balusters down to size if necessary, bearing in mind that for safety the handrail must be between 900mm and 1m above the finished deck and the base rail a maximum of 75mm. Don't forget to allow space beneath the baserail for the deck boards.

1 Decide how to space the deck posts (remembering they should be a maximum of 1.2m apart) and cut the base- and handrails exactly to length. Clamp a length of baserail in a workbench and drill pilot holes 100mm apart (or less if you decide you want your balusters more closely spaced) all the way through the rail.

2 Slot the balusters into the underside of the handrail and secure them by screwing diagonally through the baluster into the rail. For accuracy measure the intervals using a spacer made from a wood off-cut, as shown. Remember the slotted sides of both the rails are fitted facing downwards so that rainwater cannot collect in them.

3 Fit the baserail onto the balusters and screw 50mm deck screws or galvanised screws through the pilot holes into the bottom of each. Use the wooden spacer again to align the balusters precisely.

Slot a deck post in the gap between the joist support post and the corner of the sub-frame and hold it in place with a quick-release clamp. Fix the post to the sub-frame with two countersunk coach screws.

To make the corner post more secure, fit a piece of joist off-cut between it and the first inner joist, screwed to the sub-frame with deck screws. Then position the next deck post and fix it with just one coach screw for now, so that you can push it to one side while you fix the railings.

Mark a 12mm drill bit with masking tape at 38mm from the tip and drill two holes to that depth on either end of both the hand- and baserails. Fit 12mm wooden dowels into the holes and mark the corresponding positions on the adjoining posts at top and bottom. Then drill 38mm holes in each post at the four marked points.

Glue the wooden dowels into the holes and slot the railing assembly into place. Use quick-release clamps to hold the posts and railings together while the glue dries. Then add another coach screw to the base of the second post to secure it.

Laying deck boards

With the railings in place, you are now ready to lay the deck boards. Remember that they must run in the opposite direction to the joists.

Begin laying boards at the outer edge of the sub-frame and move inwards. You will have to cut notches in the first board to fit around the deck posts. Cut the board to length and clamp it in position in front of the deck posts, overhanging the sub-frame. Measure and mark the outline of the deck posts accurately on the deck board.

Remove the deck board and clamp it firmly to a workbench. Cut out the shape of the deck posts using a jigsaw.

Slot the cut deck board into position. If necessary plane or saw down its outer length to ensure that the inner edge is flush with the inside edge of the deck post – this will give you a straight edge from which to lay the rest of your deck boards. Screw the board down into each joist using 50mm or 63mm deck screws or galvanised screws (depending on the thickness of your deck boards).

Fix each deck board with two screws into every joist before moving on to the next, remembering to leave a 3mm gap between boards. Position joins exactly halfway across a joist – that way both boards can be screwed down into it. Stagger the joins, and for a professional effect arrange them in a regular pattern across the deck surface.

Working around existing features

Don't cut down a tree: build your deck around it. All you need do is include a bit more sub-structure to frame the trunk. Simply block off the area around the tree by positioning joist off-cuts between the inner joists, secured either end with two coach screws. Remember to leave enough space for the tree trunk to thicken and for it to sway in the wind. Cut and fix the deck boards to fit around the tree.

Adding a gate

If you have small children or pets, a gate will make your deck a safer place. It's best to use a lightweight gate that can hang from a deck post. If you opt for a ready-made gate this needs to be sourced and measured before you draw up your plans so that you can position the deck posts and steps to fit it. Alternatively you can make a gate yourself or have one made to fit the gap. If you choose a metal gate, these usually come complete with a hinge assembly and automatic latch. For how to fit hinges and a latch to a wooden gate, see pages 198–99.

Fitting skirting panels

On a raised deck, lattice panels can be cut to fit beneath the sub-frame, creating an attractive skirting. Attaching a wire mesh behind the lattice will stop bits of garden debris and small animals from getting under the deck.

project essentials

- **tape measure**
- **jigsaw**
- **hammer**
- **screwdriver**
- **wire cutters**
- **power drill with twist bits**

- lattice panels
- 30mm galvanised screws
- 75mm deck or galvanised screws
- fine wire mesh
- 20mm wood staples

B&Q Making it easier

Deck protection

To keep your deck looking its best, protect it from the elements and everyday use with a regular coat of stain, oil or seal. Deck stain is available in hardwood tones as well as more unusual colours, and is water-resistant and hard-wearing. Deck oil will protect and enhance the natural beauty of your wood. Colourless deck seal locks out moisture while allowing the timbers to breathe and weather naturally. You can revive older decking with specially formulated deck cleaner, which removes mildew and dirt and visibly refreshes faded timbers.

1 Measure from the bottom of your sub-frame to the ground. With a jigsaw, cut the latticed panel to fit these measurements. Remove the frame batten from the discarded section by gently knocking it away from the lattice with a hammer. Then use 30mm galvanised screws to fix it back into place on the lattice that you intend to fit.

2 Measure the lattice panel (within the frame) and cut a section of fine wire mesh with wire cutters to fit. Attach the wire mesh to the batten frame with wood staples and a hammer.

3 Drill pilot holes and screw the upper frame of the panel into the deck sub-frame.

DECKING EXTENDING A DECK

project essentials

- **screwdriver**
- **goggles**
- **gloves**
- **try square**
- **spirit level**
- **tape measure**
- **pencil**
- **hammer**
- **circular saw or handsaw**
- **mitre block**
- **power drill with twist and countersink bits**
- **2 quick-release clamps**

- joist support posts
- deck joists
- deck boards
- 50mm or 63mm deck screws or galvanised screws (depending on thickness of deck boards)
- metal joist hangers and 50mm galvanised nails
- end-grain preserver
- coach screws
- coach bolts
- deck boards

The flexibility of decking is one of its great joys. As your needs change, you might find your initial deck too small and feel it could benefit from an extension. This is simply a matter of adding on another sub-frame. If your extension runs over a downward slope, you can accommodate the change of level by adjusting the length of the joist support posts and, if you wish, by installing a set of steps to lead down to the garden (see pages 218–19). To extend up a slope, step the deck up by starting the new sub-frame on top of the last.

Extending on the same level

The most straightforward way to enlarge the area of your deck is by extending the sub-frame and boards at the same level. You may need to remove a section of balustrade first.

1 Unscrew the outermost boards along the edge you want to extend to expose two joists. To enlarge the sub-frame, you will need to erect additional joist support posts and fix to them three sub-frame joists defining the extended area. Follow the method detailed on pages 210–13.

2 Fix new deck boards across the exposed joists, staggering the joins between boards. Remember to position the joins halfway across a joist and screw both boards into it. When you reach the edge of the extension, saw off the excess deck boards flush with the sub-frame.

Extending in a new direction

If your extension changes direction or is a walkway to another section of the deck, you may need or want to change the direction of the boards.

1 Attach a new joist to the sub-frame with coach screws. Mark out the area of the extension and erect joist support posts and the remaining sub-frame joists. Nail internal joists to the connecting joist using metal joist hangers. If the deck boards are to lie diagonal to the joists, the joists must be spaced 300mm centre-to-centre; if horizontal, then 400mm centres will suffice.

2 Screw each deck board down with two screws into every joist. If they lie diagonally, clamp each onto a workbench, use a builder's square to mark the ends at a 45° angle, and cut neatly with a circular saw or handsaw. When they are all screwed down, saw the edges in line with the sub-frame.

Extending with a change in level

If you are building a deck over rising land you may need to step up part of it to accommodate the change in level. Or you might choose to add a new level as a design feature or to access a door. The higher level is achieved by building a new sub-frame on top of the existing one.

1 Centre the first joist of the new sub-frame along the edge of the deck – this will provide the step. The joist must be the length of the deck less 150mm (the thickness of two joists and two deck boards). Clamp a joist off-cut across the sub-frame and new joist and secure it with four countersunk coach screws.

2 Build the rest of the new sub-frame as described on pages 210–13. This time the new joist support posts will be higher to accommodate the stepped deck.

3 Attach internal joists to the new sub-frame spaced 400mm centre-to-centre using two countersunk coach screws at either end of each joist. Remember that the deck boards must run in the opposite direction to the joists; here the direction has been reversed for decorative effect.

4 Cut three lengths of deck board to make a fascia that will give a neat finish to the face of the step. Mitre the corner joints for a really professional finish.

5 Cut the deck boards to length and position the first board flush with the face of the step. Secure the boards with two screws into each joist along their full length.

Decking an angled corner

If you want to make your deck really stand out, an angled corner is a striking and easy-to-achieve feature. Both the outer and inner joists of the sub-frame are cut to the required angle, and the deck boards then fitted and cut to match.

ideal tool

Circular saw

A circular saw is extremely useful for cutting through timber. The cordless variety is particularly convenient. You can control the depth of the cut of a circular saw – in this instance, set the blade to cut the depth of a deck board to avoid damaging the edge of the sub-frame.

1 Using a straightedge or a long spirit level, mark the angle across the outer and inner joists with a pencil. Cut the joists along the line.

2 Measure a length of joist and cut its ends flush with the adjacent joists of the sub-frame. Then screw it to each inner and outer joist with two countersunk coach screws.

3 Lay the deck boards overhanging the angled outer joist and screw them down. Clamp a spare board to the deck to mark the line of the angled corner. Use a circular saw or handsaw to cut the ends of the overhanging boards flush with the sub-frame. Remember to coat all the sawn ends with end-grain preserver.

- **tape measure**
- **handsaw or jigsaw**
- **power drill with twist bits**
- **hammer**
- **screwdriver**
- **pencil**
- **spanner**

- concrete slabs
- step treads
- 2 step risers
- 75mm coach screws
- joist off-cuts
- 50mm deck or galvanised screws

Unless the deck is at ground level, you will need steps to give easy access to the garden or link different levels within the deck. A handrail and balusters will not only help prevent slips and falls, they will turn a functional stairway into an attractive feature. And if, as you use or extend your deck, you decide you want a balustrade after all, this is easily added on.

Coach screws

Tread

Step riser

Steps

The easiest way to build steps is to buy pre-formed components. You will need a set of two risers and as many separate step treads as you require. A basic open stair is all that's necessary but you can build a more solid construction if you prefer.

To prevent steps sinking into soft ground, you need to sit them on a durable surface. Concrete paving slabs are ideal, but any material suitable for a path or terrace will work well – block paving or a bed of gravel over weed-control fabric, for example. Remember to calculate the height of the step riser from the surface of the step support pad.

Measuring up

A comfortable width for an average stair is 900mm, but it should not be less than 760mm. If your stair is wider than 900mm you will need a central step riser to support the steps and prevent them buckling. If you do build your own riser, make sure the steps are a comfortable depth – ie not so deep that they are an effort to climb but not so shallow that you trip on them; 150mm–180mm is an ideal height.

1 Cut two sections of joist off-cut to the same width as the step treads. Attach them to the step risers at the top and bottom using two countersunk coach screws on each side.

2 Position the solid step assembly against the sub-frame of the deck and in the centre of the step support pad. Drill pilot holes through the step assembly and the sub-frame joist. Screw the step assembly securely to the sub-frame with four more countersunk coach screws.

3 Screw the treads into the riser supports at either end with two 50mm deck screws or galvanised screws to make a sturdy step.

4 If you would prefer a solid stairway to an open stair, you can fill the gaps with joist off-cuts or deck boards. Simply measure the height and depth of the gap and screw the timber into the step riser with two screws at either end.

Fitting a handrail to steps

In order to fit handrails to your steps, you first need to fix notched deck posts at the top and bottom. Drive two coach bolts through each into the step riser. Position a length of handrail on the outside face of the posts parallel with the angle of the steps and with a pencil mark the line of the outer edges of the posts. Then cut along this line with a jigsaw. When the handrail is bolted to the posts the edges should be neatly flush.

Balusters

To attach balusters, you will need to fit a baserail in the same way as the handrail. Then cut the balusters to length and screw them in place.

Fitting balustrade to an existing deck

A simple run of hand- and baserails with upright balusters will prevent falls and instantly transform a basic deck into a more elegant feature. Notched posts are specially profiled at the bottom so that they can be attached to a completed deck.

> **project** essentials
>
> - **tape measure**
> - **pencil**
> - **jigsaw or handsaw**
> - **spanner**
> - **quick-release clamp**
> - **spirit level**
> - **power drill with twist bits**
>
> - notched deck posts
> - coach screws
> - deck joists
> - hand- and baserails
> - 50mm or 63 mm deck or galvanised screws (depending on thickness of deck boards)
> - timber off-cut

1 Decide how to space the deck posts (no more than 1.2m apart) and fix the first notched post to the sub-frame with coach screws. Measure lengths of joist to sit on the outer face of the sub-frame between deck posts. Attach these with deck screws as you fix the posts. When you reach a corner, measure and cut the length of joist to the outer edge of the sub-frame. Position the corner post on the adjacent side of the sub-frame, overlapping this joist. This will keep the posts in alignment.

2 Measure and cut lengths of handrail, mitring the corners for a neat finish. Clamp a length of handrail into position with its grooved edge facing down. Check it is level with a spirit level, then drill countersunk pilot holes and screw it into the deck posts.

3 Use a baluster, aligned with the groove in the handrail, to determine the position of the baserail. Ensure any gap between the baserail and the decking boards does not exceed 75mm. Clamp the baserail in place and fix to the deck posts with countersunk screws.

4 Position the first baluster, checking it is vertical with a spirit level, and fix it to the hand and baserail with countersunk screws. Use a wood off-cut or, as here, a length of base rail as a spacer to maintain an even distance between balusters. Remember that the maximum gap by law between railings is 100mm. Ensure the spacing of the balusters and deck posts achieves a uniform design.

A well-built garden wall in brick or stone is more expensive than a fence, but it will weather attractively and last a lifetime. Planning permission is needed for any wall over 1m high on the edge of a public highway and for any freestanding wall over 2m in height. Large retaining walls may need a structural engineer's specification, and in any case shouldn't be attempted without some experience on less ambitious building projects. The techniques for building a wall are straightforward, but if it is to be strong and stable it is essential that it be properly planned and designed. The design will depend to a large extent on what it is for.

What is the function of your wall?

Garden walls may serve a variety of purposes.
- To retain earth so you can create a terraced area or to stop a steeply sloping bank from collapsing.
- To create a solid barrier adjacent to a highway or footpath, to reduce noise or for privacy.
- To divide a garden into different areas, or provide extra seating around a feature like a terrace or pond.
- To provide a low, solid base on which to erect fencing or build piers to support an overhead structure such as a pergola.

Brick-built planter

Raised patio

Retaining wall

Freestanding wall

Raised brick pond

Decorative garden walls

Garden walls can be built from bricks, natural stone or reconstituted stone. There is a large range of reconstituted stone on the market, made from concrete blocks that are finished and coloured to look like stone.

Brick wall

Bricks are the cheapest material and they come in a range of colours, depending on the type of clay they are made from and the manufacturing process. They may also be multi-coloured or mottled and have a rough or smooth texture. Second-hand bricks often have a weathered look that blends with old house walls, but they are not cheap and there is usually no way of knowing whether they are frost-resistant.

Natural stone wall

Natural stone can be bought from quarries or reclamation yards, but it is very expensive. Stone bought in its natural state is classed as random rubble or undressed stone. Semi-dressed stone is cut into fairly uniform blocks with uneven surfaces. Fully dressed stone with machine-cut faces is called Ashlar. The wall pictured above is built with semi-dressed stone.

Semi-dry stone wall

A genuine dry-stone wall is built from stones that are carefully chosen so that they are perfectly stable without needing mortar to bind them together. This wall is a semi-dry stone wall. It looks like a true dry-stone wall but it has hidden mortar joints (see page 230).

Dry-stone effect

This wall is made from reconstituted stone blocks that allow you to create the look of a dry-stone wall at a fraction of the cost or labour of the real thing.

Types of brick

Bricks come in different shapes, sizes and levels of durability. The standard size brick is 215mm x 102.5mm x 65mm, but this can vary by a few millimetres. Most bricks are solid and they may have flat surfaces or a depression, called a 'frog', on one face. Some bricks have holes through them – these are known as perforated or cored bricks.

Facing bricks

These bricks are available in a wide variety of different colours and textures. They are the type of brick most likely to be used for a garden wall.

Common bricks

There are lots of different kinds of common brick, but all are generally cheaper and less attractive than facing bricks. They are usually used where they won't be visible, though they can't be laid below ground.

Engineering bricks

These dense, strong bricks are usually used underground, particularly for foundations or manhole construction. Many facing bricks also have engineering qualities.

Wall ties

These galvanised metal or stainless steel strips (often butterfly-shaped) are used to bind sections of masonry together. They are laid in the mortar as the wall is built.

BRICK GRADING AND DURABILITY

F2 category	Completely frost-resistant
F1 category	Moderately frost-resistant
F0 category	Not frost-resistant; for internal use only
S2 category	Low salt content; suitable for most applications
S1 category	Unsuitable for foundations or retaining walls

Specials and coping

Different shaped bricks – known as specials – are made for decorative brickwork, for fitting into corners and angles and for coping, the top course of a wall. Whether of brick or stone, the coping is there not only for decorative reasons but also to ensure that water runs off the wall rather than soaking into it (where it could freeze in winter and cause serious damage). Coping bricks are available in different shapes and widths, some with attractive patterns, to suit walls of all different thickness. They usually project 25mm on each side of the wall and may slope in one or both directions. All coping bricks should be fully frost resistant.

Reconstituted stone

Reconstituted bricks and blocks are available in all kinds of colours and finishes. Buy them either as single blocks or as composite blocks that resemble a number of laid stones.

Pitched walling

These reconstituted stones have a rugged, protruding face typical of quarry-dressed stone. You can buy them in a range of natural shades.

Composite dry-stone walling

These slate-effect blocks interlock, making them very straightforward to lay.

Composite block walling

The false joints in these easy-to-lay blocks do not need pointing.

Choosing the type of material for your garden wall is the start of the process. If you are building a brick wall, you must also decide on the pattern, or bond, for your wall. And whatever material you choose, you will need to make sure you have a suitable mortar.

Choosing walling materials

Your choice of materials for building a garden wall will depend on a number of factors.

- The material your house is built from, and other houses and walls in the immediate vicinity.
- Your budget. Natural stone is by far the most expensive option and prices will vary from region to region. The amount of dressing the stone has received is also reflected in the price – perfectly cut Ashlar stone is more expensive than undressed stone. In order to calculate the cost, a rule of thumb calculation is to allow 1 tonne of stone for about 3.3 sq m of finished stonework. But this is very approximate, as stone varies in size and weight.
- Bricks demand a degree of accuracy when building a wall and are less forgiving than natural stone. Once the basic techniques are mastered, however, brick-building is much quicker than laying stone.
- Reconstituted stone is easy to lay and relatively inexpensive. The stones come in varying sizes, so estimate the number you need by dividing the area of walling by the dimensions of the blocks you plan to use.

Cutting bricks

To build any kind of brick wall you will need to get the hang of cutting bricks. It's not quite as easy as a professional bricklayer can make it look – but it's also not too hard to master. Measure the brick with a ruler and mark the cutting line on all four sides with a pencil. Tap a bolster gently with a club hammer to score along the cutting line all the way around the brick. Then lay it, frog down, on grass or sand and hit the bolster firmly to cut right through it. Always wear safety goggles when cutting bricks or blocks.

Types of bond used in brickwork

A brick wall is constructed of layers of bricks, known as courses, cemented together with mortar. The pattern in which the bricks are built up is known as the bond. The idea of a bond is to stagger the vertical mortar joints so that they are not in the same place in two or more consecutive courses. The wall load is then transmitted along its length, making it stronger and more stable. The three types of bond most often used for garden walls are stretcher bond, English bond and Flemish bond. When estimating the number of bricks for a particular bond, add an extra 5% to allow for cutting bricks and breakages.

Stretcher bond

This is used for a single-skin wall, the thickness of a single brick, and for double-skin walls when they are joined with wall ties. All the bricks are laid lengthways with the long face exposed. Half-bricks (half-bats) complete the end of every other course on a straight wall, so that each vertical joint centres on the bricks above and below. A corner is made by alternating headers and stretchers. You will need approximately 60 bricks per sq m.

English bond

This pattern is formed by laying alternate courses of stretchers and headers. Queen closers inserted before the last header are used to maintain staggered joints at the ends of the wall, and at right-angled corners. You will need approximately 120 bricks per sq m.

Flemish bond

Headers and pairs of parallel stretchers alternate on each course to make a double-skin wall. Queen closers are used on alternate courses to stagger the joints. You will need approximately 120 bricks per sq m.

Mortar and mortar additives

Mortar is what sticks the bricks or stones together in a wall. General-purpose mortars are a mixture of soft sand, lime, cement and water, or soft sand, cement, plasticiser and water. Some masonry cements have plasticiser already mixed with them.

- Plasticisers and frost-proofers create small air pockets in the mix, making it smoother. They are used as a substitute for lime in colder conditions. Frost-proofer gives some protection against freezing but only in the case of slight frosts. Don't build your garden wall in freezing conditions.
- Hydrated lime is added to mortar to slow down the drying process, thus preventing cracking. It also makes the mortar easier to use.
- Always follow the manufacturer's instructions when adding plasticisers to the mix – too much will result in a weak mortar.
- Bags of mortar ready-mixed to the correct proportions are more expensive, but are convenient for smaller jobs.
- Different coloured mortars are available to complement different walling materials.

Storing materials

It is important to keep bricks and mortar materials dry until you are ready to use them. Bricks, sand and aggregate should all be covered with a plastic sheet. Bags of cement should be raised off the ground and covered with a plastic sheet, or stored indoors.

Mortar mixes

One 25kg bag of sand, with the other ingredients mixed in the proportions shown below, is enough to lay approximately 55 bricks.

MORTAR MIXES	
General-purpose mortar (moderate conditions)	1 part cement 1 part lime 6 parts soft sand
Strong mortar (severe conditions)	1 part cement 6 parts soft sand plasticiser
Very strong mortar (exposed to snow, heavy wind and rain)	1 part cement 4 parts soft sand plasticiser

Gauging mortar

For most purposes, mortar ingredients can be measured out with a shovel. But on some types of wall, such as faced brick or pointed stonework, it will spoil the finish if the mortar varies in colour. To prevent this, the mortar is gauged – the proportions of the mix are measured more precisely, using a bucket rather than just a shovel. Draw a line on the inside of a bucket with a felt-tip marker indicating one unit of the mix. Shovel the ingredients in turn into the bucket, making sure each measure is level with the line.

Mixing mortar

Mortar can be mixed by hand or with a cement mixer; there is no advantage in mixing it by hand unless you only need a small quantity. Mortar should be used within two hours of being made, less in hot weather, so mix as much as you think you can use in that time – as a very rough guide, allow about two minutes to lay each brick. Mix mortar on a level surface, such as a sheet of plywood. If using a mixer, position it on flat ground.

Don't allow mortar or concrete to dry on your tools. Clean them with a stiff brush from time to time.

By hand

Thoroughly mix the dry mortar ingredients together. Using a shovel, make a hole in the centre of the pile and pour clean water into it (mixed with plasticiser, if you are using it). Carefully push the dry mix into the water, letting it absorb. Mix it thoroughly, adding more water as necessary. The consistency of the mortar is important – it mustn't be too dry or too runny. To test it, make a depression in the mix with a shovel – if this is easy to do and the mortar holds its shape, the consistency is correct.

In a mixer

Put about a quarter of a bucket of water into the mixer. Add half the sand, then the cement and lime if you are using it. Run the mixer, then add the rest of the sand and more water if necessary. Mix it thoroughly until you have a good consistency.

GARDEN WALLS FOUNDATIONS

Garden walls must always be built on a solid foundation, consisting of a trench filled with concrete. This is known as the footing. The importance of footings can't be overstated – the life expectancy and even the ease with which the wall is built will depend on substantial and accurate footings. When mixing concrete (see page 244), don't skimp on materials by adding large stones or blocks – this will weaken it.

Setting out the footing

Before you start marking out the position of the trench, check that the ground is firm and well drained with no obstacles such as pipes or tree roots. The position of the edges of the wall and the edges of the footing are marked with builder's lines.

1 You must use timber profiles to get the footing absolutely straight. Each one is made from three lengths of 25mm x 50mm timber: two are sharpened to a point at one end, and the third is nailed to them as a crosspiece. Hammer a profile into the ground at either end of the site, about 450mm beyond the area to be excavated. Make sure each crosspiece is level and the profiles are at the same height.

2 Gently tap two small nails into the top of the crosspiece of each profile to indicate the width of the wall (in this case, 215mm), and another two beyond these to indicate the width of the footing (in this case, 120mm beyond the wall on each side).

3 Attach builder's lines to the outer nails on the profile – the ones which mark the edge of the footings – and secure the line with pins in the ground. If the footings incorporate a right-angled corner, set two more profiles at right angles to your existing ones. Check that the lines cross at a true right-angle using a builder's square (see opposite).

4 Hold a spirit level vertically against the lines to mark the edge of the footing on the ground. Mark this edge with builder's line nailed into the ground or use spray paint or a line of nails. Remove the above-ground builder's lines so they don't get in the way while you are digging out the trench.

Digging the footing trench

The depth of the footing will depend on the nature of the ground. The chart below is a rough guide in average soil. 'Made up' ground (on a new site, with recently dug-up and put-back soil or filled holes), loose sandy soils and soft clay soils need deeper footings. Particularly soft soils may even need a layer of compacted hardcore on top of geotextile permeable fabric in the bottom of the trench. Allow an additional depth of two bricks above the concrete for replacing the top soil, or to give room to pave against the wall.

Ideal tool

Mattock
When you are digging a trench for the footing, the wide blade of a mattock makes short work of breaking up heavy soil, and it is ideal for grubbing out stones or chopping through old tree roots.

Keep it level and vertical

Use a spirit level to make sure the sides of the footing are vertical. To check the bottom is level, place a long straight piece of wood in the trench and lay a spirit level on top of it.

FOOTING DIMENSIONS			
Type of wall	Wall height	Depth of concrete	Width of trench
Single-skin	Up to 1m	150mm	300mm
Double-skin	Up to 1m	300mm	450mm
Double-skin	Over 1m up to 2m	375mm–450mm	450mm–600mm
Retaining wall	Up to 1m	150mm–300mm	375mm–450mm

Filling the trench

The footing trench is filled with concrete made with five parts mixed aggregate to one part cement. Levelling pegs are driven into the bottom of the trench as a guide to make sure that the trench is filled to the correct level.

1 Cut pegs from 50mm x 50mm lengths of timber and sharpen them to a point at one end. They should measure the depth of the footing plus enough to ensure the pointed end is solidly held in the bottom of the trench. Hammer in a peg at one end of the trench until it is level with the finished concrete height. Use a spirit level to set further pegs at the same height about 1m apart along the rest of the trench.

2 Pour the concrete and aggregate mix into the trench until it is level with the tops of the pegs. Leave it to set for 48 hours before starting to build the wall.

ideal tool

Builder's wheelbarrow
For building tasks such as moving the earth you dig out of the trench or carrying concrete you will need a heavy-duty wheelbarrow. An ordinary garden wheelbarrow is unlikely to be strong enough.

Length of wood attached to pegs

Stepped concrete footing

Plywood shuttering board

Stepped footings

When building a wall on a slope, the footing should be stepped, but the concrete must always be level. The step size depends on the slope and the material being used to build the wall; calculate it in multiples of the depth of a course. Make each step by placing a length of plywood shuttering board across the trench; secure it with a length of wood attached to pegs on either side and pour concrete behind it to make the higher step.

Make your own bricklaying guides

Gauge rod

A gauge rod is used for checking that each course of bricks is the correct height. Make one from a length of timber batten and mark it every 75mm (65mm for the depth of the brick plus 10mm for the mortar between each course).

Gauge rod

Builder's square

A builder's square is a large set square used for making sure right-angled corners in brick or stone walls are completely accurate. It is based on the simple geometry of the 3-4-5 triangle (see page 211). You need three lengths of wood about 50mm wide and 20mm thick. Mark one piece 450mm from one end, the second 600mm and the third 750mm. Nail the first two pieces at right angles, then align the third piece between the marks. Nail it in place and saw off the excess wood, then reinforce the right-angled corner with a piece of hardboard.

750mm

Hardboard

90°

450mm

600mm

Attach lines to the inner nails on the profiles (those marking the edge of the wall). Hold a spirit level vertically against the lines and mark the outer edge of both skins of brickwork on the concrete. Join the marks using a length of timber as a straightedge.

Repeat the process to set out the first course of the inner skin. Use a builder's square to check corners are true right angles.

Setting out the first course

The wall built here is a double-skin brick wall using stretcher bond. The two skins are tied together with wall or butterfly ties. Use engineering bricks for the first two courses, below ground level, and frost-resistant F category bricks above ground. Mix up the mortar (see page 223) and put it on a board supported on bricks (known as a 'spot' board) at a convenient distance from the wall. Wet the board first, to stop the mortar sticking to it.

Place a trowel full of mortar on the footing at the corner or end-of-line mark for the outer skin. Drag the point of the trowel towards you through the mortar, making a furrow in the centre. Lay the first brick, frog-side up if it has one. Level this brick along its length and across its width, using a spirit level.

Use a long spirit level to set another brick in position about a metre away from the first. This is a temporary brick and can be repositioned later. Continue along the line, checking that the bricks are level, until you can set the end-of-line brick in position.

Basic bricklaying techniques

Use your gauge rod to ensure that the mortar in every joint between the bricks is 10mm thick – you'll get better at judging this with practice. From time to time, check the wall is vertical and level with a spirit level.

Scoop up a sausage shape of mortar and shape it to roughly the size of the trowel blade. Slide the trowel underneath the mortar and transfer it to the top course of bricks. Using the flat back of the trowel, stretch the mortar along five or six bricks then make a furrow in the centre with the point of the trowel. Remove any mortar overhanging the edge of the bricks.

Pick up a brick with one hand and apply mortar to the end of it with the trowel.

Push the brick into the mortar and give it a tap with the trowel handle. Aim for 10mm-wide horizontal and vertical joints. If a brick is too low, remove it and add more mortar. Lay the top front edge of the brick to the line but not quite touching it.

project essentials

- **builder's line and line pins**
- **short and long spirit levels**
- **trowel**
- **pencil**
- **gauge rod**
- **builder's square**
- **jointing tool or roller tool and blades**
- **medium-soft banister brush**

- straight length of timber
- mortar
- engineering and frost-proof bricks
- galvanised or stainless steel wall ties (twist or butterfly type)
- thin card

Drive two line pins into the ground at each end of the wall, then stretch a builder's line between them as a levelling guide. (If you have a laser level – see IDEAL TOOL page 228 – you can use it to quickly level from one end of the wall to the other.) Then fill in the gaps in the first course, following the bricklaying techniques below. Move the temporary bricks as necessary.

Scrape away any excess mortar from the front of the wall with a quick upwards movement with the edge of the trowel.

Building corners

Once the first course is in place, the corners and ends of the wall are laid next as a series of steps.

At each right-angled corner, lay three bricks in each direction and build up the corners with a series of five or six steps. Check the height of each course with a gauge rod.

Use the spirit level to make sure the wall is vertical and the builder's square to check that the corner is a true right-angle. To tie the two skins of the wall together, lay metal wall ties at intervals in the mortar. They should be no more than 900mm apart on the horizontal plane and 450mm apart on the vertical plane. (English and Flemish bonds do not require wall ties.)

Check that the steps are aligned by holding a straightedge or spirit level against the sides of the wall. Once the corners and ends are done, you can build the straight sections. Push two line pins into vertical joints at each end of the wall, then stretch a bricklayer's line between them as a guide to level the top of the second course. Raise the line as you complete each course. Fill the join between the two skins with mortar as you lay the courses.

Builder's line
When using a builder's line, bend a small, thin piece of card in two, wrap it around the line and rest a brick on top. This will keep the line exactly on the edge of your bricks.

Pointing

The mortar between the bricks is smoothed to give it an attractive appearance – this is called pointing. It also packs the mortar into the joints and makes them watertight. There are different pointing finishes, but the most common one is the concave or rubbed joint.

Leave the mortar until it is semi-dry; test by pressing your thumb into a joint – it should leave an impression without the mortar sticking to it. Scrape a concave recess into the joint, using a jointing tool or even a bucket handle or piece of metal.

Let the shaped joints harden a little, then gently brush away any loose bits of mortar with a medium-soft banister brush. Take care not to dislodge the mortar in the joints.

ideal tool

Jointing tool
This roller tool makes it easy to achieve neat, regular pointed joints. You can also use it to rake out old mortar before repointing.

Coping and capping

Bricks, stones, slabs or special coping bricks and blocks can all be used to finish a wall. Coping is a top course that overhangs; capping is flush.

Slab coping

Slabs on a low garden wall can provide extra seating. When laying slabs, make sure they overhang the brickwork by 25mm–30mm and are firmly laid on a continuous bed of mortar. Always wet the back of the slabs, particularly on hot days, as this helps them adhere to the mortar. Use a line and spirit level in the same way as for the wall itself.

Brick capping

Bed one stretcher face of each brick into the mortar so that it spans the width of the wall and the header faces are flush with the faces of the wall. Use very strong mortar.

Building a freestanding garden wall is quite straightforward, but sometimes a wall may need extra strengthening – if it is a retaining wall holding back heavy earth, for instance, or if it is a long wall. Or you may want to build a wall attached to the house. All these call for additional wall-building techniques.

Building a brick pier

Supporting piers, spaced no more than 3m apart, are necessary in single-skin walls over 450mm high. They can also be used in double-skin brick walls as a decorative 'full stop' on which to place a statue or potted plant, or as supports for gates or uprights for a pergola. (They are essential in double-skin walls of 1.35m and above.) The piers below are built in single-skin walls. Use stretcher bond and repeat the first two courses until the pier is the required height.

Reinforcing a pier
The hole in the centre of a hollow pier at the end of a wall is filled with concrete; if the pier is going to be attached to a gate or fencing or it is going to be more than 1m high, it will need extra reinforcement. If so, build the pier around a steel reinforcing rod or bar set in the concrete footing. The rod extends up to the top of the pier and the concrete is poured into the gap around it.

Support pier

To make a solid pier that projects on one side only, lay two header bricks in place of one of the stretchers on the first course, so they project from the wall. On the second course, cover the projecting part of the headers with a stretcher and cover the inner part with two ¾ brick stretchers, with a ½ brick between them.

Solid end pier

To build a solid pier at the end of the wall, projecting on one side only, lay a header brick against the end stretcher on the first course. Place a ½ brick parallel to the stretcher, butted against the header. On the second course, lay two stretcher bricks side by side.

Centred hollow end pier

End the first course with two ¾ brick headers. Butt a stretcher against each one, flush with the outer edge, and position a ½ brick stretcher to complete the final side of the square. On the second course, lay two ¾ brick headers on that final side and butt a stretcher brick against each one, flush with their outer edges.

Movement control joints

Weather conditions and ground settlement can cause movement in a brick wall, resulting in serious cracks. Control joints help to prevent this. A control joint is a continuous vertical gap of unmortared joints, completely separating one section of wall from the next.

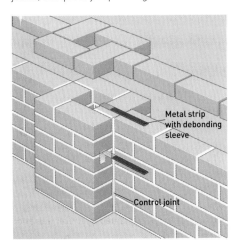

Control joints are not needed in a non-structural garden wall of less than 6m. In a wall longer than that, they should be incorporated at 6m intervals. The width of the control joint is normally 10mm, or a minimum of 1mm per metre of walling. Each joint should run right to the top of the wall, including the coping, but not into the footing.

A control joint is easier to disguise if you position it where the wall meets an intermediate pier. Build the wall and pier in the normal way, but instead of mortar insert a 10mm-thick polystyrene strip in the vertical joint between them. In the mortar of the horizontal joints embed galvanised metal strips with special debonding sleeves to allow for slight movement. When the wall is complete, run a bead of mastic masonry filler into the joint on both sides of the wall to hide the polystyrene strip.

ideal tool

Laser level and tripod
A laser level with adjustable tripod will accurately extend a level line over long distances. This is extremely useful when building a fence or garden wall.

Attaching a garden wall to a house

The simplest way to attach a wall at right angles to another is by using stainless steel connectors bolted to the existing wall. Special wall ties bedded in the new wall secure it to the connector. You will need a damp-proof course (DPC) in the garden wall or it could bridge the house's damp-proof course. Use a roll of polythene damp-proof course the same width as the wall.

project essentials

- **power drill with masonry bits**
- **trowel**

- stainless steel connectors and wall ties
- expanding masonry bolts
- mortar
- bricks
- damp-proof course

Build the first few courses of the garden wall up to the level of the damp-proof course in the house wall. Lay damp-proof polythene on the new wall at this level, sandwiched between layers of mortar, and lap it up the wall of the house by the depth of one brick.

Attach the stainless steel connector to the wall of the house just above the damp-proof course, using expanding masonry bolts (see page 199).

Mortar and lay the end bricks against the connector so that a joint is formed with the existing wall.

At every third course, hook one of the wall ties onto the steel connector and bed the other end in the mortar on the new wall.

Retaining walls

Retaining walls are used to hold back a bank of earth and, in turn, provide terracing on different levels in a garden. A steep bank can be held back by a series of small walls rather than one tall one. Retaining walls over 1m high should not be attempted without professional advice. Natural stone, bricks, concrete blocks and reconstituted stone are all suitable materials for a retaining wall. If you need a particularly strong wall, set reinforcing rods or bars in the footing concrete.

Excavate enough soil to give you room for the footing and the wall. If the soil in the bank is loose, hold it back with plywood or corrugated iron, secured with metal pegs, while you build the wall. Leave enough room to pack cleanstone – grit- and dust-free aggregate – between the back of the wall and the soil, and allow a 300mm depth of top soil.

Drainage is very important. Either leave some joints unmortared at ground level or just above to create weep holes, or fit a drainage pipe through the wall. Drainage will also be improved by a layer of geotextile permeable fabric on top of the cleanstone.

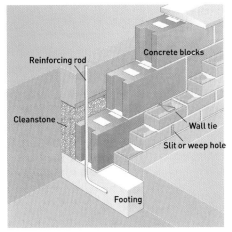

Hollow block and brick wall

This retaining wall is built with hollow concrete blocks and bricks and has reinforcing rods running through the holes in the blocks. Metal wall ties join the blocks and bricks.

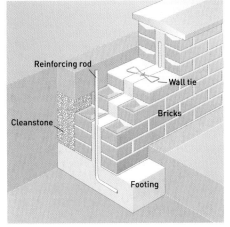

Brick retaining wall

Reinforcing rods are set between the two skins of this double-skinned brick retaining wall. Metal ties join the two skins of bricks.

Concrete block and reconstituted stone

The inner skin of this wall is concrete blocks and the outer (facing) skin is reconstituted stone. The skins are joined by metal ties and drainage pipes are fitted about 1m apart.

Proper dry-stone walling requires a great deal of skill and some wide bonding stones to span the width of the wall. An easier method, producing the same effect, is to build up the wall from both sides with a narrow layer of mortar in the centre, so that the joints look open, as if they have no mortar.

Building a natural stone wall

Lay the footing as you would for a brick wall (see pages 224–25). The minimum width of a double-faced freestanding stone wall is 450mm and the footing should extend by 120mm on both sides of the wall. Mark the footing to indicate the line each face of the wall will follow.

1 Sort through your pile of stones and pick out some likely corner stones (quoins). If there are no obvious ones, shape a stone by chipping it with a bricklayer's hammer or a stone axe. Wear gloves and safety goggles to do this.

2 Apply mortar to the footing (see Step 2, page 226) and set a quoin at each end of the footing on the marked lines.

3 Continue filling in the line of stones between the two ends. You can use a mixture of stones; they don't all have to be the same height.

5 Work on one side of the wall up to a height of no more than 500mm, then go to the other side of the wall and build that side up roughly level with the first side. Large stones, known as 'jumpers', can be introduced. These will change the height of the course. There is no need to work from one end to the other.

6 Fit metal wall ties no more than 900mm apart on the horizontal plane and 450mm apart on the vertical plane. Fill the centre with mortar and small off-cuts of stone as you go.

4 Build up the corners and ends first as you would when laying bricks (see page 227). Use a spirit level to ensure the quoins are vertical. Stretch a level line from one end of the wall to the other, 300mm–400mm above the footing. Move the line up the wall as you build, using it as a guide until you reach the finished wall height, which must be level.

Capping a natural stone wall

There are various ways of capping a stone wall, including using slab or even brick. One of the most popular methods is 'cock and hen' capping, alternating upright large and small stones. The stones are usually held in place with mortar. Before the mortar is completely dry, scrape away any surplus with a trowel and brush the stones with a medium-soft banister brush.

ideal tool

Bricklayer's hammer
A bricklayer's hammer is made of particularly hard steel with a chisel end and a square head instead of a round one, which makes it easier to chip bits off natural stones.

Reconstituted stone walls

Reconstituted stone comes in a wide range of colours, shapes and sizes (see page 221). The composite blocks used here are interlocking, making them very quick and easy to build.

1 Spread mortar on the footing and lay the first course. Build course by course, with mortar in all the joints. With these interlocking blocks there's no need to build up ends and corners first.

2 When the wall is the required height, spread mortar on the top course and fit reconstituted stone slabs or special coping stones.

project essentials

- **heavy-duty gloves**
- **trowel**
- **spirit level**
- **tape measure**
- **pointing tool**

- mortar
- interlocking blocks
- coping stones

ideal tool

Angle grinder
An angle grinder is an electric or motorised cutter that makes easy work of cutting stone slabs or bricks.

safety first

- Always wear safety goggles to cut bricks or blocks. Using an angle grinder creates a lot of dust, so you will need a gauze face mask too.
- An angle grinder continues to run for a few seconds after it has been switched off, so don't put it down until the blade has stopped turning.

Building a brick planter

A brick planter is simply four low brick walls built in a square or rectangular shape. It can be an opportunity to grow plants that need different soil conditions from those of your flowerbeds. Raised planters can also be more easily accessed by gardeners who have difficulty crouching or kneeling at ground level. Like any brick or stone wall, a planter needs a solid foundation. Rather than separate footing trenches (see page 224) it is simpler to lay a 150mm-deep concrete slab base under the planter, exending 100mm beyond each wall.

project essentials

- **spade**
- **shovel**
- **wheelbarrow**
- **heavy-duty gloves**
- **trowel**
- **spirit level**
- **tape measure**
- **pointing tool**

- concrete
- mortar
- frost-proof bricks
- coping stones

Coping stones

Multi-purpose compost mixed with horticultural grit

Brick walls

Permeable geotextile fabric

Gravel or crushed stone

1 Lay the first course of bricks on a 15mm bed of mortar, using a long spirit level to check that they are level.

2 To make sure water can drain away easily, leave a series of gaps or weep holes in the mortar in the first course of bricks – one every second or third brick should be plenty.

3 Lay the remaining courses of bricks. A good height for a planter is about 600mm (much higher and the walls may be pushed out of shape by the soil). Finish with coping stones (see page 227). Allow to dry for at least a week before filling and planting.

B&Q Making it easier

Good drainage
Help prevent plants becoming waterlogged by filling the bottom third of the planter with gravel or crushed stone. Lay a sheet of permeable geotextile fabric on top and then fill the rest of the brick planter with a mixture of compost and horticultural grit.

PAVING PATIOS AND PATHS

Patios and paths give character and definition to outdoor space. A patio designed as a sitting or dining area can be in any part of the garden, but will usually be sited next to the house for convenience. It can be paved with concrete slabs, paving blocks, reclaimed stone or even gravel, and is often connected to other parts of the garden by steps or a paved or gravel path.

Planning your garden

When you are designing major changes, it's a good idea to draw a simple plan of the house and garden to show where landscaped areas will be. It should also indicate any changes in level, because once out in the garden even slight gradients can present construction problems if they weren't thought about at the planning stage. Before you make any final decisions, use lengths of string to lay out your proposed plan on the ground.

Paving slabs

Paving slabs are straightforward to lay and come in a surprising variety of shapes, sizes and colours. Standard paving slabs are manufactured from hydraulically pressed concrete. Some have pigments added to give different colours, and you can buy them in a range of finishes: smooth, textured or moulded to resemble naturally weathered stone. Or you could opt for genuine natural stone, which is ever more affordable and popular.

House

Paved patio — Conservatory

Raised pond

Steps

Gravel path

Slab path around lawn

Concrete stepping stones

Circular paved area

Drive

Garage

Smooth

These smooth-finished slabs look great in combination with pale decorative chippings and foliage.

Wood effect

These teakwood-effect deck tiles are actually made of sawn natural sandstone, and can be used anywhere in the garden.

Textured

Textured slabs, like smooth ones, are available in a range of stones and shades.

Stepping stones

Stepping stones running through a gravel path or across a lawn will entice anyone to explore.

Coloured detail

Glass insert tiles in natural limestone slabs create a stylish contemporary look.

Woven-pattern effect

Create a design feature with the latest shaped and textured paving designs.

B&Q Making it easier

It's a wash-out

If you don't want to pave a path or drive, you can use gravel – but don't use it on a steep slope, because gravel will wash downhill in wet weather; in this situation, it is better to use concrete or tarmac.

Regular grid

Paving slab designs

You can use one size and shape of slab to make regular grid or staggered patterns, or you can combine different sizes to create a random grid design. Curved and circular slabs can be combined with rectangular ones, or used to create a stand-alone feature.

Random grid

Circular and grid combined

Circular feature

Cobbles

As well as individual cobble stones, you can buy paving slabs made to resemble cobbles. Or you can even buy cobbling by the square metre. In this case, the stones are manufactured to look like real cobble stones, but they are joined together with nylon line, so fitting them is as simple as laying a rug. They can be laid on earth, hardcore or a concrete base. Sand, gravel or soil can be brushed into the joints, or if the cobbles are laid on a concrete base (either on mortar or straight on wet concrete) they can be pointed with sand and cement. If laid on a lawn, the grass can be left to grow through the gaps. They are not suitable for drives.

Linked cobbling

Slab cobbling

Paving blocks

Brick-shaped concrete paving blocks are another alternative to slabs. In addition to standard-sized blocks, you can buy specially designed edging and corner stones. Like slabs, they are available in a range of colours and textured finishes.

Paving blocks can be laid in various patterns. Herringbone is particularly good for a drive as it can withstand the movement of cars.

Herringbone

Angled herringbone

Basketweave

Stretcher bond

PAVING SIMPLE REPAIRS

Although concrete is very hardwearing, you may sometimes need to repair paving, paths or steps. A section of paving or even a single slab may sink due to minor ground movements or heavy use, and this allows rainwater to collect in puddles. Concrete steps can wear at the edges and other areas can develop holes or cracks.

Replacing a slab

If a slab has sunk or suffered damage, it is a fairly easy matter to lift it and either re-lay or replace it.

Wearing safety goggles and heavy-duty gloves, chip out the pointing around the slab with a plugging chisel and a club hammer.

Use a bolster chisel and club hammer to break up and remove the old mortar. If the slab was laid on sand, use a piece of timber to level it and add more sand if necessary.

ideal tool

Plugging chisel
The thin angled blade of a plugging chisel is specially designed for removing mortar from joints in walls or paving.

Lift the slab with a spade, using a timber off-cut to protect the adjacent slab.

If the slab was laid on mortar, wet the back and lay it (or a new slab) in position on a fresh bed of mortar mixed with four parts sharp sand to one part cement. Make sure it is flush with the surrounding slabs. Use a timber off-cut and the club hammer to press the slab into position. Fill the joints with dry mortar (see Filling the joints, page 238).

project essentials

- **safety goggles**
- **heavy-duty gloves**
- **plugging chisel**
- **club hammer**
- **spade**
- **broom handle**
- **bolster chisel**

- timber off-cut
- sharp sand
- cement
- new slab, if required
- dry mortar of 3 parts sharp sand to 1 part cement

Insert a broom handle under the slab and roll it out of the way.

B&Q Making it easier

Slab sizes
There is a slight difference in size between older concrete slabs, produced in imperial sizes, and new metric ones, which are a fraction smaller. If you have to replace an old slab, see if it is possible to take one from somewhere else on the patio – from a position against a wall, for instance – and use that to replace the broken one. Fit the mismatched slab against the wall, where it will be less conspicuous – or you could fill the gap with earth and plants.

Repairing concrete steps

Years of use and exposure to the elements can cause concrete steps to deteriorate on the edges where the tread meets the riser. Repair the damage as soon as possible to prevent the steps becoming unsafe as well as unsightly.

Wearing safety goggles and protective gloves, chip out the loose and flaking concrete with a cold chisel and club hammer. Paint the damaged area with PVA adhesive diluted with water according to the manufacturer's instructions. Cut a piece of board to the same height as the riser and prop it against the riser with bricks.

 Making it easier

Concrete repairs
Look out for specially formulated epoxy patching mortar, which gives high-strength, durable repairs in concrete and masonry.

Let the adhesive dry to the point that it becomes tacky, then use a trowel or float to fill the damaged area with a concrete filler made by mixing three parts sharp sand, one part cement and a solution of equal parts of PVA adhesive and water mixed separately. Run an arrissing tool along the edge to create a neat, rounded front edge to the tread. Cover with polythene for three days while it hardens, then remove the bricks and board.

ideal tool

Arrissing tool

An arrissing tool is a metal float with a curved edge, which is used to round off and smooth concrete edges so they are less likely to be damaged. It also means there are no sharp edges to cause injury.

project essentials

- **safety goggles**
- **heavy-duty gloves**
- **cold chisel**
- **club hammer**
- **old paintbrush**
- **trowel or float**
- **arrissing tool**

- PVA adhesive
- piece of board
- bricks
- sharp sand
- cement
- polythene

Making it easier

Clean paving
Keeping paving stones clean will help to prevent a path or patio becoming slippery in wet weather. A pressure washer used with a chemical brick and patio cleaner will remove oil, grease and moss.

Repairing holes and cracks in concrete

Small hairline cracks in concrete are not a problem, but large cracks and holes should be repaired to prevent them filling with water, which could freeze and cause more damage. Chip away the damaged area to a depth of at least 15mm with a sharp cold chisel and a club hammer. Undercut the edge of the concrete with the chisel to hold the filler in place. Brush away any dust and debris from the hole and paint it with PVA adhesive diluted according to the manufacturer's instructions. When the PVA is tacky, fill the area with concrete repair filler mix (see above, Step 2). Use a float to level the surface with the surrounding concrete. Cover with polythene and leave to harden for three days.

project essentials

- **safety goggles**
- **heavy-duty gloves**
- **cold chisel**
- **club hammer**
- **old paintbrush**
- **trowel**
- **float**

- PVA adhesive
- sharp sand
- cement
- polythene

Undercut the edges of the crack before filling

PAVING SUB-BASE AND FALL

project essentials

- builder's line
- hammer
- builder's square
- spade
- shovel
- wheel barrow
- club hammer or rubber mallet
- spirit level
- straightedge
- earth rammer or vibrating plate compactor
- rake
- bucket
- soft brush
- heavy-duty gloves
- safety goggles
- dust mask
- bolster chisel or angle grinder
- watering can with rose attachment
- trowel

- wooden marker pegs
- hardcore
- sharp sand or all-in ballast
- 5mm spacers
- recessed manhole cover, if required
- masking tape, if required
- polythene
- wooden shims
- large-headed nails
- mortar, made from sharp sand and cement
- 600 x 600 concrete slabs
- timber off-cut

A large area of paving cannot be laid straight on soft ground. Concrete slabs, gravel, paving blocks and asphalt all need the support of a sub-base. This consists of hardcore (crushed or broken bricks, block and stone) compacted with an earth rammer (see IDEAL TOOL, page 251) or a vibrating plate compactor (which can be hired) and then topped with a layer of sharp sand or ballast – called blinding – to fill any gaps. If you are laying slabs on a drive, which is likely to have to bear the weight of several cars, the sub-base is better compacted with a single-drum vibrating roller, and it needs a layer of concrete as well.

Preparing a patio sub-base

You will need to remove a depth of top soil equal to the depth of the sub-base plus the thickness of the paving and mortar (a minimum of 25mm). In firm well-drained soil, the sub-base should be 100mm deep; in soft ground it should be deeper. Clear an area slightly larger than the paved area will be. When a patio is built next to a house, the level of the finished surface must be at least 150mm below the damp-proof course.

1 Mark out the area for the sub-base using builder's lines attached to wooden pegs. Use a builder's square (see page 225) to make sure the corners are square before you start excavating. As a final check, measure the diagonals to make sure they are the same.

2 Cut the turf in strips with a spade and roll it up. Save some of the turf in case you need to make good between an existing lawn and the paved surface.

B&Q Making it easier

How deep is your drive?
The depth of a drive sub-base depends on what you plan to pave it with. If you are laying concrete slabs, allow 150mm of compacted hardcore plus 125mm of concrete; if laying paving blocks, allow 150mm of compacted hardcore and 50mm of sand.

3 Dig the area to the correct depth and use marker pegs to mark the finished hardcore level, taking into account the required fall (see opposite).

4 Tip in enough hardcore to fill your sub-base to just above the top of the pegs.

5 Compact the hardcore with an earth rammer or a petrol-powered vibrating plate compactor, as used here.

6 Cover the surface with a thin blinding coat of sharp sand or all-in ballast and rake it level.

Setting the fall

Paved areas must have a slight slope or fall so that surface water drains away. Generally, it is only necessary to have a fall in one direction: the surface in the other direction can be level. In normal conditions, the ideal fall for a patio is 1 in 80 (that is, a 12.5mm drop in level per metre); for a path about 1 in 80 (across the width); and for a drive about 1 in 40. This is achieved in practice by using a spirit level, a 1m-long straightedge and a shim, a small strip of wood cut to the depth of the required drop in level per metre (see chart).

CALCULATING SHIM DEPTH	
Fall	Drop in level per metre
1 in 80	12.5mm
1 in 60	16mm
1 in 40	25mm

Setting the fall in the sub-base

First decide which way the paving will slope. If you are building a patio against the house, it must slope away from the walls. Cut a number of softwood pegs. Measuring from the top of each peg, mark them with the depth of the sub-base. Hammer in a row of these pegs across the high side of the site. Cut a shim to the correct size and nail it to the underside of one end of a 1m-long straightedge. Then hammer in the next row of pegs in line with the first, exactly one metre away. Place the straightedge between two pegs with the shim on the lower peg and lay a spirit level on top. A level reading means that the lower peg is deeper by the exact depth of the shim: the correct amount to give the fall you need. Repeat this process at metre intervals across the entire area to be paved.

Setting the fall in the paving

Although the fall is already established in the sub-base, it's important to run builder's lines marking the top edges of the paving to ensure you maintain the correct slope as you lay the slabs.

Mark out the edges of the patio with builder's lines attached to pegs. Use a builder's square to make sure the corners are true right angles.

Hammer pegs at the four corners of the patio to mark the finished slab height. Allow a depth of at least 25mm for the mortar. To check the fall, rest a straightedge and spirit level between opposite pegs at the high and low ends of the site. The depth of the shim on the lower peg needs to be the drop per metre multiplied by the length of the paving. Check that the pegs are level in the other direction. Fix lines between the pegs, nailed into the top with large-headed nails.

Laying the first slab

Paving slabs are bedded in mortar mixed with four parts sharp sand to one part cement (see page 223). The first slab is the key one that is the guide for all the others and it should be positioned in a corner. You may need to fit slabs around drainage gullies or manhole covers (see page 239). Arrange them so that you have to do as little cutting as possible.

Place five blobs of mortar on the ground for the slab, one at each corner and one in the middle. (If laying a drive, you need a continuous layer of mortar between the sub-base and the slab.) Wet the back of the slab with a brush – this will improve adhesion and make it easier to slide into position.

Carefully lift the first slab and lay it on top of the blobs of mortar.

safety first

Look after your back! If you are laying slabs 600mm x 600mm or larger, you must have someone to help you lift and lay them.

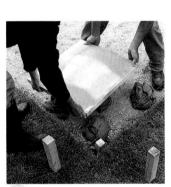

Use a piece of timber and a club hammer or rubber mallet to tap the slab into position. Take great care not to crack the slab.

Fill any gaps under the slab with mortar, cutting it flush with the edge as you go.

PAVING SLABS AND MANHOLE COVERS

Once you have positioned the first key slab, laying the rest of the slabs is quite straightforward. If there is a manhole (a drain inspection chamber) in the area you are paving, you can disguise it with a recessed manhole cover. If your finished paving is higher than the original ground level, you may have to raise an existing manhole cover.

Laying the remaining slabs

Whichever method you use to cut concrete slabs (see MAKING IT EASIER), it is difficult to achieve perfectly straight edges, so always place the cut edge against a mortar joint where it will be less noticeable.

Starting from your key slab, lay the first row of slabs in the direction of the slope. Fit 5mm spacers in all the joints to make sure they are the same size. Use a spirit level and shim to check and recheck that the surface is flat and the fall is correct. If you put a slab down and it rocks on the mortar, take it up and re-lay it; you are unlikely to be able to correct it by trying to push mortar underneath a slab once it's in position.

When the first row is complete, lay slabs along the two adjacent outer edges. If you are using a grid pattern, the first and last slabs on alternate rows will be half slabs.

Fill in the central area, working back row by row. Nail a line to pegs at either end of each row before you begin laying it. Keep checking that the fall is correct and that the surface is flat in both directions.

Cutting slabs

Cut a concrete slab on a bed of sand. Mark the cutting line in pencil on all its surfaces. Wearing safety goggles, cut a groove along the line using a sharp bolster chisel and a club hammer, cutting gradually deeper until the slab breaks.

For a quicker, cleaner cut, use an angle grinder with a stone-cutting disc. As well as safety goggles, you must wear heavy-duty gloves and a gauze dust mask while you work.

Filling the joints

Leave the mortar to set for 48 hours before walking on the slabs. Only then can the joints be filled. If the slabs are wet or it looks as if rain is imminent, wait for a drier day.

Mix a dry mortar of three parts sharp sand to one part cement. Remove the spacers and brush mortar into the joints. When all the joints have been filled, push the mix down firmly with a trowel or a piece of wood, then brush in more mortar. Repeat this process three or four times or holes will appear in the mortared joints. Finally, carefully brush away all the excess mortar – take time over this, as it's easy to end up with mortar on the slabs.

Using a watering can with a rose attachment or a spraying device, lightly wet the whole surface. This will make the mortar set.

Dry jointing compound

Alternatively you could fill the joints with dry jointing compound, shown below. Simply brush it in and compact with a jointing tool. It dries hard in a few hours – protect it from rain until then.

Skeleton manhole

If you are making a concrete path or drive, use a skeleton type of manhole cover. This is installed in the same way as a recessed cover but the tray is filled with concrete which is reinforced by a metal grid.

Bed the manhole cover on concrete, making sure the lip is 2mm–3mm below the level of the finished paved surface. Haunch the concrete around the edges with a trowel, being careful to leave room for the depth of the paving and its mortar bed.

Recessed manhole cover

A recessed manhole cover is an open tray designed to disguise a manhole in a run of paving. The paving is laid right up to the rim of the cover, then more paving is laid in the tray on a bed of mortar, retaining the paving pattern. Cobbled paving is shown here, but the same principle applies with slab paving. You can also fill a manhole cover with gravel, or buy one suitable for laying turf in. The tray can be lifted out using special manhole keys if the drain needs to be inspected.

Lay the paving right up to the cover, retaining the pattern.

Lift out the tray and cut the paving to fit inside it, still retaining the pattern. Remove the paving and spread a bed of mortar over the whole of the tray, then set the paving in the mortar. Cover the keyholes with masking tape while you fill the paving joints (see opposite).

Raising the height of a manhole cover

The surface of a new patio or drive will often be higher than the previous ground level, and the cover of any drain inspection chamber will need to be raised to the same level.

Lift off the manhole cover and lay a polythene sheet or plastic bag in the bottom of the manhole to make sure the debris does not clog the drain. Chip away the old mortar from the edge of the manhole frame with a club hammer and a sharp chisel. Take care not to hit the frame – if it is an old one it may be made of cast-iron, which cracks easily. Lift off the frame and clean away any mortar covering the top surface of the brick walls of the manhole.

Build up the manhole with engineering bricks bedded in mortar made with three parts soft sand to one part cement. If you want to raise the height less than the depth of one brick, use brick slips, which are narrow sections of brick, cut to size.

project essentials

- **club hammer**
- **cold chisel**
- **trowel**
- **spirit level**
- polythene sheet or plastic bag
- engineering bricks
- soft sand
- cement
- timber off-cut
- board

Spread more mortar on the new bricks, place the frame on top and tap it into position using a timber off-cut and a club hammer. Use a spirit level to make sure it is level across its length and its width.

If you are gravelling the area, slope the mortar around the frame to direct rainwater away. If you are laying slabs or blocks, then cut the mortar flush with the bricks so that you can pave right up to the frame. Remove the polythene and any debris from the bottom of the manhole. Cover the frame with a board weighted down with bricks while the mortar dries.

PAVING AND GARDEN DRAINAGE

Patios, paths and drives are built with a slight slope or fall so that surface water can drain away. In some instances, particularly if you have a large paved surface or live in an area of heavy clay soil, simply allowing the water to drain on to a lawn or planted bed may not be enough. You may need to build a drainage channel to collect the surface water and direct it to a dispersal point which leads into an existing surface water drain or into a soakaway.

Concrete drainage channel

If your patio isn't draining efficiently, or if you are laying a new patio or drive, one of the easiest ways to create a drainage channel along its edge is by moulding a concrete strip using a length of plastic guttering.

1 Place a length of timber the required distance from the paved surface (in this case slightly wider than the guttering used to mould the channel). Hammer in wooden pegs at intervals and nail them to the timber. The channel should run at right angles to the fall of the paving. Use a 1m-long straightedge and a 12.5mm shim to set a fall of 1 in 80 along the drainage channel (see page 237).

2 Mix concrete using four parts mixed aggregate to one part cement. Fill the channel with the concrete to a level slightly lower than the edge of the timber, and smooth it with a float.

3 Press the guttering into the wet concrete to leave a clear imprint. Remove the guttering and smooth any ridges in the concrete. Use a spirit level to make sure the fall is set at the correct angle.

Plastic drainage channel

Instead of moulding a channel in concrete, you can buy ready-made drainage channel. This may be plastic, resin-bonded or vitrified clay.

1 The channel should run at right angles to the fall of the paving and have a fall of 1 in 80. Use a 1m-long straightedge and shim of 12.5mm to achieve this (see page 237). Excavate a depth of 100mm along the edge of the patio and fill it with concrete. Place the first section of channel on the concrete.

2 Use waterproof sealant to fill the specially designed recess in the end of each section of channel. Fit the next section. Keep checking the fall and repeat all the way along the required run, cutting the channel with a panel saw, if necessary.

3 Build up or haunch the concrete on the outside of the channel, sloping away from it. Point the joint between channel and paving with dry mortar (see page 238). Finally, fit metal grating over the top.

• Check with your local
authority how far a
soakaway should be from
a building and which is
their preferred method
of construction.

• When constructing
underground drainage
systems – with the
exception of perforated
land drains – make sure
that you can rod the pipes
in case of a blockage
(see page 173).

• When working in an
excavation, you must
make sure that the soil
does not collapse into
the hole. If there is any
danger of this, shore up
the sides with plywood
boarding and stout
timbers.

Land drainage

If water builds up at the edge of a patio and takes a long time to drain away, you can install an underground drainage pipe system to cure the problem. Other wet areas of the garden can be drained the same way. However, there must be somewhere for the water to go. Rainwater should never exit into the main sewerage system. It must be diverted to a surface-water drain or, failing that, a soakaway in another part of the garden or even a river or lake (though in this case you will need permission from the local authority).

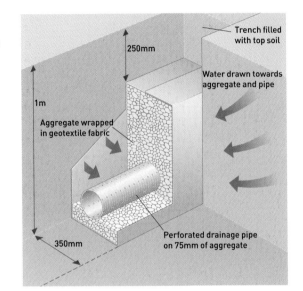

Trench filled with top soil

250mm

Water drawn towards aggregate and pipe

1m

Aggregate wrapped in geotextile fabric

350mm

Perforated drainage pipe on 75mm of aggregate

Constructing a land drain

Dig a trench about 1m deep and 350mm wide with a fall towards the outlet (to a soakaway or surface-water drain). The trench should run with the contour of the land, if possible. Line the trench with permeable geotextile fabric and lay clean aggregate (20mm–40mm) to a depth of 75mm in the bottom of the trench; the aggregate must be of a consistent depth and follow the fall. Lay a 100mm perforated plastic drainage pipe in the centre of the trench on top of the gravel bed. Work down the trench filling it with aggregate to within 200mm–300mm of ground level, being careful to keep the pipe central and running flat along the bed. Lay geotextile fabric over the aggregate and cover that with top soil.

Soakaways

Soakaways are used to disperse rainwater from drainage pipes and channels and land drains. They must not be used for household drainage or sewage and they should never exit into the sewerage system. You can buy a ready-made soakaway (right), which consists of open concrete blocks built up in rings. It has a concrete base and a manhole cover on top. It is buried underground with permeable geotextile membrane wrapped around the structure to keep soil out. Water entering the soakaway seeps out through the open blocks and membrane into the soil.

Ready-made concrete soakaway

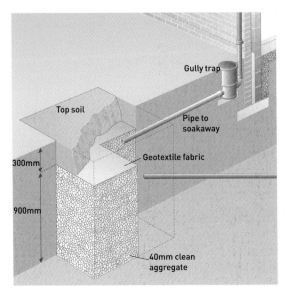

Gully trap

Top soil

Pipe to soakaway

Geotextile fabric

300mm

900mm

40mm clean aggregate

Digging a simple soakaway

A less expensive way of installing a soakaway is to dig a hole in the ground approximately 1.2m square and 1.2m deep. Break up the clay or rock at the bottom of the hole with a fork or crowbar. Cover the sides and bottom of the excavation with permeable geotextile fabric, overlapping it by 300mm where necessary. Fit a plastic underground drainage pipe from the drainage channel or rainwater pipe into the soakaway, fitting a gully trap at the top end of the pipe. Make sure that the pipe slopes towards the soakaway. Refill the hole with clean aggregate (40mm or larger), allowing for at least 300mm of top soil. Cover the aggregate with more geotextile fabric and top up with soil.

 Making it easier

Test your hole
Before excavating for a soakaway, dig a test hole at the required depth and check that it does not fill up with water from the ground. If it doesn't, half-fill it with water and check that this drains away. If the water takes a long time to drain, the soakaway may have to be bigger.

PAVING BLOCKS, GRAVEL AND ASPHALT

An edging kerb can give a decorative finish to all types of surfacing on paths, patios and drives. It is particularly useful for retaining paths of gravel or asphalt, and essential if you are laying paving blocks since these are simply bedded into a sub-base of sand over compacted hardcore. Without a securely laid kerb edging on concrete footings all around the edge, the unmortared blocks will soon fall away.

Laying paving blocks

Paving blocks are bedded into a layer of sharp sand with a light plate compactor (see page 236). You can use a club hammer and a piece of timber instead, particularly if paving a small area, but the blocks will not be so stable. Calculate the dimensions of your paving or patio in numbers of whole blocks to avoid waste and minimise cutting. Set out a sub-base at least 75mm deep in the same way as for slab paving (see pages 236–37). Allow the correct fall to ensure efficient drainage (see page 237).

(see page 236). (see pages 236–37). (see page 237).

project essentials

- **tape measure**
- **builder's line**
- **spirit level**
- **spade**
- **builder's square**
- **trowel**
- **kneepads**
- **plate compactor or club hammer and piece of timber**

- mortar, made of sharp sand and cement
- timber levelling strips
- sharp sand
- edging blocks
- paving blocks

Excavate a strip around the edge of the sub-base and lay concrete footings for the kerb. The footing should project 75mm on the outside of the edging blocks and no more than 25mm on the inside. When the concrete is dry, lay the edging blocks on a bed of mortar consisting of three parts sharp sand to one part cement. Use a line and spirit level to position them and allow for the fall across their surface. Leave the mortar to harden for three days.

Place two timber levelling strips about 1m apart to form a bay. The strips need to be as deep as the sand, which in turn depends on the size of block and method of compaction: a plate compactor will reduce the sand by 15mm; bedding in the blocks by hand will reduce it by about 10mm. Pile sand in the bay, then spread it perfectly flat and level with the tops of the strips. Check the fall as you go.

Prepare two or three bays, then remove the timber strips and carefully fill the depressions they have left with sand, using a trowel. Make sure the surface stays completely flat. Do not walk on the sand.

B&Q Making it easier

Levelling a path
When paving a path you can use the edging kerb on each side as a guide for levelling the sand. Find a length of timber longer than the width of the path and cut a notch out of either end so it will sit over the edging. The depth of board below the notches should be the depth of the paving block less 10mm or 15mm (depending on the method of compaction, see Step 2). Pull the board towards you, levelling the sand as you go.

Lay the blocks in the pattern of your choice, starting from one corner. Wearing knee pads, kneel on a length of timber to spread your weight over several paving blocks. Butt the blocks tightly against each other leaving no joints (they have small spacing nibs included in their design). Complete about 2sq m.

Press the blocks into the sand using a plate compactor, or a club hammer and piece of timber. If they drop too low, or they won't compact enough, take them up and adjust the sand bed. Continue paving in 2sq m sections.

ideal tool

Paving sealant

It's advisable to apply sealant to new concrete and brick paving. This will keep algae at bay, and help make the surface resistant to water, oil and grease.

Laying a gravel path

A loose gravel path needs a retaining edging if it is not to become dispersed through use. Set out a sub-base 100mm deep, in the same way as for slab paving (see page 236).

1 Excavate the hardcore sub-base to lay concrete footings for the kerb (see pages 224–25). The footings should be a minimum of 75mm deep and project about 75mm either side of the edging kerb line.

2 Use a builder's line to align the edging kerb as you set it on a bed of mortar (see page 226, Setting out the first course, Step 4).

5 Use a garden roller to roll in the coarse gravel and sand.

6 Cover the surface with fine pea gravel to a depth of 18mm–25mm and roll it with the garden roller.

3 Build up the mortar against the edging kerb on both sides with a trowel, keeping it lower than the path and ground level so that it will be out of sight.

project essentials

- **tape measure**
- **builder's line**
- **spirit level**
- **spade**
- **trowel**
- **builder's square**
- **rake**
- **garden roller**

- mortar
- coarse gravel and sand mix
- fine pea gravel
- hardcore
- edging kerb

4 Make sure the hardcore sub-base is firmly compacted. Cover the base with coarse gravel mixed with sand to a depth of 50mm. Rake it level.

Laying an asphalt path

Cold asphalt can be used to repair or resurface an existing asphalt surface, or to build a new path on a hardcore sub-base. It is not suitable for the construction of new drives. If you are resurfacing an old path, spray the path with weed killer about two weeks before applying the new layer. If you are building a new path, prepare a sub-base as you would for a patio (see pages 236–37) and lay edging kerb. Pick a fine day to lay the asphalt – water does not mix with bitumen emulsion.

project essentials

- **old watering can without rose**
- **stiff broom**
- **shovel**
- **garden rake**
- **garden roller**

- hardboard sheet or timber for masking
- bitumen emulsion (5kg will cover about 3sq m of hardcore or 7sq m of an existing asphalt surface)
- cold asphalt (a 25kg bag will cover about 0.9sq m)
- paraffin or white spirit

1 To avoid staining the edging kerb, cover it with some hardboard or old timber (if you do get any splashes, remove them with some white spirit on a cloth). Spread a coat of bitumen emulsion on the sub-base using an old watering can without a rose. Brush it across the surface with a stiff broom, if necessary. Let the emulsion dry for about twenty minutes, in which time it will turn from brown to black.

2 Tip or shovel the asphalt on top of the emulsion and rake it over the surface to an even thickness of about 20mm.

3 Wet the garden roller to stop the asphalt sticking, then roll in several directions to level and compact the asphalt to a depth of about 13mm. Clean your tools with paraffin or white spirit.

CONCRETE PATHS, PADS AND DRIVES

Concrete is made up of cement, aggregate (particles of stone) and sharp sand. When the ingredients are mixed with water, they bind into a solid, hard material. In different proportions, they produce concrete of different strengths for different uses. It's important to get the proportions accurate: if there is too much aggregate, you will have difficulty producing a satisfactory finish; too much sand will mean that the mix will be weak and the finished surface could be damaged by the elements. Hardening begins after about two hours and the concrete is then unworkable, but it does not become really strong for several days and continues to harden as long as there is moisture in it.

Designing with concrete

Various factors must be taken into account when designing concrete paths, pads or drives if the concrete is to be strong enough for the job.

- The mix must be determined by what the concrete is to be used for (see table below).
- The thickness of the concrete must be determined by the weight it will be supporting. A pad for a lightweight wooden shed would only need to be 100mm deep. For a stone, brick or block garage, you would need a 150mm sub-base of compacted hardcore and a 125mm concrete pad. The edges of the pad would need to be deeper (a minimum of 200mm) to support the walls.
- The surface of the concrete must form a slight slope, so that water drains off. It should slope away from buildings or, in the case of a slab used to site a shed, away from the door (see Setting the fall, page 237).
- When laid against a house wall, the surface must be at least 150mm below the damp-proof course.
- In an area that will have to withstand considerable weight, such as a drive, concrete should be reinforced with a steel grid at half its depth.

Mixing by hand

Mixing concrete by hand is only really an option for small amounts. Prepare it in the same way as mortar (see page 223), mixing thoroughly and methodically – a longer job than you might think – until it is an even consistency, neither too dry nor too sloppy. When you pick up a shovelful, it should stay on the shovel and when you drop it onto the sub-base it should spread slightly but retain some shape.

Using a mixer

Start by pouring about a quarter of a bucket of water into the mixer. Add half the aggregate and half the sand (or half the all-in aggregate), and all the cement, then check the mix to see if you need to add more water. Add the rest of the aggregate (and sand, if using it), and more water if necessary. If you find it difficult to assess a shovelful, gauge the mix using buckets (see page 223).

If the final mix is too sloppy, add more aggregate and cement in proportion. An average-sized mixer will accept 12 to 14 shovelfuls of aggregate and two to three shovelfuls of cement.

Ready-mixed concrete

If you are planning to lay a large area of concrete or have little time, ready-mixed concrete is worth considering. Depending on the access to your site, the concrete is delivered in lorries and either poured directly on to the area or wheelbarrowed from the lorry to the site. It is a much more expensive way of buying concrete, but it cuts down on labour enormously and companies will deliver any quantity. If you decide to use ready-mixed, you will need to ensure that everything is organised before the lorry arrives and that help is on hand. Ready-mixed is ordered by the cubic metre: add 10% to allow for wastage and specify the job you are doing so the right mix can be prepared.

CONCRETE MIXES

Ingredients	Amounts required for approx. 1 cubic metre of concrete
Paving mix (strong mix suitable for exposure to all weathers, including frost), using separate aggregate	
1 part cement	16 x 25kg bags
1.5 parts sharp sand	0.5 cubic metre
2.5 parts 20mm coarse aggregate	0.75 cubic metre
Paving mix (strong mix suitable for exposure to all weathers, including frost), using all-in aggregate	
1 part cement	16 x 25kg bags
3.5 parts all-in aggregate	1 cubic metre
Foundation or footing mix (and for concreting in fence posts), using separate aggregate	
1 part cement	11.2 x 25kg bags
2.5 parts sharp sand	0.5 cubic metre
3.5 parts 20mm coarse aggregate	0.75 cubic metre
Foundation or footing mix (and for concreting in fence posts), using all-in aggregate	
1 part cement	11.2 x 25kg bags
5 parts all-in aggregate	1 cubic metre
For garage or garden shed bases (not exposed to weather), using separate aggregate	
1 part cement	12.8 x 25kg bags
2 parts sharp sand	0.5 cubic metre
3 parts 20mm coarse aggregate	0.75 cubic metre
For garage or garden shed bases (not exposed to weather), using all-in aggregate	
1 part cement	12.8 x 25kg bags
4 parts all-in aggregate	1 cubic metre

Estimating the amount

To estimate the amount of concrete required for a job, you need to apply a bit of basic geometry. Measure the surface area of the site by multiplying the length by the width (in metres). Multiply that figure by the depth or thickness required (as a fraction of a metre) and you will have the volume in cubic metres. In practice, figures are rounded up and about 10% added for wastage.

For example: (width) 2m x (length) 6m x (depth) 0.15m = 1.8 cubic metres. You would round that up to 2 cubic metres of concrete.

If the site is circular, use the formula πr^2 (π = 3.14 and r^2 = the radius of the circle squared). Multiply them together to get the surface area, then multiply that number by the depth of the concrete required to get the volume.

For example: (π) 3.14 x (radius) 2m x (radius) 2m x depth 0.15m = 1.884 cubic metres of concrete. Rounded up, you would require 2 cubic metres of concrete.

Constructing basic formwork

Concrete has to be supported by a frame or edging, known as formwork, until it has set. Timber formwork is sufficient for most domestic jobs but on larger projects, such as long drives, you can hire metal roadforms. The formwork is constructed directly on a prepared sub-base (see pages 236–37). Use rough-sawn timber planks about 25mm thick and as deep as the concrete. They are held in place by wooden pegs spaced at about 1m intervals.

Irregular shapes

To work out the volume of concrete needed for an irregularly-shaped site, draw it accurately and to scale on graph paper. Each square should represent 1sq m of the site. Count the whole squares covered and roughly add up the part squares. Multiply that total by the depth of the concrete and round the figure up by 10%.

---

project essentials

- **builder's line**
- **builder's square**
- **panel saw**
- **club hammer**
- **spirit level**
- **straightedge**
- **hammer**

- 50mm x 50mm wooden pegs
- rough-sawn timber planks, 25mm thick and as wide as the depth of concrete
- 50mm nails

Set out the site using builder's lines and wooden pegs, cut to a point at one end: the lines should mark the edges of the concrete, which will be the inside of the formwork. Use a builder's square (see page 225) to check the corners are exactly 90º.

Cut a plank to length and place it in position along the high side of the site. Use a club hammer to drive a peg into the sub-base at each end, outside the area to be concreted. Hammer them in until they are flush with the top of the plank.

Use a spirit level to make sure the plank is level, then secure each end of the plank to the wooden pegs with 50mm nails.

Use a spirit level, straightedge and shim to set the fall on the two adjacent sides of the formwork. It should be about 1 in 80 for a single concrete pad (see page 237).

Attach the last plank to complete the square or rectangle. Make sure that there are pegs at the corners and that the corners are tight-fitting by nailing the planks together. It doesn't matter if the planks run past the edge of the square, as they do here.

Hammer in pegs at roughly 1m intervals along the outside of the formwork. The structure must be solid; it is very difficult to alter it once you begin concreting.

---

ideal tool

Club hammer

A heavy club hammer is needed for driving the wooden pegs into the hardcore sub-base.

Curved formwork

If you want to make a curved path or drive, you will need to bend the timber formwork to follow the curve. Do this by making a series of closely spaced parallel saw cuts across the width of the plank along the length of the curve.

project essentials

- **builder's line**
- **hammer**
- **workbench**
- **circular saw**
- **hosepipe or rope, if required**

- 50mm x 50mm wooden pegs
- 50mm nails
- bamboo cane
- rough-sawn timber planks, 25mm thick

B&Q Making it easier

Check it's firm
As a final check to make sure the formwork is solid before you start concreting, try to flex the planking by pushing it backwards and forwards with your hand. If it moves, add more pegs.

1 To mark a curve, nail one end of a line to a peg, attach a bamboo cane to the other end and use this to draw an arc in the sub-base surface. If the curve is not circular, use a hosepipe or rope to define the shape and mark it with a cane. Drive in pegs at roughly 1m intervals along the curve.

2 Hold the plank in a workbench and use a circular saw to make a series of cuts, about 50mm apart and 20mm deep, along the entire length of the proposed curve. If it is a tight curve, the saw cuts should be slightly closer together.

3 Starting in the middle of the curve, nail the plank to the pegs with the saw cuts on the inside of the curve (if it is a very gentle curve, they can be on the outside).

Driveways

Even if you intend to surface a driveway with concrete slabs, you need a sub-base that includes a layer of concrete. This is because a drive has to bear a much greater weight than a path or other lightweight structure. It should have a sub-base of 150mm compacted hardcore covered with a thin blinding coat of sharp sand, then a 125mm depth of concrete, or 150mm of concrete if the drive is going to be used by heavy vehicles. The slabs should be at least 50mm thick.

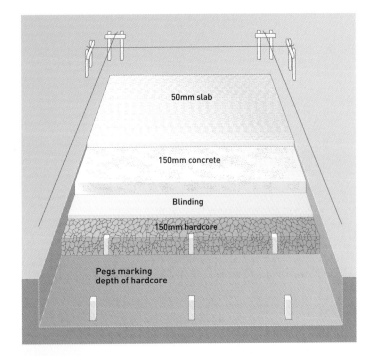

50mm slab

150mm concrete

Blinding

150mm hardcore

Pegs marking depth of hardcore

Extending a run of formwork

You may have a run of timber formwork that is longer than the length of the planks you are using. In this case, you need to butt-join two lengths very securely. Cut a section of plank about 200mm long.

Line up the two planks to be joined, end to end. Place the short length of timber across the join, outside the area to be concreted. Nail from the inside to join the short length to the long planks. Keep your feet well out of the way, and hit the spiked end of each nail when you have knocked it through to turn it safely over.

Control joints

In larger areas and along paths and drives, special control joints should be installed to allow the concrete to expand and contract without cracking as the temperature changes. Control joints usually consist of 12mm-thick bitumen-impregnated fibreboard (specially designed for the job), which is compressible and allows the concrete to expand and contract. The fibreboards are inserted as the concrete is being laid.

Control joints should be installed between concrete and a wall, between bays (see page 249), and around inspection chambers. The maximum size a concrete slab can be without danger of it cracking depends on its width and thickness: the more narrow and shallow the concrete, the more likely it is to crack (see table below). You don't need control joints in a concrete sub-base.

Installing a control joint for a path

Cut the bitumen-impregnated fibreboard to size – each joint must be the width of the slab and the depth of the concrete.

CONTROL JOINT INTERVALS			
Width of concrete	Depth of concrete		
	75mm	100mm	150mm
Under 1m	2m interval		
1m–2 m	2.4m interval	2m–3m interval	3m–4m interval
3m	3m interval	4m interval	5m interval

ideal tool

Shovel
Unlike a garden spade, a shovel has raised edges designed for transporting loose materials like sand, gravel or cement.

Place the first board on the sub-base between the formwork. Hammer nails through the formwork into the board but do not drive the nails home. This will allow you to take them out easily with a claw hammer before the formwork is removed.

Shovel concrete against the board on both sides to hold it in position.

project essentials

- **panel saw**
- **tape measure**
- **hammer**
- **shovel**

- bitumen-impregnated fibreboard
- 50mm nails
- concrete

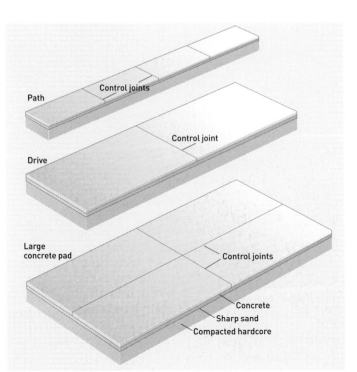

Path
Control joints
Drive
Control joint
Large concrete pad
Control joints
Concrete
Sharp sand
Compacted hardcore

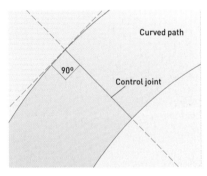

Curved path
90°
Control joint

Regular and irregular shapes

Paths need a control joint every 2m in 75mm-deep concrete. Drives and parking areas need them every 4m in 100mm-deep concrete. In large concrete pads they should be installed no more than 4m apart in 100mm-deep concrete. On an irregular-shaped winding path, control joints are inserted at 90° to the path edges.

CONCRETE LAYING AND FINISHING

Concrete starts to harden and set about two hours after it has been mixed, so it must be laid, tamped (packed down) and given its finish within that time. Divide large areas into bays or sections which can be completed one at a time before they begin to set. You can walk on the concrete after three days, remove the formwork after five days and drive on it after ten days.

Laying concrete

Concreting is a two-person job. Using ready-mixed concrete, two people can lay an area of approximately 8.5sq m before it sets. Concrete will crack if it is allowed to dry too quickly during the first few days, so keep it moist by covering it with a polythene sheet.

project essentials

- **watering can with rose attachment**
- **wheelbarrow**
- **shovel**
- **rake (optional)**
- **arrissing tool**

- concrete
- 50mm x 100mm timber longer than the width of your site
- polythene sheet
- timbers and bricks to support polythene sheet

1 Wet the sub-base and the formwork with a watering can fitted with a rose.

2 Starting in one corner, pour concrete into the formwork.

3 Push the blade of the shovel up and down in the wet concrete (particularly near the edges) to get rid of any air pockets.

4 Use a rake or shovel to spread the concrete, leaving it about 18mm higher than the top of the formwork. Fill about 1m–1.5m from the end where you started.

5 With a helper, compact the concrete using a straight piece of 50mm x 100mm timber that is longer than the width of your site (this is known as a tamping board). Start at one end and use steady blows of the plank, moving it along the site at a rate of about half its thickness at a time, until you have an even ridged surface.

6 To remove excess concrete and level the surface, go back to the end where you started and slide the tamping board backwards and forwards in a sawing motion across the site, moving it all the time away from the starting edge. Fill any depressions in the surface and repeat the procedure, if necessary, until you have an even surface flush with the top of your formwork. Continue to pour the concrete, tamp and level until you reach the end of the bay.

7 At this stage you have a rough tamped surface which can be given any of the finishes opposite. When you are happy with the finish, you can run an arrissing tool (see IDEAL TOOL, page 235) along the formwork to round off the exposed edges of the concrete.

8 Cover the concrete with a polythene sheet to slow drying and prevent cracking. Raise the sheet on wooden supports so that it does not touch the surface and weight it down with bricks around the edges.

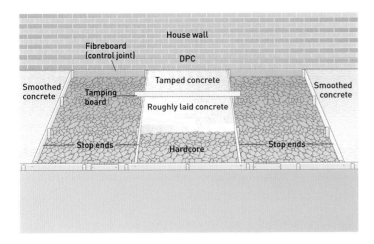

Labels on diagram: House wall; Fibreboard (control joint); DPC; Tamped concrete; Smoothed concrete; Tamping board; Roughly laid concrete; Smoothed concrete; Stop ends; Hardcore; Stop ends

Concrete bays

Try to keep bays the same size and as square as possible. Their size will vary according to the shape of the site but it is impractical to make one more than 4m wide in the direction in which you will be tamping or packing down the concrete. Position pegged boards (known as stop ends) at right angles to the main run of formwork. Remember to install a control joint against a wall and to keep the surface of the concrete at least 150mm below the damp-proof course in a house wall. The pegs must be outside the area to be concreted. Lay the concrete in alternate bays so you can stand in the empty bays to tamp it. When the concrete is dry, take out the boards and pegs and fit lengths of fibreboard in their place. Then fill the gaps, using the edges of the dry concrete pads to level the concrete in the adjacent bays.

Concrete finishes

A rough tamped finish will often be perfectly adequate, or you can use brushes or floats if you want a smoother finish. Allow the concrete to dry a little before finishing with a float or you will bring moisture to the surface, which will weaken the concrete.

Tamped finish

For a roughish finish with plenty of grip, leave the tamped surface without any extra finish.

Brush finish

Pull a stiff brush at an angle across the surface. For a softer finish, use a soft brush.

Metal float finish

Use a metal float to create a polished, glass-like finish. This is time-consuming and requires some skill to get it perfectly smooth. It is usually impractical outdoors: on a path or drive algae growth will build up as it weathers and the surface will become very slippery in no time.

Wooden or plastic float finish

Create a pattern of overlapping circles on the concrete surface, using a plastic or wooden float.

Gravel finish

Smoothed concrete can be covered with a layer of gravel. Use small, same-size gravel such as 10mm pea gravel.

Finish the surface with a float then spread the gravel while the concrete is still wet.

Lightly tamp the gravel into the surface, using a block of wood. Let the concrete harden for a day or two then lightly spray the surface, using a watering can with a fine rose attachment. Brush away any loose material with a soft brush. Let the surface dry for a day, then hose it down and brush with a stiff broom.

GARDEN STEPS ON A SLOPE

Garden steps built into an earth slope can be constructed from a variety of materials: bricks and concrete slabs, timber and gravel, concrete or large flat stones. The design will depend on the type of material you use, the gradient and the length of the slope. But the treads – the horizontal part of the step – should never be less than 300mm from front to back, and the risers – the vertical face between the treads – no lower than 100mm and no higher than 180mm. Use longer treads on a gentle slope and shorter on a steep one.

Setting out and excavating the steps

The steps shown here are built from brick and concrete slabs. The first riser is laid on a concrete footing, while the rest of the risers are bedded directly on to the tread below. The tread lengths are all the same but the excavation for the first step is longer than the others.

1 Begin by marking out the site using builder's line and pegs. Fix two parallel lines down the length of the slope, marking the outer edge of the steps, and two more to mark the top and bottom of the steps. Use a builder's square to check that the corners form a right angle (see page 225).

2 To calculate how many treads and risers are required, you need to measure the vertical height and horizontal distance of the flight of steps. Knock in a peg to mark the back of the highest tread. Then hold one end of a long spirit level (or a level and straightedge) at the top of the peg. With a helper, measure the horizontal distance to the first riser, and the vertical distance to the ground at that point.

3 Divide the vertical height by your riser height and use the tread–riser combinations chart (opposite) to find an appropriate tread length. Strip away any turf in the marked-out area with a spade.

4 Use lines to mark the back of the treads, set back an extra 50mm or so to give you enough room to work. Roughly shape the steps with a spade. Allow enough depth beneath the concrete slab treads for 100mm of hardcore.

5 Dig a trench about 125mm deep for the footing for the first riser. Drive in pegs levelled with a spirit level to mark the surface of the footing before you pour in concrete. If there is to be a paved surface leading to the steps, then dig a deeper footing and lay one or two courses of engineering bricks on top of it, below ground level. You will then be able to lay paving right up to the first riser.

6 Concrete the footing, making sure the surface is level with your pegs, and leave it to dry for 24 hours before building on it.

Concrete slab (tread)

Bricks (riser)

Hardcore

Concrete footing

Tread-riser combinations

To work out how many risers you need, divide the vertical height of the flight by the height of your riser. Then divide the horizontal length of the flight into a suitable number of treads. The combinations of tread and riser measurements given here will make attractive, safe steps. It is not always possible to follow them exactly: you may need to shorten or lengthen treads, cut bricks or build up the ground to make your flight work. But you should aim to approximate these measurements when making your calculations, and don't forget that a tread should never be less than 300mm front to back.

TREAD-RISER COMBINATIONS	
Tread length	**Riser depth**
460mm	100mm
430mm	113mm
400mm	125mm
380mm	140mm
360mm	150mm
330mm	165mm
300mm	180mm

Building the steps

It is a good idea to make a drawing showing the step dimensions once you have decided on the best tread and riser combination: you will find this a useful reference while you are building the steps. If you are using slabs that are 600mm square or larger, make sure you have a helper – they should be lifted and laid by two people.

ideal tool

Earth rammer
An earth rammer – a heavy steel club on a long handle – is ideal for compacting small areas of earth.

1 Mix a mortar using four parts sharp sand to one part cement (see page 223). Build the first riser on the concrete footing using two skins of stretcher bond bricks (see page 222). Keep checking they are horizontal with a spirit level. Leave the mortar to dry for two hours.

2 Fill behind the riser with hardcore – it should extend beyond the back of the slab when laid. Compact the hardcore with an earth rammer (see IDEAL TOOL).

3 The hardcore should rise slightly towards the back of the step. Use a spirit level and 10mm shim laid across the front of the step to achieve this (see Setting the fall, page 237).

4 Lay a continuous bed of mortar on the riser and hardcore and position the slab for the first tread on top of it. The slab should overhang the riser at both the front and sides by approximately 40mm. Place the spirit level along the front edge to check the step is in line. If you are laying two slabs side by side, apply a pointing mortar (made with three parts sharp sand to one part cement) to the edge of the first slab before you lay the second. This will make it easier to fill the joints.

5 Confirm that the treads are showing a slight fall towards their front edge with a spirit level and 10mm shim. Fill all the joints with mortar.

6 Build the next riser on the first tread. Check that its depth is the same as the first and make slight adjustments to the horizontal joints as necessary. It's very easy for slight errors to accumulate, so you should also check each riser against the overall height of the flight, measured from the top guide peg with a spirit level and tape measure. Lay the slabs of the next tread.

7 Continue building the steps, checking that the tread lengths are correct. Place a long spirit level or straightedge on the front edge of the treads to check they are in line. The slope on either side of the steps can be banked up with earth for planting or it can be grassed.

Freestanding steps constructed beside a brick wall should be built from brick and concrete, and need to be anchored to the wall to make them secure. In an informal part of the garden logs can be used to support a single step on a gentle slope, or they can be placed at intervals on a long incline.

Freestanding steps

Not all steps are built into a slope: freestanding steps can be built on a flat base alongside an existing garden wall (not a house wall, for they would breach the damp-proof course). They are supported by low walls built of bricks, which also form the risers. The walls are like a series of boxes and are filled with hardcore. For a flight of up to five steps, the supporting walls can be centred on concrete footing strips. For a longer flight, you need a concrete pad under the whole structure.

The brick risers can either be built up from ground level or you can lay a 100mm concrete footing at the back of each tread on built-up compacted hardcore before you lay the slab, and build the next riser on it. With brick steps parallel to a brick wall, the bricks in the risers should correspond to the bricks in the existing wall. The risers must be anchored, or toothed in, to the existing wall to make them more secure.

Garden wall

Raised patio

Concrete footing laid on built-up hardcore

Half brick removed for toothing in step brick

Riser built up from ground level

Hardcore infill

10mm-deep concrete footing strip

Hardcore infill

Anchoring steps to an existing wall

To anchor freestanding steps safely to the wall, the adjoining brick in every third course of their low supporting walls must be 'toothed in' to the brickwork of the existing wall. To do this half a brick is cut out of the existing wall and half of the adjoining brick is inserted and securely mortared in its place. All the appropriate half-bricks must be removed from the existing wall before you start building the steps.

Drill 10mm holes into the joints around the half of the brick that you are removing. Then drill down the centre of the brick.

Use a cold chisel and club hammer to remove the half-brick.

Build the steps and support walls up to the level of the cavity. Spread mortar on the top of the wall and into the cavity, then fit half of the adjoining brick into the cavity. Tap it into place with the trowel handle. Continue building the rest of that course of bricks and lay the tread.

ideal tool

Cold chisel

B&Q

A cold chisel, which is made from solid steel, is ideal for chopping out a brick from a wall. The plastic handle has a built-in guard to protect your hand.

Simple log step

This log step will blend well in an informal part of the garden. Instead of logs you can use railway sleepers or even sawn lengths of timber. Select one large log or two slimmer ones for each step (the logs shown here are 75mm in diameter). If you buy untreated softwood logs, be sure to give them a coat of wood preservative before you start.

project essentials

- **spade**
- **tape measure**
- **spirit level**
- **handsaw**
- **sledgehammer**
- **power drill with twist bit**
- **earth rammer**
- **hammer**
- **rake**

- 75mm-diameter logs
- wood preservative
- 125mm galvanised nails
- hardcore
- gravel

1 Excavate the ground either side of the step, roughly levelling it. Tread down the soil to compact it, if necessary. Cut your log or logs to the required length using a handsaw and paint the cut ends with wood preservative. Then lay one log in position to mark the first riser. Cut two lengths of log about 450mm long and sharpen one end of each to a point; these will be used as stakes to retain the riser. Use a sledgehammer to knock in the stakes in front of the riser at either side of the step, leaving them higher than the proposed depth of the riser.

2 Position the next log directly on top of the first and use a spirit level to ensure it is horizontal. Roll the logs away and adjust the earth below if necessary.

3 Use the sledgehammer to knock down the stakes to the level of the riser.

4 Take off the top log. Using a drill with a twist bit, drill pilot holes all the way through the lower log in line with the two stakes. Get a helper to hold the post steady from the other side with the sledgehammer and hammer in 125mm galvanised nails from the inside of the step to secure the bottom log to the stakes. Repeat with the top log.

5 Pack hardcore behind the riser to form the step tread and compact it with an earth rammer.

ideal tool

Sledgehammer
You will need a heavy-weight tool like a sledgehammer to hammer log stakes into the ground.

6 Cover the hardcore with a layer of gravel and rake it level.

Design your own steps

Reclaimed railway sleepers (left) have a rugged, weathered finish that works perfectly with the informality of simple garden steps. Fill the excavated part of the step with stones, chippings or wood bark. You could relay the turf, but it is likely to wear away with regular use. For a more hardwearing surface, let the grass grow between loose-laid log cobbles

SHEDS AND GARDEN BUILDINGS

Shed or summerhouse, playhouse or gazebo, greenhouse or simple glass lean-to: garden buildings come in all shapes and sizes, and have more potential than you might at first think. What's to stop you adding a power supply and heating to a shed or cabin and turning it into a workshop or even a home office? Do the same in a summerhouse and you can relax or entertain in it day or night, winter or summer. These structures are very affordable and are quick and easy to put together. Visit diy.com for inspiration and ideas.

Sheds and wooden outbuildings

Classed as temporary structures, sheds and wooden outbuildings rarely require planning permission, unless you live in a conservation area (see page 379). They can be sited almost anywhere, so long as they are positioned on a level, firm surface.

Whatever your needs, there is something to suit everyone. Secure storage for bicycles, garden equipment and furniture is a must. But garden buildings can also provide extra living space, work space or play space, enabling you and your family to make greater use of the garden throughout the year.

Shed

A traditional shed is the perfect storage solution for garden tools and furniture, helping you keep your outdoor space secure and clutter free. A potting shed has an additional glazed area for cultivating plants and seedlings.

Planning

Thinking through the following issues before you buy should help you make the right choice:

- What size of outbuilding do you want? How big can it be without it overwhelming your garden?
- How will you gain access to the building? Would a path protect the lawn and make it more accessible in the wet?
- Where will you put it? Don't place a building where it will create dead space, where light is blocked and access limited. It is often sensible to back a shed onto an outside wall or fence.
- Will there be enough natural light in winter? Is there a danger of overheating in summer?
- Do you want an electricity supply? How far away is the power source?
- Do you want a water supply? Is there an outside water tap from which a pipe can be run?
- What can you do to make it look good and complement your garden? You could paint it with coloured wood stain, for example, and surround it with imaginative planting.

Garage or carport

A carport or freestanding garage is a practical and affordable alternative to a conventional brick garage.

Summerhouse

A summerhouse is the perfect garden room. Providing shelter from the sun and breeze, it is ideal for lazy summer afternoons or outdoor dining. It could even double as a home office.

Wood, resin or metal?

Wood is the most popular material for sheds and outbuildings. Its natural warmth blends with the outdoor surroundings, or it can be stained or painted to give your garden a whole new look. However, you might also consider a resin shed. These are very robust and low-maintenance, needing no painting or treating. Or maybe a metal structure: usually made from galvanised steel with a paint or plastic coating, these are resistant to extremes of weather and also fire.

Shelter or loggia

An open-sided shelter is an ideal spot for a dining table and chairs, or even a hot tub. Creating welcome shade on a summer's day, it will make your garden a much more hospitable space.

Playhouse

Children love their own special garden building. See page 260 for how to construct and paint a typical playhouse.

Animal house

Hen house or dog kennel, chicken coop or pig pen – there are specially designed structures to keep all kinds of animals sheltered and safe.

Greenhouses

Greenhouses come in many shapes and sizes, with frames in timber or, more often, aluminium, which has the advantage of being maintenance-free. Choose the biggest greenhouse you can afford or have room for, as you will find that plants fill the space very quickly.

Glazing

There are three main choices: horticultural glass is most common and is inexpensive; toughened glass is a stronger alternative and safer if there will be children in the garden; even tougher still are polycarbonate panels, which diffuse sunlight and so reduce scorching.

Access

Make sure you can get all the way around your greenhouse from the outside, so that you can clean the glass each year.

Ventilation

The correct amount of ventilation is very important for temperature control and air circulation. Poor ventilation will increase humidity and encourage plant disease. Most greenhouse frames include adjustable air vents. Thermostatically controlled automatic vents can be installed inexpensively, and they don't need a power supply. Louvre windows are another option, allowing adjustable, draught-free ventilation.

Shading

Greenhouse shading is necessary in the summer months to avoid overheating and scorching plants. There are three main options:
• Special greenhouse shading paint can be applied to the exterior surface of the glass. It is weatherproof but can be removed with a duster in late autumn.
• Shading panels or woven plastic netting can be clipped to the inside of the frame.
• Internal shelving can provide shade for the most delicate plants.
It's best to avoid siting a greenhouse under a large tree, as a falling branch could shatter the glass.

Heating

For cold seasons and for growing certain plants, you may need to heat your greenhouse. Again, there are several options available:
• Paraffin heaters are cheap to buy but they consume a lot of fuel, are difficult to regulate and they encourage condensation, which can increase humidity and lead to plant diseases.
• Bottled gas heaters are thermostatically controlled but again encourage condensation.
• Electric heating is the best option, but you will need connection to a power supply. Choose between heating pipes, a fan heater or even a warming cable laid under the soil in a bed of coarse grit.

Irrigation

Capillary matting, which retains water and releases it according to a plant's requirements, is enough for most greenhouses. Alternatively you could run a pipe along the soil from an outside water tap. You could add a timer switch for automatic watering – particularly useful if you go away regularly.

GREENHOUSE CONSTRUCTION

A greenhouse will bring new life to your garden, providing a controlled environment in which to propagate plants, bring on hardy ones early, protect semi-hardy specimens from frost, and grow exotic species in year-round warmth.

Securing the base to the ground

You can buy a separate purpose-designed galvanised steel base, also available as a flatpack, on which the greenhouse frame sits, secured by frame fixings. A base will usefully raise the height of the greenhouse, and make construction easier, though it is not essential. However, the frame or base must be firmly secured onto a level surface. There are different methods of doing this:

- Push specially designed metal hooks into isolated pockets of wet concrete. These are then attached to the base, securing it to the ground.
- Or you could lay a concrete strip footing 200mm wide and 100mm deep. The base can then be anchored by drilling and bolting it into the concrete. Drill holes through the base, or directly through the bottom sill of the greenhouse frame in the centre of each bay (being careful to leave room for the glazing).
- Better still is to lay a single course of bricks on top of the concrete footing and fix the base – or the greenhouse frame without a base – to the bricks. This is the most attractive and sturdiest method, and it raises the height of the greenhouse by around 125mm.

Installing the base

This is the procedure to follow if you want to attach your base and frame to a course of bricks on a cement footing. Check the kit before you begin to make sure all the base and frame fixings are included.

If you are not using a base, the manufacturer may recommend wooden battens as a buffer between the brick/cement and the bottom of the greenhouse frame.

Laying paths

It's easiest to construct paths around and inside your greenhouse before you erect it. Watering and trampling will make soil paths in a greenhouse turn to mud, so build a path from concrete slabs or paving stones, or simply lay down gravel or coarse wood chip between retaining boards nailed to pegs hammered into the ground.

project essentials

- **tape measure**
- **builder's line**
- **spade**
- **builder's square**
- **spirit level**
- **trowel**
- **flat-head screwdriver**
- **cross-head screwdriver**
- **10mm open-ended spanner**
- **hammer action drill with masonry bit**
- **protective gloves**
- **safety goggles**

- plywood or hardboard sheets, if required
- greenhouse base kit
- foundation mix concrete (see page 244)
- bricks
- mortar
- 25mm frame fixings
- greenhouse kit

1 Construct the galvanised steel base, following the instructions supplied. It is best to work on a flat, level surface such as plywood or hardboard sheets. Make sure the site is firm and level, and lay down the base to mark out the position of the footing. The footing needs to be 200mm wide. Mark its edges by running two builder's lines parallel to each side of the base, one 50mm from the outside face, the other 150mm from its inside face.

2 Dig out the footing trench to a depth of 100mm and fill it with concrete (see pages 224–25). The surface must be absolutely level. When dry, rest the base on the concrete and pencil a line around its outside edge. Lay one course of bricks (see page 226) in the centre of the footing. The outer faces of the bricks should be flush with the outside of the frame. Leave the mortar to dry for 24 hours.

3 Lift the base onto the prepared brick foundation.

Building the greenhouse

Make sure you have the manufacturer's instructions and all the pieces to hand before you start. You need to assemble the whole frame and make sure it is straight and square before fully tightening the bolts and screws.

Lay the pieces for one gable end of your greenhouse on a flat surface. Arrange them carefully into position, with metal sections and bolts the right way round and angled pieces leaning in the correct direction.

Now use a builder's square and spirit level to check that the whole frame is straight and the corners are square.

Push and slide the thin flexible rubber line into the tiny slots all around the frame.

Bolt the pieces loosely together to assemble the first side. Follow the same procedure for the other end and then for the sides.

When you are confident that everything is level and true, tighten all screws and bolts, including those attaching the frame to the base.

Starting with the roof, place each pane of glass into the frame and secure it with clips. Be sure to wear gloves and safety goggles. Once you have the knack this process is quick and easy. Take care, be patient, and make sure you are working with the right-sized glass for the section of the frame you are glazing.

Now bolt the sides and gable ends of the frame together and screw them to the base. Leave all bolts and screws loose at this stage.

Secure the metal base to the brick plinth, using 25mm frame fixings. These must be drilled through the base and into the brickwork. Take care to drill only into brick, not cement.

Position the glazing clips according to the manufacturer's instructions. Keep them evenly spaced.

Attach the roof ridge bar, screwing it loosely between the the two gable ends. Slide on the fittings for the roof vent then screw in the roof glazing bars.

Assemble the frame of the roof vent. Once it is tightly screwed together, slide it into place along the roof ridge.

Assemble the door, fit the glass and slide it into place.

SHED CONSTRUCTION

A basic garden shed is straightforward to assemble. Or you can choose something more elaborate: extra windows and double doors for additional light and ventilation. A more substantial shed or summerhouse can be fully wired up, insulated or even heated; extra-secure locks can be fitted if you intend to store valuable items inside.

Building the shed

Lay a concrete pad (see pages 244–49) that is 25mm smaller on all sides than the base of the shed, to create an overhang and prevent water accumulating around the timber floor and runners. To ensure good drainage this should slope slightly (see Setting the fall, page 237). Centre the shed floor on top of your concrete pad, then measure and mark in pencil the centre point of each edge, and do the same on the bottom batten of each side panel.

Lift the gable end without the door into place, and use a prop to hold it upright. Lift one side panel onto the base.

Screw the gable end and side panel together along the framing battens where they meet. Drill pilot holes then fit three 50mm countersunk screws at the top, middle and bottom.

Fit the other side panel in the same way. Then fit the gable end housing the door. But don't try to fix your shed frame to the floor yet.

Fit the roof support beam across the top of the shed, slotting it into the pre-cut grooves at the top of the gable ends. Check that the shed is sitting firmly on its base and that the door opens easily. Then use 30mm screws through an L-shaped metal bracket to fix the beam to each gable end.

Lay the roof panels on the ground, one at a time, with the eave sections (wooden strips) positioned underneath flush with the bottom edge of the panel. Measure and mark six evenly spaced fixing positions. Drill pilot holes and then hammer in the nails to attach the eave sections to the roof panels.

Lift the roof panels into place one at a time. Line up the shed frame on the base using the centre markings then secure the roof panels with 30mm screws along the roof support beam. Fix them to the sides and gable ends of the shed using 40mm nails, or 30mm nails across the window heads. Check again that the shed is square on the base before finally nailing the sides and gable ends to the floor with 50mm nails.

Felting the roof

Even if your shed kit comes with a roll of roof felt, you will probably still need to cut it to size with a sharp craft knife and a straightedge.

1 Unroll the roofing felt then measure and cut three pieces: one for each roof panel, and a third strip to be laid along the apex, to prevent water seeping in. The pieces covering the roof panels should run the full length of the shed with a 50mm overhang at either end. The third piece covering the apex should be the same length and extend at least 75mm over each roof panel.

2 Lay the first piece of felt over one side panel, with a 50mm overhang at the eave. Tack it along the top edge with felt nails about 300mm apart. Then fix it down along the gable ends and eave with felt nails at 100mm intervals. Repeat the other side. Place the third strip of felt over the top of the roof and nail it along each edge at 100mm intervals.

3 Tidy up the felt at the corners: cut it to the edge, fold it neatly and tack it down (see Steps 4 and 5, page 260). Hammer the roof fascia in place using 40mm nails over the felt on the front and back gable ends. Use four nails per strip.

4 Secure each corner trim with three evenly spaced 30mm nails.

Finishing touches

Shed windows are usually made of perspex, which slides easily into the window frames. Add a bolt, and then all that remains is to decorate the shed in the style of your choosing. You could treat it with coloured wood stain, and grow plants around it to help it blend in with the garden.

1 Standing outside the shed, slot the metal window sill into position along the bottom of the window frame.

2 Still outside, nail in the window cloaks (short strips of wood), using four 40mm nails in each. This secures the sills.

3 From inside the shed, slide the perspex into place, resting it on the sill. The beading is secured with 25mm nails. Start the nails first, then position the beading over the perspex sheet at the top and sides of the frame and hammer them fully home. Finally remove the protective film from the perspex.

4 Drill pilot holes and screw in the sliding bolt. This can be padlocked for additional security.

CHILDREN'S GARDEN

Kids will play safely for hours in their own playhouse. You could stain it a cheerful colour and add features such as a sand pit, a special planting area, a shallow wildlife pond (for older children) or a climbing frame.

Building a playhouse

You can buy playhouses in a kit containing all the materials you need. Look for non-toxic wood treatments and perspex windows for added safety and peace of mind. As for a garden shed, you need to start with a firm and level base. This could be a concrete pad (see pages 244–49) or some purpose-built decking (see pages 208–9). Fit the glazing and window beading before you assemble the playhouse (see Finishing touches, Step 3, page 259).

Position the floor and erect the gable ends and sides as you would if erecting a shed (see page 258). Use a builder's square to check the corners are all 90°, then fit the roof ridge bar. Nail in the roof support block and corner trims, using 40mm nails. Lift the roof panels into position, following the same procedure as for a shed (see page 258).

Align the building and hammer in evenly spaced 40mm nails through the side frames to secure the floor. This playhouse has a small verandah: position the verandah floor at the front of the playhouse.

Secure the verandah rails onto the front of the playhouse. Screw the bottom of the rails down into the floor, and the tops into the eaves of the playhouse. Countersink all screws.

Felt the roof (see page 259). Where the gable end felt meets and overhangs the front eave, hold a piece of timber beneath the felt and use a sharp craft knife to make a straight cut from the corner of the roof to the edge of the felt.

Fold the cut flap under and nail the felt down at the corner.

Nail the fascia to the gable ends using two nails per section. If your playhouse is on a deck, you should screw it down to stop it slipping on the smooth surface. Drill 100mm countersunk screws through the runners inside the playhouse. (There's no need to fix it to a concrete surface.)

The playhouse can then be treated with wood preservative or stain. You could also paint it inside.

project essentials

- **screwdriver**
- **power drill with twist and countersink bits**
- **tape measure**
- **pencil**
- **builder's square**
- **hammer**
- **craft knife**
- **paintbrush**

- playhouse kit
- paint or wood stain

B&Q Making it easier

Keep it straight
Use a builder's square (see page 225) to make sure all the corners form true right angles.

Building a sand pit

You can make a sand pit in any shape or size, but a simple 1m x 1m square gives ample space for play.

Saw eight sections of deck joist to form two square frames or 'boxes' that will sit one on top of the other. Each box requires two lengths of exactly 1m and two of 1.056m to allow for the overlap at the corner joins. Drill pilot holes and fix the joists together at each corner using two 100mm galvanised nails.

Lay one box frame in position on the ground and mark the outer corners with canes; join the canes with builder's line or string to outline the hole. Dig the hole to the depth of the two stacked boxes. Put one box frame on top of the other and clamp them together, making sure they are flush and square. Then join them with a perforated metal plate in the middle of each side, secured with 25mm galvanised nails.

The exterior frame, made from deck boards, will rest on the ground, forming a seat around the top of the sand pit. To make it, take four pieces of 28mm x 144mm deck board. Secure each one in a workbench and cut one end to a 45° angle.

project essentials

- tape measure
- handsaw
- 4 canes
- builder's line or string
- spade
- 2 quick-release clamps
- hammer
- workbench
- try square
- power drill with countersink bits
- garden fork
- craft knife

- 8 treated deck joists, 47mm x 150mm each
- 2 treated deck boards, 28mm x 144mm each
- 75mm deck screws
- 100mm and 25mm galvanised nails
- 10mm felt nails
- perforated metal fixing plates
- heavy-duty plastic sheet or weed-control fabric
- wood filler
- exterior wood adhesive
- paint
- play sand

To cut the other ends accurately, line the deck boards up around the box, one at a time. Align the angled end with one corner and mark the point where it touches the next corner. Use this as the starting point for cutting the other end. If the box is exact, the inside, shorter edges of the frame sections will be exactly 1m long.

Working on a flat surface, glue the joints with a strong waterproof wood adhesive and then nail a perforated metal plate across the underside of each joint with 25mm nails. Wipe away surplus glue with a damp cloth, and leave to dry.

Once securely bonded, drill pilot holes and fix the seating to the top of the box with 75mm countersunk deck screws. Fill the holes with wood filler and sand smooth.

Now you can paint the frame. When it is dry, attach a sheet of heavy-duty plastic or weed-control fabric to the bottom of the box with evenly spaced 10mm felt nails.

Scatter a thin layer of sand into the bottom of the hole and lower your finished box into it.

If using plastic liner, perforate it with a garden fork. Make plenty of holes to allow for drainage and prevent your sand pit becoming soggy. Then fill it with play sand. It is best to cover a sand pit when it's not in use to stop it getting water-logged.

PONDS PLANNING AND EXCAVATING

ONE PLANET HOME®

Attracting wildlife
A pond is a wonderful way to encourage wildlife into your garden. It provides a habitat for fish, frogs, newts and all sorts of creatures to thrive.

Water has been used in landscape gardening for centuries, adding a soothing extra dimension to the garden and creating a habitat for all kinds of wildlife. Ponds and water features can range in size from small lakes to tiny self-contained pebble water fountains.

Designing a pond

Rigid pre-formed plastic ponds complete with a built-in planting shelf come in a wide choice of shapes and sizes. Installation is simple: dig a hole that is large enough to accommodate the mould, make sure the pond is perfectly level and back-fill around it. Flexible plastic liners, on the other hand, enable you to form the shape and size you want.

Fish will survive happily in as little as 400mm–600mm of water, but the heat and light from the sun will penetrate a shallow pond more easily and produce more algae growth. However, there is no need for a pond to be deeper than 1m.

The pond will need an edging. Avoid using small pieces of stone right on the edge as they may slip in. Paving slabs make one of the simplest and most effective edgings; or you can use large rounded pebbles. Alternatively, turf right up to the pond edge; if you do this, a narrow band of waterside grasses will create a more natural effect.

Where to site a pond

- Most pond plants need sun when they are growing, so you should position a pond where it will receive full sun in summer.
- Avoid windswept sites as pond plants can be dislodged in gales, and there will be increased evaporation from the surface.
- Don't site a pond on boggy or water-logged ground, unless you are prepared to install a drainage system. Water building up beneath a flexible liner can cause it to billow and come to the surface; water can also dislodge a pre-formed liner.
- A pond should be at least 5m–6m from a tree, to avoid being cast in the shade and the liner being damaged by roots, as well as the water being clogged with autumn leaves.
- Some species of tree can be harmful to ponds or pondlife: willow has a vigorous root system and its decaying leaves produce chemicals harmful to fish; water lily aphids over-winter in plum and cherry trees; laburnum and rhododendron are poisonous; horse chestnut, poplar and yew have spreading thirsty root systems; yew is also poisonous.
- Ponds need topping up from time to time, so a nearby water supply will be useful.
- Pumps and fountains need a power supply; take this into account before you decide where to position the pond. Or choose from the range of solar-powered lights, pumps and fountains now available.

Pond safety

Never forget that small children can drown in a few inches of water. Don't leave them unsupervised for a moment near a pond. For peace of mind, install a secure fence and gate around it until they are older.

Pumps

Domestic pond pumps can power waterfalls and fountains and run filters. To work out the flow rate of the pump required, you need to calculate the pond volume by multiplying average length (m) x average depth (m) x average width (m). This will give you the volume in cubic metres; to convert that to litres, multiply by 1000.

As well as the capacity of your pond, you need to know what filters you intend to use, the size of any waterfall you want to attach and the height the water will need to be pumped to reach the waterfall. As a rule of thumb, in order to run a 150mm-wide waterfall, you would need a pump with a capacity of 2750 litres per hour.

Pond filtration

It's possible to keep ponds clear and healthy without filters – by correct planting, keeping fish to a minimum and encouraging beneficial wildlife – but it is difficult and takes time. Filtration combined with planting is a better solution. There are various filters to choose from.

- **In-pond filters** consist of a plastic sponge that connects directly to the pump via a pipe. They are only suitable for small ponds up to 900 litres.
- **Tank filters** provide mechanical and biological filtration, using bacteria to remove pollutants. They come in various sizes and are sited outside the pond, either in a hole in the ground or hidden behind rocks or plants. And you can now buy them with integral ultraviolet clarifiers.
- **Ultraviolet clarifiers** (UVCs) bombard free-floating algae with ultraviolet light, killing it and causing it to clump together so that it can be filtered out by a tank filter.
- **Bioforce/Ecoforce pressurised filters** provide mechanical and biological filtration in combination with an ultraviolet clarifier (UVC). They can be buried in the ground.

Planting

Plants are essential to the health of a pond. Deep-water aquatics and lilies are submerged plants that sit on the bottom while their leaves and flowers float on the surface. Marginal aquatics are plants that line the edges of ponds, lakes and streams. Their roots need to be just below the surface so they should sit on a shelf no more than 250mm beneath the water level. In straight-sided ponds a plinth made of bricks and slabs can be built up to the required height to support them.

The most important of the submerged plants are the oxygenating ones, which absorb the mineral salts on which algae would otherwise thrive. They are usually sold as cuttings clamped together with a small piece of lead, and can be planted in baskets in the bottom of the pond. Or if there is a layer of soil on the liner, you can simply drop them into the water and they will grow until checked. In a healthy pond oxygenating plants multiply quickly and need to be thinned in summer.

Marking out a pond

Make a rough sketch of the garden and draw in the proposed outline of the pond and its surroundings, including any plants. A symmetrical shape will produce a more formal effect, or you could create an irregular, informal pond that looks natural and fits in with the surrounding landscape. Mark out the pond area with a hosepipe or length of rope, trying different shapes and sizes until you come up with something you like.

Use a spade to mark the edge of the pond clearly. Then remove the hosepipe and cut a second line beyond the pond outline to mark the outer rim of the edging. The distance from your original line should be the width of a slab less 50mm, so that the slabs overlap the pond edge by 50mm – this not only hides the liner but also protects it from direct sunlight.

project essentials

- **hosepipe or rope**
- **tape measure**
- **spade**
- **pickaxe, if required**
- **wheelbarrow**
- **wooden mallet**
- **long spirit level, or laser level**
- **trowel**
- **plastering trowel**
- **scissors or sharp knife**
- **cement mixer (optional)**
- **shovel**
- **angle grinder, or club hammer and bolster chisel**
- **protective gloves**
- **goggles**
- **dust mask**
- **jointing tool**
- **hacksaw**

- 50mm x 50mm timber levelling pegs
- soft sand
- cement
- pond underlay or old carpet, if required
- flexible plastic pond liner
- stones or bricks
- foundation mix concrete (see page 244)
- edging paving slabs
- sharp sand
- slab or flat stone
- pump with fountain head
- plastic pipe to fit the pump (in this case 25mm)
- plastic conduit
- jubilee clip
- ultraviolet clarifier
- biological tank filter

Excavating a pond

The best way to ensure the stability of a paved edging is to dig a trench around the pond before you excavate it. A concrete pad can then be laid in the trench once the liner is in place. This secures the liner and provides a base on which to rest the paving slabs. It's essential that the concrete pad and edging slabs are level, even if the ground surface is not. To achieve this you will need to cut 50mm x 50mm levelling pegs, about 300mm long, and sharpened to a point at one end. You will need enough to hammer them into the trench not more than a metre apart all around the edge of the pond.

1 Dig a trench between the two guidelines using a spade and a pickaxe if necessary. The depth should be 75mm for the concrete pad, plus the thickness of the edging slabs, plus a mortar joint of 15mm. Roughly level the trench as you go.

2 Drive a levelling peg into the centre of the trench to the finished water level. This will be lower than ground level by the depth of the edging (with a 25mm-thick slab and 15mm mortar joint, the tops of the pegs should be 40mm below ground level). Mark the first peg so you can recognise it to level all the other pegs from. Drive in pegs not more than a metre apart around the trench and level them with a long spirit level or laser level.

3 Start to dig out the pond to the level of the marginal planting shelf, using the inside line as your guide. The shelf should be about 230mm below water level and 250mm wide. For stability, the sides of the pond should not be vertical but should slope slightly inwards at an angle of 20° (or more in soft crumbly ground).

5 When all the pegs are at the right level, mix a fairly stiff mortar using three parts sand to one part cement, and lay a line of mortar around the rim of the pond. The top of the mortar line should be level with the pegs. Make sure its edges are rounded off and the surface is smooth. Use the central stake to check the level again all the way around the rim of the pond. Leave the mortar to dry for 24 hours.

6 Using a plastering trowel, cover the excavated pond with a 25mm layer of damp sand. If the ground is particularly stony or there are sharp corners, use pond underlay or lengths of old carpet on top of the sand to protect the liner.

4 Dig out the central part of the pond to the required depth, sloping the pond sides between the marginal shelf and the pond bottom at 20°. Make sure there are no stones sticking out of the ground. Hammer a stake into the centre of your pond and use a spirit level and a straightedge to set it level with your first peg (or use a laser level). Use the stake to double check that all the other pegs are level, and make slight alterations if necessary.

It takes two people to lay the liner across the excavated hole and smooth out the creases. You will not get rid of them all but, when the pond is full of water and plants have begun to flourish, they won't be visible. Once the liner is in place, the pump and filters can be fitted.

Fitting the liner

To work out how much liner you need, see MAKING IT EASIER, below. Gently stretch, smooth and fold it into position over the excavated area, leaving plenty of spare on all sides. Take great care not to puncture it on sharp stones; if you do, patch the hole on both sides with off-cuts of liner and an adhesive recommended by the manufacturer.

Lay the liner in the hole. Place some stones or bricks around the edges to stop it slipping down. Place the end of the hose in the bottom of the pond and anchor it with something heavy but not sharp. Fill the pond with water, taking care to move the stones or bricks as it fills to release the liner and allow it to fit the hole.

Smooth the liner over the mortar edge into the trench – it should cover almost half the trench. Trim off the excess with a pair of scissors or a sharp knife.

How much liner?
When calculating liner size, allow for a minimum 150mm overlap around the edge of the pond so that the liner can be secured beneath the edging. You will need a bigger overlap if you plan to bury it and turf right up to the pond edge.

- To calculate the length of the liner, measure the maximum length (including overlaps) and add twice the maximum depth.
- To calculate the width of the liner, measure the maximum width (including overlaps) and add twice the maximum depth.

Fitting the edging

Fill the trench around the edge of the pond with concrete, bringing it level with the top of the mortar rim. This will anchor the liner in place and provide a firm base on which to place the edging slabs. Leave the concrete to dry for about 24 hours.

Lay the slabs on a continuous bed of mortar on the concrete, overlapping the liner by 50mm. Mix the mortar using four parts sharp sand to one part cement. Allow a 10mm mortar joint between the slabs. For a curved pond you will need to cut each slab to fit using a club hammer and bolster chisel, or an angle grinder (see page 231). Be sure to wear heavy-duty gloves, safety goggles and a dust mask while cutting slabs.

Finally drain the pond (see below) and point the joint between the slabs and liner. Clean the liner thoroughly afterwards: mortar is poisonous to plants and fish.

Draining the pond

Once the liner is secured, you need to empty the pond again to finish the edging. Either siphon out the water with a length of hosepipe, or use the pump – simply fit a hosepipe to its outlet. The pump must be covered with water at all times when it is operating, so you will need to scoop out the last of the water.

Installing the pump and filters

Installing a pump is easier when the pond is empty. The pump must be raised off the bottom to prevent debris clogging the filter and so that you can reach it for cleaning. The pump shown here is a low-voltage pump with a fountain head. It is connected to an ultraviolet clarifier and a biological tank filter. You can connect it to the mains power as you would low-voltage garden lighting (see page 297).

Lay a piece of pond underlay on the liner to protect it and place two bricks on top as supports.

Rest a slab or a flat stone on the bricks and stand the pump on it. Use a spirit level placed on the pond edging to determine the position of the fountain head. It should be set about 3mm–5mm above the water level.

3 The pump's underground cables must be protected. The low-voltage cable shown here is run through a plastic conduit as it goes through a rockery beside the pond.

4 Attach the 25mm pipe to the pump outlet using a jubilee clip. This pipe will lead in turn to the ultraviolet clarifier and the biological filter.

5 Use a hacksaw to saw the end off the pipe attachment on the ultraviolet clarifier to fit the size of your pipe and allow you to connect it. An ultraviolet clarifier needs its own electricity supply, and it should be connected following the manufacturer's instructions.

6 Place the tank filter in a position that is higher than the pond – in this case, its outlet will feed a waterfall. Connect a pipe from the ultraviolet unit outlet to the tank inlet.

Plants for a pond

Even when a pond has filters, plants are essential for maintaining healthy water. About one-third of the pond surface should be covered with foliage during the growing season to deprive algae of the light they need to flourish. Lilies, which have large leaves, are ideal for this purpose. Deep-water aquatics and floating plants (see page 262) will starve the algae of mineral salts. Aquatic plants do not need rich soil. Use aquatic compost or a heavy garden soil; avoid sandy soils or soil containing farmyard manure.

project essentials

- **protective gloves**

- pond plants
- planting baskets
- hessian, if required
- aquatic compost or heavy garden soil
- clean gravel

1 For most ornamental ponds, plants should be anchored in special planting baskets with latticework sides, which retain the soil while allowing water to permeate. Modern baskets have micro-mesh sides that prevent the soil making the water dirty. If the basket has large holes, line it with a square of hessian before filling it with compost. If you are planting tall plants like bulrushes, try to plant them in a basket that is large enough for you to place a brick in the bottom before filling it with compost, as this will keep the plant stable.

2 If you think the pond plant you have purchased will soon outgrow its basket, repot it into a larger one. Add clean gravel as a topping around the stem to prevent loss of soil from the surface of the pot. Gently lower the plant in the pond.

Home systems and services

ELECTRICITY BE SAFE

safe electrics

Before beginning any kind of electrical work, you must always take the following safety precautions:

- Switch off the main power at the consumer unit (fuse box).
- Isolate the circuit you plan to work on by removing the circuit fuse and putting it in your pocket. Or switch off and lock the relevant circuit breaker (see page 275) and attach a very clear note to the unit stating that you are working on the circuit.
- Check the circuit is dead with a plug-in socket tester (see page 274) or, in the case of a lighting circuit, a voltage tester.

When you have completely finished, replace the fuse or circuit breaker and turn the main power switch on again. Never restore power until the faceplates and covers of all accessories have been fitted.

B&Q Making it easier

Preparation
A lot of electrical home improvements involve simple cable routing and socket fixing. These tasks require basic skills like chopping out and repairing plaster, drilling into walls and timber, or lifting and replacing floorboards. Even if you decide to play safe and employ an electrician, you will save money by doing the basic preparation and making good yourself.

Changes to Building Regulations

As of 1 January 2005, changes to the Building Regulations affected domestic electrical installations in England and Wales. You don't need to be a qualified electrician to make changes to your home's electrical system, but the work must be done in accordance with the standards in the Regulations.

You do not need to notify your Local Authority if you do minor electrical work, such as:

- replacing or repairing a socket, light or cable in any room
- adding extra spurs, sockets or lights to an existing circuit (except in a kitchen, bathroom or outdoors)
- fitting or replacing electric showers, cookers, garage doors or gates (unless a new circuit is needed)
- installing CE-marked prefabricated modular kitchen lighting systems to an existing connection unit or socket outlet
- installing security lighting or air conditioning to the outside wall of a house, provided that there are no exposed outdoor connections (unless a new circuit is needed)

However, the work must be done to the standards in the Wiring Regulations and you should consider having the work checked by a competent electrician to make sure it is safe.

Before you start other electrical work, such as:

- adding new circuits to your existing installation
- any work (other than repairs or replacements) in a room where there is water (eg. kitchen, bathroom, etc.)
- any work (other than repairs or replacements) outdoors (eg. installing garden lighting or sockets, etc.)
- replacing a consumer unit
- installing new central heating control wiring
- installing a socket outlet on an external wall

you must notify your Local Authority Building Control Department, which has responsibility for ensuring the work is inspected and tested.

Where you have any work done by a person registered with an electrical self-certification scheme prescribed in the Regulations, you do not need to notify your Local Authority.

Requirements for RCD protection
Examples where 30mA RCD protection is now compulsory include:

- all new socket outlets rated up to 20 amps (including standard 13 amp domestic sockets)
- portable electrical equipment for use out of doors
- all new or replacement cables installed less than 50mm from the surface of a wall or partition, or at any depth if the construction of the wall or partition contains metallic parts

This is not an exhaustive list. Specific locations or installations may be subject to further requirements: please refer to BS7671:2008 or consult an approved electrical contractor.

We recommend that you make yourself aware of the Regulations before you undertake any work and if you require any clarification you should contact your Local Authority Building Control Department.

Make certain your system is safe
All the advice given in these pages applies to systems that conform to the IEE Wiring Regulations for the UK only (other countries have their own regulatory organisations).

If at any time you are uncertain of your ability, or you suspect that your system has been adapted or extended in an unorthodox way, always seek the advice of an electrical contractor registered with the NICEIC (the National Inspection Council for Electrical Installation Contracting), the ECA (Electrical Contractors Association) or the Electrical Contractors' Association of Scotland (trading as SELECT). It is a requirement of the Wiring Regulations that domestic electrical systems be checked periodically by a competent person. If your house has not been checked for more than ten years, it's recommended you get your system inspected first before you start working on it – otherwise you have no way of knowing what dangers may be lurking.

Dos and don'ts of electrical safety

Making changes to electrical circuits is not as difficult as you may think, but you must always observe the safety guidelines rigorously. Electricity can cause fire, burns and in extreme cases kill. What's more, poor workmanship in an electrical job may only become apparent when a fault or overload occurs. So follow these safety tips to prevent disaster:

- Be patient and methodical, and only embark on a job that you understand from start to finish.
- If in the slightest doubt about your ability to complete a particular electrical task, call in a professional.
- Turn off the light switch before replacing a bulb.
- Always isolate the circuit you plan to work on at the consumer unit (see SAFE ELECTRICS, above).
- Wear rubber-soled shoes when working on an electrical installation.
- Use insulating tools and screwdrivers specifically designed for electrical work.
- When making connections, ensure that no cable or flex cores are damaged (see page 273); sheath the bare earth core of cable with green/yellow insulation; check that

cores are connected to the correct terminals; and tighten all terminal screws fully. Always connect the earth core to the earth terminal at fittings and appliances, unless they carry the double insulated symbol ▣ or, as with some light fittings, have no metal parts.
- Make sure circuit and appliance fuses are of the correct rating (see page 273). Never simply replace a fuse that keeps blowing with one of a higher rating; investigate the reason for the problem.
- Replace damaged electrical fittings or appliances immediately. Don't try to use anything you suspect may have a fault.
- Always ensure that any new or replacement electrical fittings have the correct IP rating for the

environment they are being installed in (see page 294).
- Never patch worn flex with insulation tape – always replace it.
- Don't overload sockets with adaptors and extra plugs. Fit additional sockets instead.
- Always unplug electrical appliances before working on them. Unplug power tools before changing blades or accessories.
- Never use electrical appliances in a damp environment and don't touch anything electrical with wet hands.
- When using electrical appliances or tools in the garden, ensure they are protected by an RCD (residual current device), either plugged in at the power socket or permanently wired into the system at the consumer unit (see page 294).

Is your system safe to work on?

There are certain sure signs that your system is out of date and unsafe to work on – old-style rubber-sheathed cable, for example. But even in a modern property whose electrical system has been professionally checked and approved in the past ten years, things can go wrong. Make sure it's safe *before* you begin work, and if in doubt, get it checked by a qualified electrician.

1 Is your consumer unit old-style or modern?
If your consumer unit cover gets cracked or broken, replace it straight away. In older houses, you sometimes find a mixture of old fuse boxes attached to the fuse board beside the electricity meter. These can be dangerous, and you are strongly advised to get a qualified electrician to change them for a modern all-in-one consumer unit (above).

2 Are the circuits labelled and fitted with fuses or circuit breakers of the correct rating?
If you are going to do electrical work in your home, you will need to isolate the circuit you are working on by removing the correct fuse or switching off the circuit breaker (see page 275). If the circuits are not already labelled, you can do this yourself. Identify each one by switching off the main power, disabling one circuit, restoring power and then investigating which sockets, appliances or lights are dead.

3 Are the cables in good condition?
Cables used to be sheathed in rubber, which perishes over time, potentially exposing bare wires. If you have rubber cabling, or if any cables are worn, get them checked by a qualified electrician and replaced if necessary. Any discolouring of modern cabling may be a sign of overheating, and should also be checked by an electrician.

4 Is the earth connection secure?
Running from the consumer unit there will be a thick cable with green-and-yellow-sheathing (or green in an older installation) which provides the vital earth connection. If this cable looks at all loose or damaged, you must get it checked straight away. See page 271 for more information on earthing.

5 Does your consumer unit have an RCD?
A residual current device, or RCD, will detect an earth leakage and isolate a circuit in milliseconds, before an accident can occur. You can test an RCD by pressing its test button.

6 How safe is your fixed wiring?
Fixed wiring runs in the walls, between floors and in the loft space. If you can get access to any part of it, check the condition. Is it rubber-insulated? Are any bare wires showing? Is it fixed securely? Does it run neatly into any junction boxes or accessories? If you have surface-mounted wiring, it should be clipped tidily to the walls, or preferably concealed behind them (see page 276).

7 Are any of your sockets damaged?
Watch out for warning signs that a connection may be loose inside. Does the socket or plug feel warm? If so, you should check the connections inside the socket and plug, or contact an electrician for advice. If it is difficult to insert a plug into a socket, it could be a sign that the socket is worn and needs to be replaced. Cracked or broken faceplates on sockets should be replaced as soon as possible. Scorching on a socket may be caused by overloading, for example by plugging in an adaptor to supply several large loads; or by loose connections in a plug. Replace the faceplate (see page 278) and investigate the cause of the problem: reduce the load and if necessary replace the plug (see page 273).

8 Are your electrical appliances connected securely?
Even if an appliance appears to be working normally, it is worth checking the wiring from time to time. Is the insulation around the flex deteriorating? Is the flex securely attached? Are there any bare wires visible? Make sure that the earth cores have green-and-yellow sleeving. If the external casing of an appliance becomes cracked or worn, it should be replaced. If the switches are not working properly, get professional help or replace the appliance. Plugs should contain a fuse of the correct rating for the appliance (see page 273).

9 Are your light fittings wired correctly?
If there isn't an earth wire inside a ceiling rose, get an electrician to check it. All wiring inside the ceiling rose should be PVC-insulated. Old-style braided flex should be replaced with the correct PVC-insulated and sheathed flex (see page 272).

10 Do you use electrical appliances outdoors?
All portable electrical appliances used outdoors must be protected by a 30mA RCD. An outdoor socket must be protected by an integral RCD, or one permanently wired into the circuit. If an indoor socket used to power appliances outdoors doesn't have RCD protection, you must use a plug-in RCD (example pictured).

ELECTRICITY THE BASICS

safe electrics

Never take risks with electrical safety. Before you start any kind of electrical work see page 268.

The consumer unit is the distribution point for the electricity supply in your home, where the flow is split to feed the various circuits. Socket outlets and fused connection units can be supplied with electricity via two types of wiring layout, known as radial and ring circuits. Your home may well have both types, since the power supply is usually split into at least two circuits.

Domestic circuits

The electrical circuits in your home all begin at the consumer unit or fuse box, where the incoming supply is split as required. The cables leading from it contain three copper wires, known as conductors or cores. The electrical current flows to the appliance or fitting along the 'live' core and then flows back along the 'neutral' core to the source. The colours of these two cores depend on when your wiring was installed. Cable in the new 'harmonised' colours, first introduced in March 2004 and compulsory in new installations since March 2006, has a brown live core and blue neutral core. Cable installed before 2004 had a red live core and black neutral core. For further information on the new colours, see page 272.

The third conductor is the 'earth' core. In two-core-and-earth and three-core-and-earth cable (see page 272) this is a bare copper wire running between the live and neutral cores which provides a safe escape route for the current should it leak from the circuit because of a fault or poor connection. Without earth protection, the metal components of appliances and fittings could give you a fatal electric shock if they were to become live through a wiring fault. Thus any metal appliance or fitting in your home that could come into contact with electricity must be earthed, and that includes the plumbing system.

The consumer unit

Also commonly known as the fuse box, the consumer unit is usually mounted close to your electricity meter and will contain the main isolating switch, which allows you to turn on and off the power to the entire house. Inside the consumer unit, the incoming current is split to feed a number of circuits – lighting, power, cooker and so on – each protected by a fuse or circuit breaker.

In addition, more modern consumer units incorporate RCD protection. An RCD (residual current device) is designed to shut off the power rapidly if an earth leakage develops, helping to prevent electrocution. Depending on the design of the installation, the RCD may operate on all the circuits or only some. Older consumer units may have a separate RCD mounted alongside. Any circuit that provides power to appliances used outdoors must have RCD protection (see page 294).

Each fuse or circuit breaker should be labelled with the name of the circuit it protects, so that you can isolate each one easily when you want to work on it.

Track your usage
The latest wireless energy monitors enable you to see at a glance how much electricity your household is using, and how much it is costing you. They don't need to be wired in: you simply clip a sensor around the main live power cable running into the consumer unit. A transmitter wirelessly relays your usage to a monitor that you can position in a convenient place. So you can instantly see how much electricity you are using, and the savings you are making by energy saving practices like washing clothes at 30° or boiling only the water that you need in the kettle.

Radial circuits

In the early days of domestic electrical systems, socket outlets were few and far between in homes, and each was supplied by an individual cable run from the fuse box. Modern circuits, whether radial or ring, can have multiple socket outlets. In a radial circuit, a single cable runs from the consumer unit and feeds a number of sockets. There is no restriction on the number of sockets fed by one circuit, but there is a limit on the floor area it can supply; a 20 amp radial circuit can supply up to 50 sq m, and a 30/32 amp circuit can supply up to 100 sq m. The cable simply runs into one socket or fused connection unit, then on to the next, until it terminates at the last socket on the line. Each radial circuit is protected by a fuse or circuit breaker at the consumer unit. This is designed to blow or trip if the circuit is overloaded.

Consumer unit

Main circuit cable

Radial circuit

Last socket on line, where radial circuit terminates

Ring circuits

In a ring circuit, the cable runs from the consumer unit, in and out of the sockets and fused connection units, and then returns to the consumer unit (rather than terminating at the last socket on the line). The electrical current can flow from either end of the ring. This has the effect of raising the current-carrying capacity of the circuit without increasing the size of cable needed, which would be the case with a radial circuit.

As with a radial circuit, there is no restriction on the number of sockets that can be wired into a ring circuit, but there is a limit of 100 sq m on the floor area served. At the consumer unit, the circuit is protected by a 30 or 32 amp fuse or circuit breaker.

Ring circuit

Consumer unit

Circuit cables connecting a single ring circuit to the consumer unit

Spur from a socket

Spur from a junction box

Spurs

A spur is a short branch cable from an existing socket outlet on the main circuit or from a connection box, known as a junction box, wired into the main circuit cable. Each unfused spur should only supply one socket outlet (single or double) or fused connection unit (used for fixed appliances). The total number of unfused spurs must not exceed the number of sockets or fixed appliances wired directly into the ring circuit. See pages 280–81 for advice on adding spurs.

Appliance circuits

Individual radial circuits are provided for appliances that require large amounts of current – cookers, immersion heaters, electric showers, storage heaters, and so on. Depending on the appliance, these may be wired in much heavier cable than normal power circuits and may be protected by a variety of fuse/circuit breaker sizes.

In most cases, the cable runs through a special double-pole switch, which interrupts the flow of current through both live and neutral cores of the cable, ensuring that the power to the appliance can be shut off completely if repairs are necessary, without the need to disconnect the wiring. Normal single-pole socket and light switches only interrupt the live supply.

Earthing

The earth is a particularly good conductor of electricity. This means that if you were to touch a live conductor, the electricity would take the shortest route into the ground via your body – with potentially fatal consequences. If a live wire in an appliance accidentally comes into contact with a metal casing, the electricity will flow to the ground – this time harmlessly – along the earth wire. This is known as an earth fault, and the sudden change of route will cause a circuit breaker to operate or a fuse to blow.

Earth wires are either insulated with green and yellow sheathing or they are bare copper wires sandwiched between the live and neutral cores in cable.

Bonding

For safety, the main gas and water pipework in your home should be connected by bonding conductors to the main earthing terminal near the consumer unit. Main bonding wires – lengths of single-core cable, usually 10mm^2, with green-and-yellow sheathing – should be clamped within 600mm of the meter or main stopcock (on the household side). In addition, there must be supplementary bonding linking all the metallic elements within a bath or shower room, since these are particularly hazardous areas. This is done with green-and-yellow-sheathed single-core cable, usually 4mm^2. If you use plastic connectors on copper plumbing pipes, you must restore the earth connection across them, or your system will not be safely earthed (see page 309).

Supplementary bonding connection

Copper plumbing pipe

Bonding clamp, which must be turned down to protect terminal screw (as below)

SAFETY ELECTRICAL CONNECTION DO NOT REMOVE

Bonding wire

ELECTRICITY CABLE, FLEX AND FUSES

safe electrics

Never take risks with electrical safety. Before you start any kind of electrical work see page 268.

Electrical current flows in the home along different types of cable and flex. You have to strip these to bare the cores before you can connect them to new terminals. Fitting new plugs is one of the most straightforward electrical jobs, but it is important to make sure you insert the correct fuse for the appliance that will be supplied.

Flex

FLEX SIZES	
Appliance rating	**Flex size**
700W	0.5mm²
1.4kW	0.75mm²
2.3kW	1mm²
3kW	1.25/1.5mm²

Flex is used to connect appliances and pendant lights to the fixed wiring. It is usually round in cross-section and normally contains three cores within a white or coloured PVC outer sheath, although non-kinking rubber-sheathed flex with a braided outer covering is also available for irons. All three cores have coloured insulation: brown for live, blue for neutral and green/yellow for earth. Two-core flex (with no earth core) is used for double-insulated appliances and some light fittings that don't have metal components. Special heat-resistant flex is available for immersion heaters. Different flex sizes are available. Check the box, left, to see the size required for different appliance ratings.

Two-core flex

Three-core flex

Cable

Cable is used for all fixed wiring, which is usually hidden behind walls, ceiling and floor. It has an oval cross-section and contains cores set side by side within a thick white or grey PVC outer sheath. The live core is separately insulated in brown sheath, the neutral core in blue sheath (note that these colours have changed: see below). The earth core is bare and runs between them. This is known as two-core-and-earth cable; special three-core-and-earth cable (with brown, black and grey cores, plus a bare earth) is used for the two-way switching of lights (again, these colours have changed: see below). When connecting cable, the exposed earth core must be protected by a length of green/yellow electrical sleeving.

Bigger cable is needed for circuits with a higher current demand. Common sizes of cable are 1, 1.5, 2.5, 4, 6 and 10mm²; the measurement represents the cross-sectional area of the individual cores. The current-carrying capacity of cable is subject to many installation design factors: if in doubt about your requirements, consult a qualified electrician.

Normal cable sheathing is not frost-resistant, so outdoors it must be protected by conduit or you must use steel-wire-armoured cable (SWA), see page 297.

Two-core-and-earth cable

Three-core-and-earth cable

Changed wiring colours

The colours of the live and neutral cores in cable have changed. The reason for this was to bring the UK more closely in line with the rest of Europe, which is why the new colours are often referred to as 'harmonised' colours. The live core, which was red, has changed to **brown**; the neutral core, which was black, has changed to **blue**. These are the colours that have been used in flex for many years. The earth core is still identified by the colour combination green/yellow. Three-core-and-earth cable colours changed from red, yellow and blue to brown, black and grey.

The new harmonised colours have been in use since 31 March 2004 and became compulsory in all new installations from 31 March 2006.

Working safely with the old and new colours

The core colour changes could cause confusion. For example, black is used for neutral in old two-core-and-earth cable but is one of the live cores in the new three-core-and-earth cable. Also, blue is used for neutral in the new two-core-and-earth cable but is one of the live cores in old three-core-and-earth cable.

Alterations or additions made to existing electrical installations will involve working with a mixture of old and new cable colours. Where old and new two-core-and-earth cables are joined at socket or junction-box terminals, it is essential to take great care to connect the cores correctly, ie old red to new brown (for live) and old black to new blue (for neutral). In addition, a warning notice like this (right) must be fixed prominently at the distribution board or consumer unit.

For further information on these changes, visit www.theiet.org/publishing/wiring-regulations/colour

> **CAUTION**
>
> This installation has wiring colours to two versions of BS 7671.
>
> Great care should be taken before undertaking extension, alteration or repair that all conductors are correctly identified.

The right fuse

These days, all appliance plugs contain cartridge fuses, normally rated at 3, 5 or 13 amps depending on the wattage of the appliance. Appliances rated up to 700 watts should be protected by a 3 amp fuse while those rated above 700 watts should have a 13 amp fuse. Some appliances, such as televisions, may require a 5 amp fuse. Always check the appliance manufacturer's instructions. A new plug will usually contain a 13 amp fuse; this may be too high for your appliance. Never fit a fuse with the wrong rating.

Changing a fuse in a plug

To replace a fuse, unplug the appliance, unscrew the cover of the plug and lift it off. Prise the fuse from its clips and insert a new one of the correct amperage. Refit the cover. (Note that some plugs are moulded in one piece with the fuse in a lever-out holder in the base. After changing the fuse, make sure this holder is pushed back fully into the plug.)

Fitting a new plug

Unscrew and remove the cover of the old plug. Turn the plug over and loosen the terminal screws so the flex cores can be pulled from the pins. Slacken the screws securing the flex clamp and pull the flex free. If the appliance was working fine, prise out and keep the fuse – but don't re-use it without checking it is the right rating for the appliance.

Make sure when you buy a new plug that the live and neutral pins are partly covered with plastic insulation. Depending on the plug's design, you may need to slide the cover over the flex before making the connections.

safety first

Not all plugs are manufactured to the same quality. A standard 3-pin plug should carry the British Standard kitemark and code BS1363 or BS1363A.

✗ Incorrect
- Earth core not connected
- Check that the fuse is of the correct amperage
- Exposed wires
- Flex clamp over cores not outer sheath

✓ Correct
- Insulation going right up to terminal
- Flex clamp gripping outer sheath

Safe stripping

To prepare flex or cable for connection, you have to strip back the plastic sheath to expose the copper cores. It is important not to damage the cores, which in flex are made up of a large number of fine copper strands. If any of these are cut through, the core's current capacity is reduced, which could lead to overheating.

Stripping flex

Mark the amount of flex outer sheath you need to remove, then bend the flex double and make a shallow cut at the mark. This will open up automatically. Repeat around the flex until you can pull the piece of outer sheath free. Cut the flex cores to length with side cutters. Remove about 10mm of the insulation from the end of each core, using wire strippers. Some wire strippers are adjustable to suit a range of core sizes; others (for example, below) have jaws with cut-outs for different sizes of core. Twist the exposed fine copper wires of each core together so that they can be inserted easily in their terminals.

Wire strippers

Side cutters

Stripping cable

Mark the amount of outer sheathing to be removed and lay the cable on a flat surface. Use a sharp knife to carefully slit the sheathing down the centre (above the earth core). Peel back the sheathing and cut it off using side cutters. Cut the cores to the required length. Use wire strippers to remove just enough of the coloured cores' insulation so that the cores extend to the full depth of the terminal, with no wire exposed. Add green/yellow sheathing to the bare copper core.

- Feed the end of the flex under the flex clamp or between the flex grips of the new plug.
- Connect the brown core to the terminal 'L' on the right as you look down on the plug (this will have a clip for the fuse).
- Connect the blue core to the terminal 'N' on the left.
- Connect the green/yellow earth core to the terminal 'E' or ⏚ at the top (the longest of the three pins). Make sure that the earth wire is longest and the live wire shortest – this way if the plug is ripped off the flex, the live wire will break away first and the earth last. If there is no earth core (the appliance is double-insulated) simply make sure that the terminal screw is tight.
- Check that the cores are pushed fully home with the insulation right up to the terminals and tighten all the screws.
- Confirm the rating of the fuse and replace it with one of the correct amperage if necessary.
- Tighten the flex clamp screws to grip the flex firmly.
- Finally, screw on the cover, ensuring that it fits properly all round.

safe electrics

Never take risks with electrical safety. Before you start any kind of electrical work see page 268.

It can be very irritating when an electrical socket or appliance doesn't work, but with a bit of logical detective work, you should be able to discover the cause of the problem and, in many cases, correct the fault yourself. But before you do any kind of electrical work, you need to know not only how to isolate a circuit, but also how to double-check that it is dead.

Checking a circuit is dead

The safest option when working on an electrical fitting is to turn off the entire household electricity supply at the mains. But if this would mean working in the dark, or prevent you from using power tools, you may need to isolate just the circuit you are working on. Do this by removing the fuse – put it in your pocket so it can't be replaced by accident – or switch off the relevant circuit breaker and lock it if you can, or failing that, leave a very clear note on the consumer unit stating that you are working on the circuit.

However it is also extremely important to check that you have turned off the *right* circuit. On a main power circuit, use a socket tester (see IDEAL TOOL) to confirm the power is off. On a lighting circuit you need a voltage tester, of which there are different types on the market. One option is a voltage meter (see page 280), which has probes that are touched to the exposed cable. This is the most reliable method of checking whether a cable is live or not, but you do have to be extremely careful while opening up the fitting, just in case it is. The alternative is a voltage tester (see page 365), which detects the presence of live wires without contact with a cable, and will even work through a fitting or faceplate. But it is vital to use it properly: always check first that it is working by testing it on a known live cable, otherwise you could get a false negative reading, with potentially fatal consequences. And be aware that a positive reading can sometimes be caused by static electricity in the environment. As always, read and follow the manufacturer's instructions.

Identifying a problem

Follow these step-by-step procedures to identify the cause of an electrical problem.

A plug-in appliance doesn't work

- If it is a plug-in light, try changing the bulb. For any other kind of appliance, first try plugging it into another socket. If it works, the original socket may be faulty and need replacing (see page 278). If it doesn't work, try again on a different power circuit (probably a different floor). If it works there, then you may have a dead circuit (see below).

- If the appliance doesn't work in a socket you know to be functioning, then check the flex connections in the plug and replace the fuse in the plug, ensuring that it is of the correct rating.

- Still not working? The appliance may have an internal fault, which will require professional attention.

A circuit is dead

- Turn off all lights or unplug all appliances on the affected circuit. Turn off the main isolating switch at the consumer unit and repair the circuit fuse/reset the circuit breaker or RCD. Then turn the main switch back on.

- Switch on each light or plug in each appliance in turn to find out which item on the circuit is causing the fuse to blow or the circuit breaker to trip. When you find it, isolate the circuit again and check the fuse, the connections and the flex (see above).

- If the fuse blows/circuit breaker trips again, the fault may lie in the fixed wiring. Call a qualified electrician.

A wall or ceiling light doesn't work

- Are the other lights on the circuit working? If not, then follow the steps for a dead circuit, below.

- If the other lights on the circuit are working, then turn off the light at the switch and replace the bulb.

- If that doesn't help, then turn off the power and check the cable/flex connections at the light. If necessary, strip back cores and remake the connections; make sure the terminal screws are tight. Still with the power off, check the condition of the flex with a continuity tester (see IDEAL TOOL, page 280), and replace if necessary.

- If that doesn't work, then turn off the power again, remove the switch cover and check the cable connections. If they are loose, remake them. If they are fine, then try replacing the switch (see page 286).

- Still not working? Call in a qualified electrician.

All circuits are dead

- If the circuits of your home are protected by an RCD (residual current device), check to see if it has tripped. If so, reset it. If it trips again, carry out the checks for faulty lights, appliances and a dead circuit. If the problem persists, call in a qualified electrician.

- Check with neighbours or your electricity supplier to determine whether the power to the neighbourhood has been cut. If not, and the problem cannot be traced within the domestic circuits, notify the electricity supplier who will check the main supply cable and service fuse.

ideal tool

Socket tester
A quick means of checking whether there is a wiring fault or incorrect connection at a socket is to use a plug-in tester. This has three pins, just like a normal plug, but on its face there are three neons. With the power to the circuit switched on, plug in the tester; the combination of neons illuminated indicates whether or not there is a fault, and if so where it lies.

Nuisance RCD tripping

To avoid nuisance tripping on RCD-protected systems you should work with the whole power supply switched off. Switching off a circuit breaker or removing a circuit fuse only isolates the L (live) side of the circuit. The N (neutral) remains connected to the mains. This is quite safe for working on the circuit, but it means that contact with the N wire will cause the RCD to trip and switch off the entire house supply. This can be irritating, even dangerous, when you are in the middle of a repair.

Fuses and circuit breakers

Each of the electrical circuits in your home is provided with a fuse or a circuit breaker: an MCB (miniature circuit breaker) or RCBO (residual current breaker with overload protection). These devices protect the circuit against overloading, which could generate heat within the wiring, melting the insulation and causing a fire. They also react to short circuits caused when the current-carrying cores of cables come into contact with each other; this can happen if they become loose inside an electrical accessory or when the cable is pierced accidentally by a drill or nail.

Fuses contain a special wire that will melt and separate, cutting off the flow of electricity, if the circuit draws too much current or a short circuit occurs. The wire may be exposed within the carrier or it can be contained within a special cartridge. Circuit breakers are trip switches that turn themselves off under the same circumstances and can be reset by pushing a button or operating the switch.

The demand placed on circuits varies – light fittings consume less electricity than most plug-in appliances, for example – so as well as having different sized cable, the circuits are protected by fuses or circuit breakers with different ratings. Lighting circuits will be protected by 5 or 6 amp fuses; socket circuits by 30 or 32 amp fuses; an immersion heater by a 15 or 16 amp fuse, and so on. It is essential that fuses of the correct rating are used. One with too low a rating will keep blowing; one with too high a rating might not protect the circuit against overloading, with potentially fatal consequences.

Cartridge fuses

RCBO (residual current breaker with overload protection)

MCB (miniature circuit breaker)

Changing a cartridge fuse

Cartridge fuses are easy to replace, but make sure you use the correct fuse rating for the circuit: fuses vary in size and colour coding according to their rating.

Switch off the power and remove the cartridge fuse. Some are simply held in spring clips and can be prised out; others require the fuse carrier to be opened by releasing a screw. Press a new fuse of the correct rating into the spring clips or insert it into the open ends of the carrier's pins. Then, if necessary, reassemble the fuse carrier. Check the main power switch is off and replace the fuse; usually the pins are offset to one side so that it will only fit one way round. Restore the power.

Changing a fuse wire

If a rewirable fuse has blown, you should be able to see that the fuse wire has melted. Replace it with new fuse wire of the correct amperage. Turn off the power, lift the fuse cover on the consumer unit and remove the blown fuse. Release the terminal screws and remove the fuse wire. Take a length of fuse wire of the correct rating and insert it in the carrier. Wind the ends of the wire around the terminals, but don't pull it taut. Cut off the excess then tighten the screws. Check the main power switch is off, and then refit the fuse. Replace the cover and turn the power back on.

 Making it easier

Connection unit fuses
Fixed appliances are permanently wired to a connection unit which has an on/off wall switch and a cartridge fuse. To replace a connection unit fuse, first switch off the connection unit switch. Then unscrew or prise out the fuse holder. Remove the fuse and insert a new one of the correct rating. Push or screw the holder back fully before restoring the power.

Spring-clip cartridge fuse holder

Enclosed cartridge fuse holder

Rewirable fuse

safe electrics

Never take risks with electrical safety. Before you start any kind of electrical work see page 268.

RCD protection

Modifications to any circuit must comply with the latest IEE Wiring Regulations. New or replacement cables or sockets may require RCD protection. See page 268.

Adding any new electrical outlet or light fitting will almost certainly involve running cable from a power source. You can simply clip cables to the surface of a wall, but it is safer and neater to conceal them. They can be run above the ceiling, below the floor, or behind walls. Where practical, mark where you run new cables for future reference.

Running cable between floors

- **Lofts** You can lay cables across the top of joists around the edges of a loft, well away from where anyone is likely to walk. Or clip them to the sides of joists, but keep them well above any thermal insulation, which can cause cables to overheat. Polystyrene insulation can also react with cable sheathing.

- **Intermediate floors/ceiling voids** Clip cables to the sides of joists, lay them on the ceiling or route them through holes drilled through the joists.

- **Ground floors** If you can gain access to the underside of the floor, clip cables beneath the joists.

- **Concrete floors** If a concrete floor has a timber sub-floor on top, you can lay cables on the surface of the concrete. But cables should only run through a concrete floor if they are passed through conduit inserted when the floor is laid, not through channels subsequently cut into the concrete.

Clipping cable to a joist

Run the cable along the centre of one side of the joist and space the clips at roughly 300mm intervals. Buy clips that match the size of cable.

Drilling through a joist

Always be cautious of drilling or cutting joists – it's very important not to weaken the structure. Drill a hole that will allow a 25% air gap around the cable – but no bigger than that. Keep to the central two-thirds of a joist's length and drill at the centre of its depth (or at least 50mm from either top or bottom) to minimise weakening and ensure you are clear of nails or fixings.

Running cable in a solid wall

You can simply mount cables on the surface of a wall with clips, or run them through plastic trunking nailed or screwed to the wall – some types are even self-adhesive. Route them along skirting boards and around door and window frames so they won't be conspicuous. But for a really neat finish you should conceal cables. In a solid wall you need to cut a channel (or chase) in the plaster and run the cable through an oval plastic conduit or, for longer lengths, 'top-hat' capping.

project essentials

- **spirit level or plumb line**
- **cable detector**
- **pencil**
- **thick gloves**
- **safety goggles**
- **bolster**
- **club hammer**
- **hacksaw**
- **screwdriver**
- **hammer**
- **filling knife**
- **sanding block**

- oval conduit or cable capping
- conduit clips or galvanised masonry nails
- cable
- filler or patching plaster
- abrasive paper

1 Always run cable vertically to a fitting in a solid wall so that you will know its approximate position when the work is finished. Plan the route of the channel using a spirit level or plumb line and mark it in pencil. Check it with a cable detector to ensure you won't accidentally damage an existing cable or pipe. Wearing thick gloves and safety goggles, cut the channel with a bolster and club hammer, making it 6mm wider than the conduit or capping. Cut away to the depth of the conduit, plus about 3mm.

2 Cut the plastic capping or conduit to length with a hacksaw and feed in the cable. Capping is fixed to the wall with masonry nails; conduit snaps into clips nailed to the wall, or can be simply held with masonry nails driven in each side. Either way, the cable will be held firm by the plaster when you fill the channel.

3 Fill the channel with patching plaster or filler to within about 3mm of the wall's surface. When it has set, add another layer flush with the wall surface. When the filler has set, lightly sand it for a perfect finish.

Top-hat cable capping

Cable in stud walls: drilling

A stud partition wall is ideal for concealing cables, but it is much easier to install them while the wall is being built, when holes can be drilled easily through the various parts of the framework (see page 70). In existing walls, it may be possible simply to drill the head or sole plate and feed the cable in, then fish it out at the appropriate spot with stiff wire. However, there may be a horizontal nogging blocking the way. One solution is to drill a passage for the cable through the plasterboard and nogging.

(see page 70)

1 Bend the end of the cable before you drop it into the wall through the head plate, as this will help you retrieve it. If you encounter a nogging, determine its precise position with a stud finder, or by tapping the face of the wall with a hammer handle – the sound will be more solid over timber. Find the edges of the nogging by pushing a bradawl through the plasterboard. Check there are no hidden pipes or cables then use a 20mm wood bit to bore at a shallow angle through the plasterboard into the nogging from above and below. The holes should meet, allowing the cable to be passed through them.

2 Bend the end of a piece of stiff wire, such as a coat hanger, into a hook shape and fish for the cable through the hole above the nogging. This is not as difficult as it sounds. Pull the end of the cable out through the hole.

3 Feed the end of the cable back into the upper hole and through the holes bored in the nogging until it emerges from the lower hole.

safety first

Over-bending cable will damage its cores, so be sure to cut off the bent section before making the connections.

4 Pull enough cable through the lower hole to reach the fitting. Take great care not to damage the outer sheathing – if you do, cut off and throw away the damaged length. Feed the cable back into the lower hole and down into the wall. Fish it out of the fitting's mounting box hole. Finally, fill the holes and sand smooth when dry.

Cable in stud walls: removing plasterboard

Another method of running a cable past a nogging is to remove a square of plasterboard then cut a shallow notch in the face of the nogging to accommodate the cable. You must shield the cable from accidental penetration with a nail or screw by screwing a flat steel plate over it, or hammer on a purpose-designed cable safeplate.

1 Before dropping the cable into the wall from above, mark its route in pencil using a spirit level or plumb line. Look for noggings with a stud detector or by tapping with a hammer handle and listening for a more solid tone. If you encounter a nogging, mark out a 125mm square at that position. Check for hidden pipes or cables and then drill holes in diagonally opposite corners. Insert the blade of a padsaw or plasterboard saw and cut out the square of plasterboard.

2 Using a chisel and mallet, cut a notch across the face of the exposed nogging, about 13mm deep and 20mm wide. Feed the cable into the wall. Protect it as it passes through the notch by screwing on a square steel plate or hammering on a cable safeplate.

3 Cut a plasterboard repair patch to fit the hole – or use the old piece if it wasn't damaged – and nail it to the nogging at each side. Fill the gaps around the edges and sand the filler when dry.

Sockets can be surface or flush mounted. Surface mounting electrical fittings is easier, but flush-mounted fittings look better and are less prone to accidental damage. Before adding a socket, you must work out whether the IEE Wiring Regulations permit it (see page 280) and establish that the circuit has RCD protection.

(see page 280)

safe electrics

Never take risks with electrical safety. Before you start any kind of electrical work see page 268.

RCD protection

Modifications to any circuit must comply with the latest IEE Wiring Regulations. New or replacement cables or sockets may require RCD protection. See page 268.

WIRING COLOURS

The colours of the live and neutral cores in cable have changed (see page 272). Take special care when working on any installation that combines old and new.

1 Isolate the circuit. Use a socket tester to double-check that it is dead. Unscrew the socket faceplate and pull it away from the wall. Keep the screws in case the new ones don't fit.

Replacing a damaged socket

Scorching of a socket, as here, will usually have been caused by overloading, or by loose connections in a plug. Don't plug it back in without dealing with the problem or it will just happen again.

2 Loosen the terminal screws and free the cable cores. If the insulation is heat damaged, cut back the cores and strip the ends. Run green/yellow sleeving over the earth core if you find it bare. Metal back boxes must be earthed: run a short length of earth cable between the earth terminals of the back box and the faceplate.

project essentials

- **screwdriver**
- **socket tester**
- **wire strippers**
- socket faceplate, same size as original
- screws
- green/yellow sleeving, if required

3 Connect the live core or cores to the live terminal (L) of the new faceplate, the neutral to the neutral terminal (N) and the earth to the earth terminal (E or ⏚). Tighten the terminal screws fully. Fit the new faceplate. If the new screws don't fit the lugs of the old box, reuse the original screws. Use the socket tester to check it is correctly wired.

Single flush socket to a double

If the socket is flush mounted, it is very easy to replace it with a surface-mounted double socket. There are special socket conversion boxes available for doing this, or you can use a standard double socket and drill and plug the wall, as shown here. If you want the socket to be flush mounted, however, you will have to remove the old box and make a larger recess for a new one (see opposite).

1 Isolate the circuit. Use a socket tester to double-check that it is dead. Unscrew the faceplate and disconnect the cables from the terminals of the single socket mounting box. Run green/yellow sleeving over the earth core if you find it bare.

2 Remove the knockout in the new surface mounting box and pass the cables through. Then mark the fixing holes on the wall in pencil. Take the box away, check for hidden pipes or cables, then drill and plug the wall behind.

project essentials

- **screwdriver**
- **socket tester**
- **pipe and cable detector**
- **hammer action drill with masonry bits**
- **wire strippers**
- new double socket
- wall plugs and screws
- green/yellow sleeving

3 Screw the new box in place and then connect the cables to the terminals (as above, Step 3). Fit the new faceplate. Use the socket tester to check it is correctly wired.

safety first

If the cable won't reach the terminals of the new socket without straining, don't pull it. Use a specially designed crimp or terminal block to attach a new short length of cable. But only do this if there is room for it inside the mounting box; all wiring connections must be accessible, not buried in the wall behind.

Flush fixing to solid walls

When flush mounting a box in a solid wall, you need to cut a neat recess through the plaster and into the masonry behind. It's dusty work, so wear gloves and protective goggles.

1 Test for hidden pipes and cables and if all is clear hold the mounting box in position. Use a spirit level to check that it is horizontal then draw its outline on the wall. Using a masonry bit and hammer action drill, make a series of holes within the outline to a slightly greater depth than that of the mounting box (use a socket template, if you have one – see IDEAL TOOL). Set the drill's depth stop, or wrap masking tape around the bit as a depth guide.

2 Chop out the plaster and masonry with a bolster and club hammer, cutting down to the bottom of the drilled holes. Brush out all the debris and check the fit of the box.

3 Hold the box in place, mark the fixing positions, and drill and plug the holes. Cut a channel for the cable (see page 276) before attaching the box. Then isolate the circuit and make the final connections (see Replacing a damaged socket, opposite). Fit the faceplate and check the wiring is correct using a socket tester.

project essentials

- **spirit level**
- **pencil**
- **protective gloves**
- **safety goggles**
- **pipe and cable detector**
- **hammer action drill with masonry bit**
- **bolster**
- **club hammer**
- **screwdriver**
- **wire strippers**
- **socket tester**

- mounting box
- adhesive tape
- plastic wall plugs
- round-head screws

ideal tool

Socket template
When cutting out a recess for a flush mounting box, a socket template will allow you to drill a series of closely spaced holes for a single or double box without the need to draw around the box first. It will also prevent the bit from wandering.

Flush fixing to a stud wall

When flush mounting a socket in a stud wall, it is simplest to use a cavity fixing box. This has a flange that sits against the face of the wall and spring-loaded or rotating lugs that press against the back of the plasterboard, giving more flexibility when you are positioning the fitting.

1 Decide where you want to put the new switch or socket. If you have a stud finder, use it to check that none of the wall's framework will be in the way. If you don't have a stud finder, tap the wall gently with a hammer handle, listening for the hollow note to change when you tap over the framework. Hold the box in place, use a spirit level to ensure it is horizontal, and then draw around it in pencil.

project essentials

- **stud finder**
- **spirit level**
- **pencil**
- **pipe and cable detector**
- **screwdriver**
- **padsaw or plasterboard saw**
- **wire strippers**
- **socket tester**

- cavity fixing box

2 Check the area is free of hidden pipes or cables, then push and twist a screwdriver through at diagonally opposite corners of the outline so that you can insert the blade of a padsaw or plasterboard saw. Cut outwards from the holes, following the box outline, and remove the waste piece of plasterboard.

3 Check that the box fits snugly in the hole. Remove the knock-out from the box. Push the box back into the hole, feeding the cable through the opening.

4 Push in or turn the securing lugs so that they grip the rear face of the plasterboard firmly. Connect the wires (see opposite) and fit the faceplate. Check the socket is correctly wired using a socket tester.

safe electrics

Never take risks with electrical safety. Before you start any kind of electrical work see page 268.

RCD protection
Modifications to any circuit must comply with the latest IEE Wiring Regulations. New or replacement cables or sockets may require RCD protection. See page 268.

Although you can increase the number of sockets in a room by converting single sockets to doubles (see page 276), there may be occasions when you need an extra socket where none exists to convert. In this case, you need to add a spur from a ring circuit. You can either run it from an existing socket or from a junction box connected into the cable run of a suitable ring circuit. The circuit must have RCD protection.

A spur on a ring circuit

The easiest way of connecting into a ring circuit is to run a spur cable from the terminals of an existing socket – but you can't connect it to just any socket you please. The IEE Wiring Regulations are very specific about this. You must not run a spur from a socket that is already on a spur, or that already supplies a spur. And the new socket must not extend the floor area served by the circuit beyond the prescribed limit of 100 sq m (see below).

If you are in any doubt as to whether the socket you plan to run a spur from is part of a ring circuit, it is essential that you consult a qualified electrician.

An alternative to running a spur from an existing socket is to run it from a 3-terminal, 30-amp junction box wired into the main circuit cable. The same regulations apply, however, so if you are in any doubt, you must consult a qualified electrician.

ONE PLANET HOME

No more stand-by
An intelligent multi-socket adapter has one 'master' and several 'slave' sockets. When the adapter detects that the appliance plugged into the master socket has been switched off, it automatically switches off the slave sockets too, so saving energy. The slave sockets switch back on as soon as the master appliance is switched on. You could, for example, plug the television into the master socket and the DVD and home cinema system into the slave sockets. Or in a home office, you could plug the computer into the master socket and printer, scanner and other peripherals into the slave sockets.

Consider the floor area

Although the IEE Wiring Regulations permit you to have an unlimited number of socket outlets on each main circuit running from the consumer unit, there are restrictions on the floor area that each circuit can supply. A 30/32 amp ring circuit can supply a maximum area of 100 sq m. However, because ring circuits serving kitchens and utility rooms are usually the most heavily loaded, it is advisable to avoid extending them into other rooms wherever possible.

You should find that the rooms of the house covered by each circuit are written inside the fuse cover of the consumer unit, but you can check this by isolating the circuit and using a socket tester on each socket to see if it works. Once you have determined the extent of the circuit, you can measure the rooms it supplies and calculate the floor area. If you have a large house and were planning to run a spur through a wall to feed a socket in a different room, you may find it will exceed the limit. If so, you must run the spur from a different circuit

New socket

Spur

Existing socket

RCD-protected main circuit cables

ideal tool

Continuity/resistance/ voltage tester
This is a battery-powered tool for testing whether a cable is part of a continuous circuit; for measuring the resistance of a component or circuit; and for testing for AC or DC voltages.

Running a spur from a socket

Install the new socket and and run a length of 2.5mm² two-core-and-earth cable from the new outlet to the existing socket (see pages 276–79).

1 Isolate the circuit and use a socket tester to double-check that the existing socket is dead.

2 Unscrew the faceplate of the new socket, feed the cable into the mounting box through a rubber grommet and connect its cores to the faceplate terminals. Don't forget to add green/yellow sleeving to the bare earth core of the new cable, and make sure the terminal screws are tight.

3 Cut the cable and do the same at the existing socket.

4 If you have metal faceplates, cut a short length of earth core from 1.5mm² cable and run it between the earth terminals of the faceplate and mounting box.

5 Replace the faceplates and turn the power back on. Check that the new socket is correctly wired using a socket tester.

Spur from socket

Labels: New socket · Mounting box · Spur · Existing socket · Mounting box · RCD-protected main circuit cable

WIRING COLOURS

The colours of the live and neutral cores in cable have changed (see page 262). Take special care when working on any installation that combines old and new.

Two-core-and-earth cable

L
N

Old colours

L
N

tools materials

- continuity tester
- side cutters
- wire strippers
- screwdriver
- socket tester

- 2 rubber grommets
- green/yellow sleeving

---

project essentials

- **continuity tester**
- **power drill with twist bits**
- **panel saw, if required**
- **hammer, if required**
- **screwdriver**
- **side cutters**
- **wire strippers**
- **socket tester**

- rubber grommet
- 3-terminal 30-amp junction box
- timber battens, if required
- 50mm nails, if required
- green/yellow sheathing

B&Q Making it easier

Know your terminals
Make sure you are connecting to the correct socket terminals – their position varies between brands. Read any instructions that come with the new socket.

Running a spur from a junction box

Install the spur socket and run a length of 2.5mm² two-core-and-earth cable back to the point where it is to be connected to the main circuit cable (see pages 276–79). The junction box should have the same amperage as the circuit.

1 Isolate the circuit and use a socket tester to double-check that it is dead.

2 Unscrew the faceplate of the new socket, feed the cable into the mounting box through a rubber grommet and connect its cores to the faceplate terminals. Don't forget to add green/yellow sleeving to the bare earth core of the new cable, and make sure the terminal screws are tight.

3 If the faceplate is metal, cut a short length of earth core from 1.5mm² cable and run it between the earth terminals of the faceplate and mounting box. Replace the faceplate.

4 Screw the base of the junction box to the side of an adjacent joist or to a batten nailed between joists so that it will be within reach of the cut ends of the main cable.

5 Cut the cable, strip back the outer sheathing (but make sure it extends a few mm into the junction box), bare the ends of the cores and connect them to the terminals of the junction box. Connect the cores of the spur cable to the matching terminals – live to live, neutral to neutral, earth to earth. Remember to add green/yellow sleeving to the bare earth cores.

6 Make sure the terminal screws are tight, then replace the cover of the box and turn on the power. Test the socket is wired correctly using a socket tester.

safety first

Grommets
When using metal mounting boxes, it is essential to fit rubber grommets to protect the incoming cable from being damaged by the sharp edges around the metal cut-outs.

Spur from junction box

Labels: New socket · Mounting box · Spur · 30-amp junction box · RCD-protected main circuit cable · RCD-protected main circuit cable

safe electrics

Never take risks with electrical safety. Before you start any kind of electrical work see page 268.

Lighting circuits are wired in two different ways, using either junction-boxes or loop-in ceiling roses. These days the loop-in system predominates, though individual circuits often combine the two for the most economical use of cable. But unlike power circuits, lighting circuits are always of the radial type: the cable leaves the consumer unit and runs to each outlet position before terminating at the last fitting on the line. Most houses have at least two lighting circuits – usually one upstairs and one down.

Junction-box circuits

The reason why the wiring of a lighting circuit is more complex than a power circuit is that each outlet or light fitting needs to be controlled by a separate switch. One way of providing for this is to install a four-terminal junction box in which the cable from a light and the cable from its switch can be connected to the circuit cable.

In practice, instead of a junction box for each lighting outlet, you may find that the cables run to a single, bigger junction-box in the attic or ceiling void, where all the connections for the circuit are made. Or there may be a combination of junction-box and loop-in wiring (see opposite) on one circuit.

Junction-box wiring

The wiring of a four-terminal junction box

Two of the cables entering the junction box are the main circuit cables. Their brown (live), blue (neutral) and earth (green/yellow-sleeved) cores are each connected to a different terminal. (In older installations these cores will be red (live), black (neutral) and green/yellow (earth). See WIRING COLOURS, right.) One

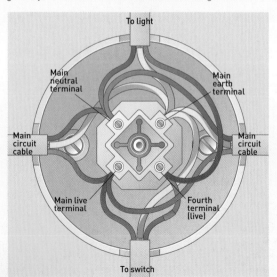

of the other cables entering the box runs to the light, the last cable to the switch. The brown core of the light cable is connected to the fourth terminal, while its blue core is connected to the main circuit neutral cores; the earth runs to the earth terminal. The brown core of the switch cable is connected to the main circuit live cores, while its blue core is connected to the light cable brown core.

Current flows from the main circuit down the brown core to the switch then (if the switch is on and the circuit therefore unbroken) back up the blue core and along the brown core to the light before finally returning through the light cable blue core to the neutral terminal in the box. Because the switch cable blue core becomes the feed to the light when the switch is turned on, it must carry a warning 'flag' of brown PVC electrical sleeving.

At the light unit itself, the current flows from the brown core of the cable into the brown (live) core of the flex, then back up the blue (neutral) core of the flex to the cable's blue core. In a pendant light fitting and some wall lights, the connections are made in the rose or base of the unit; in flush-mounted fittings, the connections must be made in a heat-proof conduit box set in the ceiling or wall.

WIRING COLOURS

The colours of the live and neutral cores in cable have changed (see page 272). Take special care when working on any installation that combines old and new.

Two-core-and-earth cable

In lighting circuits, a warning flag of brown (formerly red) PVC electrical sleeving is used to indicate that one or more cores aside from the brown live core may also at times serve as the live feed.

Loop-in circuits

With loop-in wiring, the main circuit cable from the consumer unit loops in and out of multi-terminal ceiling roses, from which individual cables run to the light switches. This type of wiring system does away with the need for junction boxes and separate cables to the lights. All the necessary connections are made within the rose. A separate terminal is provided in the rose for the switch cable neutral core, which passes current directly to the live core of the pendant flex.

Loop-in wiring

- Rose
- Circuit cable
- Switch drop cable
- Switch
- Circuit cable
- Consumer unit

Circuit capacity

A lighting circuit is protected by a 5 or 6 amp fuse or circuit breaker. This fuse size allows bulbs with a maximum combined wattage of 1150 watts (5 amps x 230 volts) or 1380 watts (6 amps x 230 volts) to be run off the circuit. In practice it is best always to restrict the number of outlets per circuit to about eight; that means that even with a 100 watt bulb at every outlet, the total wattage is comfortably within the maximum. But if you are running high-wattage floodlights, or a big multi-bulb chandelier, you will need even fewer outlets if you are to avoid overloading the circuit.

Lighting circuits are generally run in 1mm² two-core-and-earth cable, but particularly long circuits may use 1.5mm² cable to compensate for the drop in voltage experienced on long cable runs.

Two-way switching

It is common for the light in a hall or on a landing to be controlled by two-way switching, whereby the light can be switched on and off both from upstairs and downstairs. In this situation, the switch connected directly to the light (either through a junction box or loop-in rose) is linked to a second switch using special three-core-and-earth cable.

Bathroom lighting

The steamy, damp environment of a bathroom greatly increases the potential dangers of any electrical fitting. Steam can easily cause a bulb to shatter, so it is advisable always to fit moisture-proof, enclosed light fittings wherever they are positioned in a bathroom. Switches must be ceiling-mounted pull-cords; any wall-mounted switches should be sited outside the room.

The IEE Wiring Regulations divide a bathroom into three Hazard Zones. Light fittings must be suitable for the zone they are in; always read the manufacturer's instructions and measure the room carefully. A light fitting in Zone 2 must be approved as splashproof (with a minimum rating of IPX4, see page 294). A ceiling-mounted switch must be beyond Zone 2, although it is permissible for the pull-cord to dangle down into other zones.

0.6m
1
2
2.25m
0

Remember the rules

If you plan to make changes to a power or lighting circuit in a bathroom, you must inform your local authority's Building Control Department first. Any additions or alterations to circuits in a bathroom must be protected by a 30mA RCD. See page 270.

ELECTRICITY LIGHT BULBS

The world of light bulbs is changing. Old-style incandescent bulbs, which are extremely wasteful of energy, are being phased out in favour of an ever improving and widening range of energy efficient bulbs. These have a much longer lifespan and use far less electricity, saving you money and helping the environment.

safe electrics

Never take risks with electrical safety. Before you start any kind of electrical work see page 268.

Types of bulb

There is a vast range light bulbs and tubes to choose from, meeting every conceivable practical and decorative purpose. Bulbs usually have either a bayonet end cap (BC) or Edison screw cap (ES). Tubes generally have two small pins projecting from each end that fit into spring-loaded holders.

B&Q Making it easier

Dimmers

A dimmer switch will dramatically increase the potential of your home's lighting, however basic your fittings. It is wired in the same way as an ordinary switch (see page 286). Not all dimmers are compatible with low-voltage halogen bulbs or most fluorescent tubes or bulbs; check the manufacturer's instructions. Though you can now buy dimmable energy saving bulbs: see opposite.

Incandescent GLS (general lighting service)

Incandescent GLS bulbs are the most familiar and traditional bulbs in everyday use. However, incandescent bulbs are based on very outdated technology and are extremely wasteful of energy: as much as 90% of the electricity they consume is turned into heat rather than light. Because of this, they are steadily being phased out under new EU rules. In their place is an ever-growing range of high-performance energy saving bulbs that run on a fraction of the electricity and last many times longer. See opposite.

Halogen

Halogen bulbs produce crisp, bright white light – brighter than a standard bulb of the same wattage. They bring out the detail of an interior, and are also good for reading and close-work. They do get very hot, so must only be used in a suitable fitting.

Low-voltage halogen lighting uses bulbs that run at 12 volts rather than the usual 230, making them a particularly safe option in a kitchen or bathroom. The current is supplied via a transformer, which may be built into the light fitting or be in a separate location (see page 293).

Energy saving CFL and LED spotlights are also now available for use in standard halogen fittings: see opposite.

Reflector

These bulbs produce strong directional beams of light and are used in spotlight and floodlight fittings. All have some form of silvering on the bulb that helps throw the light in a particular direction. They are available in incandescent, halogen and energy saving versions.

Fluorescent tubes

These are long glass cylinders with metal end caps. Fluorescent tubes produce light ranging from a bluish white to a much warmer pinkish shade. Various lengths, and even circular versions, are available for a range of fittings. Fluorescent bulbs use less energy than incandescent bulbs to produce an equivalent amount of light, and compact fluorescent bulbs or CFLs are the most common type of energy saving bulb on the market.

safety first

All lampshades have a wattage maximum. Don't exceed it or you could cause scorching or even a fire.

The change to lumens

The brightness of an incandescent light bulb has traditionally been expressed in watts, which is the electrical unit of power. But this is much less useful now that there are so many energy efficient bulbs that produce the same amount of light using much less electricity. So from 1 September 2010, manufacturers will have to tell us how much light is produced by each bulb we buy, measured in lumens (luminous flux), as well as the equivalent incandescent bulb power in watts.

This table shows the approximate relationship between the traditional and low energy bulb types in watts and lumens.

LUMENS AND WATTS				
Lumens	Traditional bulb (incandescent GLS)	Halogen bulb	Energy saving bulb: CFL	Energy saving bulb: LED
1326–1398 lumens	100 watts	70–75 watts	19–21 watts	
702–741 lumens	60 watts	42–45 watts	11–13 watts	
410–432 lumens	40 watts	28–30 watts	8–10 watts	7 watts
217–229 lumens	25 watts	18 watts	5–7 watts	4 watts

Energy saving lighting

Energy saving light bulbs have improved dramatically in the past few years. Whatever style or level of lighting you want, and whatever your fitting, there is now an energy saving bulb to suit. They no longer need several minutes to 'warm up' – the latest CFLs light up fully in seconds or less and are as bright as a traditional incandescent bulb. They also last up to ten times longer.

Lighting accounts for a big chunk of the average UK household's electricity bill, so switching to energy saving lighting makes a big difference. Once you install an energy efficient light bulb, you start saving energy and money immediately.

Make a difference
Changing your light bulbs to energy efficient versions is a small step that will help make a big difference. Experts estimate that if everyone in the UK replaced just one of their old bulbs with an energy saving one, the amount of carbon saved would be the same as taking 70,000 cars off the UK's roads.

CFLs (Compact fluorescent lamps)

These are the most common type of energy saving bulb. They combine the technology of a fluorescent tube with the compact dimensions and standard fittings of traditional bulbs, including halogen bulbs. They produce a bright light while consuming only about 20% of the electricity of a comparable GLS bulb. You can also now buy dimmable versions.

Spotlight

GLS

Spiral

2-Pin Stick

Stick

Candle

4-Pin Stick

LED bulbs

LEDs are the latest development in energy saving lighting. Incredibly energy efficient, they are available as spotlights suitable for accent or mood lighting (see page 293), as well as bulbs for standard fittings that are bright enough for general use. And whereas many CFLs still take a couple of seconds to light up, LED bulbs reach full brightness almost immediately.

Disposal of CFLs

At the end of their life, CFLs should not be disposed of in the general household rubbish. Like many household products – including the traditional fluorescent tubes whose technology they are based on – they must be disposed of responsibly at special facilities. All local councils have an obligation to make arrangements for the disposal of this category of waste at civic amenity sites or household waste recycling centres. See www.recyclemore.co.uk to find your local facility.

Safety of CFLs

CFLs contain a very small amount of mercury – typically 3–4 milligrams per bulb (and limited to 5mg per bulb), which is just enough to cover the tip of a ball point pen. Such a small quantity of mercury is unlikely to cause harm. Nonetheless, unnecessary contact with mercury should be avoided, so breakages must be handled with care.

What to do if a CFL breaks

- Ventilate the room and vacate it of people and pets
- Scoop up the glass fragments and powder using a piece of cardboard and place them in a sturdy plastic bag
- Use sticky tape (duct tape or similar) to pick up any residual powder and dispose of the tape in the bag
- Wipe the area clean with damp paper towels or disposable wet wipes, which should also be disposed of in the bag
- Seal the plastic bag and place it inside another, sealed plastic bag
- Wash your hands well

Contact your local authority for advice on disposal of the bag, which should not be thrown away with the general waste.

safe electrics

Never take risks with electrical safety. Before you start any kind of electrical work see page 268.

RCD protection
Modifications to any circuit must comply with the latest IEE Wiring Regulations. New or replacement cables or sockets may require RCD protection. See page 268.

Light switches are functional items, and many of the cheaper varieties – made from white plastic – look strictly utilitarian, but you can choose from a range of decorative switches that will add a finishing touch to any room. If replacing a damaged switch, you could take the opportunity to improve its appearance. Another reason for changing a switch is to provide the convenience of multi-way control of a light in a hallway, landing or stairwell.

Types of switch

Wall-mounted light switch fittings (known as plateswitches) may contain one, two, three or even more individual switches (or gangs) to allow control of several separate light fittings from one position. In addition, versions are available to allow two- and multi-way switching. There's a huge range of fittings available, from functional plastic fittings to stylish metallic finishes.

Dimmers allow you to raise and lower the light level and may have a simple combined on/off and dimming control, or a separate on/off switch and dimmer control, so that you don't have to readjust the light level every time you turn on the light. They are wired in much the same way as a standard switch. Where space is limited, or for an unobtrusive installation, narrow architrave switches can be fitted into door frames. Switches generally require a 16mm-deep mounting box, although some dimmers may need deeper boxes. Ceiling-mounted pull-cord switches are required in bathrooms or shower rooms (see page 283).

Single plastic

Double brushed aluminium

Dimmer

Rotary dimmer with separate on/off switch

Narrow architrave switches

Pull-cord switch

Replacing a one-way switch

If a switch is damaged, or you simply want to update your fittings, replacing it is a fairly simple task. Just be sure to write down exactly how the old switch was wired before you disconnect it, and wire the new switch in the same way. Keep hold of the original screws – you may have to reuse them, since modern fittings will come with metric-sized screws and older fittings may have imperial threads.

1 Isolate the circuit and confirm that the power is off with a voltage tester. Then unscrew the switch faceplate and pull it forward so that you can see the connections behind. Draw a clear diagram showing the colour and number of wires connected to each terminal, then release the terminal screws and pull the cores from the terminals. If the earth core is properly insulated in green/yellow sleeving and connected to the mounting box, leave this attached.

2 Connect the cores to the correct terminals of the new switch, tighten the screws and check that they are clamping the cable cores firmly by giving the wires a slight tug. If there isn't one already, fit a length of brown PVC sleeving over the blue core (or the black core if your wiring is in the old colours) to indicate that it can be live.

3 Run green/yellow PVC sleeving over the bare earth core of the switch drop cable and connect it to the earthing terminal of the mounting box. If using a metal switch, be sure to earth the switch faceplate (see SAFETY FIRST, right).

4 Recheck that each connection is secure, then push the cable back into the mounting box and fit the faceplate.

project essentials

- **voltage tester**
- **screwdrivers**
- **side cutters**

- one-way plateswitch
- green/yellow earth sleeving
- brown PVC electrical sleeving
- screws

Two-core-and-earth switch drop cable from light

Plastic faceplate of single switch

Earthing terminal of metal mounting box

safety first

Earthing light switches
The commonest combination is a metal mounting box and plastic faceplate, as shown here, in which case the earth core or cores must be connected to the earthing terminal of the mounting box. If you have a metal faceplate, the main earth core runs to the faceplate first, and then you must also run a short length of earth core (cut from 1mm² two-core and earth cable and insulated with green/yellow sleeving) between the earthing terminals on the faceplate and the mounting box. If both mounting box and faceplate are plastic and there is no earthing terminal, run green/yellow sleeving over the bare cores and clamp their exposed ends with a connector; that way if you decide to change to metal fittings in the future, you will be able to earth them safely and easily.

Two-way switching

To change from the one-way control of a light to two-way switching you have to replace the original switch with a two-way fitting, install a new two-way switch at the second control point and link the two with 1mm² three-core-and-earth cable. Start by running the cable between the two switch positions and installing a mounting box at the new switch position (see pages 276–79).

project essentials

- **voltage tester**
- **screwdrivers**
- **side cutters**

- green/yellow earth sleeving
- brown PVC electrical sleeving

safety first

Working on multi-way installations

Be extremely cautious when opening up multi-way switches. The lights they control *should* all take their power from the same circuit, but if yours are incorrectly wired and take power from different circuits, there will still be live cables at each switch position when one circuit is isolated. Be aware also that there is more than one method of wiring multi-way lights. If yours do not match the system shown here, that doesn't necessarily mean they are unsafe.

Two-core-and-earth switch drop cable from light

Plastic faceplate of first switch

Earthing terminal of metal mounting box

Three-core-and-earth linking cable to second switch

Three-core-and-earth linking cable from first switch

Plastic faceplate of second switch

Earthing terminal of metal mounting box

1 Isolate the circuit and double-check the power is off with a voltage tester; remove the faceplate from the existing switch and disconnect the cable cores. You may find that the switch has three terminals, indicating that it is actually a two-way fitting, in which case you can reuse it.

2 Each two-way switch will have three terminals, arranged as a single and a pair. They will either be labelled Common, L1 and L2, or L1, L2 and L3. At the original switch, fit a length of brown PVC sleeving over the blue core of the switch drop cable and the grey and black cores of the linking cable to indicate that they can be live. Then connect the brown and blue cores of the existing switch drop cable and the black and grey cores of the new linking cable to the pair of terminals. Take the brown core of the linking cable to the single

terminal. Fit green/yellow sleeving over the bare earth cores and connect them to the mounting box earth terminal. If using metal switches, be sure to earth the switch faceplates (see SAFETY FIRST, opposite).

3 At the second switch, fit a length of brown PVC sleeving over the grey and black cores of the linking cable to indicate that they can be live. Then connect the cores of the three-core-and-earth cable to the same terminals as the first switch. Fit green/yellow sleeving over the bare earth core and connect it to the mounting box earth terminal.

B&Q Making it easier

Multi-way switching

The connections in two- and three-way light switches are such that the circuit can be made or broken at any of the switch points. For this to be possible you have to use cable with an extra core, so that the current can run in various directions, along various routes. Because the brown, black and grey cores (or red, yellow and blue if using cable in the old colours, see below) may all at times be live at a light switch, they must carry a warning flag of brown (formerly red) PVC electrical sleeving or tape.

Two-core-and-earth cable

Old colours

Three-core-and-earth cable

Old colours

Intermediate switching

You can control a light from more than two separate switch positions. The connections for wiring the first and final switches are the same as for two-way switching, but a special intermediate switch is wired into the three-core-and-earth linking cable between them. An intermediate switch has four terminals; fit a length of brown PVC sleeving over the grey and black cores and connect the black cores to the top and bottom terminals on one side and the grey cores to the terminals on the other. The two brown cores should be joined with an insulated strip connector. Fit the earth cores (protected by green/yellow sleeving) to the mounting box earthing terminal.

Three-core-and-earth linking cable from first switch

Plastic faceplate of intermediate switch

Insulated strip connector

Earthing terminal of metal mounting box

Three-core-and-earth linking cable to last switch

A standard single pendant light fitting near the centre of the ceiling can sometimes leave a lot to be desired. Provided you can access the ceiling void from above without too much disruption, it's not complicated to move a light to give illumination where you really need it, or to increase light levels by adding extra pendants, operated either by the existing switch or by a new one. Pre-wired lampholder-plus-flex combinations are widely available.

Identifying the circuit type

The first task is to identify the circuit type – junction box or loop-in. With the power turned off, remove the ceiling rose cover. You can't tell from the design of the rose; you need to count the cables entering it. If there is only one cable, you have junction-box wiring; if there are two or three, you have a loop-in system.

Two cables entering rose

Two cables also indicate a loop-in circuit. The last rose on the circuit will have one circuit cable plus a switch cable.

Three cables entering rose

Three cables at the rose indicate loop-in wiring; an intermediate rose on the circuit will have two circuit cables plus a switch cable.

Single cable entering rose

A single cable at the rose indicates junction-box wiring.

Moving a pendant light

Isolate the circuit, double-check it is dead and unscrew the rose cover. When you have identified the wiring type, disconnect the flex and feed cable.

With junction-box wiring

Unscrew the rose base from the ceiling and push the cable back through. Above the ceiling, connect the cable to a three-terminal junction box; run a length of 1mm² two-core-and-earth cable from the new light rose. Connect the brown core to the live terminal, the blue to the neutral terminal and the earth (insulated with green/yellow sleeving) to the earth terminal. Make good the ceiling at the old light position with filler.

With loop-in wiring

Unscrew the rose base from the ceiling and push the cables back through. Mount a four-terminal junction box (see page 282) above the original light position. Connect the live, neutral and earth cores of the main circuit cable(s) to three separate terminals. Then connect the brown core of the switch cable to the circuit lives, the earth core to the circuit earths and the blue core to the fourth (unused) terminal. Finally, add a fourth cable to feed the light, connecting its brown core to the switch blue, its blue core to the circuit neutrals and its earth to the circuit earths. Make good the ceiling at the old light position with filler.

project essentials

- voltage tester
- screwdriver
- side cutters
- sharp knife
- wire strippers
- filling knife
- sanding block
- paintbrush

- ceiling rose
- 1mm² two-core-and-earth cable
- green/yellow earth sleeving
- brown PVC electrical sleeving
- cable clips
- 3- or 4-terminal junction box(es)
- new switch, if required
- filler
- abrasive paper
- paint

safety first

Pendants

Flex can only support a very lightweight bulb and shade; fittings over 2kg must be chain-supported. Fittings with metal parts must be earthed via three-core flex unless labelled as double-insulated (▣).

Adding an extra pendant light to an existing switch

If a single pendant fitting doesn't provide enough light, you can add another controlled by the same switch without too much trouble. The one limiting factor is the number of lighting outlets already powered by the circuit; don't risk overloading the circuit (see page 283).

With junction-box wiring

Double-check the circuit is dead and cut the feed cable to the original light at a suitable position to install a three-terminal junction box. Run a length of 1mm² two-core-and-earth cable from there to the new fitting.

With loop-in wiring

1 Double-check the power is off and run a spur cable from the original ceiling rose, connecting its brown core to the same terminal as the switch drop blue core (which should carry a length of brown PVC sleeving to indicate that it can be live) and its blue core to the neutral circuit cores, the earth core going to the earth terminal – as illustrated, right.

2 At the new rose, connect the brown core to the terminal marked 'live' and the blue core to the terminal marked 'neutral'. Take the earth core to the earth terminal, covering it in green/yellow sleeving. Connect the live (brown) core of the pendant flex to the live terminal and the neutral (blue) core to the neutral terminal.

Running a spur from a loop-in rose

With a loop-in system, you can add a spur cable at the original ceiling rose to provide power to a second light controlled by the same switch.

Adding a pendant light and new switch

Whichever type of wiring you have, you may find it possible to run the switch cable back to the existing switch position, replacing the original one-gang switch with a two-gang unit. This will make for a neater installation.

With junction-box wiring

1 Double-check the circuit is dead then cut the main circuit cable and install a four-terminal junction box. Connect the live cores of the split circuit cable to one terminal, the neutral cores to another and the earth cores to a third, adding green/yellow sleeving.

2 Then run one length of 1mm² two-core-and-earth cable to the new light and another to the switch. Connect the brown switch core to the circuit lives, its earth to the circuit earths and its blue core to the fourth terminal; add a length of brown PVC electrical sleeving to this core to show that it can be live.

3 Connect the brown core of the light cable to the switch drop's blue core, its blue core to the circuit neutrals and its earth to the earth terminal.

With loop-in wiring

1 Double-check the power is off and run a spur cable from an existing rose on the circuit, connecting its brown core to the main circuit lives, its blue core to the main circuit neutrals and its earth to the earth terminal.

2 At the new light position, connect its brown core to the central bank of terminals, which may be marked 'loop', and its blue core to the neutral terminal; connect the earth to the earth terminal, adding green/yellow sleeving.

3 Then run in the switch drop cable at the new rose, connecting its brown core to the spur's brown, its blue core (flagged brown) to the live terminal and its earth to the earth terminal.

Alternatively

With either type of wiring, you have the alternative option of connecting a three-terminal junction box into the main circuit cable and running a spur from there to a loop-in rose with its own switch cable.

Running a spur from a loop-in rose to a new rose and switch

With a loop-in rose, you can add a spur cable to provide power to a second light position controlled by its own switch.

Even when controlled by a dimmer switch, a ceiling light can only produce very limited effects. For greater versatility, wall lights are hard to beat: they can be functional, providing directed light to accent particular features or to aid reading; and they can be decorative, creating pools of illumination that give a room an overall subtle glow.

Installing the lights

Fitting wall lights can be a messy, labour-intensive job, so start by planning the cable runs and connections, aiming to keep disruption to a minimum. If you have fitted carpeting on the floor above, for example, then accessing the lighting circuit cables in the ceiling void may be much more difficult than running a spur from a suitable socket within the room.

As a rule, wall lights are best placed about 1.8m above the floor. In some you can make the connections within the base of the light (using strip connectors), while for others you will need to fit a round conduit box in the wall at the end of the cable chase. In some cases, you may be able to screw the light fitting to the box; in others, it will have to be screwed to the wall.

Run all the cable first (see pages 276–79) and then fit the lights before finally isolating the supply circuit and making all the connections. If you are installing more than one wall light, you will need to cut the supply cable and install a three-terminal junction box for each additional fitting; simply connect the cores like to like and check they are secure.

Wiring options

You need to decide how you want the new lights to operate:

- Do you want wall lights that come on with the main ceiling light? If so, then you need to run a spur from the junction box or loop-in rose controlling the ceiling light.
- Do you want the wall lights to be separately switched from the main ceiling light? You need to wire a junction box into a lighting circuit and run new cable from there to both the switch and light fittings.
- Do you want the wall lights to replace the ceiling light? If so, you need to replace the rose with a junction box and run a cable from that to the new lights.

Don't risk overloading a lighting circuit (see page 283). If you want to install multiple wall lights, it may be better to power them from a spur run off a main power circuit.

Adding wall lights controlled by an existing switch

Your first task is to establish whether you have junction-box or loop-in wiring. Make certain that the circuit is dead, then unscrew the ceiling rose cover and count the cables entering it: one cable means junction-box wiring; more than one means loop-in wiring (see page 288).

With loop-in wiring ▲

If you have loop-in wiring, you can run a spur from the rose to the new wall lights. Connect its blue core to the same terminal as the blue (neutral) core of the ceiling light flex, and its brown core to the same terminal as the brown (live) core of the flex. Add green/yellow sleeving to the bare earth core and connect this to the rose's earth terminal. Make sure the blue core of the switch cable is 'flagged' with brown PVC electrical sleeving and replace the rose cover.

With junction-box wiring ▲

If you have junction-box wiring, use a cable detector to trace the cable from the ceiling rose back to the junction box where it connects with the circuit cable and switch drop. Entering the junction box, you may find three cables (one circuit, one switch and one light) or four (two circuit, one switch and one light). Remove the cover and connect the cores of the new wall light spur cable to the same terminals as the cores of the existing light cable. Remember to add green/yellow sleeving to the bare earth core.

Check that the blue core from the switch cable (which connects to the brown core of the light cable) has a length of brown PVC electrical sleeving to indicate that it can be live. Replace the cover.

Adding wall lights with a separate switch

If you want separately switched wall lights, you can take power from a nearby lighting circuit – provided you don't overload the circuit (see page 283). If possible, run the switch cable back to the existing switch position and replace the original one-gang switch with a two-gang unit; this will give you a much tidier finish.

1 First install the wall light or lights and the new switch. Run 1mm² two-core-and-earth cable from the switch back to a suitable position for cutting into the main circuit cable. Run another cable from here to the wall light, or to a three-terminal junction box from which you can run cables to two wall lights. You will need a three-terminal junction box for each additional light.

2 Isolate the circuit and check it is dead with a voltage tester. Then cut the main circuit cable, and connect it with the switch drop cable and new cable to the lights at a four-terminal junction box (see page 282).

Lighting circuit cable — New junction box — New junction box — Wall light — Wall light — New switch

Replacing a ceiling light with wall lights

The advantage of replacing a ceiling light with wall lights is that you don't need to install a new switch. If you substitute a light there is also less risk of overloading the circuit (see page 283) – but check first, particularly if installing more than one wall light. Double-check the circuit is dead, unscrew the ceiling rose, and work out whether you have junction box or loop-in wiring: see page 288.

With junction-box wiring

Disconnect the cable entering the rose, push it back through the ceiling and connect it to a three-terminal junction box. Run new cable from that to the wall lights. If there is more than one wall light, split the feed cable with one or more three-terminal junction boxes. Make good the ceiling at the old rose position with filler.

With loop-in wiring

If you have loop-in wiring there will be two or three cables entering the rose. You need to identify them before disconnecting them. Look for the switch cable, whose blue core (or black, in the old wiring colours) should be connected to the live (brown) core of the pendant flex and 'flagged' with brown sleeving. The other cable or cables will be the main circuit. Label the cables, disconnect them and remove the rose baseplate from the ceiling. Push the cables back through the ceiling and connect them to a four-terminal junction box (see page 282) from which you can run the new cable to the wall lights. Make good the ceiling at the old rose position with filler.

Connecting to a power circuit

If gaining access to a lighting circuit is difficult or adding the wall lights will overload a circuit, you can supply the new fittings from a nearby power circuit.

1 Make sure the circuit is dead and run a spur in 2.5mm² two-core-and-earth cable from a suitable socket or junction box on a main ring circuit (see pages 280–81) to a fused connection unit containing a 5 amp fuse and connect it to the 'feed' terminals. If you buy a switched fused connection unit, this can act as the on/off switch for the lights; otherwise, you will have to run a cable from the fused connection unit to a four-terminal junction box and run separate cables from this to the lights and switch.

2 The lights should be wired in 1mm² two-core-and-earth cable, which should run from the 'load' terminals of the fused connection unit. If more than one wall light is being installed, split the feed cable with one or more three-terminal junction boxes.

Junction box — Wall light — Wall light — Switched fused connection unit — Spur — Socket — RCD-protected main circuit cable

safe electrics

Never take risks with electrical safety. Before you start any kind of electrical work see page 268.

RCD protection
Modifications to any circuit must comply with the latest IEE Wiring Regulations. New or replacement cables or sockets may require RCD protection. See page 268.

For more interesting lighting effects, replace standard pendant light fittings with streamlined recessed spotlights. These are available with fittings to take a range of bulbs, including traditional incandescent, low energy and halogen. Or you could choose low-voltage halogen spotlights, which are particularly safe and practical option in a kitchen or bathroom.

Fitting ceiling spotlights

Installing recessed spotlights involves cutting holes in the ceiling, so you should always lift the floorboards in the room above to ensure that there are no joists or obstructions where you want to fit them. If you have a number of fittings to install, think about assembling a work platform – it will make the job easier, quicker and safer (see page 357).

Most recessed spotlights are supplied with a template for marking the fixing hole; if not, use a pair of compasses to draw a circle in pencil on the ceiling. Use a detector to check for pipes or cables then drill a small hole through, just inside the circle. Go back up and double-check all is clear from above, then from below insert the blade of a padsaw or plasterboard saw and cut around the marked circle. Wear safety goggles and a mask when doing this. Remove the disc of plasterboard from the ceiling. The lights usually clip in place on spring clips that grip the surrounding plasterboard.

project essentials

- **pencil**
- **compasses, if required**
- **pipe and cable detector**
- **protective goggles**
- **face mask**
- **drill with twist bit**
- **padsaw or plasterboard saw**

- spotlights

safety first

Spotlight and transformer heat
Spotlights and particularly transformers can get very hot, making them a potential fire risk if there is not adequate ventilation. Always pull any insulation material well clear of the fitting, and fit specially designed heat diffusers to downlighters (see page 337). A transformer hidden in a ceiling void must be accessible from the floorboards above or a trapdoor below. Check the manufacturer's instructions before fitting a transformer; some are not designed to operate in an unventilated ceiling void. In a loft, it's a good idea to protect fittings from accidental damage by building a plywood box around them, but be sure to leave the top open for ventilation. In some situations, the Building Regulations require all recessed ceiling lights to be enclosed in fire-proof compartments, including when installed in a multi-occupancy building. See pages 378–79 for sources of advice and further information.

Mains voltage recessed spotlights

To replace a pendant ceiling light with recessed spotlights, start by installing the lights and running 1mm^2 two-core-and-earth cable back to the position of the ceiling rose. For each additional light you will need to split the supply cable at a three-terminal junction box, connecting matching cores at each terminal. Clip the new cables neatly to the sides of the joists (see page 276).

New junction box wired into main lighting circuit cable

Recessed spotlight

Recessed spotlight

project essentials

- **voltage tester**
- **side cutters**
- **sharp knife**
- **wire strippers**
- **hammer**
- **filling knife**
- **sanding block**
- **paintbrush**

- 1mm^2 two-core-and-earth cable
- green/yellow earth sleeving
- brown PVC electrical sleeving
- cable clips
- 3- or 4-terminal junction box(es)
- filler
- abrasive paper
- paint

1 Isolate the lighting circuit and double-check the power is off with a voltage tester. Disconnect the cable or cables from the existing ceiling rose. If it is a loop-in system (284), label the cables so that you can identify which are the circuit cables and the switch drop. There should be a length of brown sleeving on the blue core of the switch drop cable (the black core, if your wiring is in the old colours), which will be connected to the live (brown) core of the flex to the light.

2 Unscrew the rose base plate and push the cables back through the ceiling.

3 If a single cable supplied the old rose, connect it to the new cable to the spotlights via a three-terminal junction box. If you find two or three cables, connect these to a four-terminal junction box as described on page 282.

4 At the spotlights, strip the outer sheathing of the supply cable, bare the ends of the cores and connect them to the light. Make sure the spring clips are positioned correctly and push the light into its hole. Check that the clips have engaged the plasterboard and are holding the light firmly in place.

5 If necessary, make good the hole where the ceiling rose was with filler, sand smooth when dry, then paint.

Low-voltage (12 volt) recessed spotlights

A relatively recent innovation in domestic lighting, low-voltage halogen lights are smaller than normal lights, with a neat, streamlined appearance. They offer a variety of lighting effects, making them useful for general lighting or picking out features in the room.

Transformers

Low-voltage lights take their power from a 12 volt transformer, which can be linked to a spur taken from a nearby power circuit (see page 280) via a 5 amp fused connection unit. If the connection unit is switched, it can be used to turn the lights on and off. Or the lights and transformer can be powered from a lighting circuit. Install a four-terminal junction box (see page 282) at a suitable position and run cables to a new switch and transformer, and from there to the lights.

The transformer output wattage must be matched to the combined wattage of the lamps that it will supply. Use 1.5mm² two-core-and-earth cable for the spur or circuit cable to the transformer. Low-voltage lights are usually supplied with cable for running between the transformer and the lights, and this should be used without modification. If a cable kit is not supplied, 1.5mm² two-core-and-earth cable can be used, provided the runs are short (up to 3m). The lights do not need to be earthed (always follow the manufacturer's instructions).

Practical and safe

Low-voltage lighting is easy to install and a safe option, particularly in an environment like the kitchen, since it carries no risk of electrocution. You can simply clip low-voltage cables along the top or underside of your units. The light is very bright and directed – perfect over a kitchen work surface.

Low-voltage lighting from a power circuit

Transformer   Recessed spotlights

Switched fused connection unit

Spur

New junction box   RCD-protected main circuit cable

Low-voltage lighting from a lighting circuit

Junction box

Transformer   Recessed spotlights

Switch

ONE PLANET HOME

LED spotlights
The latest LED spotlights are versatile, stylish, safe and offer dramatic energy savings in comparison with conventional lights. Unlike other kinds of spotlights, they are cool to the touch. Powered via a plug-in transformer, they use up to 90% less energy than traditional incandescent bulbs. They make excellent low-level lights on a kitchen plinth or staircase. And they can even be fitted in a bathroom or outdoors on a porch or deck.

If you regularly use electrical equipment outdoors, such as a lawnmower or hedgetrimmer, an external power point will make life easier and safer by removing the need to drape a lead through a window or doorway from a socket indoors.

Follow the rules

If you plan to make changes to a power or lighting circuit outdoors, you must inform your local authority's Building Control Department first. Modifications must comply with the latest IEE Wiring Regulations. New or replacement cables or sockets may require RCD protection. Be aware that additional regulations apply to any power supply to hot tubs or swimming pools. See page 268.

Adding an external power supply

You can wire an external socket in the same manner as a normal spur (see pages 280–81), running the cable from a socket or junction box on a main ring circuit (via a switched connection unit) and mounting the socket on an external wall. The circuit must have RCD protection. Proper weatherproof outdoor fittings must be used. The socket will have a weatherproof cover for when it is not in use and a surface mounting box equipped with seals to prevent moisture from entering. Some types of socket have weatherproof covers that offer protection when the socket is in use. Even so, it is wise to position it where it will not be exposed to the full force of the weather.

B&Q Making it easier

Easy living

If you plan to power outdoor lights, pond pumps or water features from your new socket, choose one with remote control on/off switching. Usable from indoors, this will make it quicker and easier to turn off the power when you don't need it – saving you effort, energy and money.

Conduit

External power socket

Socket

Switched connection unit

RCD-protected main circuit cables

Understanding IP ratings

Electrical fittings have an IP rating to tell you what environment they can be safely used in. IP stands for 'ingress protection' and is followed by two numbers: the first tells you how easily objects or dust can penetrate the fitting, the second how easily water can get in. The numbers run from 0 (or X), meaning wholly unprotected, to 6 (objects) or 8 (water). So a rating of IP68 would mean totally dust-proof and submersible.

Modern timber-framed buildings

You cannot bore a hole for a cable through the external wall of a modern timber-framed building. This is because the interior cavity is filled with insulation material and contains a vapour barrier. It is essential that the vapour barrier is not broken. However, it may be possible to supply an outdoor power point from a socket in an attached garage, provided this is not already on a spur.

RCD – a life saver

An RCD – residual current device – is a fast-acting, safety trip switch that will cut off the power within a split second as soon as it detects an earth leakage fault, reducing the risk of a fatal electric shock.

All portable electrical appliances used outdoors must be protected by a 30mA RCD. The latest IEE Wiring Regulations state that a new socket – indoors or out – can only be wired into an RCD-protected circuit. If an existing indoor socket used to power appliances outdoors doesn't have RCD protection, you must use a plug-in RCD (example pictured).

Fitting an external power point

When fitting an outdoor socket, it is essential that the installation is weatherproof, and you must always use purpose-designed fittings. Frost will damage cable insulation, so it must not be left exposed to the elements at any point. Fit the outdoor socket first then complete the installation by wiring the cable into a suitable socket or junction box on a main circuit with RCD protection, as for a spur (see pages 280–81).

(see pages 280–81)

1 Check the inside wall for hidden pipes or cables, then drill from the outside, about 50mm below the socket position, using a heavy-duty hammer-action drill and 16mm gauge bit. Angle the drill slightly upwards.

B&Q Making it easier

Running cable through an outside wall

Hold the drill at a slight upwards angle so that the hole will run uphill towards the inside. That will prevent rainwater running through and damaging the plaster inside. A normal cavity wall is about 275mm thick, excluding the interior plaster. Mark this depth on the drill bit with tape and as the hole approaches that depth, go slowly to reduce damage to the plasterwork as the drill bit breaks through. Sticking masking tape over the interior plaster before you drill will also help minimise damage. Line the hole with 16mm plastic conduit to protect the cable and ease installation.

2 Feed the conduit and cable through the wall. Leave the conduit protruding out of the wall, and sufficient cable to connect to the new socket. Remove the central knock-out from the box and fit a weatherproof grommet. Hold the mounting box in place, use a spirit level to make sure it is horizontal, and mark the fixing holes. Drill the fixing holes with a masonry bit and fit plastic wallplugs. Feed the cable and the end of the conduit through the grommet into the box and fix the box to the wall with round-head screws. A dab of silicone sealant behind each screw head will provide a watertight seal. Run a bead of silicone sealant between the wall and outer edge of the box.

ideal tool

Power hammer drill

The average hammer-action drill is not powerful enough to drill through an exterior wall and will not take sufficiently long drill bits. But heavy-duty hammer drills are now widely available to buy or hire. For the most powerful drills, look for models labelled rotary hammer or pneumatic. A slotted drive system (SDS) will give you greater holding power.

3 Strip off the outer sheathing of the cable and bare the ends of the cores. Slip a length of green/yellow sleeving over the bare earth core. Connect the cores to the appropriate terminals, making sure that the screws are tight. Then screw the faceplate to the mounting box.

WIRING COLOURS

The colours of the live and neutral cores in cable have changed (see page 272). Take special care when working on any installation that combines old and new.

Two-core-and-earth cable

L
N

Old colours

L
N

Providing some form of lighting outdoors offers a variety of benefits – it can illuminate your path to the front door; it can help you to see who is calling at night and deter criminals from lurking; it can allow you to make the most of a patio on warm summer nights; and it can create dramatic visual effects of light and shadow among the plants.

Installing a light on the house wall

Lights attached to your house walls – at the front and back doors, or on corners to illuminate pathways – can be fed by spurs from existing lighting or power circuits. When taking power from a lighting circuit, it is advisable to incorporate an RCD so that the power will shut off instantly if a fault develops. Some modern consumer units incorporate this, but you may need to wire in a separate RCD to older types. In some applications, RCD protection is now a requirement; if in doubt, check with a qualified electrician. Only fit weatherproof lights specially designed for outdoor use.

Connecting to a lighting circuit

A ground-floor lighting circuit will be the most convenient to supply outdoor wall lights, but make sure the additional fittings won't overload it (see page 283). If you want multiple outdoor lights or high-wattage floodlights, you may need to run a spur from a main power circuit (see below). Start by installing the light and switch, and run all the cables before isolating the circuit and making the final connections.

project essentials

- **heavy-duty hammer-action drill with 16mm-gauge long masonry bit**
- **screwdrivers**
- **sharp knife**
- **side cutters**
- **wire strippers**
- **filling knife**
- **voltage tester**

- exterior light fitting
- plastic conduit
- 1mm² two-core-and-earth cable
- strip connectors and PVC electrical tape, if required
- 4-terminal junction box
- brown PVC sleeving
- plastic wallplugs
- round-head screws
- silicone sealant

1 At the light position, drill a hole through the wall so that it runs downhill slightly towards the outside (see MAKING IT EASIER, page 295). Line the hole with plastic conduit and feed the cable through.

2 Connect the cable cores to the appropriate terminals within the unit or to its flex cores using strip connectors, which you should wrap tightly in PVC electrical tape to keep out damp.

3 Attach the light to the wall and seal out moisture with a bead of silicone sealant around its base.

4 Inside the house, run the light supply cable back to a suitable position for cutting into a main lighting circuit cable with a four-terminal junction box.

5 Install a switch and run a length of 1mm² two-core-and-earth cable back to the junction box position.

6 Isolate the circuit and double-check the power is off with a voltage tester. Then cut through the main circuit cable and make the connections in the junction box as described on page 282.

Running a spur from a power circuit

If you decide to run an outside wall light off a main power circuit – which you will need to do if you plan to fit a high-wattage floodlight – first identify a suitable socket from which to run a spur (see page 280). The circuit must have RCD protection. The spur must be run in 2.5mm² two-core-and-earth cable to the 'feed' terminals of a fused connection unit containing a 5 amp fuse. If this has a switch, it can be used to turn the light on and off; otherwise, you will need a separate switch. From the 'load' terminals of the fused connection unit, run 1mm² two-core-and-earth cable directly to the light (if the connection unit has a switch) or to a four-terminal junction box, from which you can run separate switch drop and light supply cables (see page 282).

Mains-powered garden lighting

Garden lights can be powered from a spur off a ring circuit (see page 280), via a 5 amp fused connection unit. Once outdoors, the lights should be supplied by 1.5mm² three-core steel-wire-armoured cable (SWA). Only fit weatherproof lights recommended for outdoor use. The circuit must have RCD protection.

Working with steel-wire-armoured cable

- The cores of three-core SWA are coloured brown, black and grey; it is essential to fit green/yellow sleeving over the black core at every connection to indicate that this is being used as earth.
- SWA should be buried: accidentally cutting through it could be fatal. Lay it in a trench at least 450mm deep under a path or driveway, or 750mm deep below unpaved areas that may be dug up at some point. Run electrical route marker tape above the cable at a depth of about 150mm as an extra precaution.
- SWA must be secured to the house wall with SWA cable clips, fixed to the masonry with suitable plugs and screws, and protected where necessary.
- Use a junior hacksaw to cut through SWA and pliers to strip back the armouring.
- Connect the SWA cores to those of 1.5mm² two-core-and-earth cable in a weatherproof adaptable box fixed to the house wall. The SWA must enter the box via a purpose-made weatherproof gland covered in a plastic gland shroud – it is essential to use the correct fittings in order to minimise corrosion of the cable armouring. Also, if the adaptable box is painted, you should clean off the paint where the cable enters it, to ensure good metal-to-metal contact and so effectively earth the armouring.
- When connecting the cable to the lights, pay particular attention to the earth connections and any waterproof seals; it is vital that the units are weatherproof. You will also need glands to protect the SWA as it enters the lights – follow the manufacturer's instructions.

RCD-protected main circuit cables

Spur

Fused connection unit

Switch

Weatherproof adaptable box

Driveway lighting

Electrical route marker tape

At least 450mm deep

SWA

WIRING COLOURS

The changes to the colours of the cores in cable (see page 272) also affect steel-wire-armoured cable.

Steel-wire-armoured cable

Old colours

ONE PLANET HOME

Solar-powered garden lights
Easy to install, with no mains wiring, solar garden lights won't add a penny to your electricity bill.

Low-voltage garden lighting

When it comes to garden lighting, a low-voltage set-up is the simplest to install and the safest. Often the light units are on spikes, which are simply pushed into the ground. The lights take their power from the transformer via ordinary two-core cable.

Socket

Transformer

Conduit

Low-voltage lights

Electrical route marker tape

450mm deep

Running the cable

The lights are fed by a 12 volt transformer, which can be plugged into a convenient socket indoors or in a shed or garage – it must be protected from the weather. The cable size depends on the circuit length and load (see page 293). It can be passed through a hole drilled in the wall and lined with conduit, or through a hole in a door or window frame. Plug the hole with silicone sealant to keep moisture at bay. Because of the low voltage, the cable can be safely laid on or just below the surface. But to avoid the trip hazard of loose cable, not to mention the sheer inconvenience of putting a garden spade through it at some future date, it is better to bury it about 450mm deep. Lay electrical route marker tape above it at a depth of about 150mm to indicate its presence.

PLUMBING COLD WATER

Your home's cold and hot water supply systems will be largely out of sight, with pipes concealed in walls and under floors. But knowing what type of system you have and the location of everything is essential for maintenance work, making improvements and, most of all, dealing with emergencies.

Your water supply

Your local water company is responsible for providing you with clean, drinkable water and for the removal of waste water and sewage. From the company's main supply pipe under the road outside your home, a branch pipe will run underground to a stop valve beneath a metal plate set in the pavement or somewhere in your front garden. This valve allows the company to control your water supply. From the valve,

the water flows along what is known as the service pipe, passing through your home's foundations before rising up through the floor, usually in the kitchen, but sometimes under the stairs or even in a garage. The rising main, as it is known, is fitted with your main stop valve at this point. From the water company's underground stop valve onwards, the entire system is your responsibility, and you must make sure that it is properly maintained. Allowing water to be wasted through leaks is an offence.

Direct cold water systems ▸

Some homes have a direct cold water system. Branch pipes lead directly from the rising main to feed all the cold taps and WC cisterns in the house at mains (high) pressure. The rising main will usually also continue up to a storage cistern in the roof, which provides a supply of water at gravity pressure to a hot water cylinder. One advantage of a direct system is that drinking water is available at all the cold taps (you should not drink water from a storage tank, which may be old and contaminated). There is also less pipework in the roof to worry about. Direct systems can expose the mains water supply to a greater risk of contamination through back-siphonage of dirty water from baths and wash basins, but this can be prevented by installing a non-return valve immediately above the stop valve supplying water to the house.

◂ Indirect cold water systems

Most houses have an indirect cold water supply system. A branch is run from the rising main after the householder's main stop valve to the cold tap at the kitchen sink to supply clean drinking water. Other branches may be taken off at this point to supply a washing machine, dishwasher or garden tap. The rising main runs up to the roof, where it terminates at a cold water storage cistern. This supplies all the remaining cold taps in the house, the WC cisterns and the hot water cylinder.

The advantages of an indirect system are that the storage cistern holds a reserve of water for washing and flushing WCs if the mains supply is interrupted, and the lower pressure of the gravity supply to most of the system causes less wear and tear and less noise as the water flows through the pipes.

Isolating pipe circuits

An indirect cold water system will have a storage cistern in the loft that is fed from the rising main through a ball valve. All the pipes that run from the cistern should be controlled by nearby stop valves, allowing individual pipe circuits to be turned off and drained for repair or maintenance work without having to empty the entire system. If there are no valves, the cistern itself has to be isolated – either by turning off a stop valve in the supply pipe or by tying up the arm of the ball valve – then drained. The cistern has an overflow pipe that runs to the outside if the water level is too high. It must have a lid to prevent anything from falling into the water and should be insulated to prevent freezing during winter.

A direct cold water system may have a storage cistern to provide top-up water for a hot water cylinder or a feed-and-expansion cistern to supply a wet central heating system. This is isolated in the same way as an indirect storage system.

Hot water cylinder vent pipe

Vent grommet

Breather filter

Ball valve

Insect screen and dip valve

Float

Stop valve

Cold water cistern

Overflow

Draining the system

The system should always be drained if you are going away for a long time in winter. You may also need to drain the system to repair or extend it. This is how to do it:

- Shut down the heating system or turn off the immersion heater.
- Close the main stop valve on the rising main, then open all taps. When the taps stop running, flush all WCs.
- Connect a hose to each draincock on the system in turn – probably above the main stop valve and at the foot of the hot water cylinder – and run it to an outside drain. Open the valve to empty any remaining water from the system. Close the draincock before removing the hose. Take care not to confuse draincocks on the heating system with those on the water supply system; there is no need to drain the former (see page 329).
- Pour a little salt down all plug-holes to prevent water in the waste traps from freezing.

Before refilling the system by opening the main stop valve, make sure that all taps and draincocks are closed. Inspect storage and WC cisterns to ensure that their ball valves have not become stuck open. Air may become trapped in the system during filling, causing taps to splutter and the water flow to be sluggish. If the problem persists, clear the air locks with mains pressure (see page 305).

Stop valve

Fitted to the rising main pipe close to where it comes into the house, the stop valve allows the entire water supply to be shut off.

Draincock

A draincock is a small tap fitted at a low point on the plumbing system to allow a pipe run to be emptied.

Ball valves

The water level in storage and WC cisterns is regulated by ball valves. These incorporate a long lever arm with a metal or plastic float (often ball shaped) at the end. When the cistern is full, the float holds the lever up, which keeps the valve closed; when the water level drops, float and lever fall, opening the valve. By altering the position of the float in relation to the valve, the point at which the valve opens and closes can be adjusted, thus varying the 'full' water level in the cistern.

The most important thing to remember about ball valves is that there are high- and low-pressure versions. High-pressure types must be used where the supply is at mains pressure (on a cold water storage cistern or WC cistern on a direct system), while low-pressure valves must be fitted to cisterns supplied under gravity pressure (WC cisterns on an indirect system).

Adjusting a ball valve

Some ball valves are adjusted simply by bending the metal float arm; others have an adjuster screw and locknut. Some have floats that can be repositioned vertically. The float should be set so that the water level is about 25mm below the overflow outlet.

Hot water for the taps and central heating system in your home is usually heated by a boiler or immersion heater. To be suddenly without hot water or heating, especially in winter, is miserable, so an understanding of the basic principles of the system could be invaluable to you. A boiler is a big energy user, so a wisely chosen, energy-efficient system is a sound long-term investment. Installing a new boiler is a professional job.

Stored hot water systems

If your water is heated by a boiler and stored in a cylinder, the chances are that the water is heated indirectly. This means that you have two hot water systems – a primary circuit and a secondary circuit. In the primary circuit, a pipe runs from the boiler to a heat exchanger (usually a coil of copper pipe) inside the hot water cylinder and then back to the boiler. When the boiler is running, hot water flows continuously around the primary circuit. As the pipes of the heat exchanger warm up, so too does the water in the cylinder, which can then be drawn off from the top of the cylinder to supply the hot taps around the house (the secondary circuit).

The hot water cylinder, usually found in an airing cupboard, is kept topped up with water from the cold water storage cistern in the roof. The primary circuit has its own top-up supply of water from a small tank in the roof known as the feed-and-expansion cistern. The cylinder's hot water draw-off pipe continues to the roof and terminates over the cold water storage cistern; the boiler's hot feed pipe to the heat exchanger terminates over the feed-and-expansion cistern in the roof. This allows any air or steam in either circuit to escape safely.

A major advantage of the indirect system is that the water that passes through the boiler does not mix with the water in the cylinder and, effectively, is recycled time and again. Consequently, there is less build-up of scale in the boiler and corrosion inhibitor can be added to the water, leading to lower maintenance costs (see page 329).

Indirect stored hot water system

safety first

If you are having a new boiler or heating system installed, it is essential to employ a qualified heating engineer. They will work to industry standards and will be able to advise on the correct and safe siting of the boiler and flue. If you are using gas as a fuel the firm must be Gas Safe registered. For other types of fuel the firm should be registered with the Heating and Ventilating Contractors' Association (HVCA).

Hot water cylinder with immersion heater

Immersion heaters

An electric immersion heater fitted into the top of the hot water cylinder provides a means of heating water during the summer without having to run the boiler. It has a long, thermostatically controlled heating element that extends down inside the cylinder. Some have two elements, a short one and a long one, allowing just the top portion of the cylinder to be heated when only small amounts of hot water are required, or the entire cylinder for bigger demands, such as filling a bath. You can also have two immersion heaters with short elements fitted in the cylinder, one above the other. An immersion heater has a thermostat to control the maximum water temperature; this can be adjusted by turning an adjuster screw with a screwdriver. For most homes, 60°C is a comfortable level.

Hot water on demand

These days people are increasingly opting for combination (or combi) boilers, which do away with the need for a hot water cylinder by heating water on demand. This can be more economical and energy efficient, as water is only heated as needed and there is no energy drain through heat loss from a cylinder. In small properties, particularly flats where there is no room for a hot water storage cylinder, an instantaneous water heater, usually gas fired, can heat the water just before it is drawn from the tap. Electric versions are also available for supplying showers.

What sort of boiler?

Standard, non-condensing boilers are run on a variety of fuels, including solid fuels. Modern fan-assisted boilers have good heat efficiency, but if your boiler is more than 15 years old, you may find that you make substantial savings on your heating bills by installing a modern version. A professional heating engineer will advise on the heat output you need, which depends on the size of your property.

Condensing boilers

For maximum efficiency and economy, a condensing boiler is the best choice. It is designed so that the water passing through the boiler extracts heat from the flue gases – which normally would be lost to the atmosphere – before entering the heat exchanger. That means less fuel needs to be burned to bring the water up to the required temperature. As the flue gases are cooled, any water vapour present condenses out and is discharged through a small drainpipe. Gas and oil versions are available, as are combi condensing boilers.

Combi boilers

If you are in a small property where it would be difficult to find space for a hot water cylinder, a combination (or combi) boiler is for you. This contains two heat exchangers – one for the central heating, the other to act as an instantaneous water heater. It is connected to the mains and is capable of supplying all the hot taps in the house. Both hot and cold water come out of the taps at mains (high) pressure, although the hot will run more slowly if more than one tap is opened. There can also be water wastage caused by the delay between turning on a hot tap and the water heating up. Fluctuations in shower temperature can be prevented by installing a thermostatic mixer shower. Gas and oil combi boilers are available, as are condensing models.

Back boilers

A back boiler is fitted behind a radiant fire, burning either gas or solid fuel. In gas-fired versions, the boiler may be operated independently of the fire, but in solid-fuel versions, the fire must be lit for water to be heated.

What sort of fuel?

If you have access to mains gas, this is the cheapest fuel for your boiler to burn. If not, the second cheapest option is oil, followed by solid fuel (such as anthracite), and then LPG (liquefied petroleum gas).

Oil and LPG can be stored in bulk tanks; LPG can also be supplied in large cylinders, but this is the least convenient and most expensive way of using the fuel. Solid fuel may be delivered loose or in pre-packed bags, but it is dirty, and you have to stoke the boiler regularly to keep it burning. That said, some solid-fuel boilers have hopper feeds that cut down on the amount of stoking required. You also need some means of disposing of the ash after burning.

In a standard boiler, the fuel is burned beneath a chamber, known as a heat exchanger, through which the water passes to be warmed. Then it is pumped around the heating circuit or circulates by gravity. This basic design can operate on gas, oil or solid fuel.

Where to install a boiler?

Standard, combination and condensing boilers may be freestanding or wall-mounted, although solid-fuel types are freestanding only. Boilers must be connected to a flue so that the gases produced by burning the fuel can be discharged to the atmosphere. In many cases, this can be an existing chimney, although it must be lined to suit the fuel being burned because the gases can have a corrosive effect on the structure. It is also essential that the room where the boiler is situated is well ventilated to ensure sufficient air for combustion and to prevent a build-up of poisonous fumes.

Fumes are not a problem if the boiler has a balanced, or room-sealed, flue. This is basically a divided horizontal duct that passes through an outside wall; air is drawn in along one passage and flue gases are discharged through the other. There are special regulations regarding balanced flues – your heating engineer will advise on this.

PLUMBING DRAINAGE SYSTEMS

Waste water is discharged from sanitary appliances in your home into a large vertical pipe or pipes, and from there into the main underground drainage system. Newer homes have a single pipe (a soil stack), whereas older ones may have separate pipes for the soil and waste water.

Where does the waste water go?

Waste water from your appliances either flows to the main soil stack and from there directly into the underground drain, or – in the case of a ground-floor sink, basin or appliance – may discharge into a trapped gully. This is linked to the underground drain and is fitted with a metal or plastic grid to prevent leaves and other debris from falling into the trap and blocking it. The drain itself may run to the main sewer or, in rural areas, to a cess pit or septic tank buried in your garden.

Rainwater drainage

Rainwater from gutters should be drained separately, as a heavy, prolonged downpour could risk overwhelming the system. Downpipes may discharge over the grid of an open gully or be connected directly to an underground drain pipe. From there, the water may run into a storm drain beneath the road or be piped to a soakaway somewhere in your garden, from where it gradually percolates back into the soil (see page 241).

Whose responsibility?

You are responsible for a substantial proportion of your home's drainage system, up to the point where it enters the main sewer; any blockages or damage must be put right at your expense. Because of the potential hazard to health presented by a drainage system, the rules concerning any changes are quite strict. Unlike the supply network, which is governed by the Water Regulations, the drainage system comes under the Building Regulations, and these are enforced by your local council, not the water company. If you are thinking about modifying any part of the drainage system, consult your council's Building Control Officer first (see page 378).

Single-pipe system

Modern domestic drainage systems are based on the single-pipe arrangement. In this, one large-diameter vertical pipe, known as the soil stack, provides the essential connection with the underground drain. The waste pipes of all upstairs basins, baths, showers and WCs will run to the soil stack. Downstairs waste pipes can also run into the soil stack but in some situations, it may be more convenient for a sink or basin to discharge directly into a gully. If this is the case, the waste pipe should terminate below the gully grid – unless the gully incorporates a special pipe connector behind the grid – and above the water level in the trap. A downstairs WC will almost certainly be connected directly to the underground drain.

In properties built nowadays, the soil stack usually runs up inside the house. At the top, the stack emerges through the roof and extends above it to vent any drain smells well clear of nearby windows and to prevent suction from occurring in the system that could empty traps of their water seals. Older systems and conversions from two-pipe systems will generally have the soil pipe on the outside of the house.

Vent pipe

Basin and bath discharge into soil stack

WC discharges into soil stack

Soil stack

Trapped gully

Inspection chamber

To sewer

Vent pipe

Basin and bath discharge into waste pipe via hopper head

WC discharges into soil stack

Hopper head

Soil stack

Waste pipe

Trapped gully

Inspection chamber

To sewer

Separate system

Traditionally, domestic drainage was provided by a two-pipe arrangement, whereby the waste and soil water were kept separate until they reached the underground drain. Although many older properties have been converted to single-pipe drainage, separate systems are still quite common.

WCs are connected to a large vertical soil pipe attached to an outside wall and extending above the roof. A second, smaller-diameter vertical pipe drains waste water. This terminates at about the level of the first floor in a funnel-like fitting called a hopper head, and all the waste pipes from the upstairs basins and baths discharge into this. At ground level, the waste pipe ends just above the grid of a gully. In most cases, downstairs fittings discharge into gullies, but their pipes terminate above the grids. This is one of the major disadvantages of the system, since grids may become blocked with sink waste, while the hopper is not self-cleansing and can suffer a build-up of soap. This can result in unpleasant odours and even overflows.

ONE PLANET HOME

Recycling your waste water in the garden
Grey water describes water that has been used for showering, bathing, handwashing, low-intensity laundry and dishwashing. It can be reused for flushing toilets and for irrigating the garden (provided it is not contaminated with excessive detergents or bleach: see page 23). You can simply collect it in a bucket, or ask your water company for information on installing a domestic grey water unit.

Joining up

If you need to run a waste pipe through an outside wall, you will need a power hammer drill, or better still a diamond-tipped core drill. Use an electronic pipe and cable detector to check there are no hidden pipes or cables behind the inside wall. Then drill from both inside and out to avoid a messy exit hole. With a core

drill you will need to drill a few cm at a time, then stop to empty the drill core and clean out the hole in the masonry with a club hammer and cold chisel. Make sure the hole runs downhill slightly towards the outside.

There may be a spare boss on the soil stack suitable for connecting a new waste pipe; or you can drill a hole and use a strap-on boss and solvent-weld fitting. Alternatively new waste pipes can be fed into an existing network of hoppers and gullies. However, there are strict rules about where you can connect pipes into a soil stack, so you must contact your local Building Control Officer before making any modifications.

Basin waste into soil stack

WC waste into soil pipe

Bath waste into soil stack

Vent pipe

Bath and sink waste into hopper head

PLUMBING PROBLEMS AND REPAIRS

Water can cause serious damage to your home, so prompt action is essential if a problem occurs in the plumbing system. Keeping a few basic repair materials in your tool kit and knowing what to do in an emergency will prevent most situations from getting out of hand.

Turn off the power and water

If you do suffer a burst pipe, a leaking cistern or flooding of any kind, the first thing to do is turn off the electricity supply at the consumer unit (fuse box) immediately. When the leak has been repaired and the water mopped up, examine all sockets, switches, ceiling roses and electrical equipment in the vicinity to make sure they are dry. If water has got into them, don't turn the power back on until they have dried out.

In such a situation, a knowledge of your plumbing system is vital: make sure you know the location of all the valves, particularly the main stop valve, which allows you to turn off the supply in an emergency or for essential work. Check valves every few months to ensure that they can be opened and closed easily. Applying a little penetrating oil to a valve shaft will help free it. Never leave a valve completely open, as this will make it more likely to seize up, preventing you from closing it when you really need to; close it by a quarter- to a half-turn.

Making a permanent repair

A burst pipe can be repaired with a burst pipe coupling provided the damaged section is no more than 40–50mm long (check the manufacturer's guidelines). Otherwise you will need to insert a new section of pipe or use a flexible hose connector (see opposite). A mini pipe cutter (see page 307) will give a far cleaner cut than a hacksaw, but you may not have space to use it.

B&Q Making it easier

Be prepared
You can buy a burst pipe repair kit that includes everything you need to fix a burst pipe: a hacksaw, burst pipe coupling, PTFE tape, wire wool and spanner. If a pipe suddenly springs a leak, you will be glad to be prepared.

Fixing a burst pipe

A pipe repair clamp is the quickest means of stopping water leaking from a burst pipe, and it doesn't require the pipe to be drained before it can be fitted. However, it should only be regarded as a temporary repair.

1 Assemble the two halves of the clamp over the damaged portion of pipe, double checking that the rubber sealing gasket is positioned correctly.

2 Fit the securing screws and tighten them fully to clamp the device firmly over the damaged section of pipe.

1 Turn off the water supply and drain the pipe (see page 299). Ideally use a mini pipe cutter to cut each side of the damaged area and remove that section of pipe. You may find that you have to free the pipe from any nearby clips so that you can rotate the cutter around it. If that is not possible, use a hacksaw.

2 Remove the burrs from inside the cut ends with a narrow file. Burnish the outside of the cut ends with wire wool or a deburring brush. Slip the capnuts and olives (metal rings) of the pipe coupling onto each cut pipe end. Wrap PTFE tape about five times clockwise around the threads of each compression joint.

3 Insert the cut pipe ends into the burst pipe coupling. Hold the coupling with a pipe wrench or waterpump pliers and tighten the nuts with an adjustable spanner.

Repairing a pipe using a flexible hose connector

It can be tricky to cut and repair a pipe that is running through noggings and cannot be released from nearby clips. A flexible hose with push-fit joints on either end may be a much quicker and easier fix than inserting a new section of pipe. Use a mini pipe cutter to remove a section of damaged pipe the length of the hose (excluding the joints). File any burrs from inside the cut pipe ends and burnish the outsides with wire wool or a deburring brush. Insert each pipe end into the push-fit joint and make sure it is pushed fully home. Take care not to stretch or rotate the hose.

Repairing a leaking joint

Remaking a soldered pipe joint that is leaking requires some skill; it's much easier to use repair putty, which will stop the leak permanently. When hard, the material can be sanded smooth for painting.

Shut off the water supply to the affected section of pipe and drain it down (see page 299). Dry the pipe, then key the area that needs to be repaired with a wire brush.

Press the repair putty around the joint, forcing it into the gap between pipe and fitting. Work quickly, as the putty dries rapidly.

Airlocks

If the plumbing system has been drained and refilled for any reason, air may have become trapped in the pipes, making taps splutter or possibly cutting off the flow completely. To cure this, connect a garden hose to the kitchen cold tap, which is on mains pressure (or any cold tap if you have a direct system: see page 298) and connect the other end to the affected tap. Open both taps and leave for a few minutes. The mains pressure should force the air out of the system, but you may have to repeat the process for a complete cure.

A frozen pipe

All pipes in lofts, under ground floors, in garages or any other areas where they will be exposed to very low temperatures should be lagged to protect them against freezing (see page 340). However, lagging will only delay the onset of freezing, and if temperatures are low enough for long enough, ice may still develop, stopping the flow of water to taps and other outlets; at worst, the ice may actually split the pipe or force apart a joint. For this reason, if you go away for a substantial amount of time in winter, you should take precautions. Set your heating thermostat at the lowest setting, or if there is one use the 'frost setting', which will cause it to come on automatically if temperatures drop near to freezing point. Or turn off the main stop valve and drain the system completely (see page 299).

To thaw a frozen pipe, warm it with a hair dryer, gradually working along its length from the tap or valve until the water starts to flow again. Alternatively, drape a hot water bottle over the pipe or soak hand towels in hot water, wring them out and wrap them around it. But whatever you do, don't use a blowtorch.

Water from a ceiling

Water storage cisterns and tanks are usually situated in the loft or on the upper floor of a house. This means that if a leak occurs, the first you will know of it is water pouring through a ceiling. You must act quickly or the ceiling may collapse.

First turn off the electricity at the main power switch and the water supply at the main stop valve. Position containers to catch the leaking water and turn on all the taps and flush WCs. This will empty the pipes and cold water storage cistern, and they will not refill while the main stop valve is off. Investigate the cause of the leak, which may be a burst pipe, a loose joint, or the cistern itself leaking or overflowing due to problems with the ball valve and overflow (see page 299). If the leak is coming from a hot water cylinder, turn off the boiler and empty the cylinder by running a hose from the draincock near its base to an outside gully. Make repairs or replace items as necessary.

No water from a tap

- Turn on the kitchen cold tap – or any other cold tap on a direct system (see page 298). If there is no flow, make sure the main stop valve is open; if the problem persists, call your water supplier.
- If the mains cold tap is working, inspect the cold water storage cistern in the loft; if it is empty, make sure the ball valve isn't jammed. Dismantle and clean the valve or replace it. If there is no flow when the valve is held open, your rising main is blocked – this can be caused by ice in winter.
- If the cold water storage cistern is full but there is no flow from the bathroom taps, there must be an air lock or blockage in the supply pipe from the cold cistern or hot water cylinder.

In an ideal world, pipe runs would be made in one piece from one fitting or appliance to another, to minimise the number of potential leak sites. In reality, this simply isn't possible – pipes are not made in infinite lengths, and the complex shapes often required would make it impossible to feed a single pipe through the structure of a house. So shorter lengths must be cut, shaped and joined together.

Pipe materials and sizes

At one time, domestic plumbing systems used iron and lead pipes. These days, copper pipes are the usual means of carrying water around the home, with plastic pipes used for waste systems. The most common size of copper pipe has an outer diameter of 15mm, although you may find smaller sizes (10mm) feeding monobloc taps (see page 313) and radiators, and larger sizes (22mm and 28mm) feeding baths, storage cisterns, tanks and boilers.

If your plumbing system was installed before the mid-1970s, the pipework will almost certainly be of imperial dimensions (½, ¾ and 1 inch inner diameter). You can join modern 15mm pipe to ½ inch imperial and 28mm to 1 inch using standard metric compression fittings, but connecting 22mm pipe to ¾ inch requires a 22mm compression fitting with a special oversize olive. For soldered joints, there are metric/imperial connectors in the relevant sizes.

Copper

Copper is strong but lightweight, solders well and can be bent quite easily. Copper pipes can take capillary, compression or push-fit fittings (see pages 308–9).

Plastic

Although plastic pipes are commonly used only for waste water, there are also types of plastic pipe that are suitable for hot and cold water supply pipes and central heating systems. They can be joined to copper pipework and are made to the same standard sizes, although the wall thickness of different makes can vary. They are easy to bend and install, are impact- and frost-resistant, and do not corrode.

Cutting pipes

It is possible – but not ideal – to use a hacksaw to cut copper or plastic pipe. Wrap masking tape around the pipe as a cutting guide, aligning its edges carefully to ensure a square cut. However, it is much easier to achieve a clean, square cut with a pipe cutter.

ideal tool

Pipe cutter

1 Measure the length of pipe required and mark with a pencil. Then place the cutter over the pipe so that the cutting wheel aligns with the mark and tighten the screw. Rotate the cutter around the pipe, steadily tightening the screw until you cut through the pipe.

2 Remove the burr around the inside of the pipe's cut end by inserting the cutter's triangular reamer and rotating the tool. Make sure that no copper fragments remain in the pipe, as they could cause damage to valves or taps on the system.

3 Clean the outside of the pipe by burnishing it with wire wool; this will provide a good surface for the joint, ensuring a watertight seal. Or use a deburring brush (shown), which will do the same job and prevent stray slivers of wire wool from sticking into your fingers or falling into the pipe.

A pipe cutter (or pipe slice) has a hardened cutting wheel and adjustable rollers that allow it to be clamped tightly around a pipe. Rotating the tool causes the cutting wheel to bite into the metal, leaving a narrow groove. By constantly tightening the rollers against the pipe, the groove can be made deeper until eventually the pipe is cut in two. Standard types have a reamer blade for removing the internal burr from the pipe. Special 'mini' versions are made for cutting through pipes that run close to a wall or other surface (see opposite).

Mini pipe cutter

This circular device has a cutting wheel that produces a clean, easy cut when rotated a few times around a copper pipe. Because of its small size, it can often be used where access is restricted, such as on pipes that run close to a wall or joist.

Plastic pipe cutter

This cutter makes a clean, square cut through plastic pipe up to 22mm in diameter. One squeeze cuts easily through the pipe. The blade is very sharp, so keep fingers clear and store well away from children.

Bending pipes

Plastic pipe can be bent into gentle curves by hand. Small-bore (15mm) copper pipe can be bent with the aid of a bending spring, which supports the pipe internally and prevents kinking. Considerable strength is needed, however; bending machines make the job much easier and are essential for larger diameter pipes.

Using a bending spring

Using a bending machine

A machine applies considerably more leverage than bending by hand. Place the pipe on the correct size of curved former (several sizes will be supplied) under the pipe stop, then insert the straight former between the pipe and roller. Draw the handles together to bend the pipe; over-bend it slightly as it will tend to spring back a little.

1 Coat the spring with petroleum jelly and slip it into the pipe. If the bend will be some distance from the end of the pipe, tie a length of cord to the spring.

2 Bend the pipe around your knee, using a pad of cloth as a cushion. Over-bend it slightly. Check that the angle is correct, then pull the spring from the pipe. If you can reach the end of the spring, inserting a screwdriver in the spring eye and turning it to tighten up the spring coils should help in its removal.

PLUMBING PIPES AND FITTINGS

The traditional methods of connecting copper pipes are capillary joints that must be soldered, and brass compression joints that are tightened with an adjustable spanner. Equally effective and much simpler are plastic push-fit joints, which incorporate rubber O-rings for sealing and can be used on both plastic and copper pipes.

Capillary joints

Soldered fittings are known as capillary joints, because, when heated, solder is drawn between the fitting and pipe by capillary action. Two types are available: end-feed and solder-ring. In both cases, a chemical cleaner, known as flux, must be brushed on to the pipe end and inside the joint before heating. Pipes must be flushed thoroughly after joining to remove all traces of flux, which is corrosive.

End-feed joint

Solder

End-feed joints

With end-feed joints, lead-free solder must be added to the mouth of the joint as it is heated with a blowtorch. These are the fittings a professional plumber would typically use.

Solder-ring joints

Solder-ring joints are made with a ring of solder already inside the mouth of the joint, so only heating is required.

Elbow

Coupling

Tee

Solder-ring joints

Compression joints

Usually made from brass, compression joints produce a watertight seal by squeezing a special metal ring, known as an olive, between the pipe and the body of the fitting. A capnut screws on to the end of the joint to provide the necessary pressure against the olive. Apply about five turns of PTFE tape clockwise around the threads of the fitting, then tighten the capnut with an adjustable spanner while holding the fitting firmly with a pipe wrench or waterpump pliers. Compression fittings are bulkier than capillary fittings, but can be more easily undone and retightened, and they need no heating.

Elbow

Coupling

Tee

PTFE tape

Tee

Coupling

Elbow

Push-fit joints

Developed originally for use with plastic pipe systems, push-fit joints are an easy and effective way of joining copper pipes too (though they can't be used with stainless steel or chrome-plated copper pipe). Cleanly cut pipe ends are essential, so be sure to use a pipe cutter rather than a hacksaw. Then simply mark the depth of the joint on the cut ends of the pipes and push them fully home. Pull to test the fitting is secure. The sharp metal teeth can cut into plastic, causing leaks, so a special protective insert is required when working with plastic pipe. They can also cut fingers, so keep yours well clear.

Plastic push-fit joints

A special plastic protective insert is required when using push-fit joints on plastic pipes to prevent the fitting damaging the pipe.

Copper push-fit joint

B&Q Making it easier

Push-fit release tool
This simple tool makes easy work of releasing a copper push-fit joint. Without it, you won't be able to undo the fitting.

Running new supply pipes

Moving or modifying elements of your plumbing system will very often involve running new pipework. There are plenty of options for doing this. Plan the route first, and try to keep bends to a minimum so that the water flows freely.

Along walls

The easiest and quickest way of running new pipework is to simply clip the pipes to a wall. They will be less conspicuous if you keep them neat, straight and parallel, and if you run them up a corner, around a chimney breast, or along the skirting. You can buy plastic ducting to hide them, or box them in with plywood and timber battens. You can also remove the skirting and build a false skirting to contain them. If you are building a stud partition wall, run any new pipework through the studs and noggings before you close off the cavity with plasterboard (see page 70).

Under a suspended floor

Clip the pipe to the side of a joist; support it on battens attached between joists; run it in shallow notches cut into the top of joists; or – if there's space to insert it – pass the pipe through holes drilled in the joists. Run pipes at least 50mm below the top of the joists to avoid them being punctured by nails driven through the floorboards. Mark the pipe runs in pencil on the boards to remind you where they are. Always be wary of cutting into joists, however, since they are essential to a building's structure. Remove as little timber as possible.

Insulating pipes

Use split foam tubes to lag any pipes that are at risk from freezing: pipes running under a ground floor, through a loft space, or against an outside wall. They could prevent a plumbing disaster. You should also lag hot water pipes to prevent heat loss (see page 339)

Pipe clips

Whether you are running pipes along a wall or concealed behind or beneath it, it is important that they are firmly clipped in place at regular intervals, otherwise they may creak or vibrate. Pipe clips come in styles and sizes to suit all situations.

Waste pipes and traps are a vital part of the drainage system of your home. Most modern systems use plastic pipes and fittings. If a sink, basin or bath is slow to drain, it is advisable to deal with the situation straight away or it may become more difficult to fix.

Waste pipes

Waste pipes are bigger than supply pipes: hand basins have a 32mm waste outlet pipe, showers, washing machines, sinks and baths a 40mm pipe, and WCs a 110mm pipe, the same size as a modern soil stack. Another important difference is that waste pipes must slope downwards at the rate of at least 20mm in every metre to ensure that the water runs away freely.

In the past, waste pipes were made of lead, but modern systems are exclusively plastic. Depending on the type of plastic used, the pipes may be joined by simple push-fit connectors containing rubber ring seals, compression-type connectors with rubber 'olives' or by solvent welding, using specially formulated solvent cement that softens the plastic and dries to form a strong, watertight joint.

Push-fit waste

Solvent-weld waste

Compression-fit waste

Cutting, jointing and fixing waste pipes

Cut plastic waste pipes with a hacksaw and then remove the burrs inside and out with a half-round file before fixing. Solvent-weld fittings are neat but permanent, so while they are ideal on visible pipework, it is better to use compression fittings under and behind sinks, so that you can take them apart again for cleaning and unblocking. When running pipes along an interior or exterior wall, hold them in place with waste pipe clips, which are available in different colours and sizes. Use wallplugs and screws to attach the clips to a masonry wall, or hollow-wall fixings on plasterboard (see pages 376–77). Don't forget to check for hidden pipes and cables before you drill.

Waste pipe

Sink outlet

Standard P-trap

Traps

A vital part of the drainage system is the trap, a water seal that prevents drain smells from entering your home through the waste outlets of sanitary appliances such as sinks, basins and WCs. Every plumbing installation that discharges waste water into the drainage system will be fitted with a trap, or incorporate one in its design. Essentially, a trap is a U-shaped loop of pipe directly below a waste outlet. Whenever you pull a plug or flush a lavatory, a small amount of water remains in the trap, providing a seal.

Traps are made from plastic and come in a variety of designs to suit different applications and situations. The most common is the P-trap, so-called because of its profile. It has a horizontal outlet. Special shallow versions of P-traps are made for fitting beneath baths and shower trays, which may have a 50mm water seal, unlike sinks and basins, which must have a 75mm water seal. Then there is the S-trap, which has a vertical outlet, and the bottle trap, which is a compact device intended for use where the trap is exposed, such as under a hand basin. However, the bottle trap is more susceptible to blockage than P- and S-traps. Some bath traps provide a connection for an overflow pipe. There are traps with connectors or standpipes for washing machines. WC pans and bidets have integral traps.

Early lead U-bend traps incorporated a threaded access plug at the bottom, which could be removed to clear blockages; modern plastic traps can be dismantled by unscrewing the capnuts that hold them together. This arrangement not only allows the trap to be cleaned completely, but also provides access to the waste pipe when a blockage occurs.

Bottle trap

S-trap

Bath trap with overflow boss

Bath/shower shallow P-trap

Washing machine standpipe and P-trap

Clearing a blocked sink

If sinks, basins or baths become slow to drain, or stop draining completely, there must be a blockage somewhere in the waste pipe. The likely cause of slow draining is an accumulation of grease in the trap, or fibres caught below the grid on the plug-hole. If water doesn't drain away at all, then there is a complete blockage and there must be an obstruction in the waste pipe. There are different methods you can try to remedy the situation.

1 If a sink is completely blocked, partially fill it with water and place the cup of a sink plunger over the plug-hole. Stuff a damp cloth into the overflow to prevent loss of pressure. Then pump the plunger up and down vigorously. Take the plunger away and see if the water drains. You may need to do this a couple of times.

2 If that fails, try using a chemical drain-cleaning product. Wear protective gloves and goggles and follow the instructions carefully, as it will be highly toxic. Do not use where other chemicals, such as bleach, may be present, as this could cause dangerous gases to be released. Smear some petroleum jelly around the rim of the plug-hole to protect it from damage.

3 If the blockage hasn't cleared, then you will have to remove the waste trap. Put a bucket under the trap to catch any spillage. Unscrew the trap, and empty the contents into the bucket. Replace the trap making sure you replace any washers or O-rings. Don't overtighten or it will be difficult to undo in the future. If there was nothing blocking the waste trap, use a drain auger to probe into the waste pipe.

ideal tool

Drain auger

A drain auger has a flexible rod that extends into a waste pipe as you rotate the handle, dislodging any blockage as it probes. The rod then winds back into the handle for hygienic storage.

Clearing a blocked lavatory

A blocked lavatory pan causes the flush water to rise almost to the rim, and then drain away very slowly. It will probably be blocked in the pan outlet, but if not then it could be a problem in the main drainage system.

1 Try pouring a bucket of warm water into the pan from a height; this often clears a minor blockage.

2 Place a large WC plunger over the pan outlet and pump the handle up and down.

3 If that doesn't shift it, use an auger designed for a lavatory. Its probe extends around the U-bend and rotates as you turn the handle, dislodging the blockage. Wear protective gloves and read the manufacturer's instructions.

B&Q Making it easier

Instant drain unblocker
Instead of harmful chemicals, this drain unblocker uses a gas that expands on contact with water, generating a strong turbulence that will clear drains up to 20 metres away by agitation, not pressure. It will remove blockages caused by hair, soap build-up, paper, grease and food particles in seconds. Use it on blocked or slow-flowing sinks, basins, baths or shower trays. With the optional plunger head it can also clear blocked and slow-flowing toilets.

PLUMBING TAPS

New basin taps are a great way to upgrade your bathroom. Look out for taps with an eco click mechanism that will help you and your family moderate your water use. Dripping taps should be fixed promptly, or they will cause staining on your bath or sink and erosion inside the tap mechanism.

Replacing basin taps

If the existing taps do not have an isolating valve, then you will need to turn off the water supply – both hot and cold – and turn on all the taps in the house until they run dry. It can be very difficult to unscrew the nuts connecting old taps to the water supply pipes. If that is the case, then use a pipe cutter to cut through the pipes and connect the new taps using flexible push-fit tap connectors instead (see MAKING IT EASIER page 316). Flexible tap connectors with isolating valves are a good idea in case you ever need to cut off the supply to one or both taps for future maintenance.

project essentials

- **basin wrench**
- **cranked spanner**
- **wooden mallet, if required**
- **wire wool**
- **pipe cutter, if required**
- 15mm push-fit flexible tap connectors
- new taps

B&Q Making it easier

Fitting an outdoor tap
You can buy a kit with all you need to fit an outdoor tap. First attach the saddle clamp to a suitable cleaned cold water supply pipe, then screw the self-cutting tap into the saddle clamp.

1 Reach up and unscrew the holding nuts of the old taps. You will need a basin wrench to release the tap connector nuts securing the taps to the pipes, and a cranked spanner to release the back nuts securing the taps to the basin.

2 Lift out the old taps. If they won't budge even after you have removed the holding nuts, they may be stuck in place with old putty. If so, tap them lightly from below with a wooden mallet. Clean the ceramic surround before fitting the new taps.

3 Secure the new taps from the underside using the washers and mounting nuts supplied. The hot tap goes on the left, cold on the right.

Insert the rubber washer and connect the hose to the tap. Check for pipes and cables, then drill a hole through the wall at a slight downwards angle towards the outside using a hammer action drill with 16mm masonry bit. Run the hose through the hole.

4 Either reattach the existing pipework or use 15mm flexible tap connectors (pictured), remembering to incude the fibre washers. Clean any paint or tarnish from the pipes using wire wool and check there is no debris in the new taps before making the attachments. Restore the water supply and check the taps are working, without any leaks.

ideal tool

Basin wrench
Use a basin wrench to release the connector nuts securing the taps to the supply pipes.

Cranked spanner
Use a cranked spanner to release the back nut attaching a tap to a basin. If the nut is stiff, try putting a screwdriver through the end of the spanner to gain extra purchase.

ONE PLANET HOME

Eco click taps
Lots of new taps now have a handy eco click mechanism that can help you and your family stick to water-wise habits. When the tap is first turned on, it flows at a rate that's ideal for rinsing a toothbrush or facecloth. If you need a higher flow, to fill up the basin for example, you turn beyond the click.

Mark suitable fixing positions for the tap. Drill holes and fix to the wall using the wallplugs and screws provided. Push the supply hose onto the tap stem and tighten the hose clip with a screwdriver.

Repairing a dripping tap

Don't ignore a dripping tap! The sooner you tackle it, the easier it will be to fix, and the less damage will be done. Even if you don't have a spare washer, take a look inside the tap – if the washer is only slightly damaged on one face, you can reinsert it the other way up. But even if that stops the drip, do remember to replace it with a new washer as soon as possible. Standard mixer taps can be repaired as shown here, but monobloc taps – often controlled by levers, and needing only a quarter turn between fully off and fully on – have ceramic disks rather than traditional washers. The disks are very hardwearing, but if one does develop a problem you will need a replacement cartridge from the tap manufacturer.

Choosing the right taps
When buying new taps, check they are the right type for your system. Fitting high-pressure (mains) taps on a low-pressure gravity-fed hot water system (see pages 300–1) could result in poor water flow, especially on a bath.

project essentials

- **adjustable spanner or pliers**
- **screwdriver**
- **pipe wrench**
- **cloth**

- tap washer
- silicone grease
- cardboard

1 Turn off the water supply and open the tap to drain water from the system. Put the plug into the plug-hole, just in case you drop any small nuts or screws. Unscrew the top plate (this has the hot/cold emblem on it). You might be able to do this with your fingers, but if not use pliers or an adjustable spanner.

2 Not all taps are made the same way so you will have to work out how the handle comes off. In the type shown, you need to unscrew the retaining screw, and pull off the handle. This will expose the headgear nut.

3 Unscrew the tap body cover. If you can't do this by hand use an adjustable spanner or pipe wrench, but protect the chrome with a cloth.

Tap body cover

Headgear nut

Jumper

Washer
Valve seating

4 Undo the headgear nut using an adjustable spanner. If the nut is difficult to turn, don't force it or you risk twisting the base of the tap and putting a strain on the inlet pipe. Instead, pad around the base of the tap with cardboard and use a pipe wrench to grip it firmly as you apply the necessary force to the nut.

5 Remove the headgear assembly by unscrewing the headgear nut. The washer sits in the jumper and is either pressed in place, often over a small button, or retained by a nut. If necessary, unscrew the nut holding the washer in place with an adjustable spanner. Prise out the old washer; use a screwdriver to dig it out if necessary.

6 Insert a new washer and push it into the jumper. Reassemble the tap in the same sequence. Apply a little silicone grease to the threads on the base of the headgear assembly before reinserting it in the tap body.

Valve seating damage
If a tap carries on dripping even with a new washer, then the valve seating is probably eroded. This can be repaired with a special grinding tool or – much more easily – with a washer and seating set. The plastic seat fits into the existing metal seat, and a washer-and-jumper unit fits on the headgear. The sooner you replace a washer, the less likely the valve seating is to get damaged.

A dual flush mechanism can lead to significant reductions in your water usage. Replacing an old lavatory is not difficult provided it can be connected to an existing branch of the soil pipe. If you want to add a new lavatory in another part of the house, however, you should get a professional plumber to connect into the main soil pipe.

Fitting a dual flush mechanism

A valve-operated flush mechanism is straightforward to install, and can replace an existing flush controlled by either a handle or a button. Flush mechanisms do vary between designs, so always read the manufacturer's assembly instructions. Shut off the water supply and flush the toilet to empty the cistern before you begin.

project essentials

- **dust sheet**
- **adjustable spanner**
- dual flush kit

1 Lift off the cistern lid and remove the ball valve, handle and existing flush mechanism. Clear any loose dirt from the tank. Unscrew the wingnuts from under the pan and remove the existing filling valve. Lay a dust sheet for protection over the toilet lid and then rest the cistern on top.

2 Clip the flush cable control to the ball float mechanism and connect this to the base of the cistern using the backnut and grommet supplied. Adjust the filter restrictor according to whether the water supply is at mains pressure or supplied from a tank: follow the manufacturer's instructions. Then insert the filter restrictor into the threaded tail of the filling valve, and attach the filling valve to the inlet pipe using the backnut and washer supplied.

3 Clip the flush cable control to the push button and secure the push button using the backnut supplied.

4 Put the cistern back in position and reattach it to the toilet pan. Reattach the tap connector that connects the water inlet pipe to the filling valve.

5 Refill and test. The amount of water per flush can be adjusted by raising or lowering the position of the float basin attached to the filling valve.

ONE PLANET HOME

Saving water
A dual flush mechanism gives the option of a half or full flush, which can save as much as 40,000 litres of water a year for a family of four.

Standard siphon flush mechanism — Ball valve, Float, Filling valve, Overflow, Water inlet pipe

Valve-operated dual flush mechanism — Ball float mechanism, Float basin, Push button, Filling valve, Flush cable control, Water inlet pipe

Standard siphon flush mechanism   **Valve-operated dual flush mechanism**

Installing a close-coupled WC

There are many different lavatory designs to choose from, to suit every style of interior. Close-coupled cisterns sit directly on top of the pan and are a particularly popular modern design. Always unpack and carefully inspect a new WC or suite before you rip out your old fittings. You don't want to discover a fault, crack or missing part once your bathroom is already out of action.

project essentials

- **adjustable spanner**
- **screwdriver**
- **pipe and cable detector**
- **power drill with twist or masonry bit**

- WC and cistern
- silicone grease
- screws
- wallplugs, if required
- push-fit tap connector
- lavatory seat

1 Follow the manufacturer's instructions to assemble and insert the flush mechanism. Make sure you include the rubber sealing rings where necessary.

2 Place the large rubber gasket into the flush entrance of the pan.

3 Insert the long fixing bolts through the holes in the cistern, using the rubber and large metal washers supplied.

4 Lift the cistern onto the pan so that the connecting bolts locate through the holes. The threaded section of the flush mechanism should go through the rubber gasket on the flush entrance of the pan.

5 Fit washers to the connecting bolts, and tighten the wing nuts. Fit securely but don't overtighten.

6 Check there are no pipes or cables beneath the fixing points, then position the WC and slide the pan outlet into the flexible connector attached to the soil pipe. A little silicone grease will ease it on. Drill pilot holes into the floor at the fixing points. If it's a solid floor you will need to drill the holes with a hammer-action drill and plug them.

7 Push plastic protective inserts through the holes in the base of the pan and screw the retaining screws through and into the floor. If the cistern has fixing holes in the back, fix to the wall by drilling and plugging; remember to add rubber washers before tightening the nuts.

8 Connect the supply pipe for the cold water feed using a push-fit tap connector.

9 Fit the hinge assembly to the seat following the manufacturer's instructions.

10 Connect the seat to the pan by securing through the holes at the back using the screws supplied. Adjust so that it sits in the correct position.

B&Q Making it easier

Changing your seat
You can replace a cracked lavatory seat without changing the whole WC. Choose an exact match or go for a contrasting effect; for example, wood-effect seats look good on plain white pans.

safety first

Use an electronic pipe and cable detector to check for hidden pipes and cables before you drill, both under the floor and behind the wall. Don't risk a flood or, worse, electrocution!

You will usually be able to use the existing water supply pipes and waste outlet when replacing an old basin or sink. Try to choose a trap similar in size to the one you have removed as this will make fitting much easier. If you want to put a sink into a new location you will have to extend the pipework, which is more ambitious (see pages 306–10).

Fitting a new kitchen sink

If you are replacing an existing sink, measure the space carefully. To cut a hole in a new work surface to accommodate a sink see page 165. If necessary, extend nearby hot and cold water supply pipes so that you can connect them to the inlet pipes of the new taps. You may also need to extend the existing waste outlet pipes to meet the trap of the new sink (see page 310). Then you can install the sink.

1 Assemble the tap according to the manufacturer's instructions, and attach the pipes to the correct inlets.

2 Insert the tap through the hole in the sink, including any washers or backing plates, according to the instructions supplied.

5 Fit the waste coupling to the outlet on the underside of each sink bowl.

6 Join the hot and cold water supply pipes to the tap pipes with flexible push-fit tap connectors (see MAKING IT EASIER). Connect the overflow pipe between the sink's overflow outlet and the inlet below the bowl. Then turn on the water supply and check for any leaks, retightening the joints as necessary.

project essentials

- **cross-head screwdriver**
- **hacksaw**
- **adjustable spanner or waterpump pliers**
- taps
- kitchen sink and waste fittings
- sanitary silicone sealant
- 15mm flexible push-fit tap connectors

3 Fit the retaining clips to the underside lip of the sink, spacing them evenly. Run a continuous bead of sanitary silicone sealant around the outer edge of the sink. Then carefully turn the sink over and rest it in the cut-out in the worktop. Working from the underside, tighten the screws on each retaining clip. Take care not to overtighten.

B&Q Making it easier

Flexible tap connectors
Flexible push-fit tap connectors are simple to fit. Some have built-in isolating valves that enable you to change a washer without turning off the whole water supply.

4 Assemble the waste pipes and trap. Place rubber O-rings onto the waste couplings.

Fitting a new basin

There are several types of basin available. Wall-mounted basins can look extremely smart, but they need very strong fixings to support their weight, and hiding pipework can be difficult. Pedestal basins are the most popular choice. The hollow pedestal supports the weight and also hides pipework, making them fairly easy to install. Pedestal basins also come as a corner fitting; these are a good space-saving option for small bathrooms.

project essentials

- **dust sheet**
- **cranked spanner**
- **spirit level**
- **pencil**
- **pipe and cable detector**
- **hammer-action drill with masonry bit**
- **pipe cutter**
- **narrow file**
- **screwdriver**
- **wire wool**

- pedestal and basin
- taps
- 15mm flexible push-fit tap connectors
- sanitary silicone sealant
- 50mm screws
- plasterboard fixings, if required
- wallplugs, if required
- waste trap
- waste pipe

1 Lay a dust sheet on the floor and rest the basin upside down. Fit the washers supplied over the tail of each tap and feed the tap through the holes in the basin. Screw the plastic nuts onto the tail end of the tap using a cranked spanner. To prevent the whole assembly from turning, hold the tap with your other hand while tightening the nut. Connect 15mm flexible push-fit tap connectors with built-in isolating valves to each tap; remember to include the fibre washers. Again, hold the tap with your other hand while tightening the nut with a cranked spanner.

2 Apply sanitary silicone sealant around the waste hole in the basin. Push the waste outlet through the hole and bed the rim of the grid into the sealant. Fit the rubber washer and plastic retaining nut. Run a bead of sanitary silicone sealant behind the washer to ensure a watertight fit. Stand the pedestal in position and put the basin on top. Adjust it until the whole unit is centrally placed over the pipework and touching the wall. Use a spirit level to get the basin level, then mark the position of the fixing holes on the wall and the floor.

3 Arrange the flexible pipe connectors so that they fit behind the pedestal, and mark the inlet pipes where they will need to be cut. They must be long enough to fully engage with the fittings on the pipe connectors. Make sure the waste pipe is in the correct position to join to the sink trap.

4 Remove the pedestal and basin. Check for hidden pipes and cables. If the area is clear, drill and plug the wall at the fixing positions. On a hollow wall, use plasterboard fixings (see pages 376–77). Check the floor-fixing positions for hidden pipes or cables, then drill the holes and, on a solid floor, plug them. Use a pipe cutter to cut the inlet pipes where you marked them, and file off any burrs. Fit the trap to the waste outlet pipe, remembering to include all rubber washers.

5 Put the unit back in position. Screw the basin to the wall and the pedestal to the floor. Don't overtighten the screws.

6 Push the flexible tap connectors onto the inlet pipes. If the inlet pipes are dirty, clean them with wire wool first. Insert the waste pipe into the trap and hand tighten the nut. Turn on the water, open the isolating valves and check for leaks. If you spot any drips, retighten the connectors as necessary.

It is fairly simple to replace an old bath with a new one, though if you are installing a bath in a completely different position, you will have to re-route the waste pipe and extend the supply pipes (see pages 306–10).

Constructing the bath

If you are replacing an old bath, the simplest thing to do is to turn off the water supply and cut right through the existing supply pipes. Carefully file off any burrs ready for reconnection. Always read the manufacturer's assembly instructions, since different designs may be put together in slightly different ways.

1 With a helper, lay the bath upside down on a dust sheet. Place the two leg cradles over the bath and fit them into their plastic mounting brackets.

2 Fix the leg cradles to the bath by inserting and tightening the locking screws into the plastic mounting brackets.

5 Screw the wall brackets to the timber frame on the sides of the bath. They should be about 150mm from each end. With a helper, turn the bath back over so it is standing on its feet.

6 Push the flexible overflow pipe into the back of the overflow hole, remembering to fit the rubber washer supplied. The other end attaches to the trap (see Step 8).

9 Run a bead of sanitary silicone sealant under the waste outlet fitting and screw it down, making sure any rubber washers are fitted according to the manufacturer's instructions.

3 Screw each leg cradle to the baseboard through the pre-drilled holes. Place the adjustable bath feet into the holes in the cradles and loosely fit the locking nuts. Roughly set each leg to the same height.

7 Insert the overflow outlet, check the washers are in place, and screw on the back nut.

project essentials

- **dust sheet**
- **cross-head screwdriver**
- **adjustable spanner or basin wrench**
- **waterpump pliers, if required**
- **spirit level**
- **pencil**
- **electronic pipe and cable detector**
- **hammer-action drill with masonry and twist bits**
- **fine-toothed saw or sharp knife, if required**

- bath and fittings
- bath trap
- bath taps
- flexible tap connectors
- wallplugs, if required
- 25mm, 40mm and 45mm screws
- 25mm x 50mm timber batten

4 Screw the centre support foot bracket to the middle of the baseboard, and screw in the adjustable foot.

8 Fit the waste trap to the bath's waste outlet.

Insert the hot and cold taps through the holes. Put on the washers and plastic nuts using an adjustable spanner or basin wrench. Don't overtighten.

Fitting the taps

Check the diameter of the inlet pipes and join them to the taps with suitable flexible connectors. This will make adjustment easier if there is any misalignment.

Fit a fibre washer to each tap connector, and screw on each tap.

Grip each tap firmly and tighten the connector with an adjustable spanner or waterpump pliers.

Put the bath in position and use a spirit level to make final adjustments to the feet. Allow for the height of the bath side and end panels. Mark the positions for the wall fixing brackets and the feet fixing screws.

Fixing the bath in place

Now you are ready to attach your bath to the wall and floor, and to fit bath panels to the sides and end. To cut the panels to fit around skirting or pipes, use a small fine-toothed saw or very sharp knife.

Lift the bath away. Remove the feet from the leg cradles. Check for hidden pipes or cables under the floor, then drill pilot holes and screw the feet down with 25mm screws. On a solid floor use a hammer drill and plug the holes.

Check for pipes or cables then drill the wall where you have marked the positions for the wall brackets. Get someone to help you lift the bath onto the feet. Double-check that the height is correct then tighten the locking nuts to secure the feet to the legs. Fix the wall brackets to a masonry wall with plugs and screws, or to plasterboard with hollow-wall fixings (see pages 376–77).

Stand a spirit level vertically against the side of the bath. Mark a pencil line against the inside of the spirit level on the floor. Do this in several positions along the side of the bath. Use a straightedge to join up the lines. The manufacturer's instructions will give you the thickness of the side panels (with profiled panels this can be tricky to measure). Use this to measure and mark the inside edge of the panel on the floor.

Cut four 150mm lengths of timber to make floor-fixing battens. Drill two pilot holes into each one and position them so that the outer edge of each is in line with the inner lines you have marked. Space them equally around the bath and fix them to the floor using 45mm screws.

Insert the top of the end panel behind the front flange of the bath and rest the bottom against the batten. Do the same with the side panel. Drill pilot holes through the panels and into the battens, and then screw them in place.

It's important to choose a shower that is compatible with your home's plumbing system (see pages 298–301 to identify the type you have). If you have a gravity-fed system – in other words you have a hot water cylinder and a cold water storage cistern in the loft – you have the most options: you can choose a mixer shower with or without a pump, a power shower or an electric shower. If you have a combination boiler or your cold water comes directly off the mains you can only install a mixer shower or an electric shower; you can't attach a pump to a combi boiler or a mains supply.

ONE PLANET HOME

Water-saving shower head
An aerating shower head gives the same invigorating shower performance with up to 75% less water. It works by injecting tiny air bubbles into the water droplets. These explode on impact, giving a great showering experience – as well as great water and energy savings.

Basic mixer

A basic mixer shower is cheap and easy to install with no new plumbing or electrical connections. The supply of hot and cold water is controlled simply by turning the bath taps. The downside is that it can be fiddly to achieve the temperature you want, and the temperature can be affected if someone draws water elsewhere in the house.

Thermostatic mixer

With a thermostatic mixer, you set the temperature you want on a manual control and the thermostat maintains that temperature to within 2°C even if water is drawn off elsewhere in the house. You can install it over a bath or in a separate shower cubicle. And if you have a gravity-fed water system, you can add a booster pump (see below).

Power shower

A power shower works just like a thermostatic mixer, with one key difference: it has a built-in electric pump to boost the flow rate. It makes an excellent choice if you have low water pressure in your home – but like any pump, it's only compatible with a gravity-fed plumbing system.

Electric shower

This kind of shower works like a kettle: it requires only a cold water supply, which is warmed by heating elements inside the unit. The higher the kilowatt rating, the more powerful the shower, though the force of its spray may weaken in winter when the incoming mains water is colder and so takes longer to heat up.

Pump it up

Adding a booster pump to a thermostatic mixer shower can more than double the flow rate. The pump can be hidden under a bath or tucked away in an airing cupboard or loft, so you will not see it though you may hear it in action. But remember that you cannot connect a pump to a combi boiler or to a cold water supply coming straight off the mains. And to get the most out of your pump, it might be necessary to install a bigger hot water cylinder.

Fitting a thermostatic mixer shower

You can supply a thermostatic mixer shower, with or without a pump, via branch pipes from the hot and cold plumbing system. Try to join them as near as possible to the cold and hot water tanks, and run them to the shower position and through the wall using the techniques described on pages 306–9.

The hot and cold water pressure in a gravity-fed system is determined by the height of the cold water tank above the shower. Without a pump, you need a minimum of 1m between the bottom of the tank and the shower head to produce a reasonable flow rate and pressure. If you don't have enough difference in height then you must either raise the cold water tank or install a pump in the system.

Cold water storage cistern

Branch pipes supplying hot and cold water

Switched fused connection unit

Spur

Pump

Hot water cylinder

Fitting the mixer valve and rail

The rail should be set high enough to accommodate the tallest user – but not so low that the shower head will dangle any less than 25mm from the spillover level of the shower tray or bath, or a nearby basin. Otherwise you risk back-siphonage of used water into your household supply.

1 Seal the hole around each inlet pipe with sanitary silicone sealant. Flush out the pipework by briefly turning on the hot and cold water supply. Then – before attaching the pipe trims – fix a coupler onto each pipe and attach the thermostatic mixer valve using an adjustable spanner. Turn on the hot and cold water to check for leaks. If all is watertight, turn off the water again, remove the mixer, fit the chrome pipe trims, and refit the mixer valve.

2 Fit the lever and holder to the slider rail. Place the brackets on the ends of the rail and mark the position of the fixing hole for the lowest bracket.

3 Check there are no hidden pipes or cables with an electronic detector, then drill where you have marked the position of the lower bracket. Insert a wallplug and squeeze onto it a spot of sanitary silicone sealant.

4 Remove the slider rail from the brackets and fix the bottom bracket to the bottom hole using the screw supplied. To find the position of the top fixing hole place the rail back onto the bottom bracket. Put the other mounting bracket onto the top of the rail. Use a spirit level to check it is vertical and mark the top fixing hole on the wall.

5 Remove the rail and drill and plug the wall as before. Screw the top bracket in with the rail in place. Finally fit bracket covers onto the top and bottom brackets.

B&Q Making it easier

Seal the joints
Sanitary silicone sealant gives a flexible waterproof seal around bathroom fittings. Run a bead of sealant around the top of the shower tray and the outside of the enclosure – but don't fill the drainage channels on the inside of a shower enclosure, or you will cause a flood.

Shower enclosures can be fitted into the corner of a room or against a flat wall. Buy one as part of a new bathroom or add one to your existing suite. The doors can be hinged, folded, sliding or pivoted. If space is tight, sliding or folding doors are the least intrusive option.

The waste pipes and trap

Before choosing a shower enclosure, you need to work out how you are going to run the drainage pipes, and check how much height you need under the tray for the pipework. You may be able to cut a hole in the floor to install the waste pipe. If so, you will also need to make an access hatch: either extend the hole for the waste trap beyond where the outside edge of the shower tray will be; or make a separate hatch nearby, within reach of the trap. If your floor is solid, or you cannot achieve enough of a fall for drainage under a suspended floor, you could opt for an enclosure with a step up to the tray; or you could raise the tray above floor level by installing it on a plinth.

If you don't have enough space under the shower tray to fit a shallow P-trap (see page 310), you could fit a compact trap (right). This is specially designed to give the necessary water seal while being shallow enough to fit under most modern shower trays. It has a removable grid for easy cleaning.

Fitting the shower tray

Once the waste pipework is prepared, you are ready to install the shower tray and connect its waste outlet to the trap. Read the manufacturer's installation instructions too, since different designs may be fitted in slightly different ways.

1 Hold the tray on its side and run a bead of sanitary silicone sealant around the waste hole.

2 Insert the waste outlet into the hole, so that it sits into the sealant. Make sure that you have fitted any washers supplied, and screw on the locking nut using an adjustable spanner. Fit the trap to the waste outlet.

3 Mix the mortar and use a trowel to lay a thin bed on the floor where the tray will be positioned. Wear protective gloves to mix and handle the mortar. Rest the tray in place.

4 Bed the tray down into the mortar and level it with a spirit level. If you can't get it exactly level you may need to take up the tray and adjust the mortar. Tidy the edges and remove any excess mortar with the trowel. Open the floor hatch and connect the trap to the waste pipe.

project essentials

- adjustable spanner
- trowel
- spirit level
- junior hacksaw
- cross-head screwdriver
- chinagraph pencil
- pipe and cable detector
- hammer-action drill with masonry and twist bits

- shower tray
- shower enclosure and fittings
- sanitary silicone sealant
- ready-mix mortar
- wallplugs

Fitting the shower enclosure

The shower tray, mixer valve and all pipework and tiling should already be in place before you fit the shower enclosure. Shown here is a corner enclosure with curved sliding doors; there are lots of designs available, each installed in a slightly different way, so do read the manufacturer's installation instructions. With any enclosure it is vital that the wall and tray are fully waterproof, and that the uprights of the frame are vertical.

1 Lie the two fixed side panels flat and run a generous bead of sanitary silicone sealant into the curved channels at the top and bottom. Then attach the head and sill rails with the screws provided; don't overtighten them.

2 Slide the plastic guide tracks into the head and sill rails.

3 Use a junior hacksaw to shorten the plastic guide tracks if they are too long.

Extractor fans
Showers generate a lot of steam and condensation, which can lead to problems with damp. So consider installing an extractor fan (see page 345) to ventilate the room.

4 Push two door stops into the guide track in the head and sill rails. Move them into the middle but don't fix them yet.

5 Stand the shower enclosure upright and slide the curved sliding doors into the head and sill rails, making quite sure that the doors are the right way around. Then insert another doorstop into both the head and sill rails.

6 Attach the wall channels to each side of the enclosure and stand it on the tray. Check it is vertical using a spirit level. From the inside of the enclosure, use a chinagraph pencil to mark the position for the fixing holes through the pre-drilled holes in the wall channels.

7 Remove the enclosure and check for hidden pipes and cables behind the fixing positions with an electronic detector. If all is clear then drill fixing holes in the marked positions. Push wall-plugs into the holes, making sure they go in beyond the depth of the tile.

8 Run a continuous bead of sanitary silicone sealant down both wall channels. Put the enclosure onto the base, and screw in the fixing screws. Remove any excess sealant. Refer to the instructions to make final adjustments to the sliding doors.

9 From the inside, drill through the holes in the wall channels and into the frame. Secure with the screws provided and cover the heads with screw caps. Drill through the plastic track and inner head channel then screw the doorstops in position.

10 Seal the join between the tray and the tiled wall with a continuous bead of sanitary silicone sealant. Do the same around the outside edges of the enclosure.

safe electrics

Follow the rules
If you plan to make changes to a power or lighting circuit in a bathroom, you must inform your local authority's Building Control Department first (see page 268).

An electric shower has an element like a kettle that heats the water as it passes through. You control the temperature by modifying the rate that the water passes over the element. As most don't have a thermostat, if the temperature of the incoming water varies, then so too will the temperature of the shower. An electric shower can be mounted over the bath or set in a cubicle.

Preparing the pipework

Before you fit the shower you need to prepare the pipework and install an electricity supply. Run a single 15mm pipe from the cold water supply near the storage tank to the wall where you intend to fit the shower. Hold the shower unit in place and mark the position for the inlet pipe and power supply cable. Use a pipe and cable detector to check there are no hidden pipes or cables before drilling into the wall. Run the pipe through the wall at the marked position. Fit an isolating valve in the pipe and fit the correct connector for the unit.

Fitting an electric shower

When you decide on the position of the shower unit make sure you leave enough room around the shower to remove the front cover, as it may need servicing some time in the future. Depending on the type of unit, the water supply pipe may enter from the top, bottom or rear. Make sure you have the recommended amount of cable emerging from the wall to connect to the terminal block. The instructions with the shower will tell you how to do this. Before you connect the unit, turn on the water to flush any debris from the water inlet pipe, as any small particles could damage the new shower. Then turn the water off and drain the pipe.

safe electrics

- Never take risks with electrical safety. Before you start any kind of electrical work, see page 268.
- All new or modified installations must comply with the latest IEE Wiring Regulations. New or replacement cables or sockets may require RCD protection.
- Remember that different rules of electrical safety apply in a bathroom. If in doubt, always consult a qualified electrician.

project essentials

- **chinagraph pencil**
- **pliers**
- **pipe and cable detector**
- **hammer-action drill with masonry bit**
- **screwdriver**
- **pipe wrench**
- sanitary silicone sealant
- 15mm compression fitting
- electric shower and fittings
- masking tape
- wallplugs

Providing the power supply

Drill a hole in the wall for the electric cable. The size of cable required will depend on the length of the run and the kilowatt rating of the shower unit: check the manufacturer's instructions. Run cable from the shower unit position to a ceiling-mounted double-pole pull-cord switch. This should have an on/off indicator and must not be sited in Hazard Zones 1 or 2 as defined by the IEE Wiring Regulations (see page 283). An electric shower needs its own dedicated circuit from the consumer unit, and for safety you must get an electrician to make the final connection for you. The circuit must be protected by an RCD (residual current device, see page 294).

Cold water storage cistern

Cold water supply

Pull-cord switch

RCD

Consumer unit

Rising main

Save water and energy
Electric shower units are both economic and energy efficient. They use less water than any other system and because the water is heated as you need it there is no wasteful storage of hot water.

Hold the shower unit in position and mark the fixing holes with a chinagraph pencil. Drill holes at the marked positions with a masonry bit. On a tiled surface use a tile bit or stick masking tape on the tiles to stop the bit slipping. Fit wallplugs and squeeze a little sanitary silicone sealant onto each one.

Feed the pipe and electric cable through the backplate of the unit. Screw it to the wall using the screws supplied.

Connect the inlet pipe to the shower unit using a pipe wrench to tighten the compression fitting.

Connect the cable to the unit by connecting its live and neutral cores to the terminals marked 'load' and its earth core to the earth terminal.

Fit the cover according to the manufacturer's instructions, ensuring that the rubber seal is in place.

To fit the rail, follow Steps 1–5 on page 321. Don't forget to position it high enough that the shower head cannot dangle less than 25mm from the spillover level of the bath, shower tray, wash basin or bidet, otherwise you might get back-siphonage of dirty water.

Screw one end of the hose to the handset, making sure to include any washers supplied. Follow the procedures described in the instructions to check the shower is working correctly before finally screwing the other end to the shower unit.

In a central heating system, heat is produced from a single source – usually a boiler – and distributed through the house, either in the form of hot water or hot air. Most homes now have central heating systems and while you need a qualified professional to install them, there is a lot you can do to maintain them yourself if you understand the basic principles.

Wet central heating

In a wet central heating system, a boiler heats water, which is usually pumped around a circuit of pipes to radiators fitted throughout the house. Each radiator has valves that control the rate at which water flows through it, thus controlling the amount of time the water spends in the radiator and the amount of heat that is given off. When the water leaves the radiator, it is piped back to the boiler for reheating.

Although some heat is lost from the pipes as the water flows around the system, their narrow diameter and the speed of the flow keeps this to a minimum. A well-designed system may have several short circuits radiating from the pump, rather than one large one, ensuring that the last radiator on each circuit heats up just as efficiently as the first.

Two-pipe system

Microbore pipe system

Pipework

The radiator circuits in most modern wet central heating systems are run in standard 15mm copper pipe, while pipes linking the boiler and pump and the points where the circuits split off will be 22mm or 28mm diameter. Soldered capillary joints are best (apart from connections to boiler, pump and valves), as these are least likely to leak. Plastic pipes have been developed for use in wet central heating systems, but they can't be connected directly to a boiler; a short length of copper pipe must be used instead.

Two-pipe and single-pipe systems

More modern systems have a two-pipe layout, where hot water is carried from the pump to the inlet valve of each radiator by a flow pipe, which terminates at the last radiator on the circuit. A second pipe, the return pipe, collects the cooled water from the radiators and carries it back to the boiler for reheating. In the older single-pipe layout, the hot water passes through one radiator, then is returned to the flow pipe to be carried on to the next and so on around the circuit, losing some of its heat each time. Consequently, radiators towards the end of the circuit have to be bigger in order to give off the same amount of heat.

Microbore pipe system

A variation of the two-pipe layout uses small-diameter microbore pipe, which is available in 8mm and 10mm sizes. It is supplied in coils and is very easy to bend, so you can feed the pipe through cavities and around corners without the need for joints. These narrow pipes only carry enough water to heat one radiator at a time, so each radiator must have its own circuit. These radiate out from fittings known as manifolds. The flow pipes to several radiators are connected to one end of the manifold and the returns to the other. Both feed and return microbore pipes are connected to the same end of the radiator.

Dry central heating

In a dry central heating system, air is warmed by a single heat source and blown through a series of large ducts to heat the rooms of the house. Each duct terminates in a floor or wall grille, which can be opened and closed to control heat output. Some systems rely on an electric storage heater to warm the air; others use a fuel such as gas. You can use overnight off-peak electricity to heat firebricks in an electric storage heater, and then use their stored heat to warm the house during the day.

Depending on the type of heater, some systems are also able to provide hot water. This type of heating system is only really suitable for installation when the house is being built, since the ducts are very bulky and must be incorporated into the structure if they are to be unobtrusive.

Other forms of heating

Although strictly speaking not central heating, there are other dry systems that can be employed to heat a whole house. These include individual room storage heaters, which use off-peak electricity to heat firebricks that give off heat during the day.

Another option is underfloor heating, in which hot water pipes or electric elements are laid under the floors. These are designed to produce enough heat to warm the air of the room without making the floor uncomfortable underfoot.

Types of radiators

A wet central heating system delivers its heat by radiation and convection. You can feel radiation as heat emitted from a hot surface, but convection warms the air and, in doing so, sets up a gentle circulation centred on the heat source – the warm air rises and cooler air flows in to take its place; in this way, the temperature of the whole room rises gradually.

The simplest form of heat emitter is the panel radiator. Although called a radiator, in fact over half of its heat output occurs through convection. It has a corrugated body to increase its surface area and ensure maximum heat output. Where space is limited, double-panel radiators are ideal. Another means of improving output is to use a convector radiator, which has a number of fins on the back to increase convection.

Radiator valves

Radiators normally have a threaded hole, or tapping, at each corner. The bottom two are for the valves – a manual or control valve to adjust the incoming flow of water (this is used to turn the radiator on and off), and a lockshield valve to control the outgoing flow of water (this is normally left fully open). One of the top tappings will be fitted with a bleed valve, a simple tapered screw that allows you to remove air from the system; the other has a blanking plug.

Radiator design

Radiators and towel warmers needn't just be functional heat providers. These days there are lots of stylish options to complement every interior – see diy.com for ideas.

Heating controls

The more you are able to programme and control your heating system, the more energy efficient and economical it will be to run.

Roomstats

Many systems incorporate a room thermostat, or roomstat, which switches the heating on and off in accordance with the temperature you have selected. It is normally sited in the living room or hall, and it operates on the assumption that a rise or drop in temperature in its vicinity will be matched by a corresponding rise or drop throughout the house. A programmable roomstat gives you greater control, enabling you to set different temperatures for different times of day. These are available in wired or wireless versions.

The problem with a roomstat is that it doesn't accommodate local temperature variations – caused perhaps by the sun shining through windows or an open fire in a living room.

Thermostatic radiator valves

You can reduce the heat output of an individual radiator by closing a manual radiator valve, but much more efficient is to install thermostatic valves, which will do this automatically for you and then open again when the room temperature drops (see page 330). Even better are programmable thermostatic radiator valves, which will maintain the desired temperature of individual radiators at set times of the day.

Time switches and programmers

A simple time switch will turn the system on and off at pre-set times, but a programmer allows independent operation of the heating and hot water circuits at different times of the day. Even greater flexibility is provided by a controller, which operates the system at set times and also responds to temperature fluctuations, while a boiler manager ensures that the boiler only runs when necessary by sensing a variety of conditions, including outdoor temperature.

Cylinder thermostats

The temperature of water required to heat radiators is much higher than that needed at the taps (82°C as opposed to 60°C), and a cylinder thermostat will prevent overheating of the hot water supply. When the temperature in the cylinder reaches the set limit, the thermostat operates a motorised valve, shutting off the flow to its heat exchanger. When the water temperature drops, the valve opens again.

Zone valves

Motorised valves, known as zone or mid-position valves, can also be used to shut off parts of the system at specific times of the day when heating is not required in certain rooms. This can be useful in a large house, where you may not want to heat all the bedrooms on upper floors during the day, and is a requirement in systems heating more than 150m².

Different makes and models of boiler have different controls, so keep your boiler operating instructions in a handy place in case of trouble. Many faults have simple solutions, which you should be able to do yourself – but if in doubt, call in an engineer.

Noisy system

Hissing/banging

- The water level in the system might be low. Turn off boiler and pump, and examine the feed-and-expansion cistern in the loft; if it's empty, check that the ball valve is not jammed closed and that the water supply has not been turned off or supply pipe frozen. If you can identify and fix the cause yourself, you can then top up the system water level again, following the boiler operating instructions.
- Substantial deposits of scale can build up in the system in hard-water areas – call an engineer to clean it out. They may decide to fit a hard water filter to stop it happening again.
- It could mean that your boiler thermostat is faulty – call an engineer.
- If you have a solid-fuel system, it could be that the chimney is blocked – try sweeping it (see page 141).
- In a solid-fuel system, noises could indicate that the pump is not working. You can check this yourself, using the boiler operating instructions. Shut down the boiler; check that the pump is turned on and the impeller running by feeling the casing for vibration; if the switch is set to on, but the pump is not running, turn off the power at the mains and check that none of the wiring connections has come loose. If the pump is running, but the outlet pipe is cool, open the bleed valve to release trapped air. If the problem persists, call an engineer.

Creaking from pipework
- This could be caused by hot pipes expanding and rubbing against floor/wall structure or other pipes. Widen pipe notches in joists (but don't deepen them, as this will weaken the joists); clip unsupported pipe runs; and pack insulation around and between pipes.

Humming in pipes

- It could be that the pump speed is too high or that your pipes are too narrow for the system flow – call an engineer.

Rushing sound in pipes

- Probably caused by air or gas bubbles in the system. Bleed the radiators (see page 330); if the problem persists, call an engineer.

Boiler not working

- Check if the pilot light is extinguished. If it is, re-light it in accordance with the boiler manufacturer's instructions.
- It may be that the temperature setting on the roomstat or boiler thermostat is too low. Check and reset as necessary.
- The system timer/programmer may be incorrectly set or faulty. Check and reset the timer/programmer, as necessary. If the problem persists, call an engineer.
- Overheating caused by the pump shutting down may have caused the thermostat to shut down the boiler too. Confirm the pump is running and restart the boiler. If the problem persists, call an engineer.

Cold radiators

All radiators cold when boiler running

- This could mean that your pump is not working: see under Hissing/banging, left.
- It may be that your pump thermostat/timer is incorrectly set or faulty. Check and reset, if necessary. If the thermostat/timer is set correctly, turn off the power and check wiring connections, following the operating instructions. If the problem persists, call an engineer.

Some radiators cold

- First you should check if the zone valve thermostat/timer is incorrectly set or faulty; reset it, if necessary. If set correctly, switch off the power and check the wiring connections, using the operating instructions. If the problem persists, call an engineer.
- The zone valve itself may be faulty, or the system may need 'balancing'. Call an engineer.

Single radiator cold

- It may simply be that the radiator's manual control valve is turned off – if so, open it.
- The thermostatic radiator valve could be incorrectly set or faulty. Check and reset, if necessary. If the valve is set correctly but the radiator still doesn't work, try replacing it (see page 330).
- You may have an incorrectly set lockshield valve (see page 327). Open the manual valve fully, then remove the plastic cap from the lockshield valve and use an adjustable spanner to open the valve until the radiator warms up. Next time you have the system serviced, ask the engineer to balance the radiator.
- Heavy corrosion deposits may be blocking the inlet and outlet. Remove the radiator and flush out or replace it, as necessary; add corrosion inhibitor to the system (see opposite).

Top of radiator cold

- This means there is air trapped. Open the bleed valve so that air can escape (see page 330); if the problem persists, call an engineer.

Centre and bottom of radiator cold

- Corrosion is probably restricting the water flow. Remove the radiator and flush out or replace it, as necessary; add corrosion inhibitor to the system (see opposite).

- There may be a problem with the electricity supply. Check some other electrical circuits and if there is a power cut, wait for power to be restored. If a fuse has blown, repair it.
- With combination boilers, it's possible that the water pressure is at an incorrect level. Refer to the operating instructions for the correct figure and check the boiler pressure gauge; if it is too low, you may be able to top up the system at the mains water filling point; otherwise, call an engineer.

Overflow in the roof dripping

- The water level in the feed-and-expansion cistern may be too high, due to a leaking ball valve float or an incorrectly adjusted or faulty ball valve. Turn off the water supply and empty the cistern to below the level of the valve; examine the float and replace, if necessary. Bend the float arm or adjust the valve stop, if necessary. If the float arm/valve is adjusted correctly, fit a new washer to the valve; if the valve is in poor condition, fit a new valve (see page 299).

Preventing the system from freezing up

If you go away during the winter and turn off the heating, a severe drop in temperature could cause the water in the system to freeze and burst the pipes, even if they have been lagged. To prevent this you can take one or more of the following steps:

- With gas- and oil-fired systems, turn the roomstat down to its minimum setting so that the heating will come on when the temperature falls.
- If you regularly go away in the winter, have a frost thermostat fitted; this will switch the system on when the temperature drops to freezing and off again when it rises.
- Pipes that are particularly susceptible to freezing may be wrapped with trace heat tape. This is used in conjunction with a frost thermostat; when the temperature drops low enough, the thermostat switches on the tape, which heats the pipe.

Leaks

- Leaks could be caused by loose pipe connections. Shut down the boiler and pump; tighten leaking compression fittings, but no more than a quarter-turn; if the problem persists, or soldered joints leak, drain the system (see below) and remake the joints completely (see pages 308–9).
- A pipe may be damaged. Shut down the boiler and pump, drain the system (see below) and replace the damaged section of pipe (see page 306–9).
- If a corroded radiator is leaking, replace the radiator and add corrosion inhibitor to the system (see below).

Adding corrosion inhibitor

Corrosion inhibitor should be added to a system when it is installed, but it can also be added later if required. Make sure you buy a product compatible with the materials your boiler, pipes and radiators are made of; if in doubt, get expert advice. With an older installation, it is a good idea to flush the system first to remove any build-up of corrosion sludge, which can eventually cause the pump to fail. Turn off the heating and allow the water to cool, then drain the system completely (see below). Refill and drain again. Carry on in this way until the water runs clear. Partially fill the system, pour the correct quantity of corrosion inhibitor into the feed-and-expansion cistern (5 litres should be enough for most domestic systems, but check the manufacturer's instructions) and allow the system to fill completely. Turning the boiler and pump back on will cause the corrosion inhibitor to be mixed thoroughly with the water.

Alternatively, you could use a product designed to be injected from a cartridge straight into one of the radiators. This removes the need to drain down the system.

Draining and refilling the system

All wet central heating systems will be provided with at least one draincock to allow the system to be emptied for maintenance or repairs. Usually, this will be in the return pipe close to the boiler. However, where a solid ground floor prevents pipes from being run below it, the pipes will drop down from the ceiling void to supply ground-floor radiators. These sections of pipework will remain full of water when the system is drained from the boiler draincock and will have their own draincocks, allowing them to be emptied separately.

When refilling the system, make sure all draincocks and radiator bleed valves are closed before restoring the water supply to the feed-and-expansion cistern in the loft. As water flows into the system, air will become trapped in the radiators, so bleed each by opening the bleed valve about half a turn, starting at the bottom of the house and working upwards (see page 330). Before turning the pump back on, bleed this too.

1 Before draining the system, switch off the boiler, but allow the pump to run for ten minutes to cool the water. Then turn off the pump and close the stop valve in the pipe supplying the feed-and-expansion cistern. If there is no valve, place a batten across the top of the cistern and tie the ball valve arm to it to prevent the valve from opening. Push one end of a hose on to the outlet of the draincock. Run the hose to an outdoor drain.

2 Use an adjustable spanner to open the draincock, but do not remove the square valve shank completely. When the feed-and-expansion cistern has emptied, work down through the house, opening radiator bleed valves to release any remaining water trapped in the radiators.

HEATING RADIATORS

Keeping your radiators well-maintained will save energy as they will function more efficiently. They should be bled from time to time to release trapped air, so that they heat up evenly. If a radiator has become corroded or damaged, replacing it with one of the same style and size is a simple job. Another easy improvement is to fit thermostatic radiator valves, which will provide automatic adjustment of each radiator's heat output, ensuring better temperature control throughout your home.

Bleeding radiators

All radiators are provided with a bleed valve in one top corner to allow trapped air to be released, ensuring that the radiator heats up evenly. The valve takes the form of a square shaft inside a threaded plug. Turn off the heating and use a radiator bleed key (or in some cases a flat-head screwdriver) to turn the shaft anti-clockwise by between a quarter- and a half-turn to open the valve – don't unscrew it by more than one complete turn. You will hear the trapped air hissing as it escapes. Hold a cloth beneath the valve to catch any water, and as soon as the first trickle appears close the valve. If you find you have to bleed your radiators frequently, have the system checked by a heating engineer, as there is likely to be a fault somewhere.

Fitting a thermostatic radiator valve

Many central heating systems are controlled by a single thermostat, usually sited in the hall. Unfortunately, this arrangement doesn't take into account local variations in temperature, and some rooms may become too hot or cold unless you keep adjusting the manual radiator valves. The answer is to fit thermostatic valves, which open and close automatically in response to room temperature. In many cases, a thermostatic valve will be a straight replacement for an existing manual valve, but do check first to ensure that it will fit.

project essentials

- **adjustable spanner**
- **wire wool**

- thermostatic radiator valve
- new connector, if required
- PTFE tape

1 First drain the heating system (see page 329). Disconnect the valve from the radiator by unscrewing its capnut, but before releasing it completely, slacken the nut holding the valve to the pipe. Then unscrew both nuts fully and lift the valve together with its capnut and olive from the end of the pipe. The radiator here has been removed, but you can replace a valve without taking the radiator off the wall.

2 Clean the end of the pipe with wire wool and slip the capnut and olive of the new valve on to it. Hold the valve in place and screw the capnut on to the valve, making sure the olive is seated properly. Don't tighten the capnut fully at this stage.

3 Fit the radiator with a new connector if necessary, wrap a few turns of PTFE tape around its threads, align the valve and start turning the capnut onto it. Then tighten both capnuts fully. Refill the system, checking for leaks, and finally set the thermostatic valve in accordance with the manufacturer's instructions.

ideal tool

PTFE tape
This is used by plumbers to ensure a watertight joint on threaded fittings. Wrap around the threads about five times clockwise before you screw the fitting together.

ONE PLANET HOME

Get the most from your radiators
Thermostatic valves allow much more efficient control of your heating system. The position of radiators can also make a big difference to their effectiveness. If they are screened by big pieces of furniture, they will heat a room much less efficiently. If you want to change the room layout, you can reposition radiators by running extra lengths of copper pipe. If your radiator is on an outside wall, up to 25% of its heat can be absorbed into the wall. To avoid this, fit radiator foil behind it to reflect heat back into the room (see opposite).

Replacing a radiator

You don't have to drain the entire heating system to replace a radiator, just turn off the heating and isolate the radiator by closing off the valve at either end. Turn the manual valve clockwise until it won't turn any further. Pull off the plastic shield of the lockshield valve at the other end and turn the square shaft clockwise with an adjustable spanner. Count the number of turns so that you can reset the new radiator at the same flow rate. If replacing several radiators, you will lose corrosion inhibitor from the system and should drain it down and add more (see page 329).

With both valves turned off, use an adjustable spanner to slacken the capnut holding one of them to the radiator. You may need to hold the valve body with a second spanner or pipe wrench to prevent it turning and buckling the pipe.

Place a tray beneath the valve to catch the water as it drains out. Open the bleed valve at the top of the radiator and loosen the capnut. When the tray is nearly full, re-tighten the capnut and empty the tray. Be ready with cloths to mop up any spillage – the water will be filthy. Repeat until all the water has drained out then disconnect the other valve.

Lift the radiator from its brackets and tilt to drain any remaining water. Get a helper to stuff tissue into the outlet the other end to stop it leaking. If the existing brackets don't suit the new radiator, unscrew them and fit those supplied with the new radiator. Check for pipes and cables before drilling new fixing holes.

Remove the valve connectors from the old radiator, using an adjustable spanner or large allen key. Clean the threads with wire wool and wind PTFE tape around the threads about five times to ensure a good seal. Screw the connectors into the new radiator, making sure they are tightened fully. Hang the radiator. Connect the valves and reset them, allowing water to enter the radiator. You will need to open the bleed valve about half a turn so that air can escape; close it when water starts to appear.

project essentials

- **2 adjustable spanners**
- **drain tray**
- **radiator bleed key**
- **bucket**
- **electronic pipe and cable detector**
- **large allen key, if required**
- **hammer-action drill with masonry bit**
- **wire wool**

- cloths
- PTFE tape
- new radiator and brackets

Fitting reflective radiator foil

Available as a roll or tiles, reflective radiator foil can reduce your heating costs by reflecting heat into the room that would otherwise be lost through the wall. It is particularly effective for radiators on cold outside walls.

Measure the height and width of the radiator, and the distance of the wall brackets from its top and side edges. Cut a piece of foil 50mm smaller than the radiator in both directions so that it won't be visible once installed.

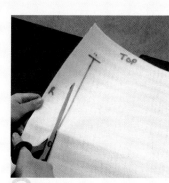

Mark the position of the wall brackets on the reverse of the foil, and also make a note of which side is top. Using scissors make a vertical cut from the bottom of the foil to the upper bracket on each side.

project essentials

- **tape measure**
- **marker pen**
- **scissors**
- **wallpaper brush, if required**
- **radiator paint roller**

- reflective radiator foil
- wallpaper paste or sticky pads

To stick the foil to the wall you can use either sticky pads or wallpaper paste. If using paste, protect the wall above with some paper as you position the foil.

Use a radiator paint roller to stick the foil to the wall.

A towel radiator is a luxurious addition to any bathroom. There are many designs available, from simple ladders in white or chrome to stylish designer models. They are installed in the same way as a standard radiator.

Fitting a new towel radiator

The easiest way to install a new towel radiator is to replace a radiator of the same width. In that case there's no need to drain the system, nor to take up flooring and skirting boards. You simply turn off the heating then isolate the old radiator by shutting off the valves on either side before removing it from the wall (see page 331). The new towel radiator is connected to the existing pipework.

However, if you want to run chrome pipes to match a new chrome radiator, or your new radiator is a different width from the old one,

you will need to drain the system and make alterations to the pipework. This will enable you to choose from a much wider range of replacement radiators, and is straightforward using modern plumbing fittings, which are very easy to work with and need no heating or soldering. Drain the system before you begin (see page 329) and remove flooring and skirting as necessary in order to gain access to the pipework.

Mounting the new towel radiator

Remove the old radiator (see page 331) and brackets and fill the fixing holes. The wall and new fixings must be strong enough to hold the weight of the towel radiator when filled with water. Leave at least 20cm between the bottom rail and the floor.

1 Screw in the bleed valve and blank plug of the new towel radiator. Protect the chrome with a cloth and tighten with an adjustable spanner.

B&Q Making it easier

Warm and dry towels all year round
Some towel warmers can be fitted with an optional electrical element. This means you can have warm, dry towels all year round – even when your central heating is switched off. Remember that different rules of electrical safety apply in a bathroom (see page 268). The electrical installation should be done by a professional electrician.

2 Align the radiator to the pipework and mark the fixing positions of the new brackets. If fixing to a tiled surface, attach a horizontal strip of masking tape to the tiles at the upper and lower fixing positions: this will be easier to mark with a pencil, and will also help prevent the drill bit slipping.

3 Check the bracket positions are vertically and horizontally aligned, and that there are no hidden pipes or cables, then drill. Remove the masking tape, insert wallplugs, and screw the bracket bases to the wall using the screws and washers provided. Take care not to overtighten, as this can crack the tiles.

4 Attach the bracket stems to the towel radiator, then push the assembled radiator onto the bracket bases, following the manufacter's instructions. Check the radiator is level. Don't fully tighten the bracket screws yet – you may need to dismount the radiator again before you finish.

Connecting to the pipework

For the best result when installing a chrome towel radiator, use chrome-plated copper pipe to match. You can snap a chrome-effect pipe cover (see MAKING IT EASIER) over the section of visible pipe that you are not replacing. Telescopic extending radiator tails make it easier for the novice plumber to get a precise fit.

1 Fit telescopic extending tails to the towel radiator inlet and outlet. It may be easier to take the radiator off the wall to do this.

2 Fit a compression elbow joint to the telescopic extending tail on the radiator inlet. Cut a length of pipe to run from the new elbow to the existing radiator valve. Remember to apply PTFE tape to the threads of compression fittings.

3 Unscrew the old valve head and replace it with the new one. Remount the radiator. Use a suitable compression fitting to attach the radiator outlet to the pipework on the other side. Only fully tighten the joints once all the pipework is in place and fitting accurately. Hold each fitting steady with a pipe wrench or waterpump pliers and tighten the compression nuts using an adjustable spanner. Take care not to overtighten.

Upgrade your pipes
Give old radiator pipes an instant makeover with chrome-effect plastic pipe covers. Simply cut to length and snap in place.

Upgrade your valve
Even if you are not replacing the valve, you can often unscrew the old valve head and replace it with a new one.

Running new pipework

If you are planning to run new pipework to the radiator, the system needs to be drained (see page 329) and the pipes exposed. Make sure all new pipe fittings are below floor level. Once you have connected each side of the radiator, turn on the water and heating and check it is working with no leaks before replacing flooring and skirting.

1 Wrap PTFE tape around the threads of the radiator valve compression joint and attach it to the radiator. It may be easier to take the radiator off the wall to do this. Remount the radiator.

2 Use a mini pipe cutter to cut through the hot water supply pipe. Clean the cut end with wire wool.

3 Attach a push-fit straight coupler. Measure and cut a short length of pipe to extend the supply pipe as far as the inlet of the new radiator.

5 Connect the horizontal and vertical sections of the new inlet pipe using a compression elbow joint. Remember to apply PTFE tape to the threads. Repeat to connect the radiator to the pipework on the other side.

4 Measure and cut a section of chrome-plated pipe to run from the radiator inlet down to the supply pipe.

project essentials

- **tape measure**
- **mini pipe cutter**
- **wire wool**
- **pipe wrench or waterpump pliers**
- **adjustable spanner**

- PTFE tape
- 2 copper push-fit straight couplers
- 15mm copper pipe
- 15mm chrome-plated copper pipe
- 2 compression elbow joints

Without proper insulation, as much as 50% of your heating could be disappearing straight through the walls and roof. Leaking heat means leaking money! Loft insulation is surprisingly quick and easy to install, and is one of the most effective steps you can take to make your home more energy efficient and bring down your bills.

ONE PLANET HOME

Retain heat and save money
Without loft insulation, you could be losing as much as 15% of the money you spend on heating straight through the roof. If every UK household fitted loft insulation to the recommended thickness it would save enough energy to heat 750,000 homes each year.

B&Q Making it easier

Bats in your roof?
Bats and their roosts are protected by law. But this does not necessarily mean that you can't work in your loft. Contact the Bat Conservation Trust (see page 379) for advice.

How much insulation?

Most homes have some insulation, but it may not be as effective as it could be. A minimum of 270mm insulation is recommended for loft floors, but it is common to find as little as 25mm, particularly in older houses. Sometimes existing insulation has been compressed by storage boards laid over the top: this makes it much less effective.

Insulation can easily be topped up using blanket insulation (also known as loft roll).This is available in different thickness and widths designed to be laid between and on top of joists. However, if you want to be able to walk in the loft or store boxes, then you will need to lay solid polystyrene board insulation on top of the insulated joists and secure chipboard loft boards on top (see page 338).

Rafter insulation

Fitting insulation at the joists (on the loft floor) reduces the amount of heat rising into the loft space, so in winter it will get colder up there than it used to. If you use the space for storing perishable items such as books or photographs, you can insulate the sloping roof to keep more heat in the loft. The insulation can either be expanded polystyrene panels fitted between the rafters or reflective foil stapled to the rafters. Alternatively you could install a multi-foil insulating quilt at the rafters. Although more expensive than conventional products, it's far more efficient and gives a much higher level of insulation than equivalent thicknesses of conventional insulating material.

However, rafter insulation should be used as a top-up only: you also need 270mm insulation at the joists otherwise you will be wasting energy and money to heat an uninhabited loft space.

If you convert a loft into a room, the insulation requirement is different and you will need professional advice as well as Building Control approval.

The 'R' value

The insulating properties of a material are described by the thermal resistance or 'R' value. This is how much the material stops heat passing through it. The higher the 'R' value the better the insulation. A minimum 'R' value of 6.1 is recommended in a loft, and preferably up to 7.0. Simply add the 'R' values of different products together to get their combined 'R' value. To work out the approximate 'R' value of your existing insulation, see the table below.

'R' VALUES	
Depth of existing insulation	**Approximate 'R' value**
25mm	0.5
50mm	1.1
100mm	2.2
150mm	3.4
200mm	4.5

50mm air gap

Insulated cold water cistern

Insulated feed-and-expansion tank

Reflective foil

Rafter panel

Foam lagging on cold water pipes

Chipboard loft boards

Polystyrene board insulation

170mm blanket insulation

100mm blanket insulation

25mm air gap

Insulated loft trap door

Blanket insulation

Blanket insulation is traditionally made from glass mineral wool. It is sold in rolls, usually 100mm, 150mm, 170mm, 200mm or 270mm thick, and is available ready perforated to cut and fit between widths of 400mm, which matches the joist spacing in older houses, and 600mm for more modern houses. It is compression packed for easier handling and will expand to the required thickness when unwrapped. Glass mineral wool is irritating to the skin, so gloves and protective clothing are essential. Alternatively you could choose an encapsulated or non-irritant blanket insulation, see right.

Polystyrene loft board

If you need to install storage boards in your loft you should combine blanket insulation laid between the joists with extruded polystyrene loft boards laid on top. These are quick and easy to cut and fit, have a high compressive strength, and can also be installed over existing timber loft boards. Chipboard loft boards are finally laid on top and secured to the joists.

Types of insulation

Insulation designed for lofts comes in the form of blanket rolls, boards, panels and foil. It may be made from glass mineral wool, rock mineral wool, polystyrene, recycled plastic bottles or natural fibre products such as sheep's wool.

Encapsulated insulation

This consists of glass mineral wool encapsulated between thin plastic on the bottom and a part-metallised polythene film on the top. It is a light, quilt-like insulation packaged in a roll. Because the glass mineral wool is encapsulated, it is much more comfortable to work with, though gloves and protective clothing still need to be worn when cutting and handling. It is available in dimensions suitable for laying between and on top of joists.

Reflective foil

Reflective insulating foil roll can be rolled across the rafters and secured with a staple gun. Each row is butted up against the next and the join taped together. This is only a top-up insulation product: you also need adequate insulation at the joists (see opposite).

Slab insulation

Semi-rigid rock mineral wool slab insulation is designed to be friction-fitted between rafters, which means it is quick and easy to install without the need for additional fixing. It also has acoustic insulation properties, and can be used to insulate and soundproof a stud partition wall by fitting it between the timber or metal studs (see page 68).

Rafter panels

These expanded polystyrene panels are simply squeezed in place between the rafters. Like reflective foil, they are suitable as a top-up insulation but you will also need adequate insulation at the joists (see opposite).

Recycled plastic bottle insulation

Insulation made from 85% recycled plastic bottles is available in 150mm and 200mm thicknesses. It is totally itch-free, which means you can lay it easily and comfortably without the need for protective clothing, mask or gloves.

Sheep's wool insulation

Made with wool from British sheep, this blanket insulation takes very little energy to manufacture. It is also non-irritant, clean and easy to install.

safety first

When working in a loft, be sure to have a sturdy ladder that is long enough to reach into the loft. Only stand on the ceiling joists or use walkboards: the plasterboard in between will not bear your weight. You need good lighting; if there is no fixed light, use a work lamp that can be clipped to the rafters. It is likely to be dusty up there, so wear protective overalls or loose clothing with long sleeves, protective gloves, safety goggles and a face mask.

Rolls of blanket insulation are easy to lay and fit. To calculate how many rolls you need, measure the length and width of your loft. This may be difficult to do in the loft area. If the ground floor is the same size as the loft, you can measure that instead, or even measure around the exterior walls of the house. Multiply the length by the width to determine the area, and then divide that figure by the coverage per pack of insulation to work out how many packs you need.

Clear the loft as much as possible to give yourself a large safe work area. Remove any old storage boards. Use planks to create a flat storage area for a few rolls close to where you are working. Make yourself one or more walkboards, long enough to span three or four joists and wide enough to kneel on (see MAKING IT EASIER).

Once you have unrolled your first length, lightly push the insulation down against the joists so there are no gaps, taking care not to compress it. Carry on across the complete loft area.

Laying blanket insulation

The rolls can be heavy, so if you are using the larger ones either have someone pass them up to you or cut them to size before taking them into the loft area. Once the second layer of insulation is down, you can no longer see the joists, so this method is only suitable for a loft, or part of a loft, that does not need to be walked on or used for storage. If laying mineral wool insulation, as here, you will need protective clothing and gloves.

Start in one corner and work back towards the hatch. Position your walkboard along the adjacent joists. Begin laying the first roll at the eaves, leaving a 25mm gap for ventilation. Use 100mm insulation between the rafters.

For narrower areas, cut the insulation to the required width and lay it between the joists in the same way. Do not pack or compress insulation into awkward corners.

Continue unrolling between the joists across the loft floor area. If one roll isn't long enough to reach to the other side, start a new roll and butt the joints closely together.

When you reach a cross beam, cut the insulation flush with the beam (see opposite) then start again on the other side, working in from the eaves.

project essentials

- **ladder**
- **walkboards**
- **protective gloves**
- **dust mask**
- **knee pads**
- **tape measure**
- **handsaw**
- **long sharp knife**
- **scissors**

- 100mm blanket insulation
- offcuts of wooden board
- downlight heat diffusers, if needed
- 170mm blanket insulation

B&Q Making it easier

Walkboards
Make yourself a couple of walkboards to lay across the joists so you can safely work in the loft area. It's useful to have more than one walkboard so you can stand on one while you move the other; three when working in larger lofts. Use a strong piece of sheet timber – 18mm ply or chipboard is perfect. Don't make the boards too large or they will be difficult to manoeuvre. Most ceiling joists are fitted at 400mm centres so a walkboard 1700mm long and roughly 500mm wide is ideal. Avoid having too much overhang either end as the board will be unstable if you stand close to the end.

Cutting insulation

Rolls of blanket insulation come in different widths and can be easily cut with a handsaw. It may be easier to cut them before taking them into the loft. Once rolled out in the loft, insulation can be cut with a long sharp knife such as a bread knife, or a pair of scissors in tricky areas.

1 Cut large rolls using a handsaw. They may be perforated so they can be cut easily and without any need for measuring. They can also be cut in their packaging, following the pre-marked lines. The roll should be left uncut when laying the insulation across the top of the joists.

2 Blanket insulation can be cut by sandwiching it between two offcuts of board. Using the top board as a guide, run a sharp knife along the edge for a straight cut.

3 For small, difficult cuts or cuts near power cables, use a pair of sharp scissors for accuracy and safety.

Insulated loft trap door
Don't forget to insulate your loft trap door. You can insulate an existing door by sticking solid insulating board cut to size on its upper side. Better still, replace it with an insulated trap door. This is a drop-down door with insulation attached to the reverse. Most modern homes have a standard size loft opening so you can simply screw a new trap door in place.

Cables and downlights

In your loft you may have electrical cable and downlights for the room below. In older homes cable should not be covered with insulation as it may overheat; lay it under the cable or re-route the cable if necessary. In most new homes cable is rated such that you can cover it, and you will most likely find it clipped to the joists; you can leave it clipped and carry on insulating. If in doubt, always consult an electrician.

Downlights generate considerable heat and can be a fire risk. If you have a downlight fitting, you must leave a 200mm gap either side of it if laying encapsulated insulation, or any other insulation except glass mineral wool, between the joists. Standard glass mineral wool insulation can be laid over the light fitting as long as a cylindrical heat diffuser is fitted to the light fitting to create a gap around the fitting.

safety first

Protect yourself
Wear a dust mask, protective gloves and knee pads when working in a dusty loft.

1 If cables in your loft are not clipped to the joists, carefully lift the cable while you lay the insulation underneath.

2 If using glass mineral wool insulation, cut it either side of a downlight fitting. Fit a heat diffuser to the fitting from the room below, following the manufacturer's instructions. Push it back through the hole into the loft. A second layer of insulation can be laid over the top of the heat diffuser.

Second layer

Once you have laid insulation between the joists, unroll a second layer of 170mm blanket insulation at a 90° angle to the first layer. Use wider rolls to speed up the process. It is dangerous to walk in the loft once the rafters are invisible, so only cover them in parts of the loft that will not be walked on; otherwise lay polystyrene board insulation (see page 338).

If you want to use part of your loft for storage you need to insulate this area in a different way. You can't put heavy boards or boxes on top of blanket insulation because this will compress the material, reducing its 'R' value and effectiveness. Instead, high performance extruded polystyrene board insulation can provide an insulated storage deck in your loft. Cover with chipboard loft boards to protect from wear and tear.

Laying board insulation

This rigid polystyrene board insulation is designed to fit over joists with 100mm loft roll or blanket insulation between the joists underneath. With a double layer of this board insulation on top, you will have the same 'R' value as a 270mm double layer of blanket insulation. Your storage area should be directly accessible from the loft hatch, and should also give access to a water tank if you have one. If installing blanket installation in the remainder of the space, lay board insulation in your storage area before hiding the surrounding joists with a second layer of blanket insulation.

Make sure blanket insulation is installed between and flush with the top of the joists. Loose lay the board insulation across the joists. Each 1200mm board should typically fit across three joists. If you have downlights, install heat diffusers (see page 337) and cut a hole in the board insulation to accommodate them.

Boards can be cut to size using a handsaw. Mark a straight line using a marker pen and straightedge. If cutting the boards in the loft, be very careful not to cut through any pipes or loose cables.

Mark the joist centres on the boards with a marker pen.

Join up the joist centre marks with a straightedge.

Loose lay a second layer of board insulation in same way, at 90° to the first layer. Transpose the joist centre lines onto the second layer. If you have any downlights, cut the board insulation around them following the manufacturer's recommended guidelines.

Lay chipboard on top of the board insulation and secure it to the joists along every joist centre for a firm fixing. Drill small pilot holes through the chipboard flooring in line with the joist centre marks at each corner and in the centre of each long edge. Screw through the chipboard and both thicknesses of board insulation into the joist using 150mm screws.

Once the storage area is complete, lay blanket insulation over the joists across the rest of the loft to a combined thickness of 270mm.

Lagging pipes

Lagging pipes is simple with split foam tubes. Lag cold water pipes in the loft to prevent them freezing and lag any exposed hot water pipes running through unheated areas of the house to retain their heat.

Open a split foam tube and slide it onto the pipe. If you have pipes coming up through the loft floor or running along the joists, fold back the loft insulation, fit the pipe tube and then put the insulation back in place.

If you have a stopcock or tee joint, the simplest way to insulate it is make a cut to one side of it, then make a horizontal cut so the foam tube can wrap around the object.

Continue insulating the whole length of the pipe run. When you come to a bend in a pipe, cut a 45° mitre join in the foam tube using a small mitre block and small saw.

Cut and place a small length of pipe tube over the tap handle and cover it with tape to hold it in place.

Tape the join using heatproof aluminium tape.

Carry on lagging all the pipes. If the pipes run across a joist, lag them before covering them with a second layer of insulation.

project essentials

- **small saw**
- **mitre block**
- **tape measure**
- **protective gloves**
- **knife**
- **scissors**

- split foam tubes
- heatproof aluminium tape

B&Q Making it easier

Foil rafter insulation
To top up your insulation, or prevent the temperature in a loft storage space dropping too low in winter, a quick and easy option is to fit insulating thermal foil to the rafters. Wear safety goggles and a dust mask for protection against dust.

It will be easier if you get someone to help unroll the foil. Staple it to the rafters with a staple gun.

Each row should be butt-joined. Tape each join with aluminium joining tape.

Rafter panel insulation

Expanded polystyrene panels fitted in the rafters are a very easy way to add top-up insulation. They are easy to cut with a small saw and are fitted by simply squeezing them between the rafters. Protect yourself from falling dust and debris with safety goggles and a dust mask.

Rafter insulation needs a 50mm air gap between the insulation and the roof felt. Attach 50mm battens in line with the top edge of the rafters using screws.

The rafter panels have pre-formed grooves so they can be bent and slotted in between the rafters. They stay in place without the need for extra fixing.

Cover the whole area leaving a 25mm gap along the bottom, at the eaves.

project essentials

- **tape measure**
- **power drill with twist bits**
- **small saw**
- **pencil or marker pen**
- **safety goggles**
- **dust mask**

- 50mm timber battens
- 40mm wood screws
- expanded polystyrene insulation panels

INSULATION AROUND THE HOME

The average uninsulated house loses about 35% of its heat through the walls, 25% through the roof, 25% through draughty doors and windows, and 15% through the floor. Fixes such as draughtproofing windows and doors are simple, cheap and quick. Others, such as insulating walls, are more expensive but worth it in the long run. You can also use acoustic insulation to soundproof your home if you are troubled by noise from traffic or neighbours.

Secondary, double and triple glazing

Adding a second sheet of glass or plastic to a window traps a layer of air, which acts as an insulator and also reduces draughts, condensation and noise. It doesn't have a dramatic effect on overall heat loss – only about 5% – but does make rooms warmer and quieter near the windows.

With secondary glazing, a frame containing a pane of glass (or plastic) is fixed over the existing window frame, leaving an air gap between. Simple secondary glazing kits, usually made from aluminium and plastic, are available in a range of sizes.

Sealed double and triple glazing consists of two or three panes separated by spacing strips, bonded together and hermetically sealed at the factory before being fitted into the window frame. Inert gases that give extra sound and heat insulation may be sealed inside the gap.

Secondary glazing

Double glazing

Triple glazing

Insulating walls

Insulating walls to reduce heat loss is a bigger, more expensive job than insulating the roof. Newer houses may have had insulating panels inserted between their cavity walls as they were built. This is less likely in older properties. Cavity walls can be insulated – the insulating material is blown through holes drilled in the outside wall – but this is a job for a professional.

You can insulate solid walls by dry-lining them, that is, by adding an extra layer of plasterboard to their inner faces. Plasterboard with thermal and acoustic properties is available for this purpose (see page 369). It is up to 50mm thick, so you will reduce your room space by this amount. The plasterboard is simply cut to size and glued or screwed to the existing wall. You may have to move and reinstall electrical wiring, sockets and switches, radiators, doors and windows.

Lagging cylinders, tanks and pipes

It is well worth lagging your hot-water cylinder by fitting it with a jacket made from mineral-fibre insulation. If you are buying a new cylinder, choose one with foam insulation already fitted. Lag cold water pipes in the loft and any exposed hot-water pipes running through unheated areas of the house with split foam tubes. You should also insulate the cold-water cistern and the small feed-and-expansion tank (if you have one). The cistern can be wrapped in a purpose-made jacket or a glass-fibre blanket. But don't insulate the area underneath it – any heat rising from the room below will help to prevent the tank from freezing.

Hot water cylinder with insulating jacket

Cold water cistern

Feed-and-expansion tank

Foam lagging on cold water pipes

Insulating floors

In new houses the floors have to be insulated. With existing uninsulated floors, a good-quality carpet combined with underlay is often sufficient to minimise downward heat loss. Gaps below skirtings can be filled with flexible sealant or covered with wooden beading pinned to the skirting. Alternatively, the floorboards of a suspended floor can be lifted and blanket or sheet insulation laid between the joists. If you have a concrete floor, an insulated suspended floor can be built on top of it. See pages 30–31.

ONE PLANET HOME®

Draught excluders for windows and doors

Brush strip
This strip of flexible bristles screws onto the bottom of a door to keep draughts out.

E profile seal
Made from long-lasting rubber, this draught excluder for doors and windows fills gaps of 1.5–3mm. Its self-adhesive backing makes it easy to fit.

Sliding seal
This hard-wearing polypropylene brush pile draught excluder for doors and windows has a self-adhesive backing and fills gaps of 1.5–4mm.

Foam seal
Foam seal expands to fill gaps of 1–5mm, so is ideal for variable gaps around windows and doors. It has self-adhesive backing.

Compression door seal
Heavy-duty draught excluder threshold bar with a low profile that allows easy access for prams and wheelchairs.

Draughtproofing windows

Fitting draught excluders to all gaps around doors and windows will keep warm air in and cold air out, making your home warmer and reducing fuel bills. Self-adhesive foam strips of draught excluder are inexpensive, easy to fix in place and suitable for casement windows and interior doors. Make sure you don't stretch the strips when fitting them as this impairs their efficiency.

1 Clean off all dirt and any loose paint from the window frame, using a damp cloth.

2 When the frame is dry, peel off the backing paper from the self-adhesive foam draught excluder a little at a time. Press it on to the outside of the window frame where the opening casement window will press against it when closed. Cut the ends of each length at a 45° angle to form a neat join at each corner. Close the window to press the strip firmly in place.

Draughtproofing external doors

For external doors there are different coloured draught excluders to fit to the door or on the floor in the threshold, as well as strips and seals for the door frame (see opposite). For extra insulation, you can also fit a letterbox cover and a key hole cover that drops a metal disc over the hole.

1 Fit a brush strip across the bottom of the door on the inside using the screws provided.

2 Screw a letterbox cover over the inside opening of the letterbox.

Draughtproofing internal doors

Draughtproof internal doors to unheated rooms by fitting a brush strip to the bottom of the door and a self-adhesive foam seal strip all the way round the door frame. Draught excluders come in various sizes for different-sized gaps. If you are not sure about the size of the gap, squash a small piece of reusable tack into the door frame and shut the door. Open it again, remove the tack and measure it.

1 Clean off all dirt and any loose paint on the door frame rebate using a damp cloth. When the frame is dry, apply self-adhesive foam draught excluder all the way around the edge in the same way as for a window and cut it to the correct length with scissors.

2 Make sure you attach the strip to the frame rather than the door stop, or it will be rubbed off when the door closes.

Sound insulation

Noise from neighbours can be a problem, especially in modern buildings and in properties converted to flats. There are various ways you can soundproof your home.

Soundproofing doors, windows and walls

A draughtproof exterior door and secondary or double glazing in entrance-hall windows will reduce noise levels. The joints between exterior and interior door frames and the masonry can be sealed with decorator's caulk. Lightweight interior doors can be replaced with heavier ones. Fitting double glazing is the best way of soundproofing windows.

A party wall can be soundproofed by fitting a detached insulated lining, rather like a stud partition wall, directly in front of it. The gap between the lining and the party wall is filled with acoustic insulation and then the lining is clad with acoustic-check plasterboard (see page 369). This does reduce the space a little, but is effective.

Soundproofing floors and ceilings

A floor covering may not deaden the noise between the floors of a house, which can be a particular problem in properties converted into flats. Mineral-fibre insulating blanket can be laid under a suspended wooden floor to help deaden the sound.

A ceiling can be soundproofed either by adding a suspended grid-like ceiling of acoustic panels or by building a suspended ceiling from a timber frame of joists and battens with acoustic-check plasterboard fixed to it.

DAMP PREVENTION AND TREATMENT

Don't ignore damp: it can do serious damage to the structure of your house. Lots of different factors can cause it, however, and you need to find out what they are before you try to cure it, or you may treat the wrong thing and make the situation worse. Remedies that involve opening up external cavity walls or fitting a new damp-proof course should be left to the professionals. If your home is in an area prone to flooding, there are a number of precautionary measures you can take to protect it.

Diagnosing damp

There are three main kinds of damp: penetrating damp, rising damp and condensation. If you're not sure which kind you have, check the symptoms against the chart opposite and gauge moisture levels using an electronic moisture meter.

Penetrating damp ▸

Penetrating damp is caused by water seeping through the walls at any point (as opposed to rising damp, which is confined to the lower part of ground-floor walls). Damp patches may be visible when strong winds drive rain against the house wall and disappear when the weather improves. A semi-permanent damp patch may be caused by a leaking gutter or a crack in the render; if a whole wall is showing signs of damp, it may mean that old bricks have lost their weatherproof facings and become porous.

Penetrating damp is less likely to affect houses with cavity walls. If water does cross the cavity, it is usually because mortar has spread onto a wall tie.

Rising damp ▸

Rising damp is confined to the lower part of walls – up to a height of about 1m – and to solid floors, and is caused by water soaking up from the ground. Modern houses are protected by a waterproof barrier built into the walls 150mm above the ground (the damp-proof course) and another laid under concrete floors (the damp-proof membrane).

Water from the ground will be drawn up into the structure of the house through any gap or breach in the damp-proof barrier. This can happen if the plastic membrane under the floor is torn by sharp stones, for instance. Very old houses built without damp-proof barriers frequently suffer from rising damp. The problem is aggravated by wet weather, but even in summer it never completely dries out, and you may require professional help to determine the cause and remedy it.

Condensation

The warmth of a house causes moisture to evaporate into the air. If windows and doors are always kept shut, fresh air is unable to replace this water-laden air. When humid air comes into contact with a cold surface, it cools and condenses, depositing droplets of water. In cold weather the temperature of the external walls and windows is lower than the air indoors, so moisture condenses and runs down window panes and into the wallpaper and plaster.

Damp in a modern house in good condition is nearly always due to condensation. To reduce condensation, you can extract the moist air with an extractor fan, reduce the moisture in the air by improving ventilation, and add double glazing and insulation so that the inner surfaces of walls and windows don't get so cold.

Flood prevention

More and more houses are prone to flooding as the frequency of severe wet weather appears to be increasing and because many homes have been built on flood plains. Apart from keeping your flood insurance up to date, there are several practical measures you can take.

- Check for and fix any leaks in walls, floors, windows or foundations.
- Keep gutters and downpipes free of leaves and debris. If surface-water doesn't drain freely, get a drainage specialist to check for blockages.

- Make sure that the outside ground surface slopes away from the house walls, and choose porous surfaces next to the house, that will allow rainwater to soak into the ground, rather than concrete.
- If you suffer from repeated flooding, your insurance company or drainage specialist will advise on installing a pump to redirect the water.

In the event of a flood, turn off gas and electricity supplies straight away. Keep sandbags or heavy boards to hand with which to block doorways and airbricks. Store the numbers for the emergency services and your insurance company in a safe, accessible place, along with a torch.

Symptom	Likely cause	Treatment
Penetrating damp		
Damp patches on the ceiling around the chimney breast.	The flashing sealing the joint between the chimney stack and roof (see page 189) may have cracked or become dislodged, allowing water through the joint.	Refit loose flashing; replace damaged flashing with the same type of flashing or with a self-adhesive flashing strip.
Damp patch or mould forming at the top of an upstairs wall.	Blocked or broken gutters will send water gushing down the wall and possibly saturate it.	Clear gutters or repair damaged ones (see pages 170–73).
Damp patch appears on upstairs ceiling when there is heavy rain.	A slipped, broken or missing roof tile or slate will allow water through the roof.	Replace the tile or slate (see pages 192–93).
The inner side of an external wall shows signs of widespread damp, which spreads even further in wet weather.	Old bricks can become porous and allow water though the wall.	Replace bricks or repoint and treat the area with exterior silicone water-repellent fluid (see page 177).
An isolated damp patch on an inner wall.	Cracks in brickwork or damaged pointing in the joints will allow water through the wall.	Replace damaged bricks and fill any gaps in the mortar (see page 177).
Damp patch appears on the inner wall of a cavity wall after heavy rain.	If the brickwork is not causing the problem, mortar on a wall tie in the cavity could be bridging the gap and allowing water to cross to the inner wall.	The only way to solve this is to remove some bricks, inspect the cavity and rake out or chip off any mortar on the wall ties.
Damp patches around windows.	Mortar may have fallen out of the gap between the wall and the window frame.	Seal any gaps with flexible frame sealant.
Damp patch along the underside of the window frame.	The exterior window sill should have a drip groove on the underside to stop rainwater running under the sill and into the wall. If the groove is filled with layers of paint, water can run on to the wall.	Clear the groove; if there is no groove, glue and nail a hardwood strip (about 6mm square) to the underside of a wooden sill about 35mm from the front edge to stop water reaching the wall. Paint it to match the sill.
Signs of rot at the base of an external door, or damp patches on the floor just inside the door.	A door in an exposed position is more weatherproof if it is fitted with a weatherboard (see page 179).	Repair any rotten parts of the wood and if necessary fit a weatherboard.
Rising damp		
Damp rising to about 1m up the wall.	If it is an old house, there may not be a damp-proof course or it may be damaged.	Repair or install a damp-proof course: call in a professional.
Damp concrete floor.	If there is no damp-proof course, a house is unlikely to have a damp-proof membrane under the floor. If there is a membrane, it may be damaged.	Paint the floor with two coats of bitumen latex waterproofing emulsion. For added protection, lay reflective foil building paper, foil side up, on the second coat before it has completely dried.
Widespread damp at skirting level.	The problem could be caused by render on the outside wall extending below the level of the damp-proof course.	Hack off render to a level just above the damp-proof course.
Damp at skirting level where there is a raised path beside the outside wall.	The damp-proof course should be 150mm above ground level. If it is closer than this – where a raised path has been built, for instance – water can splash above the damp-proof course and soak into the wall.	The ground outside needs to be lowered; re-lay the path; or dig a channel about 150mm wide between the wall and the path then fill it with gravel to aid drainage.
Damp spreading from the skirting level where earth has been heaped up against an outside wall.	Earth against a wall will breach the damp-proof course, allowing water to seep through.	Remove the earth and let the wall dry out.
Condensation		
Pools of water at the bottom of the windows or condensation on the glass.	The windows get colder than other parts of the room because they are thinner than the walls, so condensation will form on the glass first.	If better ventilation (see page 345) doesn't help, double-glaze the windows (see page 340).
General condensation in a room in winter.	This can happen if a room gets too cold and the air cannot absorb the moisture.	Turn up the heating so the air can absorb more moisture, and increase ventilation so the damp air can escape.
Widespread damp or mould on upstairs walls and ceilings.	Lack of loft insulation.	Install loft insulation (see pages 334–39) and apply fungicidal paint, which will prevent mildew.
Damp on the chimney breast of a sealed fireplace.	A sealed-off fireplace should always be ventilated or air will not be able to circulate inside the flue (see page 140); instead moisture in it will condense and saturate the brickwork.	Remove any wall covering on the chimney breast, make sure the wall is clean and sound, and fit an airbrick just above the skirting level. Then apply two coats of a damp-proofing liquid suitable for inside walls. Redecorate when the area has completely dried out.
Water dripping from cold-water pipes that are not leaking or damp patch on a wall or ceiling along the line of pipes.	Unlagged cold-water pipes in cold areas such as the loft can suffer from condensation.	Insulate the pipes with split-foam lagging tubes.
Mould on the timbers in the roof space.	If there is no ventilation to let air circulate around the roof space, condensation will form and, in time, lead to damp and mould problems.	Clear any blocked air vents. If there is no ventilation, fit soffit vents or tile or slate vents (see page 344).

VENTILATION FITTING VENTS AND FANS

Installing ventilation in parts of the house without windows can prevent serious problems developing in the future. Condensation in an unventilated roof space, for example, can cause timbers to become damp and develop wet rot, and insulating material to become wet and useless. This in turn can lead electrical wiring to short-circuit. Steam in bathrooms and kitchens can also lead to damp if the ventilation is poor; in these cases, fitting an extractor fan is an effective way to reduce condensation.

Ventilation in the roof space

The simplest method of ventilating a standard pitched roof is to fit plastic vents in the soffit board. If the roof insulation is likely to block the passage of air from soffit vents, eaves vents can be fitted between the rafters and joists to make a passageway for the air.

When there is an attic room with a sloping ceiling, tile or slate vents may be fitted near the ridge, and ridge vents can be fitted on the ridge itself, so they draw air over the ceiling in the roof space. Tile or slate vents may also be fitted where a solid wall, such as a party wall, is built across the loft space, stopping air flowing from the eaves on one side of the house to the eaves on the other side.

If a flat roof – on an extension, for example – is insulated, vents called over-fascia ventilators can be fitted at the eaves and where the roof meets the house's external wall (see page 191).

Soffit board

Air vent

Slate vent

Tile vent

Ventilation under the ground floor

The external walls of a house contain airbricks to ventilate the space below suspended wooden floors. With a cavity wall, an airbrick is built into each side of the wall and a telescopic sleeve bridges the cavity between them.

Airbricks should never be blocked; check them regularly for leaves and other debris. Replace a broken airbrick immediately to prevent mice gaining access to the area under the floor.

Types of airbrick

Ground-level airbrick below level of a suspended floor

Airbrick with telescopic sleeve through cavity wall

Extractor fans

There are two main types of extractor fan: axial fans, which can be fitted in an exterior wall or in a window, and centrifugal fans, which are usually ceiling mounted. They may be operated by a pull-cord or a pull-switch in a separate location; some can be wired to the light switch and will switch on with the light and stay on for a timed period after the light is switched off; others come on when the humidity in the room reaches a certain level. Modifications to any electrical circuit must comply with the latest IEE Wiring Regulations: see SAFE ELECTRICS, right. It is advisable to get an electrician to run the cable and make the final connections for you.

Different rooms need different rates of air flow so choose a fan that is suitable for the room where you want to install it. If there is a boiler in the room there must be sufficient ventilation for it when the fan is on.

Ceiling mounting

Wall mounting

project essentials

- **pipe and cable detector**
- **dust mask**
- **ear defenders**
- **heavy-duty gloves**
- **safety googles**
- **stepladder**
- **pencil**
- **heavy-duty hammer drill**
- **holesaw**
- **screwdriver or drill driver**
- **small saw**

- extractor fan kit
- flexible hose or ducting
- exterior filler
- exterior wall grille

Fitting an extractor fan

A wall-mounted fan should be positioned as high as possible on the wall, preferably opposite a door that can supply fresh air to replace the air extracted when the fan is running. In a kitchen the best place for a fan is close to the cooker to prevent steam being drawn across the room. Rigid ducting is suitable for a wall-mounted fan if the outer hole is directly in line with the inner hole; in other cases, use flexible hose.

1 Mark the fan position and use a pipe and cable detector to check for hidden pipes and cables. Check no pipes on the outside wall will block the fan, and that the outlet is not directly below a window. Wearing ear defenders, dust mask and heavy-duty gloves, use a power holesaw to drill though the wall. Angle the drill slightly upwards towards the inside.

2 If necessary, cut the ducting to length with a small saw, then screw the fan body to the ducting.

3 Push the fan and ducting into the hole, making sure the electrical cable is threaded through according to the manufacturer's instructions.

4 Mark and drill fixing holes, then screw the fan in place. Remove the central safety cover in order to expose the electrical connections. It is advisable to get an electrician to make the final connections for you, in accordance with the manufacturer's instructions.

5 Fit the internal grille cover, with slats parallel to the ceiling.

6 Make good the outside wall with exterior filler. Fit the external grille.

safe electrics

- Never take risks with electrical safety. Before you start any kind of electrical work, see page 268.
- If you plan to make changes to a lighting or power circuit in a bathroom or kitchen, you must inform your local authority's Building Control Department first.
- Modifications to any circuit must comply with the latest IEE Wiring Regulations. New or replacement cables may require RCD protection (see page 268).
- The IEE Wiring Regulations divide a bathroom into hazard zones (see page 283). Choose a fan that is suitable for the zone where you want to position it.

The
basics

FIRE SAFETY BE PREPARED

Every home contains potential sources of fire – such as cookers, electrical equipment or candles – so it makes sense to be fire aware, to fit smoke alarms and to keep fire-fighting equipment to hand. Check your equipment regularly to make sure it is working; test the battery of a smoke alarm weekly, and be sure that your extinguisher is charged and hasn't passed its use-by date.

Smoke alarms

Fumes produced by a smouldering fire can kill you without you even waking up. This is where smoke alarms offer vital protection, giving early warning of trouble. They are very reasonably priced, but remember to check that your device carries the British Standard kitemark.

The more alarms you have around your home, the safer you will be. If you live on one level, fit a smoke alarm in the hallway between the living and sleeping areas. This will allow you to hear it throughout your home, particularly when you're asleep. The ideal site for a smoke alarm is on the ceiling, at least 300mm away from a wall or light fitting. On a wall the alarm must be 150mm–300mm below the ceiling. It is pointless installing an alarm in a kitchen or bathroom, as steam will set it off. If your house has more than one storey, fit one alarm at the bottom of the staircase and further alarms on each stair landing.

There are two types of smoke alarm. An ionisation alarm is very sensitive to particles of smoke from a fast-raging fire. Photoelectric alarms are good for detecting the large quantities of smoke given off by smouldering or slow-burning fires. Also described as 'toast proof', they are less sensitive to everyday cooking fumes, and so nuisance triggering is less of a problem.

Most of the less expensive alarms are battery powered, so it's important to check the batteries regularly. Better still, choose an alarm with a 10-year lithium battery. You can also buy mains-powered smoke alarms that are wired permanently to the household electricity supply.

Ionisation smoke alarm

Photoelectric 'toast proof' smoke alarm

The 10 commandments of fire safety

- Teach your family all the dangers of fire, and practise your fire-escape plan thoroughly.

- Fit a smoke alarm on each level of your home. Test the batteries regularly, and always replace a dead battery immediately.

- Be prepared: install an all-purpose fire extinguisher in a prominent position, and a fire blanket close to (but not over) the hob.

- Unless a fire is very small and can be put out with a domestic fire extinguisher, do not tackle it yourself.

- Unplug all electrical appliances before going to bed, and keep them correctly maintained: no electrical flexes under carpets!

- Never leave a chip pan unattended. If a chip-pan fire starts, contain it by turning off the heat source then covering the pan with a damp cloth or fire blanket. Leave it there for at least 30 minutes while the heat subsides.

- Keep matches, lighters and candles out of sight and out of the reach of children.

- Do not plug electric blankets into multi-adaptors, or you risk switching them on accidentally.

- Never dry clothes or materials by the fire.

- In the event of a fire, get everyone out, shutting all doors behind you, and call the Fire Brigade.

No fire, no smell – but beware!

Carbon monoxide is a colourless, tasteless, odourless gas produced whenever a fossil fuel is not burned efficiently. It can be emitted from inadequately maintained or badly fitted domestic heating appliances, such as wall heaters, fires and boilers. Carbon monoxide cannot escape from your home if the flue or chimney has a blockage, and it is well known that it can be fatal in high concentrations. Official figures indicate that in the UK over 50 people a year die from exposure to this dangerous poison within their own home. The symptoms of exposure often mimic many other common ailments, and so are easily misdiagnosed as flu, headache, fatigue or food poisoning.

Your best protection is to install a domestic carbon monoxide or combined smoke and carbon monoxide alarm that carries the British Standard kitemark, and test it regularly. Coal-burning and natural gas appliances should have their flues and chimneys swept regularly to ensure that blockages are identified and cleared. You should also have all your fuel-burning appliances serviced by a qualified installer every 12 months. Ensure there is adequate ventilation in each room. Air vents should be kept clear and never wallpapered over.

Fire extinguishers

Fire extinguishers over 1kg must comply with European Standard BS EN3. Extinguishers have all-red bodies with a band of colour to indicate the contents. You should make yourself aware of the different colours used for the different types of fire – see below.

Using an extinguisher safely

Before tackling even the smallest fire, ensure that everyone has been evacuated and the alarm has been raised. Take up a position where access to the fire is unrestricted, but where a quick and safe retreat is possible. Crouching will help you keep clear of smoke, avoid heat and allow a closer approach to the fire. Always ensure that a fire is completely extinguished and not liable to re-ignite or continue smouldering.

Do not continue to fight a fire if:

- It's dangerous to do so
- Your escape route may be cut off by fire or smoke
- The fire continues to grow despite your effort
- There are gas cylinders threatened by fire

As you withdraw from the scene, close windows and doors behind you whenever possible.

Do not use an extinguisher to put out burning gas. Turn off the gas supply, if it is safe to do so, and call the Fire Brigade.

Water (red body)

Ideal for freely burning materials, such as paper, cloth and wood. Some contain water plus a special fire-inhibitor that prevents materials burning. These extinguishers are not suitable for flammable liquids or fires involving electrical appliances.

Foam (red body with yellow band)

Multi-purpose foam extinguishers are suitable for fires involving freely burning materials such as paper, cloth and wood, plus most flammable liquids.

Powder (red body with blue band)

Suitable for flammable liquids and electrical apparatus and most freely burning materials. But remember that powder smothers rather than cools the flames, so a fire may re-ignite.

Carbon dioxide (red body with black band)

For fires involving flammable liquids or electrical equipment like computers, photocopiers or generators. Not to be used in confined spaces where the fumes could be inhaled.

B&Q Making it easier

Fire ladder

For peace of mind, consider keeping compact escape ladders in your upstairs bedrooms. These can be stored in a roll that fits under the average bed. Escape ladders are lightweight but strong, flame-resistant, and easy to use, and are available in different lengths.

Fire blankets

A fire blanket is the simplest and safest way to extinguish a cooking-oil fire. Turn off the heat source, hold the blanket so that your hands are protected behind it, then drape it over the pan. Flames will be smothered immediately, but you mustn't remove the blanket for at least 30 minutes to allow the heat to decrease. Never pick up a blazing pan and run outside with it; flames blowing back could make you drop the pan and you could get burned.

Most modern fire blankets are made of woven glass; some are coated to ensure oils and fats can't penetrate. If someone's clothes are on fire, wrap a fire blanket around them to smother the flames.

HOME SECURITY DETERRING BURGLARS

We all want to keep our homes, our valuables and our families safe from loss and harm, yet few would want to live in a fortress. Happily there are low-cost and easy-to-fit security devices that will significantly reduce the risk of burglary. These, combined with sensible precautions, will make your home more difficult to break into. Consult your local Crime Prevention Officer via your local police station for further advice and information.

How secure is your home?

Alarms

One of the most effective burglar deterrents is an intruder alarm system with a bell box and strobe light at the front of the house. See page 353 for advice on the types of systems available.

Side gates

Secure a side gate with strong bolts and locks and make sure it is difficult to vault over.

Doors

A front door should be fitted with a mortise lock that carries the British Standard kitemark, rack bolts top and bottom, a viewer and door chain (see pages 352–53). Fit a light in the porch or by the front door. If you live in an apartment, consider fitting an internal entrance door with a bolting system that secures the door to the frame on all four sides.

In fact burglars generally prefer to break and enter through side or back doors, where they are less likely to be seen. Security lighting will deter them – whether operated manually, automatically or on a time switch – but make sure it does not irritate your neighbours. Back doors should be secured with mortise locks and bolts.

Check with your insurance company – they may stipulate that particular kinds of locks must be fitted on exterior doors. Don't leave keys in the lock or on view, especially not lying around in the hall where they could be reached with a long implement inserted through the letterbox.

Windows and glass

Fit window locks to all frames – particularly if they are easy to access. Laminated glass or double glazing are more difficult to break through quietly. Make sure your putty or glazing beads are in good order so that a pane of glass cannot be easily removed. Metal grilles and rolldown shutters are good, if conspicuous, deterrents.

French windows

Each closing door should be fitted with locking bolts top and bottom. Make certain that sliding doors cannot be sprung or lifted off their runners.

Attics and skylights

If you live in a terrace or semi-detached house with a common loft, you are at risk from burglars breaking in from between houses and down through loft hatches or skylight windows. Fit bolts to your loft trap door and suitable skylight locks.

Understanding burglars

The last thing any common burglar wants is to find the house occupied. Most burglars will make themselves familiar with your routine before attempting to break in. Early-to-mid afternoon is the favourite time for break-ins; night-time burglaries are comparatively rare. Burglars like to get in and out as quickly as possible, so anything that delays them, such as locks and bolts, will be a deterrent. They will also be put off by alarm systems and tend to avoid houses with barking dogs.

Once inside the house, they will head for the master bedroom first to look for personal possessions, such as jewellery. Your living rooms will be next, where they will seek out electronic and camera equipment.

If you surprise a burglar in your house, never confront him – just let him go. Don't risk your personal safety for the sake of a few possessions.

Garages and outbuildings

Garden machinery is attractive to thieves. Lock sheds securely with a robust hasp and padlock – but even so, remember that a shed is a lightweight construction and can be broken into with ease.

Tools

Any tools and equipment left lying around may be useful for breaking and entering, particularly a ladder. Lock away all tools and chain a ladder to a wall fixing.

Hedges and fences

Don't forget that if you create privacy with a solid wall, tall hedge or fence, you also provide cover for a burglar to work in peace.

Neighbourhood Watch

Active community awareness and cooperation does reduce local crime. Consider joining or setting up a Neighbourhood Watch scheme.

Taking sensible precautions

When you are going on holiday:

- Cancel milk and newspaper deliveries and ask the post office to hold mail for you.
- Buy timed light fittings that switch on and off automatically, making it look as though someone is at home.
- Driveway empty? It would be better to park a friend's or neighbour's car there.
- Portable valuables may be best transferred to your bank or safety deposit centre, or install your own safe.
- Tell a neighbour that you are away.
- Ask a friend or neighbour to visit from time to time to change the appearance of the home, for instance by opening or closing curtains or fitting time-switches to different lamps.

Marking and cataloguing

Write your postcode on your possessions with a UV pen, make a note of the serial and model numbers of electrical and camera equipment and keep a photographic record of jewellery and other valuables.

Doors are a burglar's favourite entry and exit point, so it's important to make sure that yours are fitted with good-quality locks and security devices. Windows are also vulnerable – match the lock or locking system to the style or type of window. The new generation of alarm systems are effective and easy to fit, and can be adapted to suit your home, while intercoms and CCTV cameras are additional means of keeping intruders out.

Door locks

Mortise locks ▶

These are the most secure type of lock you can fit to any door. As the name implies, they fit in a slot called a mortise formed in the edge of the door, and shoot a hardened steel bolt into a keeper recessed in the frame when the key is turned. Make sure that any lock you buy is made to British Standard BS3621 and carries the British Standard kitemark. Versions with three, five and seven levers are available; pick one with at least five for greater security.

Mortise sashlocks ▶

A side or back door is often used during the day to allow access to the back garden from the house. The best security lock for these doors is a mortise sashlock, which combines a mortise lock and a handle-operated latch mechanism so the door can be opened and shut without the need to operate the key. The door can then be securely locked at night or whenever you leave the house.

Mortise sashlocks are left- or right-handed to suit the way the door opens, or may have a reversible latch bolt to enable the lock to fit either edge of a door.

◀ Cylinder locks

The locking mechanism of a cylinder lock is contained in a brass barrel that fits in a hole drilled through the door. On the inside there is a surface-mounted lock body fitted with a knob or lever so the door can be opened from inside without having to use a key. There is also a knob called a night latch that you can operate to prevent the latch being forced, but do remember that a night latch does not provide adequate security on its own.

Deadlock cylinder lock ▶

The most secure cylinder locks have a deadlocking facility that locks the latch securely with a key, used from inside at night and from outside when you leave the house. Again, make sure you buy a lock made to BS3621.

Patio door locks ▶

Sliding patio doors are relatively easy to force unless they have been designed with integral multi-point locking and anti-lift devices. Many older doors do not have these features, so it's wise to add a pair of key-operated surface-mounted locks to each sliding door, installed either at each side of the door or at the top and bottom. The lock body is screwed to the door frame or sill, and the bolt engages in a hole drilled in the door itself.

Bolts ▲

You can improve the security of any door by adding bolts, either surface-mounted bolts or concealed mortise rack bolts (above), which fit in a hole drilled in the door edge and are operated by a special key.

◀ Door chains

To restrict the door opening to a few inches, fit a door chain; this will prevent a caller from forcing entry as you open the door.

Hinge bolts ▸

These are fixed steel pegs that fit into holes drilled in the hinge edge of the door and engage in holes drilled in the door frame as the door closes. They prevent the hinged edge of the door from being forced.

Window locks

The type and positioning of suitable locks depends on the type of window.

Casement windows ▸

Casement windows may have locking catches or stays, or you can fit special locks or rack bolts to secure the casement to the frame.

Alarm systems

There are several choices when it comes to installing security alarms in your home. Infrared movement detectors known as PIRs fitted high up in the corner of each room will activate the alarm if they sense a door opening or an intruder walking across the room. Magnetic contact detectors installed on doors or windows trigger the alarm if the magnetic plates are disturbed. Most alarm systems use a combination of these elements with an interior control panel and an exterior casing containing the bell or siren.

CCTV and intercoms

CCTV cameras

No criminal wants to be captured on camera, so cameras are an extremely effective deterrent to intruders. An automatic system can be connected to your home video or DVD player. When the PIR sensors positioned around the perimeter of the property detect a visitor or intruder, the CCTV cameras are activated and begin recording.

Door viewers ▸

You can fit this small lens in a hole drilled through a solid front door, to allow you to see who the caller is before you open the door.

Sash windows ▸

Secure the sashes to each other with dual screws that clamp the rails together, or surface-mounted rail locks. Sash stops permit ventilation but prevent the window from being opened wide.

Wirefree or wired?

Wirefree alarms are much easier to install than wired alarms, but you will have to change the batteries from time to time. You can add as many PIR sensors or magnetic contact detectors as you wish to wirefree systems, while there are limits to the number of accessories that can be added to a wired system. All the components of wired alarms need to be linked and the control panel needs an electricity supply. It is possible to have wired alarms monitored by a security company, who will alert the police if they go off.

Zones

Some alarm systems allow you to isolate different zones in the house. For example, at night you can turn on the alarm downstairs but leave it off upstairs so you don't set it off on trips to the bathroom. If you have a cat or dog, you might choose to leave one room free of movement detectors, where your pet can be left when the alarm system is switched on.

2-way intercom

Built-in speakers and microphones allow you to check who is at the gate or front door before you let them in. Some systems incorporate security cameras so that you can see as well as hear your caller.

SAFE HOME IMPROVEMENTS

Plan ahead

Before you tackle any home improvement job, think it through from start to finish. Read all the instructions and make sure you understand them fully. Check you have all the necessary tools and materials to hand. Consider any heights or weights you will have to deal with; will you need someone else to help? How long will it take, and will a room in the house be uninhabitable while you are working there? What are the possible consequences of the work you are planning? If you are in any doubt whatsoever about your capabilities, call in a professional to do the whole job, or just the parts of it that you are unsure about (see pages 380–81).

 Making it easier

Seek advice

If you hit a snag in the middle of a project and can't decide how to proceed, visit B&Q's website **diy.com** – you'll find a wealth of useful advice.

When embarking on a home improvement project, we take precautions to reduce the mess and disturbance that will inevitably result. We move furniture or possessions from the work area or lay dust sheeting in the room, even though this can be a painstaking and laborious process. But how much time do we spend protecting our own well-being, or that of our families and pets? One glance at the home accident statistics makes the answer all too clear: not enough!

Be aware that home improvement projects are almost always messy, often noisy, and sometimes dangerous. Take time to assess the risks. Protect yourself and, if necessary, those around you, and consider whether your activities may be disturbing others too.

Personal safety

What to wear for the job? The uniform of most builders is a pair of worn jeans, tough boots and either a T-shirt in summer or a sweatshirt in winter. Cheap, easy to replace and comfortable, this is sensible clothing for home improvement activities too. You may be in a hurry to get started, but do pause, change into old clothes or cover up with a set of overalls, many of which come with useful pockets for small tools and sundries.

Do consider buying and wearing:

- Purpose-designed workwear. This should be reasonably close-fitting to reduce the risk of interfering with machinery.
- Sturdy 'safety' boots or shoes with toe-cap reinforcement. These will protect your feet when you are handling heavy materials, such as bricks or stone slabs, as well as plasterboard, wooden sheets or large sections of timber. Wear rubber-soled shoes when working on electrical installations.
- A tool belt is very handy for holding your most useful and easily mislaid tools, such as a tape measure and claw hammer. And it can speed up repetitive tasks such as fixing with nails or screws, since you can have all that you need right there at hand.

Do not wear:

- Loose clothing, especially big sleeves or accessories such as a tie or jewellery. These may get entangled with a power tool, or snag on a ladder or workbench.
- Anything that restricts your movement.
- Very woolly sweaters when decorating – you will be amazed how many fibres are left stuck to the surface if you do.

Always essential:

- Good lighting. Make sure you can see your work clearly; poor lighting is hazardous and tiring.
- A mobile phone is advisable whenever you are working alone, in case of an accident.
- A first-aid kit, either bought or compiled according to your own needs. Include plasters and antiseptic salve as an absolute minimum, and consider reading an approved first-aid manual too. There is a Health and Safety executive standard for workplace use: if planning heavy work, check out their recommendations first.
- Beware of fatigue. You will need to concentrate and not rush, especially when working with electricity, using power tools, or beginning any new and costly job. Take frequent breaks.

Safety of family and pets

If you are going to make a lot of noise and mess, do take into account your family and pets. Keep them well clear of wet paint or cement until it is fully dry. Seal off the work area if you can and make certain that all tools and materials are out of reach of children.

Be a good neighbour

Late-night drilling and hammering may get the job done more quickly, but could ruin your relationship with those around you. Be aware of the regulations concerning nuisance, and if in doubt about your rights, contact your local Environmental Health Department.

Asbestos in the home

The mineral asbestos was used extensively in building materials from the 1930s through to the mid-1980s, particularly from the 1960s onwards. It added rigidity and fire-resistance, and was used in materials for the home including gutters and downpipes, fire blankets, floor tiles, garage and shed roofs, linings for walls, ceilings and doors, insulation panels in some storage heaters, bath panels, central heating flues, and loose packing used between floors and in partition walls.

Undisturbed asbestos usually poses no problems. However, fibres and dust from damaged asbestos materials are potentially very dangerous if inhaled in higher concentrations over a period of time, when they can cause serious lung diseases. The symptoms of these diseases often do not appear until 20–30 years after exposure. Therefore great care must be taken to prevent the release of fibres.

Essential gear for specific tasks:

- A hard hat is absolutely essential when there is any danger of either bumping your head or from falling objects. If you find a hard hat cumbersome, get a bump cap (this looks like an oversize baseball cap), which will give some protection from a knock.
- If you are going to put down any quantity of flooring, buy a pair of good-quality knee pads. Without them, laying a floor is a painful job.
- Always protect your hearing. Even if the noise is not loud enough to damage your ears, you will find yourself becoming tired more quickly. Ear defenders will reduce the impact, but remember to be extra vigilant while wearing them.
- Wear the right gloves for the task – if exposed to liquids, protect your skin with throwaway thin rubber gloves. When doing work or handling materials that might damage your hands, wear cotton and leather reinforced gloves.
- Impact-resistant clear goggles will protect your eyes from dust and flying debris: another cheap but significant piece of safety gear.
- Protect your lungs from dust as well as from invisible fumes. There are breathing masks designed to provide different degrees and types of protection, from a simple gauze to screen out fine particles to a full facial respirator to isolate the wearer from poisonous fumes. Match the mask to the task!

Stay tidy

It is important to clean your tools and keep your work area tidy as you go along. Paint, adhesive and mortar will be much harder – and in some cases impossible – to clean off when they have dried. Sharp tools, such as saws and chisels, must be hung up after use or the edges can become blunt. Safety guards should be replaced on power tools. Anything left lying around is a potential hazard.

Be especially careful when working with toxic substances. Follow the manufacturer's instructions to the letter and never decant substances into containers that are not clearly labelled.

If you suspect asbestos may be present in your home:
- Leave it alone: asbestos is safe unless damaged or disturbed.
- Avoid creating or breathing asbestos dust. Never sand, drill or saw asbestos materials.
- Do not attempt to remove asbestos lagging, spray coatings or insulation board yourself.

Visit www.direct.gov.uk or contact your local authority, which can provide advice and carry out an inspection.

LADDERS FOR DIFFERENT TASKS

Always select the right equipment for the height and nature of the task. Stepladders and multi-purpose ladders are ideal for indoor and light outdoor jobs, reaching up to 3m. Beyond that height, it's best to use ladders and scaffold towers.

Step-ups ▶

If you need a steady platform to work just above head height, a simple step-up is a good solution; easy to handle and sturdy, some are available with a handle – ideal if you feel unsteady when raised off the floor.

Stepladders ▶

Choose a stepladder that will allow you to reach the ceiling and to the top of the ground-floor windows outside. All will have a locking mechanism to stop the two halves sliding apart – be sure to use it.

- Not sideways! Set the stepladder facing the work area, otherwise it will be unstable.
- Firm ground? If you are working outside make sure you are standing on firm, level ground. If the surface is soft, lay down a large wooden board to spread the load.
- No over-reaching! If you have to reach out or stretch, you need to move the ladder.
- Keep one hand on the guard rail and both feet on the treads while you work.
- One person at a time. Never let someone else climb on a stepladder while you are on it.
- Never, ever stand on the top platform. If you need to go higher, use a ladder or a platform.

◀ Ladders

Once you need to go beyond the reach of your trusty stepladder it is time to buy, hire or borrow a ladder. The most popular buy is an extension ladder, and in particular a pair of ladders that can be used separately, or joined together for reaching up high.

Choose a ladder to match the dimensions of your home. Allow for at least 1m above the highest point at which you expect to work. A ladder that will extend to 7–8m will probably be ideal. A double-extending ladder will measure up to 4.5m long when closed; if storage space is limited, look for a triple-extending ladder.

If you need to put your ladder on an uneven patch of ground, bolt stabilisers to the bottom on both sides to stop it rocking. It is very dangerous to rest a ladder against guttering. Hook a metal stand-off to the top of the ladder to hold it away from the wall, so its weight is not resting on the gutter.

Ladder stand-off

Stabiliser

Roof ladders ▶

A proper roof ladder is essential for even minor repair work on a roof. It has wheels on one side and hooks on the other. Standing on an ordinary ladder, you push the wheeled side of the roof ladder up the roof then turn it over and slide the hooks down onto the ridge tiles to hold it in place. Don't be tempted to walk across the tiles or slates: this will damage them, and you may slip off. For more extensive work on a roof, you must by law install proper scaffolding.

Multi-purpose stepladders and ladders ▼

Many aluminium stepladders also convert to a small extending ladder. An aluminium combination ladder can be arranged in different configurations for use as steps, a short ladder, a stairwell work platform or low-level staging, making it an ideal choice if you need access in a variety of different situations.

If you are using a combination ladder on a staircase, set the ladder in place and then, if possible, nail strips of scrap wood across the stair treads to prevent the ladder feet from slipping off the treads.

Work platforms and scaffold towers ▼

When you need access to a large area of wall or roof up to about 9m high, consider buying or hiring a tower made of lightweight alloy sections that clip together, framing a set of boards and guard rail that form a safe working area. The components, complete with lockable wheels, can be used to make a variety of mobile work platforms for inside and outside the home. Once a tower is erected, use the stabilisers to keep the structure solidly in place.

- Never build a tower beyond the specified dimensions.
- Only move a tower, once erected, when you are on completely level, solid ground. Once you remove the stabilisers the structure can become top-heavy.

Ladder safety

Ladders are one of the biggest common factors in accidents during home improvement activities. Be safe: don't add to the statistics.

Firm footing?

Always inspect the surface on which you intend to erect a ladder. If it is not level or firm, lay down a sturdy piece of board with a length of batten nailed in place to act as a stop, or find a ready-made ladder safety foot. If you can, use ladder stabilisers too; if not, drive stakes into the ground on either side of the feet and lash the ladder to these. On hard ground, lay a heavy sandbag over the bottom rung to prevent slipping. Finally – as ever – if in doubt, find a helper to stand on the bottom rung and hold on to the sides.

Get a grip and don't go too far

Climb the ladder by holding the rungs, not the ladder sides. Don't press against the ladder; climb with your arms straight and your body upright. Use the top four rungs of any ladder as handholds only.

Be safe

- Wear thick-soled flat footwear, particularly if you'll be standing on one rung for long periods, and make sure that your shoelaces are securely tied. You can fit a hook-on foot platform to save your feet. Ensure that your shoes are free of mud or grease, to prevent slipping.
- Wear a helmet and do not wear loose clothing that might be snagged on the way up or down.
- Go slow – never rush when working at height.
- Do not climb the ladder with your hands full – use a tool belt, apron or shoulder bag. Haul up materials in a bucket or on a rope.

- Don't lean sideways or backwards from the ladder. Keep your centre of gravity inside the stiles. Keep both feet on the rungs – not one foot on the wall!
- When working on gutters and underneath eaves fit a ladder stand-off or stay (see opposite) before you erect the ladder – this is clipped to the top two or three rungs. Never, ever rest a ladder against guttering.
- Don't use a ladder in high winds or when it is raining.
- Always hold on to a rung with one hand when working.
- Fit a tool tray to keep the items you need to hand.
- Use cordless power tools wherever possible.
- Never leave a ladder unattended.

Be secure

- Always store ladders and stepladders under cover, particularly if they are made of wood.
- Store stepladders standing against the wall, not suspended by a rung.
- Hang ladders horizontally on strong brackets.
- If you have to store a ladder outdoors or in view, make sure it is securely chained and padlocked to a well-fixed bracket. Don't give a leg-up to a thief!
- Never paint a wooden ladder – you may hide dangerous defects. Always use clear varnish or clear wood preservative. Be wary of buying or even borrowing a wooden ladder: the paint may be covering up potentially dangerous defects.

Modern tools and equipment allow you to complete home improvement projects more easily than ever before. Yet despite all the new technology and design, the basic principles and techniques have not changed. With these essential tools you will be able to measure, cut, fix, assemble and finish most jobs.

Maintain order

◄ Tool box

Most of us buy tools haphazardly, as and when we need them. It doesn't take long to find that you need a storage box to keep them all safely in one place. Tool boxes, bags, belts or trays make it easier to carry and protect your tools. Be particularly careful how you store cutting edges in a tool box – keep and use the plastic guards that are usually fitted to new saw and chisel blades.

Storage box ►

Every fixing requires a specific nail, clip, screw or bolt, often in combination with matching plugs, washers and nuts. If you keep them sorted in storage drawers, they will be easy to find when you need them. Many tool boxes have combination tool trays, compartments and drawers.

Hold firm

◄ Workbench

A secure working surface is essential for many tasks, and a portable workbench allows you to establish a solid platform in the house or garden. Workbenches are popular with professionals and home improvers alike.

Sawhorses ▲

A pair of lightweight plastic sawhorses will support materials while you cut them. Inexpensive and easy to store, these are a simple evolution of the carpenter's wooden sawhorse.

Clamps ►

Hold materials securely in place while you work with modern spring-loaded or ratchet clamps, whose clever design makes them incredibly easy to use. They can also be a good substitute for an extra pair of hands.

Measure and mark up

Accurate measuring is essential when working on home improvement tasks. And don't forget: always measure twice and cut once.

Retractable tape measure ▲

Buy a robust retractable tape measure – you will need it more than you might think.

Combination square ►

The combination square can be used for measuring; for marking angles of 90° or 45°; and also has a small spirit bubble for levelling and a scribe for marking.

Steel rule ►

Use a 300mm steel rule for accurate line drawing and measuring. When marking out over greater dimensions, use a wooden batten as a straightedge.

Spirit level ►

Another must-have tool is a good-quality spirit level, designed to show you a true horizontal or vertical. This is essential when lining up shelving or cabinets on a wall, for instance. Spirit levels come in all lengths and prices. For more ambitious projects, a laser level (see page 364) will also prove invaluable.

Pencils ►

Soft black pencils for marking cutting and drilling positions are one of the most useful tools of all.

Bradawl ►

The bradawl is a perfect tool for marking drilling positions on plaster, as well as for boring pilot holes in wood.

Cutting tools

Handsaw ▸

A handsaw will come in useful for many jobs. The panel saw is the most versatile, cutting sheet materials and timber well. As with all saws, the fewer teeth per inch (TPI) the more aggressive the cut, the more teeth the smoother the cut.

Hacksaw ▴

A good hacksaw will cut anything metal. It takes different blades, with different numbers of teeth per inch (TPI); for example, you might use 24 TPI to cut a thin metal sheet, 16 or 18 TPI for coarse metal.

Junior hacksaw ▴

For small-scale metal-cutting tasks, a junior hacksaw is an inexpensive and useful tool.

Grip and wrench

Combination pliers ▸

For everyday tasks such as gripping, twisting and cutting, a pair of combination pliers is invaluable.

Self-grip wrench ▸

The best general-purpose wrench, useful for basic plumbing tasks too, is the mole or self-grip wrench, which is available in different sizes.

Multi-purpose strap wrench ▸

More versatile than a standard wrench, a flexible strap wrench will grip, twist, tighten or unscrew any shape or material, without scratching.

◂ Adjustable spanner

Always keep an adjustable spanner handy, to grip nuts of all different sizes.

◂ Socket set

When securing and releasing nuts and bolts you will find a simple socket set very helpful. It includes a range of different socket sizes which can be attached to a fixed rod or ratchet. Modern sets are not expensive.

Craft knife ▸

Every tool box should include a craft knife; it can be used to cut many different materials. The simplest versions store spare blades in the handle. For safety in your tool box, buy a craft knife with a retractable blade.

Chisels ▸

A sturdy chisel with a synthetic handle that you can hit with a wooden mallet is essential for most woodworking jobs, such as fitting new door locks. Chisels need constant sharpening with a sharpening stone. Never use one to open a tin of paint!

Hit it home

There are different hammers for different jobs, but if you buy only one hammer in your life, make it a claw hammer.

Claw hammer ▸

This will drive in all but the smallest nails, hammer in wall plugs and generally knock things together and apart. Thanks to the curved claw opposite the hammer head, it will also pull out nails and can, at a pinch, be used as a small crowbar.

Cross-pein ▸

When you need to drive home lots of small nails – for instance, when securing hardboard to the floor – use a cross-pein or Warrington hammer.

Driving

Match your driver to your screw! Obvious but true – you will quickly strip the head from a screw if you use the wrong screwdriver.

Screwdrivers ▸

Manual screwdrivers have moved on from simple wooden-handled tools; the new plastic and hard rubber handles are much easier to grip. But when you have a lot of screwdriving to do, a power screwdriver or drill-driver will save you time and effort (see page 360).

Power tools are constantly being developed to be more effective and versatile than ever before – and at the same time cheaper and more reliable. This section will help you make the right purchasing decisions; visit diy.com for further information and advice.

Power drills

The most useful of all power tools is undoubtedly the drill. No other single tool can make so many tasks – particularly the repetitive ones – less of a chore. When you drill, or drive screws, you will want speed and control as well as accuracy. To help your selection, take a moment to consider your future drilling priorities:

Where will you drill?

If you buy a mains powered tool, you will also need to use an extension lead. A cordless drill will give greater mobility, although the most powerful cordless tools are more expensive than their corded equivalents. For maximum versatility, combination cordless and corded power tools are available, complete with easy-change adaptors for drilling, screwdriving, sawing and sanding.

What are you going to drill into?

Sooner or later you will almost certainly need to drill into masonry. To do this you will need a power drill with hammer action. If you wish to drill large-diameter holes in masonry, select a corded drill with a low speed gear. If you envisage drilling into a variety of materials – such as wood, plastic or metal – you should choose a drill with a multiple speed feature.

Electronic pipe and wire detector ▾

Never drill blind into a wall or floor – you might hit gas or water pipes or electrical wires. A pipe and wire detector is inexpensive and essential for making sure it is safe to drill. A triple detector will also find wood, so is extremely useful for locating studs in a partition wall.

How much power do you need?

The motors of power drills are rated in watts, typically ranging from 400 watts for basic models to around 1080 watts for the biggest hammer drills. The more powerful the motor, the faster it will drill. However, for most basic jobs, a 450–500 watt drill is adequate.

Do you want a screwdriving function?

If so, look for a drill that has variable speed or torque control and is also reversible, so that it will not only drive in but also remove screws.

Basic mains drill ▶

If all you ever want to do is to drill small holes in wood and occasionally masonry, the best choice is an inexpensive single-speed drill with hammer action. Pick one with an input power of at least 400 watts and a chuck size of 13mm – this means it will take drill bits of up to 13mm in diameter. Some of them have an old-fashioned chuck that needs to be tightened with a key, so always buy a spare key in case you lose the original.

Advanced mains drill ▲

More power means bigger drilling capacities – up to 40mm in wood, 26mm in masonry and 13mm in metal. Additional features include reverse gear and torque control, so the drill can do double duty as a power screwdriver. The most expensive models offer rotary hammer or percussion action – very useful if you do a lot of drilling into masonry.

Basic cordless drill ▶

The obvious advantage of a cordless drill is that you can take it anywhere without having to tow an extension cable behind you. The slow chuck speed, compared with mains drills, also makes it ideal for driving screws, and with a reverse gear it's easy to undo them as well. You can change drill bits by hand, but most have a maximum chuck capacity of just 10mm. Get a drill with variable speed and hammer action, allowing you to tackle masonry as well as wood and metal. A drill with a 12 volt battery is suitable for most jobs.

Advanced cordless drill ▶

As with mains drills, paying more for a cordless drill buys you a bigger chuck and more drilling capacity, as well as a longer battery life. Models with batteries up to a massive 24 volts are now available, offering drilling capacities of up to 30mm in wood, 13mm in metal and 20mm in masonry if the drill has hammer action. Many have two speed ranges and torque control that allows them to be used as power screwdrivers.

Drill bits

A range of different sizes and types of drill bit is available, and they are often designed to make specific jobs easier and safer. For best accuracy when you start to drill a hole, select a bullet-point drill bit if there is one for your task. The sharp point will allow you to position the drill exactly on the right spot.

High speed twist ▲

For wood, metal and plastics, in sizes of 1mm–13mm.

Countersink ▶

These bits are for creating a shallow circular recess in wood to ensure that the head of a flat screw is set just below the wood surface to avoid snagging.

Screwsink ▶

These are designed to allow you to drill pilot and countersink holes in one operation, without needing to change bits.

Tile and glass ▶

The sharp tip and curved spade of these bits allow you to position and cut through glass and tiles with ease.

Screwdriver ▲

For drills that also drive screws, these bits come in a range of sizes, often double-ended, like these.

Masonry ▲

Hardened with a shaped tip of tungsten carbide, these are made specifically for boring into masonry when using a hammer-action drill. Sizes range from 6mm upwards.

Flat wood or spade ▲

For boring holes larger than 13mm in wood. Available in sizes 8mm–40mm.

Hole saw ▶

For making holes larger than 40mm in wood, plastic and light metal. Hole saws are available in 35mm–152mm sizes.

Sanders and planers

When you need to remove layers of varnish, stains, paint or rust, or you want to create a fine finish over a large area, a power sander is invaluable. There are many different types available. And a power planer will make easy work of reducing and smoothing timber.

◀ Orbital and sheet sanders

Ideal for light sanding work, such as finishing. Here the abrasive paper is stretched across a foam pad. Smaller versions are known as orbital palm sanders.

Belt sanders ▶

Perfect for heavy-duty shaping, preparing and finishing on large areas of timber. The continuous abrasive paper sheet is held in position by two rollers.

Delta sanders ▶

Use a delta sander, which is shaped with a triangular base plate, to finish tight corners.

Rotary sanders ▶

A simple, inexpensive fitting for a power drill, this is suitable for small-scale tasks.

Electric hand sander ▶

A small hand sander can help you work in less accessible areas where orbital and belt sanders can't reach. It can be fitted with various grades of abrasive paper to ensure a fine finish.

Electric planer ▲

A superb tool for shaving and smoothing sawn timber, this is quick and easy to use. You adjust the depth of cut by turning a knob.

Abrasive papers

Select the appropriate type of abrasive paper for the power sander you are using and use the grade of paper recommended for the work in hand. The golden rule is to work through the grit sizes, from coarse to fine. Note that the grit specification is common to all abrasive papers: 400 grit is finer than 200 grit.

Power tools reduce your labour but they also demand respect and careful operation:

- Read and observe the safety instructions for each type of tool you use
- Always work in good light and wear clear goggles when using powered cutting tools. Wear protective gloves when using a power saw to protect you from hot blades and sharp edges.
- When using power tools outdoors, you must have RCD protection against electrocution (see page 294). This is also a very good idea when using a power saw, or any tool that could cut into an electrical cable.

There are many other power tools apart from drills and sanders that will make your home improvement work easier, quicker and more accurate. The new generation of power saws is designed and built to be more sophisticated and easier to use, and you'll find that they are very affordable as well.

Jigsaws

These are highly portable, and there are now cordless versions available too. Select the right cutting blade and a jigsaw will cut through metal, timber, plastics, laminates and ceramic tiles. They are ideal for cutting curves and awkward shapes.

B&Q Making it easier

Biscuit jointer
This powerful tool is used to create joins between two surfaces, for example between planks or boards being fixed side by side. It cuts matching pockets or biscuit slots into the underside of the planks. A wooden tab or biscuit is then glued across the slots, holding the planks securely together.

Standard jigsaw ▶

A jigsaw has a slim reciprocating blade that cuts on the upstroke as you feed it into the edge of the wood or board (except for a laminate cutting blade, which cuts on the downstroke). If you do little more than the occasional sawing job, a single-speed jigsaw with an input power of 350–400 watts is ideal. Depending on the size of blade fitted, it will cut wood up to 50mm–55mm thick, and a model with an adjustable soleplate will allow you to make bevelled cuts at angles of up to 45°.

Advanced jigsaw ▶

More money buys you a range of additional features, including more power and a faster, deeper cutting performance. You can also expect variable speed control, pendulum action and an anti-splinter device for smoother, chip-free cutting – essential if you're cutting faced boards and laminated worktops. Dust extraction is a standard feature.

▾ Reciprocating and multi-saws

These saws are good for general and rough cutting. The pointed blade comes in different lengths up to 300mm, and is ideal for cutting through solid timbers like stud partitions during demolition work. With the correct blade it can also cut through metal pipework.

Jigsaw blades ▶

There are wood-cutting jigsaw blades for coarse, medium and fine cutting – the closer the teeth, the finer the cut – and the same blades will also cut plastic. Blades for metal have much finer teeth and should also be used for cutting wood that contains nails or screws. There are special blades for cutting ceramics, glass-reinforced plastics (GRP) and laminates. Laminate blades cut only on the downstroke, allowing you to work with laminated materials the right way up without damaging the surface. The toothed section of the blade typically ranges from 50mm–105mm in length.

◀ Rotary cutter

This is a more precise cutting tool that will cut perfect circles or curves in a variety of materials, from ceramic tiles to wood and MDF. The cutting depth is adjustable.

Circular saws

The disc-shaped blade of a circular saw makes professional-quality straight cuts in man-made boards and timber. It can be used freehand, guided by a parallel guide fence, or it can be mounted in a saw table with the blade projecting upwards through a guarded slot.

Advanced circular saw ▲

More powerful saws take larger 180mm blades and will cut deeper and faster. Other features include adjustable cutting depth, a mitre and bevel facility for angled cutting, sight liner, adjustable fence guide and a vacuum cleaner attachment or dustbag.

Standard circular saw ▲

The cheapest models take blades around 150mm in diameter and have a maximum cutting depth of about 45mm. When selecting a blade for a circular saw you need to take three things into account:

- Pick the correct blade diameter for your saw.
- Select the right bore size (the diameter of the hole in the centre); this may be 12.7, 16, 20 or 30mm.
- Choose the tooth size and number to suit the job. A blade with a few large flat teeth will give a fast, coarse cut, while a blade with a larger number of alternately-offset teeth gives a medium or fine cut. Lots of small, flat, trapezoid-shaped teeth will give you the cleanest cut. All these blades have tungsten-carbide-tipped teeth for long life.

◀ Compound mitre saw

With the right blade, a power mitre saw will make clean and precise cross, mitre and bevel cuts in hard- and softwoods, plastic, alloys and non-ferrous metals. Additional features may include a laser guide for cutting accuracy, extension wings for larger materials, and dust extraction for cleaner operation.

Types of blade

Pointed tooth blade – suitable for cross-cutting solid timber, giving a reasonable finish.

Fine tooth blade – for fine cuts in chipboard and laminated board.

Ripsaw blade – rips through softwood, hardwood and man-made boards, leaving a rough-edged finish.

Chisel tooth blade – universal blade for soft- and hardwoods.

Carbide-tipped universal blade – top-quality blade, cutting with a fine finish through all materials, including laminates.

Router ▲

A router is used for accurate cutting in wood, such as shaping, edging, rebating, making grooves and decorative mouldings. This is a specialist tool, which is only essential for advanced home improvers, woodworkers, joiners and cabinet makers. But if you do a lot of wood machining, a router is for you. It will pay to take advice from an experienced user before you start, and practise first on some scrap wood. Wear a breathing mask, ear defenders and goggles or safety glasses.

Angle grinder ▲

Designed to cut and grind metal, as well as to cut stone, slabs, blocks, brickwork and concrete, an angle grinder is a powerful addition to a tool kit. Choose the right disc for the size of the grinder and for the job in hand: buy a metal cutting disc for metal, and a masonry cutting disk for masonry. Particle diamond discs are effective at cutting through blocks and brickwork. Do not cut or grind with excessive pressure, and wear heavy-duty gloves, ear defenders, a breathing mask and goggles.

Tool care

To keep tools safe and effective, they must be well looked after. All tools must be kept clean and stored in a secure place, out of reach of children. Paintbrushes and rollers should be cleaned straight after use. Cutting tools, such as saws, planes and chisels, must be sharpened regularly and stored hanging up so the blade is not blunted. Badly maintained tools can cause accidents, so don't take shortcuts with tool care.

Your general tool kit will provide most of what you need on a day to day basis, but for specific home improvement tasks you will need to purchase, hire or borrow other tools and equipment. Some tools, like a creosote paintbrush, are cheap enough to use once and throw away; others will last for a lifetime if they are properly looked after.

Building and landscape gardening

For building and outdoor projects you will need a mixture of specialist builders' tools and general-purpose gardening implements.

Cement mixer

If you are concreting or mixing mortar on a large scale, consider buying or hiring a cement mixer. Be sure to wash the drum thoroughly after use.

Wheelbarrow

For heavyweight tasks, such as moving rubble or sand, you will need a robust builder's barrow. An ordinary lightweight garden wheelbarrow is not strong enough.

Extension reel

Essential when using power tools without a nearby power point. Make sure you keep your extension reel away from water, and if the electrical load is heavy, unwind the reel so that the wires do not overheat. You must have RCD protection when using electrical devices outdoors (see page 294).

Laser level

Extremely useful when building a fence or garden wall, a laser level will accurately extend a level line over long distances.

Soft short-handled brush

A handbrush with soft bristles is perfect for finishing off mortared joints in bricks and stone.

Long bar

The long bar is good for prising, levering and also breaking up surfaces.

Tape measure: 30m

An extra-long tape measure is essential for jobs like fencing or building a garden wall.

Straightedge

Any straight piece of rigid and easy to handle timber will make a good straightedge.

Builder's line and pins

This nylon line is an essential guide for lining up and maintaining a level when building a structure of blocks or bricks.

Cold chisel

This is used for cutting through masonry. Strike it with a club hammer, and get one with a plastic safety sleeve to protect your hand from misplaced hammer blows.

Bolster chisel: 100mm

Use this to cut bricks and concrete blocks as well as for general levering.

Club hammer

Use a club hammer for small-scale demolition work, or for jobs like driving lightweight posts into the ground.

Bricklayer's trowel

Builders use 300mm-long trowels but you will find it easier to use a shorter trowel until you are more experienced.

Pointing trowel

This small-bladed trowel (between 75mm and 100mm long) is handy for repairing and shaping mortar joints in bricks.

Builder's float

For finishing concrete or applying render and plaster to walls.

Pointing hawk

This lightweight handheld platform is ideal for carrying small quantities of mortar to the wall when pointing.

Jointing tool

This is used to shape neat mortar joints in brickwork, and also to rake out old mortar ready for repointing.

Bucket

Choose a sturdy one, preferably with measurements marked inside.

Pickaxe

Break up ground with a pickaxe or long bar rather than a spade or shovel, especially if there is buried rubble and rocks.

Sledgehammer

This is the tool for smashing up hardcore or slabs, and is also good for driving in fenceposts and stakes.

Shovel

The curved edges of a shovel make it ideal for moving aggregates as well as mixing and shifting mortar or concrete.

Spade

Dig holes and trenches with a spade. Steel alloy is good, and stainless steel best.

Garden rake

A common garden tool, useful for smoothing and spreading sand and gravel into place.

Post-hole borer

Use this to make neat holes in the ground for fence and gate posts.

Electrics and wiring

Besides general building tools, electrical and lighting improvements require a few specialist electrician's tools. It is also a sensible idea to keep a group of essential electrical tools together for emergencies, and store it in an easily accessible place.

EMERGENCY KIT

- Small terminal screwdriver
- Medium-sized flat-head screwdriver
- Pliers
- Retractable-blade knife
- Torch (with fresh batteries)
- PVC insulating tape

- Replacement 3–13 amp fuses

- Replacement cartridge fuses or fuse wire

- Spare bulbs

Side cutters
The best tool for cutting cables to an exact length.

Wire strippers
Remove the insulation from cables and flex cores with a wire stripper. The jaws will accommodate most core diameters.

Long-nosed pliers
For bending, twisting and positioning cable cores. Available with insulating handles for extra safety.

Terminal screwdriver
For tightening small terminal screws only – the driver blade is too delicate for anything else.

Socket template
Useful for installing flush-mounted socket boxes. The hard plastic guide provides an easy-to-use drilling template.

Continuity/resistance/ voltage tester
Battery-powered tool for testing whether a cable is part of a continuous circuit; for measuring the resistance of a component or circuit; and for testing for AC or DC voltages.

Socket tester
A plug-in tester that confirms that a circuit is dead – and so safe to work on – and also whether a socket is wired correctly.

Voltage tester
Test that a lighting circuit is dead with a voltage meter or tester (pictured). Either way, be sure to use it properly and safely (see page 274).

Hand lamp or torch
Whenever you have to work without light or power, you will need a good battery-powered torch or lamp.

EMERGENCY KIT

Pipe repair clamp
For instant but temporary repairs to pipes, clamp this rubber-lined collar over the leak and tighten the screws to seal it.

Freezing kit
When you want or need to do plumbing work without draining the system, use a freezing kit to create temporary ice plugs in the pipework.

Epoxy putty
For patch repairs to all types of leaking pipework

- Short lengths of copper pipe

- Push fit couplings for joining pipes

- Tap washers
- Plunger
- Adjustable spanner
- Self-grip wrench
- Pliers
- Junior hacksaw
- Screwdrivers

Plumbing

Plumbing repairs and improvements require a few specialist items and a variety of general-purpose tools as well.

Pipe cutter
It's possible to cut copper pipe with a hacksaw, but you will do a more accurate and neat job with a pipe cutter. Some come with a built-in reamer to remove burrs and rough edges from the inside of the pipe.

Mini pipe cutter
Works like a pipe cutter, but is circular-shaped and ideal for working in confined spaces.

Bending springs
You can bend copper pipes up to 28mm in diameter by hand. To stop the pipe kinking, insert a bending spring; they are available in 15mm and 22mm sizes.

Pipe bending machine
If you are running a lot of new copper pipes, this tool is invaluable. Its levers make easy work of bending pipes to the profiles you require.

Pipe or Stillson wrench
Designed for gripping pipework, the jaws of the wrench self-tighten as you apply force.

Slip-joint or waterpump pliers
With long handles and an easy-to-adjust slip jaw, these pliers are a useful tool for undoing fittings. But if you want to avoid damaging the finish, use a precision spanner instead.

Pipe cleaning rods
Flexible 1m-long polypropylene rods that screw together so you can reach blockages in drains and inspection chambers. There are a range of cleaning heads, including scrapers, plungers and corkscrews.

Radiator bleed key
For releasing trapped air from a radiator.

Basin wrench or crowsfoot spanner
This has a pivoting jaw that can be set for tightening or loosening tap connectors.

Cranked spanner
Double-ended wrench, also for use on tap connectors.

Half-round metal file
For removing burrs inside the ends of cut copper pipe.

Plunger
The traditional device for clearing a blocked sink, basin or bath; pump up and down to create pulses of air and water.

Lavatory auger
Insert the wire and rotate the handle to clear the blockage.

Woodworking

Lots of home improvements involve simple carpentry tasks, and these tools will help you work accurately and effectively.

Try square

To mark up and cut timber square, or to check the accuracy of right angles, use a try square (or a combination square, see page 358).

Sanding block

To smooth flat surfaces or square edges, wrap abrasive paper around a flat-based sanding block, often made of cork, and grip the paper with your fingers as you work.

Jack plane

The jack plane is a good all-purpose plane, used for shaving fine layers off the surface of wood to smooth and reduce it.

Smoothing plane

Larger than the jack plane, a smoothing plane gives a finer finish.

Carpenter's mallet

Often made from solid beech, a carpenter's mallet is specially designed for use with a chisel.

Pincers

The broad jaws of pincers are perfect for removing nails; grip and roll the nail out of the surface. Some pincers are also equipped with a tack lifter in the handle.

Padsaw

A padsaw or keyhole saw is used for cutting curves and enlarging holes in timber. Some have interchangeable blades for cutting plasterboard too.

Tenon saw

One of the backsaw family, all of which have a stiffened metal top edge, the tenon saw has fine teeth, making it ideal for precision workworking and joinery.

Floorboard saw

Designed to cut accurately into or across floorboards, a floorboard saw is invaluable when renovating a home with old wooden floors.

Mitre box

The perfect device for cutting 45° and 90° mitres in all types of wood and plaster mouldings. Available in plastic or wood, and different sizes too. Use a tenon saw in a mitre box.

Painting

Manufacturers are constantly introducing new tools and equipment (as well as materials) that can reduce the labour of painting and speed the process.

Paintbrushes

A good-quality bristle brush that is well looked after will give the best results over the years, but the new generation of synthetic bristle or mix-bristle brushes are great value and also give an excellent finish, particularly with water-based paints. Smaller brushes (12mm or 25mm) are for fiddly work; 50mm for doors and skirtings; 100mm and 150mm are ideal for walls and ceilings.

Cutting in (sash) brush

The angled cut of these bristles helps you get a neat result in the corners and inside edges of window frames.

Paint kettle

Life is easier if you carry around small quantities of paint at a time – so decant into a plastic or metal paint kettle.

Special effects brushes, sea sponge, rags

Some paint effects can be created using everyday objects like a clean cotton rag, but others – such as sponging – require specific tools.

Roller handle

When you want to paint walls and ceilings quickly, a roller is the answer. Buy a durable roller handle with wire cage, which makes it easy to change the sleeve, but also makes the sleeve less likely to slip off than cheaper push-fit roller handles.

Roller sleeves

Suit your roller sleeve to your type of paint or the desired effect. The most common sleeves are finished with cropped wool or synthetic pile – ideal for painting smooth surfaces with a water-based paint.

Tack cloth

This will remove all traces of dust before you apply a final coat of paint or varnish.

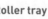

Roller tray

A metal or plastic roller tray is essential when painting with a roller. Pour paint into the deep end of the tray and roll the roller across the ribbed surface so that the paint is applied evenly across its sleeve.

Corner roller

A normal roller will not reach into corners. You will need a corner roller to finish the job, or use a brush.

Radiator roller

A special long-handled roller designed for painting behind radiators.

Telescopic pole

You can extend your reach to the ceiling with a telescopic pole that slips onto the handle of a roller or paint pad. Or look out for rollers with a shorter but still useful built-in extension handle.

Paint shield

A paint shield or 'george' can be used to create a clean edge at skirting boards and cornices, or for keeping paint off windows when you are painting the frames.

Paint pads and trays

Often sold in kits complete with trays or a roller applicator tray, paint pads are quick, light and easy to use, particularly on large areas with a smooth, flat surface. Paint pads designed for fence panels are much quicker than using a brush.

Paint sprayer

Ideal for covering large surfaces such as a fence.

Paintbrush cleaning kettle

Looking after good, and expensive, paintbrushes is well worth it – and now you can buy cheap and easy-to-clean pots to store and clean all types of paint and brushes.

Wallpapering

Having the correct tools will make the job simpler and the finished result much neater.

Paste brush
You can use any 100mm or 125mm paintbrush to apply paste, but a paste brush has a thicker wedge of soft bristles and is easier to use.

Paper hanging scissors
The extra-long blades make it easier to cut wallpaper in straight lines.

Wallpaper table (pasting table)
Higher than a kitchen table and just wider than a roll of wallpaper, this lightweight folding platform is perfect for measuring, cutting and pasting paper. W-leg tables are more stable than cheaper versions, and plastic ones are sturdiest of all, as well as being the easiest to clean and store.

Plumb line/chalk line
Use a plumb line – a weight on the end of a string – to establish a vertical. For drawing a straight line on most surfaces, snap a chalk line.

Paper hanging brush
The soft bristles on this brush are designed to smooth wallpaper by squeezing out bubbles and excess paste. Wash the bristles in warm water when you've finished.

Seam roller
Smooth the seams between lengths of wallpaper with this tiny roller – but don't use it on embossed or fragile papers.

Wallpaper scorer
When soaking wallpaper ready for stripping, score the surface first with a rotary scorer to enable the water to penetrate. Then use a scraper to lift the paper off the wall.

Wallpaper steamer
Steaming is the fastest way to strip wallpaper. It makes good sense to buy a steamer when you have a lot of paper to strip.

Combination smoother/cutter
Smooth the wallpaper into place then cut around obstructions with the retractable snap-off blade. Don't press too hard on fragile papers.

Tiling

When using tile-cutting and snapping tools, don't forget that you will need safety goggles and gloves to protect you from flying fragments and sharp edges.

Tile scorer
Get a clean break in a tile by scoring first through the glaze using a tile scorer with either a tungsten carbide tip or steel wheel.

Tile saw
Used for cutting curved lines through a tile. You can also use a jigsaw or rotozip with a ceramic blade for this task.

Tile file
Removes rough edges from a cut tile.

Tile snippers or nibblers
For very narrow cuts, score first and then nibble to the line with these tungsten carbide-edged pincers. Also ideal for cutting mosaic tiles.

Tile snapper
Snap a tile in two by scoring and then squeezing the marked line between the jaws of a tile snapper. Some have an integral scoring blade too.

Diamond-wheel tile cutter
The rotary blade on this machine will cut through all types of tiles; if you are tiling a large area, it's worth buying this relatively inexpensive power tool.

Flat-bed tile cutter
Lever-actioned tile cutters, which score and snap, are available for both wall tiles and thicker floor tiles.

Profile gauge
Mould the profile of an obstruction onto this tool and then transfer the pattern to your tile, or any floor covering.

Notched spreader
A notched spreader will give you the correct depth of adhesive, evenly spread. Buy one for either wall or floor tiles, or choose a multi-toothed tool for both surfaces.

Grout spreader
Designed to spread grout across tiles and into the joints; you can buy different sizes of spreader for wall and floor use.

Sponge
Synthetic and tough, a decorator's sponge is useful for wiping and mopping up after decorating tasks.

Stripping and filling

Choose your stripping method with care so as not to damage the surface (see pages 128–29).

Wire brush
A good stiff wire brush will loosen flaking paint and surface rust from metalwork.

Hot-air gun
A safer alternative to the old-fashioned blowtorch, a hot-air gun lets you control the heat easily when softening paint before stripping.

Scraper
A must-have for preparing any surfaces – particularly removing old paint or wallpaper. Scrapers have stiff blades, and though they can be used to apply filler, you will get a neater result with a filling knife.

Combination shavehook
For use with chemical paint stripper or a hot-air gun. The blade is designed for scraping paint from flat, concave and convex surfaces.

Glass scraper
If you accidentally spatter mirrors and glass with paint, scrape it off when dry with this scraper.

Putty knife
Shaped to allow you to smooth and finish putty in window frames.

Filling knife
This has a similar appearance to a scraper, but the flexible blade makes it ideal for forcing filler into cracks and crevices in walls.

Cartridge gun
Tubes of various types of sealant or grab adhesive will fit this easy-to-use spring-loaded applicator.

ONE PLANET HOME

Timber falls into two categories – softwood and hardwood. It is generally more expensive than man-made boards, of which there are many different kinds with different uses. Skirting and mouldings have a whole range of uses, including holding glass in place in doors and windows, hiding expansion gaps and joins, or just adding a decorative touch to an interior.

Responsibly sourced wood products
diy.com.forestfriendly

Hardwoods

Hardwood can be bought machined or as whole planks cut from the log and seasoned. The colour can vary even between trees of the same species. Tools need to be sharp for cutting hardwood and screw fixings require pilot holes to be drilled first. Brass or plated screws should be used in oak – the acid in the wood will turn steel screws black.

Hardwood veneers are thin sheets of wood used to cover softwood or man-made boards such as plywood and chipboard. Nowadays there is a wide range of veneers, and you can buy several sheets or single pieces.

Softwood

Softwood is sold as rough (sawn) or smooth (planed) timber. Use planed timber when the appearance of the wood matters; it is often sold as the size before planing, and if so you need to take this into account when planning a job as planing can remove 4mm–6mm. When buying softwood, avoid timber with black knots (unlike brown ones, they will shrink and may drop out), warping, splits and wide cracks.

Wood is sold in standard thicknesses and widths, ranging from 12mm x 25mm to 75mm x 225mm. It can also be bought as tongue-and-groove boards for flooring and panelling. Wall panelling may be flush tongue-and-groove or V-jointed (known as TGV) to emphasise the junction between the boards. Buy all the TGV boards you will need at the same time as batches can differ slightly.

MDF

MDF, short for medium-density fibreboard, is the best known type of fibreboard, which is a type of board made from wood fibres that are compressed and stuck together under pressure. MDF comes in a range of thicknesses in a sheet size of 2440mm x 1220mm. Cut edges can be painted; they don't need to be covered with veneer or wooden lipping.

Man-made boards

Plywood

Plywood consists of thin wooden sheets bonded on top of each other, with the direction of the grain alternating at right angles in each layer. Edges are smooth enough to leave plain or they can be covered with a thin strip of veneer or wooden lipping. Thicknesses range from 3mm–18mm and the standard sheet sizes are 2440mm x 1220mm, 1220mm x 1220mm and 1220mm x 610mm.

Chipboard

Chipboard is manufactured by bonding small chips of softwood together under pressure. Standard chipboard and moisture-resistant chipboard are available. Melamine- and wood-veneer-coated chipboard are popular for shelves and kitchen worktops. Chipboard is sold in thicknesses of 9, 12, 15 or 18mm and a standard sheet is 2440mm x 1220mm.

Hardboard

Hardboard is made from compressed softwood pulp. The thin sheets are easy to cut, but they are not as rigid or strong as other man-made boards. However, hardboard is a cheap alternative, ideal for drawer bottoms or as underlay for some floor coverings. Standard hardboard is 3.2mm thick and shiny one side, textured the other.

Plasterboard

Plasterboard is the most common material for covering walls and ceilings, giving them a clean flat surface for painting or papering. It is made by covering gypsum plaster with heavy-duty paper on both sides, and it comes in a variety of types and sizes. Standard plasterboard is usually grey on one side and ivory-coloured on the other side. Fit it with the ivory side outwards. You can decorate straight on to the ivory side or give it a coat of finishing plaster first. Plasterboard can be fixed to masonry using plasterboard adhesive, timber studs using plasterboard nails, or metal studs using special self-tapping dry-wall screws.

PLASTERBOARD FOR DIFFERENT USES

Standard plasterboard
Suitable for all applications where normal structural and insulating levels are required. Choose between tapered-edge and square-edge boards according to how the wall is to be finished. Tapered-edge boards can be finished either with jointing tape and compound (see page 75) or with a skim coat of plaster; square-edge boards need to be plastered over for a smooth finish.

Thermal-check plasterboard
Plasterboard with a bonded layer on the reverse side which gives improved thermal insulating properties.

Vapour-check plasterboard
Plasterboard with a vapour control membrane. Used for wall and ceiling linings where vapour control is required, including ceilings beneath a loft space.

Moisture-resistant plasterboard
Plasterboard with water-repellent additives in the core. Suitable for occasional wet areas such as a kitchen or bathroom, or as a backing for ceramic tiling in a shower cubicle.

Cement board
Made from cement rather than plaster, this strong, moisture-resistant board will not rot or degrade in damp or wet areas. Ideal as a backing for wall or floor tiles in a bathroom, shower, kitchen or utility room.

Acoustic-check plasterboard
A high-density plasterboard designed for use in wall linings and partitions where sound insulation is required.

Fire-check plasterboard
Plasterboard with glass fibre and other additives that give it greater fireproofing qualities.

SKIRTING, MOULDINGS AND COVING

Chamfered skirting
Skirting is sold in a variety of heights, profiles and finishes, including chamfered, ogee, torus, bevelled and ovolo.

Ogee skirting

Torus skirting

Bevelled/rounded reverse skirting

Ovolo skirting

Architrave
Used to hide the join between a door frame and the wall.

Picture rail
Positioned on the upper part of a wall, it may be used to hang pictures from or serve simply as a decorative feature.

Dado rail
Divides the lower (dado) and upper area of wall.

Quadrant
Covers the gap between skirting and floor, and between wooden windows and the window sill.

Scotia
A more decorative moulding that is used like quadrant.

Triangle moulding
Used as a finishing for internal corners.

Square or rectangular moulding
Used as retaining beads for glass panels in doors or for finishing the edges of shelves.

Glass beads
Used to hold glass in place on doors and window frames.

Staff and parting beads
Used in sash windows to keep the sashes in place.

Half-round moulding
Gives a curved finish to man-made boards like chipboard.

Dowelling
Ranges in size from tiny dowels for plugging screw holes to diameters suitable for use as curtain poles.

Coving
Prefabricated plaster or polystyrene decorative moulding fitted at the wall/ceiling junction in a room.

Cornice
A highly ornate form of coving found in period houses.

Masonry

The term masonry refers to the stone, brickwork or concrete from which the walls of a house are built.

Stone

Few houses are built of natural stone these days, though there are plenty of old stone houses around, many coated with render on the outside to make them more weather-resistant. Stone may be used for building garden walls but it is far more expensive than other building materials.

Glass

Glass is sold by its thickness in mm. Most glass in domestic doors or windows is 4mm thick.

Float glass

The modern method of making glass involves floating a layer of molten glass on a bath of liquid tin to produce a flat sheet with no distortion. Known as float glass, this has now replaced plate glass, which was made by casting glass on a flat surface and then grinding and polishing both surfaces. Float glass is made in thicknesses of 3mm–25mm and is very strong, so is used for picture windows and glass items such as tabletops.

Safety glass

The term safety glass refers to any kind of strengthened glass, including toughened, laminated and fire-resistant wired glass. It is used for glazed doors, low-level windows and shower screens.

Toughened or tempered glass

To make toughened glass, ordinary glass is cut to shape, heated and then cooled rapidly. This makes it more shock-resistant and much stronger. The glass breaks into granules rather than sharp shards, making it suitable for doors or other areas that could be subject to sudden impact.

Fire-resistant glass

A steel mesh is sandwiched between two layers of glass during manufacture so that if the glass cracks, the mesh holds it in place for a time, helping to prevent the spread of fire and smoke.

Laminated glass

Two or more layers of glass are bonded together with clear plastic film between them. The film helps to hold the glass in place if it is broken.

Brick

Bricks are made from baked clay and their colour varies according to the type of clay used. They come in a standard size of 215mm x 112.5mm x 65mm and various special shapes are available for decorative brickwork.

There are three varieties: facings, commons and engineering bricks. Facings are used for exposed brickwork because of their attractive appearance as well as their structural qualities. Commons are general-purpose bricks that are not as finely finished as facings, so they are used for building walls that will be plastered or rendered or for the inner leaf of cavity walls. Engineering bricks are extremely strong bricks which are impervious to water. They are usually used underground for constructions like manholes. Bricks are made with differing levels of frost-resistance (see page 221).

Concrete blocks

Cast-concrete blocks are widely used in house-building. Lightweight concrete blocks are made from aerated concrete so they are easy to cut and drill. They are used for both internal and external walls, and are good for acoustic and thermal insulation. Dense concrete blocks, also known as medium-density or dense-aggregate blocks, are heavier and less common. Frost-resistant, moisture-proof blocks are used for foundations and walling below ground level. Blocks measure approximately 450mm x 225mm (length and height) while the thickness can vary from 75mm to 230mm.

Patterned or obscured glass

One side of the molten glass is given a textured surface or a decorative pattern with a special roller. Patterned glass is available in plain or tinted versions and in thicknesses of 3mm and 5mm. It is used for decorative effect and for privacy, such as in bathrooms.

Low emissivity glass

This is ordinary glass with a special chemical coating on one side that helps prevent heat loss. It may be used in double glazing or in greenhouses.

Non-reflective glass

Mainly used in picture frames, this glass looks clear but has a slightly textured surface that reduces reflections.

Solar-control glass

Laminated or patterned glass can be tinted or coated to reduce heat penetration in summer and heat loss in winter.

Choosing tiles

Wall tiles can vary in size from 25mm-square mosaic tiles up to 600mm x 300mm tiles. Tiles can resist fairly high temperatures without cracking, but if you are tiling around a cooker or fireplace, check that the tiles you plan to use are suitably heat-resistant.

Standard field tiles

There is a huge choice available of ceramic wall tiles, in different colours, patterns and sizes, including hand-painted ones. Standard tiles have square edges, but you can buy tiles with two rounded glazed edges for using at the corner of a panel, and tiles with one rounded edge for panel borders or for turning external corners.

Mosaic tiles

These tiny tiles are usually sold in sheets on a mesh backing or with a paper facing that holds them together while laying.

Inset tiles

Some tiles are printed with a decoration that coordinates with a border – these are known as inset tiles and can be used to add pattern and colour. Look out too for inset tiles with a hole cut into them: these are sold with various decorative pieces designed to be set in the hole.

Borders

Borders can be used to add extra colour and decoration to your walls. Many come with coordinating inset tiles.

Tile adhesives, grout and sealants

Tile adhesives, available as a powder or ready-mixed, are used to stick tiles to the wall. Grout, also available as powder or ready-mixed, fills the gaps between tiles, and sealant is used to give a waterproof seal. Grout reviver will clean up dirty old grout to look like new. As well as general-purpose grouts, there are now many grouts on the market specially formulated for tiling over different surfaces and working with different kinds of tile. These can both improve the durability of the tiled surface, and make the job of tiling easier.

Natural tiles

Sourced from quarries all over the world, natural tiles such as slate, limestone and travertine are becoming increasingly popular. They are very versatile: most can be used on walls or floors in any part of the house, including outdoors. All natural products need to be sealed before and after grouting and periodically thereafter. Some natural stone tiles such as marble can be expensive, but many convincing imitations are available in ceramic. These are more affordable and easier to care for than natural tiles.

Polished porcelain tiles

Polished porcelain tiles need a little extra care to stay looking their best. It's essential that they are sealed to prevent staining by dirt or spilt liquids. They must be sealed on the face and all edges (including any cut edges) before fixing and again across the surface of the tile and grout lines after grouting. Unless the tiles have been pre-sealed by the factory (which will be indicated on the tile pack) you will need to do this using a suitable sealer specifically formulated for polished porcelain.

Before sealing, the tiles should be thoroughly cleaned to completely remove their protective wax coating and any dirt using a specially formulated heavy duty tile cleaner. Always follow the instructions on cleaning and sealing products carefully.

Occasional cleaning and resealing of the tiles will be necessary. How often will depend on the amount of wear your tiles get.

FINISHES PRIMERS, PAINTS, WALLPAPER

Interior walls are most often finished with paint or wallpaper, and there are endless colours and styles to choose from. Before you start, you may need to prime or seal the surfaces.

Primers and sealers

On bare wood, plaster or metal surfaces you will get a better result if you use a primer first. The primer provides a surface to which the paint can bond, and will stop paint being absorbed. There are primers to suit different surfaces, inside and outside the house. See also page 83.

PRIMERS AND SEALERS

Type of surface	Primer/sealer	Use
Bare plaster or wood	All-purpose primer, or wood or plaster primer	Seals porous surfaces and gives the paint a surface to grip.
Stained walls or plaster, or areas treated with preservative	Stain block primer	Has aluminium scales which form a barrier, sealing in the stain. Two coats may be needed.
Knots in wood	Knotting solution	This is a shellac (resin) solution which prevents the resin in the wood from bleeding through and discolouring the paint. Coat with primer when dry.
Interior or exterior surface with mould, algae or lichen	Fungicidal wash/mould killer	Kills the spores. Brush them away and apply a second coat.
Flaking external walls (usually render but can be used on exposed brick and stone)	Stabilising solution/primer	Binds chalky/flaky surfaces to make a sound base for paint. If there is any sign of mould, apply fungicidal wash first.
Metal	Metal primer	Contains zinc to help prevent rust. Different types available for different metals. Rusted metal should be cleaned and primed with a rust-inhibiting primer.

Choosing the right type of paint

Paint comes in two main types: oil-based and water-based. Oil-based paints need an undercoat; with emulsion paint the first coat acts as an undercoat. When painting large areas like walls and ceilings, you should only use water-based paint. Oil- and solvent-based paints give off fumes that are harmful to your health and to the environment, so use them only on small areas like woodwork and trims, and make certain there is very good ventilation both while you apply them and while they dry. Even better, use water-based alternatives. The chart below covers general-purpose paints and where to use them. You can also buy specialised paints, such as floor and radiator paint.

CHOOSING THE RIGHT PAINT

Paint	Surface	Use
Undercoat	Interior and exterior surfaces. Apply over primer, where necessary, and before the top coat.	Apply a second coat if colour underneath shows through.
Vinyl or acrylic emulsion (interior)	Walls and ceilings.	Water-based paint that does not need separate undercoat. Available as matt, silk or soft sheen finishes.
New-plaster emulsion	Newly plastered walls and ceilings.	New plaster takes months to dry out fully; this type of emulsion is more permeable than ordinary emulsion, allowing moisture to pass through and evaporate.
One-coat emulsion	Walls and ceilings.	Better coverage than ordinary emulsion.
Anti-condensation emulsion (also called kitchen and bathroom paint)	Bathrooms and kitchens.	Semi-porous emulsion that reduces condensation by preventing water droplets forming on the surface of the wall.
Emulsion (exterior)	Exterior walls.	Hardwearing water-based paint.
Multi-surface acrylic emulsion	Walls, ceilings, wood, metal and radiators.	Water-based paint similar to emulsion. Available as matt and satin finishes.
Gloss paint (water-based)	Interior wood and metal.	Fast-drying, high-sheen paint.
Gloss paint (oil-based)	Any undercoated surface.	Oil-based paint that is slow to dry but very hardwearing.
Non-drip one-coat gloss paint	Woodwork.	Combines undercoat and top coat.
Masonry paint	Exterior render.	A stronger exterior emulsion paint. Paint walls first with stabilising solution and a fungicide, if necessary.
Textured paint	Uneven plaster surfaces.	Much thicker than ordinary paint so can hide cracks. Can be over-painted with emulsion.

How much paint do you need?

Manufacturers specify on the paint container the area that the paint will cover; this varies according to the surface you are painting. To calculate your surface area, measure the height and width in metres, then multiply the figures together to get the area in square metres.

To calculate the total wall area of a large room, or more than one room, break it down into smaller areas, multiply the height by the width of each area, then add all the numbers together.

Choosing healthier paints

The main environmental impact of paint is the release of VOCs (Volatile Organic Compounds), primarily solvents, into the atmosphere. These contribute to atmospheric pollution, smell unpleasant and can be harmful to people with respiratory problems.

B&Q has developed a VOC labelling scheme – now adopted across the UK paint industry – and has encouraged the development of water-based technology to provide alternatives to traditional products. All paint products, stains, varnishes and decorative sundries such as white spirit are now labelled to give information on VOC concentration, so low-VOC products are clearly identifiable.

safety first

Paint with a high lead content can cause poisoning. Most paints are now lead-free but before stripping old paint, always check it first with a lead-testing kit (see page 128). If the result is positive, you must use a special chemical stripper and take all the precautions advised by the manufacturer.

Choosing wallpaper

Wallpapers come in numerous finishes and range from everyday, hardwearing, economical papers to very expensive hand-painted ones that need to be treated with care. If your wall surface is imperfect, you will achieve a better result by applying lining paper first. Porous surfaces should be coated first with wall size, a special sealer that prevents them soaking up the paste.

CHOOSING THE RIGHT WALLPAPER

Paper	Description	Uses
Lining paper	Plain undecorated paper.	Hung on bare wall surfaces under wallpaper. Can be papered or painted over.
Standard wallpaper	Flat wallpaper with a design machine-printed on its surface.	Price and quality vary. Cheap papers tear easily, making them harder to hang.
Woodchip	Small chips of wood glued between two layers of paper.	Hides rough wall surfaces. Should be painted with emulsion.
Vinyl	A printed PVC surface laminated to a paper backing.	Water-resistant, so wipes clean. Heavy-duty vinyls are good for kitchens and bathrooms.
Blown or textured vinyl	Screen-printed and then heated to create a textured effect that can also be painted.	Covers uneven surfaces and cracked walls. Flat underside means it is easy to paste and easily peeled off. Relief doesn't crush, as embossed paper can.
Embossed	Raised pattern is imprinted in the paper during manufacture.	Must be hung with care to avoid flattening the relief pattern.
Flock	Fibres such as velvet pile are bonded in patterns to the surface of the paper.	Expensive paper; hung the same way as standard paper.
Hand-printed/ screen-printed	Screen-printed or block-printed paper that is printed one roll at a time.	Attractive but expensive paper. Hand prints are very delicate and need expert hanging.
Paste the wall	Wide variety of printed and textured papers.	Special backing that doesn't expand when wet, so paste can be applied straight to the wall. Quick and clean to hang. Can be trimmed with a knife.

FIXINGS NAILS, SCREWS, GLUES

Whether you want to put up shelves or ceiling coving, fit a new kitchen or lay floor tiles, you will need some kind of fixing. There is a vast array of nails, screws and glues to choose from: those shown here are some of the most useful for general domestic jobs.

Nails

Steel nails come in all shapes and sizes. Outdoors, use zinc-plated galvanised nails to delay rusting.

Plain-head wire nail

General-purpose round nail. Can sometimes cause wood to split.

Cut floor brad

Nail with a rectangular cross-section used to fix floorboards to joists.

Oval wire nail

Oval shape helps to prevent wood splitting as it is hammered in.

Ring-shanked nail

Round nail with rings around shank that make the fixing more secure.

Lost-head nail

Round nail that can be punched below the surface with a pin punch.

Plasterboard nail

Jagged shank helps it to grip plasterboard.

Clout nail

Used for fixing slates and window sash cords.

Masonry nail

Grips well in bricks and breeze blocks and is used for fixing wood to masonry.

Panel pin

Small, slim nail, easily punched in. Used for mouldings, joinery and general carpentry.

Felt nail/large-head clout nail

Shorter than the clout nail; used for attaching roofing felt.

Screws

Screws provide a stronger fixing than nails and most of them can be unscrewed again. They are usually made of mild steel, but hardened steel, stainless steel, solid brass and steel plated with chromium or brass are also available, as are galvanised rust-proof screws for outdoor use.

A screw consists of the head, the shank and the thread. Its length is measured from the pointed tip of the thread to the part of the head that lies flush with the surface it is screwed into. The gauge is the shank diameter. Screws can be raised-head, which means the head sits above the surface, or countersunk, when the head is flush with or sinks below the surface. They can have either a slotted-head or a cross-head, which requires a cross-head screwdriver. Cross-head screws are easier to drive in than slotted-head ones, especially with a power screwdriver.

Pilot and clearance holes

Screws go in more easily and accurately if you drill a narrow pilot hole to guide them. When you are screwing one thing to another you will need to drill a clearance hole through the top layer so that the screw thread cuts only into the lower one.

Countersunk screws

To countersink a screw, use a countersink drill bit to drill a shallow crater at the top of the pilot hole so that when you screw it in the head lies flush with the surface of the wood. For a completely smooth finish, fill the recess with wood filler and sand it when dry.

Screw gauges

The imperial system of screw gauges ranked the shank diameter as a number from 1 to 20 – the higher the gauge, the bigger the screw. Their metric equivalents are not nearly so user-friendly, but they are the way screws are now increasingly sold. The table below will help.

SCREW GAUGES			
Gauge		**Clearance hole**	**Pilot hole**
Metric	Imperial		
2mm	2	2.5mm	1.6mm
2.5mm	3	3mm	1.6mm
3mm	4	3.5mm	2mm
3.5mm	6	4mm	2mm
4mm	8	5mm	2.5mm
5mm	10	5.75mm	3.5mm
5.5mm	12	6.5mm	3.5mm
6.5mm	14	6.5mm	4mm

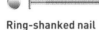

Countersunk woodscrew

The traditional unhardened woodscrew has a single thread. A pilot hole and a shank-clearance hole need to be drilled before it is fitted.

Raised-head woodscrew

Used for decorative hardware fittings, this screw is countersunk to the rim of the head.

Hardened-steel woodscrew

Double threads enable fast insertion with no need for a pilot hole if screwing into softwood.

Round-head woodscrew

Used for fitting decorative door furniture.

Chipboard screw

Deep threads extend right up to the head of this screw. It can be used in wood as well as chipboard.

Dry-wall screw

A twin-threaded screw used for fixing plasterboard or fibreboard to timber studs.

Masonry screw

A strong screw that can be driven into masonry without using a wallplug.

Coach screw

This has a square or hexagonal head that is driven with a spanner. It gives a very strong, heavy-duty fixing.

Carcass screw

With a thick shank and coarse thread, this can be useful for securing chipboard.

Self-tapping screw

Cuts its own thread in thin sheet metal and plastic.

Security screw

The shape of the countersunk head prevents the screw being removed once it is in place.

Coach bolt (cup square bolt)

Coach bolts have a square neck under a domed head that locks into the wood as the nut is tightened.

Fitting wallplugs to solid walls

A normal screw won't stay in masonry without a wallplug. The wallplug expands to grip the sides of the hole when the screw is driven in, so holding the screw securely in place. To drill into masonry, you need a power drill with hammer action and masonry bits. Make sure your wallplugs, screws and bit are of matching size.

B&Q Making it easier

Hold the power

If you don't have much experience using a drill, you may find it easier to achieve a neat, accurate result if you start the hole without the hammer action turned on.

Select the correct size of plugs and drill bits for your screws. The yellow plugs here take 4mm gauge screws, the red take 5mm and the brown take 5.5mm (but note that wallplug colours can vary).

Hold the plug up to the drill and mark its length on the bit with tape. You should drill into the wall slightly deeper than the length of the plug.

Check for hidden pipes and cables (see SAFETY FIRST) then use a hammer setting to drill the hole. Keep the drill square to the wall and hold it steady or you will end up with a tapered hole.

The wallplug should only require finger pressure to insert, but it should be a firm fit. Lightly tap the plug with a hammer to level it with the wall, if necessary.

Wallplugs

Moulded plastic wallplugs are produced on plastic 'trees' and the size of drill bit will be printed on the tree. Some manufacturers make different-sized wallplugs in different colours, but colours are not standard across all brands.

Straight plastic plugs

These are tubes with ribs running lengthways. They take the screw thread only, so they have to be cut shorter than the depth of the hole.

Moulded plastic wallplugs

These have a split end and take a range of screws.

Hammer-in plugs

Hammer-in plugs are the alternative to wallplugs and screws, good for fixing timber battens to masonry. One type has a wallplug with a ready-fitted screw. It is inserted into a drilled hole with a hammer and the screw then driven home. There is also a version of this designed for plasterboard. The other type has a flanged expansion sleeve fitted with a masonry nail.

Hammer-in screw fixing

Hammer-in nail fixing

Heavy-duty fixings

Expanding masonry bolt

This is an extremely strong fixing for attaching heavy items like fence posts to masonry walls. A bolt is screwed into a metal or plastic segmented shield which fits into a drilled hole. As the bolt is tightened, the segments are forced apart to expand and grip the sides of the hole.

Frame fixings

Plastic frame fix

Metal frame fix

These are long plastic or metal fittings which can be used for fixing wood, metal or plastic window and door frames to the wall. They fit into a hole drilled through the frame into the wall.

Knock-down fixings

You can't screw into the sides or ends of laminated board with an ordinary screw or it will split. Knock-down fixings are used for secure fixings in laminate that give strength and avoid splitting.

Chipboard fastener

This nylon plug has a thread on the outside which grips the board to make a secure fixing for woodscrews.

Tee nut

The projecting prongs of this metal nut grip into the wood. It is stronger than a chipboard fastener, but shows both sides.

Screw socket

This is a threaded metal plug into which a screw is fitted. It is slightly less strong than a block joint, but much neater.

Cross dowel

A cross dowel consists of a steel dowel with a hole drilled through it and a screw. The screw fits through the dowel, which has a slot so it can be turned with a screwdriver to align it correctly. This makes a strong fitting for joining the ends of rails to side panels.

Block joints

These fittings are plastic blocks in two sections, which are used to join panels of man-made boards, such as chipboard, at right angles to one another. One block is screwed to each of the sheets being joined, then a longer screw joins the two plastic blocks together.

Hollow-wall fixings

When fixing screws into hollow walls of plasterboard, you must use specially designed fixings. The strongest kind open up once they are inside the cavity. None, however, are strong enough to take a heavy load; for this, you need to locate the timber wall studs with a detector and fix the load with wood screws.

Nylon petal plug anchor

This has nylon wings that open out like petals to grip the back of the plasterboard.

Gravity toggle

This is a screw with a swinging metal bar (toggle) attached. When inserted, the toggle swings down and grips the back of the wall. The toggle is lost in the cavity if the screw is removed. A gravity toggle is a strong fixing for plasterboard or lath-and-plaster walls.

Plastic anchor

This has a plastic anchor with segments that open out once it is in the hollow wall.

Metal anchor

This has metal segments that open out in the hollow wall.

Spring toggle

This screw has a spring-operated toggle bar that folds flat for insertion and springs open inside the cavity. As the screw is tightened the bar is pulled tight against wall. The toggle is lost in the cavity if the screw is removed. This is a strong fixing for plasterboard or lath-and-plaster walls.

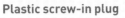

Plastic screw-in plug

This has a coarse thread designed to cut through plasterboard.

Metal screw-in plug

This has a coarse thread on the outside and a sharp point that cuts its own hole in plasterboard.

Adhesives and sealants

There are many good general-purpose adhesives on the market, but for some materials you need a specific product. Whatever surfaces you are sticking, make sure they are clean and free of dust, and not damp or wet. If necessary, hold them together with tape, clamps or even temporary nails until the adhesive has dried. Check the recommended setting times and note that they may vary in summer and winter, due to differences in temperature and humidity.

PVA (Polyvinyl adhesive)

Polyvinyl adhesives, commonly known as PVAs, are available in a range of general-purpose formulas, as well as wood adhesives and building adhesives. Some PVAs are waterproof. They are milky white when squeezed from the tube, but dry transparent.

Rubber-based contact adhesives

These are used for gluing synthetic laminates to wood, man-made boards and plaster. Adhesive is normally applied to both surfaces before they are pressed together.

Epoxy resin adhesives (two-part adhesives)

Metal, ceramic, stone, glass and rigid plastic can be glued to materials such as wood and glass with these adhesives. Always check the product label as some adhesives will not join all the materials. Two-part epoxy resins can be used outdoors or for joints that need to be waterproof; take care because in powder form these can be toxic.

Flooring adhesives (rubber resin adhesives)

These, and synthetic latex adhesives (see below), are used to stick floor coverings to floors. They are able to withstand a certain amount of water and they are slightly flexible, so they will not crack when you walk or put furniture on the floor.

Tile/coving adhesives (synthetic latex adhesives)

These adhesives will fill gaps, which makes them good for fixing expanded polystyrene ceiling tiles and coving to plaster or plasterboard. They are also used for floor tiles. Like rubber resin adhesives, they allow a certain amount of movement without cracking.

Grab adhesives (acrylic polymer adhesives)

These adhesives can be used instead of nails and screws to fix wooden mouldings and skirting-boards.

Filler adhesives (polyurethane-foam adhesives)

Sold in pressurised cans, these adhesives make good gap-fillers in wood, masonry, plaster and stone because the foam expands when dispensed. To remove them you need a specially formulated solvent.

Super-glues (cyanoacrylates)

These fast-working glues will stick all kinds of small household objects, including metal, glass, ceramic and plastic. Special super-glue remover is needed to prise apart any items that are accidentally bonded. Use with great care as super-glues will also glue skin.

Mastics

Mastic sealants are available in different colours, for sealing around window and door frames to prevent water leaking into cracks and rotting the wood. They are usually sold in a cartridge that fits in a mastic gun. Use flexible acrylic mastic to fill joints subject to cracking, such as along skirting boards.

Roof and gutter sealants

Repair small cracks in asphalt roofs and plastic gutters quickly and easily with the appropriate type of sealant.

Silicone sealants

These form a waterproof seal around wash basins, baths and shower cubicles.

REGULATIONS BUILDING AND PLANNING

What are planning and building controls, and why do they exist? Can you sort it out yourself or is it best to consult a specialist (see page 380)? As with any task, you can decide that for yourself once you know what's involved. First of all, it's important to understand what planning and building regulations do, as it's easy to think of them as restrictive and bureaucratic tools put in place purely to thwart your ambitions. In fact, they are essential safety mechanisms devised to protect you, your neighbours and the local environment. The regulatory bodies will grant permission for you to carry out your plans unless there are very sound reasons for refusal, in which case they must explain their decision. If you disagree, you do have a right to appeal against it.

Planning permission and Building Regulations

Planning permission

Planning permission regulates the use, siting and appearance of buildings and other structures. What to a homeowner might seem a minor alteration can have far-reaching implications. A structure that could obscure a driver's vision near a junction, for instance, might constitute a traffic hazard. Equally, a local authority may refuse planning permission on the grounds that the proposed scheme would not blend in with its surroundings. If you live in a listed building, you will need listed building consent for any significant exterior or interior works. Conservation areas are also subject to stricter rules than normal.

Building Regulations

Building Regulations are concerned with structural integrity and the suitability of the materials used. Most building works, including alterations or extensions, have to meet certain standards to safeguard public health and safety, and also – increasingly – to guarantee satisfactory levels of insulation and energy efficiency. It's important to note that even when planning permission is not required, Building Regulations might well need to be taken into account.

How can I learn more?

It's a very good idea to consult a representative of your Local Planning Authority and the Building Control Officer before you submit a planning application. They will be happy to discuss your proposal and offer advice about the best way to comply with the rules. They will also know from experience whether it is necessary to approach other authorities about related aspects of your project, such as sanitation and fire escapes. Such consultations can save you time and money.

Information on planning permission and Building Regulations is also available from www.planningportal.gov.uk, where you can apply online. Planning requirements can be complex and may require detailed drawings, but there is nothing to prevent you doing them yourself if you feel you are capable.

Permitted development rights

You can make certain changes to your home without needing to apply for planning permission. These permitted development rights were clarified and extended in October 2008 to cover a range of household building projects that used to automatically require an application for planning permission. These projects can now be carried out without formal permission provided they meet a range of key conditions (for example relating to the size and height of an extension, and its proximity to a highway). Projects include:

- extensions, conservatories, garages and outbuildings
- loft conversions
- solar roof panels
- roof alterations
- patios and driveways

For full details of the conditions that apply in each case, see www.planningportal.gov.uk.

Note that permitted development rights for houses differ from those for flats, maisonettes, commercial premises and other buildings. Listed properties are also subject to different rules, as are those on 'designated land', which includes national parks, conservation areas and Areas of Outstanding Natural Beauty. Planning rules do also differ across the UK. So you should always seek advice from your Local Planning Authority when considering undertaking any work, just to be sure.

Liability

It is crucial, and your responsibility, to be aware of any relevant regulations, because if you proceed without permission you might later be forced to restore the property to its original state – probably at considerable expense – or face prosecution. It can also be difficult to sell a property if you have made alterations without the necessary authorisation.

Hiring a specialist

If you prefer, you can employ a builder or preferably an architect to handle your application. Even so, it is still your responsibility and in your interest as the owner of the property to keep an eye on developments. For example, do not ignore a request from the Building Control Office's surveyor to inspect the site, or you could incur the cost and inconvenience of having to expose covered work at a later stage.

PLANNING PERMISSION AND BUILDING REGULATIONS*

Project	Is planning permission necessary?	Do Building Regulations apply?
Interior painting and decorating	No	No
Kitchen and bathroom improvements	No	Yes. Seek advice.
Electrical work	No	Yes. All electrical work must comply with the latest IEE Wiring Regulations. See page 268.
Removing or creating openings in internal walls	No	Yes. Internal walls may be loadbearing, and their removal could affect the stability and safety of the building. Seek advice.
Replacing or fitting a new floor	No	Yes. Factors to consider include loadbearing capacity, sound insulation and fire safety. Seek advice.
Installing or replacing a staircase	No	Yes. Safety standards apply. Seek advice.
Replacing radiators	No	No
Installing or replacing central heating	No	Yes. A new gas boiler must be installed by a Gas Safe registered fitter. Electrical work must comply with the latest IEE Wiring Regulations. Energy efficiency standards apply. Seek advice.
Repairing and replacing windows	No	Yes. If you are replacing a whole window, or creating a new window opening, standards relating to thermal performance, air supply, means of escape and ventilation apply.
Decoration or repairs to an external wall	No	Yes. If you want to re-render, re-clad, replaster or re-line internally more than 25% of an external wall, thermal insulation will normally also have to be improved. Seek advice.
Paving more than 5sq m of a front garden	Yes if the surface is impermeable and rainwater will run off onto a road	No
Adding a fence, wall or gate	Yes if it will be over 1m high and is next to a highway used by vehicles (or the footpath of such a highway); or over 2m high elsewhere	No, but gates, walls and fences must be structurally sound and properly maintained.
Converting a house to flats or business premises	Yes	Yes. Seek advice.

* This information is for general guidance only. Planning and Building Regulations differ across the UK, and are stricter for listed properties and those in conservation areas, national parks or similar. Your Local Planning Authority and Building Control Department are the best sources of advice.

safety first

New electrical regulations
Since 1 January 2005, new laws have been in place requiring anyone carrying out electrical work in a home or garden in England or Wales to inform their local authority's Building Control Department. See page 268 for further details and exemptions.

Independent advice and further information

Architects Accredited in Building Conservation (AABC)
01625 871 458 www.aabc-register.co.uk

Association of Building Engineers (ABE)
List of members 0845 126 1058
www.abe.org.uk

Bat Conservation Trust
If you have bats in your attic, you must call the Bat Conservation Trust before working in there.
Helpline 0845 1300 228 www.bats.org.uk

British Standards Institute (BSI)
Tests materials and practices and defines product and industry standards
020 8996 9001 www.bsigroup.co.uk

Builders Merchants Federation (BMF)
List of builder's merchants
020 7439 1753 www.bmf.org.uk

Building Research Establishment (BRE)
Research on building techniques and problems
01923 664 000 www.bre.co.uk

Centre for Accessible Environments (CAE)
Advice on accessibility for the disabled
020 7840 0125 www.cae.org.uk

Chartered Institute of Building
List of members
01344 630 700 www.ciob.org.uk

Electrical Contractors' Association (ECA)
List of members
020 7313 4800 www.eca.co.uk

Electrical Contractors' Association of Scotland (SELECT)
List of members
0131 445 5577 www.select.org.uk

Energy Saving Trust (EST)
Gives advice and administers grants on energy conservation
0800 512 012 www.energysavingtrust.org.uk

Environment Agency
Government body responsible for controlling air, land and water pollution in England and Wales
08708 506 506 www.environment-agency.gov.uk

Federation of Master Builders (FMB)
List of members and guarantee information
020 7242 7583 www.fmb.org.uk

Gas Safe Register
Replaced the CORGI gas register in April 2009. Find a registered gas business in your area.
0800 408 5500 www.gassaferegister.co.uk

Glass and Glazing Federation (GGF)
List of members
020 7939 9100 www.ggf.org.uk

Health & Safety Executive (HSE)
Advice on safety at work in construction
0845 345 0055 www.hse.gov.uk

Heating and Ventilating Contractors' Association (HVCA)
List of members
020 7313 4900 www.hvca.org.uk

Institution of Gas Engineers
List of members
0844 375 4436 www.igem.org.uk

Institution of Structural Engineers
List of members
020 7235 4535 www.istructe.org.uk

National Access and Scaffolding Confederation (NASC)
List of members
020 7822 7400 www.nasc.org.uk

National Federation of Roofing Contractors Ltd
List of members
020 7638 7663 www.nfrc.co.uk

The National Inspection Council for Electrical Installation Contracting (NICEIC)
Independent electrical safety regulatory body
0870 013 0382 www.niceic.com

Office of Fair Trading
Protects consumers and ensures that businesses operate fairly
0845 7224 499 www.oft.gov.uk

Ricability
Information on products and services for older or disabled people
020 7427 2460 www.ricability.org.uk

Royal Institute of British Architects (RIBA)
List of members
0207 580 5533 www.architecture.com

Royal Institute of Chartered Surveyors (RICS)
List of members
0870 333 1600 www.rics.org

Scottish Office
Advice on environmental and building regulations in Scotland
0131 556 8400 www.scotland.gov.uk

WORKING WITH SPECIALISTS

The golden rule of home improvements is be realistic. Most of us love to feel a sense of achievement but even the most gifted amateur cannot hope to complete every task alone. Beware: if you allow your enthusiasm to run away with itself, you are likely to take on too much! There are some circumstances – such as buying a home – in which you may have no choice but to call in a professional. And remember too that some home improvement work can be physically demanding. Don't let determination override common sense. Be kind to yourself!

Getting help from the professionals

If a potentially dangerous task requires more skill than you can realistically offer, then do play safe and call in an expert. But it's not only health and safety concerns that may lead you to call in a professional: timing, budget or even the law may require it.

Buying a home

When buying a property you will need to complete a survey, and you will have no choice but to call in an expert. If you need a mortgage, a survey will be a condition of the loan. If you are a cash buyer, it is highly recommended, whether in the form of a valuation, a 'home-buyer's report' or a full structural survey. If you opt for the full survey, every accessible nook and cranny of the property will be checked. However, those parts too difficult to reach during the inspection can be overlooked, and although surveyors point out major and minor pitfalls, you should not assume a report is a legally binding guarantee.

Spend wisely

With larger jobs you will probably be making a considerable investment in materials; it would be foolish to waste this because of inexperience. If you run into difficulties during a job, specialists at your local B&Q store will be able to advise you about the best way to proceed.

Know your limitations

Be honest with yourself. If you don't feel confident, or you will need to invest huge amounts of time acquiring skills that you might never use again, then surrender, and take the well-trodden path to the door of the tradesmen.

Share the task

If time is a constraint then consider calling in a contractor to do the major work in order to let you get on with smaller tasks that you know you can complete on schedule.

Know the law

Any maintenance or installation work on a gas appliance must by law be carried out by a qualified fitter on the Gas Safe Register. Do not attempt it yourself.

New regulations in force since 1 January 2005 impose much stricter controls on electrical work in the home or garden. See page 268 for details. Failure to comply with the new rules could lead to a heavy fine.

Using architects

Complicated projects such as extensions benefit from the overview, draughtsmanship and management of an architect. An architect, particularly a local one, will be able to prepare and adapt the plans in order to maximise your chances of success in securing the permission of local authorities, with whom they will have had previous contact. They will also make up a budget for you and oversee the work of any other professional tradesmen you are using.

Which professional?

Some jobs require a combination of professionals – a kitchen or bathroom makeover, for example.

Plasterer: It takes a minimum of six months (and a maximum of a lifetime) to acquire the skill needed to create a smooth, even surface ready for painting.

Plumber: Always be cautious where there's any risk of flooding.

Electrician: Put safety first at all times. Never forget that electricity is potentially lethal. To find an approved contractor, get in touch with the NICEIC or ECA, or in Scotland SELECT (see page 379 for contact details).

Builder: Essential if major structural alterations are required. The Federation of Master Builders has a strict code of conduct for members.

Surveyor: A qualified professional – always go for a 'chartered' or listed surveyor when you need a report.

Carpenter: Joinery can be a highly skilled craft. Use a professional if a neat and accurate job is essential.

Estimates and quotations

Always get at least two estimates for the job, and remember the cheapest is not always the best – low prices may indicate cutting corners, poor-quality materials or shoddy workmanship; decide how much you value a good finish.

Peace of mind

Make sure that as many separate tasks are itemised as possible. An 'estimate' is not legally binding, since it is just an approximate cost, so you will need a 'quotation' to get a fixed price. Some builders' estimates will include 'provisional sums' to cover work they intend to subcontract and do not have a firm quote for. Insist that you are consulted before any final sums are agreed.

Schedules and contract management

Having determined the principal tasks and the individual prices, then it's a very good idea to agree a 'schedule of work'. This is an important document allowing both you and the expert to see clearly what is involved and when it is to be completed. A schedule should be a statement of agreement for both parties, and it is a good idea on larger jobs to tie payments to agreed completion dates.

When to give the go-ahead

Once both parties are happy, a contract should be drawn up that includes all of these elements. This should help ensure that nothing is left unplanned or uncovered. It should set out clearly exactly what is expected of you and of the professional you are hiring.

When to pay

With small jobs, most professionals will accept payment on completion, so long as they don't have to buy any special materials. With larger jobs it is normal for a builder to ask for an initial payment on receipt of materials and further interim payments to cover outlays until completion of the job. Never pay for the entire job in advance. If the job requires 'making good' or involves decoration, it is sensible to hold back some of the funds until after completion. You should also allow for 'snagging', when the builder returns after a six-month settling period; hold back a significant sum (5–10% is the accepted norm) to ensure a happy return. Make sure this final sum is mentioned in the contract, to insure you against any defects that may arise.

B&Q installation services

Our experienced teams offer a free planning and design service either in store or in your home. They will take you through over 40 ranges and details, from worktops to appliances, bathroom suites to taps, to help you create a kitchen, bathroom or bedroom perfectly tailored to your needs and budget.

Our national network of local installation centres means that our experienced trades people from your area will be on hand to manage all the elements of your project, including plumbing, electrics and lighting, and even tiling and decorating if you need it.

- There are no hidden costs: our full service quote includes everything from the products and labour to the gas, plumbing, tiling and plastering
- Products are quality checked before being delivered in one go ready for the fitter
- We can remove your old kitchen or bathroom, as well as any packaging, and dispose of them responsibly
- All our kitchens and bathroom furniture are from sustainable timber sources
- B&Q installers are fully qualified for whatever aspect of the installation they work on, from electrics to gas to plumbing, and our fitting service is independently audited through relevant bodies
- In addition to any product guarantees, all fitting work carried out by our installers is guaranteed for two years

GLOSSARY

Aggregate
Mixture of small stones and particles of stone used in making concrete or in decorative finishes.

Architrave
Wooden moulding fixed around a window or door frame to hide the join between frame and wall. There is a variety of architrave mouldings available to suit the style of your home.

Arris rail
Timber beam, triangular in cross-section. The vertical timbers of a closeboard fence are attached to horizontal arris rails.

Balustrade
Protective railing along a stairway, landing or deck. It consists of a handrail and a set of vertical posts or balusters.

Batten
Any narrow strip of sawn timber. A length of straight batten used as a straightedge is surprisingly useful for measuring and marking out.

Beading
• A painting technique for achieving a clean, sharp edge where two colours meet.
• A type of moulding, often semi-circular in cross-section. Wooden beading is used to hold panes of glass or door panels in place. Metal or plastic corner beading is used to reinforce repairs to crumbling plaster at an external corner.

Blown
• A surface layer such as plaster or cement render that has begun to separate from the wall behind.
• A fuse wire that has melted and broken an electrical circuit due to overloading.

Building membrane
Water-permeable sheeting used in outdoor construction projects, usually to keep materials – for example earth and gravel – separate from one another.

Burr
Rough edge left behind after cutting a piece of wood or a copper pipe, for example.

Butt joint
Joint in which the two elements are cut square and fastened end to end without overlapping or interlocking.

Chalk line
Length of string or cord saturated with brightly coloured chalk, used to mark out a straight line on walls, floor or ceiling.

Circuit breaker or miniature circuit breaker (MCB)
Trip switch in a consumer unit that operates automatically to cut off the power to a particular electrical circuit in the event of a short-circuit or fault. Once the problem has been remedied, power can be restored by simply resetting the switch – much easier than old-fashioned fuses which, once blown, had to be replaced or rewired.

Cleanstone
Grit- and dust-free aggregate, used for example in the construction of garden retaining walls or when laying land drains.

Clearance hole
When screwing one thing to another, drill a clearance hole right through whatever you are fixing. This must be big enough to take the unthreaded part of the screw (the shank). *See also* pilot hole.

Consumer unit
The point from which mains electricity is distributed to the various circuits around the home. It contains a set of circuit breakers or fuses that protect the circuits against overloading.

Control joint
Helps prevent cracking caused by slight movement, expansion or contraction in a garden wall or concrete pad. In a wall a control joint consists of a continuous vertical row of unmortared joints; in a concrete path or pad it is a strip of compressible fibreboard inserted at intervals within the concrete.

Coping
The top course of a garden wall. Often sloping or overhanging, it helps direct water away from the body of the wall, as well as providing a decorative finish.

Cornice
Decorative moulding running along the joint between a wall and ceiling.

Countersink
A countersink screw has a head designed to lie flush with the surface it is fixed to. As well as a pilot hole, you have to drill a slight recess in the surface to take the screw head using a countersink bit. Or use a screwsink bit to drill a countersunk pilot hole in a single operation.

Coving
Moulding running along the joint between a wall and ceiling. Modern coving may be made of plaster or polystyrene.

Cross-head
A type of screw with a cross-shaped recess on the head rather than a single slot. Cross-head screws include Phillips and Pozidriv, and need a compatible screwdriver. They are the best type of screw to use with a power screwdriver since they are easy to locate and the screwdriver is less likely to slip.

Dado
The lower portion of an internal wall. Because it is the part most subject to wear and tear, the dado was traditionally protected with wallpaper or panelling. A wooden moulding dividing a wall horizontally at about waist height is known as a dado rail.

Damp-proof course
Layer of waterproof material that stops moisture rising up and into a wall.

Damp-proof membrane
Layer of waterproof material that stops moisture rising through a solid floor.

Distemper
Traditional water-based paint that is powdery to the touch and wipes off with a damp cloth. To redecorate, you must first scrape or wash off distemper completely, or seal it with a special stabilising solution; otherwise the new paint will not stick.

Dowel
Cylindrical wooden peg used to secure butt joints in wood.

Flashing
Thin metal strip used to seal the junction between a chimney and a roof, or along the valley between two sloping roofs.

Flatpack
Self-assembly (or knock-down) furniture is supplied by the manufacturer as a flatpack.

Flue
Passage in a chimney that allows the escape of smoke, hot air and gases.

Flush
Two surfaces that are perfectly level with each other are flush.

Formwork
Temporary timber frame that shapes and supports concrete as it sets.

Gauge rod
Purpose-made measuring rod used in tiling and bricklaying for setting out and for maintaining regular joints.

Geotextile permeable fabric
Hardwearing, long-lasting sheeting available in various thicknesses. Used in outdoor construction projects, for example to keep earth out of land drains and soakaways, or to stabilise soft ground before building a sub-base.

Grommet
A protective ring of rubber or plastic used to line the knockout hole through which an electrical cable enters a fitting.

Grout
Fills and seals the joints between tiles. Used to finish the tiled surface once the adhesive is dry. Available in different colours and formulas suitable for wall and floor tiles.

Hardcore
Crushed or broken bricks, block and stone, used in the construction of foundations and sub-bases.

Housing
Slot or hole made in one timber to receive another.

Insulation
• Non-conductive protective covering of electrical flex or cable.
• Material that inhibits the passage of heat or sound.

Joist
Horizontal beam supporting a roof or floor. Joists are usually timber, but may also be made of reinforced concrete or steel.

Junction box
Electrical fitting used for making connections between cables on a power or lighting circuit. Usually plastic with a screw-on lid, junction boxes are normally hidden from view behind the ceiling, walls or floor. They contain varying numbers of terminals.

Key
To key a surface is to roughen it either by scoring or by rubbing it over with abrasive paper so that plaster, adhesive or paint bonds more effectively.

Lagging
Insulating material that reduces heat loss. It is fitted over a hot water cylinder, or over pipes and tanks in unheated spaces to protect them from frost.

Laths
Narrow strips of wood that the plaster is stuck to in a traditional lath-and-plaster wall.

Melamine
Tough synthetic resin used to coat man-made composite boards such as chipboard.

Mitre
Corner joint made by cutting two pieces of material at an equal angle.

Mortise
Slot or recess cut to receive a matching projection or tenon in a mortise-and-tenon joint.

Moulding
Shaped strip usually made from timber or man-made board that is used for interior trims such as dado rails and skirting, as well as in the construction of glazed and panel doors and many types of window.

Nogging
Short horizontal reinforcing timber fixed between the vertical studs in a wood-framed partition wall.

Olive
Sealing ring in a compression plumbing fitting.

Pilot hole
Drilling a pilot hole helps to prevent wood splitting when you drive in a screw. It must be of a smaller gauge than the screw so that the thread bites into the wood. When fixing one thing to another, drill a clearance hole for the screw shank through whatever you are fixing and a pilot hole into whatever you are fixing to.

Plinth
Detachable panel that covers the feet and base of self-assembly units such as kitchen cabinets.

Primer
Substance applied to a surface to seal it in preparation for subsequent decoration. Metal primer prevents rust; plaster and wood primers make a surface less absorbent.

Render or rendering
Thin layer of cement-based mortar coating the surface of an exterior wall.

RCD or residual current device
Fast-acting trip-switch that cuts off the power in the event of an earth leakage.

Riser
The upright part of a step or stair that rises from the back of a tread.

Scribe
Score a line with a pointed instrument.

Sheathing
Insulating outer covering of electrical cable and flex.

Shim
Thin wooden strip used as a measure to establish a fall across a surface. Cut a shim of the right size from any scrap of timber.

Size
Sealer used to coat plastered or papered surfaces in preparation for wallpapering. It prevents the surface from absorbing the paste, which means the paper sticks better and is easier to hang.

Slot-head
Traditional screw with a single slot into which the flat blade of a screwdriver is fitted.

Soakaway
Rubble-filled pit or underground receptacle into which water is drained, and from which it soaks away into the surrounding earth.

Spur
Branch cable that extends an existing electrical circuit.

Straightedge
Long metal ruler, or any long straight piece of timber. Use it to check that something is flat or straight, or as a guide when drawing a line.

Striker plate
Plate set in a door frame containing a cutout into which the latch fits when the door is shut.

Stud
Vertical timber support in a wood-framed partition wall.

Sub-base
Layer of compacted hardcore that provides a stable base for a patio or path.

Tamp
Pack down by repeated blows to the surface.

Tenon
Projecting peg that fits into a matching mortise in a mortise-and-tenon joint.

Terminal
The connection to which the bared cores or conductors of flex or cable are attached inside an electrical fitting.

Trap
U- or S-shaped waste pipe fitting attached to the outlet of a sink, bath, washing machine or lavatory. The shape means that it always retains water, which acts as a seal, preventing insects, bacteria and smells re-entering your home from the drains.

Tread
The horizontal part of a step or stair – the part you tread on.

Tongue-and-groove
Type of joint between boards in which a projecting tongue along the edge of one board fits into a corresponding recess or groove along the edge of the next.

Wall tie
Metal connector used to bind different sections of a masonry wall together.

INDEX